Until recently Consultant Editor of the *Observer* and now a Contributing Editor of *The Atlantic* (Boston), Dr Conor Cruise O'Brien has had a distinguished diplomatic, literary and journalistic career for many years. He entered the Department of External Affairs of Ireland in 1944 and was Head of the UN Section and Member of the Irish Delegation to the UN from 1956 to 1960; he then served as Representative of the UN Secretary-General in Katanga in 1961, when he resigned from the UN and Irish service. He has since been Vice-Chancellor of the University of Ghana (1962–5); Albert Schweitzer Professor of Humanities, New York University (1965–9); Member of the Dublin parliament (1967–77); Minister for Posts and Telegraphs (1973–7); Member of the Irish Senate (1977–9); Pro-Chancellor of Dublin University since 1973; Visiting Fellow of Nuffield College, Oxford (1973–5); Fellow of St Catherine's College, Oxford (1978–81); Editor-in-Chief of the *Observer* (1978–81); and Montgomery Fellow, Dartmouth College, New Hampshire (1984–5). His many publications include *The Shaping of Modern Ireland* (ed.), *To Katanga and Back, Conflicting Concepts of the UN, Writers and Politics* and *A Concise History of Ireland.*

CONOR CRUISE O'BRIEN

The Siege

The Saga of Israel and Zionism

PALADIN
GRAFTON BOOKS
A Division of the Collins Publishing Group

LONDON GLASGOW
TORONTO SYDNEY AUCKLAND

Paladin
Grafton Books
A Division of the Collins Publishing Group
8 Grafton Street, London W1X 3LA

Published by Paladin Books 1988

First published in Great Britain by
George Weidenfeld & Nicolson Ltd 1986

ISBN 0-586-08645-5

Printed and bound in Great Britain by
Collins, Glasgow

Set in Caledonia

ACKNOWLEDGMENTS

I thank Elaine Greene and Ilsa Yardley for their encouraging interest in this project from the beginning; George Weidenfeld, who welcomed the idea with imaginative sympathy, and helped to shape it, through his deep knowledge of the subject matter; Alice Mayhew for her close, kind and wisely critical attention to the book at every stage in the publication process; and to Linda Osband at Weidenfeld and Nicolson, and Henry Ferris, Pat Miller and Maria Iano at Simon and Schuster, for their sympathetic and systematic contributions to the same process; and to Professor Ross Brann for his discriminating help with problems of transliteration of Hebrew and Arabic names.

I also wish to thank the directors and staff of the various repositories in which I worked, or with which I corresponded, including the Library of Trinity College, Dublin, and the National Library of Ireland; the Library of the Hebrew University and the Central Zionist Archives, Jerusalem, and also the newspaper archive of the *Jerusalem Post;* the British Library, the Library of the School of Oriental and African Studies, the Library of the London School of Economics, the Public Records Office, and the Wiener Library, London; the New York Public Library; the Baker Library, Dartmouth College, Hanover, New Hampshire; and the Library of Edinburgh University.

Thanks to Isaiah Berlin, who kindly read the first two chapters, and whose wise and learned comments helped me also with the general orientation of the book. And thanks to Mel Lasky for a memorable discussion, and for referring me to important sources which I might otherwise have overlooked.

My thanks are due to more friends in Israel than I can easily list, but in particular to Teddy Kollek, Mayor of Jerusalem, on whose Jerusalem Committee I have had the honor to serve since 1982, to the members of the Committee, and to Tom and Susan Sawicki, for much kindness and help in understanding contemporary Israel. Thanks also to Michael and Joan Comay, Gideon and Nurit Rafael, and Arieh and Roisin Eilan, all friends from United Nations days; to Yehuda Litani of Ha'ariz; to Ari Roth and Alex Berlyne, of the *Jerusalem Post;* to Shlomo Avineri, Meron Benvenisti, Meron Medzini, and to Wim and Leah Van Leer, in whose delightful home I have often had the benign illusion of finding myself simultaneously in Jerusalem and in Dublin. Through Wim's intercession, I was admitted to a Talmudic *Heder* in Jerusalem conducted by the eminent scholar Rabbi Adin Steinsaltz; my thanks to the Rabbi and the other participants for a unique intellectual and moral experience.

5

Part of the work for the book was done in the delightful surroundings of the Mishkenot Shaananim, Jerusalem, in the kindly care of Ruth Bach and the other members of the Mishkenot staff. I gratefully record here my indebtedness for their contribution to this book.

Thanks too to Shula Eisner and Sezana Merin for friendly help in getting around, and understanding, Teddy Kollek's Jerusalem.

I also owe a very special debt to Cindy Offenbacher, whose painstaking researches on my behalf, and creative follow-up on inquiries of mine which were sometimes rather vaguely formulated, were of inestimable value toward the preparation of this book. My thanks also to Akiva Offenbacher, both for his patience with this time-consuming project, and for his own judicious comments and analysis.

Thanks to Kitty Quinn of Dublin and to Gail Patten of Dartmouth College, for much detailed help in the preparation of the book, and for their friendly interest in it.

And now a category of people to whom I owe, and offer, heartfelt thanks, but to whom my thanks, to be generally acceptable, must be offered in such a way as to exclude firmly even the faintest implicit claim on my part to any kind of endorsement on their part, of my book. I refer to those scholars in Israel who have read, from the point of view of their specialist interest, the different chapters of *The Siege*.

When I told an Israeli diplomat of what I was doing in the way of consultation, he raised his eyebrows and said: "You are sending chapters of your book to be read by *specialists*, in *Israel*? Dr. O'Brien you are a very brave man!"

Nothing so dramatic as bravery was required. All the same, there were one or two moments when I seemed to get an inkling of what my diplomatic friend meant. All the scholars whom I consulted gave me freely of their time and of their learning. All of them offered factual corrections, which I was most happy to have, and to embody. But some of them—by no means all—also, courteously but firmly, conveyed to me that factual corrections would never be enough; that my interpretation was wrong. Rightly or wrongly, I stuck to my own interpretation wherever—as for the most part happened—it did not appear to me to be invalidated by any factual corrections. But I owe it to the scholars concerned to make clear in this acknowledgment that the inclusion of their names in the list of those who have helped me does not imply any endorsement on their part of *The Siege*. The point is the more important as the list of those who have helped includes a number of the leaders in the relevant Israeli scholarship. So, having given that Health Warning, let me offer my profound thanks to the following scholars: Dr. Yehuda Bauer—Jonah M. Machover Professor of Holocaust Studies and head of the Division of Holocaust Studies at the Institute of Contemporary Jewry, Hebrew University of Jerusalem; Dr. Gabriel Cohen—Professor of History, Tel Aviv University; Mr. Yehoshua Freundlich—General Editor of the Documents of the Foreign Policy of Israel, at the Israel State Archives; Mr. Mordechai Gazit—Senior Fellow at the Truman Institute and at the Leonard David Institute for International Relations at the Hebrew University; Dr. Abraham Haim—Scientific Coordinator at *Misgav Yerushalayim*, the Institute for Research on the Sephard and Oriental Jewish Heritage; Dr. Michael Heymann—Deputy Director of the Central Zionist Archives; Dr. Hedva Ben-Yisrael Kidron—head of the Department of History, Hebrew University; Dr. Moshe Lissak—Professor of Sociology at the Hebrew University; Dr. Moshe Maoz—Chairman and Professor of the Department of Islamic and Middle Eastern Studies, Hebrew University; Dr. Meron Medzini—visiting Senior Lecturer at the School of Overseas Students, Hebrew University, specializing in Israeli foreign policy; Dr. Dan Schueftan—Research Fellow at the Truman Institute and at the Yad Tabenkin Institute for Defense Studies; Dr. Moshe Shemesh—of Ben-Gurion University of the Negev, Beersheva, and the Ben-Gurion Research Center, Sde Boker; Dr. Emmanuel Sivan—Professor of History and Middle East politics at the Hebrew University, and editor-in-chief of *The Jerusalem Quarterly;* Dr. Matti Steinberg—Lecturer in Middle East Politics at the Hebrew University and a Research Fellow at the Harry S. Truman Research Institute for the Advancement of Peace, the Hebrew University; Mr. Shmuel Toledano—adviser to the prime minister on Arab affairs under Eshkol, Golda Meir, and Rabin (1966–1977); Mrs. Dvorah Barzilay-Yegar—of the Israel Academy of Sciences and Humanities, Jerusalem; Dr. Ronald W. Zweig—Senior Lecturer in the Department of Jewish History, Tel Aviv University, and editor of *Studies in Zionism* (Institute for Zionist Research, Tel Aviv University).

I am also indebted, for general analytical comment, to several senior serving officials of the Israeli Foreign Office, and other Israeli public servants. Having been a Foreign Office official myself (of Ireland) at one time, I believe that, in a book which may well prove to be somewhat controversial, both inside and outside Israel, thanks due to serving officials of the State is most appropriately conveyed through a general acknowledgment, respecting the anonymity of those concerned.

The same principle applies, *mutatis* very much *mutandis*, to those officials of the P.L.O. with whom I was in contact in Southern Lebanon, in 1981.

My thanks are also due to David Richardson, of the *Irish Times* and the *Jerusalem Post;* to Colin Smith, of *The Observer;* and especially to Eric Silver, long a correspondent in Israel for *The Guardian* and *The Observer,* and generous, like Edmund Burke, with the fruits of his experience.

Thanks also to those Middle Eastern experts, outside Israel, who have helped me in various ways, and notably to Professor P. J. Vatikiotis, of the School of Oriental and African Studies, London, and to Professor Elie Kedourie, London School of Economics; and also to other scholars, with relevant expertise, notably Professor Edward Alexander, of Washington University and Professor Michael Curtis, of Rutgers University. Special thanks to Bat Ye'or and David Littman for generous and valuable help, especially in questions related to the Oriental Jews.

Thanks to Ian Lustick, of the Department of Government, Dartmouth College. Ian was my colleague at Dartmouth during 1984–1985, and many discussions and friendly arguments with him helped to enlarge my understanding of Arab-Israeli relations. That it could do with further enlargement, I do not dispute.

My longtime friend Owen Dudley Edwards, of the Department of History, Edinburgh University, read a number of the chapters, and helped to correct a number of errors, in fact and in perspective, especially in relation to the British and American aspects. He also made me laugh, while showing me where I was wrong, which is quite a trick. With him, no Health Warning is necessary.

Thanks to Ken and Harle Montgomery, of Chicago, for their friendly interest in the progress of the book, and in issues relating to it, during my time as Montgomery Fellow at Dartmouth College (1984–1985). And thanks also to Arthur Hertzberg, whom I got to know while we were both Visiting Fellows at Dartmouth. If I had known him earlier, this would have been a better book.

Thanks also to a number of friends, in Ireland, Britain and the United States, who helped by stretching my mind and keeping me on my toes in relation to relevant topics and other topics. Some of these friends are academics, some journalists; some a bit of both, like me: *en Amérique professeur, en Angleterre, journaliste*. Some resist categorization. I thank in particular John Cole, Tony Howard, Terence Kilmartin, Colin Legum, Jonathan Mirsky and John Silverlight, formerly my colleagues on *The Observer*, London; David Astor and Arnold Goodman, London; Vivian and Eilis Mercier, of Dublin and Santa Barbara; Marysa Navarro, of Dartmouth College; Patrick Lynch of Dublin, and Sheila and Valentin Iremonger, also of Dublin; Thomas and Jean Flanagan, of Stony Brook, New York; Deirdre and Alan Bergson, New York City, and Leonard and Jean Boudin also of New York City; Bob and Roisin McDonagh, Dublin and New York; Darcy O'Brien, Tulsa, Oklahoma; Wilton Dillon, Washington; Izzy Stone, Washington—Health Warning there, on this particular subject; Judy Stone, San Francisco; Bob and Treasa O'Driscoll, Toronto; Bill Dunphy, Toronto; Brian Garrett and Martin Dillon, Belfast; Muiris and Maire MacConghaile, Dublin; Jack and Doreen Brennan, Dublin; Derwent May, London; Marty Peretz and Leon Wieseltier, Washington; Jack Beatty, Boston; Alan Bloom, Chicago.

Finally, I want to thank my family: my wife Maire; my children and their spouses, Donal and Rita Cruise O'Brien, Fedelma and Nicholas Simms, and Kate and Joseph Kearney; my younger children, Patrick and Margaret; all of whom contributed much indispensable encouragement, along with some penetrating criticism.

Kate has a special connection with *The Siege*. She typed it all out from an appalling tangle of longhand, encouraging and criticizing as she went along in a most helpful way.

In Memory of
Bethel, Edward and Vicky Solomons

CONTENTS

PROLOGUE
How This Book
Came to Be Written

IT IS NOW nearly thirty years since I first became involved, as a minor participant, in the international debate over the Arab-Israeli conflict.

My country, Ireland, had become a member of the United Nations in 1955, and took part in the General Assembly debates for the first time in the autumn of 1956. I represented Ireland on the Special Political Committee, the organ of the Assembly which was seized of the item known as "The Question of the Palestine Refugees," the rubric under which the Arab-Israeli conflict was annually debated.

As delegates sit in alphabetical order, I found myself seated between the delegate of Iraq, on my left, and the delegate of Israel, on my right. Both delegates greeted me cordially; it took me a few moments to realize that my seating had relieved each of them of an extremely uncongenial neighbor.

The debate on "The Palestine Refugees" took up several weeks of the committee's time each autumn, and I attended and took part in it for five successive years. It was a bitter, sterile and static debate, taken up in the main by heated attacks on Israel by every Arab delegation—often in speeches delivered by Palestinians attached to different delegations—and by cool, unyielding Israeli replies.

Ireland—like, I suppose, other small European countries—did not at that time think of Middle Eastern affairs as matters of close practical concern to it. This was long before the Yom Kippur War and the use of the oil weapon. The "pro-Arab" posture (or rhetoric) of the European countries—including Ireland—was then far in the future. My own contribution to the debate, accordingly, was emollient and "balanced"; something in it for both sides, but not much.

As I came out of the debating chamber after my first intervention on this item, I met a friend, an American newspaperwoman. She asked me how my speech had gone over. I told her I had been thanked by both my neighbors, the delegates of Iraq and of Israel.

"Christ!" she said. "Was it as bad as that?"

I have often thought of that comment since, on reading some judicious article or editorial explaining, for example, how the positions of Israel and of the P.L.O. are to be reconciled.

In that autumn of 1956, the debates in the plenum of the General Assembly were taken up mainly with Suez. Britain and France had agreed, under American and Soviet pressure, to withdraw their forces from the Suez Canal. Israel now came under almost universal pressure to withdraw from Sinai. Britain joined in the pressure. The British delegate, Commander Noble, told the Assembly that Britain "could not condone" Israel's attack on Egypt, and called on Israel to withdraw.

It was generally assumed at that time—and is now universally admitted—that Britain, France and Israel had been acting in collusion in their concerted attacks on Egypt. So Commander Noble was a bit hard to take. Irish people, for historical reasons, have a rather low threshold of tolerance for manifestations of British official hypocrisy. (We can live very comfortably with our own peculiar forms of hypocrisy, but that is another matter entirely.) So I took some pleasure in drafting our delegation's statement, which opened with the words: "Far be it from our delegation to be any less censorious, about an attack on Egypt, than the distinguished delegate of the United Kingdom judges it appropriate to be."

That statement went down rather well with our neighbors on our right, and in general a good working relationship—and in some cases a joking relationship—built up between the delegations of Ireland and Israel in those years. The relationship was better than might have been expected, indeed. Relations between Ireland and Israel from 1948 on had been bedeviled—though that is perhaps not the *mot juste*—by the "Vatican factor," and the question of Jerusalem. Ireland had followed the Vatican line, calling for the placing of Jerusalem under international control, and this had impeded the growth of diplomatic relations between Ireland and Israel. However, a number of us were not all that keen on the Vatican factor, and it was not allowed to disturb relations between the two delegations at the United Nations.

The relationship on my left did not, unfortunately, flourish to the same extent, or so long. In the first years—1956 and 1957—I had many talks with our Iraqi neighbors, and learned quite a lot about Middle Eastern affairs, as these appeared to "pro-Western" circles around Nuri Pasha. But then came the Iraqi revolution of July 14, 1958, and when the General Assembly convened in September of that year, there were no familiar faces to my left. Rather naïvely, no doubt, in the circumstances, I asked my new neighbor, the head of the new Iraqi delegation on the committee, whether he had any news of his predecessor. Without moving a muscle, and with his gaze firmly directed into space, my new neighbor pronounced the single word: "Hanged!"

It was the only word he ever addressed to me, if it was addressed to me. For social purposes my only neighbors were now those on my right. The blockage, or chasm, to my left did not prevent good relations with other Arab delegates, and those of Egypt and Tunisia in particular. My wife, who represented Ireland in the more relaxed atmosphere of the Third Committee—Social, Cultural and Humanitarian—alias "the women's committee," had a number of Arab friends, including her Iraqi neighbor, a strong-minded aristocratic lady—Mrs. Bebia Afnan—whose well-established radical opinions had enabled her to survive the revolution. But one of my wife's Arab friends was warned by Arab colleagues to see less of my wife. "The Irish are too friendly with the Israelis."

II

The comment was, at least, understandable. I found my neighbors on my right invariably interesting, informative and instructive, not merely about the Middle East, as seen by Israelis, but also about international politics generally, as reflected in the United Nations. Israelis, even in those days, didn't care for the United Nations—though it was a far less hostile environment for Israelis than it was to become by the mid-seventies—but they understood how the United Nations worked, far better than anyone else did. They were a first-rate professional team—much the best in the place, not excluding the superpowers—and I liked to pick their brains, to put it at its lowest. But also there were several of them—I think of Michael Comay, Arieh Eilan, Gideon Rafael[1]—whose company as neighbors was particularly enjoyable because of their quick wit, and pungent pithy asides, when something odd came up, every now and then.

My last memory of the United Nations General Assembly is of one such occasion. It was a dark, miserable morning early in 1961, and Adlai Stevenson was addressing us, in the First Committee, at great length. What Adlai was saying did nothing to raise the spirits of delegates, especially those who—like myself—had been among his admirers. Adlai was talking about the Bay of Pigs, and about how the United States had had absolutely nothing to do with it. This was, as it had to be, a dreadful speech, full of the kind of official lies that stick out in an unappetizing fashion. Adlai himself was clearly conscious that this was not his finest hour. He tried to distance himself, as a human being, from what he had to say. He personally was noted for his fastidious choice of words, and frequent felicities. But the speech he read out consisted exclusively of great gobbets of untreated bureaucratic prose. And Adlai read this stuff as if he had never seen it before, frequently stumbling over words, as he never stumbled over words of his own.

While this performance dragged on, Gideon Rafael, in the chair beside me on my right, was doodling on his pad, his face impassive. The Caribbean is not a region of the highest priority for Israel. When the time came, Gideon would cast his vote with the United States, keeping his personal opinion about the Bay of Pigs to himself.

Adlai's peroration was even more embarrassing than the rest of his speech. "I have told you," he said, "of Castro's crimes against *man*. But there is even worse: the record of Castro's crimes against *God*."

Several delegates looked faintly sick.

"Fidel Castro has"—Adlai here turned his page and peered at the new one—"Castro has . . . *circumcised* the freedoms of the Catholics of Cuba . . ."

Gideon looked up sharply and turned to me. "I always knew," he said, "that *we* should be blamed for this, sooner or later."

It was a ray of light on that dark morning. That was the kind of thing that made it a privilege to have been, for a time, a neighbor of Israel.

III

In 1961—known to my children as "the year the bed fell on father"—I severed my connection with the United Nations and with Ireland's foreign service.[2] For the next sixteen years or so, the Middle East was not high among my preoccupations. For the first half of the sixties, I was concerned mainly with African affairs. Then after a few years of university teaching in New York, I went into politics in my own country, spending four years in parliamentary opposition and four as a member of Government. My Irish political career came to an end in 1977, and in 1978 I became editor in chief of *The Observer*, of London.

It was through *The Observer* that I had to renew, professionally, a concern with the Middle East. "Editor in chief" has a nice ring to it, but it really worked out as one of those *primus inter pares* affairs—with the *pares* not necessarily paying all that much attention to the *primus*. *The Observer* is a paper of collegiate tradition. In practice, this meant that editorial policy in relation to particular areas was largely shaped by the specialists in those areas.

As regards the Middle East, the editorial philosophy of *The Observer* at that time was quite close to the philosophy of the Brookings Institution. We believed—collectively and collegiately—in the possibility and necessity of a comprehensive settlement, by treaty, embracing both Israel and the P.L.O. We advocated such a settlement eloquently, in editorials and leader-page articles, especially at this period, toward the end of the seventies, when all Western discourse on the subject was full of the Camp David Framework for Peace, and the need to fill it in.

My trouble was that I couldn't, for the life of me, believe in such a settlement. Even with all the deference felt to be due to the expertise of the senior colleagues specializing in the region—the colleagues who had formed *The Observer*'s policies in this matter—I couldn't imagine a settlement concluded between representatives of Israel and the P.L.O., and then ratified, by both the Knesset and the people of Israel and also by a convention of the P.L.O. membership.

Nothing I remembered from my U.N. days—whether of public debate or private discussion—suggested to me that such a thing could be;[3] nor did my reading of the news from the area in the years since then convince me that such a thing had become any more likely than it would have been in those days.

However, I left the Middle East, rather uneasily, to our pundits on the subject, as long as I was editor in chief. But when I retired from that agreeable but rather hazy eminence, in 1981—while continuing to contribute to *The Observer*—I decided to go to the region and have a look for myself and form my own opinions, without undue deference to the opinions of specialists, or any deference at all to collegiate opinions. I visited the region several times from 1981 to 1984, spending most of my time in Israel itself, and in different parts of distracted Lebanon. I wrote on the subject, from time to time, for *The Observer*.

Then, around the beginning of 1982, I decided I would have to write a book. I won't say I decided to write *this* book, because what I had in mind then was rather different. It was to have been a fairly short book, of "current affairs" type. There was to have been a short prologue dealing with Zionism, before 1948, in quite a summary way.

But then, when I came to read about Zionism, I found the subject, and its leading personalities, taking a grip on me in a way I had not expected. This was partly because the story is inherently astounding, and I hope some of its power to astound comes through in my first four chapters. But there were also special reasons derived from my own religious, national and family background that made the themes of Zionism reverberate in my mind and imagination in (for me) a peculiarly poignant and haunting way.

IV

The central mystery of Zionism, it seems to me, is the relation within it of religion to nationalism, with the suspicion, within the mystery, that religion and nationalism may ultimately be two words for the same thing. The early Zionists were mostly avowed secularists, but their enterprise derived most of its power, and all of its territorial orientation, from a religious book, and the ancient longing it inspired.

For as long as I can remember, religion and nationalism have been a puzzle to me—one puzzle or two? Most Irish Catholics (I believe) have always felt their religion and their nationality to be essentially the same thing. In modern times, however—and partly in an effort to *be* modern—they have generally proclaimed the opposite: religion and nationalism entirely distinct, the Irish Nation consisting of Catholics and Protestants, without distinction. This was more a matter of theory than of feeling, and Ulster Protestants rejected even the theory, holding themselves to be alien, both by religion and by nationality, to Irish Catholics, whether of North or South. The "war" in Northern Ireland, smoldering away now for nearly fifteen years, is assuming more and more openly the character of a Holy War, with nationality and religion inseparable.

I was brought up on the fringes of the Catholic nation, and with ambivalent feelings toward it. My family background was entirely Southern Irish Roman Catholic, but my father was what would be called, in the Jewish tradition, a *maskil*. That is to say he was a person of the Enlightenment, an avowed agnostic. To the Catholic Church, however, he wasn't a person of any enlightenment whatever: he was "a lapsed Catholic," not a good thing, and I was headed that way too. Confusingly, I had been sent to a Catholic school—which I disliked—during my father's lifetime, but after my father's death, my mother, who was a believing Catholic, sent me to "a Protestant school," out of respect for my father's memory. This proved an excellent formula for producing ambivalence and alienation, conditions which—in order not to get downhearted—I like to think of as stimulating to the intelligence and to the imagination. (Also a consideration not irrelevant to the story of the Jews and of Zionism.)

Actually, the school I went to—and which I liked—was not exactly a Protestant school. It was a liberal, nondenominational school, but of mainly Protestant ethos, attended by Catholics, Protestants and Jews in approximately equal numbers. We were conscious of the differences between us, but also conscious of a bond between us, as boys whose parents chose to send us to that school, so untypical of the new and overwhelmingly Catholic State—then called the Irish Free State—in which we were being brought up. All around us was the ocean—as it seemed to us—of our contemporaries, all good Catholics going to good Catholic schools, and being indoctrinated like mad. From our tiny island of Enlightenment (Haskala), we could peer out into that possibly enviable fog. And to be at that distance from the religion was to be at a corresponding distance from the nation, not in theory, but in feeling.

As I said, these things form a certain bond. I knew, for example, that if I heard a Catholic priest or layman referring to Jews in a hostile manner, that person would be likely to be no friend, either, to our family—to my father, as a lapsed Catholic; to my mother, as a disobedient Catholic; and to myself, attending a non-Catholic school, along with Jews as well as Protestants. So a chance anti-semitic remark could be a red light to me too. That is to say, I had to possess something of the same kind of wary alertness that Jews have always had to have within a Gentile society.

•   •

V

Coming from that background, I found in Zionism much that was partly familiar. Pinsker's idea of "the stranger" was something with which I could empathize, to a certain extent. The mutations of religion and nationalism (within Zionism) were not entirely unexpected. It didn't seem altogether surprising to me that when religion and nationalism seemed to be *di*verging—as among the Zionist *maskilim* of the late-nineteenth century—they might also be *con*verging, on a different plane—as the Mizrachim realized.

There was another connection. Those who belong to the Irish Catholic people—whether holding to their Faith or not—have a certain atavistic understanding of what it means to belong to a stigmatized people. Too much should not be made of that point, and too much sometimes has been.[4] It remains true that Irish Catholics, over a period of some centuries in the early part of the modern era, have had a greater experience of persecution, oppression and stigmatization than any other people in Western Europe *except* the Jews. The position of the Irish Catholics at the nadir of their fortunes, in the first half of the eighteenth century, resembled that of the Jews shortly before their emancipation in Europe. The laws in force in the British Isles at that time "presumed no such person as an Irish Roman Catholic to exist."

Some leading Jews and Catholics in the United Kingdom of the nineteenth century were aware of the similarity of the predicaments of the two stigmatized peoples. Daniel O'Connell—the greatest, in my view, of all the leaders of the Irish Catholic people—when he had won for Catholics the right to sit in Parliament, helped and advised the leaders of the British Jews in their struggle to win the same right, which they did less than twenty years later.

VI

These connections may perhaps seem rather tenuous to some readers. I mention them—without overestimating their significance—both because they have in fact been important to me, in approaching this subject, and writing this book, and because I think it may be useful to the reader to know where the author starts out from, and what sort of baggage he carries with him.

This is the work of an outsider. An Israeli scholar to whom I showed one of the earlier chapters told me that it lacked a "true sense of the inwardness" of the Zionist experience. It certainly does lack that, and of necessity. But I was grateful for the comment, because it helped me to bring into focus what my book is about.

The Siege is not about the inwardness; it is about the outwardness. In the foreground always is the play of forces *around* the Jews, around the Zionists, and then around the Israelis: the siege, in fact. The book is not a history of Zionism and of Israel, though it is constantly concerned with that history. It is the story of a siege, and especially of the international, cultural, political and diplomatic aspects of the siege.

Above all, I have tried to tell a story, or rather to disengage from clutter what is inherently perhaps the greatest story of modern times, and to allow it to reach the reader.

I hope that something of the awe and wonder—the sense of "What hath God wrought?"—that beset me so many times as I was reading for this book, and writing it, may come through, here and there, to the reader too.

I must confess that there were moments as I worked on this book when I literally felt the hair rise on the back of my neck: when, for example, I read Vladimir Jabotinsky's letter about the "little track," or when I contemplated George Curzon bringing to birth the Jewish National Home, for the idea of which he personally entertained such a cordial detestation.

"News," a great journalist once said, "is anything that makes the reader say 'Gee whiz!'" I found myself saying the equivalent of "Gee whiz!" quite often during my work on this book. And I don't mind if I make my readers too say "Gee whiz!" occasionally.

VII

This book is not at all intended for scholars or specialists in its field, as a number of these will, no doubt, in due course confirm. *The Siege* is intended for the general reader, thought of as not necessarily knowing much more about the story than I did when I started to work on this book, which was not a great deal. I don't know whether this will be a popular book, but I hope it will be, and intend it to be.

Yet I don't want to overstress that aspect either. I was trained as a historian, and have not altogether run amok. The story I tell is a

true story, told with due respect to chronology—master of all things—
without invention, or propagandist intent, or added color: there is
color enough there, in the material, without need of addition.

What I have aimed at is what the French politely call *un ouvrage
de haute vulgarisation*. Insofar as I have had a model in mind, it is in
the writings of Edmund Wilson, and in particular *To the Finland
Station*.

VIII

This is a highly personal book, and necessarily so, through the
principle of selection involved. I put in the things and people that
seemed to me interesting and significant, in the belief that these
would also interest and instruct my reader. This meant leaving out a
lot of other things and people. For example, there were many people
who played important parts in the history of the Zionist movement
whose names do not figure in *The Siege*. But I thought I could best
tell the story of Zionism through the great archetypal figures: Herzl,
Weizmann, Jabotinsky, Ben-Gurion. And similarly with the history of
Israel itself.

I have not tried either to indict or to flatter modern Israel, or to
exhort or admonish it; there are plenty of others to do all these things.
I have just tried to tell the story of *The Siege* as best I can.

But I hope that the reader, having followed the story of *The Siege*,
may feel that he or she now has a somewhat better idea of how Israel
came to be what and where it is, and why it cannot be other than
what it is.[5]

BOOK ONE

1

THE STRANGER

The Jew is the stranger *par excellence*.
— LEON PINSKER

Anti-semitism continues to grow—and so do I.
— THEODOR HERZL

There was the boot; but there was also the longing.
— RABBI ADIN STEINSALTZ

DOES ISRAEL have a right to exist?

The State of Israel has lived since its birth—and even before its birth—under the pressure of that question. And that question was preceded by another question: Do the Jews have a right to exist?

Hardly anyone would deny, I think, that there is some connection between the two questions. Some Zionists, perhaps most Zionists—and so most Israelis—believe that the two questions are really one. Chaim Weizmann (1874–1952), the negotiator of genius who won the Balfour Declaration—and so the Jewish political foothold in Palestine—sometimes used language that seems to depict anti-Zionism and anti-semitism as one thing. "The real opponents of Zionism," Weizmann wrote in his autobiography, "can never be placated by any diplomatic formula: their objection to the Jews is that the Jews exist, and in this particular case, that they exist in Palestine."[1]

That seems too neat.[2] Weizmann himself knew better than anyone that some of the most dangerous opponents of the Zionist movement were not anti-semitic at all. They were Jews, and strongly anti-anti-semitic. As Arthur Balfour's first biographer recalls: "In England the most formidable foes of Jewish nationalism were themselves Jews."[3] These Western Jews detested Zionism, precisely because they thought Zionism made a present to the anti-semites of a devastating argument. Assimilated English Jews like the philanthropist Claude Montefiore (1858–1938) and the Liberal politician Edwin Montagu (1879–1924) passionately felt that there was no contradiction between being a good Jew and being a good nationalist of the land where you lived.

The assertion of the absence of such a contradiction was as old as the earliest emancipations of the Jews in Europe. In 1807, the Great Sanhedrin—the first since the destruction of the Temple, eighteen hundred years before—which Napoleon convened in Paris, declared Jews to be not a nation but a religion, and similar declarations, in all the countries of Western Europe, had accompanied every phase of the process of Jewish emancipation in Western Europe up to around 1870.

The anti-semites had rejected all these declarations as insincere. They had affirmed that the Jews were not just people with a distinctive religion, who could share fully in the nationality of the lands where they lived; that they were, in reality, a distinct and alien people.

"It is impossible," the German nationalist Paul de Lagarde (1827–1891) had proclaimed, "to tolerate a nation within a nation; and the Jews *are* a nation, not a community of co-religionists." Another leading German nationalist, Heinrich von Treitschke (1834–1896), warned the Jews that if Jewry were to demand the recognition of its nationality, then the lawful basis of emancipation collapses.[4] Accordingly, Jewish leaders in Europe, working for the emancipation of their people—not completed in most of Western Europe before the 1870s—asserted that a community of coreligionists, and not a nation, was what the Jews were.[5]

Now up came the Zionists with the message that the supposedly assimilated Western Jews were wrong, and the anti-semites were right: there *was* a distinct Jewish nation, with a right to a National Home in Palestine.

The wealthy English Jew Claude Montefiore—like many other successful Jews in the West—felt very much in no need of a National Home in Palestine.[6] He had, he deeply felt, a national home right where he was, in England, and he wanted no other. The Zionists were not providing him with a National Home: they were helping his enemies try to put him out of the only national home he had or wanted. In a last desperate effort to avert the coming of the Balfour Declaration, he wrote a letter to the War Cabinet in October 1917. This plea against a National Home for the Jews in Palestine included the words: "It is very significant that anti-semites are always very sympathetic to Zionism."[7]

Always? Hardly. But some anti-semites were certainly pleased about Zionism. In the early years of the National Home, G. K. Chesterton made that much clear in his book *The New Jerusalem* (1921). He and his friends, he said, had been rebuked for "an attitude" of theirs. What was that attitude? "It was always called anti-semitism," wrote Chesterton, "but it was always much more true to call it Zionism. It consisted entirely in saying that Jews are Jews; and that as a logical consequence they are not Russians or Roumanians or Frenchmen or Englishmen."[8] And again more brutally: "For if the advantage of the ideal to the Jews is to gain the promised land, the advantage to the Gentiles is to get rid of the Jewish Problem. . . ."

Exactly what Montefiore had feared. And indeed the element of truth in what he feared may have been among the reasons why he failed. There are some grounds for believing that the architects of the Balfour Declaration liked the idea of a National Home for Jews in Palestine as one means of keeping down the number of Jews in Britain. "It may as well be frankly recognized," wrote Leonard Stein, the first historian of the Balfour Declaration, "that among the most ardent gentile pro-Zionists were some who, until they came into contact with Zionism, had no particular affection for Jews."[9]

Stein includes in this category Arthur James Balfour himself. It was Balfour's Government which in 1904—more than thirteen years before the Declaration—had introduced the Aliens Bill in order to control immigration into Britain more strictly, after the wave of immigration associated with the second series of violent anti-semitic outbreaks in Russia in the early years of the century, and the imposition of conscription during the Russo-Japanese War.[10] At the end of the debate on the Second Reading, Balfour tried to separate his Government's bill from the Jewish question. He spoke of the bigotry, the oppression, the hatred the Jewish "race" has too often met with in foreign countries:

> The treatment of the race has been a disgrace to Christendom, a disgrace which tarnishes the fair fame of Christianity even at this moment, and which in the Middle Ages gave rise

to horrors which whoever makes himself acquainted with them even in the most superficial manner, reads of with shuddering and feelings of terror lest any trace of the blood-guiltiness then incurred should have fallen on the descendants of those who committed the deeds.[11]

For that cool, fastidious patrician, this was extraordinary language—emotional, fanciful, rambling and tangled, almost ungrammatical. I infer that Arthur Balfour did have strong feelings about the Jews, and that these included guilt. Only the guilt is rather unlikely to have had much to do with thoughts of what medieval Balfours may possibly have been up to in their day. It is much more likely that Balfour was expressing some feelings of revulsion at what he was up to, on that May evening of 1905 at Westminster, winding up for His Majesty's Government on the Second Reading of the Aliens Bill.

Balfour went on: "This [bill] is a question wholly alien to and distinct from the Jewish question; and it has to do with a much wider problem—the problem whether an individual country has the right to decide who is to be added to its community from outside, and under what conditions."

In short, the bill was not about Jews, it was about keeping them out. Major W. Evans Gordon, who spoke earlier in the debate, had made essentially the same point more plainly: "Our desire is not to exclude undesirable aliens because they are Jews but because they are undesirable aliens."

The whole course of the debate showed that speakers were preoccupied with Jews: the vast and poor Jewish population of Eastern Europe. The intensified persecution of those Jews, around the turn of the century, increased both Jewish emigration and resistance, in the host countries, to Jewish immigration.

There was a fear that if the persecution got worse, this population might move in very large numbers—perhaps in millions—and the Western world would be swamped with poor Jews. The British Government was concerned, in particular, about developments in America. America had absorbed most of the Jewish emigration up to that time, but by 1905 it began to seem as though America might cease to be receptive. There was pressure inside America for the introduction of effective immigration restrictions—not just against Jews—and the British Government[12] hastened to anticipate these, lest masses of desperate Jews and others turn away from closing doors in America to seek a home in Britain.

That was what Balfour's Aliens Bill was designed to stop.[13]

There was, of course, a paradox in that. The man who put the brake on Jewish immigration into Britain was also the man who twelve years later made provision for large-scale Jewish immigration into Palestine, under the "national home" provision of the Balfour Declaration.

From the point of view of an Arab of today, looking back on the history and prehistory of Israel, this may seem an odious piece of hypocrisy: the British, who themselves excluded Jews, under the guise of "undesirable aliens," deflected them instead into an Arab land, under a specious pretext of humanitarianism.

Balfour was not really a hypocrite. He was sincerely ambivalent on the Jewish question. He agreed with G. K. Chesterton on the one basic point that Jews were Jews, Englishmen were Englishmen, and Jews were not English. So he didn't want more Jews in Britain, and didn't much care for British Jews.[14] But he could like Jews who were not British, and did not claim to be British. He very much liked Dr. Weizmann, and Dr. Weizmann, who understood him very well, was able to pass on to Balfour a considerable part of his own enthusiasm for the Zionist cause.[15] For Balfour, who was somewhat anti-semitic where Britain was concerned, was philo-semitic where the world was concerned. He was an intellectual, with a strong sense of the tremendous Jewish contribution to religion and morals, philosophy, science and the arts. His niece and biographer, Blanche Dugdale, recalled: "I remember in childhood imbibing from him the idea that Christian religion and civilization owes to Judaism an immeasurable debt, shamefully repaid."[16] He didn't see a Jewish Palestine primarily as a refuge for suffering human beings. What attracted him was the idea of a Jewish Palestine as the focus for a new blaze of human creativity, a new enrichment of the culture of the world. To the romantic in him, the epic concept of the Great Return, after nearly two thousand years, had an inherent appeal.

Was he also affected by a concern cognate with the Aliens Bill, the need to find a place, other than Britain, where the Jews of Eastern Europe could go? There are some indications that he was affected in this way. He did feel guilty about the Jews, for he was conscious of the danger they were in, in Eastern Europe, and he was looking, as early as 1903, for some place where they could go, away both from Eastern Europe and from Britain. In that year, his Government had offered the Zionists land in East Africa for settlement.

The Zionists had been tempted (see Chapter 2), but eventually turned the offer down. Balfour was anxious to know why. He was still anxious to know in January 1906 and he asked to see Dr. Weizmann. This was during the General Election of that year. Balfour was running in East Manchester, and Winston Churchill in Northwest Manchester. (The elections resulted in a general Liberal landslide; Balfour lost his seat, and Churchill won a spectacular victory.) Churchill had opposed the Conservative Aliens Bill, and had become "highly acceptable to the powerful Jewish community in Manchester."[17]

Weizmann was a member of that community, and Winston's son and biographer, Randolph Churchill, lists Weizmann among Winston's leading supporters. It is not clear that that was so, but Churchill was anxious to have his support. So presumably was Balfour, especially as he needed to mend fences, after his Aliens Bill; but that motive is not incompatible, in Balfour's case, with genuine intellectual curiosity and sympathy with Zionism.

Weizmann—who, with other Russian Jews, had been primarily responsible for the Zionist rejection of the East African offer—gave Balfour, in memorable words, the reason for that rejection:

"I said [Weizmann later recalled], 'Mr. Balfour, if you were offered Paris instead of London would you take it? Would you take Paris instead of London?' He looked surprised. He: 'But London is our own!' I said: 'Jerusalem was our own when London was a marsh.'"[18]

Balfour was profoundly impressed. The seed of the Balfour Declaration had been sown.[19]

Balfour knew that Palestine was already inhabited, although he does not seem to have referred to the Arab question specifically until 1920, by which time Arab resistance to the National Home policy had become abundantly clear. In a speech to a Jewish audience in London, in July 1920, he expressed the hope that the Arabs—"a great, an interesting, an attractive race"—will remember "that it was the British who freed them from Turkish tyranny" and that "remembering that they will not grudge that small notch in what are now Arab territories being given to the people who for all these hundreds of years have been separated from it."[20]

Balfour must have known that those to whom that advice was (rhetorically) offered would have been most unlikely to accept it, but he would have been philosophical about that. Balfour had governed Ireland, quite sternly, as a Tory Chief Secretary in 1887, just after the defeat of Gladstone's first Home Rule Bill, and an Irishman complained to Balfour that his policies constituted a denial of justice for the Irish people.

"Justice?" said Balfour thoughtfully. "There isn't enough to go round."

And indeed there wasn't enough to go round, for both Jews and Arabs, or for either of them.

II

Anti-semitism and anti-Zionism are not to be equated. But it is clear, as a matter of history, that it was anti-semitism in Europe that turned Zionism into a political force, preparing the ground for the emergence of the State of Israel.

"The story of Israel in the Middle East," as a contemporary writer has said, "stems directly from the history of Israel in Europe."[21]

Before 1880 the Jewish population in Palestine was less than 25,000 people, two-thirds of whom were in Jerusalem, where they made up half the population (and from about 1890 on, more than half the population). These were, in general, people without political ambitions or interests: pious Jews who wanted to die in Jerusalem. These Jews were supported by the alms—*halukkah*—of other pious Jews, in the Diaspora, some of whom looked forward to a similar journey, and to a similar death. To the Arabs, the Jews of Palestine were known in those days as "children of death." But after 1881, other Jews began to arrive in Palestine, not in order to die there, but in order to live. This was the movement of population known as the first Zionist *aliyah*, the first Zionist ascent to the Land of Israel.[22]

The first *aliyah* arose in consequence of the resurgence of anti-semitic persecution, with official backing, in the Russian Empire, following the assassination of Tsar Alexander II, on March 1, 1881 (O.S.).[23] This return of persecution directly affected most of the world's Jews, since most of them—more than five million—lived at this time in the Pale of Settlement, on the western fringes of the Russian Empire, between the Baltic and the Black seas. Many of these Jews seem to have reached these regions in the centuries after the original dispersion following persecution in the newly Christianized Roman Empire.[24] "The Jewish population in all these regions," writes Salo Baron, "increased considerably after each of the recurrent Byzantine persecutions and particularly after the total outlawry of Judaism, promulgated in each of the four centuries between the seventh and the tenth."[25]

With the Christianization of the regions where Jews had taken refuge, Christian anti-semitism caught up with the Jews, and fluctuated in intensity over the centuries. By the beginning of the nineteenth century, Enlightenment ideas were starting to affect Russian official attitudes and practices, also in a fluctuating manner. Gavriil Romanovich Derzhavin (1743–1816), who had been Catherine the Great's court poet, and who was to be Alexander I's Minister of Justice, surveyed the Jewish situation in the western provinces for Tsar Paul (reigned 1796–1801).

"Since Providence, for the realization of some unknown purpose," wrote Derzhavin, "has left this dangerous people on the face of the world and has not destroyed it, the government under whose rule it lives ought to tolerate it. It is also their duty to take care of them in such a manner that the Jews be useful to themselves and to society at large in whose midst they live."

The Empire's first fundamental law regarding Jews, Alexander I's decree of November 9, 1804, was liberal and assimilatory (in a secular way) in its general tendency, although cautious in practice. It opened all schools up to university level to Jews, and stipulated that Jewish students were to be safeguarded against any violation of their faith.

The liberal momentum was not, however, sustained, even under Alexander I (reigned 1801–1825). The Jews suffered from the Russian patriotic reaction to the Napoleonic Wars. Even as early as 1807, a little more than a year after Russia's defeat at Austerlitz (December 1805), the Holy Synod—shrewdly, from its point of view—was turning Russian nationalism to Orthodox ends, by playing up Napoleon's philo-semitism. As the Holy Synod proclaimed:

> To the greater shame of the Church he assembled in France Jewish synagogues, ordered to pay honour to the rabbis, and re-established the great Jewish Synedrion [Sanhedrin], that same godless congregation which once dared to condemn to crucifixion our Lord and saviour Jesus Christ. He [Napoleon, not Jesus] now attempts to unite the Jews scattered by divine wrath over the whole world and to lead them to the overthrow of Christ's Church and to (O horrible impudence overstepping all his wickedness!) the proclamation of a false messiah in the person of Napoleon.[26]

The Jews, who had suffered for so long as enemies of Christ, were now beginning also to be cast in what was to prove an even more dangerous role: enemies of the nation. Yet most of the Jews of the

Pale, far from rallying to Napoleon in the War of 1812, helped the Russian Army for religious reasons. As a leading Hasidic rabbi said at the time, "If Napoleon should be victorious, the Jews would become richer and their [civic] situation will advance, but their hearts will drift away from Father in heaven. But if our Tsar Alexander were to triumph, Jewish hearts would draw nearer to our Father in heaven, although Jews would become poorer and their status lower."[27] The latter was what happened.

The effect of the Napoleonic invasion, and its debacle, was to weaken the liberal, Westernizing forces in the Russian ruling class, and to strengthen the patriots and the Orthodox, the enemies of the Jews. The slogan of the next tsar, Nicholas I (reigned 1825–1855), was "Orthodoxy, Autocracy and Nationality." He disliked the Jews, "Zhids . . . leeches," "the ruin of the Western provinces." His dislike, however, was mitigated by a memory, which he noted in his diary: "Surprisingly . . . in 1812 they were very loyal to us and assisted us in every possible way even at the risk of their own lives."

Possibly mindful of that loyalty, Nicholas removed, in 1828, the old exemption of the Jews from military service. Differently handled, this might have been a measure of liberalization. As applied by Nicholas, however, this *Rekrutchina* was an instrument of suffering and death, especially for children of the Jewish poor. Jews could be conscripted, legally, as early as twelve years of age, and in practice often as early as eight or nine, for twenty-five years of military service. Conscription was used for the purpose of forced conversion of the children, many of whom submitted to baptism in order to live; some committed suicide.

Alexander Herzen's haunting picture of a group of child conscripts whom he saw in Vyattka province is well known:

> Pale, worn out, with frightened faces, they stood in thick, clumsy soldier's overcoats, with stand-up collars, fixing helpless, pitiful eyes on the garrison soldiers, who were roughly getting them into ranks. The white lips, the blue rings under the eyes looked like fever or chill. And these sick children, without care or kindness, exposed to the icy wind that blows from the Arctic Ocean, were going to their graves . . . boys of twelve or thirteen might somehow have survived, but little fellows of eight or ten . . . No painting could reproduce the horror of that scene.[28]

Yet the policies of Nicholas I, cruel though they were, were not yet those of "stimulated exodus," as became the case under Alexander

III; that genocide could be the solution had not yet occurred to anyone. Nicholas aimed at the assimilation of the Jews, through making them Russian Orthodox Christians, and Russian-speaking. In the case of the conscripts he attained this object by force. In the case of others—the great majority—he pursued it by guile, through educational policies whose veneer of liberalism attracted some liberal Jews; after all, assimilation was what they wanted, and they were being offered it, in a way. Most Russian Jews, however, saw Nicholas's policy as one of Christianization, parallel with the conscription measures, and refused it accordingly. Under Nicholas's iron rule, there was no question of mass pogroms, Government-tolerated or Government-inspired. That was to come later. Under Nicholas, the peasants, as well as the Jews, were kept in order.

The accession of Alexander II (reigned 1855–1881) brought some relief to the Jews. Nicholas's conscription policy was replaced with the submission of all, including Jews, to general draft laws. Nicholas's conversionist policies were relaxed, and various petty restrictions were removed. The fruits of Alexander II's liberalism, as far as the Jews were concerned, were very meager indeed.[29] Still, the general tone and tenor of Alexander II's reign, at least in its early years, encouraged educated Jews to hope that the setback under Nicholas I had been an aberration; that the norm for the nineteenth, and especially the twentieth, century would be in Russia what it seemed to have been in the West. Liberalism would win out in Russia as elsewhere. Everywhere in Europe, Jews would be citizens, equal before the law with other citizens, and equally protected by the laws.

To all such hope, the accession of Alexander III (reigned 1881–1894) dealt a savage blow. The pogrom was back on a scale not known since the mid-seventeenth century.[30] The authorities condoned it, may have encouraged it, certainly did nothing to stop it, and it became horrifyingly apparent that what most united the Russian people—peasant, middle class and Tsar—was a hatred of Jews.

The assassination of Alexander II is one of the great turning points in world history, and especially in the history of the Jews. It is the moment in which the notion of the inevitable and universal triumph of liberal ideas receives its first great setback. That notion had dominated the thinking and expectations of most educated middle-class people throughout the nineteenth century. It drew strength also from the intoxicating notion of *progress*, the fixed idea that the passage of time and the spread of liberal ideas were inherently identical. And it drew strength from the overwhelming nature of past successes, the

English Revolution, the American Revolution, the French Revolution. Liberal, secular, universalist ideas were unstoppable; their victory everywhere was only a question of time; the only important questions concerned the social and political forms which that victory would take.

Western Jews had benefited enormously, up to the late nineteenth century, from the spread of Enlightenment ideas and from their political, social and legal consequences. By 1871, Jewish emancipation in most Western countries was an accomplished fact, for most practical purposes. Western Jews were now citizens, with the same rights (or almost the same rights) as other citizens; they were no longer in a special stigmatized category, as Jews had been in all the centuries before the great revolutions, and as Jews still were in Eastern Europe. Western Jews were acutely conscious that anti-semitism was still an important social force, even in the West, but the whole spirit of the age encouraged their natural wish to believe that anti-semitism was vestigial. It would inevitably fade away, along with the whole bad dream of the past of the Jews in Europe.

In Eastern Europe, of course, that past still lingered, and Jews were still treated largely as they had been in medieval Europe. But educated people in the East, including educated[31] Jews, were powerfully affected and often dominated by Western ideas associated with the vast prestige of Western success. Within that system of ideas Russia was "backward." That was a powerful word, charged with the notion of linear progress.

Russia would have to catch up, and then it would be exactly like the Western countries, and Russian Jews would be Russian citizens, living securely under the rule of law. So educated Russian Jews had tended to believe in the seventies and eighties, before the assassination of Alexander II.

III

The new reign began with a series of pogroms. The first large pogrom occurred at Elizavetgrad (now Kirovo) at Easter, in April 1881. After that, all the major Jewish communities in the Russian Empire, and a great many minor ones, came under attack. By the end of 1881, pogroms had hit 215 Jewish communities in southern and southwestern Russia, where most Jews lived.

A contemporary estimate put the numbers of homeless at 20,000, those ruined economically at 100,000, the value of property destroyed at $80 million.[32] Not many Jews were killed—though some usually were in the course of each pogrom. The general pattern was one of looting, on a huge scale, arson, drunken brutality, rape and physical injury, pushed in relatively few cases to the length of murder.

Alexander III and his principal adviser, Konstantin Petrovitch Pobedonostsev, were not, or at least did not admit that they were, in favor of instigating pogroms. Some of those around them were, and did so, and local officials who encouraged pogroms went unpunished. But the peasants didn't really need instigation. They only needed to know what they could get away with, and that they did know. The general pattern—from 1881 to 1884, and again in the early years of the twentieth century—was to let the peasants have their fling, and then use the Cossacks to disperse them when they had gone far enough. Some of the Jew beaters—the *pogromshchiki*—could then be tried, and some of them even punished. The Tsar and his advisers were conscious of public opinion in the West, and needed to show that Russia too was a civilized and modern country.[33] But the trials of the *pogromshchiki* generally turned into trials of the Jews. The Jews, so the ostensible prosecutors of the *pogromshchiki* would say, were the people who were really guilty of all the disorders, since their exploitation had given the peasants unbearable provocation. And of course some Jews—shopkeepers, tavern keepers and moneylenders—*had* exploited the peasants.

But others—including the class to which the prosecutors belonged—also exploited the peasants. Prosecutors, peasants and the Jews themselves all knew that the Jews belonged in a special category. Of all the people whom the peasants had a grudge against, or fancied robbing, the Jews were the only ones they could attack and rob and get away with it. Any offense against a landowner, or an official, or even an Orthodox shopkeeper or rich peasant would bring savage punishment.

These were mild manifestations of anti-semitic opinion, by twentieth-century standards. By nineteenth-century standards, they were extraordinary and shocking. All sorts of public people in the West denounced the outrages. But for all Jews—not just Jews in Russia—the phenomenon that declared itself in that spring of 1881 was not just shocking. It was terrifying, in an intimate and existential way, as the diagnosis of a grave and possibly terminal disease is to an individual.

That disease—of which the actual pogroms were merely the ugliest and most distressing surface symptoms—was modern aggressive anti-semitism. In its Russian form, which was to remain the most virulent until the end of the First World War, the disease had three main aspects, all of which were to have an important bearing on the emergence of Zionism, the Balfour Declaration and the creation of the State of Israel.

The first of these aspects consisted in the normality of the new anti-semitic regime combined with the centrality of its anti-semitic policy. This was no passing whim of some mad despot. Alexander III was a big, stolid, rather folksy man, a Mr. Average Russian who would fit quite well into the Politburo today. Nor was there anything crazily fanatical about Alexander's principal adviser, and mentor in this matter, Konstantin Petrovitch Pobedonostsev (1827–1907), Ober-Procurator (Director-General) of the Most Holy Synod, tutor to both Alexander III and Nicholas II, and creator of what became under his influence the governing ideology of the Russian Empire.

Pobedonostsev was an intellectual, the most distinguished Russian jurist of his day, and author of a vast number of learned works. He was pompous and priggish, but formidably competent, and he achieved a complete ascendancy over the Tsar and the Russian Church.

Pobedonostsev derived his ideas from the French counterrevolutionary thinker Joseph de Maistre (1753–1821) and applied them to Russian conditions. For both Pobedonostsev and Alexander III, the great enemy was liberalism, and the principal carriers of liberalism were the Jews. Liberalism, for more than two hundred years, had been challenging traditional authority, in Church and State, with revolutionary consequences, experienced in France, and feared in Russia. Liberalism's progress in the West had first undermined the social authority of the Catholic Church and had then gone on to destroy the ancien régime. Liberalism had infected even Russia. The first contagion had come with Catherine the Great; it had spread more widely under Alexander I; Nicholas I had given it a temporary check, but even he had paid at least lip service to it. Finally, liberalism had reached epidemic proportions in the reign of Alexander II, where it had opened the way to all kinds of revolutionary and terrorist activity, and eventually cost the life of the Tsar himself. If Holy Russia was to be saved—a purpose to which Pobedonostsev had long ago dedicated his whole life—then the liberal rot in Russia would have to be stopped, and in order to stop it, the first thing necessary was to stop the insidious progress of the Jews, the progress behind all liberal progress, in Pobedonostsev's opinion.

The reasons for that, Pobedonostsev set out very clearly on August 14, 1879, in a letter to Dostoevski—yes, *that* Dostoevski.[34]

> What you write about the Yids [Zhidi] is extremely just. The Jews have engrossed everything [wrote Pobedonostsev], they have undermined everything, but the spirit of the century supports them. They are at the root of the revolutionary socialist movement and of regicide, they own the periodical press, they have in their hands the financial markets, the people as a whole fall into financial slavery to them; they even control the principles of contemporary science and strive to place it outside Christianity.[35]

It is customary to acquit Pobedonostsev of any personal responsibility for the pogroms. His biographer says that he was "resolutely opposed to pogroms and popular violence."[36] He was certainly concerned about what would now be called Russia's "image" in the West, and he was afraid that some of his colleagues were going too far, too obviously. He also, however, took pains to disseminate, and advertise, in Church and Synod publications, writings accepting the medieval "ritual murder" legend.[37] It must be assumed that the Orthodox clergy knew, through him—the designated representative of the head of their Church, the Tsar—that preaching in this vein had the approval of the Tsar. Not a very effective way of opposing pogroms.

It has been alleged—and widely repeated—that Pobedonostsev said that the Jewish problem was to be solved by the conversion of one-third of the Jews to Orthodoxy; the emigration of one-third; and the deaths of the remaining third.[38]

It is highly unlikely, given the man's circumspect character, and concern for Western opinion, that he ever said anything of the kind, nor do I believe that he even intended anything as drastic. It is probable that what he intended was what occurred: the intimidation of most Jews, the emigration of a great many, and the deaths of a few.

Anti-semitism was now the settled official policy, controlling the whole human environment in which the Jews of Russia had to live. In the early eighties, that must have seemed to most people less important than the brute fact of the pogroms. But the pogroms stopped in 1884, not to resume during the nineteenth century. Anti-semitism, however, as a central factor in official policy, continued throughout the century, and into the next one. There was nothing dramatic about it, for the most part. It manifested itself in such steps as the progressive reduction in the quota of Jews to be accepted for higher education. But it had a very clear meaning. The assumption by many Jews that emancipation must inevitably come in the East, however slowly, just as it had come in the West, no longer held. What was happening was not slow emancipation. It was slow *de*-emancipation.

As a modern historian of Zionism, David Vital, has written:

> So far as the general approach of the Russian Government towards the Jews was concerned, it was soon evident that policy . . . was now in the process of being reformulated in much harsher terms than had ever been conceived and pronounced upon in Russia since the first partition of Poland. And it was perhaps this intensification and consolidation of the overtly anti-semitic character of Russian policy on the Jews and the particular terms in which it was to be publicly rationalized and proclaimed, rather than the material brutalities inflicted by the Russian mob, that at first bewildered the Jews, and then horrified them, and finally caused vast numbers of them actively to seek a decisive remedy.[39]

The normality and centrality now acquired by anti-semitism constitute—in terms of our analysis—the first aspect of the new phenomenon. The second aspect was the overwhelming popularity of anti-semitism. The cautious liberalizations of former tsars had not been popular—which is why they were cautious—but the new line went down very well. Its popularity among the peasants—the great bulk of the population—was obvious, but it was also popular with the ruling classes generally. In Russian terms, it was sound Machiavellian policy, tending to unite all classes in what was otherwise a deeply divided society.

Hindsight tends to make us look at the anti-semitic policies of Alexander III (and after him, Nicholas II) as an aberration, the last, desperate expedient of a doomed regime. But it wasn't like that. What doomed the regime was not the unpopularity of its domestic policies. What doomed it was what has doomed so many regimes: military incompetence. Under Nicholas II, the regime failed in two wars— 1904–1905 and 1914–1917. It tottered under the first failure and collapsed altogether because of the second. Before the military failures, the people never rejected the anti-liberal and anti-semitic domestic policies of the regime. The course adopted by Alexander III in 1881 was popular and successful, in its own terms, including, and especially, its anti-semitism.

The third significant aspect of the new phenomenon was its general acceptability in the West. True, there was public outcry in the West about the actual pogroms, and about obvious official complicity in these. This may have contributed to the temporary cessation of the pogroms in 1884. But the anti-semitic system—what Vital has called "the constriction of the Jews by administrative and police measures"— pursued relentlessly from 1882 on, did not arouse any significant revulsion in the West. In France, Alexander was feted and courted. French money financed Russia's industrial revolution. In 1893, Alexander concluded the military alliance with France that was to seal (as it happened) the doom of his successor, and his dynasty.

Anyone inclined to meditate on Western rejection of anti-semitism, how deep it goes, and does not go, might give a thought to the architecture of the city of Paris. In Paris, there stands a splendid monument to the greatest persecutor of the Jews in modern times, up to the advent of Adolf Hitler. The most exuberantly triumphal of the many notable bridges that span the Seine is the Pont Alexandre III.[40]

IV

Russian Jews, contemplating the dreadful turn their history had taken from March 1881, had only one basic choice: to stay and endure, with little hope for the future, or to go.

Tragically, the great majority of Jews chose to stay and endure. They were inured to suffering and accepted persecution as their ancestors had done in so many lands over countless generations as an aspect of the will of God.

A fairly large number of Jews, however, did not resign themselves to what now looked like a hopeless future in Russia. Russian-Jewish emigration to the United States—which was where most of those who left Russia wanted to go—had been rising even before 1881. In the period 1871 to 1880 it was over 40,000; in the 1880s it rose to 135,000; in the 1890s, to 279,811; and to 704,245 in the first decade of the twentieth century.[41] It continued at a high rate after 1910 until the outbreak of the First World War made emigration from Eastern Europe almost impossible.

There were other Jews—a very small but significant minority— who wanted to leave Russia, but were not content to settle, yet once more, in someone else's country. These men conceived the astonishing design of leaving in order to create a country for Jews.

These people were a minority of a minority—Jews with a secular education—those who knew Russian. The educated, to a greater extent than the majority of Jews, were thrown into near despair by the new turn. The hope of their lives had been the thought that Russia was evolving, however slowly, into a society of liberal character, in which Jews would have equal rights, and play a full part in Russian society. It was for that that their education had been seen as a preparation. But suddenly, from March 1881, they came under notice that they had to abandon that hope. Things were not going to get better, even very slowly, for the Jews of Russia. Things were going to get worse; slowly over a long period, and horribly fast at certain times.

For those Jews of the Russian Empire who had been assimilationists up to 1881, there were only three courses that held any promise after 1881. The first course, favored by many of these Jews, was to go to a Western country, in the hope of being assimilated there. The second course, also favored by many, was to stay in Russia and work for the Revolution, expected to solve the Jewish problem, along with all other problems. The third course, Zionism, was favored only by a fairly small minority, even within the minority of Jews who had had a Western education. There were already Russian Zionists before 1881—Eliezer Ben Yehuda (1858–1922), for example—who had decided before that date to go to Palestine with the object of making modern Hebrew the vernacular there and initiating the renascence of Israel on its ancestral soil. But it was not until 1881 that sufficient support for Zionism emerged to make possible an organized movement. Small but determined groups of Jewish students began to meet, after March 1881, in Moscow, St. Petersburg, Kharkov and other cities to discuss Zionism. That they should be meeting at all was significant. Before March 1881, Jewish students would not have wanted to meet in a way that suggested consciousness of their own distinct identity within the general student population. But from the spring of 1881 on, that kind of consideration was no longer important, as far as Western-educated Jews living in the Russian Empire were concerned. They didn't have to worry anymore about their future in Imperial Russia. There was no such future for them.

It was out of these meetings that the movement grew that was known as Hovevei Zion: the Lovers of Zion. A witness of one of these meetings, in Moscow, later described it:

The meeting, which was in secret of course, because of the police, was held in a fairly large hall on Karetnyi Row. It

was very crowded. The throats of the speakers were sore from
excess of talk and excess of smoke. The discussion was very
stormy and went on for four to five hours. Students of several
schools of higher education participated, among them a few
women. All the discussions were in Russian, of course. We
two, as mere gymnasium students, had not the right to join
in. We stood near the doorway and listened. The meeting
was presided over by a medical student called Rappaport
who later served as a doctor in Nikolaev for many years.
Those participating in the discussion were solely concerned
with the choice of the country of migration; there was no debate on whether or not Russia should be left for some other
country in which an independent state would be established;
it was not an issue. The meeting did not vote on a clear-cut
resolution. But by the time we left the hall we ourselves were
already enthusiastic *Hovevei Zion* and had already formed
the simple and absolute decision to found a society of young
people who would go to Eretz-Israel[42] and settle there.[43]

Hovevei Zion did not publicly proclaim a political objective.[44]
To do so would have antagonized the Ottoman authorities, to whom
Palestine belonged, and thus would endanger the settlement. Even
greater dangers could arise should a political purpose come to the
notice of the Russian authorities. If the Tsar's Government had come
to believe in the existence of a Jewish plot to gain control of the Holy
Places, and if the Government had disclosed that idea to the peasants,
no Jew's life would be safe anywhere in Russia. Hovevei Zion hoped
that its migrations would look, to the authorities, both in Constantinople and in St. Petersburg, much the same as earlier migrations of
religious Jews to Palestine.

There is no doubt, however, that the full objective of political
Zionism—a Jewish State in Eretz Israel—was already gripping the
minds of a number of participants in Hovevei Zion. Very early in the
first *aliyah*, in November 1882, Ze'ev Dubnov (1858–1940?), a member of Bilu—a group which differed from other Hovevei Zion groups
in that its members personally pledged themselves to emigrate to
Palestine—wrote from Palestine to his brother, Simon, the historian
(1860–1941), as follows:

My final purpose is to take possession in due course of Palestine and to restore to the Jews the political independence of
which they have now been deprived for 2,000 years. Don't
laugh, it is not a mirage. The means to achieve this purpose

could be the establishment of colonies of farmers in Palestine, the establishment of various kinds of workshops and industry and their gradual expansion—in a word, to seek to put all the land, all the industry, in the hands of the Jews. Furthermore, it will be necessary to teach the young people, and the future young generations, the use of arms (in free and wild Turkey everything can be done) . . . Then there will come that splendid day whose advent was prophesized by Isaiah in his fiery and poetic words of consolation. Then the Jews, if necessary with arms in their hands, will publicly proclaim themselves master of their own, ancient fatherland. It does not matter if that splendid day will only come in fifty years' time or more. A period of fifty years is no more than a moment of time for such an undertaking.[45]

It took sixty-six years for Dubnov's amazing prophecy to be fulfilled.

The idea of the Jewish State was itself, even then, not altogether novel. Twenty years before, Moses Hess[46] (1812–1875), a German Jew and Socialist comrade of Karl Marx (who sneered at him for his sentimentalism), wrote a book called *Rome and Jerusalem* (1862). In that book, Hess proposed that Jews should follow the example of the Italians and set up their own state: "As Rome is being reawakened by the Risorgimento, so Jerusalem too will awake." Hess had no doubt at all where he stood: "Jews are not a religious group, but a separate nation, a special race, and the modern Jew who denies this is not only an apostate, a religious renegade, but a traitor to his people, his tribe, his race."

Hess, a man of extraordinarily deep insight (though not given to understatement), clearly understood that it was not true, as most Jews then comfortably assumed, that anti-semitism was on the wane. The diffusion of Enlightenment ideas, and the weakening of religious faith, did not involve the gradual disappearance of anti-semitism. It simply meant that anti-semitism was taking a new form,[47] a "scientific" form in tune with the spirit of the age: racism. Hess put the whole thing in a nutshell: "The Germans hate the peculiar faith of the Jews less than they hate their peculiar noses."

It sounds funny, the way Hess put it, but it was not funny at all. The distinctive characteristic of the new anti-semitism was its inescapable and implacable character. A Jew could escape the old anti-semitism (though never totally) by changing his religion, but there was no escape from the new one. As a historian of Zionism, Walter

Laqueur, has said: "The new anti-semitism meant the end of assimilation, the total rejection of the Jews. For racial characteristics, according
to the new doctrine, were unchangeable: a change of religion did not
make a Jew into a German, any more than a dog could transform itself into a cat."[48]

The truth that Moses Hess had seen, the growth whose malignancy
he had diagnosed, was to destroy, eighty years later, almost all the
Jews of Europe.[49]

V

For German Jews in the 1860s the Hess message was utterly unacceptable, and must have sounded crazy. Things had never been as
good for German Jews as they were in the 1860s and they were
confident about the future. Anti-semitism was still present in the society, but it was easy to assume that it was a vestigial anti-semitism.
Most German Jews did not feel in the least like leaving their comfortable, interesting and civilized places of residence, especially not
in order to go and try to scratch a miserable living as farmers in the
dry and rocky soil of Palestine, with barbarous neighbors, living under
a decrepit and benighted despotism. Moses Hess went unheeded.

The predicament that educated Russian Jews found themselves
in twenty years later, from March 1881 on, was such that the general
drift of the message that Moses Hess had tried in vain to deliver became intelligible to many Jews, and attractive to some. But the Russian
Jews had to reinvent Hess's message, and formulate it in their own
terms. The men who did most to formulate it, the men who founded
Zionism, as a doctrine with followers and practitioners, were Moshe
Leib Lilienblum (1843–1910), Leon ("Yehuda Leib") Pinsker (1821–
1891) and Peretz Smolenskin (1842–1885).[50]

Pinsker, by both background and inclination, had been an assimilationist. He was from Odessa, the most secular and cosmopolitan of
Russian cities. His father, and he himself, belonged to the Haskala
tradition—whose followers were known as the *maskilim*—the Jewish
expression of the European Enlightenment. Leon Pinsker, as Vital says,
was "in every way a striking exemplar of all that the Russifying wing
of *Haskala* Judaism wished for at a time [the early years of Alexander
II's reign] when its ambitions for all the Jews were greatest and its
hopes highest and seemingly most reasonable."[51] Pinsker wanted Rus-

sian Jews to learn Russian—most of them spoke only Yiddish—as the first step on the road to full integration. He helped to found the first Russian-language Jewish journal.

To understand the life and hopes of people like Pinsker, one has to keep in mind that nineteenth-century Russia was, in some of its aspects, extremely attractive. The attraction of the Russian language and of Russian literature was powerful. This was the Golden Age of Russian literature, and a time of feverish mental and imaginative activity in the great Russian cities. It was natural for people like Pinsker to feel that Jews should be playing a full part in all that, and moving in the mainstream of Russian creativity.

From March 1881 on, however, it became clear that Jews were not going to be allowed into that mainstream. True, some of the leading Russian intellectuals—the kind of people whose activity attracted Pinsker and his followers—did protest against the new anti-semitic trend. The poet and philosopher Vladimir Sergeevich Soloviev (1853–1900) drew up a petition to Alexander III which carried one hundred distinguished signatures, including that of Tolstoy.[52] The petition did honor to its signatories, but it did no good for the Jews. To Pobedonostsev, the petition could only come as confirmation of his suspicions. Liberal intellectuals were sympathetic to the Jews because Jews were carriers of liberalism, which aimed at the ruin of Holy Russia. The Government ignored the contents of the petition and suppressed its publication.

After March 1881, Pinsker altogether renounced his former hopes. In September 1882 he published his great manifesto, *Autoemancipation!*, one of the seminal documents of Zionism. It is written in German, addressed to Western Jews and signed simply, "a Russian Jew." Pinsker's message to the Westerners is that their hopes, following emancipation, of being fully integrated into various European nation-states rest on an illusion. Jews will always remain strangers in these societies. Strangers are not much liked anywhere and: "The Jew is the stranger *par excellence.*" But other strangers have homes to go back to. The Jew has no home of his own and, because of this, is an object of peculiar aversion in other people's homes. Jews must realize that that aversion is permanent.

> With unbiased eyes and without prejudice we must see in the mirror of the nations the tragicomic figure of our people which, with distorted countenance and maimed limbs, helps to make universal history without managing properly its own

little history. We must reconcile ourselves once and for all to the idea that the other nations, by reason of their inherent natural antagonism, will forever reject us. We must not shut our eyes to this natural force which works like every other elemental force; we must take it into account. We must not complain of it; on the contrary, we are duty-bound to take courage, to rise, and to see to it that we do not remain forever the foundling of the nations and their butt.[53]

For Pinsker, the Jews in the Diaspora form the ghost of a nation that has died and cannot find a home, and wanders and frightens everyone.

Pinsker's solution is that Jews must acquire a territorial base somewhere, and on it set up their own nation-state. He appealed therefore to Western Jews to take the lead in convening a national congress of Jews, which would set up a directorate to make the financial and other arrangements necessary to bring the Jewish nation-state into being.

Western Jews of the time paid little or no attention to Pinsker, just as they had paid little or no attention to Moses Hess in his time; and for the same reasons. The manifesto addressed to the Western Jews found its main audience among Russian Jews. Among these, it was widely discussed and played a considerable part in the general ferment of Zionist ideas in the Russia of the eighties.

But in terms of what was to become Zionism, Pinsker's manifesto suffered from a huge defect; it did not clearly point to Eretz Israel as the land where the Jewish nation-state must be built. This defect was made good by Moshe Lilienblum and Peretz Smolenskin.

Significantly, both Lilienblum and Smolenskin, unlike Pinsker, had been brought up in an atmosphere of strict religious orthodoxy. Lilienblum, born at Kaidan, in Lithuania, was known as a scholar in terms of the traditional learning. But he had broken with that tradition and moved toward the Haskala and assimilation, the position in which Pinsker had found himself from the start. Lilienblum also moved to Odessa. After March 1881, his mind began to turn in the same direction as Pinsker's. Jews were strangers in the nation-homes of others and must find a place where they would be citizens and masters of the land themselves. Lilienblum knew that land was Eretz Israel, "to which we have a historic right, which was not lost along with rule of the country."[54] Both Orthodox Jews and secular Jews should make common cause and create again in Eretz Israel a Jewish State.

Smolenskin has been described as "one of the archetypal members of that generation whose hopes were kindled and then extinguished after 1881."[55] Born, like Lilienblum, in the Pale of Settlement, Smolenskin had been a student at the yeshiva (center for Talmudic studies) at Shklovi, in Lithuania. He too moved to Odessa, then to Vienna. In a series of Hebrew essays published from 1875 to 1877, under the title "It Is Time to Plant," Smolenskin had argued that the Jews were a nation only in the spiritual sense:

> In practical reality every Jew is a citizen of the land in which he dwells, who accepts all the obligations of citizenship like all other nationals of the country. The land in which we dwell is our country. We once had a land of our own, but it was not the tie that united us. But Torah [the spiritual core of Judaism] is our native land which makes us a people, a nation only in the spiritual sense, but in the normal business of life, we are like all other men.

All that was changed in 1881. Those who had tried to be "like all other men" fell victim to the pogroms, just as the Orthodox Jews did, and were the *main* victims of the new official policies of exclusion. In a new essay, "Let Us Search for Ways" (1881), Smolenskin now argued in favor of collective emigration, based on national solidarity. And: "If the wave of emigration is to direct itself to one place, surely no other country in the world is conceivable except Eretz-Israel." Smolenskin gave as the first reason for that choice its appeal to "those who cherish the memories of their ancestors."

VI

This linkage of secular and Orthodox Jews was a crucial factor in the development of Zionism. Zionism as a political program took off among the *maskilim*, but it derived its vital force and its orientation toward Palestine from the religious life of the Orthodox Jewish population of the *shtetl*,[56] the typical Jewish village or small town of the Pale of Settlement, in which most Jews lived. The state of mind of the *shtetl*, in relation to Palestine, is brilliantly expounded by Maurice Samuel:

> Half of the time the *Shtetl* just wasn't there: it was in the Holy Land, and it was in the remote past or the remote future, in the company of the Patriarchs and Prophets or of the Messiah. Its festivals were geared to the Palestinian climate and

calendar; it celebrated regularly the harvests its forefathers
had gathered in a hundred generations ago; it prayed for the
Zoreh and Malkosh, the subtropical [early and late] rains,
indifferent to the needs of its neighbors, whose prayers had a
practical, local schedule in view.[57]

The two great leaders who brought Zionism to fruition in the
twentieth century were both born in such a nineteenth-century *shtetl:*
Chaim Weizmann at Motol, in western Russia, near the Polish border,
in 1874, and David Ben-Gurion at Plonsk, in Russian Poland, not far
from Warsaw, in 1886.

As Weizmann recalls his childhood (in *Trial and Error*):

We were strangers to their ways of thought [those of the non-
Jewish neighbors], to each other's dreams, religions, festivals,
even languages. There were times when the non-Jewish world
was practically excluded from our consciousness, as on the
Sabbath and, still more, in the spring and autumn festivals.
My father was not a Zionist, but the house was steeped in
rich, Jewish tradition, and Palestine was at the center of the
ritual . . . the return was in the air, a vague deep-rooted
Messianism, a hope which would not die.

Yet, Zionism as a practical program—distinct from a hope—never
took a grip on the masses of the *shtetl* population. Partly, this was due
to habit, especially the Jewish habit of resignation, together with the
relatively low appeal of Palestine for the practically minded. Partly, it
was due to the discouraging attitude toward Zionism of most rabbis,
fearing the ravages of false Messianism. But also the Russian Zionists
themselves—as distinct from the later, Western Zionist leadership—
were not trying to precipitate immediate mass migration, which would
have ended in disaster. What they looked for initially was the migration of an elite, to prepare the way for later migration of large numbers.

Such an elite could be drawn only from the ranks of the *maskilim,*
those who had been working away from Orthodox Judaism and toward
assimilation. For some of these, Zionism came as a bold and dazzling
solution to a problem that had become heartbreakingly baffling: how
to adapt to the modern world without ceasing to be a Jew. The
maskilim who chose Zionism were reintegrating their personalities, an
aspect on which the German Zionist leader Kurt Blumenfeld dwelt at
length, using the phrase "Zionism as a problem of personality." Paradoxically, Zionism, in one of its aspects, is a collective form of assimilation; for Jews to have their own country—territorially, not just spiritu-

ally—is to become "like all other men," in having a country like other countries. But this is radically different from individual assimilation into Gentile nations. The pre-1881 *maskilim* had required of themselves to renounce the *shtetl*, with its insistence on difference, its obsession with a long-lost land. The Zionists required of themselves to take pride in precisely these things, and to act on them. For the *maskilim* born in the *shtetl*, or near to it, Zionism closed a schism in the soul. This was a fusion that released a formidable outburst of intellectual and moral energy, expressed through the lives and actions of Weizmann, Ben-Gurion and their followers.

Under the immediate shock of 1881, some of the *maskilim* recoiled in the direction of Orthodox Judaism. In Kiev in the early eighties, a student addressed the synagogue congregation: "We regret the fact that we regarded ourselves as Russians and not as Jews. The events of the last years have shown us that we were sadly mistaken. Yes, we are Jews." And the poet J. L. Gordon (1831–1892) seemed for a time to repudiate everything the *maskilim* had stood for: "I believed that *Haskala* would surely save us, but that blessing was turned into a curse, and the golden cup of which we drank was flung into our faces."[58]

For the most part, those Zionists who were *maskilim* did not repudiate the modern, scientific, secularizing tendency of the Haskala together with what they did reject of it: its tendency to individual assimilation.

Although most of the leaders of Orthodox Judaism repudiated Zionism, not all did so. There was a tradition of practical Zionism among certain of the Orthodox. This appears in the teaching of two rabbis in the first half of the nineteenth century: Rabbi Yehuda Alkalai (1798–1878) and Rabbi Zevi Kalischer (1795–1874). Alkalai, born in Sarajevo, was a Sephardi; Kalischer, who officiated in the small town of Thorn, in the province of Posen, was an Ashkenazi.

Alkalai had developed a medieval Jewish tradition about the Messiah, giving it an essentially Zionist interpretation. According to this tradition, the appearance of the actual Redeemer, the Messiah, Son of David, will be preceded by the appearance of a forerunner, a Messiah who will be called the Son of Joseph (Mashiah Ben Yosef), who will conquer the land of Israel. According to Alkalai's interpretation, the Mashiah Ben Yosef symbolizes a process, the emergence of a political leadership among the Jews that will prepare "the beginning of the Redemption": "The Redemption will begin with effort by the

Jews themselves: they must organize and unite, choose leaders and leave the land of exile."[59]

Kalischer's book *Derishat Zion* was published in 1862, the same year as Moses Hess's *Rome and Jerusalem,* and was prompted by the same phenomenon, the Risorgimento. While Italians and others give their lives for their country, he says: "We, the children of Israel, who have the most glorious and holiest of lands as our inheritance are spiritless and silent. We should be ashamed of ourselves."

Theologically, Kalischer argues that "the Redemption of Israel will come by slow degrees and the ray of deliverance will shine forth gradually. These things will be accomplished by the return of the Jews, by degrees, to the Land of Israel, and their settlement on the land." Kalischer's book, unlike Moses Hess's, ran into a number of editions in his lifetime, so it is likely that it helped to prepare the ground, in Russia, for the Lovers of Zion.

The general viewpoint shared by Alkalai and Kalischer was represented in the eighties by Rabbi Samuel Mohilever (1824–1898) and by Rabbi Isaac Jacob Reines (1839–1915), both children of the *shtetl,* from Poland and Belorussia, respectively. Both immediately joined Hovevei Zion and both rallied to Herzl nearly twenty years later. Mohilever stressed the importance of *rapprochement* between the Orthodox and the *maskilim,* as a prerequisite to the unity of the Jewish people, necessary for the rebuilding of the Jewish heritage. Reines was later to found—at Vilna, in 1902—the movement known as the Mizrachi ("spiritual center"), which might be defined as the main religious lobby within Zionism. It has wielded, and continues to wield, a notable influence over the development and social life of Israel.

From the beginning, the Zionist movement had its religious as well as its secular side. But it might be more illuminating to speak of aspects rather than sides. Weizmann, Ben-Gurion and other Zionist leaders in the *maskilim* tradition could not be "religious Jews," in the sense of accepting for themselves the network of prescriptions and proscriptions that covers the daily life of the Orthodox Jew. But in a wider sense, they could not be anything else but very religious Jews indeed. Not only were their imaginations saturated in the Bible, but their burning faith in the restoration of the Chosen People to the Promised Land—even if they chose not to put it that way—made them, if not religious leaders, at least men fitted to lead those who saw their movement as essentially religious, and secular only in outward form.

Rabbi Abraham Isaac Kook (1865–1935), who became Chief Rabbi (Ashkenazi) of Palestine under the British Mandate, saw the secular aspect of Zionism as merely a cover for a divinely willed purpose. What Jewish secular nationalists want, wrote Kook, "they do not themselves know: the spirit of Israel is so closely linked to the spirit of God that a Jewish nationalist, no matter how secularist his intention may be, is, despite himself, imbued with the divine spirit even against his own will."[60]

The "secular" leaders could not take issue with that view of the matter—even if they really differed from it, which is doubtful—because it served their purpose, of uniting Orthodox and *maskilim* in the common Zionist effort which spread throughout Russia in the 1880s.

Local societies along Hovevei Zion lines now sprang up all over the Jewish-populated areas of Russia, and Pinsker and Lilienblum, working together, set about organizing communications between these societies. Lilienblum persuaded Pinsker that he ought to take the lead in convening the National Congress, for which he had appealed to the Western Jews. As the Westerners had failed to respond to that appeal, the congress would have to be one of Russian Jews.

The congress met on November 6, 1884, in the Silesian town of Kattowitz, just outside Alexander III's dominions, but near to the homes of most Russian Jews. Thirty delegates attended and Pinsker took the chair. He was an uninspiring chairman and leader, and it was a low-key conference. The ultimate objective of the movement—the establishment of a Jewish State in Eretz Israel—could not be publicly alluded to, for fear of the Tsar and the Sultan. The conference confined itself to detailed matters affecting emigration and settlement.

By 1891—after a decade of Zionist ferment in Russia—the results on the ground in Palestine may have seemed meager enough. Ten thousand new, politically oriented settlers—the first *aliyah*—had established themselves in Palestine, most of them in agricultural settlements such as Rishon le-Zion and Gedera, others in new quarters of Jaffa and Jerusalem. The numbers were tiny, set against the great majority who had stayed in Russia and endured, or against those, the great majority of all emigrants, who had gone to the West. Also, those who had settled in Palestine would probably not have survived if they had been dependent on the meager trickle of aid that reached them from the Russian Zionists. What enabled the settlers to survive were the benefactions coming from Paris, from Baron Edmond de Rothschild (1845–1934), who was not a declared Zionist at all, in a political sense. (Rothschild did not declare himself publicly to be a Zionist until 1917, after the Balfour Declaration. But he had played a large part in the building of the Jewish nation in Palestine.)

All in all, Zionism did not seem to have a great deal to show for those first ten years of feverish activity. Yet, when we look back on it, the first *aliyah* does constitute a decisive step on the road. Zionism had established a bridgehead in Palestine. Now for the first time there was a Jewish population there committed to a territorial (though not for all of them purely territorial) objective, the eventual establishment of a state (or commonwealth, or "home") in which Jews would no longer be strangers, dependent on the tolerance or intolerance of others.

VII

In Western and Central Europe, too, anti-semitism rose sharply in the last decade of the nineteenth century. But whereas the anti-semitism of the Russian ruling class was largely motivated by fear of liberalism, Western anti-semitism was a middle-class affair, and largely motivated by resentment of consequences of the triumph of liberalism. The most resented of these consequences—especially in France, Germany and Austria—was the greatly increased participation, and competition, of Jews in many spheres of middle-class urban life, especially in the professions, in business and finance, in the press and in the arts. The emancipation of the Jews was completed in the main countries of Western and Central Europe by 1871. It was a consequence—and for some liberals an unintended, unwelcome and significantly delayed side effect—of the general laicization of Western society during the nineteenth century, leading to the removal of all religious tests and exclusions affecting secular life.

There were two main currents in the Western anti-semitism of this period. These currents often intermingled and both together affected many anti-semites. It is important, however—for reasons which will be examined later—to distinguish between them. The two currents are Christian resentment and nationalist resentment. Christian resentment drew its strength from the centuries of Christian teaching—as strong in the Lutheran tradition as in the Catholic—which portrayed the Jews as a people uniquely set apart and accursed: the people chosen by God, who had then rejected and crucified His Son. But to that ancient layer, new motives for resentment, and the expression of resentment, were now added. Christians blamed the Jews for the dissemination of Enlightenment ideas, for the weakening of Christian faith and Christian power. (There was a curious symmetry in this, since leading Enlightenment writers—Voltaire, most notably—had made use of anti-Jewish feelings in order to discredit Christianity.) And they knew also that to blame the Jews for those things was a good way of discrediting Enlightenment ideas, which had benefited the Jews in a more obvious way than they had benefited anybody else. Christian writers invited people to return to the good old days when all power had been in Christian hands, and the Jews knew their place.

Nationalist resentment was aroused by the idea of the Jews as an international people, something which should not be. French Jews said they were Frenchmen, but German Jews said they were German. How could the same people be both German and French? The thing was contrary to nature. Jews were really aliens, and consequently any power acquired by Jews was an alienation of national power, something not to be tolerated. The more European nationalisms became excited—as they did from the seventies, following the Franco-Prussian War—the more obsessed they became with the image of the hostile alien, and the more racist they became.

Christian resentment was becoming a recessive strain in the West, although still very important up to the First World War. But the emergence—not completed until after the First World War—of nationalism as the dominant strain was an event of terrible significance. As P. G. J. Pulzer, an authority on nineteenth-century Germanophone anti-semitism, has said:

How important, in its practical effect, was the change from pre-liberal, backward-looking to post-liberal mass-based anti-semitism? The audience's vague and irrational image of the Jew as the enemy probably did not change much when the orators stopped talking about "Christ-slayers" and began talking about the laws of blood. The difference lay in the effect achieved. It enabled anti-semitism to be more elemental and uncompromising. Its logical conclusion was to substitute the gas chamber for the pogrom.[61]

Anti-semitism in its various forms was an all-European phenomenon. But the anti-semitism of three countries—Germany, Austria and France—was of crucial importance for the development of Zionism, and the creation of the State of Israel. The anti-semitism of these three countries therefore needs to be examined here, briefly.

VIII

German anti-semitism, as contrasted with the French and Austrian varieties, was much more strongly affected, from very early on, by the nationalist/racist component, and less by the religious one. It was also established quite securely near the center of the national culture. Already by the mid-century the writings of Richard Wagner (1813–1883), notably *Das Judentum in der Musik* (1850), and of Heinrich von Treitschke had done much to make nationalist anti-semitism respectable among cultured Germans.

The racist theories of the Englishman Houston Stewart Chamberlain (1855–1927) and the Frenchman Comte Joseph Arthur de Gobineau (1816–1882) caught on more strongly in Germany than anywhere else. Chamberlain, who married a daughter of Wagner's, thought that King David, the Prophets and Jesus were all Germans. Gobineau offered to his German readers the congenial thought that of modern peoples only the Germans had preserved their ethnic purity as an Aryan race.

It was in the 1870s that German intellectual, and racist, anti-semitism became insistently articulate in the writings of a number of journalists and academics. A basic reason for that is given by one of the historians of anti-semitism in this period, R. F. Byrnes: "As the liberal movement spread through the Germanies in the nineteenth century, complete emancipation of the Jews followed, until with the formation of the Empire in 1871 they had obtained complete equality. This achievement was, of course, one of the principal reasons for the attack against the Jews which began almost immediately."[62]

The reaction after 1870 was colored in Germany by the feeling that the liberal values, which had led to Jewish emancipation, were themselves of particularly obnoxious foreign extraction in that they were imported from France.

The word "anti-semitism" occurs for the first time (as far as is known) in a book called *Der Sieg des Judentums über das Germanentum* by the German nationalist-racist journalist Wilhelm Marr (1818–1904). The book had gone into twelve editions by 1879. Marr is described as having been "the first to appreciate the possibilities opened by propaganda on racial lines and the advantage of using extreme and unscrupulous rather than polite and respectable methods in a matter which appealed, in essence, to extreme and unscrupulous sentiments."[63]

Marr was, however, eclipsed in violence by Eugen Duehring (1833–1921), a blind lecturer in economics and philosophy at Berlin University. It is in Duehring's writing that the potentially genocidal element in German anti-semitism made its first, though fleeting, appearance. As early as 1865, in a philosophical work called *Der Wert des Lebens,* Duehring had advocated solving the Jewish question by "killing and extirpating" (*durch Ertötung und Ausrottung*). Theodor Herzl later recalled reading this book, at the age of twenty-two: "The effect of Duehring's book upon me was as if I had suddenly been hit over the head." (*Zionist Writings,* Vol. II, p. 111.)

In Germany, and even more in Austria, and to a lesser extent in France, the great increase in westward emigration from the Russian Empire after 1881 stimulated and exacerbated anti-semitism.

It was inevitable that this should be so. The basic concept was that the Jews were strangers, and the newcomers, emerging from their isolated existence in the Pale of Settlement, seemed to the Westerners very strange indeed. Their movement to the West, out of the Russian Empire, in large numbers, in the late-nineteenth century, seemed to make plausible the notion that the Jews were taking over everything, that the homeland was no longer safe.

The reaction of many Germans to the immigration was well summed up by Treitschke:

> Year after year there pours over our Eastern frontiers . . .
> from the inexhaustible Polish cradle, a host of ambitious,
> trouser-selling youths, whose children and children's children
> are one day to dominate Germany's stock exchanges and
> newspapers. . . . Right into the most educated circles, among
> men who would reject with disgust any thought of ecclesiasti-
> cal intolerance or national pride, we can hear, as if from one
> mouth, "The Jews are our misfortune."[64]

Treitschke's anti-semitism was both nationalist and Christian, and this was the brand of anti-semitism that became politically significant in Germany in the eighties. (Radical anti-semitism, non-Christian or anti-Christian, was already intellectually influential, but did not become politically powerful until the twentieth century.)

Adolf Stoecker (1835–1909), whose Christian Social Party became anti-semitic in the eighties, was chaplain to the Imperial court. His political movement was for a time discreetly favored by Bismarck, because of its potential for undermining the Progressives and Social Democrats in Berlin, but Stoecker was not a brilliant political leader, and anti-semitism never really took off as a distinct political movement in Germany before the First World War. What happened was that anti-semitism became widely diffused throughout society, including the political parties.[65] In its milder Christian or semi-Christian (Wagnerian) forms, it was generally acceptable, and there was also a considerable middle-class following for the more manic forms.

There were some anti-anti-semites, even among German nationalists. The historian Theodor Mommsen (1817–1903) resigned from the Prussian Academy in 1895 on learning of Treitschke's election to it. "Next to him," said Mommsen, "I cannot remain." But in this transaction it was Mommsen, not Treitschke, who seemed eccentric to contemporaries. In Germany in the eighties and nineties, as in contemporary Russia, the local form of anti-semitism had become normal and central. The German form, being both unofficial and restrained by law, was, of course, much more tolerable to Jews than the Russian form. But the ominous common factor was the normality of anti-semitism, both in a country where emancipation had never come and in a country where it had been fully achieved.

But there was also already something special, and particularly ominous, about German anti-semitism. As we have seen, genocide had been advocated by one writer, Eugen Duehring, in the 1860s. But it was not until the 1880s that the potentially genocidal strain in German culture became clearly isolated: *anti-Christian anti-semitism,* dominant in the works of one of the greatest of German writers, by far the most influential European mind of the late-nineteenth century.

Christian anti-semitism, throughout the centuries, had always recognized a limit. This is acknowledged by the *Encyclopaedia Judaica:*

> The persistence of Judaism, seemingly a contradiction of the Christian conception of Church as *Verus* Israel, the true Israel, led the great theologians, notably Augustine, to elaborate the doctrine that represents the Jews as *the* nation which was a witness to the truth of Christianity. Their existence was further justified by the service they rendered to the Christian truth, in attesting, through their humiliation, the triumph of Church over the Synagogue. "Unintelligent, they possess in-

telligent books"; they are thus doomed to perpetual servitude. A further variation, reversing a biblical image, depicts the Jews as Esau and the Christians as Jacob. They are also Cain, guilty of fratricide, and marked with a sign. However, the hostility of allegorization also implies a nascent tendency on the part of the Church to protect the Jews, since: "if someone killed Cain, Cain could be revenged seven-fold." . . . Thomas Aquinas considered [the Jews] condemned to perpetual servitude because of their crime, but "they were not to be deprived of necessities of life."[66]

That was the Christian limit. Both the depth of Christian hostility and the existence of a limit to its expression were consecrated in the Liturgy of Good Friday: "O God who in thy goodness dost not even deny mercy to the perfidious Jews." Derzhavin acknowledged the Christian limit in the eighteenth century; Pobedonostsev respected it in the nineteenth. But what if the Christian limit were to be removed?

Eugen Duehring, as a racist anti-semite with genocidal proclivities, wanted to remove the Christian limit. "Those who wish to cling to the entire Christian tradition," he wrote in *Die Judenfrage* (1881), "are in no position to turn against Judaism with sufficient force." But Duehring and his like did not have the nerve, or the capacity, to mount a full-scale attack on Christianity and its inhibiting ethics. That was to be the work of Friedrich Nietzsche (1844–1900). Nietzsche, through his work in replacing Christian (limited) anti-semitism with anti-Christian (unlimited) anti-semitism, played a large part in opening the way for the Nazis and the Holocaust.

I am well aware that that will seem to many people an extravagant, to some even outrageous, statement. The current[67] academic convention regarding Nietzsche is to treat Nazi admiration for this thinker as due to a misunderstanding. As far as anti-semitism is concerned, it can be shown that he condemned it, occasionally. Since the Second World War there has been a consensus for excluding him from the intellectual history of anti-semitism, in which, in fact, his role is decisive.

It is true that Nietzsche detested the vulgar (and Christian)/anti-semitism of his own day, especially of his brother-in-law, Bernhard Foerster. It is also true that the main thrust of Nietzsche's writing was not directed against the Jews. It was directed against Christianity. But the way in which it was directed against Christianity made it far more dangerous to Jews than to Christians.

Anti-Christian anti-semitism in itself was nothing new. The most anti-Christian of the *philosophes* of the eighteenth century—Voltaire especially—were also anti-semitic, though not consistently so.[68] What was new in Nietzsche, however, was the ethical radicalism of his sustained onslaught on Christianity. The Enlightenment tradition, on the whole, had respected, and even to a great extent inculcated—through its advocacy of tolerance—the Christian ethic, the Sermon on the Mount.

Nietzsche's message was that the Christian ethic was poison; its emphasis on mercy reversed the true Aryan values of fierceness; "pride, severity, strength, hatred, revenge." And the people responsible for this transvaluation of values (*Umwertung des Wertes*), the root of all evil, were the Jews.

In *The Antichrist* he writes about the Gospels:

> One is among Jews—the first consideration to keep from losing the thread completely—Paul and Christ were little superlative Jews. . . . One would no more associate with the first Christians than one would with Polish Jews—they both do not smell good. . . . Pontius Pilate is the only figure in the *New Testament* who commands respect. To take a Jewish affair seriously—he does not persuade himself to do that. One Jew more or less—what does it matter?

Nietzsche's real complaint against the vulgar Christian anti-semites of his day was that they were not anti-semitic enough; that they did not realize that they were themselves carriers of that semitic infection, Christianity.[69] "The Jews," he wrote in *The Antichrist*, "have made mankind so thoroughly false that even today the Christian can feel anti-Jewish without realizing that he is himself the *ultimate Jewish consequence*."

Amid the excited vulgar anti-semitism of the late-nineteenth century, the reminder that Christianity was a Jewish thing was the most effective argument against Christianity. And to weaken Christianity, especially by this route, was to move toward the abolition of the Christian limit.

Nietzsche went mad in 1889, the year Hitler was born. In the 1890s Nietzsche's writings became a dominant intellectual influence throughout Western Europe, and in the first decade of the twentieth century his works were available (especially in Germany and Austria) in large, cheap editions. His main themes—especially the notion of Christianity as a Jewish corruption of proper Aryan ferocity—were widely diffused. It is not known whether Hitler actually read Nietzsche, but he certainly took in his anti-Christian message, and his license for ferocity. Hitler did not need to learn anti-semitism from Nietzsche; that was in the air all around him. What he learned from Nietzsche, directly or indirectly, was that the traditional Christian *limit* on anti-semitism was itself part of a Jewish trick.[70] When the values that the Jews had reversed were restored, there would be no limit and no Jews.

IX

It was in Germany that anti-semitism made its most fatal intellectual breakthrough in the 1880s. It was not in Germany, however, but in Austria, and specifically in the city of Vienna, that anti-semitism registered its first major political success, and found its first great political leader.

In Austria, as in Germany, the political anti-semitism of the eighties took both nationalist/racist and Christian forms. The original—though not the great—leader of the Austrian anti-semites, Georg von Schoenerer (1842–1921), was a doctrinaire racist (as well as the leading exponent of Pan-Germanism of his day). He used to go around Vienna with a bodyguard of Jew-baiting students, chanting the jingle: "*Was der Jude glaubt ist einerlei, in der Rasse liegt die Schweinerei*"—"What the Jew believes is neither here nor there. In the Race lies the Swinishness."[71]

Schoenerer, like Stoecker in Germany, took up the cause of prohibiting Jewish immigration. This was a popular cause, especially in Vienna, where the number of Jews, as a proportion of the total population, doubled between 1869 and 1890, mainly because of immigration from Eastern Europe. In May 1887, Schoenerer introduced in the Reichsrat an anti-immigration bill. When the vote was taken, he had the support of only a small minority, nineteen deputies, an indication of how strong the liberal tradition in parliament still was in the eighties. But among the nineteen was a serious and ambitious politician: Karl Lueger (1844–1910). Lueger's speech on Schoenerer's bill was his first anti-semitic utterance, and it was made with the shrewd calculation that there were votes in anti-semitism, and more to come, under the expanding franchise of the late-nineteenth century. As he observed rather cryptically in the debate on Schoenerer's bill: "Whether Democrat or anti-semite, the matter really comes to the same thing."[72]

Starting from that perception, Lueger built up, in the nineties. a spectacularly successful political career. But, in taking up anti-semitism, Lueger took care not to follow Schoenerer down the racist path. His movement was a populist reaction of "ordinary Viennese" against the city's glittering cultural elite. As one of Lueger's followers put it, speaking in the Vienna City Council: "I am fed up with books, you find in books only what one Jew copies from another."[73]

Lueger was aware that many voters in Vienna were still Catholics, and that mainstream Austrian anti-semitism was Catholic. Accordingly, the party which Lueger founded in 1893 was the Christian Social Party, appealing to Catholics, to social reformers and to anti-semites. That was a sure-fire combination in Vienna. The C.S.P. won a landslide victory—92–46—over the Liberals in the municipal elections of 1895. That victory in Vienna, together with another event that happened in the same year in Paris, was to constitute, as we shall see, a decisive stage in the emergence of Zionism, and the creation of the State of Israel. Lueger proved to be an immensely successful, reforming mayor. He was also a charmer in the Viennese manner. As a historian of the Austrian Empire says of him: "His integrity, his handsome appearance and homely humour won for him an immense personal following; he was also both an administrator of genius and an unscrupulous and ruthless political tactician."[74]

By personal inclination, Karl Lueger may not have been an anti-semite at all. He was an anti-semite in practice, perhaps simply because most Viennese were. In Lueger's Vienna, as in Pobedonostsev's St. Petersburg—though in a widely different political context—what is striking, once more, is the normality of late-nineteenth-century anti-semitism. In German-speaking lands, Liberals who opposed anti-semitism were swept aside, as in Vienna. Other Liberals came to terms in the nineties. Thus in Germany, the Liberal program in 1885 had "condemned most decisively all loathsome agitations against individual classes . . . but especially the anti-semitic movement unworthy of a civilized society." In 1891, however, the Liberal program falls silent on these matters.[75]

That Liberal silence of 1891 is like the death of a white mouse in a mine shaft, signaling that the poison in the air has attained a critical strength.

Under the surface of normality, abnormal forces were already stirring. Adolf Hitler first came to Vienna in 1906, just after his seventeenth birthday, spent some time there in 1907 and 1908, and lived there from 1909 to 1913. The years 1906 to 1910 were the last years of

Lueger's extremely successful political career (he died in 1910). The young Hitler was enormously impressed by Lueger: "the best Mayor we ever had."[76] Hitler did not learn anti-semitism from Lueger. What he learned from Lueger was pragmatic politics: how to make use of anti-semitism in order to win political power.

Ideologically, Hitler—whose father was a supporter of Schoenerer's—was much closer to Schoenerer's fanatical racist anti-semitism than to Lueger's relatively mild, and ostensibly Christian, version. But politically, it was Lueger, not Schoenerer, whom Hitler approved. It was Lueger, not Schoenerer, who had won power by going for where the votes were. That was more important than ideological purity.

Hitler acknowledged learning two great political lessons from Lueger: first, the wisdom of appealing to classes which are threatened and will therefore fight vigorously, instead of to established and cautious classes, and, second, the determination to use existing instruments, such as the Church, or the Army, or the bureaucracy, for whatever political power they might provide.[77]

The career of Adolf Hitler, after the First World War, was to show what the lessons and methods of Karl Lueger could accomplish when—instead of using anti-semitism with cynical opportunism, as Lueger apparently used it—they were applied in the service of a sincere, passionate anti-semitism; not only anti-liberal, but radically opposed to the Christian ethic, and therefore, without ethical inhibition or limit of any kind.

X

In France, the emancipation of the Jews, dating from the French Revolution, was the oldest and most complete in Europe. French anti-semitism up to the eighties was marginal; it existed mainly on the Left. Writers in the Proudhon tradition "identified capitalists with bankers and bankers with Jews." In other words they tried to use the "strangeness" of Jews, like the Rothschilds, to bring capitalism itself under suspicion. But their efforts did not catch on. Nowhere else in Continental Europe did the Jews appear so secure as they did in France, and nowhere else was there more ground for confidence that anti-semitism was a vestigial thing, disappearing when civilization reached a certain point.

The emergence in the 1880s of French anti-semitism as a major force, with a vast clientele among the middle class, shook that confidence badly, without altogether dispelling it. To some extent, the rise of anti-semitism may have been stimulated in France—as it certainly was in Austria—by the arrival of victims of anti-semitism from Russia. According to a historian of the Dreyfus case, "The Eastern European Jews, who spoke only Yiddish, were not easily assimilated."[78] But the new anti-semitism was stimulated mainly by the general politics of cultural conflict within France, which became particularly bitter in the decades following France's military debacle of 1870.

The new French anti-semitism was mainly nationalist, Catholic and right-wing, even counterrevolutionary, but it also had a distinctly populistic streak, again in the Proudhon tradition. The new anti-semitism drew much of its strength from French Catholic resentment of the Third Republic, and particularly of the anti-clericalism dominant in the Government of the Republic from 1877 on.

Up to the 1880s, French Catholics had tended to blame their troubles on the Freemasons. But they had found that other people were not particularly interested in Freemasons, and especially not interested in Catholic theories about Freemasons. In the 1880s, however, it became clear that Jews were much more interesting than Freemasons. Were not Jews—now one came to think of it—the main beneficiaries of the French Revolution, and of the educational policies of the Third Republic? And had not Jews taken part in anti-clerical politics and journalism? Might it then be they, rather than the Freemasons (or along with them), who were behind it all? The course of French Catholic right-wing politics and journalism in the 1880s was set into the anti-semitic channel in which it was to flow for sixty years.

French anti-semitism never found a political leader of the stature of Karl Lueger. The political leadership of the French Right during this period was absurdly inept. But what France did produce was the greatest popularizer of anti-semitic ideas and emotions who ever lived (up to the advent of Adolf Hitler): Édouard Drumont (1844–1917). Drumont has been described as a "sociologically typical anti-semite." Up to the publication of his spectacularly successful anti-semitic tract *La France Juive*, in 1886, he had been "a hard-working, respectable, ambitious but frustrated journalist who believed that his great talents had been blunted and ignored because of forces beyond his control."[79]

Drumont had not, however, shown any sign of anti-semitism before the mid-eighties. It seems possible that, like Lueger, he was not driven on by anti-semitic passion but was professionally attracted by the possibilities inherent in exploiting rising anti-semitism. As in Lueger's case, the variety of anti-semitism Drumont opted for was a version of Catholic anti-semitism (though it was a version with more nationalism in it than Lueger's). Catholic anti-semitism was where the votes were in Austria, and it was where the sales were in France. *La France Juive* ran into 121 editions within a year of its publication. It was the most widely read book in France.

La France Juive established the tone for more than two generations of right-wing French journalism: feverish, prolix—the pamphlet runs into two volumes octavo—gossipy, scurrilous, paranoid, spasmodically devout—and not without its moments of genuine eloquence and wit.[80] Drumont, like Pobedonostsev, accepted and popularized the ritual-murder story. His main theme, however, is that the Jews not merely crucified Christ in the past but are continuing to crucify Him today, in France. In the course of his peroration, Drumont presents "Christ insulted, covered with opprobrium, torn by the thorns, crucified. Nothing has changed, in eighteen hundred years. It is the same lie, the same hate, the same people."

Drumont followed up *La France Juive* with a series of other anti-semitic tracts, almost equally successful, and in 1892 he founded a successful anti-semitic daily newspaper, *La Libre Parole*.

French anti-semitism never attained the same general diffusion, the normal status, of Austrian or German anti-semitism; it remained (generally speaking) the property of a politico-religious sect: right-wing, Catholic, anti-Republican. And that sect was itself extremely unpopular with many other French people. The fact that the Catholics became so rabid about the Jews, in the eighties, caused the Left, on the whole (and after a while), to drop its own Proudhonist (or Marxist) variety of anti-semitism and even tend, under favorable conditions, to defend the Jews. In France, attitudes to Jews became much more politically polarized than they were in Austria or Germany.

Also in France—unlike Russia and the Germanic lands—national pride had an unusual tendency to work in favor of the Jews. The Great Revolution, which had liberated the Jews, was a French world-historical achievement, of which most French people were proud. So when the French Right attacked the Jews and the French Revolution, in the same breath, they were doing the Jews some good, in the eyes of most French people.

Among the large and influential, though frustrated, minority which did take it up, however, French anti-semitism tended to be more virulent and even hysterical than was generally the case in Austria and Germany in the late-nineteenth century. And it completely dominated some sections of society. One of these was the Army. The newspaper to which most Army officers subscribed in the nineties was Drumont's *La Libre Parole*. Many of these officers liked to flaunt this organ of opinion in the presence of their Jewish colleagues, of whom there were about three hundred. One of these was Captain Alfred Dreyfus (1859–1935).

XI

On Monday, October 29, 1894, a short notice appeared in Drumont's *La Libre Parole:* "Is it true that recently a highly important arrest has been made by order of the military authorities? The person arrested seems to be accused of espionage. If the information is true, why do the military authorities maintain a complete silence?"[81]

Two days later, *La Libre Parole* was able to run the headline it wanted: "High Treason. Arrest of the Jewish Officer, A. Dreyfus."

On December 21, a court-martial found Dreyfus guilty of treason, largely on the perjured evidence of Major Hubert-Joseph Henry (1846–1898). (Henry committed suicide four years later, on the exposure of forgeries he had committed in support of his original perjury. Apostrophizing Henry, after his death, the right-wing writer Charles Maurras [1868–1952] declared, "Your unlucky forgery will be acclaimed as one of your first deeds of war.") On Dreyfus's conviction, Drumont wrote: "He committed no crime against his country. To betray one's country, one must first have one. [*Pour trahir sa Patrie, il faut en avoir une.*]"[82]

Dreyfus was sentenced to deportation for life, to forfeiture of his rank and to military degradation. The degradation ceremony was set for January 3, 1895, in a courtyard of the École Militaire in Paris. "Though crowds gathered in the streets," writes Chapman, "only a few favoured journalists were given permission to watch the spectacle."[83]

One of these favored journalists was the Paris correspondent of the *Neue Freie Presse*, of Vienna, Theodor Herzl (1860–1904). In the following year, 1896, with the publication of his book *Der Judenstaat*—which he wrote in the summer of 1895—Herzl was to emerge as the intellectual leader of world Zionism. Immediately after the publication of his book, he went on to found, animate and preside over the international Zionist movement. He is therefore accepted as the founder of Zionism, though he was, of course, not the first Zionist.

But in the early 1890s—and probably as late as January 1895— Herzl had not been any kind of Zionist. Europe had been good to Theodor Herzl. He was a distinguished member of his chosen profession, foreign correspondent of a great European newspaper, in a great capital. He was brilliant, handsome, beautifully dressed, ebullient, imaginative, bursting with life.

It went without saying that a man like Herzl—or Dreyfus for that matter—was an assimilationist, thinking of himself as assimilated. In the early nineties, in his reports for his paper, Herzl had tried to minimize the importance of anti-semitism (minimization was the policy of the Jewish proprietors of his paper). Most assimilated Jews did that, for as long as they could—Hess did, and Pinsker, Lilienblum and Smolenskin; and Herzl. (Herzl had carried into assimilation his characteristic exuberance and sense of theater. He had proposed the conversion of the Jews *en masse* to Catholicism, at the call of the Pope, in St. Stephen's Cathedral, "amidst the pealing of bells.")[84] In 1892, Herzl had even denied the existence of French anti-semitism; "the French people remain strangers to, and without understanding of, anti-semitism."

If the French were strangers to anti-semitism, one wonders why *La France Juive* and its successors had been selling like hot cakes— and why it was possible, in that same year, 1892, for Drumont to found in Paris a successful anti-semitic daily newspaper. Clearly the assimilationist Herzl had gotten himself into a precarious intellectual and emotional position on the eve of the Dreyfus case.

It is usually said that the conviction and degradation of Dreyfus converted Herzl to Zionism. David Vital, a historian of Zionism, appears to cast cold water on that. "The evidence does not," he says, "support the theory that it was the Dreyfus Case . . . that changed the essentially conventional man of letters into a dissentient and an *exalté*."[85]

Herzl himself, however, a little more than four years later, said that "what made me a Zionist was the Dreyfus trial" and that *The Jewish State* was written "under the shattering impact of the first Dreyfus trial."[86] Herzl was a most impressionable man, with a powerful dramatic imagination—he was a playwright as well as a journalist—and the conviction of Dreyfus followed by the scene in the École Militaire made up a ritual drama of grisly potency.

Together with Herzl, in that little group of favored journalists, in the courtyard of the École Militaire that January morning, was a brilliant young French nationalist and racist writer, Maurice Barrès (1862–1923). Barrès has left the following remarkable report of what they both saw and heard:

As nine o'clock struck, the General drew his sword, the commands rang out, the infantry presented arms and the cavalry flashed their sabres, the little platoon detached itself from the angle of an immense square. Four men, in their midst the traitor, marching stiffly, on one side the executioner, a veritable giant. The five or six thousand people who were present and moved by the tragic waiting period had only one thought: "Judas is marching too well."

A spectacle more exciting than the guillotine, set up on the cobblestones, early in the morning, on the Place de la Roquette. He was one of the happy men of this world, despised, abandoned by all: "I am alone in the universe," he might have cried.

In this desert, he marched firmly, his jaw kept high, his body well held, his left hand on the grip of his sword, his right hand swinging. Could his dog have licked those hands? Taking a diagonal line the sinister group arrived four paces from the General astride his horse and halted brusquely. The four artillerymen retired, the clerk of the court spoke, the rigid silhouette did nothing, except to raise an arm and let go a cry of innocence, while the Guards Adjutant, terrible in his size and magnificent in his bearing, tore off so quickly and so slowly the buttons, the chevrons, the epaulettes, the red bands, manhandled him, stripped him, put him in mourning. The most terrible moment came when he broke the sword on his knee.

After some seconds when he had been left disgraced and disarmed, the instinctive cries of the crowd insisted, with a fury that outdid itself, that this HOMUNCULUS in gold, who had become a homunculus in black, should be killed.

But the law protected him in order to subject him to the prescribed humiliations.

Judas up to that time had been a little immobile speck, beaten by all those winds of hatred. Now, like a marching pillory, he had to meet the looks of all.

He marches off.

The military wall round which he marches represses its rage, but seems ready to burst with fury. At every moment I

Above left, Moshe Leib Lilienblum (1843–1910). "We have a historic right [to Eretz Israel] which was not lost along with rule of the country."—(1881).
Above right, Leon Pinsker (1821–1891). "We must reconcile ourselves to the idea that the other nations, by reason of their inherent natural antagonism, will forever reject us."—*Autoemancipation!* (1882).
Below right, Moses Hess (1812–1875). "Jews are not a religious group, but a separate nation, a special race, and the modern Jew who denies this is not only an apostate, a religious renegade, but a traitor to his people, his tribe, his race."—*Rome and Jerusalem* (1862).
Below left, Peretz Smolenskin (1842–1885). "If the wave of emigration is to direct itself to one place, surely no other country in the world is conceivable, except Eretz Israel."—*It Is Time to Plant* (c. 1876).

Above, Richard and Cosimà Wagner. The great composer was also a pioneer of modern German anti-Semitism, with his *Das Judentum in der Musik* (1850) and other writings.

Below left, Fyodor Dostoyevski. The great novelist was also a pioneer of modern Russian anti-Semitism and a close friend and admirer of its chief official ideologue, Pobedonostsev.

Below right, Friedrich Nietzsche. "The Jews have made mankind so thoroughly false that even today the Christian can feel anti-Jewish without realizing that he is himself the *ultimate Jewish consequence*."—*The Antichrist*.

Drawing from Édouard Drumont's *La Libre Parole*, 1903. Édouard Drumont (1844–1917) was a spectacularly successful journalist, whose *Libre Parole* was the newspaper to which most French army officers subscribed in the 1890s when the Dreyfus case began.

The degradation of Captain Dreyfus, January 5, 1895. The event was personally witnessed by Theodor Herzl, who wrote *The Jewish State* in its immediate aftermath.

imagine that a sword will be lifted. The crowd on the railings and on the rooftops is still calling for his death.

As he came towards us, his cap pressed on to his brow, his pince-nez on his ethnic nose, his eye furious and dry, his white face hard and defiant, he shouted—what do I say?—he ordered, in an intolerable voice: "You will tell the whole of France that I am innocent!"[87, 88]

"Judas!" "Traitor!" It was a storm. Through the fatal potency which he bears, or the potency of the ideas associated with him, the unfortunate forced from us all a discharge of antipathy. That countenance of a strange race, that impressive rigidity, his whole *mien* revolted the most self-possessed spectator. When I saw Emile Henry, his feet tied, his hands tied, being dragged to the guillotine, all I had in my heart was a sincere sympathy for an unfortunate of my race. But what had I to do with him who was called Dreyfus?

"In three years," someone said, "he will be a captain of Uhlans." Oh no! Surely there is not a group of men in the world who would accept this individual. He was not born to live socially. Alone, in a condemned wood, the branch of a tree reaches out to him. So that he can hang himself. . . .

And since he appealed to the witness of those who were there, we must complete the degradation of Judas for the benefit of our brother Frenchmen, rob him of something more, better than an epaulette or a chevron, of the truth which seems to have escaped him. [*La vérité qui semble lui avoir échappé.*][89]

Chapman records a detail which Barrès omits: "The soldiers were silent but the *pressmen* [my italics] and reserve officers who had been admitted to the atrocious ceremony shouted abuse at [Dreyfus]." I infer from Barrès's words "forced from us all a discharge of antipathy" that the distinguished and refined author of *Sous L'Oeil des Barbares* joined in the yelling.

Herzl had to feel the full force of "all those winds of hatred," proceeding not only from the silent soldiers, the shouting reserve officers and the screaming mob outside, but also from the group in which he himself was standing.

What Herzl was looking at was a scene such as he could have imagined only in his worst nightmares: the elaborate and sacralized rejection of an assimilated Jew, amid calls for the death of all Jews. Herzl, who wrote about French culture for his Austrian readers, certainly knew *Les Fleurs du Mal*. There is a line there about what

Herzl was looking at: *"Un gibet symbolique où pendait mon image.* [A symbolic gallows on which my image hung.]"

There was surely enough power in the scene in the École Militaire to generate a conversion. In any case, that message was reinforced, a few months later, by a second rejection, this time at the hands of Herzl's adoptive city.[90] As mentioned earlier, Karl Lueger's anti-semitic Christian Social Party won the local elections in Vienna in May by a landslide. The liberal reformist current of the nineteenth century, in which the Western Jews had put all their trust, had finally brought democracy to Vienna. And Viennese democracy had made it plain that it had no use for the Jews.

In Herzl's mind, Lueger's victory and the Dreyfus case were part of one phenomenon. In November 1895, a young French Jew, talking to Herzl, "emphasized his French nationality." "I said: 'What? Don't you and I belong to the same nation? Why did you wince when Lueger was elected? Why did I suffer when Captain Dreyfus was accused of high treason?' "[91]

XII

The central message of *Der Judenstaat* was identical with the argument of Moses Hess and Leon Pinsker, although Herzl had not yet read either of them. The message was that there was no room or hope for the Jews in Europe; that the Jews must acquire a territory on which to build a nation. And Herzl—this is his great strength—is confident that this extraordinary, impracticable thing can be done: "The Jews who wish for a State shall have it, and they will deserve to have it."[92]

Herzl's book made few converts, but it did arouse interest. The idea that had seemed simply eccentric when Moses Hess had put it forward now touched a nerve zone of concern among Western (as well as Eastern) Jews. Most Jews in the West still held to assimilation, but few (probably) could altogether convince themselves, by the mid-1890s, that anti-semitism was vestigial, or the victory of assimilation inevitable. The idea of a Jewish State—the idea of an alternative, if things got very much worse—was inherently interesting, even if one thought it impracticable. And Herzl was interesting, and saw to it that he remained so.

For Herzl, the publication of *Der Judenstaat* was not an end in itself; it was the start of a campaign. Herzl now threw himself heart and soul into Zionism. He established contact in the spring of 1896 with Hovevei Zion in Russia and Poland. He knew little about the groups, and their leaders were inclined to distrust him, but all the same the contact was to prove vital for the future. In the early days, Herzl possibly undervalued such contacts, and overvalued other, more exalted ones. Herzl wanted to meet kings and princes and dukes, and he did meet some—beginning with the Grand Duke of Baden in April 1896. None of these meetings led to anything, other than a perception that they had occurred. But that perception itself was important, as Herzl knew. It suggested that Zionism had "arrived" socially and was on its way politically; it was no longer just a creed for obscure, poor, powerless Russian Jews. That established Herzl's credentials as a leader, and that also is what he intended.

Herzl in fact was a great showman—or impresario, as people said then—something Zionism badly needed; in the hands of men like Pinsker and Lilienblum, it had looked sad, and drab. He also brought to Zionism something else of importance: *presence*. He was a big, well-made man with a head like an Assyrian god's and a stately demeanor.

He was just such a leader for the Jews as had been imagined by a character in an English novel published twenty years before. The dying Mordecai in George Eliot's *Daniel Deronda* had described what the Jew who was to bring the fulfillment of his life's hopes must be like: ". . . his face and frame must be beautiful and strong, he must have been used to all the refinements of social life, his voice must flow with a full and easy current, his earnestness be free from sordid need, he must glorify the possibilities of the Jews. . . ."[93]

Poor and oppressed people who long to assert their dignity love a leader like that. The Irish nationalists, in the previous decade, loved Charles Stewart Parnell, for being on their side, and for looking and behaving like a king at the same time. The Zionist rank and file loved Herzl, for the same reasons.

Herzl himself was conscious of the parallel: "I shall be the Parnell of the Jews."[94] But Herzl was more than Parnell, for he was felt to have a religious, as well as a national, significance.

In the summer of 1896, Herzl traveled to Constantinople, on the *Orient Express*, to try to negotiate with the Sultan. On the way out, when the train stopped at Sofia, Herzl got his first whiff of what his message already meant to poor Jews in the East. His diary, for June 17,

1896, records the scene in Sofia Station: "Beside the track on which our train pulled in there was a crowd of people who had come on my account. . . . There were men, women and children, Sephardim, Ashkenazim, mere boys and old men with white beards. . . . I was hailed in extravagant terms as Leader, as the Heart of Israel. . . . People cried 'Leshonoh Haboh Birusholayim' [Next year in Jerusalem]. The train started again."[95]

In Constantinople Herzl failed, on his first visit, to see the Sultan, but he saw the Grand Vizier, talks resembling negotiation occurred, and he got an Ottoman decoration. On the whole, it seemed not a bad start.

On his way back, Herzl addressed the congregation in the synagogue at Sofia (June 30, 1896). As his diary records: "I stood on the altar platform. When I was not quite sure how to face the congregation, without turning my back to the Holy of Holies, someone cried: 'It's all right for you to turn your back on the Ark, you are holier than the Torah.' "[96]

No wonder that the rabbis were worried.

On his return to Western Europe, Herzl made his first major contact with the poor immigrant Jews from Eastern Europe. He addressed an audience made up of such Jews in Whitechapel, London, in July 1896, and wrote in his diary: "As I sat on the platform of the workingmen's stage on Sunday I experienced strange sensations. I saw and heard my legend being born. The people are sentimental; the masses do not see clearly. I believe that even now they no longer have a clear image of me. A light fog is beginning to rise around me, and it may perhaps become the cloud in which I shall walk."[97]

There had been a messianic feeling in the Zionist movement from its earliest manifestations. It is explicit in the writings of Alkalai, and it has been seen as permeating the whole of a superficially secular movement. According to the *Encyclopaedia Judaica*, "Zionism and the creation of the State of Israel are to a large extent secularized phenomena of the messianic movements."[98] But it was only now that this feeling found a personality capable of inspiring it, and disposed to do so. Herzl, in the last year of his life, confided that as a boy he had had "a wonderful dream" about Moses and the Messiah: "The Messiah called to Moses: 'It is for this child that I have prayed!' And to me he said: 'Go and declare to the Jews that I shall come soon and perform great works and great deeds for my people and for the whole world.' "[99]

According to Joseph Nedava: "The combination of Moses and

Messiah is a recurring theme throughout Herzl's life and should be considered the *élan vital* of his historic mission."

Herzl never allowed any trace of Messianism or mysticism of any kind to appear in his public statements, which are entirely secular. He may have taken to heart a warning he had received from an Austrian Jewish friend, toward the end of 1895, not to "come forward in the role of Messiah"; and the advice from the same friend: "The Messiah must remain a veiled half-hidden figure."[100]

In his own mind Herzl seems to have entertained both the possibility that he might be the Messiah, or a precursor of the Messiah, and other possibilities. He sometimes compared himself with the seventeenth-century false Messiah Shabbetai Zevi (1626–1676). In Russia, the year before his death, he was to say, "Our people believe that I am the Messiah. I myself do not know this, for I am not a theologian." That last sentence is characteristic of Herzl in its unique combination of irony, awe and exaltation.

Herzl was right about what people believed about him. Belief in Herzl as the Messiah spread with extraordinary speed, among poor Jews, after the publication of *The Jewish State*. Long afterwards, David Ben-Gurion, then aged eighty, recalled that when he was ten years old, in the *shtetl* where he lived, "a rumour spread that the Messiah had arrived—a tall handsome man—a 'doctor' no less—Dr. Herzl."[101]

It may be well to put Christian readers on guard against a possible misconception. The Messiah, in Jewish tradition, is not expected to be the Son of God, or any form of Divine Incarnation. He is to be a mortal man, an agent of God's will. Insofar as Herzl and his followers thought of him as the Messiah, their belief was of the same order as the belief of Oliver Cromwell and his followers that Oliver was the chosen instrument of Divine Providence.

The very fact of Herzl's messianic appeal among the masses of poor Jews tended to put more sophisticated Jews against him. Jews established in the West—apart from the recent immigrants—were already mostly against him for assimilationist reasons. He had a few converts in the West, due to the recent rise in anti-semitism, and these included two distinguished writers—Max Nordau (1849–1923) and Israel Zangwill (1864–1926)—but he soon knew that it was the Eastern Jewry he must have if Zionism was to make progress. And the leaders of Jewish thought in Eastern Europe—both Orthodox and *maskilim*—were repelled, though in different ways and degrees, by Herzl's messianic appeal to the masses. They feared the consequences of mass enthusiasm. They too thought of Shabbetai Zevi, of the frenzy of his followers, and how it had all ended: in the apostasy of the Redeemer to Islam, at the bidding of the Sultan. Even the leading Lovers of Zion, whose whole purpose in life was a Jewish State, were angry with Herzl not only for behaving like a Messiah but for stealing their idea and blurting it out in public and going on about it. Who knew what that might not provoke in Turkey or in Russia?

XIII

By the autumn of 1896, Herzl was rather depressed by these negative reactions, but he soon rallied and took a decisive initiative. On March 7, 1897, after conferring in Vienna with a group of Hovevei Zion from Berlin, Herzl decided to convene a congress of Zionists to meet in Switzerland. Herzl now applied his energies to the congenial task of organizing this dramatic event, the event that had eluded Pinsker and his friends, in the days before Dreyfus and Lueger. Zionists everywhere could have gone on discussing Herzl endlessly. But now they had to make a decision. ". . . a question had been posed to which the answer was reducible to a simple yes or no. This was new in modern Jewish affairs."

The invitation provoked a major controversy throughout the Jewish world. Most of the published reactions were unfavorable, but Herzl had already made his impact. The Congress would be an Event. The most fateful of the responses to Herzl's invitations came from Russia. The key figures among Hovevei Zion, despite deep reservations, and after long controversy, decided to attend Herzl's congress. It was the Russian Zionists who were to shape the future of the movement that Herzl had begun.

The Congress opened on Sunday morning, August 29, 1897, in the concert hall of the Basel Municipal Casino. More than two hundred men and women attended—some as delegates of groups, others as individuals—from twenty-four states and territories.

By a seeming paradox, although Herzl's personal popularity was greatest among the masses, his congress was a very middle-class affair. But it was a special kind of middle class, drawn mainly from those *maskilim* of the Russian Empire who would have been assimilationists before 1881. As the Congress itself would show, most of the participants were emotionally close to the people of the *shtetl*—the Jewish villages and districts of the Russian Empire—in their response to Herzl.

Although only half of the participants actually came to the Congress from the East—mainly from the Russian Empire—a high proportion of those who came from Western countries were really Easterners; half of those from Germany, for example, came originally from Russia. And most of them were Hovevei *Zion*. The *Jewish Chronicle* (September 10) commented, "It seemed that Dr. Herzl had come to their Congress and not they to his."

Herzl himself took care not to appear to dominate the Congress, but he looked after every detail of the staging. He told Max Nordau, who had come in a frock coat, to go home and change into tails. "Externals," Herzl believed, "increase in importance the higher one climbs, for everything becomes symbolic."[102]

The most eloquent and moving speech came not from Herzl but from Nordau, who evoked the situation of European Jews at the end of the nineteenth century, the predicament which called for the Zionist answer:

> After a slumber of thirty to sixty years, anti-semitism broke out once more from the innermost depth of the nations, and his real situation was revealed to the mortified Jew. . . . He has lost the house of the ghetto, but the land of his birth is denied to him as his home. He avoids his fellow Jew because anti-semitism has made him hateful. His countrymen repel him when he wishes to associate with them. He has no ground under his feet and he has no community to which he belongs as a full member. He cannot reckon on his Christian countrymen viewing either his character or his intentions with justice, let alone with kindly feelings. With his Jewish countrymen he has lost touch. He feels that the world hates him and he sees no place where he can find warmth when he seeks it.[103]

The Congress was deeply moved by Nordau's speech, which was the high point of the Congress. As he told his wife afterwards, "Old men cried like children."

Herzl himself held back from any bold effects. His speech was solemn and dignified, on a keynote of reassurance. Zionism, he told his hearers, is not a "chiliastic horror" but "a civilized, law-abiding, humane movement towards the ancient goal of our people."

However low-key Herzl might pitch his words, the impact of his personality on this great occasion of his creation was overpowering:

Above, Theodor Herzl (dark-haired, at center) greeting Max Nordau at the First International Congress of Zionists at Basel, 1897. About Herzl, a participant in the Basel Congress wrote: "It seemed as if the great dream cherished by our people had come true at last and Messiah, the Son of David, was standing before us."

Below, Herzl on boat to see Kaiser Wilhelm II in Jerusalem, 1898. Herzl wrote at this time: "Strange ways of destiny. Through Zionism it will again be possible for Jews to love this Germany to which our hearts have been attached despite everything."

When I went to the Casino [wrote a member of the Odessa committee, Mordecai Ben-Ami (1845–1932)] I was so excited my legs were weak and I stumbled. . . . The delegates greeted each other warmly. They conversed quietly. Tremendous anticipation. . . . Suddenly the hall was quiet. . . . Old Doctor Lippe of Jassy mounted the rostrum, covered his white head with his hat and made a blessing. . . .

Many eyes filled with tears. . . . Herzl mounted the rostrum calmly. . . . Not the Herzl I knew, the one I had seen only the previous evening. Before us was the splendid figure of a son of kings with a deep and concentrated gaze, handsome and sad at one and the same time. It was not the elegant Herzl of Vienna, but a man of the house of David risen all of a sudden from his grave in all his legendary glory. . . . It seemed as if the great dream cherished by our people for two thousand years had come true at last and Messiah, the son of David, was standing before us.[104]

It is this notion of the resurrection of the Jews, symbolized by the Biblical person of Herzl, that makes the Basel Congress a quasi-liturgical affair, a secular ritual of great power, bonding together religious and nonreligious Jews; a bonding which had to happen if Israel were to come into being.[105]

Even for some Jews who were never themselves to become Zionists, Basel had a tremendous significance, in its reaffirmation of Jewry as a distinct nationality. The historian Simon Dubnov wrote: "Ever since the Sanhedrin of Paris, Jews in Western Europe had continued to reiterate that they no longer aspired to the claim of nation: but now a call to national reconstitution suddenly sounded. *Basel of 1897 expiated the sin of Paris in 1807* [author's italics]."[106]

There was an inner Congress paradox, however. The creation of a Jewish State was what the Congress was all about, but there could be no mention of a Jewish State at the Congress—any more than there had been at Kattowitz, thirteen years before—mainly because mention of it might endanger the Jewish settlers in Palestine, and prejudice future settlement. Hovevei Zion, the predominant element in the Congress, were particularly conscious of this. True, Herzl had originally dreamed of a Jewish State to be achieved by agreement with the Sultan; if that were a serious possibility, there would be no harm in public reference to it. But it was never a serious possibility. Abdul Hamid, a Muslim ruler of Muslims, had no intention of handing over Palestine to the Jews. And even if he had been inclined to do so, he would have had reason to fear Russian opposition, and intervention. Rothschild had explained this to Max Nordau in May 1896, when he was giving his reasons for refusing to back Herzl's enterprise, although he must have been basically in sympathy with it. The Sultan feared Russia, Rothschild told Nordau, "and Russia would never allow Palestine to fall under Jewish influence."

Rothschild was right, if Palestine is thought of as including Jerusalem. The idea of the Jews' becoming masters of Jerusalem would be an abomination to any Russian Orthodox Christian who could imagine such a possibility. If the Sultan had consented to such a thing, the Tsar would almost certainly have gone to war with him, with the enthusiastic support of his Orthodox people, and to the acclaim of much of the Christian world. It would have been a Crusade. And, in the course of that Crusade, what would happen to the Jews of Russia? What happened to them in the earlier Crusades was frightful, but those Crusades were primarily directed *against Muslims*. In this one, the Jews would be identified as the prime enemy, laying their sacrilegious hands on the Holy Places. It seems unavoidable that the consequences of that would have been far, far worse for the Jews than the pogroms of the 1880s and the early 1900s, and that something like a general massacre would have taken place. The idea of the Holy Places in Jewish hands could break the "Christian limit."[107]

In view of these fearful possibilities, latent in the fulfillment of Zionism, it is remarkable that so many Russian Jews should have traveled to Basel and there publicly assembled under the chairmanship of the man who had invited them, the famous, or notorious, author of *The Jewish State*.

What is also remarkable is the complaisance of the tsarist regime toward Zionism. Zionists were not persecuted in the nineteenth century to any greater extent than other Jews were, and Zionism was tolerated, though never officially legalized. True, the Zionism that was legal was the public, or ostensible, Zionism: the Zionism of settlements, with no mention of a Jewish State. But the authorities must have known that the idea of a Jewish State was in the air. Herzl at least wore his heart on his sleeve, and any Jews who went to Basel at the invitation of the author of *The Jewish State* were likely to be attracted by that concept. It would appear that the Russian authorities—understandably—must have regarded the whole notion as too chimerical to take seriously. They had also a practical reason for tolerating Zionism. Zionism drew Jews away from the revolutionary movement in Russia itself—intelligent, educated, energetic Jews, the very type most likely to become revolutionary. As far as the authorities were concerned, a Zionist was a neutralized Jew.

He wasn't really, though. Logically, the emergence of a Jewish State in Palestine depended on the collapse of both the Ottoman and the Russian empires. Such a state could not come into being, by the nature of the case, without Ottoman disintegration. But if Russia—Holy Russia—were still a Great Power when that happened, it would insure that the Holy Places, including Jerusalem, would come under the protection of a Christian power or powers, preferably Russia itself, but in the last resort any form of Christian power rather than Jews.

Leon Trotsky (1879–1940) and Rosa Luxemburg (1870–1919) were not Zionists (although the British Foreign Office, in 1917, seems to have imagined that they were). They were among the many Jews, in Russia and elsewhere, who were bitterly opposed to Zionism. All the same, the work of revolution they set their hands to, in the two decades that followed the Basel Congress, was a work that was (by no intent of theirs) essential for the attainment of Herzl's purpose. Without the destruction of the Russia of the Romanoffs—Holy Russia—the State of Israel could not have come into existence.

The sort of things that had to happen, if the Jewish State was to become a reality, were not of a nature to be publicly discussed in the casino at Basel. There were radicals who wanted a frank proclamation of Zionist aims; and this point of view was given a limited hearing and expressed in rather abstract language, calling for frankness, rather than exhibiting that dangerous quality. The program of the Congress, however, which the Congress adopted by acclamation, omitted reference to a Jewish State. Instead it used the formula: "Zionism aims at the creation of a national Home [*Heimstaette*] for the Jewish people in Palestine to be secured by public law."[108]

After the Congress, however, Herzl noted in his diary: "Were I to sum up the Basel Congress in a word—which I shall guard against pronouncing publicly—it would be this: 'At Basel I founded the Jewish State.' . . . Perhaps in five years, but certainly in fifty, everyone will know it."[109]

The fulfillment of Herzl's prophecy took nine months longer than his projected term. On May 14, 1948, David Ben-Gurion in the Tel Aviv Museum made his historic announcement: "The State of Israel has arisen." On the wall behind him hung the portrait of Theodor Herzl.

2

A HOME?
1897-1917

His Majesty's Government view with favour the establishment in Palestine of a national home for the Jewish
people, and will use their best endeavours to facilitate
the achievement of this object, it being clearly understood that nothing shall be done which may prejudice
the civil and religious rights of existing non-Jewish communities in Palestine, or the rights and political status
enjoyed by Jews in any other country.

—*Balfour Declaration,*
November 2, 1917

AFTER BASEL, there were two Zionisms in existence, working together uneasily. There was the Zionism of Herzl, which came to be
known as "political Zionism," and there was "practical Zionism," the
policy of the Russian Lovers of Zion.

After Basel, as before, the Lovers of Zion continued with small-
scale settlements in Palestine; settlements tolerated by Turkish officials,
partly because they were small-scale, partly because they superficially
resembled the older, religious immigration and partly because the
officials in question were bribed.[1]

"Practical Zionism" was, of course, "political" as well. For its
practitioners, the ultimate objective was essentially the same as
Herzl's: a country that Jews could call their own, which meant in
practice a Jewish State. But practical Zionists thought that the ground-
work for that state had to be laid by inconspicuous stages, over many
years.

Herzl rejected that approach, partly because its undramatic nature was uncongenial to his temperament, but more fundamentally because he sensed, as Russian Zionists on the whole did not at this time, that the problem of the European Jews was urgent, that time was running out. As Walter Laqueur said: "Herzl felt—and in this respect the fin-de-siècle Austro-Hungarian background is of importance—that the Jews could simply not wait."[2]

At the time of the First Congress of Zionists, Adolf Hitler was eight years old. By the time of the Balfour Declaration, Hitler was twenty-eight, and conscious of his mission.

Herzl wanted to save the Jews in one spectacular stroke. He wanted to negotiate, at the highest level, a grant of land adequate to accommodate Jews in great numbers. He wanted to win financial support on a scale adequate to develop this land into a home for all Jews who either could not or would not be assimilated, which meant the great majority of Europe's Jews. In that home, they would build their own state.

It was a colossal project, and as we look at it now, it seems almost a crazy one. But it was a time of large, bold projects, and Herzl succeeded in interesting some powerful people in his ideas.

II

The Second Zionist Congress was held, also at Basel, at the end of August 1898. The attendance was almost double that at the First Congress, and there was progress to report. The number of Zionist societies had increased ninefold since the previous year: there were now 913 such societies in the world, most of them in Russia (273) and Austria-Hungary (250). Significantly for the future, there were 25 societies in Britain (more than there were in Germany) and 60 in the United States. The total membership of these societies was not divulged. Vital believes that "the movement's total membership at the time of the Second Congress was well under 100,000, or roughly 1% of all Jewry."[3] All the same, even these numbers must have been far in excess of the Zionist strength before Herzl.

Although the proceedings at the Second Congress were inevitably somewhat repetitive of the first, and so anticlimactic, the growth of the Zionist movement between the two congresses was impressive enough to allow Herzl, and Herzl's form of Zionism, again to dominate the Congress. Herzl, in his opening address, hammered home his central message:

> From that emancipation, which cannot be revoked, and from anti-Semitism, which cannot be denied, we were able to draw a new and important conclusion. It could not have been the historical intent [*der geschichtliche Sinn*] of emancipation that we should cease to be Jews, for when we tried to mingle with the others we were rebuffed. Rather, the historical intent of emancipation must have been that we were to create a homeland for our liberated nation. We would not have been able to do this earlier. We can do it now, if we desire it with all our might.[4]

Herzl did not consult the Congress about just how this object was to be achieved. In effect, he assumed that the Congress would leave that to him, and the Congress, as a whole, was content to do just that. He handled the Congress with his usual self-confidence, style, adroitness and imperious dash. He snubbed the Russians by condemning "the smuggling in of settlers" to Palestine without a formal agreement with the Turkish authorities. He snubbed the Orthodox rabbis who opposed his movement: "It will always be one of the great curiosities of our period that these gentlemen should be praying for Zion and working against it."[5]

This won warm applause from a gathering which was almost entirely secular, or deemed itself to be so. A young chemistry student, Chaim Weizmann (1874–1952), was in that gathering. Weizmann was to be Herzl's successor, not formally, but in the actual leadership of Zionism, and he was to win, in 1917, the breakthrough that eluded Herzl. The Second Congress was the first attended by Weizmann; he had missed the 1897 Congress, although he had helped to organize it and had been a fervent Zionist since he was eleven years old.

In his old age, Weizmann wrote rather disparagingly, and sometimes unjustly, about Herzl,[6] but at Basel he must have been learning from him. Many of Weizmann's most quotable remarks in later years ring like Herzl's challenge to the rabbis: tough, sardonic, neat, concise, funny and a little unfair—and by that combination maddening to the adversary, and meant to be so.

Born at Motol, near Pinsk, in the Russian Pale, Weizmann identified with the Russian group—a caucus in the Congress, and a distinct entity between congresses—within the Zionist movement. He always remained a Russian Jew, wholly comfortable only among Rus-

sian Zionists. But he was Western-educated, a student at the time of
the Second Congress, and his future career was to lie in the West,
first in Switzerland and then in Britain. He constituted a link between
the Russian Zionists and those in the West with whom their hopes lay.
There were, as Weizmann observed, two leaders of Russian Zionism:
a "spiritual" one and a "political" one.

The spiritual leader was Asher Ginsberg (1856–1927), known to
all Zionists as Ahad Ha'am ("One of the People"), the name he wrote
under. It was through his writings, and especially through the
distinguished Hebrew-language periodical *Ha-Shiloah,* which he
edited from 1896 on, that he was heard. Ahad Ha'am preached cultural Zionism. He wanted to see a Jewish Home in Eretz Israel, not as
a haven for the Jewish masses, but as a spiritual center for the Jewish
people, most of whom would go on living in the Diaspora. That it
might become impossible for many of them to go on living there was
not an idea that impressed him. Of all the Zionists, he was the least
possessed of any sense of urgency where settlement was concerned.
He was at the opposite pole from Herzl; for him, even the practical
Zionists were going too far too fast. Educational preparation for the
future spiritual center was all-important. The key to that was the development of Hebrew, spoken and written, as a modern idiom. Ahad
Ha'am (Hebrew scholars agree) did not merely preach that doctrine,
but set a critically important example.

"He introduced—it might almost be said, invented—a Hebrew
style that serves to this day as a model of clear, astringent writing,
sparing of ellipsis, and almost devoid of the then customary Scriptural
and Talmudic allusions."[7] His writings serve as such a model in the
schools of Israel today, from elementary level up.

The description "one of the people" does not fit its wearer very
well. Ahad Ha'am was a remote, fastidious, scholarly figure. By social
origin, he belonged to the small upper class of Russian Jews, though
not to its tiny topmost tier. His father had farmed an estate leased
from a member of the Russian nobility near Berdichev, in the Ukraine,
and the Ginsberg family "lived in a style and on a scale analogous
to that of the Russian gentry."[8] His style was correspondingly aristocratic. He practiced an unremitting courtesy, which bordered on the
faintly offensive. Western Zionists, many of whom at this time knew
little Hebrew—Herzl knew hardly any—and were not particularly anxious to learn more, must have found Ahad Ha'am hard to take.
Herzl's Western Zionists, who were literally in a desperate hurry, must

have been exasperated by Ahad Ha'am's insistence on the meticulous sorting, mending and packing of the cultural baggage.

Just before the First Congress—which Ahad Ha'am attended aloofly, "a mourner at the wedding," as he said—Herzl wrote, in a moment of bitterness, about himself, that he was heading "an army of boys, beggars and prigs."[9] Ahad Ha'am was a prig, as even David Vital, who greatly admires him, acknowledged: "It cannot be denied that he was something of a prig; there are, perhaps, few confirmed and self-conscious intellectuals who are not; and he was nothing if not deliberate and self-conscious in his intellectualism."[10]

So I think it is permissible to speculate that when Herzl wrote the word "prigs" there may have floated before his mind's eye a thin, pale face with a lofty brow, a small beard and pince-nez on a black silken cord: the face of Ahad Ha'am.

Apart from other differences, Herzl and Ahad Ha'am were working to different time clocks. The anti-semitism that Ahad Ha'am was familiar with was *Christian* anti-semitism, unexpectedly reintensified in Russia, but in essence the same kind of anti-semitism that Jews over so many of the centuries had known only too well. But Herzl, and with him other Westerners—Nordau and Zangwill—were aware of the new strain of anti-semitism: racist, "scientific," post-Christian in spirit, and now beginning to reach for an anti-Christian ethic. By the late nineties, Western European culture, especially the culture of German-speaking Europe, was saturated with Nietzsche.

Ahad Ha'am was more sensitive to cultural strains than Herzl was. Had he lived in Paris or Vienna in the early nineties, Ahad Ha'am would surely have sensed, well before Herzl did, the sinister possibilities of Western anti-semitism. In his writings about Zionism, Ahad Ha'am shows a pessimistic lucidity that borders on masochism. It is impossible to imagine him living in the Paris of Édouard Drumont and writing (as Herzl did in 1892) that the French were "strangers to . . . anti-semitism." Had he lived in the West he might well have been in even more of a hurry than Herzl was. Living in Russia—and far more *directly* threatened than Herzl in the West[11]— Ahad Ha'am is faintly ironic about the hurry that Herzl seems to be in.

The political leader of Russian practical Zionism was Menachem Ussishkin (1863–1941). Like Ahad Ha'am, Ussishkin belonged to a higher social class than most Zionists. He had been born in the Pale, but his family, during his childhood, moved to Moscow, a certain sign of social success and of as much official acceptance as was attainable by Jews in Russia. He was unusual among Zionist leaders in that he was an Orthodox Jew, though equipped with a modern technological education (as an engineer). This combination made him a pivotal figure in the Zionist movement, acceptable both to secular leaders, like Pinsker and Lilienblum, and also to a section of the Mizrachi, around Rabbi Mohilever. He was able to devote a great deal of his time to Zionism, especially to the practical work of settlement and backing up the settlers.[12] He had a powerful personality which was reinforced by his massive physique. Weizmann, who was to cross his path, wrote of him that his bearing "suggested a mixture of Turkish Pasha and a Russian governor-general." "His skull was round and massive; you felt that he could break through a brick wall with it."[13]

Ussishkin deferred to Ahad Ha'am on cultural matters, but ignored him on practical matters, notably the pace of settlement. Both men were skeptical about Herzl, but acknowledged his usefulness to the movement: not quite the kind of usefulness that Herzl sought. Ahad Ha'am had welcomed the First Congress as "a great public statement before the world that the Jewish people were still alive and wanted to go on living." It was welcome, not (as Herzl wished) "so that other nations hear it and grant us our desire, but, before all else, so that *we ourselves* hear the echo of our voice in the depths of our soul which might then awake and shake off its degradation."[14]

Ussishkin was making much the same point, in his own very different way, when he wrote, after leaving Herzl's house on his first visit: "His greatest deficiency will be his most useful asset. He does not know the first thing about Jews. Therefore he believes that there are no internal obstacles to Zionism, only external ones. *We should not open his eyes to the facts of life so that his faith remains potent.*"[15]

The man who didn't know the first thing about Jews did know that the leaders of the Russian Zionists lacked faith in him and his great project. But he knew also—and it meant more to him—that their followers did have faith, almost as in a Messiah. They looked to him, simply, to lead the Jews out of bondage, and he hoped to do just that. His hopes never looked nearer fulfillment than they did in the period immediately after the Second Congress.

III

In his address to the Second Congress, Herzl had alluded—as proof of the importance of Palestine—to the impending visit to Jerusalem of Kaiser Wilhelm II. It was to the Kaiser, and to this visit, that Herzl now pinned his hopes. This was natural, because if any human being could have delivered Palestine to the Jews, in Herzl's lifetime, the Kaiser was the man.

Imperial Germany was now emerging as the patron and protector of the Ottoman Empire under Abdul Hamid II, and the Kaiser's visit to Constantinople, Jerusalem and Damascus in October and November 1898 was intended to symbolize and strengthen this relationship. Herzl saw this visit as his opportunity, and he grasped it energetically. Through the aristocratic contacts he had already established in Germany—primarily the Grand Duke of Baden, the Kaiser's uncle— Herzl managed to get through to the Kaiser and to kindle his imagination. For a short time, in the autumn of 1898, the Kaiser became an enthusiastic Zionist. He agreed to receive Herzl, with a Zionist deputation, in Jerusalem itself, and he agreed to intercede with the Sultan on behalf of the Zionists.

Like many of his contemporaries, the Kaiser was accustomed to thinking about the Jews *en bloc,* and he therefore imagined that support for Herzl would enlist "the tremendous power represented by international Jewish capital in all its dangerousness" in support of Imperial German penetration of the Middle East.[16] Herzl was adept at encouraging notions of this kind.

Herzl knew that what the Kaiser had in mind implied that the Jewish State would be, initially at least, a German protectorate, and he was ready to accept this, even with enthusiasm: "To live under the protection of this strong, great, moral, splendidly governed, highly organized Germany can only have the most salutary effect on the Jewish national character. . . . Strange ways of destiny. Through Zionism it will again be possible for Jews to love this Germany to which our hearts have been attached despite everything. . . ."[17]

The Kaiser received Herzl, first, in Constantinople, on October 18, 1898, at the Yildiz Kiosk, where the Kaiser was staying as the Sultan's guest. "I felt," wrote Herzl afterwards, "as though I had entered the magic forest where the fabulous unicorn is said to dwell. . . . He has truly Imperial eyes. I have never seen such eyes. A remarkable, bold, inquisitive soul shows in them." Herzl kept his gaze on those eyes, feeling that the Kaiser must be sensitive about his withered arm.

After a rambling conversation, in the course of which the Kaiser discussed the Dreyfus case—assuming Dreyfus's innocence—and mentioned the desirability of getting "elements among your people," such as the usurers of Hesse, to settle in Palestine, the Kaiser asked Herzl to tell him exactly what he was to ask of the Sultan. "A chartered company," Herzl replied, "under German protection." "Good! A chartered company!" said the Kaiser and departed.[18] Prince von Bülow later recalled that "the Kaiser was at first fired with enthusiasm for the Zionist idea because he hoped by this means to free his country of many elements that were not particularly sympathetic to him."[19]

But when, in Jerusalem, on November 2, 1898, the Kaiser received the Zionist delegation, headed by Herzl, nothing was said about the charter or intercession with the Sultan. There were some vague remarks about agriculture. The Kaiser had dropped the role of protector of the Jews as suddenly as he had taken it up.

Pondering that failure nearly two years afterwards, Herzl felt that it lay in lack of symbolism, through the prosaic use of a delegation: "My greatest mistake so far was not waiting for the Kaiser at the entrance gate of the Jews. For the Kaiser who has a penchant for symbolic acts, it would have been the right thing if I, whom he regarded as the head of all Jews, had waited for him at the threshold of our City of Jerusalem and had greeted him there. That is when he may have turned away from me."[20]

However that may be, the Kaiser had indeed turned away. He was about to cast himself in a different role, indeed a contradictory one. At Damascus, at the conclusion of his tour, the Kaiser emerged as protector of Islam: "Let me assure His Majesty the Sultan and the three hundred millions of Moslems who, in whatever corner of the world they live, revere him as their Kalif, that the German Emperor will ever be their friend."

The Kaiser had raised the question of a chartered company with the Sultan, but had met immediately with a polite but terminal Oriental negative. A German courtier later recalled that when the Kaiser twice attempted to raise the matter, the Sultan showed "a complete and ostentatious lack of understanding."[21]

Abdul Hamid told the Kaiser that he did not like the idea "but that as there could be no question of the German Emperor backing a project likely to cause the Turkish people harm, he would nonetheless have his ministers examine it." The Germans took the hint and dropped the subject. It was to become the settled policy of the Wilhelmstrasse that "intervention by Germany in favour of Herzl's 'Jewish State' would inflict irreparable damage on all our interests in Turkey."[22]

In retrospect, there is a ghastly, cosmic irony about this episode. Although the Kaiser dropped Zionism altogether, his visit to the Middle East was nonetheless a link in the chain of events that led to the National Home, and the creation of the State of Israel—among other things. A diplomatic historian, analyzing the foreign policy of Wilhelmine Germany, has written:

> If Weltpolitik was to be the order of the day, two courses lay open—the exploitation of Asiatic Turkey, and the creation of a first-class fleet. The former was bound to alarm Russia; the latter, however legitimate, would inevitably estrange England. The maxim of limited liability pointed to a choice between the two. The wise tradition was flung aside, and the rulers of Germany, overestimating their strength, determined to pursue both policies at once.[23]

For both parts of this policy, 1898 was the crucial year. In March of that year the new German naval law prepared for the creation of the first-class fleet. The Kaiser's flamboyant Oriental tour at the end of 1898 expressed the second half of the reckless new policy in a style which was itself singular and alarming. His final proclamation at Damascus was bound to offend, simultaneously, Britain, France and Russia, all of which—unlike Germany—ruled over substantial Muslim populations. (State Secretary—later Chancellor—von Bülow, who accompanied the Kaiser on this tour, saw this, and disapproved of the proclamation.[24]) But it was not just a matter of symbols and gestures. The visit, once the Jewish idea was dropped, produced important concessions for Germany in Turkey. Abdul Hamid in November 1899 announced his decision to award to the Deutsche Bank the concession for a railway to Baghdad and the Persian Gulf. A bloc was beginning to take shape, though as yet indistinctly, consisting of Germany, Austria-Hungary and Turkey. Imperial Germany's Middle Eastern ambitions—the *Drang nach Osten*—linked its fate more closely to that of Austria-Hungary and the Balkans as well as to Turkey, alienating Russia and helping to establish the fatal new Europe of the Central Powers versus the Entente.[25]

The tour was in fact an outstanding example of a pattern of behavior which played a leading part in bringing about the First World War. Herzl's "fabulous unicorn," as well as being spectacular, was a stupid, hyperactive and enormously dangerous animal.

The "ways of destiny" were stranger, and vastly more sinister, than even Herzl supposed. The Imperial tour, from which he hoped so much, proved to be a link in the infernal chain that led to the First World War: the war that gave the Zionists the Balfour Declaration, but that also made possible the rise of Adolf Hitler, the Second World War, the Holocaust, and only after that, the State of Israel.

IV

As far as the immediate future was concerned, Zionism had gained something from Herzl's Imperial interviews, though far less then Herzl had hoped for. Anything that interested the Kaiser, even temporarily, necessarily aroused the interest of all the other Powers. The Kaiser had contemplated the Zionist option and he might do so again. So Zionism became a recognizable subject for diplomatic consideration, and possible use. Herzl had noted that at the worst "our idea, as the jilted darling of the German Kaiser,"[26] would attract others.

In particular, the Kaiser's interest necessarily stimulated British interest, and so helped to prepare the way for the real breakthrough, which came thirteen years after Herzl's death.

At the Third Zionist Congress, again in Basel, Herzl inevitably ran into more criticism than before, but not more than he could tackle. The fact that Herzl had met the Kaiser—and more than once—offset the (more obscure) fact that the meetings had produced no tangible result. Ahad Ha'am acknowledged this, in his backhanded way, when he wrote: "No doubt, in itself, it [meeting with the Kaiser] makes a good impression; although what benefit may result from it is far from clear."[27] In short, the Russians grumbled, but did not attack. Herzl had a breathing space.

Herzl was now bent on winning, directly from the Sultan, what he had hoped to win through the Kaiser. "Our efforts," he told the Third Congress, "are directed at obtaining a Charter from the Turkish Government, a Charter under the sovereignty of His Majesty the Sultan." The charter would enable the Zionists "to begin large-scale practical settlement."

Herzl had not grasped that it was the Sultan, to whom he was now appealing, who had killed the Kaiser's interest in the charter. Herzl underestimated the Sultan, and what the Sultan stood for. Herzl knew that the Turks took bribes, and he jumped from that to the false conclusion that "a golden key" could open Palestine to officially approved large-scale settlement by the Jews.

In fact, the Ottoman authorities had been interested in Zionism long before Herzl had taken any interest in it. By the astonishingly early date of autumn 1881, at the very beginning of Russian Zionism, and before the arrival of the first Zionist groups in Palestine, the Ottoman authorities had decided to oppose Jewish settlement in Palestine, though not elsewhere in the Empire. The Sultan was absolutely clear about what the Zionists were up to. In 1891, he had expressed the fear that "Jewish emigration may in the future result in the creation of a Jewish government."[28] On the occasion of Herzl's earlier overtures, in 1896, the Sultan had tried to make clear to him that nothing of the kind would be allowed as long as the Ottoman Empire existed: "'When my Empire is partitioned, [the Jews] may get Palestine for nothing. But only our corpse will be divided. I will not agree to vivisection.'"[29] But Herzl, in this matter, was not capable of taking no for an answer.

Abdul Hamid never had the slightest intention of granting the only thing that Herzl was interested in: the charter for Palestine. He was interested in Herzl both because, making the same *en bloc* assumption as the Kaiser, he thought Herzl must represent important financial interests, as indeed Herzl claimed to do, and because he thought that Herzl, as a well-known correspondent of one of the leading newspapers of Europe, would be able to do something to help what would now be called the Sultan's "image." The image in question was at this time about as bad as it was possible to be. The massacres of Armenian Christians in various parts of the Ottoman Empire in the two previous years had horrified much of Europe and had earned Abdul Hamid, in Britain, a name that was to stick in history: Abdul the Damned.

Herzl was hardly more in a position to give the Sultan what he wanted than the Sultan was to give Herzl what he wanted. Herzl had no significant financial backing at any time, and by the end of the century, he had little journalistic influence, or power, and none at all in relation to the Middle East. His Zionist commitment had alienated the Jewish-assimilationist owners of the *Neue Freie Presse*, which ignored Zionism on principle. He was not in a position to influence his paper's editorial policy (though he did write some favorable signed articles) on Ottoman affairs.

Herzl's principal intermediary in this fantastic negotiation was an appropriately improbable, but very remarkable, man: Arminius Vambery (1832–1913). Vambery, like Herzl himself, was by origin a Hungarian Jew. He had also been a tailor's apprentice, a tutor at the

Ottoman court, and a British secret agent; he had passed as a dervish in Central Asia and as a Protestant in England. He was now established as "a master linguist, a particular expert on the peoples and languages of Central Asia, and an occasional adviser to Abdul Hamid with whom he had been on unusually close terms for a great many years."[30] Vambery and Herzl took to each other, as one might expect.

It was Vambery who arranged for Herzl to meet Abdul Hamid, and it is also Vambery who has left us the most convincing assessments of the man whom Herzl was to meet. Vambery's feelings about the Sultan were strong and contradictory. The first reference to the Sultan in Vambery's autobiography is like an officially commissioned portrait: "A watchful and intelligent ruler, full of national pride, although perhaps a little too anxious and severely absolute." A few pages later on, the "official" tone begins to slip a little: ". . . a skillful diplomatist and discerner of men, one of the most cunning Orientals I have ever known."[31] Twenty pages after that, the watchful and enlightened ruler becomes simply "the imperial rogue." In his correspondence with Herzl, Vambery called the Sultan "that *mamser*" (bastard).

The audience with the Sultan took place on May 17, 1901, in the same place, the Yildiz Kiosk, where Herzl had met the Kaiser more than two years before. Herzl has left us a portrait of the Sultan—"the Master" as he calls him ironically—which is in marked contrast with his idealized portrait of the Kaiser: "Small, shabby, with his badly dyed beard which is probably freshly painted only once a week for the *selamlik*. The hooked nose of a Punchinello, the long yellow teeth with a big gap on the upper right. . . . The feeble hands in white, oversize gloves, and the ill-fitting, coarse, loud-coloured cuffs. The bleating voice, the constraint in every word, the timidity in every glance. And *This* rules! Only on the surface, of course, and nominally."[32]

Although Abdul Hamid's powers, both mental and political, were already slipping at this time, Herzl's disdain was excessive, and revealingly "European" in character, reflecting even something of European anti-semitism. Zionists, acutely conscious of their Oriental origin, were bent on returning to the land of their ancestors, but they could not help bringing with them, in their efforts to regain that land, attitudes prevailing in Europe, where they had sojourned so long, toward the Orient and Oriental peoples.

The interview led nowhere, except to further contacts and correspondence, also leading nowhere. Herzl was to return to Constantinople—"that den of Ali-Baba and the forty thieves"—with a growing consciousness of being up against an impenetrable barrier, whose nature he never seems to have fully understood.

The Sultan's objection to the project was the fundamental one that it tended, in two major ways, toward the breakup of his dominions. It did so directly by increasing the number of inhabitants of his dominions who were not under his rule, but were protected by the consulates of European countries, under the regime of the Capitulations, which remained in force up to September 1914.

Very few Zionist immigrants became Ottoman subjects; most chose the protection of one or the other among the European Powers: Austria, Britain, France or even Russia. Because of the Capitulations, the Sultan was averse to the immigration of any Europeans, including Jews. But also, in admitting large numbers of *Jews* into *Palestine,* there was the danger of creating alarm and unrest among Muslims.

The Sultan was also, of course, the Caliph: Commander of the Faithful. That was indeed his only real title to the consent of the governed throughout vast dominions which the Sublime Porte could hardly have held down by force alone. His right to the title was disputed by many Muslims, but on the whole the title did work, certainly better than anything else in the Ottoman Empire. Non-Turkish Muslims might not like Turkish rule, but at least it seemed preferable to being ruled by infidels—as in Egypt, India, North Africa and Central Asia.

To give the Zionists what they were looking for would have been at odds with the basis of the Sultan's popular acceptance as sovereign. Herzl and other Zionists thought they could get around this by dissimulating their ultimate object—the Jewish State—and concentrating on the innocuous-sounding project of a chartered company. But Ottoman diplomats saw clearly what the Zionists were aiming at. Reporting on the Sixth Zionist Congress (1903), the Ottoman ambassador to Berlin, Ahmed Tevfik (1845–1936), told his Government that it was urgently necessary "to draw up special laws prohibiting the purchase of land in Palestine by the Zionists under any name whatsoever, so preventing the colonization of that country, the purpose of which colonization is first to attain autonomy and [then] employing all political or other means, form an independent state there.

"That is the essential aim of the Zionists."[33]

Ambassador Tevfik had understood the Zionist program. And no Sultan could enter into any agreement tending toward the fulfillment of that program—aimed ultimately at putting Jerusalem, third holiest

Muslim city, in Jewish hands—without endangering his own rule, and his own life as soon as what he had done was understood by his subjects. That was why the barrier was impenetrable, as long as the rulers of Palestine were Islamic rulers.

Herzl spent much of 1902 in the Yildiz Kiosk, knocking on that barrier with feelings of growing despair. The Yildiz had been built to Abdul Hamid's own designs. It consisted of a cluster of apparently unrelated small houses with small rooms, and exits by way of subterranean passages, some of which debouched far away from the buildings. Fear was the animating principle, and the Yildiz has been described as "a portrait of its owner such as no artist could better."[34] The Yildiz was built over a Jewish cemetery,[35] although Herzl, in the long hours he spent there, seems never to have known this. It could only have deepened the peculiar sense of oppression he felt, as it was, in the Yildiz.

Herzl's diaries for this period (Vols. III and IV) are particularly eloquent:

> Yildiz the capital of Wonderland . . . these horrible hours of waiting . . . a hazy, blurry, cigarette-smoke-enveloped coffee confabulation which was supposed to constitute negotiations. The anxiety of Yildiz which increases with the hours of waiting. . . . They are like sea-foam. Only their expressions are serious, not their intentions. . . . Loathsome meals with these innumerable barbaric dishes which, according to the Oriental custom, have to be forced down with exclamations of delight. Veritable snake food!

Herzl's constant companion at Yildiz was his interpreter at court, the Court Master of Ceremonies, Dragoman of the Imperial Divan, Ibrahim Bey. "A sincere, smooth gentleman . . . with a full grey streaked beard." Herzl found him *relatively* congenial: "To the extent that a Yildiz courtier can be a better type of person, he is one. I do have a certain liking for him." Ibrahim Bey explained certain advantages of Ottoman over Western culture. There was, for example, "a Christian play called *Le Marchand de Venise*. We have no theatre. Therefore no such inflammatory play can be performed here."

Ibrahim Bey had his own opinion about Herzl's negotiations. A German diplomat who noted Herzl's presence at the Yildiz Kiosk in February 1902 asked Ibrahim Bey what Herzl wanted.

"Des choses impossibles," said Ibrahim Bey.[36]

V

Though Herzl never altogether abandoned hope where Palestine was concerned, he now seriously considered the possibility—left open in *Der Judenstaat*—of establishing the Jewish State in another part of the world.

As a general idea, this had occurred to him as early as July 1898, even before the disappointment with the Kaiser. "I am thinking of giving the movement a closer territorial goal, preserving Zion as the final goal." At another level of his mind, this seemed to be linked with Moses, about whom he thought of writing a Biblical drama: "He does not care about the goal, but about the migration."[37]

After his disappointment with the Kaiser's Germany, Herzl turned to Britain for help. The location of the Fourth Zionist Congress was switched from Basel to London. Herzl began to think in terms of a chartered company in British territory—Cyprus or Egypt—near Palestine. "I would be a serious but friendly neighbour to the sanjak of Jerusalem, which I shall somehow acquire at the first opportunity."[38]

Two factors worked in Herzl's favor where Britain was concerned. One was the desire to deflect Jewish emigration away from Britain itself. The other was the desire to promote European settlement in the Empire.

Herzl gave evidence before the Royal Commission on immigration, the body whose deliberations were the prelude to the Aliens Act, and so a stage in the incubation of the Balfour Declaration. Herzl told the commission that nothing

will meet the problem: except a diverting of the stream of migration that is bound to go on with increasing force from Eastern Europe. The Jews of Eastern Europe cannot stay where they are—where are they to go? If you find that they are not wanted here, then some place must be found to which they can migrate without that migration raising the problems that confront them here [in England]. These problems will not arise if a home be found them which will be legally recognized as Jewish.[39]

Herzl's argument was taken seriously. Joseph Chamberlain (1836–1914), a member of Balfour's Conservative Government, and leading Imperial thinker, became interested in the idea of Jewish settlement in the Empire. Herzl met Chamberlain in October 1902, and Chamberlain agreed—as far as he personally was concerned—to a Jewish settlement at El Arish, in the Sinai peninsula, bordering on Palestine. But Egypt (including Sinai), being nominally independent, was the domain of the Foreign Office, and in particular of the powerful resident British Agent, and *de facto* governor, Lord Cromer. The Foreign Office at the time did not care for the idea—"very visionary"—and Lord Cromer was definitely opposed. Like the Sultan, he had to think about millions of Muslim subjects. A technical committee found that the idea was feasible—provided that large-scale irrigation works were undertaken. But Lord Cromer made it clear that, as ruler of Egypt, he was not about to divert the waters of the Nile to meet the needs of a Jewish colony in Sinai. By May 1903, Herzl was forced to realize that the El Arish idea too was "simply all over."

Herzl was now suffering from terminal heart disease. His race against time was entering a nightmare region. The Russian pogroms, after a lull of nearly twenty years, were starting up again, on an even more frightful scale than in the early eighties. For two days—April 19–20, 1903—the Jews of Kishinev, the capital of Bessarabia, were left to the mercy of a mob that had been worked up by semiofficial anti-semitic propaganda, including, as well as an Eastertime blood libel, an early version of what was later to become famous as the *Protocols of the Elders of Zion*. Vital writes:

> In cold figures, and by the standards of our times, the Kishinev pogrom was a nasty, but not outstanding case of licensed brutality: 32 men, 6 women, and 3 children killed outright, 8 persons who later died of wounds, 495 injured, of whom 95 heavily, many (mostly unreported) cases of rape, some mutilation of individual victims, some desecration of sacred objects, much blood and gore, innumerable roving and ecstatic mobs forming and reforming continuously, and vast heaps of debris and filth left over to be cleaned up after the troops had finally moved in and peace had descended on the streets. Damage to property was in due proportion: some 1,500 homes, workshops, and stores looted and destroyed and a large proportion, possibly a fifth of the city's Jewish population, rendered homeless and destitute. There were too some touches of that blocking-off of moral sensitivity which typically accompanied a hammering of the Jews.

The better class of the Christian public behaved dis-

After the Kishinev pogrom (April 1903), the first major physical attack on European Jews in the twentieth century.

The Kishinev pogrom received worldwide publicity, which the author ascribes to "the sharpness of the contrast between these ugly and obstinately archaic events and the bright progressive ideas which were expected to dominate the new century."

TWO PHOTOS: YIVO INSTITUTE

gracefully (the semi-official St. Petersburgskiye Vedomosti reported). They did not raise a finger to put a stop to the plunder and assaults. They walked calmly along and gazed at these horrible spectacles with the utmost indifference. Many of them even rode through the streets in their carriages in holiday attire in order to witness the cruelties that were being perpetrated.[40]

Kishinev created more of an international stir than the pogroms of the 1880s had done. Partly, this was due to improvements in communications, and expansion of the press and of reporting arrangements. Also, it was due to the sharpness of the contrast between these ugly and obstinately archaic events and the bright, progressive ideas which were expected to dominate the new century.

The events at Kishinev could not have taken place without encouragement, incitement and collusion on the part of the Russian authorities. In London, *The Times* pinned personal responsibility on the Tsar's Minister for the Interior, V. K. Plehve (1846–1904). *The Times* published a document that purported to be Plehve's instructions, twelve days before the outbreak, to the governor of Bessarabia, informing him of impending attacks on the Jews, and warning him not to use armed force against the *pogromshchiki*. Whether the document was genuine or not, it was generally accepted at the time as being so. Plehve became universally regarded as the man primarily responsible for what had happened at Kishinev, and for the new pogrom policy.

Herzl's response to Kishinev was to go to St. Petersburg to see Plehve. Herzl, though extremely romantic, was entirely without sentimentality, where his great purpose was concerned. Most other Zionists, and most other Jews, would have recoiled with horror from the thought of meeting the butcher of Kishinev. For Herzl, Plehve was interesting, as a man whose purposes had something in common with his own. Plehve didn't want the Jews in Russia. Herzl wanted to get the Jews out of Russia. Something might be arranged.

Herzl traveled to St. Petersburg, arriving on August 7, 1903. He met the Finance Minister, Count S. Y. Witte (1849–1915). Witte was a liberal by Russian standards. He told Herzl he was "a friend of the Jews." "The Jews are too oppressed," he said. "I used to say to the late Czar Alexander III, 'Majesty, if it is possible to drown the six or seven million Jews in the Black Sea, I would be absolutely in favour of that. But as it is not possible, one must let them live.'"

The reactionary Plehve, by contrast, was civil, even friendly and, it seemed, extraordinarily accommodating. Plehve was a big man, who cultivated an English phlegm, ill-matched to his hyperactive temperament. According to Herzl, he had energetic brown eyes, and a logical mind. Plehve was an industrious and feverishly inventive bureaucrat, creator of the system known as "police socialism": the attempt to control the revolutionary movement by pervasive infiltration, into working-class and revolutionary activities, of syndicated manipulators, spies and *agents provocateurs*. Police socialism by this time had attained such dimensions that it was impossible for anyone to know where the Tsar's bureaucracy ended and where the revolutionary movement began. Among the police socialists was Joseph Stalin.

Plehve was interested in Jews, not precisely for Pobedonostsev's reasons, but partly in consequence of Pobedonostsev's policies. Jews now bulked large in the revolutionary movement. Out of 5,426 political exiles under surveillance in Siberia, 1,676, or 31 percent, were Jews, although Jews were only 4 percent of the population of the Russian Empire. Jews, in consequence, played significant parts in the ambiguous, underground empire of Plehve's police socialism. One of Plehve's "secret assistants," the Jew Yevno Azeff, was chief of the Socialist Revolutionaries' fighting organization, or terrorist wing.

As Herzl had surmised, Plehve's interest in Jews led him to take an interest in Zionism, as something to divert some Jews from revolutionary activity, and to take some Jews out of Russia. But Plehve went much further, in words at least, than Herzl can ever have expected. Plehve emerged as even more of a Zionist than the Kaiser had been five years before. Plehve told Herzl that Russia was in favor of a Jewish State in Palestine. He promised that Russia would intervene in Constantinople to support the creation of such a state.

Herzl, sick and in desperate need of a breakthrough, seems to have convinced himself that Plehve meant what he said.

The Russian ambassador to Constantinople was instructed—after much prodding from Herzl—to make a *démarche* to the Porte. But the instruction made no mention of anything resembling an independent Jewish State. The ambassador was instructed to inform the Porte of Russia's sympathy with "the Zionists' project to return their co-religionists to Palestine." That was all, and even that was too much. The ambassador made no *démarche* and there was no follow-up from his authorities.

The idea of the Tsar bringing pressure to bear on the Sultan to

turn Palestine into a Jewish State is improbable. That Plehve himself
did not take it seriously can be inferred from his failure, in conversation with Herzl, even to refer to the Holy Places.[41] If the project had
had any reality at all in Plehve's mind, he would have been looking
for ways to circumvent the formidable opposition to such a project
that would be certain to come from the direction of the Orthodox
Church—and Ober-Procurator Pobedonostsev, who had refused to
see Herzl—and personally from the Tsar, who saw himself as Protector of the Holy Places.

If Plehve felt he could afford to disregard opposition of that
order, then he had no intention, in reality, of arousing it. The Russian
Zionists were almost certainly right, and Herzl wrong, about Plehve.
Plehve needed Zionism as diversion. And Plehve needed Herzl for the
same reason that Abdul Hamid had needed him: in order to palliate
his own sinister image in the West. To these ends Plehve, unlike Abdul
Hamid, was prepared to promise *des choses impossibles.*

In any case, what Plehve intended or did not intend was not to
matter very much longer. Plehve, the Sorcerer's Apprentice of the
Russian Revolution, was assassinated at the end of July 1904, by
agents of the terrorist organization headed by his own "secret assistant" Yevno Azeff. But by that time, Herzl too was dead.

VI

On his way back from St. Petersburg, on August 16, Herzl stopped
at Vilna, in Lithuania, an important Jewish city and center of rab-
binical learning. The Jews of Vilna thronged to see and hail him. As
a colonel in Plehve's police reported to the governor of Vilna:

> The influence the doctrine of Zionism has had on the Jewish
> people was plain to see during the brief stay here in Vilna of
> Dr. Herzl. For Vilna, in which there are 100,000 Jews, it was a
> holiday: crowds of Jews in their holiday clothes received him
> as a king would be received, and it was necessary for the
> police to take particularly cunning steps to prevent the visit
> from leading to nationalist demonstrations on the Jews' part.[42]

There was a dinner in Herzl's honor, at a summer house near
Vilna. Herzl was delayed.

> We walked about in the garden in the afternoon waiting for
> Herzl [recalled one of the guests]. Three o'clock already, then

half past three. Still no Herzl. Then four o'clock. The suspense grows; then tension: a minute is like an hour, an hour like a day. We watch all the paths in the forest leading to Verki.

Suddenly, at about half past five, Herzl appears among the trees, alone—he had gone ahead of his group and the trees had hidden his companions. Herzl, straight and tall, magnificent to see as he approaches the first line of trees against the background of nature, a picture of glory that lasts a few instants until his companions emerged from the forest to join him, but which I shall never forget.[43]

The dinner itself was interrupted by a crowd of Jewish youths who had walked from Vilna—a walk of about six hours, there and back—to see Herzl. One young worker drank a toast to the time when King Herzl would reign. "This absurdity," Herzl noted in his diary, "produced a remarkable impression in the dark Russian night."

After Kishinev, and after what he called "the day of Vilna"—his first serious contact with the Jews in the Russian Empire—Herzl was more than ever gripped with a sense of the urgency of getting the Jews out of Russia, and Europe, and into a home of their own. But, even in his own highly optimistic interpretation of his meetings with Plehve, Herzl realized that Palestine would not open soon to major Jewish colonization. Herzl knew the procrastinations of Constantinople too well for that, even if he never fully acknowledged the inflexible refusal behind them. His mind remained open therefore to the idea of a Jewish National Home elsewhere in the world, where the Jews could stay, more safely and honorably than in Europe, until the doors of Palestine should open.

And now new doors appeared to open: those of East Africa, now a British Protectorate. On his African journey of 1902–1903, Chamberlain had been impressed by the possibilities of the East African highlands—later part of Kenya, then referred to generally as Uganda—for European settlement and development. He thought the Jews might contribute to that. The Colonial Office did not yet—until 1905—have formal authority over the area, but unlike Egypt it fell broadly within Chamberlain's sphere of influence. On Chamberlain's urging, the Foreign Secretary, Lord Lansdowne, told the Zionists, on August 14, 1903, that if a suitable site could be found, he would "be prepared to entertain favourably proposals for the establishment of a Jewish colony or settlement, on terms which will enable the members to observe their national customs." Lansdowne invited the Zionists to send a delegation to East Africa to look at the possibilities for themselves. This offer Herzl now decided to take up. In doing so, he brought upon himself great, but illuminating, trouble.

Herzl crossed the Russian frontier on August 17. After one day's rest in the Austrian mountains, he went on to Basel, where delegates were beginning to gather for the Sixth Congress of Zionists, which was to be the last Congress in Herzl's lifetime.

Delegates were shocked by the changes in Herzl's physical appearance. "He looked old and worn. There were brown and grey streaks in his erstwhile black beard." Many delegates were also shocked by what Herzl had to tell them about what he called his "greatest accomplishments to date": the undertaking from Plehve and the invitation from Lord Lansdowne.

Russian delegates, in particular, did not trust Plehve's undertaking and deeply disapproved of Herzl's meeting with Plehve. They were also strongly opposed to the acceptance of Lansdowne's invitation, as a diversion from what should be the sole objective of Zionism, a National Home in Palestine.

The Plehve undertaking, whether reliable or not, did not require any decision from the Congress. Lansdowne's invitation, however, did, and opened a great debate within the Zionist movement, both inside and outside the Congress.

At the Congress itself, Herzl's proposal for sending an investigative expedition to East Africa carried by 295 votes to 178, with 99 abstentions. But the apparent victory, on so modest a proposal, was really a defeat for the project itself. Herzl was interested in East Africa as a place of refuge—a temporary one—for the persecuted Jews of Russia. But it was the Russian Zionists who passionately opposed this diversion of Zionism, who voted against even studying it, and who walked out when Herzl's motion was carried.

One of those who took part in that vote was a man then twenty-three years old, who was later to play a leading and controversial part in Zionism, Vladimir Jabotinsky (1880–1940). Although he admired and trusted Herzl, he was among those who voted against even looking at an alternative to Palestine. "I don't know why," he wrote later, "simply because this is one of those 'simple' things which counterbalance thousands of arguments."[44]

Herzl's opponents included the delegates from Kishinev. As Herzl said: "These people have a rope round their necks and still they refuse." And as Weizmann said, "The people *for* whom British East Africa was to be accepted, the suffering oppressed Russians did not want it. They would not relinquish Zion."[45]

Herzl protested that he was not relinquishing Zion. At the end of his speech closing the Congress, he raised his right hand and pronounced the words, in Hebrew: "If I forget thee, O Jerusalem, may my right hand lose its cunning."

Herzl, who seems to have suffered two minor heart attacks during this grim last Congress of his, thought that he must "obtain Palestine" before the Seventh Congress, or submit to that Congress his resignation from the leadership.

From Russia, in the wake of the Congress, came signals of implacable opposition to the slightest deviation from the objective of Zion. Menachem Ussishkin, who had stayed in Eretz Israel during the Congress, now circulated an open letter to delegates rejecting the majority decision. "Just as no majority in the world," Ussishkin wrote, "can cause me to apostatize from the faith of Israel or the law of Israel, so no numerical majority at the Congress will detach me from the Land of Israel."

One thing the East Africa debate revealed was how thin the secular covering was over the sacred core of Zionism.[46] The Russian Zionists met at Kharkov in November 1903. The meeting was dominated by Ussishkin, and the spirit of Ussishkin. An ultimatum was sent to Herzl. He was required to withdraw the East Africa project "totally" and "in writing" and no later than the Seventh Congress. If Herzl failed to comply, steps would be taken "to get up an independent Zionist Organization without Dr. Herzl."

At a Zionist Committee meeting in Vienna, in April 1904, the confrontation took place between Herzl and Ussishkin. Herzl once more appeared to dominate the proceedings by force of his personality and eloquence. Ussishkin, by contrast, was heavy, dour and dull, but it was Ussishkin who had won. Herzl defended his past conduct effectively, but conceded to the Russians the central point:

> No one could rightly reproach me with disloyalty to Zionism were I to say: I am going to Uganda. It was as a Jewish-state man [*Judenstaatler*] that I had [originally] presented myself to you. I gave you my card: Herzl, *Judenstaatler*. I learned a great deal in the course of time. I got to know Jews—and sometimes it was a pleasure. But, gentlemen, I also learned that the solution for us lies only in Palestine.[47]

The East African project had not yet been formally dropped, but from now on, it was Palestine or nothing. And Herzl knew that that meant nothing for many years to come. Certainly there was no prospect of any news from the Yildiz Kiosk that could gladden the hearts of the Seventh Congress.

To the end, Herzl never lost confidence in the value to Zionism of face-to-face encounters with the great. In January 1904, he went to Rome and saw the King of Italy and the Pope. King Victor Emmanuel III (1869–1947) spoke of Messiahs "with understandable roguishness," according to Herzl, and asked whether there were still Jews who expected the Messiah.

Herzl replied: "Naturally, your Majesty, in the religious circles. In our own, the academically trained and enlightened circles, no such thought exists of course. . . . Our movement is purely nationalist." Herzl adds: "And to his amusement I also told him how in Palestine I had avoided mounting a white donkey or a white horse, so no one would embarrass me, by thinking I was the Messiah."[48]

Appropriately, the last of Herzl's great interviews was with the Pope, the saintly Pius X, "a good, coarse-grained village priest," Herzl thought him. The Pope was polite, but implacable, and honest. "The Jews have not recognized Our Lord, therefore we cannot recognize the Jewish people." Herzl told the Pope: "We are not asking for Jerusalem—only the secular land." The Pope was not mollified: "We cannot be in favour of it." Only if the Jews were prepared to be converted to Catholicism could the Pope support their return to the Holy Land. "And so," said Pius X, "if you come to Palestine and settle your people there, we shall have churches and priests ready to baptize all of you."[49] It was a strange, ironic echo of Herzl's 1893 proposal for the conversion of the Jews *en masse* to Catholicism "amidst the pealing of bells."

Herzl knew it was now time for him to leave the stage. "Let us not fool ourselves," he told a doctor friend on May 9, "with me it is after the third curtain." A week later, his diary breaks off. On July 3, 1904, Herzl died, at the health resort of Edlach. He was forty-four years old.

Ahad Ha'am, no mean stylist himself, appreciated the ending. "He died at the right time," wrote Ahad Ha'am, with something less than his usual degree of acidity. "His career and activities over the past seven years had the character of a romantic tale. If some great writer had written it, he too would have had his hero die after the sixth congress."[50]

Herzl was buried in Vienna, provisionally, as he had stipulated: "until the day when the Jewish people transfer my remains to Palestine."

Jews came to the funeral from all of Europe. More than six thousand people followed the hearse. Among them was the Austrian writer Hermann Bahr (1863–1934), a friend of Herzl's since their undergraduate days (oddly, since at that time Bahr had been a Wagnerian anti-semite). Bahr wrote that it was only at the funeral he realized who Herzl really had been: "I realized I was moving in an alien world. The dark mass of people . . . whispered sounds I could not comprehend; it rolled through the streets of Vienna on its way to the promised land. This is Herzl's deed. He gave his people the feeling that they had a homeland once again."[51]

VII

The Seventh Congress of Zionists (Basel, July–August 1905) turned down the East Africa project once and for all—to the great relief of the British Colonial Office[52]—and declared the movement's final and exclusive commitment to a Jewish National Home (meaning, ultimately, State) in Eretz Israel. But the doors of Palestine remained closed to large-scale Jewish immigration, and no Zionist in the period from Herzl's death to the First World War tried to renew his heroic efforts to fling those doors open. The Zionist movement as a whole now followed the tactics of the Russian Lovers of Zion: practical Zionism, piecemeal settlement, infiltration in small numbers through the corrupt cracks in the Ottoman wall of exclusion.

Herzl's political Zionism seemed to be dead; it was in fact dormant. Herzl had impressed the international diplomatic world. He had made Zionism a recognizable counter in the diplomatic game; something one might want to make use of some day; or something that other Powers might use, and which it might be prudent to deny them. This may seem strange in view of the largely chimerical nature of Herzl's actual negotiations. As one reads the series of Herzl's diplomatic encounters—with grand dukes and grand viziers, with Imperial statesmen, with the Kaiser, with the Sultan, with the King of Italy, with the Pope—one can sometimes have the feeling of watching a sort of Peer Gynt conducting a high quest, through a series of dialogues at cross-purposes, with a succession of crowned and masked trolls.

But the fact that the meetings had happened made its mark. The masters of temporal and spiritual empires had met Herzl, who was master of nothing, and who represented only an idea. That was enough to insure, for the idea, interest and guarded respect. It is doubtful whether the British War Cabinet in 1917 would have taken Zionism as seriously as they did if they had not known that the Kaiser had taken up Zionism before (in 1898) and thought that he might do so again.

Within Zionism itself, the Herzlian idea went into eclipse for a while, but did not die. The man who did most to keep it alive was Chaim Weizmann. During Herzl's lifetime, Weizmann had aligned himself with the Russian Zionists, stressing practical Zionism as against Herzl's political Zionism. But after Herzl's death, there came a subtle change. At the Eighth Congress (The Hague, 1907), Weizmann proposed what he called "synthetic Zionism," a synthesis between the practical and the political. Although Weizmann put the case for his synthesis primarily in practical rather than in political terms, the very concept of a synthesis had a tendency to rehabilitate political Zionism, then in discredit. There was room for "diplomatic work" and "the tribunals of the world" once the way had been prepared by practical work in immigration, colonization, education.

Thus unobtrusively and obliquely—and so appropriately—Weizmann made his bid for the diplomatic mantle of Herzl, something by which few Zionists, at this point, would have set much store. (Vladimir Jabotinsky is the principal exception.) Zionism's diplomat would have to wait his hour. As long as the international political world remained broadly the same as the one Herzl had explored in vain, there was no hope at all of a Herzlian solution. But large changes were expected, sometime. No one believed the Ottoman Empire could last very long. And after 1905 the Russian Empire too seemed to be cracking. There would be opportunities. Weizmann could wait. Weizmann did not possess, at this time, the Herzlian sense of desperate urgency. In any case, there was hardly as much sense of urgency among Zionists in Western Europe in the middle of the first decade of the twentieth century as there had been ten or more years before.

In Germany and Austria, anti-semitism had not gone away, but neither had it noticeably increased since the mid-nineties. In Germany, it was very widely diffused, but rather academic in expression, and apparently harmless; in Austria, it was still the more or less *gemütlich* anti-semitism of Karl Lueger; many Jews considered it quite possible to go on living with anti-semitism of that order. And in France, the scene looked positively bright. The anti-semites had overreached themselves over the Dreyfus case and had taken a terrible beating through Dreyfus's rehabilitation. In 1906, General Gillein conferred the Legion of Honor on Alfred Dreyfus, in that same court-yard where, eleven and a half years before, Herzl and Barrès had witnessed the ceremony of the degradation. Assimilated Jews through-out Western Europe could take that rehabilitation as confirming their own accepted status, and as signaling the final defeat of anti-semitism. Those who had thought all along that the Zionists were panic mongers felt themselves to have been proved right.

In Russia, however, the pogroms continued, and mass emigration grew. Yet even in Russia, among many Jews, a kind of catastrophic optimism was prevalent at this time. The violent anti-semitism of the first decade of the twentieth century could be seen, especially after the revolutionary upsurge of 1905, as part of the death throes of the tsarist regime. Understandably, many young Jews felt that the right response was to stay and work for the Revolution, which would bring about, so they assumed, the end of anti-semitism, along with all other social evils.

But those Jews who were neither confident of salvation by revolu-tion nor religiously resigned to the acceptance of persecution now left Russia in huge numbers. Emigration from Russia had been running around 50,000 at the turn of the century; in 1905 it jumped to double that figure, and by 1907 it had tripled. The movement was escalated by the intensification and extension of the pogroms that followed the Revolution of 1905.

Most of this vast movement of people went toward America, then still open to mass immigration. But the rate of emigration to Palestine was increased, on its miniature scale, proportionately to the main emigration. In the years from 1882 through 1903, the first *aliyah*, 25,000 emigrated to Palestine. In the ten years from 1904 to 1914, the second *aliyah*, 40,000 emigrated there. Y. H. Brenner, who was him-self part of the second *aliyah*, wrote: "It was only world-upheavals such as there were in 1905–6, shaking and boiling the ice-age formula-tions of our Pale of Settlement and throwing tens of thousands of our people overseas at a single blow that led to some bits and pieces be-ing cast up on Eretz-Israel itself."[53]

The last part of that metaphor is misleading. The "bits and pieces" were not "cast up" on Eretz Israel. They chose to go there, when they could have gone to America. And many of them made that choice not with the eager encouragement of the Russian Zionists but to some extent against their discouragement. Men like Ussishkin were "ap-palled at the prospect of anything like a mass movement of people" into Palestine.[54] Their reasonable fear of that was one of the reasons why they had disliked the spectacular and quasi-messianic appeal of Herzl's version of Zionism. Many of that minority who chose the daunting option of Eretz Israel, as against the relatively easy option of America, were, like Ben-Gurion, under Herzl's spell.

Many of these immigrants (as Ussishkin had foreseen) could not stand the hardships of their new environment and left again in a hurry. As Ben-Gurion later wrote, they "took one look and caught the same ship back again." But those who stayed raised families. In 1880, 20,000–25,000; by 1914—the end of the second *aliyah*—the total was 85,000, with of course a far higher proportion of young people.

Eighty-five thousand was 12 percent of the population of Palestine in 1914, as against about 5 percent in 1882. We now come to the fateful question of how members of the Arab majority felt about this development at this time.

VIII

Whatever they felt—and their feelings were mixed, in this early period—there was not much they could do about the immigration. The Ottoman Empire was not a democracy, and it was dominated by Turks, not Arabs. Also—and this was a crucial point—the Ottoman authorities, under the system known as the Capitulations, had conceded a special status, with immunity from local jurisdiction, to the subjects of the European Powers. The Zionists benefited from this system; indeed in the early years, they could hardly have established themselves without it. The European Powers collectively upheld the privileges of all Europeans living in the Ottoman Empire. The European Powers competed among themselves for subjects to protect. Thus Russia, while persecuting Jews at home, protected them in Palestine (from 1890). Few chose to be Ottoman subjects.

There was, of course, a certain tragic irony about all this. The Zionists saw themselves as the native children of Eretz Israel, returning to their original home. And they saw themselves as shaking off the dust of the European lands of their long sojourn. Yet to the authorities in Palestine, and to its native-born inhabitants, they appeared as Europeans. This was helpful, and probably indispensable, to their establishment in Palestine, but it also meant that the general Arab resentment of European power and influence, which was to grow in proportion as that power and influence declined, would apply to the Zionists, along with other resentments.

These resentments were to rise to a frenzy when it came to be widely realized that this was one category of Europeans who were not going to go home, because they regarded themselves as having *come* home.

It was not until after the Balfour Declaration that realization of the meaning of Zionism became widespread among Palestinian Arabs generally, and among other Arabs. For most of the period before the First World War, Arab hostility to the new settlers had relatively little to do with Zionism. It was a matter of resentment and suspicion of Jews, and it was confined—as far as overt manifestations were concerned—to two relatively restricted categories of Arabs: Christians and the commercial classes. But some exceptional Arabs, even before the nineteenth century was over, had seen Zionism as a great danger, against which they tried to warn their compatriots.

The first Arab protest against modern Jewish settlement in Palestine came as early as 1891, and reflected fear of competition on the part of merchants and craftsmen in Jerusalem. It took the form of a telegram to the Grand Vizier, in June 1891, protesting against an expected wave of further Jewish immigration. It called for a stop to this, and to Jewish acquisition of land. Thus, as a historian of the period has written, this first protest, entered even before Herzl's conversion to Zionism, "spelt out the two basic demands which the Arabs never abandoned thereafter: a halt to Jewish immigration into Palestine, and an end to land purchase by them."[55]

Ahad Ha'am paid his first visit to Eretz Israel in that same year, 1891. He believed that Arabs were generally quiescent at that time because "they see no future danger to themselves in anything we do," and some of them (landlords and some peasants) profited from the Zionists. "But," he warned, "if ever there comes a time when we shall have developed our life in Eretz Israel to the point where we shall be encroaching upon them in a greater or lesser degree, [then we should not expect them] to yield their place easily."[56]

That was not an insight shared (or at least acknowledged) by any other Zionist, either at that time or for long afterwards. Officially, the Zionist position was that there was no conflict of interest, but only a community of interest, between Arabs and Zionists. That long remained an article of faith to Zionists in the Diaspora. But among the Yishuv[57]—the Jews actually settled in Eretz Israel—there was a growing realization of the truth Ahad Ha'am had divined.

The protests of 1891 were probably initiated by Muslims, but a disproportionately large part of the early Arab agitation against Jewish settlement—and later against Zionism—was carried out by Christian Arabs. This was inevitable, since Christians made up so large a proportion of the educated and articulate class, the people most likely to feel, and to be able to express, resentment of encroachment. The resentment would have arisen in any case, even if there had been no Christians around, but the Christian element worked to give a special character to the resentment: one marked by the anti-semitism of European Christians.

In Europe, one of the sections of the population most strongly affected by anti-semitism was the Christian clergy. Naturally the Christian clergy was strongly represented in the Holy Land. The Russian Orthodox clergy were there in strength, as were the French, Austrian, and German Catholics, and German Protestants. All these bodies of men and women had to carry with them their portion of the prejudices and stereotypes current in their homelands and in their own order, including prejudices and stereotypes about Jews.

The French were traditionally the most influential power in Greater Syria—the Syria, Lebanon and Palestine of today. The French clergy, on the whole strongly anti-semitic in the last decade of the nineteenth century, had additional reasons for being so in the first decade of the twentieth. The Dreyfus case, so unwisely exploited by so many Catholics, had rebounded against them, and the Catholic religious orders fell under heavy pressure from a militant, secular retaliation. This they interpreted as "the revenge of the Jews." There is clear evidence that anti-Dreyfusard clergy transmitted their interpretation of "the Jewish problem" to Arabs—principally Christian Arabs, but also Westernized Muslims.[58]

The naturalization in the Arab world of a European variety of anti-semitism seems to have had four main kinds of effect. First, it legitimized (as European and therefore "modern") the anti-Jewish feeling that was already there and growing. Second, it tended to intensify that feeling, since European anti-semitism had a hysterical, obsessional edge to it, lacking in the more placid forms of anti-Jewish feeling that were traditional in Islam and the Middle East. Third—and this was the most important in practical terms—it conveyed the message that the European Jews now immigrating into Palestine were not regarded by other Europeans as really European, or as desirable immigrants. In that light, the Jewish immigrants could be seen as isolated, vulnerable, not like other Europeans, who were sure of the unvarying support of the Powers.[59] And finally there was the European stereotype of the Jew as essentially a parasite: lacking in moral fiber, incapable of standing on his own feet, above all, no fighter, or even capable of being one.

The most likely combined effect of all this on the Arabs was surely to encourage them in their resentment of the Zionists, while encouraging them also in their propensity to underestimate both the Zionists themselves and the probable cost to the Arabs of an attempt to extirpate the Zionists by force.

The net result of the importation of European forms of anti-semitism into the Middle East was to prove even more damaging to the Arabs than to the Jews.

IX

Six months after the First Zionist Congress a reader in Frankfurt wrote to the Arabic paper *al-Muqtataf*[60] to ask what the Arabic press had to say about Zionism. It replied that the Arabic press had simply mentioned the Congress, without paying any special attention to it. This provoked a leading Arab thinker, the Lebanese Rashid Rida, into the first published protest against the programs of Zionism. Rashid Rida roundly assailed his compatriots:

> You complacent nonentities . . . look at what people and nations do. . . . Are you content for it to be reported in the newspapers of every country that the penniless of the weakest of peoples [the Jews], whom all governments are expelling, have so much knowledge and understanding of civilization and its ways that they can take possession of your country, establish colonies in it, and reduce its masters to hired labourers and its rich to poor men? Think about this question, and talk about it.[61]

Rashid Rida was affected by some Western stereotypes, but he was far too intelligent and well informed to underestimate the Zionists.[62] He thought that nothing prevented the Jews from becoming "the mightiest nation on earth" except statehood (*mulk*), and they were well on their way to achieving that, through their powers of organization. He advised his compatriots "to take note of the Jews."[63]

Rashid Rida was not the only Arab intellectual to be troubled by the progress of Zionism by the turn of the century. On March 1, 1899, a leading member of one of the outstanding Muslim families in Jerusalem, Yusuf al-Khalidi, wrote a historic letter, in French, to Zadoc Kahn, Chief Rabbi of France, an acquaintance of Herzl's (and a fence-sitter where Zionism was concerned). Yusuf al-Khalidi was an enlightened and traveled liberal who had been a member of the short-lived Ottoman parliament in the seventies, and was then expelled from Constantinople by Abdul Hamid.

In theory, wrote Yusuf al-Khalidi, the Zionist idea was "completely natural, fine and just." "Who can challenge the rights of the Jews in Palestine? Good Lord, historically it is really your country."

But in practice the Jews could not take over Palestine without the use of force (cannons and battleships), which they did not possess. Turks and Arabs were, at present, well disposed to Jews, but they could be aroused against them.

> [Christian] fanatics . . . do not overlook any opportunity to excite the hatred of Muslims against the Jews . . . It is necessary, therefore, for the peace of the Jews in Turkey that the Zionist Movement, in the geographic sense of the word, stops . . . Good Lord, the world is vast enough, there are still uninhabited countries where one could settle millions of poor Jews who may perhaps become happy there and one day constitute a nation. That would perhaps be the best, the most rational solution to the Jewish question. But in the name of God, let Palestine be left in peace.[64]

Zadoc Kahn passed the letter to Herzl, who sent a soothing reply. The Jews were supported by none of the Powers, and had no military intentions of their own. There need be no difficulty with the local population. Nobody was trying to remove non-Jews. The local population could only benefit from the prosperity the Jews would bring.

> Do you believe that an Arab who has a house or land in Palestine whose value is three or four thousand francs will greatly regret seeing the price of his land rise five- or tenfold? For that is necessarily what will happen as the Jews come; and this is what must be explained to the inhabitants of the country. They will acquire excellent brothers, just as the Sultan will acquire loyal and good subjects, who will cause the region, their historic motherland, to flourish.[65]

About the landowners at least, Herzl was right. He could have added what was still true at this time—that the peasants benefited materially too, because the early Zionists paid good prices and gave employment.

In general, however, it is easy to see in retrospect that al-Khalidi was raising real difficulties, and Herzl, returning unreal answers. Did he simply have his tongue in his cheek? On one point, he certainly did. When the author of *The Jewish State* assured his correspondent that the Zionists would be "loyal and good subjects" of the Sultan, he was saying what he knew to be untrue and intended to be untrue.[66] For the rest, he was saying how he hoped—and intended—things would turn out. He did not wish to remove non-Jews, nor had he any use of force in mind. What would happen, if the things he hoped would happen did not happen, was not something Herzl ever much cared to contemplate. It is a pity Zadoc Kahn did not pass al-Khalidi's letter to Ahad Ha'am.

In the five years following Herzl's death, things happened, both on the Zionist side and on the Arab side, which made Herzlian optimism increasingly hard to sustain.

On the Jewish side, the new factor was the emergence, at the heart of the second *aliyah*, of a new strain of Zionism: harder, more puritanical, more ruthless. Like so much else in the prehistory of Israel, this new strain was a product of Russian conditions. The men and women of the first *aliyah* had grown up in relatively benign, and still apparently hopeful, conditions for Jews, under Alexander II. The men and women of the second *aliyah* grew up in the shadow of the harsh and menacing Russia of Alexander III and Nicholas II. Most of them grew up having to cope with—at best—permanent, cold, systematic rejection on the part of the Gentile world. They were Pobedonostsev's children.[67]

Pobedonostsev's policies turned young Jews, in large numbers, into revolutionaries. Most of them became Russian revolutionaries. Others brought a revolutionary hardness into Zionism. Some were not sure whether to be Russian revolutionaries or Zionists. Members of Po'alei Zion (Workers of Zion) took part in the Russian revolutionary movement, while remaining Zionists (which was what Plehve had complained about to Herzl). One of these, Izhak Ben-Zvi (1884–1963), recalls how he resolved the conflict inherent in that. In October 1905, when the revolutionary parties emerged for a time into the open, Ben-Zvi addressed a mass meeting in Poltava:

It was I who spoke to the crowd of ten thousand souls—in Russian, of course. I spoke as a Jew—on the Russian revolu-

tion, on the participation of the Jews, and on our own aspirations to the life of a free nation in Zion. But then, as I was
speaking from the theater balcony, I saw in my mind's eye a
living image of the holy city of Jerusalem, in its ruins, empty
of its sons, as I had seen it a year earlier on my first visit to
the land in the summer of 1904. And I asked myself: *to whom
am I speaking?* Will my listeners here in Poltava understand
me, will they believe? Are we, the Jews, *true partners* in this
revolution and in this victory? Will this revolution which
heralds salvation for the Russians bring the hoped-for salvation to us Jews as well? Why am I here and not there? Why
are we all here and not there? And once these questions had
sprung to my mind I was unable to shake free of them: and
when I had finished speaking my thoughts were not on the
demonstration and on the victory of the Russian revolution,
but on *our own Jerusalem.* I decided absolutely that my place
was in Eretz Israel and that it was for me to go there and to
dedicate my life to its reconstruction and without delay.[68]

The people of the second *aliyah,* people of particularly strong
character, made a very great contribution to the shaping of the New
Yishuv. Many of its innovations, including the cooperative farming settlements, the *kibbutzim,* were their creations. The second
aliyah was also decisive in making Hebrew the day-to-day language
of the Yishuv.[69] But, without intending to do so, the people of the
second *aliyah* increased the antagonism of Arabs to the Jewish settlers.
The impact of the new type of Zionist was felt most critically in two
related fields: employment and defense.

The older Zionists, those of the first *aliyah,* had been (generally)
content to employ Arabs, both for manual labor and as armed watchmen. The new Zionists—members of Po'alei Zion, and other groups
participating in the second *aliyah*—rejected this whole system. Zionists, these socialists[70] thought, should be entirely self-reliant, working
their own land, cooperatively, themselves, and defending it themselves.

These conceptions brought nearer a conflict with the Arabs, which
was probably inevitable in any case. Under the earlier forms of Zionism, the purchase of an Arab estate often meant, for many of the
Arab peasants concerned, only a change of employers (or masters)
and generally a change for the better, as far as conditions of employment (or tenure) were concerned. Thus, in this early period, the
concept that Zionism brought benefits to both Jews and Arabs was not

unfounded. But wherever the *new* Zionists were in control, transfer of land from an Arab landlord to a Zionist cooperative meant that the Arabs on (and now *from*) the land became landless and unemployed. It is not surprising that many such Arabs should also have become fanatically anti-Zionist.

The Russia from which the new Zionists came was an increasingly violent place: anti-semitic violence, revolutionary violence, and especially revolutionary preparation against inevitable counterrevolutionary violence were all part of their background. The new Zionists were all people who had a horror of the age-old nonviolent tradition of Diaspora Jewry: the submission to violent oppression as a manifestation of the will of God. In the Russian pogroms of the opening years of the twentieth century, Jews resisted, as they had not done in earlier times. At Gomel, in the summer of 1903, Jews organized their defense and beat off the *pogromshchiki,* whereupon the Tsar's police abandoned their traditional neutrality and intervened to crush the Jews.

The New Zionists were determined that the Jews should organize their own defense, and successfully this time, in Palestine. General conditions on the land in Palestine were fairly lawless, and there had been attacks on Jewish settlements as early as 1886; not, at that date, reflecting any kind of political reaction to Zionism but part of a general pattern of frequent agrarian violence, usually over grazing rights. The earlier Zionists had thought it an adequate response to this to hire local watchmen, Arab or Circassian. The new Zionists now challenged this.

In September 1907, there was a historic meeting in Jaffa, in the attic of a rooming house kept by Izhak Ben-Zvi—the same Ben-Zvi who, speaking of Palestine, had asked himself the question: "Why are we all here and not there?" The meeting heard a young man from Gomel, Israel Shochat (1886–1961), speak of the organization of Jewish self-defense in his native town. The ten young men present resolved to accept employment themselves as guards, and to promote the concept of self-defense within the Yishuv. This little enterprise developed into Ha-Shomer (The Watchmen), numbering one hundred highly efficient armed men by 1914. This was the tiny nucleus of the future Israel Defense Forces.

New-style Zionism pointed in the direction of a completely self-reliant and self-contained Jewish community—and eventually Jewish State—in Palestine: a community, and state, which would have no need of Arabs. The new Zionists were neither hostile nor particularly friendly toward Arabs. They were prepared to tolerate Arabs as neighbors, having their own separate and distinct life—neither exploited by Jews nor in control of them—but they realized that Arabs might not be prepared, for long, to tolerate *them*. If there were to be *pogromshchiki* in Palestine, a hundred Russian Zionists were putting themselves on a footing to repel them.

The Arabs were not yet in any mood to attack. Few understood what Zionism was about. Only in a few areas, and by those immediately affected, had the impact of the new, self-reliant Zionism been experienced. Dr. N. J. Mandel writes of "generally good day-to-day relations" between Jews and Arabs in Palestine as late as the summer of 1908. During this period, he says, "It is clear that Arab anti-Zionism had not yet emerged. On the other hand, there was unease about the expanding Jewish population in Palestine and growing antagonism towards it."[71]

The whole relation of Jews and Arabs in Palestine was altered, however, by the Turkish Revolution of July 1908. In that month Abdul Hamid, Sultan and Caliph, ceased to be an absolute ruler, having been forced by the Revolution of the Young Turks to "restore the Constitution." In the following year Abdul Hamid was deposed and exiled. From now until the outbreak of the World War, the Ottoman Empire was governed, under constitutional forms, by a Westernizing oligarchy of middle-class officers.

In relation to Zionism, the oligarchy continued to pursue the same line as the deposed Sultan; that is, it was against Jewish settlement in Palestine but incapable of altogether preventing it. But as regards the Arab world, the new regime had revolutionary effects.

The main instrument of revolutionary change, in the world of ideas, was the press. "Constitutionalism" could not, in most fields, mean anything very precise in the conditions of the Ottoman Empire, but one precise result of it was a relatively free press: a press whose freedom reflected not only constitutional and Western ideas but also the weakness of the military oligarchy in Constantinople.

The Zionists, whose hopes were generally high in the early months of the Ottoman Revolution, were the quickest to take advantage of the new press freedom. For a time, they had a significant influence over the press in postrevolutionary Constantinople. The most gifted and most militant of Zionists, Vladimir Jabotinsky—later founder of the Irgun and spiritual father of Menachem Begin—became the deputy editor of the organ to which people turned first when they wanted to know the thinking of the Turkish Revolution: *Le Jeune Turc*.[72]

It was a rare interlude of farce in what is generally a tragic story: Jabotinsky as a Young Turk is a lot less convincing than Herzl's friend Vambery dressed as a Central Asian dervish or an English Protestant.

Neither Zionist influence nor a free press lasted long in Constantinople. It was in the Arab world, and especially in Palestine, and at the expense of the Zionists, that freedom of the press—while it lasted—was to make a historic impact.

The free press was both a factor in the dissolution of the Ottoman Empire and an influence over the manner and—perhaps most important—the consequences of its dissolution. By nature, free newspapers were bound to appeal to *linguistic* groups, to cater to their likings and resentments, to flatter their collective pride, and to articulate their hopes. Thus a free press, in the Arabic lands, naturally became a vehicle of Arab nationalism.[73]

By its linguistic nature, the Arabic press expressed—and therefore emphasized—the difference between Arabs and other Ottoman subjects, and specifically the difference between Arab Muslims and other Muslims. Arab Christians, being a minority, thought they had a special interest in stressing the linguistic and cultural distinctiveness of all Arabs and in fostering the Arabic bond and the growth of Arab nationalism. And Christian Arabs—with the special educational advantages they enjoyed from their relations with the West—played the leading part in the building of the Arabic press.

Before 1908, there was no Arabic press in Palestine. As soon as such a press appeared, it began to attack the Jews. As the first Arabic paper in Jaffa published:

> They harm the local population and wrong them, by relying on the special rights accorded to foreign powers in the Ottoman Empire and on the corruption and treachery of the local administration. Moreover, they are free from most of the taxes and heavy impositions on Ottoman subjects. Their labour competes with the local population and creates their own means of sustenance. The local population cannot stand up to their competition.[74]

This succinctly articulates the principal grievances of Arabs against Jews in Palestine at this time. It was also the Arabic press which first conveyed to the Arab population not just a protest against

Jewish immigration but an accurate warning about the comprehensive nature of the Zionist grand design. *Al-Karmil,* in Haifa, published in December 1910 an "open letter" from an eminent Arab nationalist of Damascus, Shurki al-Asali, which gives a remarkably clear picture of the state of political development of Zionism in Palestine at this period, as seen by a hostile Arab eye:

> They do not mix with the Ottomans, and do not buy anything from them. They own the Anglo-Palestine Bank, which makes loans to them at a rate not exceeding one percent *per annum.* Every village has set up an administrative office and a school, every kaza a central administration, and every district has a general administrator. They have a blue flag in the middle of which is a "Star of David," and below that is a Hebrew word meaning "Zion," because in the Torah Jerusalem is called the "Daughter of Zion." They raise this flag instead of the Ottoman flag at their celebrations and gatherings; and they sing the Zionist anthem. They have deceived the Government with lying and falsehood when they enroll themselves as Ottoman subjects in the register, for they continue to carry foreign passports which protect them; and whenever they go to the Ottoman courts, they produce their passports and summon foreign protection; they settle their claims and differences amongst themselves with the knowledge of the administrator, and they do not turn to the Government. They teach their children physical training and the use of arms; you see their houses crammed with weapons, among them many Martini rifles. They have a special postal service, special stamps, etc., which proves that they have begun setting up their political aims and establishing their imaginary government. If the Government does not set a limit to this torrential stream, no time will pass before you see that Palestine has become the property of the Zionist Organization and [its] associates or of the nation mentioned above (the Jews).[75]

Together with penetrating, and largely realistic, criticism of this order, the Arabic press increasingly carried an inflammatory and contemptuous anti-semitic message.[76] As this tended to reproduce European stereotypes of Jews, it probably also tended to offset such warnings as that of al-Asali by causing people to underestimate Zionism's inherent fortitude, vigor and determination.

Although the Arabic press and Arab public representatives were generally hostile to Jewish immigration, and at least uneasy about

Zionism, there was still some feeling that some kind of entente between Arabs and Jews might be possible. As the disintegration of the Ottoman Empire progressed and the idea of an Arab State (or Arab states) began to loom larger, some Arab nationalists toyed with the idea of such an entente.[77]

It came to nothing, because underlying it, on the Arab side, was the idea that the Jews would accept Arab (initially, "Ottoman") nationality, and assimilate. As these particular Jews were in Palestine because they were Zionists, rejecters of all assimilation, they were inherently incapable of agreeing to an entente on anything resembling these terms. Complicated discussions, and indirect negotiations, around the idea of entente went on right up to the outbreak of war, but they really only served to demonstrate that there was no basis for such an entente. One of the participants in the talks soon went over to radically different ideas. Haqqi Bey al-Azm, secretary of the Decentralization Party—the Arab nationalist group which had originated the entente idea in 1913—was writing as follows to one of his associates by mid-1914:

> Understand, dear brother, that [the Zionists] are marching towards their objective at a rapid pace, thanks to the help of the Government and the indifference of the local population. I am sure that if we do nothing which is demanded by the present situation, they will achieve their objective in a few years in [Palestine] where they will found a [Jewish State]. Then they will gravitate towards Syria, next towards Iraq and thus they will have fulfilled their political programme. . . . But by employing means of threats and persecutions— and it is this last means which we must employ—by pushing the Arab population into destroying their farms and setting fire to their colonies, by forming gangs to execute these projects, then perhaps [the Zionists in Palestine] will emigrate to save their lives.[78]

By the outbreak of the First World War, Arab nationalism was already a force in Palestine, and using the description "Palestinian." Arab nationalists were already aware that the new Jewish immigrants to Palestine were not just immigrants: they were Jewish nationalists. And since the two nationalisms laid claim to the same land, they were incompatible. As the Christian Arab nationalist George Antonius was later to say in the concluding words of his famous book *The Arab Awakening* (1938): "No room can be made in Palestine for a second nation except by dislodging or exterminating the nation in possession."

It was not really as symmetrical as that. The Jewish nation in Palestine was made up of people who had volunteered to be a nation, returning to its native soil. They had undergone great hardships together and were animated by a common, conscious passionate purpose. Nothing equivalent faced them on the other side; at least not yet, and not for a long time. There was no Palestinian Arab nation then. There was an Arab world, in which Arab nationalism was beginning to stir and of which Palestine was part. A Palestinian nation was not something which the Zionists found awaiting them; it was something that came into being, first slowly and then frantically, in response to Zionism itself. That response was already beginning to appear, among the youth of Palestine, just before the First World War. At the end of June 1914 an anonymous General Summons to Palestinians—signed by "a Palestinian"—was circulated in Jerusalem. It is the first clear expression of a distinct Palestinian nationalism, within Arab nationalism—"in the name of Arabia, in the name of Syria, in the name of our country Palestine"—and it is also an explicitly Muslim document, with a theological basis.

> Men! Do you want to be slaves and servants to people who are notorious in the world and in history? Do you wish to be slaves to the Zionists who have come to expel you from your country, saying that this country is theirs? Behold, I summon God and his Messenger as witnesses against them that they are liars. They dwelt in this holy land in former times and God sent them from it and forbade them to settle in it. Therefore why are they now craning their necks towards it, wishing to conquer it, after having deserted it for two thousand years? The Zionists desire to settle in our country and to expel us from it. Are you satisfied with this? Do you wish to perish?[79]

The General Summons is impressive, because, unlike earlier and later Arab manifestos, it clearly addresses only those people it claims to address, and in concepts familiar to them. The identification here of the Arab cause with Islam is notable: there is no trace of the Arab nationalism "transcending religious difference" of an earlier (and not yet ended) Christian-led phase or of the ostensible secularism and democratism of a later period. There is a genuine effort here to reach the mass of Arabs, whose Muslim faith was the most important thing in their lives.[80]

And by this time, there was already some awareness among the mass of Arabs of what Zionism—as distinct from Jewish immigration—meant. A non-Zionist Jew was asked by a peasant "if the Jews had really prepared a Jewish king for Jerusalem."[81]

It was a strange echo, from the other side of Palestine, to a scene eight years before in Vilna, where the dying founder had heard from a Jewish workman, "in the dark Russian night," the salutation: "King Herzl."

X

"It was between 1905 and 1914," writes a historian of Israel, "that the foundation of the Jewish National Home was laid."[82] It was the Russian Zionists, not Herzl, who had done most to lay the foundations in Palestine. But the First World War was to create, at last, the conditions for the realization of Herzl's dream: the establishment of the National Home itself, under the initial protection of a Great Power, and with international acceptance.

With the outbreak of war, Zionism, as an international movement, had to suspend its activities. The secretariat of the Zionist International moved from Berlin to Copenhagen, so as not to appear to take sides. But it was clear that the only Zionists who would have any influence by the time of the peace settlement would be Zionists who had taken a side: the one that proved to be the winner. As an international movement, Zionism was intrinsically suspect (on both sides) as a possible channel of communication with the enemy. So, paradoxically, the only Zionists who counted now were Zionists who threw in their lot, for the duration, with the country they lived in, in the Diaspora. In this situation, the country that counted most was Britain, and the Zionist who counted most was Chaim Weizmann, a chemist working in Manchester.

Britain counted most because it was the only Great Power already solidly established in the region of which Palestine was part. Few expected the Ottoman Empire to survive the war, and Britain's control of Egypt, since 1882, implied that, in the event of either an Allied victory or a negotiated peace, Palestine would be likely to fall, in whole or in part, within the British sphere of interest. Palestine was too near the Suez Canal for the British Empire willingly to allow it to fall into the hands of another Power. And Britain's interest in Palestine implied some interest—negative or positive—in Zionism.

Britain was also much better disposed to the Jews than any other major European Power, and had been a protector, under the Capitulations system, of Jews in Palestine.

Zionists were correspondingly interested in Britain. "From the first moment I entered the movement," wrote Herzl in 1898, at the time of the London Zionist Conference, "my eyes were directed towards England because I saw that it was the Archimedean point where the lever could be applied."

From the very start of the war, Chaim Weizmann was conscious that the time for the application of the lever had come. As early as September 1914, he was writing to a correspondent in America: "We should prepare ourselves for the future peace conference!"[83] In the following month: "I have no doubt that Palestine will fall within the influence of England. . . . We (given more or less good conditions) could easily move a million Jews into Palestine within the next 50–60 years. . . . I'm writing to you now in the most solemn moment of my life. . . ."[84] And a few weeks later: "Turkey has come in, and no doubt this will have fatal consequences for her."[85]

In December 1914, Weizmann met Arthur Balfour again. He found that Balfour "remembered everything we discussed eight years ago."[86] Weizmann reported to Balfour on the progress of the Yishuv in the interim: ". . . the Technical College, the University project, the Secondary school." Balfour said: "*You may get your things done much quicker after the war.*"[87] Balfour talked at large about the Jewish question. He told Weizmann of a long talk he had in Bayreuth with Richard Wagner's widow, Cosima, and that he shared her anti-semitic ideas. "I [Balfour] pointed out to him that we too are in agreement with the cultural anti-semites, insofar as we believe that Germans of the Mosaic faith[88] are an undesirable, demoralizing phenomenon but that we totally disagree with Wagner and [Houston Stewart] Chamberlain as to the diagnosis and the prognosis. . . ." Weizmann warned against "the fatal error" of Western statesmen in despising Eastern Jews: "Our bodies are in chains, but we are trying to throw off our chains and save our souls. At the end of this long talk, Balfour saw me out into the street, holding my hand in silence, and bidding me farewell said very warmly: '*Mind you come again to see me.* I am deeply moved and interested, it is not a dream, it is a great cause and I *understand it.*' "[89]

Balfour's interest in Zionism was at this time a personal one, and did not imply any official commitment. British interest in Palestine, dating from before the war, was a strategic interest. Imperially minded Britons—like Lord Kitchener—thought it a British interest to secure Palestine, in British hands, as a northern barrier protecting the Suez Canal. The British Zionists, of course, supported this conception, with the addendum that the barrier would be greatly reinforced by the setting up of a Jewish National Home.

The predominantly Liberal Asquith Government, in office in the early part of the First World War, did not want exclusive responsibility for Palestine, and was not collectively interested in any Jewish National Home—an idea which Asquith considered "fantastic." One Jewish member of the Government—Herbert Samuel—was a Zionist sympathizer and in touch with Weizmann, and submitted a memorandum to the Government, with a Zionist project. Asquith's Foreign Secretary, Sir Edward Grey, at least toyed with these ideas, but Asquith never took them seriously, and they came to nothing under his Government. The Sykes-Picot agreement of February 1916—officially the Asia Minor Agreement—proposed to partition the Middle East into French and British Zones of Control and Influence. It would have placed Palestine under an Anglo-French condominium, without any commitment to the Jews. Earlier, in fomenting the Arabian revolt against the Turks, Asquith's Government had committed itself, through the Hussein-McMahon correspondence of the autumn of 1915, to "recognize and support the independence of the Arabs." Palestine was apparently not intended to be covered by this commitment, but Arab commentators have not accepted any such limitation.

The fall of the Asquith Government, at the end of 1916, altered the situation radically, in favor of the Zionists. In the new Government, headed by David Lloyd George, Arthur Balfour was Foreign Secretary. The Tories and Imperial thinking were in the ascendant— and much more attracted to British control over Palestine than to an Anglo-French condominium. Lloyd George was determined, as early as March 1917, that Palestine should become British, and that he would rely upon its conquest by British troops to secure the abrogation of the Sykes-Picot agreement as it related to Palestine.[90]

A great expeditionary force had been built up in Egypt, throughout 1916, for a decisive attack on Turkey. Geography dictated that Palestine would be the first main theater of war.

Zionism had a potential role to play in the postwar settlement, but it also had a relevance to the far more immediate problem of winning the war. The arguments that eventually convinced the War

Cabinet in favor of the Balfour Declaration were not related to the postwar settlement; they were arguments related to winning the war. The arguments were advanced by Balfour's Foreign Office in the context created by the huge events of early 1917: the first Russian Revolution (February, O.S.) and America's declaration of war on Germany (April) as a result of Germany's unrestricted submarine warfare. The most vital interests of Britain (as well as of France) in the summer and autumn of 1917 were to keep Russia in the war for as long as possible and to get America fully committed to the war as fast as possible.

As it happened, in relation to both these vital interests, Zionism looked a promising card to play. In both the countries concerned, public opinion was deeply divided about the war, and in both also Jews appeared to have a significant influence over the forming of opinion. (The February Revolution had emancipated the Russian Jews, and the interval between the February and October revolutions was a period in which it seemed meaningful to talk about Russian public opinion.) But in Russia and America, a great many Jews—perhaps most Jews—were (in some degree) Zionists. As far as America was concerned, the rising strength of Zionism had been attested at the end of 1915 by a distinguished British anti-Zionist Jew. "In America," Lucien Wolf reported to the Foreign Office, "the Zionist organizations have lately captured Jewish opinion."[91] So it did seem reasonable to suppose that a pro-Zionist declaration, on the eve of Britain's invasion of Palestine, could swing more support behind the war effort, where it counted most.

It was subsequently argued, on many occasions, that the Balfour Declaration was a mistake. About the promise of a Jewish National Home, Elizabeth Monroe says: "Measured by British interests alone, it was one of the greatest mistakes in our imperial history."[92] But it surely wasn't a mistake at all in terms of British interests *as these stood in 1917*, at a most difficult and critical period of the war. To the War Cabinet, the main criterion about any proposition was: Will it help the war effort? The War Cabinet thought the Declaration would help, and it did. True, it didn't help as much as they hoped it would. The "Russian" part of the calculation went wrong very early. The Bolsheviks seized power in Petrograd within a few days of the issue of the Declaration, and the Bolshevik leaders were radically hostile to the war, to the Entente Powers, and also to Zionism.

On the other hand, the "American" part of the calculation went right. American Jews warmly welcomed the Declaration. Jews in America had generally opposed American entry into the war, on the side of an alliance which included the Russia of Nicholas II. Even before the war, the British ambassador to the United States, Sir Cecil Spring-Rice, had ascribed to Jewish influence the rejection of a projected treaty between the U.S. and Russia: "No sooner was the President's statement made—recommending such a treaty—than a Jewish deputation came down from New York and in two days 'fixed' the two houses [of Congress] so that the President had to renounce the idea." Sir Cecil inferred that the Jews in America were worth cultivating. "They are far better organized than the Irish and far more formidable. We should be in a good position to get into their good graces."[93] But after the outbreak of the World War, Sir Cecil had to report that Jewish influence in the United States, both in banking and in the press, was damaging to the Allied war effort, and worrying President Wilson, who, in a conversation with the ambassador, had quoted the text: "He that keepeth Israel shall neither slumber nor sleep."[94] The February Revolution removed the principal causes of Jewish aversion from the Allied cause, but Jewish *support* was still an uncertain quantity. By making a project dear to the heart of many Jews into an Allied war aim, the Declaration swung much new support behind the Allies. Far from being a mistake, it was one of the greatest propaganda coups in history.[95]

The German Government recognized this, with alarm. The Germans in the early years of the war had recognized the potential value, to their side, of the Jewish community in the United States, with its hatred of Russia. Imperial Germany had stressed its own role as a civilized power, friendly to the Jews. It had scrupulously protected the Jews in the territories occupied by its forces in Central Europe. It had made repeated diplomatic interventions in Constantinople, to protect the Yishuv from the harassment, and the persecuting tendencies, of the Ottoman military governor in Palestine, Djemal Pasha. It has been reckoned that without Germany's persistent interventions—especially when the danger was at its greatest, toward the end of 1917—the Yishuv might not have survived the war at all.[96]

German officials, as well as publicists, had been attracted to the idea of a German pro-Zionist statement, but had feared offending their Ottoman ally. (The possible imminence of such a German declaration was a major argument used by Balfour to influence the War Cabinet. It carried weight, though it was without foundation.)

After the Balfour Declaration, when the enthusiasm of American Jewry was manifest, the Germans tried vainly to regain lost ground. They got the Turks, in December 1917, to agree to remove restrictions on Jewish immigration, provided the Jews accepted Ottoman nationality, and the Germans then tried to make the best of that. But they were unable to steal the Balfour thunder. "We are trailing behind, as usual," noted the Kaiser.

The Balfour Declaration may perhaps not have helped the Allies to win the war, but at the time, both the Allies and the Central Powers thought that it did.

For the British War Cabinet as a whole, the Declaration's value as wartime propaganda was what mattered. To Balfour, the Jewish National Home itself mattered. To Lloyd George, the Declaration had other propaganda uses besides the wartime one. It could be used to promote a postwar settlement which would, as he intended, give Palestine to Britain. It would create a lobby in favor of that in America. Lloyd George also knew that the Zionists with whom he was in contact, and most English-speaking Zionists, wanted Britain, not France, as the protecting power.[97] The Jews would help Lloyd George to keep the French out of Palestine. And the Jews, and Balfour's Zionism, could help him to overcome the scruples of the Foreign Office about the supposed need to honor the Sykes-Picot agreement. Balfour didn't particularly want Palestine for Britain; he wanted it for the Jews. But if he didn't help Lloyd George get it for Britain, he wouldn't be able to do anything for the Jews.

How much did Balfour's personal commitment to Zionism have to do with progress toward the Declaration? Quite a lot, I think, but a case to the contrary has been argued. Isaiah Friedman, a writer who has studied this period in detail, says that Balfour had no share in drafting the Declaration "and the records show how irresolute and cautious he was. He preferred to act in unison with his colleagues, even to be pressed by the Foreign Office rather than to lead it."[98]

I suspect this judgment may not do justice to the subtlety and economy of Arthur Balfour. Records don't show everything. Balfour helped to establish an atmosphere favorable to Zionism at the Foreign Office. He saw that Weizmann got to see the right people. And he saw that the arguments of officials who had been listening to Weizmann got up to the War Cabinet. He had to be very careful not to make Zionism sound like a bee in his personal bonnet. It was much better to make it sound as if the Foreign Office was pushing him, but that was not necessarily the reality. If the Foreign Office had gone to someone else in 1917—say to George Curzon—the Foreign Office arguments that decided the War Cabinet in favor of the Declaration might never have reached the War Cabinet.

After the Declaration had gone out, and when it was becoming apparent that it had come too late to be much help in Russia, a Foreign Office official said it was a pity it hadn't come four months earlier. "Not my fault," said Balfour laconically. Allowing for the idiom, I infer that he had done all in his considerable power to make possible the Declaration that bears his name.

The Declaration itself was not issued until near the end of 1917, but the Zionist option had come to the fore almost as soon as the Lloyd George Government was formed.

By April 1917, Weizmann and Zionism were high in favor with the War Cabinet. On April 3—as it happened the day after President Wilson committed the United States to entering the war—Weizmann and his friend C. P. Scott, the famous editor of the *Manchester Guardian,* breakfasted with Lloyd George and Lord Curzon (1859–1925), a member of the War Cabinet, and a former Viceroy of India. After breakfast, Lloyd George and Curzon saw Sir Mark Sykes (1879–1919), then about to leave for the East as Chief Political Officer on the staff of the Commander in Chief of the British Army then operating in Palestine. Sir Mark was coauthor of the Sykes-Picot agreement, and was now helping Lloyd George to nullify that agreement, as far as Palestine was concerned. The two are recorded as having "impressed on Sir Mark the importance of not prejudicing the Zionist movement and the possibility of its development under British auspices."[99] Sir Mark said that the Arabs probably realized that there was no prospect of their being allowed any control over Palestine. From this time on, until the end of the war, and during the peacemaking process, Zionism—Weizmann's Zionism—is tacitly recognized as an important auxiliary of British policy.

In the spring of 1917, the obstacle of Anglo-Jewish opposition to the Jewish National Home idea was largely removed, through the disavowal by the Board of Deputies (the representative body of British Jews) on April 17, 1917, of any such opposition. In this summer, also, an important further step was taken, implicitly linking Britain and the Zionist cause. At the end of July, the War Office announced its intention to form a Jewish regiment, with the Shield of David for its badge. This idea, originally the brainchild of Vladimir Jabotinsky, proved to be extremely controversial, largely because of the obvious danger it presented for the Yishuv, in a Palestine still under Turkish occupation. The idea, in the form announced, did not take shape, but three battalions, consisting mainly of American Jews, were set up and took part in the fighting for the Jordan Valley in the summer of 1918.

The month of September 1917 was a crucial one for the future of the National Home. It opened in a most discouraging way for the Zionists. On September 3, when the question came before the War Cabinet, in the absence of both Lloyd George and Balfour, Edwin Montagu fought a fierce rearguard action against any National Home declaration, a concept which he described as "anti-semitic." Although the case Montagu argued—the anti-Zionist assimilated case—had been already rejected on behalf of British Jews by the Board of Deputies, it shook the War Cabinet, which made no decision, except to ascertain President Wilson's views. Lord Robert Cecil, for the Foreign Office, cabled to President Wilson's closest adviser, Colonel House: "We are being pressed here for a declaration of sympathy with the Zionist movement and I should be very grateful if you felt able to ascertain unofficially if the President favours such a declaration."[100]

Considering the strong official commitment of the Foreign Office, under Balfour, to the National Home idea, this is a curiously neutral formulation, and may reflect some official second thoughts (in Balfour's absence). House saw "many dangers lurking" in a declaration, and his reply to Cecil, received on September 11, represented Wilson as cooler than tepid: "The time was not opportune for any definite statement further, perhaps, than one of sympathy, provided it can be made without conveying any real commitment."[101]

Weizmann, naturally, did not take that reply as final. He cabled (September 19) the text of the draft declaration, on which he and the Foreign Office had been working—essentially the Balfour Declaration that was to be—to Supreme Court Justice Louis D. Brandeis (1856–1941), leader of the American Zionists. Brandeis went speedily to work, and within a week was able to send the following reply, through House and the British War Office, to Weizmann: "From talks I have had with President and from expressions of opinion given to closest advisers I feel that I can answer that he is in entire sympathy with declaration quoted in yours of 19th as approved by Foreign Office and Prime Minister. I of course heartily agree.—Brandeis."[102]

This is an astonishing reversal, within a fortnight, of a presidential position on a major issue. Leonard Stein says that "there are no means of telling how Brandeis put the Zionist case, or what arguments he used that carried weight with House,"[103] and through House to Wilson. House's own impression of the Zionist pressure is on record: "The Jews from every tribe descended in force, and they seemed determined to break in with a jimmy, if they are not let in."[104] House's "jimmy" is another word for Herzl's "lever," which now, in the hands of Weizmann and Brandeis, had indeed found its "Archimedean point."

We can infer, from House's soreness, that Brandeis and his friends had brought all the leverage they had to bear on *him*. The leverage of Brandeis was partly moral, partly political. Brandeis, as is abundantly attested, was an extremely impressive character, both intellectually and morally. He was one of Wilson's closest advisers, and Wilson was bound to listen carefully to his argument in favor of the Jewish National Home. But Wilson was a practical politician, and he knew that there was a political force behind Brandeis's argument. If it became known that the British were seriously considering setting up a National Home for the Jews in Palestine and that Wilson had discouraged them from going ahead, then resentment of Wilson's attitude could turn many American Jews against the Democrats. The formula in which House eventually conveyed Wilson's approval of the proposed declaration officially to the British seems to suggest that such political considerations were predominant. On October 16 the British intelligence chief in New York wired London: "Colonel House put formula before President, who approves of it but asks that no mention of his approval shall be made when His Majesty's Government makes formula public, as he has arranged that American Jews shall then ask him for his approval, which he will give publicly here."[105]

The British had now every incentive to press ahead with the Balfour Declaration, not merely because they had the President's "entire sympathy," with all that implied for the concert of the Allied and associated Powers and the war effort, but because that expression of sympathy was the best guarantee of American support for a British protectorate over Palestine, as part of the peace settlement. Lloyd George saw Weizmann briefly at the end of the month and "immediately ordered that our case be placed on the agenda of the next meeting of the Cabinet."

The decisive meeting of the War Cabinet occurred on October 31, with Wilson's approval of the Declaration assured in advance. The only serious obstacle now was the opposition of Lord Curzon, who had been appointed in March as chairman of a Cabinet committee on Middle East acquisitions. Curzon thought that the Jewish National Home idea was unrealistic, since Palestine was already inhabited by some half a million Arabs who "will not be content either to be expropriated for Jewish immigrants or to act merely as hewers of wood and drawers of water for the latter."[106]

It is not known how Balfour answered that particular objection or even whether he answered it at all. At the War Cabinet, he rested his case mainly on the propaganda value of the Declaration, both in America and in Russia, and on the danger that Germany might preempt the British, by being first with its own declaration in favor of a National Home. The points about Russia and Germany were questionable, though they seem to have been uncontested. The point about America had great substance, and on that, Wilson's approval was decisive. Curzon did not press his objection, and the War Cabinet approved the Balfour Declaration.[107] Weizmann was waiting outside the Cabinet Room when Sir Mark Sykes came out with the text. "Dr. Weizmann," said Sykes, "it's a boy."

Arthur Koestler held that the British Government's motives for issuing the Balfour Declaration were "romantically sentimental" and not "cynical," the men responsible being "Bible-lovers."[108] There is some truth in this, at least where Balfour himself is concerned, and without Balfour at the Foreign Office there might well have been no Declaration. But there were also strong pragmatic reasons, from both wartime needs and postwar aims. As regards the wartime needs, Winston Churchill was to tell the Peel Commission nearly twenty years later that the Balfour Declaration "arose because we gained great advantage in the War. We did not adopt Zionism entirely out of altruistic love of starting a Zionist colony: it was a matter of great importance for this country. It was a potent factor in public opinion in America. . . ."[109] As regards postwar aims, once Lloyd George had decided that he wanted Palestine for Britain, without France, Weizmann could show that he was in a position to help him get it. And in the event, Weizmann and Brandeis between them did more to make the British Mandate eventually part of the peace settlement than the orthodox channels of British diplomacy could have done.

By whatever mixture of sentiment and calculation, and with

much more short-term than long-term awareness of what it was about, Britain was now on its way to acquiring "the terrible gift of Palestine to rule for the Jews."[110] The Zionists had won at last the Herzlian opportunity to build a National Home in Palestine, and turn it into a Jewish State. The British Government was not committed to that last objective—though both Balfour and Lloyd George approved of it, as an ultimate goal. At some stage conflict was probable, between the country which had promised a National Home, without quite knowing what it meant by that, and the people who understood that promise as meaning eventually a Jewish State.[111]

3

A HOME
CONTESTED
1917-1933

> One fundamental fact—that we must have Palestine if
> we are not going to be exterminated.
> —Chaim Weizmann
> *November 26, 1919*

On December 9, 1917, five weeks after the Balfour Declaration, British forces took Jerusalem from the Turks. On December 11, General Allenby made his official entry into Jerusalem, through the Jaffa Gate, on foot. This was a snub to the Kaiser, who had entered the Holy City nineteen years before, mounted on a white horse, under a triumphal arch, practicing

> *Such boastings as the Gentiles use*
> *And lesser breeds without the law.*

The original Muslim conqueror of Jerusalem, Caliph Omar, had adopted a median position, between the extremes of pride and humility, when he made his solemn entry into the city, 638 A.D. "In the chronicles he is described as riding a white camel, dressed in worn and torn robes, as he came to pray at the place where Mahommed dreamed he had ascended to Heaven. . . ."[1]

Under British rule, the Muslim conquest was about to be undone, in a far more fundamental way than Allenby, or anyone under his command, could possibly have guessed. What Herzl had hoped for from the Kaiser, his successors were to win from the conquerors of the Kaiser.

The population of Palestine—Muslims, Christians and Jews alike—had suffered terribly from the consequences of the war, through conscription, deportations, famine and other disasters. The total population is believed to have fallen from about 800,000 in 1914 to about 640,000 at the end of the war. The composition of the population by December 1918 was as follows:

Muslims	512,000
Christians	61,000
Jews	66,000[2]

There had been 85,000 Jews in Palestine in 1914. In absolute terms, the Jewish population had declined sharply. As a proportion of the total, however, the Jewish population had not declined; in fact it may have risen slightly. And it was a younger population, in its internal composition. The Old Yishuv, preponderantly elderly, was harder hit by wartime privations, which included the cutting off of the alms from overseas, the sole livelihood of many of the pious Jews of Jerusalem. The New Yishuv had also suffered, from conscription and deportation in particular, but it survived, as a hardened core, around which the third *aliyah* could form in Palestine under the promise of the National Home.

Most of Palestine, and in 1918 all of it, came under British military rule, and so remained until military rule was replaced by civil administration in the summer of 1920.

It was not until that date that agreement was reached between France and Britain on the final terms of modified Sykes-Picot: Britain was to get Palestine and Iraq, and France to get Syria. But, as a result of the resurgence of Turkey, under Kemal Ataturk, the Treaty of Sèvres, of which these arrangements were to be part, was never ratified, and agreements on the forms of the League of Nations Mandates were not finally reached until the summer of 1922.

The Balfour Declaration was included in the terms of the British Mandate for Palestine. Even before that, it was understood—incontestably from 1920, with the formation of the civil administration—that British rule in Palestine was to be conducted in terms of the policies and principles of the Balfour Declaration. Whatever that might mean.

The ground was littered with contradictions from the beginning:

a contradiction inside the Balfour Declaration (and so also inside the Mandate); contradictions between this particular Mandate and the rest of the Mandatory system of which the Palestine Mandate was supposed to be an integral part; and contradictions between parts of the Balfour Declaration and different policy statements made at various times under British Government authority.

The contradiction inside the Balfour Declaration is between what His Majesty's Government "view with favour"—"the establishment in Palestine of a national home for the Jewish people"—and what it wants to be "clearly understood"—that "nothing shall be done which may prejudice the civil and religious rights of existing non-Jewish communities in Palestine . . ." In theory, this contradiction is reconcilable, in one of two ways. You could scale down the concept of a "national home" until it is indeed no longer felt to "prejudice the civil and religious rights" etc. of Arabs, as Arabs understood these rights, in which case the national home would turn out to be identical with the Old Yishuv, at most. Or you could scale down the concept of "civil and religious rights" for Arabs until these no longer conflict with the "national home," as envisaged by Zionists, in which case the civil and religious rights in question would—ultimately—be those guaranteed to Arabs by a Jewish State. In the first case, you would be doing the Jews out of what they thought they had been promised. In the second case, you would be doing the same to the Arabs.

What the British saw themselves as having to do was to avoid either extreme and to be fair to both sides. Naturally, this annoyed both sides. That would have been so even if only the Declaration and the Mandate had been involved. But the British had also produced—after the Declaration—statements aimed at Jews, which confirmed the Zionist interpretation of that document, and statements aimed at Arabs, which were incompatible with the creation of a Jewish National Home in Palestine.

II

It had been primarily in terms of its wartime propaganda value that Balfour, as Foreign Secretary, had commended the Jewish National Home to the War Cabinet.[3] The Foreign Office was thus committed, from the beginning, to propagandist exploitation of the

Declaration, for the duration of the war. The propaganda was aimed at Jews, and concentrated on what His Majesty's Government "viewed with favour"—the National Home. It ignored those matters which were to be "clearly understood"—by persons other than those to whom the propaganda in question was addressed.

A special branch for Jewish propaganda, set up by the Foreign Office within the Department of Information, produced and distributed suitable literature. Literature circulated among Jewish soldiers in Central European countries after the fall of Jerusalem included the following flat statement: "The Allies are giving the land of Israel to the people of Israel."[4] The propaganda circulated, as it was meant to do, along Jewish grapevines in Central and Eastern Europe, and grew as it went. Writing to Weizmann from Odessa in December 1918, Menachem Ussishkin said he had heard news of "the formation of a Jewish government in Palestine of which I am one of the members."[5]

The contrast between the Jewish National Home, as depicted in British propaganda of the last year of the war, and the realities of Palestine under British rule was particularly striking in the period of military rule (1917–1920). The administrative military authorities—O.E.T.A., Occupied Enemy Territory Administration—did not even allow the Balfour Declaration to be published in Palestine.[6] But they did publish a document which legitimized aspirations and demands running contrary to the whole idea of a Jewish National Home. This document was the Anglo-French Joint Declaration, issued after the Armistice with Turkey, on November 6, 1918. The Joint Declaration said:

> The object aimed at by France and Great Britain, in prosecuting in the East the war set in train by German ambition, is the complete and final liberation of the peoples who have for so long been oppressed by the Turks, and the setting up of national governments and administrations that shall derive their authority from the free exercise of the indigenous populations. . . .
>
> In order to carry out these intentions, France and Britain are at one in encouraging and assisting the establishment of indigenous government and administrations in Syria and Mesopotamia now liberated by the Allies. . . .
>
> Far from wishing to impose on the populations of those regions any particular institutions, they are only concerned to

secure by their support and by adequate assistance, the regular working of Governments and administrations freely chosen by the populations themselves.[7]

The object of the Joint Declaration was to consolidate what was left of the Sykes-Picot agreement: the division of the Arab regions of the Ottoman Empire between Britain and France, with Syria going to France, and Iraq to Britain. The language in which the concept is embodied is the language of Wilsonian idealism, and so contrary to the spirit of Sykes-Picot, as Balfour was quick to acknowledge.[8] This contradiction seemed to be required by the necessities of the Western alliances. The Bolsheviks, at the end of 1917, had published the Entente's secret wartime agreements and promises—including Sykes-Picot. This publication had greatly embarrassed both the European Allies—especially in their relations with America—and President Wilson, in his relations with the American public.[9] Wilson's Fourteen Points, in January 1918, signaled America's rejection of that sinful old diplomacy whose devious tracks the Bolsheviks had brought to light. The old diplomacy continued, but felt the need, both in the last year of the war and as the tasks and costs of reconstruction loomed, to propitiate the United States. The pressure at work has been called "the strange Western fatality made irresistible by America's entry into the War. . . ."[10] So in November 1918, the Sykes-Picot idea—and the Anglo-French rivalries which were modifying Sykes-Picot—put on the sheep's clothing of "self-determination," a truly Orwellian word for a policy of annexation.

The British were quicker than the French, naturally enough, to learn the new Wilsonian language, and they used it against the French to break the original version of Sykes-Picot. It was the British negotiator of that agreement, Sir Mark Sykes, who used it in order to put his French opposite number, Georges Picot, in his place. Picot came to London in early July 1918, at the request of Sykes, who explained to Picot that the agreement as it stood did "positive harm" to the Allies because "democratic forces" regarded it as an instrument of aggression and as "contrary to President Wilson's foreign policy." Moreover, the agreement had "a very unsettling effect on the Arab-speaking peoples, giving them the impression that we were intent upon annexation." As Sir Mark's biographer notes: "Picot had heard all this before . . . but had to listen, as the British still held all the military cards in the Middle East and might otherwise order Allenby not to continue his offensive into Syria"—which the French hoped to acquire whether by Sykes-Picot or by Wilsonian Mandate.[11] Sykes went on to draft the Joint Declaration, in the same high-minded vein. It suited the British, at this time, to stress the sanctity of "President Wilson's foreign policy," in order to get out of the British commitment (original Sykes-Picot) to let the French have part of Palestine. It was "Wilsonian" for the British to be in Palestine because President Wilson had personally approved the Balfour Declaration. But for the *French* to be there would smack of the wicked "old diplomacy." Picot, having weak cards, went along with Sykes, in the hope of getting Syria.

As a British historian has said, the Joint Declaration was "a crowning piece of insincerity."[12] In terms of Western diplomacy, and Western public opinion, it made sense, of a cynical sort.

In terms of the attitudes of the peoples over whom the British and French proposed to rule, it did not make so much sense. But then neither the British nor the French, at this time, were greatly preoccupied with these attitudes. What both had in mind was direct rule, leading to indirect rule; that is, to something resembling British practice in Egypt, parts of India, and northern Nigeria, and French practice in Morocco and Tunisia. What the idea of free choice for Arabs meant to the British administrative mind at this period was breezily expounded by a former Viceroy of India in a private letter: "It really would not matter if we choose three of the fattest men in Baghdad or three of the men with the longest beards who would be ruled by the resident and a certain number of advisers."[13]

As Balfour himself said, commenting on the Sykes-Picot agreement: "Now by an adviser, these documents undoubtedly mean—though they do not say so—an adviser whose advice must be followed."[14]

In Baghdad a version of that system was to last—though rather bumpily, and growing more attenuated—for forty years. In Palestine, it never came into being. The Joint Declaration was not intended, by the British Government, to apply to Palestine at all, but it was difficult for them to formulate this exclusion explicitly. The French thought of the Joint Declaration as expressive of the full original Sykes-Picot agreement, under which Palestine was to be an Anglo-French condominium. For the British, the Joint Declaration meant *modified* Sykes-Picot, with no role at all for the French in Palestine. The Balfour Declaration, and the Jewish National Home in particular, had been intended to make sure of that. The French, having no alternative, were prepared to swallow that modification, but they had not yet got around to doing so explicitly. The idea that "the complete and final liberation of the peoples who have for so long been oppressed by the Turks" was not applicable to Palestine—still thought of as part of Syria—would have been hard to formulate in any case, officially and publicly; in the context of an Anglo-French declaration, in 1918, it was impossible. In Anglo-French relations, Palestine at this time had become an area of awkward silence. Such areas, not being understood, or intended to be understood, by underlings, often give rise to administrative errors. So the Joint Declaration was sent to Jerusalem, where it was not intended to go.

In Jerusalem, Zionists had just finished celebrating the first anniversary of the Balfour Declaration, amid Arab protests. Arabs knew about the Balfour Declaration, although they had not been told about it officially. Instead, they now got the Joint Declaration. Colonel Storrs—then Military Governor of Jerusalem, later Sir Ronald Storrs (1881–1955)—reported the distribution and reception of the Joint Declaration:

> Hardly had the excitement caused by the Zionist celebrations died down, when in accordance with orders received from G.H.Q. I distributed . . . the eighteen copies of the Anglo-French Declaration respecting the inhabitants of Syria and Mesopotamia. The result was instantaneous, but I fear hardly that anticipated by the authorities. On returning to the office the next day I found a large deputation of Muslims and Christians combined, who announced that they had come to speak to me. I received them in my office when they began with offering to the Allies their sincere thanks for the Declaration. They then asked me, formally (a) whether Palestine formed or did not form part of Syria, (b) whether if so Palestinians came under the category of those inhabitants of the liberated countries who were invited to choose their own future, and (c) if not, why the notices had ever been sent to them at all? I replied to them in general terms, and they left apparently satisfied . . . but I have since learnt that there have been further meetings in one of the Arab schools, the Muktataf al Drus, attended by Muslims, Latins and Orthodox Christians. It is their intention to visit reciprocally each other's churches and mosques as proof of solidarity, and this demonstration once made before the world, to put forward officially their acceptance of the Anglo-French declaration and their desire for a Sherifian government.[15]

"The winter 1918–19," writes Wasserstein "witnessed the first stir-
rings of organized Arab opposition to the Balfour Declaration."

If the British military authorities in Palestine had consciously intended that result, they could hardly have promoted it more effectively
than by their initial failure to acknowledge, in Palestine, the existence
of the Balfour Declaration—combined with the proclamation, in
Palestine, of a policy radically incompatible with the establishment
of a Jewish National Home. As Jabotinsky wrote to Weizmann about
O.E.T.A.: "The official approach is to apologize to the Arabs for a
slip of the tongue by Mr. Balfour."[16]

III

Some Zionist writers have suggested that British administrators
in Palestine, both in the military and later in the civil government,
did consciously intend to stir up opposition. Certainly, most of the administrators disliked the Jewish National Home idea from the start,
and warned that it would lead to trouble. It is human, if you have
given a warning, not to be too displeased if it looks as if you are going
to be proved right. Also, if you give the impression to those you
govern that opposition to the policy you are supposed to implement
is expected and justifiable, you are likely to stimulate the opposition—
and to look as if you were looking for it.

Zionists in Palestine thought anti-semitism was at work, and it
was, mainly at the lower and middle levels, but on occasion at the top.
The first Chief Administrator in Palestine, General Sir Arthur Money
(1866–1951), publicly rejected charges about the existence of anti-
semitism in the military administration but privately complained about
"Balfour, Lloyd George and their long-nosed friends."[17] In a tradition
of the Indian Army, in which he had served, Money preferred Muslims
to other varieties of natives, including Christians, but he preferred
even native Christians to Jews. His successor, General Sir Harry Watson (1866–1945), was a man of similar outlook, though he expressed
himself more discreetly: Jewish "clannishness," General Watson
thought, was at the bottom of much of the trouble. Watson's successor, General Louis Bols (1867–1930), was at least as firmly "anti-
Zionist" as his predecessors.

Zionists sometimes thought that British anti-Zionism derived from
a tendency to romanticize the Arab, in the manner of T. E. Lawrence.
There was almost nothing in this. Where such a tendency existed, it

was the desert Arab, the Bedouin, who got romanticized. There was nothing romantic about the settled Arabs of Palestine, and nobody imagined there was. Those who had any tendency to romanticize Arabs called the Palestinians "so-called Arabs"—as Curzon did.

Such sympathy with Palestinians as existed was that general, vague sympathy with the underdog that formed such a significant and paradoxical characteristic of British imperialism, distinguishing it from other imperialisms. As one young officer in Palestine put it, "The Jews are so clever, and the Arabs so stupid and childish, that it seems only sporting to be for the Arabs."[18]

Antipathy to Jews seems to have played a more important part than sympathy with Arabs. More important than either, however, was the natural resentment of administrators against the extraordinary and unprecedented policy requirement of setting up a Jewish National Home in Palestine. Since that was opposed by those among the existing population who knew what was going on, and was bound eventually to be opposed by almost all of that population, it was obviously going to make Palestine harder to govern. In most other parts of the Empire, British administrators traditionally sought to hold the balance even between the different peoples and religions, and to preserve the essentials of the *status quo*. In Palestine, policy pointed toward overthrowing the *status quo*, and tilting the balance in favor of people most of whom weren't even there yet. True, that was also the policy at the time in Kenya and Rhodesia—as it had been in the old Dominions—but those were straight cases of favoring Britishers as against natives, which seemed inherently right. In Palestine, it was a case of favoring foreigners—mainly Russian Jews—against natives, and that seemed quite wrong. It is hardly surprising that most of the administrators, from the beginning to the bitter end, thirty years later, emphatically did *not* view with favor the establishment of a National Home for the Jewish people in Palestine. In the beginning, under the military administrators (1917–1920), this was so also at the top. At lower and middle levels it remained so throughout. And both Jews and Arabs knew this.

IV

Sir Ronald Storrs, who was for eight years (1917–1925) Governor of Jerusalem, first under the military and then under the civil administration, was a lover of the *status quo*. He was also an intellectual, and aesthetic, and erudite. Christopher Sykes says of him, prettily, that "he carried his learning lightly but with ostentation."[19] Sanders adds that Storrs's blond moustache perhaps gave a hint of dilettantism in the way it curled up slightly at the ends.[20] He was not an antisemite or at any rate not to begin with. Norman Bentwich (1883–1971), a British Jew who, as attorney general in the civil administration (1920–1931), was to have a rough time from both British and Zionists, wrote about Storrs: "He appreciated, better than most British officials, the Jewish talent and love of the arts, their philanthropy for good causes, and the intellectual power of Weizmann and [Sir Herbert] Samuel."[21] Storrs even, in the early days, described himself as a committed Zionist—*sioniste convaincu*—but that notion must have rested on a misunderstanding: no man, in the early days of Mandate Palestine, could be both a Zionist and a lover of the *status quo*. It was the love of the *status quo* that was real in Storrs's case. Storrs's excellent autobiography, *Orientations*,[22] is full of delight in the quaintness and deviousness of the Orient, the delicate ironies of its traditions. He savors such anomalies as the fact that the custodian of the Church of the Holy Sepulchre in Jerusalem has to be a Muslim (because all the Christian sects regard that as a lesser evil than letting the job go to a member of a rival sect). Respecting the fine intricate contours of a *status quo* made up of such anomalies was, for Storrs, central to the wisdom of government in the East. It was also a sensuous pleasure.

Storrs, just before coming to Jerusalem, had served for eight years as Oriental Secretary in Britain's Cairo Residency. He had been concerned in the negotiations with Sherif Hussein of Mecca over the Arab Revolt, and he was a friend of T. E. Lawrence's. Because of this background, Weizmann and others suspected Storrs of romanticizing Arabs. This was understandable, but wrong. Storrs was a romantic all right, but what he tended to romanticize was not Arabs, but himself dealing with Arabs. Storrs was a clever man—Pembroke College, Cambridge, first class in Classical Tripos, 1903—and what he enjoyed about Arabs was the comedy of their courteous deviousness, and his own courteously superior manipulations of their deviousness. He spoke of himself as *anima naturaliter Levantina*, and then he was surprised when nobody trusted him.

For such a man, holding the gorgeous East in fee was fun, or had been, before the war.

The Zionists were not fun. They were serious. They were not devious—at least in minor transactions—and they were seldom courteous, and often rather rude. Storrs was to remember "the mystic, the almost frightening, metallic clang of Zion."[23] Nothing in Storrs's administrative career, or privileged youth, could have prepared him for the tempered hardness, the total concentration of purpose, of Russian-born Zionists like Weizmann and Ussishkin. Storrs was not as frivolous as he sometimes makes himself sound; he was in many ways a good governor of Jerusalem—the fine appearance of many sections of Jerusalem today is largely due to his ordinance that all new buildings in the city should be in stone. But in comparison with these Zionists, Storrs was frivolous; most people were, and Storrs was a little more frivolous than most people. He was intelligent enough to realize that—and he also knew to what purpose these people were applying their formidable gifts. They intended to make the whole system and context, which Storrs so appreciated and enjoyed, disappear with a metallic clang.

Storrs was, if anything, naturally inclined to philo-semitism. He was a cosmopolitan by taste, who had enjoyed the company of the rich Sephardic ladies of Cairo. But, whatever he might say, he was existentially anti-Zionist, as a cat is anti-dog.

Ronald Storrs must have been well aware of what he was doing when he bustled around Jerusalem with his aides on that November day in 1918 obediently distributing those eighteen copies of the Anglo-French Joint Declaration. General Money ("recreation, duck-shooting") might not have appreciated the full significance of that document. But Storrs was an experienced political specialist chosen, because of proved skills, to take charge of an excruciatingly sensitive city. He had to know there had been a slipup, that this pseudo-Wilsonian Anglo-French extravaganza was intended for Damascus, Baghdad, London, Paris and Washington, but never for Jerusalem, after the Balfour Declaration. As Military Governor, he certainly had the authority to query such an instruction. After all, people like him were paid to reason why. If he raised no question, but simply put the blunder into execution, it is hard not to infer that he liked the blunder's unintended but probable consequence: the encouragement of Arab resistance to the Jewish National Home. The wording of Storrs's own report tends to confirm that. There is an unmistakable Storrsian sniff behind the sentence: "The result was instantaneous, but I fear hardly that anticipated by the authorities."

We are not to understand that Storrs himself was taken by surprise. As he said, with deadpan and detached sagacity: "It was a singularly unhappy moment for such a pronouncement to be made."[24]

Of Storrs, Christopher Sykes writes: "He became the central subject of the anti-British propaganda campaign of the Zionists. A legend of his wickedness and anti-Semitic conspiracy grew round him and is believed to this day in Israel."[25] Sykes dismisses the legend altogether. It was all due, in Sykes's opinion, to "this maddening British gift of fairness," which Storrs possessed, in unusual combination with "a somewhat extravagant show of diplomatic good manners."

Perhaps so. Sykes mentions the Anglo-French declaration, but does not refer to the circumstances of its promulgation in Jerusalem. That promulgation necessarily tended to undermine the Jewish National Home, as Storrs certainly knew it would. Storrs may well have thought that fairness required that. But Zionists at the time could hardly be expected to agree. They classed Storrs as the cleverest and the civilest—and therefore the worst—of their many enemies in British Palestine:

> *By merit rais'd*
> *To that bad eminence*

V

During 1919, matters moved visibly toward some kind of showdown between Jews and Arabs in Palestine, and also between the British military administration and the British Government. While tension mounted between Jews and Arabs—especially in the spring of 1919—the military administration clamped down on Zionism. There was a series of official decisions whose cumulative effect was "to provoke Zionist fury."[26] These measures included the prohibition of Jewish immigration and the withholding of authorization for land transfers—which were held to be a breach of the *status quo*—the nonrecognition of Hebrew as an official language and the banning from public performance of the Zionist anthem, "Hatikvah." Understandably, the Zionists felt that the promise of the Balfour Declaration was being broken, while the Arabs felt that the Jewish National Home might be aborted through resolute action.

At the same time, the military administration continued to press the British Government both directly and indirectly for, in effect, a reversal of the Balfour Declaration.[27] The semiofficial mission of the Americans Henry King (1858–1934) and Charles Crane (1858–1939), who visited Palestine in the summer of 1919, noted "the practically unanimous feeling of British officers that the Zionist programme in anything like its full form could not even be initiated by force of arms."[28]

The last months of 1919 saw a great increase in Arab nationalist activity, not only in Palestine, but also in neighboring Syria. Much of this was due to the consequences of the areas of conflict between Britain's promises of the period 1915–1918. The Hashemites—the family of Sherif Hussein of Mecca, the men who had raised, at British instigation, the standard of the Arab Revolt against Ottoman rule—believed themselves to have been promised, through the Hussein-McMahon correspondence of 1915, a throne in Syria, then generally assumed to include Palestine. But the Sykes-Picot secret agreement (1916) awarded Syria to France, while by modified Sykes-Picot (1917), Britain awarded Palestine to itself, and then, by the Balfour Declaration of the same year, awarded a National Home in Palestine to the Jews. Finally, the Anglo-French Joint Declaration, at the end of 1918, appeared to promise self-determination and independence to Syria (as well as Iraq), and possibly to the Palestinian Arabs as well.

Small wonder that Arthur Balfour about this time made his celebrated judgment that "so far as Palestine is concerned, the powers have made no statement of fact that is not admittedly wrong, and no declaration of policy which, at least in the letter, they have not always intended to violate."[29]

At an earlier period—June 1918—Faisal (the Hashemite claimant to a Syrian throne), on British advice, had reached agreement with Weizmann, and had actually endorsed the Balfour Declaration, receiving in return assurances of protection for Arab rights in Palestine. But that agreement came to nothing.[30] Once Faisal and his followers realized, in the second half of 1919, that the British were not really backing his claim to a throne in Damascus, the Hashemite claim to a united Syria, including Palestine, revived, and Arab nationalism took a Pan-Syrian and very militant turn.[31]

There had been a time, not many months before, when Britain might have recognized Faisal, at least in Syria. During the British military occupation of Damascus (1918–1919), General Allenby—who in Palestine had vigorously adhered to a *status quo* policy, as alone appropriate to a military administration—had allowed Faisal the symbols of sovereign rule, including the use of his Sherifian flag on public buildings. The fiction, encouraged by both Lawrence and Allenby, was that the Arabs themselves had liberated Syria. The basic idea was to keep out the French.[32] But by the autumn of 1919, the British Government had decided to let the French have Syria. They needed to cut back on overseas expenditure; their military resources were overtaxed. Also, mistrusting the Americans, they felt they needed to reaffirm the French Alliance.[33]

So by the end of 1919, the British had withdrawn from Syria (exclusive of Palestine). But the French had not yet come in (except in Lebanon), and Faisal had not been explicitly repudiated by Britain. In March 1920, a General Syrian Congress, meeting in Damascus with Palestinian participation—and taking the Anglo-French Joint Declaration seriously—elected Faisal king of a united Syria, which included Palestine. The British military administration still hoped it might be possible to use Faisal to frustrate both the French and the Zionists. They tried to back Faisal, both for Syria and for Palestine. They encouraged Faisal to claim Palestine, and then urged London, unsuccessfully, to accept his claim.[34] The officers saw this as a clever move to achieve indirect rule over all Greater Syria.[35] In conditions of indirect rule, with Faisal as nominal sovereign, the promise of the National Home could have been held not to apply.

In Palestine itself, Arab hopes soared, and Arab anti-Jewish agitation increased in the early months of 1920. The agitation was organized by the Muslim-Christian Association, which had been founded immediately after the promulgation of the Anglo-French Joint Declaration in Jerusalem, in November 1918. Both Jews and Arabs believed that the military administration was sympathetic to the association and to the agitation. Ronald Storrs was cheered by a demonstration in Jerusalem which presented him with a declaration including the words:

> Palestine, where the Messiah was born and crucified, and which is considered as a fatherland by all the world, refuses to be a National Home for the people who did evil unto the Messiah and to the whole world. Which people, among whom the Jews have dwelt, has not witnessed massacres and shedding of blood? History shows what Russia did, and Spain, Germany, France and England against the Jews. Palestine . . . by no means consents to its mountains being converted

into volcanoes spitting fire, and the waters of its Jordan being turned into blood which will blacken the face of humanity.[36]

Storrs had exhorted the demonstrators to remain peaceful, but when agitation is conducted at that pitch, and is apparently condoned by the authorities, violence becomes probable.

From April 4 to 8, 1920, Arab rioters attacked the Jewish Quarter of the Old City of Jerusalem. The Arab police sided with the rioters and had to be withdrawn and disarmed.[37] The Army did not enter the Old City, and forbade the Jews to organize their own defense. Vladimir Jabotinsky, who tried to do so, was arrested. In the four days of bloodshed, 9 people died (5 of them Jews) and 244 were wounded (211 Jews). Most of the victims were old men, women and children.[38]

The fury of the Jews in Palestine, in the wake of these events, was directed mainly against the British—whom the Jews had earlier tended to idealize. A few days after the riots had died down, Ronald Storrs called on Menachem Ussishkin, acting chairman of the Zionist Commission. A record of their conversation is preserved in the Central Zionist Archives.[39] It begins:

> COL. STORRS: I have come to express my grief to Your Honour over the catastrophe which befell us.
> MR. USSISHKIN: . Which catastrophe?
> COL. STORRS: I am referring to the saddening events which took place here in the last few days.
> MR. USSISHKIN: Is Your Honour referring to the pogrom?
> COL. STORRS: (*Emotionally*) It was not a pogrom! It is impossible to call these riots a pogrom!
> MR. USSISHKIN: You, Colonel, are an expert in administrative matters and I am an expert in the laws of pogroms; I can promise you that there is no difference between the Jerusalem pogrom and the Kishinev pogrom. The organizers of the local pogrom did not show any originality; they followed, step by step, in the ways of the perpetrators of the Russian pogroms.

Later, in the course of his long and increasingly emotional speech, Ussishkin said: ". . . Czar Nicholas also did not interfere with the pogroms, he also oppressed us. Yet does Your Honour see what befell him? In his place sits Trotsky. All our enemies in the world and in the land of Israel will also meet such an end."

In Cairo, Weizmann spoke to Allenby, also in terms of a pogrom, and wept.

It was inevitable that the Russian (and Polish) Jews who made up most of the population of the New Yishuv should see the situation in that light—seeing the administration, Russian or British, as helping to inflame a population to riot and then failing to protect the victims. If the military administration had been left to itself, that parallel was getting close.[40] But the military administration was not left to itself. What the military administration had achieved was the reverse of what it had intended. As a result of the riots, a reaction set in in Whitehall in favor of the Zionists and against O.E.T.A.

At the San Remo Conference, at the end of April 1920, final agreement was reached between France and Britain on modified Sykes-Picot. The French were assured of Syria, and drove Faisal out of Damascus in the summer; the British provided him with a throne in Iraq a year later. Britain, assured of Palestine, decided to replace the military administration there with a civil one, and to put at the head of that administration Sir Herbert Samuel, who was both a Jew and a convinced (though gradualist) Zionist.

What the Arabs who sacked the Jewish Quarter had in fact helped to bring about was the replacement of a Palestinian administration opposed to the Jewish National Home by an administration committed to the Jewish National Home. Again and again, in the following six decades, the forms taken by Arab resistance to Zionism were to have similar self-defeating effects.

VI

In retrospect, what is remarkable is not so much the (localized) attempt to jettison the Balfour Declaration in the period 1918–1920 as the degree of fidelity to the Balfour Declaration shown by the British Government, in the teeth of such determined opposition from most Britons on the spot, as well as from some Arabs, and in a political context radically different from that in which the Declaration was launched.

In the postwar context, the arguments originally advanced by Curzon against the Balfour Declaration, in terms of Imperial interests in the Arab and Muslim world, appeared as strong as ever. Telling on the same side of the question, the degree and extent to which Zionism complicated the problem of governing Palestine were far more formidably apparent by 1920 than they could ever have been, amid quite different and vaster dangers, in 1917.

The arguments in favor of the Declaration looked seriously weakened. The urgencies of war propaganda had disappeared with the war. There was no need now to preempt a possible German bid; no relevance in the possible appeal of Zionism to Russian public opinion. By 1920, if not earlier, Britain's acquisition of Palestine was a *fait accompli*, in no real need of idealistic sweetening. There was no need now for a Jewish lobby working for a British Palestine. America was now withdrawing into isolation;[41] the Mandate system, that great sop to Wilsonian idealism, was no longer subject to Wilsonian scrutiny.

The weight of argument, *in terms of British interests,* seems to tilt decisively, in the postwar period, against the Jewish National Home. The Balfour Declaration itself could not have been disavowed, but it could have been interpreted (as was later attempted) in such a way as to reduce the National Home to a token. In this context, the wording of the actual Mandate becomes important. The Mandate would be the governing document for Britain in Palestine. In theory, the Mandate represented the standing instructions to the Mandatory from the League of Nations. In fact the Mandatory, as one of the two dominant partners in the League in the immediate postwar period, was in a position to draft its own instructions, and did so. Any diplomat could recognize the possibilities inherent in that situation for the blameless attenuation of an existing unilateral commitment. For example, the Declaration could have figured in a historical section of the Mandate, without being actually integrated into the preamble to the Mandate itself. And so on.

In the event, however, the Mandate in no way attenuated the Balfour Declaration. As the Peel Commission later noted: "Unquestionably . . . the primary purpose of the Mandate, as expressed in its preambles and its articles, is to promote the establishment of a Jewish National Home."[42] Not only did the Declaration become an "integral part of the Mandate," but the Mandate actually reinforced the commitment to the Jewish National Home in Palestine.

At San Remo in April 1920, the Allied Powers agreed to entrust "administration to a mandatory, whose duties are defined by a verbatim repetition of Mr. Balfour's declaration of November 1917."[43] But in its final form, when it was issued in the summer of 1922, the Mandate for Palestine went further than that. Having noted that "the Principal Allied Powers have . . . agreed that the Mandatory should be responsible for putting into effect the declaration originally made on November 2, 1917 . . ." and having recited the text of the Balfour Declaration, the Mandate added: "Whereas recognition has thereby been given to the historical connection of the Jewish people with Palestine and to the grounds for reconstituting their national home in that country . . ."[44]

When Palestinian Arabs protested against that last recognition, they succeeded only in getting something even worse than what they had originally protested against. "It is essential," the Colonial Office told them in what became known as the 1922 White Paper,[45] "that it [the Jewish Community] should know that it is in Palestine as of right and not on sufferance. That is the reason why it is necessary that the existence of a Jewish National Home should be internationally recognized and that it should be formally recognized to rest upon ancient historical connections."

The White Paper also contained some reassurance for the Arabs. As the Duke of Devonshire—Churchill's successor at the Colonial Office—would explain it in the Lords, it did not mean a Jewish State: "The intention from the beginning has been to make a National Home for the Jews, but every provision has been made to prevent it from becoming in any sense a Jewish State, or a State under Jewish domination."[46] This assurance was of course unwelcome to Zionists. But both Zionists and the Arab leadership well understood that, in the here and now, the vital issue was not the imagined ultimate form of a Palestinian polity, but Jewish immigration. On that point the White Paper, with its "as of right," satisfied the Jews, not the Arabs. The White Paper did say that immigration would be governed by the "absorptive capacity" of the country, but that was not seen as presenting any serious barrier to immigration until many years later.

The Mandatory provisions quoted are all from the preamble, but the articles contained one provision that was even better for Zionists: the recognition of an institutional role in Palestine not merely for some Jewish body but specifically for the Zionist organization. Article 4 of the Mandate said: "An appropriate Jewish agency shall be recognized. . . . The Zionist organization . . . shall be recognized as such an agency."

Surprise has often been expressed at the original British commitment to the Jewish National Home. But that commitment, in the circumstances of November 1917, seems considerably easier to explain than the deepening and strengthening of the commitment, in apparently much less propitious circumstances, from three to five years later. Not merely were the external circumstances less propitious, but changes inside the British Government and in the Foreign Office appeared to be distinctly unfavorable from a Zionist point of view. Balfour left the Foreign Office in October 1919—though he remained in the Government—and he was replaced by Curzon, who had been opposed to the Balfour Declaration from the start. Foreign Office officials who, in 1917, had helped Balfour convince the War Cabinet of the need to announce the Jewish National Home had departed, or changed their minds. One of them told Ronald Storrs that "our friend Weizmann . . . sold us a pup."[47] The Foreign Office, after Balfour, began to take on an anti-Zionist tone from which it has seldom since departed. "By the end of 1919," writes a historian, "the honeymoon period in Anglo-Zionist relations was over."[48] Zionist writings give the same impression of a weakening of the commitment. Thus Leonard Stein writes: "Once the terms of the Mandate began to be seriously considered in 1919 the British Government moved progressively further away from any commitment to the idea of a Jewish State or Commonwealth in Palestine."[49]

But the British Government had never given any such commitment.[50] The commitment was to the National Home, and it was a qualified one. It is true that Weizmann's first draft of the Mandate had included a commitment to a "Jewish Commonwealth," and that Balfour personally may well have assented to this. Curzon, when he succeeded Balfour at the Foreign Office, objected to this and managed to get it out. But that did not represent a withdrawal, or a depreciation: it meant a setback, on this particular point, to the Zionist effort to *deepen* the commitment. On other points, as we have seen, they succeeded. And it is Weizmann's success, in 1920–1922, in bringing about, in most unfavorable circumstances, the consummation of Zionist policies that constitutes the most astonishing—and least acknowledged—achievement of his astonishing career.

It is in 1920–1922 that the policy of the National Home begins to come into existence. From this time on, for nearly two decades, the British—though not without some wavering—allowed the Zionists to get on with the job of building the National Home—which would be the basis, as friends and foes both recognized, of the eventual Jewish State. It is from this point that Jewish immigration into Palestine proceeds on the principle that the Jews are in Palestine "as of right and not on sufferance." It is at this moment that Herzl's dream begins to turn into reality. The Balfour Declaration up to 1920 was a unilateral promise. In 1920, the promise begins to be kept; in 1922 it becomes part of an international commitment. If the promise was later broken—

with the White Paper of 1939 and its postwar sequels—this should not obscure the fact that it was kept by the generation which gave it, and kept to an extent which made possible the emergence of the State of Israel.

Not the least extraordinary part of the story is that the legal foundations for the future State of Israel should have been completed by that sardonic anti-Zionist George Nathaniel Curzon. Curzon had disliked the idea of the Jewish National Home from the beginning, and in 1920, when he was helping to build it, he seems to have disliked it more than ever. Balfour had not consulted him about earlier phases in the drafting of the Mandate, and when Curzon saw the then current draft, in March 1920, he exploded:

> I think the entire conception wrong.
>
> Here is a country with 580,000 Arabs and 30,000 or is it 60,000 Jews (by no means all Zionists). Acting upon the noble principles of self-determination and ending with a splendid appeal to the League of Nations, we then proceed to draw up a document which reeks of Judaism in every paragraph and is an avowed constitution for a Jewish State.
>
> Even the poor Arabs are only allowed to look through the keyhole as a non-Jewish community.
>
> It is quite clear that this mandate has been drawn up by someone reeling under the fumes of Zionism. If we are all to submit to that intoxicant, this draft is all right.
>
> Perhaps there is no alternative.
>
> But I confess I should like to see something worded differently.[51]

"I am quite willing," wrote Curzon, "to water the Palestine mandate, which I cordially mistrust." He did get some water into it. He got out the reference to a Jewish Commonwealth. He also objected, with partial success, to the phrase (in the draft), "Recognizing . . . the historical connection of the Jews with Palestine, and the claim which this gives them to reconstitute it as their national home." Curzon disliked the whole phrase: "I do not myself recognize that the connection of the Jews with Palestine, which terminated 1200 years ago, gives them any claim whatsoever. On this principle we have a stronger claim to parts of France."

Curzon added: "I greatly dislike giving the draft to the Zionists, but in view of the indiscretions already committed I suppose that this is inevitable."

Curzon managed to get rid of "claim," but Weizmann—"this

rather unquiet spirit," as Balfour calls him at this time[52]—managed to hold on to "historical connections."

Weizmann was "quite pleased about it," and so well he might be. He had managed to get something a bit better than the Balfour Declaration out of George Curzon.

If the document originally submitted to Curzon "[reeked] of Judaism" and was the product of a brain "reeling under the fumes of Zionism," the document Curzon eventually sanctioned reeled and reeked only slightly less. Curzon hated what he had to do, but he did it, under protest.

Reading Curzon's protestations, and looking at Israel's legal foundation stone, as it left Curzon's hands, I found a line of Racine's coming into my mind:

> Le cruel Dieu des Juifs l'emporte aussi sur toi.
> (The cruel God of the Jews has you beaten too.)[53]

Curzon and others who, in the postwar years, disliked the whole idea of the Jewish National Home justified perseverance with it on the ground that it was a binding national commitment. But the British Government of which Curzon was a member had given other—*ex parte*—commitments in the Middle East—to the French in the Sykes-Picot agreement, and to the Arabs in a number of statements, including the Anglo-French Joint Declaration—and it was only the commitment to the Zionists that was treated as binding, modified in a sense favorable to those to whom the original commitment was given, and enshrined in an international instrument. The promise that was honored was the promise to the Jews.

If a Zionist, of the pious sort, were to tell me that the true explanation of this phenomenon was that God had decided that it was time for His people to come home, I should no doubt express polite skepticism. But if the same pious Zionist were then to ask me whether I can discern any explanation, in terms of Britain's material interests, for the British Government's reinforcement of the Balfour Declaration, in the circumstances of the early twenties, I should have to say that I can't find any such explanation.[54, 55]

This doesn't mean, of course, that one has to look around for miracles. It means that the mainspring of action in this matter seemed to come from moral, spiritual and aesthetic forces, rather than calculations of material interest. The Zionist idea was and is a power. For Herzl, it opened the doors of King and Emperor and Pope. For Weizmann, it was opening the doors of Palestine itself.

As the doors of Palestine opened, Weizmann's language, in writing to Zionist friends, takes on a note of mystical exaltation, similar to many passages in Herzl's diaries. As he prepared to present the Zionist case to the Paris Peace Conference, Weizmann wrote: "I am living like Moses on Mount Sinai . . . 'on fire' . . ."[56]

Later Weizmann addressed the Peace Conference, saying that the Jewish National Home should ultimately become a nationality "as Jewish as the English nation is English." When this address was well received, Weizmann wrote: "I think that the God of Israel is with us."[57]

The power of the Zionist idea is primarily the power of the Bible over human imaginations together with the power, over others, of imaginations strongly affected in this way. The second and third decades of the twentieth century in Britain were hardly an Age of Faith, but men's minds were still full of the Authorized Version—and this was especially true of the most important Britons involved, Lloyd George and Arthur Balfour (and Curzon too, irrelevant though he believed that fact to be). There were plenty of others who cared little for that sort of thing, but those who did care counted for more. Curzon, on the essentials of this matter, did Balfour's bidding, even after he had succeeded Balfour at the Foreign Office. Lloyd George and Balfour were for giving Weizmann what he wanted, knowing that was, eventually, a Jewish State.[58]

Curzon was Foreign Secretary, and responsible for Palestine,[59] in 1920—Weizmann's *annus mirabilis:* the year of the dismantling of the military administration, of the appointment of Herbert Samuel as High Commissioner, and of San Remo, and the commitment to make the Balfour Declaration part of the Mandate—all amounting, as has been said, to "a great victory for Zionism."[60]

Zionism has shown a capacity to make its opponents do some very strange things. This capacity should be ascribed not merely to the power of the Zionist idea over certain (Gentile) minds but also to the intensity with which that idea burned in the minds of the Zionists themselves; to their tireless ardor in its pursuit, and to the way in which it concentrated their faculties. Their opponents seem, in comparison, made of some lighter and less durable material. At times also, the opponents seem even to lack the will to oppose as distinct from carping, or grumbling, like Curzon.[61]

Deep down, I suspect that there was at work a feeling that it would not be lucky to break a promise to the Jews to help them return to the Promised Land.

Efforts were made at the time to show that the Balfour Declara-

Above, As British Governor of Jerusalem (1917–1925) the gifted aesthete Ronald Storrs experienced what he called "the mystic, the almost frightening, metallic clang of Zion."
Below, Sir Herbert Samuel, first British High Commissioner (1920–1925) in Mandate Palestine. Also described as "the first Jewish ruler of Palestine since Hyrcanus II"—whose reign ended circa 40 B.C.

tion was, or was not, in conformity with the Covenant of the League of Nations. What mattered far more was that it was felt to be in conformity with a far older Covenant, between God and the Jews, over Eretz Israel.[62]

VII

On June 30, 1920, Sir Herbert Samuel arrived in Palestine as High Commissioner: "the first Jewish ruler of Palestine," as his biographer said, "since Hyrcanus II, that last degenerate Maccabean. . . ."[63] As Hyrcanus had been replaced as king of Judea by the Edomite Herod the Great around 40 B.C., the interval in question here is of 1,960 years.

Ronald Storrs, as military governor of Jerusalem, met Sir Herbert in Jaffa Harbor. When he went aboard the High Commissioner's cruiser, H.M.S. *Centaur*, Storrs "was delighted to find Sir Herbert in white Diplomatic uniform wearing the Star and purple ribbon of the Empire together with the (far prettier) Star of the Belgian Order of Leopold."[64]

Generally speaking, the military, from whom the new High Commissioner was taking over supreme control, were not delighted. In May, before Sir Herbert left London, Curzon had informed him of Allenby's reaction to his appointment. Allenby had said that he feared the appointment of "any Jew as the first Governor" would be the signal for widespread disturbances, murders, attacks on Jews and the Jewish colonies, and Arab raids across the border; though he added, "if a Jew were to be appointed, Samuel would be the right man."[65]

Curzon, naturally, was impressed by Allenby's warning, and thought it was "a heavy responsibility" for both Samuel and himself "if lives were lost." There was "no question of withdrawing the appointment"—Samuel remembered Curzon telling him—but "someone else should go to Palestine for the first year to relieve me of the brunt of the difficulties."

Samuel, having his appointment from the Prime Minister, resisted Curzon's suggestion, which was eventually overruled by Lloyd George. But it was clear that the military were not completely reconciled either to Samuel's appointment or to giving up the substance of power in Palestine. The Foreign Office letter (June 19, 1920) formally notifying Samuel of his appointment as High Commissioner and Commander in Chief in Palestine contained a potentially ominous paragraph:

> The Army Council have approved the assumption by you of the title of Commander-in-Chief of the troops in Palestine, with the proviso that the possession of this title will not give you any right of interference in details of movements of troops, but will merely allow you to indicate the general policy to be pursued by the Military forces.

The early months of Samuel's tenure went, however, without trouble, and he succeeded in getting the administration, including Storrs, generally on his side. "The Jews received him with an enthusiasm appropriate to a herald of the messianic dawn; the Arabs with an unexpected restraint, bordering even on respect."[66] The restraint may have been connected with the pricking, by the French, of the Faisal bubble in Damascus, a month after Samuel's arrival.

Samuel was a shrewd, capable and determined man, the first non-baptized Jew to attain Cabinet office in Britain (1909). He was generally regarded as prosaic and unimaginative, but he was a Zionist. He had tried to convert Asquith to Zionism, and succeeded only in bringing to Asquith's mind Disraeli's dictum that "race is all." The fervor of Samuel's Zionism had astonished even Chaim Weizmann. Reporting on a conversation with him, Weizmann wrote: "He also thinks that perhaps the Temple may be rebuilt, as a symbol of Jewish unity—of course in a modernized form. After listening to him, I remarked that I was pleasantly surprised to hear such words from him: that if I were a religious Jew I should have thought the Messianic times were near."[67]

As well as being a Zionist, Samuel was also a conscientious and liberal British High Commissioner. He believed that Zionist aims could eventually be fulfilled through a harmonious process, with the progressive enlisting of Arab goodwill, and to the satisfaction of Arab aspirations. This was still a general belief among Zionists in the Diaspora, but in Palestine itself it had few adherents among the Jews, and even fewer among the Arabs.

Samuel's first major acts were Zionist. In August, a Land Transfer Ordinance made possible sales of land to the Zionists, and in September an Immigration Ordinance opened Palestine, for the first time, to legal Jewish immigration. Visas were to be granted to all persons recommended by the Zionist Organization. These two ordinances brought into effect the substance of the charter which Herzl had dreamed of and worked for.

Samuel tried, and with some apparent initial success, to reconcile the Arabs to these major Zionist measures. He pardoned (as well as Jabotinsky and his comrades) the ringleaders of the Arab riots of April 1920, including Haj Amin al-Husseini, now beginning to emerge as leader of Arab nationalism in Palestine. He also brought into being a nominated Advisory Council, with an Arab majority in the non-official membership, announcing that "this is to be regarded only as a first step in the development of self-governing institutions."[68] Arab nationalists were neither mollified nor interested, and anti-Zionist agitation resumed in the winter of 1920–1921.

Samuel, being a convinced Gladstonian Liberal, as well as a Zionist, was unwilling to limit freedom of speech. Men like Ussishkin, brought up under non-Gladstonian conditions, could not understand this, and neither could the Arabs. For men who had been subjects of the Russian Empire, as for men who had been subjects of the Ottoman Empire, freedom of expression had been unknown as a general concept. It had been known as a specific phenomenon occurring in particular contexts for particular purposes. Where the authorities permitted it, it was for some purpose which they, or some of them, had in mind. Freedom to agitate, that is to say, implied some considerable official sympathy with the agitation. (And there was such sympathy in Samuel's entourage, as we shall see.) Also, tolerated verbal violence implied, in the experience of men like Ussishkin, the imminence of physical violence, with some degree of official complicity.

Under the rule of a benevolent and respected Jewish and Zionist governor, the Jews of Palestine in the winter of 1920–1921 felt themselves to be "on the edge of a volcano."[69]

Samuel was now menaced by contradictions between the Britishness and the Jewishness in his role and in his feelings; contradictions bafflingly multiplied by the contradictions inside the Mandate, and those between the general Mandatory concept and the particular concept of the Jewish National Home. On the one hand, Samuel opened the doors wide to Jewish immigration and land acquisition; on the other hand, he promised representative institutions, which, if they had emerged in the 1920s, would have had as their first objective the slamming of those doors.

It was symptomatic that Samuel, the exalted Zionist, should have appointed a bitter and fanatical *anti*-Zionist, Ernest Richmond (1874–

1955), as his principal adviser on Arab affairs. Richmond had been introduced to Palestine, and brought on in its administration, by that *sioniste convaincu*, Ronald Storrs, whose intimate friend he was, and whose house he shared.[70] Thus the High Commission was to pursue a Zionist policy, through the High Commissioner, in relations with the Jews, and an anti-Zionist policy, through the assistant secretary (political), Ernest Richmond, in relations with the Arabs.

Perhaps, in the circumstances, it was the only thing that could have worked at all.

In January 1921, a change occurred which was helpful to Samuel, and to the Zionists. Palestine was transferred from the care of Curzon's Foreign Office to that of the Colonial Office under Winston Churchill. Curzon in a letter to Samuel announcing the change said "it was a put up job between L.G. and Churchill." He added, with Curzonian tact: "I have seen Storrs once or twice and he tells me of the many excellent things that you have done. I view with some apprehension the reported tramp of crowds of seedy Jews toward your shores from Central Europe."[71]

Winston Churchill, as Christopher Sykes said, "wished Zion well from his heart." He was also influenced by T. E. Lawrence, and by the idea of ruling the Arab Middle East through the Hashemite dynasty, which had legitimized the British-instigated "Revolt in the Desert" against the Turks. The Colonial Office now had Iraq as well as Palestine in its care.

Having set up a Middle East Department in the Colonial Office, Churchill convened a conference of senior British officials in the Middle East at Cairo, in March 1921, in order to reach a settlement with the leaders of Arab nationalism.[72] For the purposes of the Cairo conference, these alleged leaders were the Hashemite dynasts, Faisal and Abdullah, sons of Sherif Hussein. Churchill explained that Faisal was to be king of Iraq, and suitably "elected."[73] Abdullah was to be emir of Transjordan, a kingdom to be made for him by detaching the whole territory east of the Jordan from the rest of Mandate Palestine.

From Cairo Churchill went on to Palestine, where, in spite of these concessions to "Arab nationalism," he was welcomed by the Jews and largely boycotted by the Arabs.

A focus of Palestinian Arab unrest, growing in the spring of 1921, was the advent of relatively large-scale Jewish immigration, no longer as a fear but as a fact. By April 1921, nearly 10,000 Jews had entered Palestine, under Samuel's Immigration Ordinance of September 1920.

These immigrants were, in the main, highly committed young Zionists, who had been eagerly awaiting a long-withheld opportunity. Their immigration is part of what is known in Zionist history as the third *aliyah* (1919–1923). They played a particularly important role in the development of agriculture by the Yishuv: "It was the third *aliyah* that revived collective farming and provided it with an idealized image as the emergent trend of Jewish agriculture in Palestine."[74] These immigrants, unlike their predecessors, had received a careful advance training, and were well prepared for the social and technical conditions of Palestine. The people of the third *aliyah* and second *aliyah*, taken together, have been described as "the founding fathers of Israel."[75] The third *aliyah*, like its predecessors, was bound to be resented by Arabs. But there were other factors at work now, tending to produce more serious consequences.

One of these was the knowledge both of the Balfour Declaration and of serious British opposition to it. A further factor, and probably the most incendiary, was a politico-religious dispute over the election of the Grand Mufti of Jerusalem. Under the Ottoman Empire, it does not seem that the post of Mufti had been important or sensitive: the Sultan was the supreme religious as well as temporal authority. But under, or facing, a Christian temporal power, the post of Mufti took on a different significance, as the supreme representative of Muslim Arabs, threatened by alien infidelity. It was under the British—with the deferential and ecclesiastically susceptible Storrs as governor of Jerusalem—that the Mufti was allowed to style himself Grand Mufti.

The post of Grand Mufti, which fell vacant at this time, was to be filled in accordance with Ottoman legal procedures, which provided for the election, on a limited franchise, of three persons from whom the ruling power could then take its pick. The elections occurred in mid-April. The most conspicuous and controversial candidate was Haj Amin al-Husseini, a member of a powerful Jerusalem clan, and a principal instigator of the anti-Jewish riots of Easter 1920. However, Haj Amin came in fourth in the elections, and therefore was not among those whom the Government had the right to nominate. Haj Amin and his followers then claimed that the elections had been rigged by the Jews, in furtherance of a scheme "to have a Jewish Zionist Mufti."[76] Richmond argued in favor of the invalidation of the elections. Samuel hesitated.

While the matter of the Mufti hung in the balance, the second major outbreak of Arab anti-Jewish violence took place on May 1, not in Jerusalem, but in Jaffa, the main center of Jewish immigration. After a fight broke out between two factions of Jews—far Left and moderate Left—Arab rioters, joined by Arab police, attacked Jewish shops and a shelter for immigrants. By the end of the day 27 Jews and 3 Arabs had been killed and 104 Jews and 34 Arabs wounded.[77]

In the following days, the violence spread to other coastal centers. The new civil administration—unlike the former military one—authorized armed Jewish self-defense. By May 7, the violence came to an end, leaving a total of 47 Jews killed and 146 wounded, and 48 Arabs killed and 73 wounded.[78]

Samuel felt a need to try to calm the Arabs. To this end, he took two main steps. He introduced a temporary suspension of immigration (May 5), and he yielded to Richmond's argument in the matter of the Grand Mufti. One of the elected and unwanted trio was induced to stand down, and on May 8, Haj Amin was appointed Grand Mufti of Jerusalem.

These moves infuriated the Jews, who saw them as putting a political premium on Arab aggression. But there was little the Jews could do about it, since they still needed the Mandatory power. They knew also that Samuel was in danger, not for his recent concessions to the Arabs, but for having favored the Jewish National Home. They felt Samuel had let them down, but they still needed him.

In 1921, the military made yet another attempt—the last for a number of years—to break the Balfour Declaration. General Sir Walter Congreve (1862–1927), commander of British forces in the Middle East, went to London at the end of June to argue against Zionism and Samuel, adding for good measure, in a conversation recorded by a Colonial Office official, that "all his officers were certainly under the impression that H.M.G. were in the hands of the Zionist Organization."[79]

Not satisfied with the results of the London talks, General Congreve's headquarters, in October 1921, issued a circular to officers under his command, which actually evoked the specter of the famous prewar Curragh Mutiny in Ireland:

Whilst the Army officially is supposed to have no politics, it is recognized that there are certain problems such as those of Ireland and Palestine in which the sympathies of the Army are on one side or the other. . . . In the case of Palestine these sympathies are rather obviously with the Arabs, who have hitherto appeared to the disinterested observer to have been the victim of the unjust policy forced upon them by the British Government.[80]

Whether conscious of where military sympathies lay or not, Arabs in Jerusalem, shortly after the Congreve circular, attacked Jews celebrating the fourth anniversary of the Balfour Declaration. The Jews resisted; five Jews and three Arabs were killed.

As often was to happen, the zeal of the anti-Zionists, both British and Arab, now produced a grave setback to their cause. On Christmas Eve, 1921, shortly after receiving from Weizmann a copy of Congreve's circular, Churchill, as Colonial Secretary, invited the Air Ministry to assume responsibility for the defense of Palestine. A squadron of the Air Force was stationed in the area, and a small British Gendarmerie was set up.

British military attitudes toward the policy of the Jewish National Home were not the only reason for the change: Air Force control was cheaper, which was a major objective. But, whatever the reason for it, the change was decidedly favorable to the emergence of the National Home. There was no longer—as there had been from the beginning to now—a British military policy on the ground in Palestine, at variance with the civil policy of His Majesty's Government.

It is a remarkable fact that for nearly eight years following that change—from the end of 1921 to the summer of 1929—there was no serious outbreak of violence in Palestine. This does not "prove" the truth of the opinion generally held among Zionists—that the military encouraged Arab resistance to the Balfour Declaration—but it does suggest that the opinion may not have been without foundation. There were, however, other reasons conducive to a period of tranquillity.

VIII

During this crucial period, 1920–1922, the future of the National Home seemed at high risk, from the potential consequences of Sir Herbert Samuel's genuine commitment to liberalism. Backed by Churchill, Samuel at this time worked hard to favor the emergence of representative institutions in Palestine—a central element in the policy announced in the White Paper of 1922. It was difficult for Zionists to contest openly a project so clearly in accordance with the Covenant of the League, and the Mandatory system, the juridical framework within which the Balfour Declaration became part of the law of the land for Palestine.[81] But Zionists feared the notion of representative institutions and with good reason.[82] The census of 1922 showed Jews—84,000 in all—as about 11 percent of the population of Palestine. Immigration in the early twenties was running at about 8,000 a year. The Arab birthrate was higher than that of the Jews. In these conditions, an Arab majority in any representative institutions that might emerge in Palestine, in, say, the next quarter of a century, seemed virtually certain. Zionists feared the Arab majority in any such institution would be used to block Jewish immigration.

As against that, Samuel, and Churchill also, had a vision of an eventual Middle Eastern Federation, of which the Jewish National Home would be a part, accepted by the Arabs. Some Zionists in the Diaspora were attracted to such visions; and Weizmann gave some encouragement to them, perhaps partly for tactical reasons. To the leaders of the Yishuv, on the other hand, in daily touch with the realities of Jewish-Arab relations in Palestine, such notions seemed illusory. Their fear of death to their cause, through the emergence of Arab-majority representative institutions, was correspondingly great, and surely realistic.

From this peril, as from so many others, the Zionists were rescued by the Arabs.

Samuel's first step in the direction of representative institutions had been the modest one of the establishment, in October 1920, of a nominated Advisory Council, with a narrow majority of Arab notables among its nonofficial membership. After the riots of May 1921, Samuel proposed the development of the Advisory Council into an elected body, which would be advisory, but "a further stage on the road to self-government."[83] In public, Samuel at this point infuriated and alarmed the Zionists by declaring that the Balfour Declaration did *not* mean the setting up of a Jewish government to rule over the Muslim and Christian majority and that "the British Government, the trustee under the Mandate for the happiness of the people of Palestine, would never impose upon them a policy which that people had reason to think was contrary to their religious, their political and their economic interests."[84]

In the, to them, propitious atmosphere created by that declaration, an Arab delegation visited London in August 1921. They were offered an elective assembly for Palestine. But since they could not immediately get such an assembly with legislative and executive powers, or explicit control over immigration, and since the Balfour

Declaration was not repudiated forthwith, they turned down the proffered advisory assembly altogether. Samuel and Churchill nonetheless persevered with the idea. After the passing at the League of Nations Council meeting in London of the Mandate for Palestine (July 24, 1922), the Government promulgated a Palestine Constitution on September 1, 1922. The Constitution established a Legislative Council. The Legislative Council was to have a majority of nonofficial members, most of whom would be elected. In its representative aspect—the only one that mattered—the council would have been a predominantly Arab body.

All the same, the Palestine Constitution was accepted by the Jews and rejected by the Arabs. Weizmann—taking a calculated risk—had notified his acceptance of the Constitution in advance, in June. Immediately after the promulgation of the Constitution, a Palestine Arab Congress, meeting at Nablus, rejected it *in toto*.

The Government decided, even in the teeth of this opposition, to go ahead with the elections. The Palestine Arab Executive—elected by the Nablus Congress—decided on a boycott of the elections. The boycott was a success. The Legislative Council died. Samuel then tried a reconstituted Advisory Council, which also succumbed to Arab hostility, and a proposed Arab Agency—intended to be symmetrical to the Jewish Agency recognized under the Mandate—met with the same fate. At this point the Arabs were committed to a policy of total noncooperation in the Government of Palestine, as long as the Balfour Declaration was not expressly repudiated.

This policy, on the part of the Arabs, suited the Zionists very well indeed. The British Government could not go that far to meet the Arabs, since the Balfour Declaration was now enshrined in the Mandate, and therefore part of an international system. Britain could not expressly repudiate it without relinquishing its title deed to Palestine.

This, then, was the point at which the Arabs missed their chance to stifle the National Home idea in its cradle. No doubt there were many reasons for that lost opportunity. Neither the Arabs nor anyone else under the Ottoman Empire had had any serious opportunity to get to know the working of representative institutions. A newfound freedom of political expression lent itself to rhetorical competition, and the prestige of the absolute. As factional leaders maneuvered for support, uncompromising positions were the only ones safe against being denounced—and punished—as treachery. These facts have proved remarkably durable, and pernicious to the Arab cause. So

also has another factor: impolitic encouragement by Western sympathizers. Former O.E.T.A. officials helped the Arab leaders prepare
their disastrous positions in 1921–1922, and the increasingly anti-
Zionist tone of much of the British press fed the illusion that the Balfour Declaration could be boycotted to death.[85]

The same illusion was further stimulated by the fall of the Lloyd
George Government in October 1922. It was natural to hope that a
new Government, not responsible for making the Balfour Declaration,
could be pressured into repudiating it. But, as we have seen, the Lloyd
George Government had lasted just long enough to shape the Mandate, stitching the Balfour Declaration very firmly into it. Neither the
new Government—of Bonar Law, rapidly succeeded by Baldwin—
nor any of its successors was in any position to repudiate the Mandate.
The Mandate itself was not reversible without the consent of the
League Council (Article 27). Such consent could no doubt have been
obtained, had the British Government been willing to abandon Palestine. The Baldwin Government—in which Curzon again served as
Foreign Secretary—did consider this option in the summer of 1923,
but decided against it on the advice of the Navy and the Air Force
that retention of Palestine was strategically imperative.[86] (The Army,
having been relieved of responsibility for the area by Churchill,
thought it was *not* needed.) In theory, it would have been possible
to get the Mandate amended, reducing or abandoning the commitment to the National Home. In practice, this course would have been
conspicuous, embarrassing and politically divisive within the Conservative Party. It was Curzon who solemnly ruled it out, thus render-
ing the last of his reluctant but notable services to the Zionist cause:
"It is well nigh impossible for any Government to extricate itself
without a substantial sacrifice of consistency and self-respect, if not
of honor. Those of us who have disliked the policy are not prepared
to make that sacrifice. Those of us who approved the policy throughout would, of course, speak in much less equivocal terms."

But there were good hopes, from an anti-Zionist point of view,
within the letter of the Mandate, of bringing about the euthanasia of
the National Home, under the care of representative institutions. Some
British Governments, in the late twenties and in the thirties, would
have liked that option very much. But the Arabs kept that option
firmly closed, preferring to go on banging their heads against the very
structure of the Mandate itself.

The Zionist position, by contrast, looked impressively reasonable at this time. There had indeed been elements in the Yishuv which, at one point, had seemed about to take up the boycott option themselves. But the Zionist leadership, under Weizmann's firm guidance, kept their heads. By his cool intrepidity in accepting the Palestine Constitution, intrinsically so alarming from a Zionist point of view, Chaim Weizmann rendered the third of his vital services to the Zionist cause. "Representative institutions" were, in due course, killed off, and the Zionists could not be blamed for their death.

As for Sir Herbert Samuel, the outcome of his efforts to establish representative institutions in Palestine is said to have constituted a "humiliating setback"[87] for him. No doubt it did, but it was also a salutary setback. That rejection saved him from himself, or rather from his selves. There was never any real hope of bringing into reality the dream of reconciling Zionism with Arab aspirations. If Samuel had succeeded in bringing about representative institutions in the Palestine of his time, these would have applied all their energies and influence to the throttling of Zionism. Because of Samuel's deep emotional commitment to the Zionist idea, this would have been a personal tragedy for him. Because of the passionate and militant commitment of the Palestinian Zionists, and their resistance to being throttled, the growth of representative institutions would have been likely to involve far greater disturbances in Palestine than those of 1920 and 1921.

As it was, Samuel's setback had a notably sedative effect on Palestine. The Arabs loudly hailed it as a great victory for their cause, while the Jews quietly appreciated their deliverance, at the hands of their deluded enemies, from their dangerous friend.

Palestine, after the collapse of the bid for representative institutions, was necessarily a land governed by the High Commissioner and his officials, without any form of joint consultation with the two communities. But the communities developed or were given institutions of their own, powerful within each community, and consulted by the Government about the affairs of their community.

On the Jewish side, the supreme body was the Zionist Executive (formerly the Zionist Commission and later the Jewish Agency), an authority which had official recognition under the Mandate (Article 4). The Executive was responsible to the Zionist movement as a whole, and tended to reflect the views of Diaspora Zionism. Another body, the Va'ad Leumi (National Council), represented the Yishuv, grew in importance along with the growth of the Yishuv and was capable on occasion of challenging the Zionist Executive. Within the

Yishuv also, two powerful specialized organs developed, the Histadrut and the Hagana. The Hagana, the Jewish armed force, grew out of local self-defense units, which had existed in rudimentary form since the first decade of the century. In 1920, following the first major Arab attacks, those in the Yishuv concerned with defense—members of Ha-Shomer and the Jewish League—"came to realize that it was impossible to depend upon the British authorities . . . and that the Yishuv must create an independent force, completely free of foreign authority"—in a word, an underground.[88] This new nationwide organization was named the Hagana.

The Histadrut was founded in December 1920. It was a unique organizational complex, embracing both trade unionists and the cooperative movement (including the *kibbutzim*) in what has been called "a parliamentary community on an unacknowledged federal basis."[89] It was in fact the organizational embryo of the nascent Jewish State. The Histadrut, at its foundation conference, decided to accept responsibility for the Hagana on behalf of the Yishuv as a whole. The Zionist Executive also fostered the Hagana, while officially not wishing to know of its existence. In this period, the Hagana was a small force, numbering only a few hundred part-time members.

On the Arab side, a quite different form of organization emerged. The main component in this was a remarkable concentration of personal politico-ecclesiastical power in the hands of Haj Amin al-Husseini. Haj Amin had become Grand Mufti of Jerusalem in May 1921. In January 1922 he became—again with British support—president of a newly founded Supreme Muslim Council to which the British Government handed over the powers of patronage in Muslim financial and legal affairs, which had belonged to the Ottoman rulers. As these powers were very great, this made Haj Amin by far the most important Arab in Palestine, in political as well as in religious affairs. Indeed, the idea that the religious sphere is distinct from the political one is a Western idea, not generally accepted in the Islamic world.

The Yishuv were angry and apprehensive about the accession of Haj Amin to such an unprecedented eminence. They knew him to be their enemy, and believed him to have instigated the attacks on them in 1920, and perhaps in 1921 also. Haj Amin was to prove, years later, that the Yishuv's apprehensions about him were amply justified. But in the early years of his preeminence—after he had become president of the Supreme Muslim Council—this did not seem to be the case. Samuel seems to have hoped that power would bring responsibility, on a "poacher-turned-gamekeeper" basis—and this hope seemed to be fulfilled throughout the remaining years of Samuel's term and the full term of his successor.

Thus, by 1923, there had emerged in Palestine that tripartite system which was to endure throughout the Mandate period. The Mandatory Power left each of the major communities[90] to look after its own affairs in its own way. This has been variously described as "internal partition" and as a system of "parallel Governments." As one writer put it, both the Jews and the Arabs succeeded "in growing crocodile skins round their respective communities, through which the rule of the government of Palestine hardly penetrated at all."[91]

This system has been severely criticized, but it is not easy to see in what other way Palestine could have been run under the Mandate, once the idea of cross-community representative institutions proved to be unattainable. The Mandate—with the Jewish National Home and the Zionist Executive as integral parts of it—required a considerable measure of autonomy for the Jewish community. For the Mandatory to respect that autonomy while conceding nothing comparable to the Arabs would hardly have been tenable. Also the Mandatory, as a Christian power, could hardly undertake to exercise the powers which it inherited—in reality by conquest—from an Islamic power, in respect of Muslim affairs in general, and Muslim Holy Places in particular.

In any case the tripartite system—once Samuel had stumbled on it by trial and error—worked considerably better than either military administration or civil-administration-in-quest-of-representative-institutions had been able to do. This was most clearly seen in the last year of Samuel's administration, 1925. In that year, two events took place which might have been expected, in the light of previous experience, to cause great disturbance. Both in fact passed off with not much more than a ripple.

The first, and major, event was a very large increase, for that year, in the volume of Jewish immigration into Palestine. From 1920 to 1923, immigration had been running at an annual rate of about 8,000. In 1924 the rate jumped to around 13,000, and then, in 1925, it attained over 33,000. This last, as it turned out, was to be by far the highest immigrant total for any year before the coming to power of Hitler in Germany, and even then it was to be exceeded by only two post-Hitler years—1934 and 1935—during the entire period of the Mandate.[92]

The influx of 1924–1925 was due to three factors. The first was a politico-economic crisis in Poland, where the Government of Wladislav Grabsky nationalized those branches of industry in which Jews were most heavily represented, then dismissed Jewish employees in favor of Christian Poles.[93] As a result, fully a third of the nation's Jewish merchants were driven to bankruptcy, and emigration soon became their only hope.

The second factor was a temporary relaxation in Soviet emigration controls. The third was the hugely significant event of the final closing, in 1924, of America to mass immigration. For the first time, Jews were coming to Palestine not primarily by religious or political choice but because there was now no longer any other place where Jews could go, in large numbers, in an emergency.

This immigration is the fourth *aliyah*. It differed in character from the three previous ones, as it seems probable that many of those concerned might have chosen America, had that option been still fully open. But the fourth *aliyah*, like the previous ones, played an important part in the growth of the Yishuv. It "laid the basis for [the growth of] the Yishuv's urban economy."[94] Within five years, the Jewish population of Jerusalem and Haifa doubled, and the fourth *aliyah* was largely responsible for making a city out of Tel Aviv.

What is remarkable is the complete absence of militant response, on the Arab side, to this unprecedented mass immigration.[95] In 1921, immigration at less than a quarter the 1925 volume was believed to have caused widespread and lethal violence. The absence of any such reaction in 1925[96] may suggest that there was some truth in the Zionist impression that the earlier violence was not so much spontaneous from below as fomented from the top: by British officers and Arab notables, especially Haj Amin. By 1925, Churchill's decision had eliminated the British military factor. As for Haj Amin and his friends on the Supreme Muslim Council, they now had a lot to lose, and seem to have felt the time was not ripe for high risks. London's determination, in the matter of the National Home, had proved to be much stronger than had seemed to be the case in 1918–1921. The generals who had tried to beat the Balfour Declaration were all gone.

The second event which might have been expected to lead to serious Arab disturbances in 1925, but did not, was the visit of Arthur Balfour, in March, to open the Hebrew University. The first anniversary of the Balfour Declaration (November 2, 1918) had elicited the first[97] incident—a minor one of violence by Arabs against celebrating

Above, Arthur Balfour speaking at the opening of the Hebrew University in March 1925. Seated on Balfour's left is Chaim Weizmann. The meeting of minds between Balfour and Weizmann had been central to the emergence of the Balfour Declaration, eight years before.
Below, Jewish immigrants arriving in Palestine, circa 1920.

Zionists. In 1921, that same anniversary had provided the occasion for the last outburst of lethal violence in Palestine (before 1929). Yet now, in 1925, the eponymous (and rightful) author of that detested Declaration was able to appear in Arab-majority Palestine, at a time of rapidly increasing Jewish immigration, without the slightest breach of the peace. There were protests in the Arab press, and the Arabs put on "a display of public mourning."[98] But that was not particularly noticeable; Balfour no longer held public office, the occasion he had come for was a Jewish one, and the Jews welcomed him warmly.

Balfour was seventy-seven at this time, and this was his first and only visit to Palestine. He either ignored or did not notice the Arab display of public mourning: "He passed through silent streets in the old city of Jerusalem and assumed that friendly salutations addressed to his companion, Ronald Storrs, were addressed to him."[99]

IX

But the most significant event of the mid-twenties, in relation to Palestine, was one that happened far away from Palestine and without specific reference to it. That event was the closing of America to mass immigration in 1924.

This is one of the decisive events in the history of Zionism, and the prehistory of Israel. Had those doors remained open, great numbers of European Jews would have found refuge in America between 1933 and 1941, and also after the Second World War. Immigration to Palestine in the same period would have been likely to be much less; the pressure toward the creation of the State of Israel would have been proportionately lessened; and it is possible that the British might have succeeded in scaling down the Jewish National Home to some kind of guaranteed enclave within an independent and predominantly Arab Palestine. In that case, the Yishuv—if its resistance had proved unsuccessful—would probably have migrated *en masse* to the United States.

The closing of the doors of America, in 1924, was thus hardly an event of much less significance toward the creation of the Jewish State than the coming to power in Germany, nine years later, of Adolf Hitler.

As is well known, it was an American Jewish poet, Emma Lazarus (1849–1887)—moved by reports of the anti-Jewish pogroms in Russia—who wrote, in 1883, the words now universally associated with the Statue of Liberty:

> Give me your tired, your poor,
> Your huddled masses yearning to breathe free,
> The wretched refuse of your teeming shore,
> Send these, the homeless, tempest-tossed, to me:
> I lift my lamp beside the golden door.

This had nothing to do with the intentions of the sculptor, the French-man Frédéric Auguste Bartholdi, who was thinking not of a welcomer to an asylum, but of a symbol of Republican Enlightenment, *La Liberté Éclairant le Monde*. At the dedication ceremonies, in 1886, Emma Lazarus's words, and concept, were (apparently) ignored. As John Higham puts it: "By 1886, when the New Colossus was finally unveiled upon her completed pedestal, there was already considerable alarm about the huddled masses streaming through the golden door. The lavish dedication ceremonies took place without a single reference to Miss Lazarus's sonnet."[100]

In 1903—possibly as a result of the great expansion in Jewish numbers and influence in New York since 1886—the sonnet was for the first time officially associated with the statue. But it was an inconspicuous association at this stage: a bronze tablet with the poem was placed on an interior wall of the pedestal. It was not until *after* the closing of the immigration doors, in 1924, and after the beginning of the agony of the European Jews in the 1930s, that the poem, with its encouraging but now misleading message, came to be conspicuously associated with the statue, in the late thirties of this century. John Higham describes the process that led to this macabre outcome:

> The event that called [the poem] forth from obscurity was a recurrence of the very problem that had moved Miss Lazarus in the first place: the plight of Jewish refugees. . . . Although the Statue of Liberty was not intended to beckon the tired and the poor, they had come to it. Because it received them no longer in significant numbers, it could enshrine their experience in a transcendental national way. Because Jewish Americans now were immigrants, all Americans could think of themselves as having been "immigrants."

In short, once the golden door was safely closed, the lines celebrating its openness could at last be prominently affixed to it.

To the European Jews, the verbal message on the door had no

significance. All that mattered was that the door was closed. And its closing greatly enhanced the significance of the doors of Palestine.

X

In June 1925 Samuel retired and in August of that year Baron—later Viscount—Plumer of Messines (1857–1932) became High Commissioner.

The Yishuv, despite its disturbing experiences under Samuel, was disappointed at the replacement of a Jew by a non-Jew, and of a civilian by a soldier. Some feared a recurrence of official anti-semitism, as manifested in the period of military rule. Nothing of the kind occurred.

Plumer had been perhaps the most respected of Britain's military commanders during the First World War, and his tenure in Palestine was one of almost unqualified success. He was a man of order and of a *status quo* which included the growing and developing Jewish National Home, whose legitimacy he accepted as part of the Balfour Declaration and the Mandate. He did not, like the military rulers, declare the National Home incompatible with the preservation of peace and order in Palestine, and he preserved peace and order, throughout his tenure, as the military rulers had failed to do. Plumer made no attempts at reviving representative institutions, nor did he attempt to reconcile Jews and Arabs. His main objective was to insure civil peace, through firm and fair government. In this, he was successful so far as his own period of tenure was concerned. The period of Plumer's High Commissionership (1925–1928) was a time of peace in Palestine, continuing the peace of the last years of his predecessor.

This period has been called one of "equilibrium," and also one of "negative equilibrium,"[101] between Jews and Arabs in Palestine. Understandably, this was a time of some optimism among Zionists about future relations with Arabs. It seemed as if the Arabs, having failed to avert a Mandate containing the Balfour Declaration, might be resigning themselves to the National Home as a *fait accompli*.

Optimism on that point was more marked in the Diaspora, and in public declarations, than among the Yishuv, and in private. The Yishuv knew full well that the Arabs continued to be basically hostile, both to Zionism and to Jews. There were two main views in the Yishuv as to what should be done about that. One was that advantage should be taken of the conditions of outward peace to move toward genuine conciliation. The other was that the Arabs were fundamentally irreconcilable to the Zionist objective, and that realism required preparation for a coming armed showdown between Jew and Arab for the land of Palestine.

Those who favored some kind of conciliation can in turn be distinguished into two groups: pragmatists and idealists (though the membership of the two groups overlapped). Among the pragmatic conciliators, the leading figure was the Polish-born agronomist H. M. Kalvaryski (1867–1947). Kalvaryski, within the Zionist movement and the Yishuv, was a kind of unofficial "Minister for Arab Affairs" between the wars. For Kalvaryski, a main objective was to discover "moderate Arabs" and encourage them to speak out. Unfortunately there were virtually no Arabs who were spontaneously attracted to anything which Zionists could perceive as moderation. In these conditions, Kalvaryski's "Arab work" came to depend very largely on bribery. As one of those closely associated with Kalvaryski in the "Arab work" told the Va'ad Leumi, the representative body of the Yishuv: "We all know that the moderates . . . are the baksheesh-takers who will oppose us if we don't pay them."[102] Leonard Stein—the author of *The Balfour Declaration*—was sent by Weizmann to Palestine "to study possibilities for the formation of a moderate Arab party with which we could really cooperate politically and economically."

This was of course precisely what the unfortunate Kalvaryski had been trying to do, by the only means available for doing it. Stein's report was highly unfavorable, in an oblique fashion, to the results obtained by "Arab work" on behalf of the Yishuv. Stein wrote: "The signature of the professional petition-monger or the temporary benevolence of a venal editor have no appreciable effect on the situation; and in general little can be done by the mere distribution of casual bribes, except, perhaps, on a vastly larger scale than it is possible to contemplate."[103]

Stein's comment was probably justified, yet he himself could offer no practical suggestions as to how to move toward the desired end by means more effective and reputable than Kalvaryski's.

Kalvaryski had succeeded in establishing—at least on paper—a "moderate Arab" party, the Muslim National Association (M.N.A.). But the results of the Legislative Council elections of February–March 1923, and the overwhelming success of the Arab nationalist boycott of those elections, demonstrated that the M.N.A. had no popular base whatever. The "Arab work" conducted to date had proved an expensive failure. Opinion in the Yishuv turned against this kind of work, as a wasteful use of the Yishuv's scarce resources.

Yet some Zionists—in the Yishuv, quite a small minority—still hoped that Jewish-Arab cooperation, and an agreed policy for Palestine, could be attained, on a solider base than that of the old, discredited "Arab work." In 1925, a group of (mainly Western European) intellectuals, whose most eminent associate was the American-born chancellor (later president) of the Hebrew University (and a disciple of Ahad Ha'am's), Dr. Judah Magnes (1877–1948), founded the society known as Berit Shalom (The Covenant of Peace). Unlike the previous "Arab work," Berit Shalom wanted to seek peace through Zionist concessions to the Arabs, leading perhaps to the establishment in Palestine of a binational state. But Berit Shalom remained a small and rather unpopular minority in the Yishuv, and its overtures evoked no significant response on the Arab side. Probably no such response would have been attainable under any conditions, but the chances of winning disinterested Arab support for the binational concept can hardly have been enhanced by the reputation which the "Arab moderates" had acquired through the previous years of "Arab work."[104]

Berit Shalom, and later organizations on similar lines—such as Ihud, during the war years—seemed unconvincing to most people in Palestine, Jews and Arabs alike. The main objections to it were crisply formulated in a letter published in its own magazine, *She'ifotenu:*

> You are in favour of a democratically elected legislative assembly. But how do you know that this assembly, with a clear Arab majority, will not spell the doom of Zionism? You are in favour of negotiations with the Arabs, but you also know that the mufti and his party are not willing to negotiate; they regard any talks on the basis of mutual concessions as an act of national treason.[105]

At the other extreme of the Yishuv political spectrum, but much more influential within it, were those who argued that a clash with the Arabs was inevitable before the Jewish State could come into being. From the very beginning of the National Home a few voices had been raised to this effect, with harsh eloquence and scornful vigor. Thus, the agronomist Y. A. Wilkansky (1880–1955) had told the Conference of the Yishuv in 1918 that

it was impossible to evict the fellahin, even if we wanted
to. . . . Nevertheless, if it were *possible*, I would commit an
injustice towards the Arabs. . . . There are those among us
who are opposed to this from the point of view of supreme
righteousness and morality. Gentlemen . . . if one wants to
be a 'preventer of cruelty to animals,' one must be an extremist in the matter. When you enter into the midst of the Arab
nation and do not allow it to unite, here too you are taking its
life. The Arabs are not salt-fish; they have blood, they live,
and they feel pain with the entry of a 'foreign body' into their
midst. Why don't our moralists dwell on *this* point? We must
be either complete vegetarians or meat-eaters: not one-half,
one-third, or one-quarter vegetarians.[106]

The most pertinacious and effective advocate of hard-line doctrine, during the entire period between the wars, was Vladimir Jabotinsky, who had become a hero to the Yishuv, because of his role in
the defense of the Jews of Jerusalem (during the riots of April 1920)
and his jail sentence for that. It was impossible, according to Jabotinsky, "to bridge this contradiction between us and the Arabs with
words, gifts or bribery." What was needed was an "iron wall"—it became a famous phrase—of armed force. The Arab had to be made to
say to himself: "Here stands an iron wall; the Jews are coming and
will keep on coming; we are unable to prevent this; we cannot kill
them."[107] And again, two years later:

But the Arabs loved their country as much as the Jews did.
Instinctively they understood Zionist aspirations very well,
and their decision to resist them was only natural. Every
people fought immigration and settlement by foreigners, however high-minded their motives for settling. *There was no
misunderstanding between Jew and Arab, but a natural conflict*. No agreement was possible with the Palestinian Arab;
they would accept Zionism only when they found themselves
up against an "iron wall," when they realized they had no
alternative but to accept Jewish settlement.[108]

In the troubled period of 1920–1921, Jabotinsky's doctrine struck
a responsive chord in the Yishuv, as it was again to do much later,
especially from the late thirties on. In the peaceful period that opened
up from 1922, however, neither Jabotinsky's saber rattling nor the
differing forms of "Arab work" seemed particularly relevant. The
Yishuv, within its own particular "crocodile skin," was preoccupied

with its own internal tasks and problems, which were considerable, and varied.

These were years of considerable economic growth and strengthening of the infrastructure in Palestine. As Bentwich writes:

> Economically, apart from the temporary trouble of Jewish unemployment, the period was one of prosperity and steady expansion. The exports were doubled, largely because of the great increase of the citrus crop. The Government revenue showed a substantial surplus over the expenditure, enough to pay off Palestine's share of the Ottoman public debt. A Palestine Government loan of £4,500,000 was authorized by the British Government, and fully subscribed; and the Administration repaid from it to the British Government the advances made for public works. It began also the enterprise of building a modern naval and mercantile harbor at Haifa, which was to revolutionize the maritime importance of Palestine.[109]

The massive Jewish immigration, from Poland and Russia, in 1925, was followed by a period in which immigration almost dried up. Between the end of 1926 and the end of 1931, the Jewish population of Palestine increased from 149,640 to 174,606, representing an annual increase of about 2.7 percent. In the same period, the Muslim population increased from 675,450 to 759,700, representing an annual increase of about 2.2 percent.[110] Assuming a continuation of these comparative growth rates, the narrow Jewish "edge" (0.5 percent) would not produce a Jewish majority in Palestine until well into the twenty-first century. The Jewish State seemed remote indeed, if one were to go by statistical indications.

The late twenties were also a time of economic distress and depression for the Yishuv. The Zionist movement at this time seems to have been almost broke. There was a certain irony in this, as it had been part of the mystique of Zionism, from Herzl's day, that it could somehow dispose of vast financial resources. That had never been really true, but by the late twenties it seemed a mockery. Most European Jews were poor, and most of those who were not poor were not interested in Zionism. Most Jews with money were in the United States, and Zionism in the United States was going through a bad period. This was partly due to the generally isolationist mood of American opinion at this time, but it was also partly due to a difference between Weizmann and Louis Brandeis, which led to a serious division within American Zionism. Weizmann, president of the World Zionist Organization since July 1920, insisted, in effect, on controlling the Zionist Organization of America through his nominees, who—because of Weizmann's immense personal prestige—were elected to control of the organization at the Cleveland Conference in June 1921. The Cleveland result led to the withdrawal from active involvement in the Zionist movement of Brandeis, along with a number of the most eminent and respected names in American Zionism. As we have seen, Brandeis's contribution to the securing of the Balfour Declaration had been second only to Weizmann's own.

As the Cleveland split gravely weakened American Zionism for many years, Weizmann's judgment on this occasion is open to question. It might be said that Weizmann's extraordinary diplomatic talents seem to have failed him in his relations with the Americans. But that would be a misconception. Weizmann did not regard relations *between Zionists* as an object of diplomacy at all. He insisted that, with the National Home at stake, Zionism must again be one world movement, under one leader, as in Herzl's day. As has been well said, Weizmann "could not compromise with the concept of organizational centrality: unless the Jewish people were a single historical unit, there could be no reason to justify its specifically national claim."[111]

"Organizational centrality" implied one leader, and that leader could only be Weizmann. The more "American" American Zionists were, the more securely established in American society, the harder they found it to accept the notion of subordination to a "foreign" leader. Brandeis and his friends were very American indeed.

(Curiously enough a very similar split had developed, in the same postwar period, between the Irish-American leaders John Devoy and Daniel Cohalan, on the one side, and Eamon de Valera, as "President of the Irish Republic" [still unrecognized], on the other.)

Among the Zionists, the "organizational" or "leadership" difference was at the root of the dispute. Formally, however, policy differences were salient. These differences took place along an old line of fault in the Zionist movement: that between political Zionism and practical Zionism. In this matter, Weizmann was subject to oscillation. In Herzl's day, he had tended to side with the Russian practical Zionists against Herzl's dramatic political Zionism. After Herzl's death, Weizmann had begun to edge in the direction of political Zionism (through synthetic Zionism), and during the war he became the master political Zionist, and architect of the Balfour Declaration. In

1921, he threw the great prestige which that had won for him into the scales against Brandeis's emphasis on practical Zionism—the building up of an adequate infrastructure in Palestine, with a major public-health program, and priority given to the elimination of malaria. Yet within a few years of the defeat of Brandeis, Weizmann himself was putting the emphasis back firmly on practical Zionism, and going further than Brandeis in that direction, by playing down the Jewish State, and (eventually) expanding the Jewish Agency to include non-Zionists.[112]

The sequence of events suggests that Weizmann did not in fact disagree with Brandeis on the policy matter so much as over the organizational one. Weizmann prevailed, but the American Zionist Organization shriveled, in consequence, for a time. Only the women's organization, Hadassah, flourished in the twenties, under the inspiring leadership of Henrietta Szold (1860–1945). Hadassah neither split nor subordinated itself to the (male) Zionist Organization of America (in its post-Cleveland Weizmannized form) but continued to develop its practical-Zionist public-health program in Palestine, with results of lasting importance.[113]

Even the coming to power of Adolf Hitler failed to reunite the movement which split in Cleveland, and languished thereafter. It was not until 1942, when most of the Jews of Europe were already doomed, that the Jews of America rallied as a major political force.

XI

At the end of July 1928, Lord Plumer retired from the High Commissionership and left Palestine. Within a month of his departure, an incident in the Old City of Jerusalem started a train of events which would lead to mass violence by Arabs against Jews in the following year, ending nearly eight years of peace in Palestine.

The peace seems rather mysterious; the breakdown of the peace not less so.

Concerning the peace, one writer on the Mandate period does offer an explanation: "The real reason for peace lay in the decline in Jewish immigration and in the economic troubles which had brought the progress of the National Home almost to a standstill."[114]

Unfortunately, the explanation fails to fit the known facts. The years 1924, 1925 and 1926—at the very center of the peace period—

were all years of exceptionally high immigration, and were not years of depression. In those years, 62,000 Jewish immigrants entered Palestine: a total equivalent to one-third of the entire population of the Yishuv as it stood at the end of the decade. On the other hand, the year 1928 had the lowest immigration figure of the decade—2,178—and it was the year of deepest depression. It was also the year in which overt friction between Muslims and Jews began again. And the year 1929, which saw the first recrudescence of major violence, was also a year of a degree of economic recovery and of relatively low immigration: 5,249, the third-lowest figure of the decade, after 1927 and 1928.

Clearly there is no simple correlation between the volume of Jewish immigration and the intensity of Arab reaction. As Laqueur says: "It is a moot point whether there was any direct connection between Jewish immigration and the situation of the Arabs."[115] Other factors have to be allowed for, including Arab perceptions of the attitude (or attitudes) of the Mandatory Power, and of its capacity to impose its will. Competition in anti-Zionism between Arab elites has also to be allowed for.

Plumer had made one decision which was to cost his successor dear. He had cut back severely on the armed forces—mainly Gendarmerie, and partly recruited from the old Royal Irish Constabulary (and Black and Tans)—available to the Mandatory in case of trouble. He seems to have assumed that there would not be any trouble: a strange assumption, given the circumstances of the case, but one which lasted out Plumer's time, perhaps due to his personal authority, prestige and self-confidence.

Plumer's successor, Sir John Chancellor (1870–1952), was a colonial administrator of some distinction but not an eminent public figure, as his two predecessors had been. He also lacked the luck that, on the whole, had favored his predecessors. Chancellor, though later execrated by the Zionists, was certainly not an anti-Zionist appointment. He had been appointed by Leopold Amery, "the last Colonial Secretary to have had a major involvement in the negotiations leading to the Balfour Declaration, the final text of which, he claimed, had followed his draft."[116]

There was a hiatus of nearly six months between Plumer's departure (July) and Chancellor's arrival (December). During this critical period, which saw the beginning of renewed trouble between Arabs and Jews, the Government of Palestine was in the hands of H. C. Luke (1884–1969) as Officer Administering. Later, Luke was Chief Secretary in Chancellor's administration.

Luke had been assistant governor of Jerusalem under Storrs, who had procured his appointment to that post,[117] and Luke is said to have "shared Storrs's genuine interest in and knowledge of the social and religious peculiarities of Palestine": he also shared Storrs's worldliness, ambitiousness and penchant for name-dropping."[118] What is more directly to the point, however, is that Luke, as he states in his memoirs, considered the Balfour Declaration "a contradiction in terms."[119] This is a very defensible opinion, but hard to reconcile with the holding of high executive office under a Mandate based on the contradiction in question. What this opinion involved in practice was an effort to placate Arab opinion, and to distance the administration from the Jews.[120] This was the general tendency of the administration, from middle levels down, throughout the Mandate. After Plumer's departure, it was for a time the dominant tendency at the top. It then became established under Luke, and Chancellor, when he arrived, took his cue from Luke, with results which were unfortunate for him and others.

It was under this new dispensation, and in this climate of enhanced sensitivity to Arab opinion, that the troubles began again. They began in Jerusalem, at the Wailing Wall, on the eve of Yom Kippur, in September 1928. Douglas V. Duff, the police officer in charge at the time—and who was to become, because of that, detested by the Jews—has left an account of how it all started. He and the District Commissioner of Jerusalem—Ronald Storrs's successor—Edward Keith-Roach (1885–1954), having taken a walk around the Old City of Jerusalem, visited the Mahkama al-Shariya, the religious court attached to the area of the Dome of the Rock, the chief Muslim Holy Place in Palestine, the Haram esh-Sharif, or Noble Sanctuary. From this vantage point, they looked down on the Western Wall (often called the Wailing Wall). The Wall is sacred to Orthodox Jews—and venerated by other Jews—as being all that is left of Herod's Temple, the last Temple of the Jewish nation. But the area of the Wall is also sacred to Muslims, because it was here that the Prophet tethered his miraculous horse, Buraq, after his flight from Mecca to Jerusalem, and before his ascent to Heaven.[121] Muslims call the area al-Buraq, after the horse. Jews have prayed at the Wall since the destruction of the Temple, but their approach to it had been strictly regulated in the period of Muslim rule, and remained so under the Mandate: part of the Anglo-Ottoman *status quo* for the Holy Places.

Looking down on the area in front of the Wall, the District Commissioner noticed an object "made of lath and cloth exactly like an ordinary bedroom screen." A screen in fact it was, having been put there by the Jews to separate men and women at prayers. The District Commissioner asked Duff whether he had seen such a screen there before; as a matter of fact he had, but he didn't say so. The District Commissioner then spoke words that were, in this context, explosive: "This is an infringement of the status quo ante."

"Some of the religious sheikhs belonging to the Mosque," writes Duff, "had entered the room, and the District Commissioner turned to them and asked them whether they had noticed the screen. The crafty old gentlemen had not, but, always willing to make capital at the expense of the Jews, immediately assumed miens of righteous indignation."[122]

As Christopher Sykes observes: "The fat was now in the fire, and this scruffy little piece of furniture was destined to be the starting point of a long and terrible feud of Arab and Jew."

On the following day, Yom Kippur, Duff and his police duly removed the infringement of the *status quo*. They had to disrupt prayers in order to do so, and they were assaulted by some of the worshipers. This incident caused widespread fury among the whole Jewish population of Palestine against the Mandatory Power. Jewish fury was stimulating to the Arabs. As Sykes says, Jewish accusations against the British "had the unlooked-for effect of putting confidence into the Arab leadership. It opened up new possibilities to their eyes. Suppose these accusations were true, they asked themselves, then, if they were, what were Arabs waiting for? Perhaps the British were their friends after all."[123]

Such was the general mood when Sir John Chancellor made his delayed entry into Palestine in December 1928. Chancellor was a colorless figure. One writer about the Mandate period says that he "left curiously little impression behind him either in memory or in print."[124] Another, who served under him, found him "rather detached and not anxious to consult me about the Jewish community."[125] A third gives a harsher verdict: "A discontented, self-pitying, lonely, suspicious man, aloof towards his subordinates, and hypersensitive to criticism, Chancellor possessed neither the resourceful political brain of Samuel, nor the benevolence and stolidity of Plumer."[126]

In terms of policy, what Chancellor did was to follow the course which the administration had already adopted in the interregnum, under Luke. Chancellor's first significant move on entering office was

to announce—January 3, 1929—that he would consider the establishment of a legislative council.[127] Thus the population was put under
notice that the Plumer policy—of *status-quo*-with-National-Home—
was no longer in operation.

Chancellor and Luke had some reason to feel that this announcement was well timed. Some leading Arabs—including the Nashashibi
clan, contending with the Husseini for power in Jerusalem—had come
to realize, with encouragement from British officials, that a great mistake had been made in boycotting the elections of 1923. They saw, as
was the case, that participation in representative institutions offered
the best hope of blocking future Jewish immigration, and of killing off
the National Home. This viewpoint had prevailed at the Seventh
Palestinian Congress, meeting in Jerusalem in June 1928. The Congress passed a resolution calling for the establishment of a representative legislative body. It also elected a moderate Arab Executive, committed to the same program.[128]

Chancellor and Luke, in their quest for legislative institutions,
now had what had eluded Samuel in his equivalent quest six years
before: Arab interlocutors, with impressive credentials, calling for
these institutions, and willing (apparently) to work for them. A
change of Government in London at this time was also favorable to
the project. In June 1929, the Conservative Government fell, and was
replaced by a Labour Government under Ramsay MacDonald. For
the first time, there was a Government in Britain with no past ties
with the Balfour Declaration. And the new Colonial Secretary, Lord
Passfield (Sidney Webb), had little sympathy with the concept of the
National Home. This was the most dangerous conjuncture that the
Zionists had had to face since the end of military rule.

Through the first half of 1929, Luke was carrying on negotiations
with the two main leaders on the Arab Executive: Musa Kazim al-
Husayni and Raghib al-Nashashibi. In June they reached agreement
on the form of a legislative council—it would have contained, in addition to officials, fifteen "appointed representatives" of the populace
(ten Muslims, three Jews and two Christians).[129] But although the
two Arab leaders agreed to the proposed council, and agreed to serve
on it, the value of their agreement was considerably lessened by their
insistence on keeping their agreement secret, even from the Arab
Executive itself. They were afraid of being outflanked. Specifically,
they were afraid of the Grand Mufti, Haj Amin al-Husseini. Porath
speaks of "a new arrangement of forces" among the Palestinians, with

"Musa Kazim al-Hussayni and Raghib al-Nashashibi on one side and al-Hajj Amin al-Husseini, Mufti of Jerusalem and President of the [Supreme Muslim] Council, on the other."[130]

It was to prove an uneven contention. The Mufti was not to be drawn into the delicate—though potentially rewarding—strategy of "representative institutions": Harold Luke's chess game, designed to end in a quiet checkmate to the policy of the National Home. The Mufti chose different ground, that of religion, where his own authority was acknowledged as supreme. In practice, of course, it was ground where religion and politics are inseparable.

What the Mufti did was to raise the cry of the Holy Places in danger from the Jews. After the Yom Kippur incident, the Mufti launched a fierce campaign of propaganda to this effect, in the mosques and in the Arab press. He was reverting in fact to his tactics of 1920, before he became Mufti, and throwing away the restraint which he had practiced in all the years till now, in which he had held the great power of Mufti and president of the Supreme Council.

Why did the Mufti take this fateful turn at this moment? He was always, of course, sincerely anti-Zionist, and no doubt he did feel that the Holy Places were in some kind of ultimate danger from the National Home. But the Jews hardly looked a greater danger, and they possibly looked a lesser one, in 1929 than they had in, say, 1925.[131] Haj Amin was too intelligent a man to believe in the threat of that screen.

A large part of the answer may be that Haj Amin saw that he could get away with such a course of action in 1929, as he could not in 1925. The Yom Kippur incident had shown a marked sensitivity on the part of the Mandatory to Muslim religious sensibilities, and a corresponding lack of sensitivity to Jewish religious sensibilities. Taken together with the noises about "representative institutions" now coming strongly from the direction of the Mandatory, all this might imply that the British were seriously thinking of handing over power to the Arabs. The whipping up of Arab feeling against Jews might contribute to that process. Also, it might leave the whipper-up in a stronger position than his rivals, if it did come to a transfer of power.

The Mufti, who knew his British officials rather well by now, knew that he was probably not running any immediate risks, even if it should turn out that the British were not leaving, after all. British officials liked him, and liked to think they could trust him. Christopher Sykes, who knew him, refers to:

. . . the extraordinary British misconception of the Mufti's character, an aberration of judgment that continued for many years. This, in so far as it was the Mufti's work, was in all probability a triumph of discretion and personality. He was an impressive man to meet, and unlike many impressive men he had an infectious personal charm. He did not appear to be secretive and left whomever he met in no doubt that he would strive to the last for the preservation of Jerusalem and Palestine as a Moslem city and land, first and foremost. It was impossible not to believe in his sincerity. He had natural dignity. He was handsome though very slight in build, and, an Oriental of Orientals, he never wore European clothes but the becoming habit of a Moslem doctor of Theology. His voice was soft and he had the trick of sitting as still as a statue. He never gesticulated or raised his voice. He made other people seem vulgar. It was difficult to think of him as blood-thirsty.[132]

Looking at a photograph of Haj Amin, I can see what Sykes meant. Haj Amin looks like Alec Guinness dressed as a sheikh. One can understand how such a man could deny incitement, while practicing it, and be believed.

The incitements themselves were no laughing matter. The Jews, well aware of what Haj Amin's incendiary propaganda was likely to portend for them, organized counterdemonstrations at the Wall, and these in turn were interpreted by the Muslims as corroborating the threat to the Muslim Holy Places.

About the wrangling over the Wall, Walter Laqueur judiciously writes:

This propaganda [on the Arab side] was part of the contest between the party of the Mufti and its rivals, the former trying to outbid the latter with the extremism of its slogans. There was a similar development on the other side. For the main outcry did not come from those directly affected, the orthodox and ultra-orthodox Jews, but from the revisionists [Jabotinsky's followers] for whom the Wall was a nationalist rather than a religious symbol.[133]

In August 1929 things came to a head. It began with a Jewish boy kicking a ball into an Arab garden. A brawl followed in which the boy was stabbed to death. After the boy's funeral there was a Zionist demonstration at the Wall, followed by an inflammatory sermon from the Mufti in the Mosque of al-Aqsa. Then, on August 22

Above, Haj Amin al-Husseini, Grand Mufti of Jerusalem (1920–1937) under the British Mandate and leader of Palestinian nationalism, with Adolf Hitler. In exile after 1937, he helped foment the anti-British revolt in Iraq in 1941 and after its failure went to Berlin, whence he returned to the Middle East at the end of the Second World War.

Below, Chaim Arlosoroff (1899–1933), head of the political department of the Jewish Agency. Murdered in June 1933, probably by Jewish extremists, for his part in negotiations with the Nazis for the purpose of getting Jews out of Germany.

ZIONIST ARCHIVES AND LIBRARY

and 23, large crowds of Arab peasants started coming into Jerusalem, armed with clubs and knives. Marlowe finds it "almost impossible to believe that they had not been summoned thither."[134]

Douglas Duff, as Chief of Police in Jerusalem, did not have enough reliable men—i.e., non-Arabs—to disarm these people. So, instead he went to the Mufti. As Sykes tells it:

> With his habitual and charming air of innocence the Mufti replied that recent events had made them afraid of the Jews. There was no need to worry, he said. The Chief of Police was convinced of his good faith. Later in the morning the Mufti and one of his colleagues of the Supreme Moslem Council addressed a mass meeting in the noble sanctuary. They said nothing that could be called incitement but at the conclusion of the meeting the mob rushed out into the streets of Jerusalem and attacked every Jew they could see. They murdered several. And now violence broke out on a more terrible scale than had yet been seen in the country.[135]

Partly because of Plumer's reduction in the armed forces, and partly because of the failure of Chancellor and Luke to read danger signs that had been obvious for months, the British authorities, while awaiting reinforcements from Egypt, did not have enough men to control the situation. Yet they refused the request of the Zionist authorities for the arming of a large number of Jews, and they also refused the use of Jewish police.

The ensuing violence continued for several days and spread to other centers. Some of the most horrible slaughter occurred at Hebron, a town sacred to both Muslims and Jews as the burial place of their common ancestor Abraham.

Of the attacks generally, Sykes writes "that it is difficult to believe that this sudden outbreak of savagery was unplanned."[136]

By the time reinforcements arrived and the attacks on the Jews were brought to an end, 133 Jews had been killed by Arabs and 339 wounded.[137] In the repression of the attacks by the reinforced police, 110 Arabs were killed and 232 wounded. Six Arabs were killed by Jewish action in a counterattack near Tel Aviv. The terrible events of August 1929 left lasting marks on both sides in Palestine.

Among the Jews, the idea of looking for a settlement to which Arabs could agree became utterly discredited. Men like Arthur Ruppin, who had helped to start Berit Shalom, now gave up all hope of peaceful settlement. As he explained his position a little later: "What

we can get today from the Arabs—we don't need. What we need—
we can't get. What the Arabs are willing to give us is at most minority
rights, as in eastern Europe. But we have already had enough experience of the situation in eastern Europe."[138] On the other hand, Jabotinsky's tireless preaching of armed preparedness now seemed fully
vindicated. David Ben-Gurion, who, as secretary of the Histadrut, had
by now become a central figure in the Yishuv, was opposed to Jabotinsky, whom he considered to be almost a Fascist. But Ben-Gurion
agreed—in substance though not in language—with Jabotinsky's basic
doctrine of the "iron wall." Confrontation with the Arabs seemed inevitable. The essential thing was for the Jews to insure that they would
be the winners when the confrontation came. The events of August
1929 had shown how alarmingly inadequate Jewish defense measures
had been. Arms and training in the use of arms were now a top
priority.

The events of August produced both a reorganization of the
Hagana and a split in its ranks. Supporters of the Hagana pointed out
that it had averted far worse disasters: "The meager number of Hagana volunteers with their limited supply of arms filled the gap and
saved the Jewish communities of Jerusalem, Tel Aviv and Haifa from
mass slaughter."[139] Others were more impressed with what the Hagana
had failed to prevent. A major reorganization ended the Histadrut's
monopoly of control over the Hagana and brought an equal number
of nonlabor members onto the Defense Committee.

But even this reorganization failed to avert a split. The political
leadership of those who split away from Hagana at this time was furnished by the group known as Betar. Betar was an activist Zionist
movement founded in 1923 in Riga, Latvia, under the influence of
Jabotinsky. The Betar immigrants to Palestine, from 1925 to 1929,
joined Histadrut and Hagana as a matter of course. But after August
1929, Betar increasingly diverged from the Hagana majority leadership. In 1931, a group of Hagana comrades left Hagana in protest
against its "defensive" orientation and joined forces with Betar, in
order to set up a new and more militant armed underground organization, the Irgun. The first Betar congress meeting at Danzig in 1931
elected Jabotinsky as *Rosh Betar* (head of Betar). Betar and Irgun rejected the Histadrut/Hagana doctrine of Havlaga (self-restraint) and
favored retaliation.

The political life of the Yishuv, from 1929 on, was powerfully
marked by the contest between the Histadrut-Hagana movement, led

by Ben-Gurion, and the right-wing militarist Revisionist movement, based on Betar and Irgun, and led by Jabotinsky. And the Revisionists were a rising force: in 1925 they had elected four delegates to the Zionist Congress; in 1929, twenty-one; in 1931, fifty-two.

The events of August 1929 made the Yishuv more inclined to self-reliance, and less inclined to look to Britain, or even to the world Zionist movement. There was intense resentment at Britain's role, and even Weizmann became unpopular, for encouraging reliance on Britain.

On the Arab side, one immediate result was a great increase in the prestige and influence of the Mufti. Haj Amin's decisive role in this affair led to his being regarded as the most important Arab-Palestinian leader. "The conflict itself emphasized the religious significance of the anti-Zionist struggle, while the course of its development demonstrated that [Haj Amin's] strength and influence were incomparably greater than those of the other Arab leaders."[140]

Haj Amin's theme, the defense of the Muslim Holy Places, was readily intelligible, and charged with emotion, not only in Palestine but throughout the Muslim world. The Wall, with Buraq encroached upon, was a powerful symbol. "The Wall affair marked the beginning of the development of the Palestinian question from a local question into a Muslim pan-Arab one."[141] Haj Amin was already becoming an international figure. And there were good grounds for the admiration which his fellow countrymen felt for him. The manner in which he had built himself a power base, and the manner in which he had managed to use that power base, and the impunity with which he managed all that, were all remarkable.

He had acquired power from the hands of a Mandatory committed to the establishment of a Jewish National Home in Palestine. He had used that power to precipitate a massacre of Jews in Palestine. And he remained Mufti.

In general, the Arabs had apparently good grounds for confidence, following the events of August 1929. The Jews had been saved, it seemed, not by themselves, but by the British. So it seemed that if the British were to go, it would be quite easy to get rid of the Jews.[142]

And the British, in the wake of these events, still sounded as if they were going. The lesson that the ruling triumvirate of the time—Passfield, Chancellor and Luke—drew from all this was that they themselves had been right all along. The National Home was impossible, because of the fury it aroused among the Arabs. And this was, of course, precisely the message that Haj Amin had intended to convey.

Weizmann, on learning of the massacres, hastened to London, from Switzerland, to a cold reception. Passfield at first would not see him, but Weizmann saw Lady Passfield (Beatrice Webb). According to him, she said: "I can't understand why the Jews make such a fuss over a few dozen of their people being killed in Palestine. As many are killed every week in London in traffic accidents, and no one pays any attention."[143] Passfield, when he did see Weizmann, made it clear that he was against "mass immigration," and Weizmann knew he was up against an enemy of the National Home.

Passfield's strategy for disencumbering Britain of the National Home commitment consisted mainly of two Royal Commissions and a White Paper.

The first Royal Commission, headed by Sir Walter Shaw, was concerned with the events of August 1929. It found that the attacks on the Jews were "unpremeditated." It blamed the Mufti for "not having done more to stop the riots," but declined to believe that he had instigated them. Its principal general recommendation was that the administration should strengthen its control of Jewish immigration so as to prevent a repetition of the mass movements of the 1920s.

As Sykes notes, all the Shaw Commission's recommendations "have something of a pro-Arab, anti-Zionist tendency."[144] This is rather remarkable, given the fact that what the commission was actually inquiring into was a massacre of Jews by Arabs. But the commission's report was in line with the Colonial Secretary's thinking.

On May 12, 1930, following the publication of the Shaw Report, the Colonial Office instructed the Mandatory to suspend the latest Jewish immigration schedule of 3,300 Labour Certificates.[145]

Passfield's second Royal Commission was headed by Sir John Hope Simpson. What it did was to apply the criterion of "absorptive capacity"—laid down in Churchill's White Paper of 1922—in a very much more restrictive sense than had ever been applied before. Hope Simpson found, or divined, that Palestine could not absorb more than a total of 50,000 extra Jewish immigrants. This finding, if accepted, would of course have put a stop to the whole Zionist enterprise.

Passfield now prepared the League of Nations for major change in the spirit in which the Mandatory interpreted the Mandate. In a report to the Permanent Mandates Commission of the League, the British Government noted the existence of "a twofold duty" and of "a conflict of interests. . . . The absence of any measure of self-govern-

ment in Palestine is not due to any lack of goodwill on the part of the
Mandatory Power. . . . It must be a primary condition of constitutional change that Mandatory Government should reserve to itself the
power of carrying out the obligation imposed on it by the Mandate."
It ended by appearing to promise "a further, and more explicit statement of policy."[146]

On this report, Marlowe makes the just comment: "The British
Government, whose predecessors had in fact drafted the Mandate in
cooperation with the Zionist Organization, had now begun to use, and
were to continue to use, language which implied that the Mandate
was an onerous obligation imposed on Great Britain by the League of
Nations. . . ."[147]

Passfield next incorporated the essential elements in the Shaw
and Hope Simpson reports into a White Paper ("Statement of Policy")
published on October 21, 1930. The White Paper also embodied proposals for a legislative council, and suggested that Britain's commitment to a Jewish National Home had already been discharged. The
White Paper failed to make any mention of the Balfour Declaration.
It looked at this point as if British policy was moving in the direction
of an independent Arab Palestine, no doubt with some form of "guarantees" for the Jews already there.

Up to this point, the anti-Zionists had been having it all their own
way. But with the publication of the White Paper, things began to go
wrong. Most Labour members did not have much idea of what the
White Paper was supposed to be about. The Conservative and Liberal
opposition was much better informed in the matter, and well supported from outside the House. These were conditions propitious for
lobbying. Weizmann led the attack.

Weizmann had been deeply troubled by the course of events since
August 1929—by the revival and extent of Arab attacks, by the weakening of British support for the National Home, and, perhaps above
all, by the rising influence of Jabotinsky and Revisionism. He feared
that the clamorous insistence of the Revisionists on the Jewish State
might frighten British opinion and endanger the National Home itself. For a time, he himself despaired of achieving a Jewish State at
all: "The Jewish State will not come about, whether we want it or
not—unless some fundamental change comes about which I cannot
envisage at present."[148]

Shaken though he might be, in relation to the Jewish State, Weizmann summoned up all his old fighting spirit for the defense of the
National Home. He opened his campaign with his own resignation as

president of the Zionist Organization, on the day of the publication of the White Paper. His resignation personalized and dramatized the conception of the betrayal of the Balfour Declaration, and became a rallying point for the parliamentary opposition to the White Paper. Weizmann's resignation was, at this stage, a formality only, and he remained the effective leader of Zionism throughout the White Paper crisis.

When the White Paper was debated in the Commons, in November 1930, it came under formidable attack, led by Lloyd George, Samuel and Amery. Some Labour members indicated strong misgivings. MacDonald's minority Government needed to placate part of the opposition—the Liberals in particular—not to draw fire from Liberals and Conservatives together. MacDonald realized that the White Paper was a political blunder.[149] He defended the White Paper, in the House, with a propitiatory vagueness, and prepared to jettison it.

It was agreed that he would jettison it by means of a letter "of clarification" addressed to Weizmann. At first MacDonald tried to equivocate, by asserting that the letter would not have the same "legal-political status" as the White Paper. Weizmann, because of Mac-Donald's parliamentary weakness, was in a strong enough position to insist that the Prime Minister give way. The letter of "clarification" (by means of retraction) would have to be communicated to the League of Nations as an official document; it would also have to be included in a dispatch to the High Commissioner in Palestine; and it would have to be made clear that it constituted an "authoritative interpretation" of the White Paper.

This was the most impressive example to date of Zionist influence over the British Government and Parliament; and it was to be the last.

On February 13, 1931, the Prime Minister read to the House his letter to Weizmann, duly underlining its status as "authoritative interpretation." And he said: "The obligation to facilitate Jewish immigration and to encourage close settlement by Jews on the land remains a positive obligation of the Mandate and it can be fulfilled without prejudice to the rights . . . of all sections of the population of Palestine."[150]

This interpretation of the White Paper naturally caused consternation among those who had welcomed the document so interpreted. MacDonald's letter to Weizmann became known among the Arabs of Palestine as the Black Letter.

Officially, all the Prime Minister was doing was "explaining and elucidating the policy already announced by His Majesty's Government." But a little earlier, at question time, the Prime Minister had blurted out the truth. Asked "whether there has been a complete change of policy with regard to the White Paper, he had replied: "Yes, my honourable and gallant friend may accept that assurance."[151]

Lord Passfield, like Lord Curzon before him, and a long line of British enemies of the Balfour Declaration, had been overruled.

As it happened, this was the last great victory which Zionism won by purely diplomatic means, and from a position of virtual impotence, materially speaking. It was a victory that came at a most crucial time.

XII

When Weizmann, in 1919, wrote the words quoted as epigraph to this chapter—". . . we must have Palestine if we are not going to be exterminated"—most Jews, and even most Zionists, would have thought them absurdly exaggerated. The Jews of Eastern Europe had suffered greatly during the war—especially when Russians recaptured territory from the Germans—and also, and to an even greater extent, in the Russian civil war, and in the fighting which preceded the stabilization of the western borders of the Soviet Union. But extermination—even in the milder sense of a general driving out—hardly seemed a threat; and, even if it were, Palestine hardly seemed much of an answer. The doors of America were still open at that time. And for about five years after those closed (to mass immigration) in 1924, the danger in Europe seemed to have receded.

In Germany in particular, in those years, danger seemed remote. The Weimar Republic was a liberal state, in which Jews were free to rise to the top, and did so, in almost every branch of activity, but especially in the sciences and in the arts, in business and in the media. The Jews of Germany were becoming fast assimilated, as they believed. "In the period 1921–7, 44.8% of all Jewish marriages were mixed."[152]

The year 1929 was a hinge year in this matter, as in many others. It was in that year that Adolf Hitler began his comeback from failure and obscurity. His skillful demagogic exploitation of the "reparations" crisis of the summer of that year brought him back into public prominence. The Great Depression, whose catastrophic effects hit Germany toward the end of 1929, gave Hitler his great opportunity, as he himself immediately recognized. In the general elections of September 1930—the month before the publication of the Passfield White Paper—the vote of the Nazi Party rose to nearly 6.5 million, more than seven times its previous level, thus raising the party's strength from 12 Reichstag seats to 107, making it the second-largest party, instead of the ninth and smallest.[153]

Anti-semitism was nothing new in Germany, or in Hitler's native Austria. But Hitler's kind of anti-semitism was new. From the German tradition of academic and artistic anti-semitism he took the notion of racial science, as well as the contempt for the Christian ethic and its "limits." Out of the Austrian tradition of Karl Lueger he drew the demagogic populism and the skillful electoral exploitation of anti-semitic potential. But he was unlike Lueger in that the force he exploited was one which also dominated him; part of his own demon. And his demon had scope. Anti-semitism in Germany and Austria before the First World War had been, relatively, abstract and muted. But when, under the Weimar Republic, defeat, economic disasters, national and military humiliation for the Germans were seen to combine with total emancipation, and many kinds of brilliant success, for the Jews, then German anti-semitism fully took on that manic and pathological character which had been previously present only in prophetic voices.

From September 1930 on, it became clear that it was possible Hitler could take over the German State. That possibility did not yet evoke much alarm, in Britain at any rate. In the debate on the White Paper, two months after Hitler's sensational electoral advance, no speaker suggested that European Jews might soon be looking for some place to go.

But Weizmann was always haunted by that thought. The National Home was a far more urgent matter than the Jewish State.

In retrospect, Weizmann's feat of converting the White Paper into the Black Letter seems an extraordinary one. But Zionists at the time were not impressed. They carped: Weizmann should have gotten a whole new White Paper; a mere letter was not enough. Zionists—and those of the Yishuv in particular—were bitter against Britain after the events of 1929 and 1930, and Weizmann, as "Britain's friend," came in for a share of that bitterness. He had a grim time at the Seventeenth Zionist Congress, held in Basel, June–July 1931. Having resigned as president—over the White Paper—he no longer appeared invested with all his old authority. Jabotinsky, at the head of his fifty-two delegates—a nearly doubled representation since 1929—seemed the rising star. And Jabotinsky, with his reckless brilliance and flamboyant maximalism, had the gift—and probably knew he had—of stinging Weizmann into unpopular rebukes. "The aim of Zionism," said Jabotinsky, "is the formation of a Jewish majority in Palestine on both banks of the Jordan."

Weizmann rose to this. In an interview, he said: "I have no understanding nor sympathy with the demand of a Jewish majority in Palestine. A majority does not guarantee security, a majority is not essential for the development of a Jewish civilization and culture. The world will interpret the demand for a Jewish majority that we want to achieve it in order to drive the Arabs from the country."[154]

There seems something slightly irrational—to an outsider—about this Jabotinsky-Weizmann clash. Majorities are not created, or removed, by debating about whether they ought to be there. Jews at this date were far from achieving a majority between the sea and the Jordan: in the Emirate of Transjordan there were no Jews at all. Against that background, Jabotinsky's demand for a Jewish majority "on both banks" seems absurd. But Weizmann's position too is strange. Nothing in his past, or future, career suggests that he would have been against a Jewish majority, if he could get it. No doubt he was particularly anxious—after the hairbreadth escape with the White Paper—to hold on to Zionism's vital remaining support in the British Parliament, and fearful that this might be alienated by Jabotinsky's extremism; fearful also of what the truculence and arrogance of the Revisionists might represent for the future of Zionism.

However that may be, Weizmann's disparaging words about a Jewish majority were altogether out of tune with the mood of the Seventeenth Congress. A vote of censure—moderately worded, but unmistakable—was moved: "The Congress expresses its regret at Dr. Weizmann's statement in a J.T.A. interview and regards his reply as inadequate." This motion was carried by 123 votes to 106.

After that vote, it was no longer possible for Weizmann to resume, at this Congress, as president of the Zionist Organization, as he had no doubt intended and expected, after the triumph of the anti–White Paper campaign. The Revisionists did not gain control of the Executive, as was Jabotinsky's aim; a relatively colorless compromise figure, Nahum Sokolow, became president. All the same, the Seventeenth Congress was a notable victory for Jabotinsky and the forces he represented.

For Weizmann, the Seventeenth Congress was hardly less bitter an experience than the Sixth Congress had been for Herzl, twenty-eight years before. In a letter written shortly after the Seventeenth Congress, Weizmann described it as "a nightmare. It was all so tricky and treacherous and beastly"; it represented, he thought, a victory for "the enormous deterioration in the movement."[155] Years afterwards, in his memoirs, he recalled his feelings after the decisive vote: "When it was finished, and some tactless person applauded my so-called downfall, the feeling came over me that here and now the tablets of the law should be broken, though I had neither the strength nor the moral stature of the great law-giver."[156]

For a time, Weizmann thought of turning his back on all political activity, but he soon rejected that course. He retained a significant power base as president of the English Zionist Federation (from 1932 on), and he was to return to the presidency of the World Zionist Organization in 1935. He had still to render great further services to the Zionist cause, but his authority over the movement as a whole—including the Yishuv—never fully recovered from the events of 1929–1931. Yet, in terms of Jewish lives saved, Weizmann never rendered greater service than during this period of his partial repudiation.

It is to Weizmann, above all, that the Jews owe the fact that the doors of Palestine were still open when, on January 30, 1933, Adolf Hitler became Chancellor of the Reich.

4

DEATH AND BIRTH
1933-1948

Have we the right to live?
—Chaim Weizmann *to the Peel Commission,* 1936

Between 1933 and 1938, Nazis and Zionists cooperated in organizing the emigration of Jews, with some of their property, from Germany to Palestine. This was the program known among Zionists as Ha'avara ("transfer").

On August 25, 1933, Eliezer Siegfried Hoofien (1881–1957), general manager of the Anglo-Palestine Bank (now Bank L'umi L'Yisrael), agreed with the German Ministry of Economics to use Jewish assets (otherwise blocked) for the purchase of goods needed in Palestine.[1] This arrangement became the basis of an official Jewish emigration plan.

In 1933 the Anglo-Palestine Bank established in Tel Aviv the Trust and Transfer Office Ha'avara Ltd. A corresponding body was set up in Berlin with the assistance of two leading Jewish bankers, Max Warburg of M. M. Warburg, Hamburg, and Dr. Siegmund Wassermann of A. E. Wassermann, Berlin. The Berlin company, known as Palästina Treuhandstelle zur Beratung Deutscher Juden ("Paltreu"), assumed responsibility for negotiating with the German authorities the settlement of bills of German exporters and contracts with German Jews wishing to leave for Palestine. As the policy of the

Above, Warsaw, February 1940. Jewish women already marked with a yellow triangle sewn on the back of their garments.
Below, Warsaw, 1943.

Mandatory permitted unrestricted immigration—in excess of the normal quotas—of Jews with assets of £1,000 and over, the funds transferred were used for the creation of the highest possible number of "capital" lots per immigrant. Most of the 50,000 Jews who left Germany between 1933 and 1939 used the services of Ha'avara. This number included children sent to Palestine ahead of their parents and war veterans and civil servants who had been forced to retire and whose pensions had been paid by the German authorities to Ha'avara for transfer to Palestine.

Understandably, these arrangements were questioned and criticized publicly by Jews—both Zionist and non-Zionist—and privately by Nazi officials.

Apart from the general Jewish revulsion from any kind of dealings with the Nazi rulers of Germany, there was a strong specific objection to these particular economic and financial arrangements. The arrangements broke the boycott of German exports: a boycott which had sprung up spontaneously among Jews throughout the world after Hitler had come to power, and especially since Hitler's proclamation, on April 1, 1933, of a national boycott of Jewish shops.[2]

In Britain, even before Hitler's national boycott officially came into force, the *Jewish Chronicle* reported a "flood of letters" coming into its office on this subject and it editorialized: "Let Jews, here and in every land, borrow from the Germans their weapon of the boycott and turn it against them. . . . Not an ounce of German goods! . . . till the Nazis desist from their devilries."[3] On the same day, in New York, also in protest and retaliation against the coming Nazi boycott, Rabbi Stephen Wise (1874–1949) addressed an overflow Madison Square Garden rally of more than 50,000 people.

Inevitably, the practical arrangements of Ha'avara let down this protest-and-boycott movement: "Nowhere were Jewry's weaknesses and the inherent contradictions of the boycott more cruelly exposed than in the confusions of the 'Transfer Agreement' . . . A festering sore on the body of Jewry, the 'Agreement' added insult to injury, and self-disgust to the rage against the common enemy."[4]

Both in the Yishuv and in the Diaspora, Jabotinsky and his Revisionists, and his youth organization, Betar, took up these themes, denouncing Ha'avara, and the Zionist leadership which had agreed to it.

It was easy to denounce the "festering sore." It was less easy to answer the arguments in favor of Ha'avara. With the Nazis in total control of Germany, what other means were there of getting considerable numbers of Jews out of Germany except by agreement with the Nazis, and how could you get agreement unless the Nazis got something in return? Chaim Arlosoroff (1899–1933), who, as head of the Political Department of the Jewish Agency, had gone to Germany to prepare the ground for Ha'avara, said: "Up to now 40,000 Jews have turned to Palestinian offices. . . . It would be crazy to think that this problem could be solved without the consent of the German government."[5]

The issue was debated at the Eighteenth Zionist Congress in Prague (August–September 1933). It was an exceptionally well-attended meeting because international support for Zionism had greatly increased: 535,193 electors, as against 233,730 at the Seventeenth Congress in Basel in 1931. Jabotinsky had a resolution down calling for a worldwide boycott of Germany. But the majority mood of the expanded Congress was hostile to Jabotinsky and his group.[6] On June 16, 1933, more than two months before the Congress opened, Chaim Arlosoroff had been murdered on the beach at Tel Aviv, where he was walking with his wife, just after his return from Germany. Revisionists were accused of his murder, the Labor Zionists believed the charges were true and the Congress majority seems to have believed the Labor Zionists.[7] Jabotinsky and his friends were ostracized.

The call for a world boycott of German goods—a call which would of course have invalidated Ha'avara—was nonetheless taken up by a number of delegates, especially among those from the United States. Ha'avara was effectively defended, however, not only by the Zionist leadership, inside and outside Palestine, but also by the German Zionists, and by the most effective and admired of American Zionists, Henrietta Szold, head of Hadassah. The boycott resolution was not put to the vote. Congress officially adopted the Ha'avara policy and put Ha'avara under the control of the Zionist Executive.

The Revisionists continued to attack Ha'avara, and to seek to impose a boycott of their own. But Jabotinsky was here showing much less than his usual consistency.[8] Jabotinsky loved to present himself as the true heir of Theodor Herzl. But in this matter, it was his opponents who were following a clear Herzlian precedent. In enlisting Nazi cooperation in order to save German Jews, they were acting precisely as Herzl had done, after Kishinev, when he had traveled to Russia to try to save Russian Jews, with the help of Plehve.[9]

II

The attempted Jewish boycott of Nazi Germany was a failure, as most international boycotts are. Paradoxically, the most notable result was in the contribution it made toward the relative success of the opposing policy, Ha'avara.

In the early months of the new regime, the Nazis had been somewhat apprehensive about the possible consequences of the international Jewish protest and boycott movement. In March 1933, a German Jewish delegation, sent by Goering, arrived in London. The delegation had been "instructed to deny newspaper accounts of persecution of German Jews and to persuade the American Jewish Congress to cancel its upcoming demonstration in New York on March 27."[10] In fact, they reported objectively on the situation in Germany, but the nature of their report was such as to discourage protest and boycott and to encourage support for Ha'avara, the great boycott weakener.

Hitler's acquiescence to the Transfer Agreement in 1933 has been ascribed to "the pressure of circumstances—international Jewish boycott, German isolation in the international arena, unemployment, etc."[11]

The Nazi idea of the Transfer Agreement as defense against Jewish boycott survived, even after the boycott itself had lost credibility. As late as 1936, Dr. Reichert, Gestapo agent in Palestine, maintained that the correct course was to do nothing to "strain the relations between Germany and Palestine Jewry" but rather "to use the Jewish community in Palestine as a means against the economic boycott of Germany by world Jewry."[12]

All this was neither very easy, nor very hard, to reconcile with Nazi ideology. There is only one reference in *Mein Kampf* to Zionism. It runs:

> . . . while Zionism tries to make the other part of the world believe that the national self-consciousness of the Jew finds satisfaction in the creation of a Palestinian State the Jews again most slyly dupe the stupid *goiim*. They have no thought of building up a Jewish State in Palestine, so that they can inhabit it, but they only want a central organization of their international world cheating, endowed with prerogatives, withdrawn from the seizure of others: a refuge for convicted rascals and a high school for future rogues.[13]

Hitler's interpretation of Zionism was not original; it seems to have been a cliché among anti-semites of the less subtle variety. Thus

General Money, the first British administrator of Palestine, suspected in 1918 that the whole Zionist enterprise from the beginning might be no more than some get-rich-quick scheme of the Jews. Pinsker and Lilienblum might have gotten in, as it were, on the ground floor.[14]

Baron von Neurath, Hitler's Foreign Minister, put his master's theory into more sophisticated dress, and translated it into terms of policy:

> The formation of a Jewish State or a Jewish-led political struc-
> ture under British Mandate is not in Germany's interest, since
> a Palestinian State would not absorb world Jewry but would
> create an additional position of power under international law
> for international Jewry, somewhat like the Vatican State for
> political Catholicism or Moscow for the Comintern.[15]

From this, Neurath drew the conclusion that it was in Germany's interest to strengthen the Arabs. That was the theory of the thing. In practice, the *policies* actually pursued by Nazi Germany from 1933 to 1939 tended to strengthen the Jews in Palestine, as against the Arabs, although the *fact* of the rise of Nazi Germany, and its effects on Britain, encouraged the Arabs, but not to their benefit.

The strengthening of the Jews in Palestine was a marginal, unintended—but not strongly regretted—by-product of the Nazi persecution of the Jews in Germany, in its prewar, less-than-genocidal phases. The victory of a violently anti-semitic leader and party in Germany rejoiced and stimulated anti-semitic movements everywhere in Europe, especially in Eastern Europe. This was especially so since—contrary to widespread Western assumptions before and into 1933—Hitler soon made clear that his anti-semitism was settled policy, and not just rhetoric. As early as the end of 1933, most Jews had been excluded from public office, the civil service, all branches of the media, and teaching. They were also victims of a general boycott, officially encouraged, and enforced by the public. The Nuremberg Laws (September 15, 1935) deprived the Jews of citizenship. By 1936—the year of the Berlin Olympic Games—it has been reckoned that at least one half of German Jews were without means of livelihood.

It was Nazi policy, during this period, to permit, and even to encourage, emigration, where this could be made to pay, from the point of view of the German Government, as under the Transfer Agreement. Many Jews of the salaried classes, once put out of their jobs, lacked means to buy their way out. Of those who were able to get out at this time, from both Germany and its emulous Eastern

neighbors, more found their way to Palestine than to any other country. The official statistics on Jewish immigration into Palestine tell the
most crucial part of the story:

1931	4,075
1932	9,555
1933	30,327
1934	42,359
1935	61,854

The Jewish population of Palestine, which had stood at around
84,000 in 1922, had reached around 400,000 by 1937. Nearly half the
increase resulted from the emigration of European Jews during the
first three years of Hitler's power in Germany.

The immigration policy of the Mandatory from 1932 to 1935 was
relatively generous from a Zionist point of view—and much more so
than some Zionist retrospects would suggest. Yet it remained rather
closely restrictive as regards the largest category of would-be immigrants: those without capital, who could only come in on Labour Certificates issued by the Mandatory. In the period 1933–1939, the Jewish
Agency applied for 171,430 of these certificates; of these, the Mandatory granted 59,180, or little over one-third. The Mandatory justified
this policy in terms of the criterion of economic "absorptive capacity"
laid down in the 1922 White Paper.[16] It appears that this was indeed
the real, as well as the nominal, criterion applied up to about 1936.
Thereafter, it was more a question of *political* absorptive capacity.

The barriers against immigrants without capital concentrated
much Zionist attention on the quotaless immigration of Jews *with
capital*, and helped to overcome the revulsion felt against the Ha'avara
arrangements. It was also hoped that the volume of new investment
so obtained would, by enlarging economic "absorptive capacity," later
make possible increased immigration of propertyless Jews.

Between 1933 and 1939, about £63,000,000 of Jewish capital was
imported into Palestine. It has been estimated that the total amount
of capital imported in 1934 was £10,000,000 and in 1935 £16,000,000.
"While a part of this capital was kept in the banks for future use, considerable amounts were invested in industry and served to create a
remarkable expansion of the country's machinery of production."[17]
The variety of industrial skills brought by the immigrants from Germany contributed to the same effect.

The Yishuv, by the end of 1935, was much larger, much wealthier
and developing much more rapidly than it had been five years be-

fore.[18] The idea of a Jewish State could no longer be dismissed as unattainable. Many Jews in the Diaspora, who had never before seen any need for a Jewish State, had their minds changed for them by the events in Germany. And the same events made Zionists more determined than ever before not to accept any compromise that could endanger the emergence of the Jewish State.

All the great Zionist leaders were occasionally visited by flashes of prophetic lucidity. David Ben-Gurion had one such flash in January 1935:

> The disaster which has befallen German Jewry is not limited to Germany alone. Hitler's regime places the entire Jewish people in danger, and not the Jewish people alone. . . . Hitler's regime cannot long survive without a war of revenge against France, Poland, Czechoslovakia . . . and against Soviet Russia. Germany will not go to war today for she is not ready, but she is preparing for the morrow . . . Who knows; perhaps only four or five years, if not less, stand between us and that awful day.[19]

Considering that Hitler, at that date, had not yet made any aggressive international move, this is an astonishingly accurate prediction, as regards both the scope and the timing of Hitler's aggression. Ben-Gurion drew a conclusion, for Palestine: "In this period"— the four or five years remaining—"we must double our numbers, for the size of the Jewish population on that day may determine our fate at the post-war settlement."

III

Christopher Sykes, an English writer who was fruitfully ambivalent about Zionism,[20] was in Palestine at this time and gives a vivid picture of the arrival of immigrants:

> There was no more moving sight in those days than the arrival at Haifa or Jaffa of a Mediterranean ship carrying Jews from Europe: the spontaneous cries of joy at the first sight of the shore, the mass chanting of Hebrew hymns or Yiddish songs usually beginning raggedly over all the boat and sometimes swelling into a single harmony; the uncontrolled joy of these returning exiles (for so they thought of themselves); a man seizing hold of a stranger and pointing with tears of joy

to the approaching land crying "Zion! Zion!" and "Jerusalem!" Such scenes made many of those who saw them recognise as never before that the human spirit cannot be destroyed, and the Jewish inspiration is among the sublimest expressions of the unconquerable soul. Zionism showed itself at its very finest in these years. Enthusiasm went hand in hand with practical sense. The Zionists remembered how the mass-migrations of the mid-twenties had endangered their purpose, and they succeeded in settling the thousands of newcomers with extraordinary skill. Unemployment crises inevitably arose on several occasions, but they were always kept under control, and the control was largely Jewish. Palestine was the answer to Hitler![21]

But Sykes adds: "The Arabs looked on with dismay. Seen through Arab eyes, this great work of rescue and redemption had nothing beautiful about it and seemed on the contrary to be a stark act of oppression against themselves."[22]

Many writers ascribe the outbreak of the Arab Revolt, beginning in April 1936, to resentment and despair at the growth of the Yishuv from 1933 on. Certainly, the growth of the Yishuv evoked precisely those feelings, and those feelings were not at all mollified by Zionist demonstrations that Arabs also benefited economically from the prosperity of the Yishuv. Palestinian Arabs did see the progress of Zionism as a burning grievance, justifying revolt against Britain. There are good reasons, however, for questioning the tendency to identify the increased immigration as the sole and sufficient cause of the revolt. Other factors can also be seen at work.

First of all, there was resentment at Western rule, in itself, and especially Muslim resentment at being ruled by Christians. It is a strange fact that of the three main Middle Eastern Mandates—Palestine, Iraq and Syria—the one *slowest* to revolt against its Mandatory was Palestine. It took Britain an estimated 90,000 men and £40,000,000 to crush the Iraqi tribal revolt of the summer of 1920. The French, from their arrival in 1920, had over 50,000 troops in Syria, and even larger numbers following the rebellion of 1925–1927.[23] That was at a time when British forces in Palestine, never very large, were being brought down to a few hundred gendarmes, and Palestine remained at peace, despite the Balfour Declaration, and (in 1925) by far the highest Jewish immigration yet recorded under it. As it seems absurd to suppose that the Balfour Declaration, and Jewish immigration into Palestine, were more strongly resented in Syria and in Iraq than in Palestine itself, it is misleading to isolate these factors as (together) the sole cause of disturbance during the Mandate period. As Arab violence in Palestine, in the pre-Hitler period, was directed exclusively against Jews, the Balfour Declaration may have served, to some extent, to deflect resentment away from the Mandatory Power.[24]

Following the affair of the 1930 White Paper and the 1931 Black Letter, the resentment began to cease to be deflected. Arab leaders (in Palestine), including Haj Amin—though with some vacillation—began, for the first time, to make the British, and not only the Jews, a main target for denunciation. In October 1933, the first anti-British disturbances—as distinct from anti-Jewish disturbances, subsequently repressed by British forces—broke out in Palestine: at Jaffa, Nablus, Haifa and Jerusalem. But the disturbances were quickly and firmly repressed. Twenty-six Arabs were killed, and one Briton; no Jews. There were no more major disturbances for some time. Haj Amin drew back. As Christopher Sykes notes: "The year 1934 was relatively peaceful by Palestinian standards and extraordinarily so when the enormous immigration of that year is taken into account."

The real Arab Revolt in Palestine did not break out until April 1936. But between October 1933, and April 1936, other important and relevant things had happened, in addition to the increasing Jewish immigration.

On October 3, 1935, Mussolini invaded Ethiopia. At the League of Nations, Britain took the lead in announcing a firm stand against Italy. On the eve of the invasion, the then British Foreign Secretary, Sir Samuel Hoare (1880–1959), had stated: ". . . The League stands, and my country stands with it, for the collective maintenance of the Covenant in its entirety, and particularly for steady and collective resistance to all acts of unprovoked aggression."

In practice, however, the conduct of Britain's policy was governed by a determination to avoid any risk of war in the Mediterranean.[25] As the Italian dictator's prestige was riveted to his Ethiopian adventure, there was no possibility of deterring him without risk of war. By the end of 1935 it was obvious that League sanctions had failed. By February 1936, Mussolini was clearly winning his war in Ethiopia. In March 1936, Hitler, having considered the demonstrated extent of Western determination to avoid the risk of war, sent his troops, then very few in number, into the demilitarized Rhineland.

The contrast between Britain's words and actions during those fateful months was clear throughout the world, but it was especially glaring in the region of which Palestine was part. The Suez Canal was the lifeline of Mussolini's whole enterprise. As has been authoritatively stated:

> The closing of the Suez was never proposed by any government. . . . Its effect would have been crushing . . . the bigger the Italian force in Africa, the sooner Mussolini would have had to come to terms with the League. For just this reason it was never seriously considered by the British government which had despatched a part of the fleet to Alexandria, but was resolved to run no risk of an Italian attack upon British bases or ships in the Mediterranean. And no other power could propose a measure which only the British could execute.[26]

Although Mussolini's adventure could not have been carried through without British acquiescence, he chose to depict Britain as his determined adversary. In this way, he could be seen as triumphing not merely over backward tribesmen but over a mighty, or once-mighty, Empire. And this was the message that Italian radio, in the early months of 1936, was broadcasting from Bari in Arabic to the Eastern Mediterranean. The impact of the broadcasts was greatly increased by the knowledge that a Power so openly hostile to Britain was able to use the Suez Canal, in the heart of the British sphere, for a purpose to which Britain declared itself strongly opposed.

The Arabic press echoed the Italian broadcasts and responded to them with enthusiasm. The wish for a war, with the defeat of Britain and France, was openly expressed: "There is not a single Arab who does not fervently pray for the coming war which will free us of the yoke of the Western powers."[27] That was in 1935. For 1936, Chatham House's annual *Survey of International Affairs* reports: "In the Arab World, a triplex blend of Fascism—anti-French, anti-British with anti-Jewish—was running like wild-fire across North Africa, and Southwest Asia, from Morocco and Algeria and Tunisia through Egypt and Palestine and Syria to Iraq."[28]

The Arab Revolt of 1936 has to be seen in the context not only of the local situation in Palestine but also of the world situation, which changed drastically from 1933 to 1936, to the detriment, first of the Jews, and then of the Mandatory. The arrival of large numbers of German Jews did more than anger the Arabs; it carried a message of the vulnerability of the Jews, through the advent, for the first time on the world stage, of a modern Power fully committed to outlawing the

Jews. And the events of 1935–1936 suggested that Britain—the Power seen as the protector of the Jews, as well as an infidel ruler over Muslims—might itself now be vulnerable.

To some extent, that last impression was corroborated by the contradictory policies pursued by Britain in Palestine under the High Commissionership of Sir Arthur Wauchope (1874–1947), who succeeded Chancellor in 1931 and remained until February 1938. Wauchope was a kindly and honorable man but seems also to have been muddled, obstinate and weak.

In retrospect, few will probably dispute the verdict on him by a member of his administration: "His greatest desire was to grant everyone's request or to let him think that he intended to do so. . . . In the end he pleased and satisfied no one."[29] A later writer diagnosed his trouble in more sympathetic words, describing Wauchope as "a man unwilling to jeopardize his admittedly substantial achievement with the two communities in Palestine."[30] So Wauchope attempted to combine the permitting of unprecedentedly high Jewish immigration with the pursuit of a Legislative Council on which Jews and Arabs would serve together.

Basically, there were only two serious options the British could consistently pursue in Palestine. One was to let the Jews get on with building their National Home and to achieve, if they could, a Jewish majority, and then a Jewish State, in Palestine, or part of Palestine. That was what Balfour and Lloyd George had originally had in mind, although without unambiguous public commitment to it. This policy was not consistent with representative institutions in Palestine—in advance of a Jewish majority—and consequently not consistent with even an attenuated Legislative Council, invariably seen as the harbinger of representative institutions.

The second option was to abort the Jewish National Home, through the early development of Arab-majority representative institutions. The logical first step in that direction was the Legislative Council.

The first option had been pursued through most of the twenties: *faute de mieux* in the second half of Samuel's tenure, and then under Plumer, apparently without reservation. Whether by coincidence or otherwise, this was the period of the greatest peace experienced in Palestine under the Mandate.

The second option had been seen as desirable—although it could not then be legally attempted—in the days of the military administration. The option was first consistently attempted from 1928 to 1931, under the triumvirate of Luke-Chancellor-Passfield. That option reached its culmination in the White Paper of 1930, and then was blighted by the Black Letter of 1931.

Sir Herbert Samuel, in the early part of his tenure, sought to combine the development of the National Home with the proposed establishment of a Legislative Council. Samuel was saved from some of the consequences of this contradiction by luck, which took a paradoxical form. The Jews accepted, and the Arabs rejected, a proposal which was full of negative potential for the Jews and of positive potential for the Arabs.

Again, whether by coincidence or not, all the periods in which British policies seemed to offer the hope of ending the Jewish National Home were periods of high Arab turbulence and violence. This was true of the military administration period, of "first Samuel," and of the triumvirate. Sir Arthur Wauchope's tenure as High Commissioner did nothing to refute the apparent correlation.

Sir Arthur attempted to repeat the policies of "first Samuel," but in vastly more discouraging and dangerous circumstances, due mainly to the combination of far higher Jewish immigration with greatly diminished British prestige and authority (from the end of 1935 on). This time, it was the Jews who rejected the Legislative Council and any present move toward self-government. Being now in a far stronger position on the ground in Palestine than they had been in 1921, and at the same time in a far weaker position in the world outside, and far more in need of Palestine as a refuge, they were in no mood to make even tactical concessions that might endanger their position in Palestine.

The idea of a Legislative Council was formally rejected by the Nineteenth Zionist Congress, meeting in Lucerne in 1935. Weizmann—who returned to the presidency of the Jewish Agency following this Congress—endorsed the rejection but warned against turning "our non-cooperation into a general policy of non-cooperation with the British Government." But even Weizmann responded negatively when Wauchope urged on him the wisdom of voluntarily restricting immigration. "I appreciate the sagacity of your advice," said Weizmann, "and we might take it if it were not that at this moment we are being harried by the Furies."[31]

On the Arab side there was some cautious interest in the idea, on the part of moderate notables, who were, however, not disposed to commit themselves too far, fearing to be outflanked by Haj Amin. Haj Amin, while prepared to explore the idea (and expose its limitations), had some reason to fear being outflanked by members of a rising and more militant generation. By now fifteen years of Western-endowed education, interpreted by Arab teachers who were mostly nationalists, had radically politicized a large section of the young.[32] At the same time, a more militant mood declared itself among devout Muslim *fellahin* in some regions of Palestine, mainly as a result of the preaching of the fierce and saintly Sheikh Izz al-Din al-Qassam (1871–1935).

Al-Qassam was president of the Young Men's Muslim Association in Haifa, and became, in 1932, acting president of the national conference of the Y.M.M.A. in Palestine. He combined this role with being the head of a secret terrorist society against Jews and Jewish settlements in the north. In the course of one such operation, he and his band were surrounded in the Jenin hills in November 1935. Refusing to surrender, they fought to the death. On each body, a Koran was found. The martyred al-Qassam immediately became a hero to the Muslim youth and center of a cult. The excitement was all the greater because the news of the deaths followed closely on the discovery of a Jewish attempt to smuggle arms (October 1935).

During al-Qassam's lifetime, Haj Amin's relations with him had been equivocal.[33] But al-Qassam's heroic death greatly increased the pressure on Haj Amin to raise the standard of the Muslim revolt. It was to be Muslim this time, rather than Pan-Arab. The Muslim-Christian associations, which had played such an important part in the earlier phases of Arab resistance to the Zionist enterprises, faded out once it began to be a question of actually fighting no longer just the Jews but the primarily Christian Power which held the Mandate.

In the inflamed mood which now gripped the Muslims, the Legislative Council proposal could have little intrinsic appeal, especially when it became apparent that there was to be no immediate check on immigration. Even such Muslim minds as were not particularly inflamed had to be skeptical, remembering the fate of the 1930 White Paper. But the pertinacity with which the High Commissioner pursued the idea of the Legislative Council, in the teeth of so much discouragement, was more interesting than the idea itself. It suggested divided counsels, the possibility that the British might, after all, yet be induced to fall back on their second option. As Christopher Sykes writes: "[Wauchope] persisted in the [Legislative Council] attempt

for over three years, and the more the proposal led to rage and dis-
cord and even bloodshed in Palestine, the more sure he seemed to be
that Palestine needed a Parliament."[34]

Dangling the Legislative Council before the Arabs created the
impression that the British were about to give in on the National
Home. Then, when the council proposal stalled, the Arabs felt they
had been betrayed. After debates in the Lords and Commons in February–March 1936 had shown almost no parliamentary support for the
council—mainly because of sympathy for Jewish refugees from the
Nazis—the Colonial Office backed away from the idea.[35] The Arab
reaction was much the same as over the Black Letter of February
1931; they felt that promises to them had been broken as a result of
hidden Jewish influence, and that political negotiation was hopeless.
But Britain's general political and military position in the spring of
1936 now looked far weaker than it had five years before.

IV

By the beginning of April 1936, the Yishuv was aware of serious,
impending trouble in Palestine. On April 5, Jabotinsky, then in London, cabled to Wauchope about

> alarming reports from Palestine voicing acutest apprehen-
> sion of anti-Jewish outbreaks. . . . Reports affirm agitation
> furthered by circles hoping to force Zionists . . . accept Legis-
> lative Council. . . . Authorization specific Arab manifesta-
> tions unprecedented scale appears being exploited to revive
> ominous battlecry Eddowleh Maana [The Government is
> with us]. . . . Experience shows such developments inevit-
> ably result bloodshed especially considering scarcity imperial
> troops inefficient police[36] . . . Together with all Jews I re-
> spectfully await denial of danger or decisive action.[37]

The troubles broke out ten days later. On April 15 a group of
armed Arabs took two Jews off a bus in the Nablus mountains and
murdered them. Two days later members of the "nationalist Hagana"—parent body of the Irgun Zvai Leumi—murdered two Arabs
near the Jewish settlement of Petah Tikvah. These events were followed by major Arab disturbances in Jaffa, Nablus and elsewhere, by
the establishment of Arab strike committees and by outbreaks of armed
violence in many parts of the country.

The murders of the two Arabs, which helped to spread the violence, were committed by ideological supporters of Jabotinsky. In issuing his prophetic warning, Jabotinsky may have had in mind not only the need for the British to prepare against the threat of Arab violence but also—in case the British did not effectively so prepare—the advance justification of Jewish self-defense, including the version of self-defense that was special to the Revisionists: retaliation.

Jabotinsky's foresight was remarkable, but there was often something sinister about it. However, acts of Jewish retaliation did not in fact become a regular feature of the troubled period from 1936 to 1939. In general, the Yishuv at this time followed Ben-Gurion's policy of Havlaga, self-restraint, and confined itself to the successful defense of the Jewish settlements. Throughout this period, it was the Arabs, not the Jews, who were on the attack. In the first weeks, it was the Jews who were the main targets of attack—as had been generally the case up to this time—but after that the movement took on the character of an insurrection against British rule, although attacks on Jews also continued throughout the period. Arabs perceived as supporters of the British or of the Jews were also frequently attacked.[38] Some hundreds of Arab volunteers from outside Palestine took part in the revolt.

The shift from an entirely anti-Jewish movement to a primarily anti-British one was awkward for Haj Amin. If he went along with this, he risked losing his position of power as head of the Supreme Muslim Council. On the other hand, if he failed to go along with it, he might lose the base on which he had built his power: his prestige as the leader of Muslim nationalism in Palestine. So in the beginning he temporized. He gave in to the demands of the young militants, so far as to agree to becoming head of the Higher Arab Committee set up at the end of April to lead a general strike. The H.A.C. was also there to coordinate the Arab rising—or as much of it as was willing to be coordinated. But the violence could be disavowed, as well as coordinated. In theory, the H.A.C. was a lawful body, there to express Arab political demands—principally the stoppage of Jewish immigration—and to back those demands by the lawful method of the withdrawal of labor. So Haj Amin's position as head of the Higher Arab Committee, leading those Arabs who were now in revolt against British rule, was still—just—reconcilable with his position as head of the Supreme Muslim Council, appointed by the power against which his followers were in revolt.[39]

But Haj Amin was well aware that his position as president of the S.M.C. had become precarious. During the first two months of the revolt, Haj Amin "did his best to convince the Government that he had nothing to do with the rebels and that he was a moderate factor."[40] This was even partly true at this time. Haj Amin, during these months, did not use the mosques to inflame the Muslim crowds as he had done to such effect in 1928 and 1929. There was, of course, less need for such incitement now.

During the month of June, a change occurred. Muslim functionaries began to call on the people in the name of Islam to join the rebels. The Supreme Muslim Council, still headed by Haj Amin, threw its weight behind this new policy. The Jews—as the S.M.C. informed the High Commissioner on June 26—had refused offers of a National Home in other places only "for a religious idea which they maintain and which aims at the reconstruction of the Jewish Temple of Solomon" in the place of the Mosque of al-Aqsa.[41] Britain, in refusing the Muslim demands, was seen as supporting the Jews in this endeavor, and the network of Muslim functionaries throughout the land was used for the supply of money, arms and information to the rebels. All this activity was directed and organized from the Mufti's sanctuary, the Haram esh-Sharif, which—once more—he represented as the chief target of Zionism.

Various reasons have been offered for this change in the direction of open defiance of Britain on the part of the Mufti and his colleagues.[42] It seems likely that among the reasons was the fact that the prestige and apparent strength of the Power defied underwent a further steep decline during the period of May–June 1936.

On May 3, Emperor Haile Selassie, fleeing from Ethiopia, reached the French colony of Djibouti. On May 4, he embarked on the British cruiser *Enterprise* for Palestine, to pray at Jerusalem. On May 5, Marshal Badoglio made his triumphal entrance into Addis Ababa. On May 6, the Foreign Secretary, Sir Anthony Eden, spoke in the Commons. He said that the situation was "difficult and disappointing" but that Britain had "taken the lead" throughout the dispute. As regards suggestions of military force, he warned that "you cannot close the Canal with paper boats."[43] On May 9, Mussolini, from the balcony of the Palazzo Venezia, announced that the King of Italy was now Emperor of Ethiopia. On May 10, Haile Selassie, from Jerusalem, addressed a forlorn appeal to the League "to pursue its efforts to ensure the respect of the Covenant." On May 11, the League Council met and adjourned its deliberations on "the dispute between Italy and Ethiopia" until June 15. In fact the Council never again considered the substance of the dispute, but transferred the matter to the Assembly, which did not get around to it until June 30. In the meantime, the Baldwin Government had decided to "take the initiative in proposing the raising of sanctions," which were accordingly raised in the following month.

Haj Amin and his colleagues had before their eyes that May, in their own city, the spectacle of the chief of a people whose cause Britain had "taken a lead" in upholding, and who was now utterly defeated, suppliant and ignored. From the standpoint of the Haram esh-Sharif—bent on the elimination of a people who looked to Britain for protection—Haile Selassie in exile must have been an encouraging and stimulating sight.

With increasingly open religious encouragement, and in the teeth of a greatly increased British military presence, the revolt spread in the summer of 1936. Throughout June, attacks increased along the roads and against the Haifa-Lyddah railway line. The first fairly large-scale engagement between British troops and Arab bands took place near Tulkarm. During July, the disturbances intensified, and continued on a similar scale throughout August. The strike which accompanied these activities was only partly successful—mainly because so much of the work of the country was done by the Jews, who undertook more of it while the Arabs were on strike. In the port of Haifa, the key to the country's economy, the Arabs, as well as the Jews, remained at work. But the combination of violence and even a partial strike was sufficiently formidable to make its essential point: that there did indeed exist strong and widespread opposition among the Arab population to continued Jewish immigration.

The reaction of the British authorities to all this was marked, as often, by hesitations and inconsistencies, but it was on the whole far from discouraging from an Arab point of view throughout 1936.

First of all, there was, in this stage, no attempt at a general repression of the revolt. British forces defended themselves and kept lines of communication open, and little more. These forces were increased in number until they reached more than a division by the beginning of August—six or seven times the strength in April. As a soldier sardonically observed: "The civil power in Palestine seemed to require a great deal of aid."[44] One reason for this was the unusual restraint with which the aid was used. It was apparent, by early summer, that the Government would greatly prefer a political solution to a military one. And this meant treating the Arab leaders, as well as those of their followers who were not in the act of shooting, with care and respect. The Mufti remained at large—and in possession of his two great offices. A contemporary British observer—no Zionist—compared the Palestine Government's performance at this time to "a figure in a dressing-gown and bedroom slippers, pathetically padding along in the dusty wake of the Arab Higher Committee."[45]

A political solution to an Arab Revolt required concessions to Arab demands, and important concessions were forthcoming. The main Arab demand, and the key to everything else, was cessation of Jewish immigration. Immigration was not stopped, but it was sharply cut back. The half-yearly immigration quota of April 1936 had been 4,500. In November 1936, it sank to 1,800, and in May 1937, to 770. The total authorized immigration into Palestine in 1936—quota and over quota—was 29,727, less than half the figure for 1935, and the lowest since 1932, although the plight of the Jews in Europe was no less grave.

One important element in the new tilt in the direction of a settlement on Arab lines was the growing ascendancy of the Foreign Office. Palestine itself still came under the Colonial Office, but the Foreign Office had an increasing role, because of the emergence to sovereignty, in the early thirties, of certain Arab states. The sovereignty of these states, being subject to British "advice," was partly real and partly fictitious, but either way, it was now an affair for the Foreign Office. So the repercussions, and alleged repercussions, of events in Palestine, as affecting, or seeming to affect, the sovereign Arab states, were also of concern to the Foreign Office, whose prestige and seniority of course overshadowed those of the Colonial Office.

In the old days of the Empire and up to about 1930, the attitude of British rulers toward vassal princes had been generally condescending, cynical or peremptory. But conditions in the mid-thirties greatly altered this relationship, especially after the dismal course of international affairs from the autumn of 1935 to the summer of 1936. The British Government was acutely aware of the vulnerability of the Empire, of the limited resources available for its defense and of the pacific attitudes of the contemporary British public. They were also aware of new factors—development of air communications, growing dependence on oil—increasing the importance and vulnerability of their Middle Eastern domains. In these conditions it seemed essential to hold the goodwill of the Arab rulers, and try to make them more popular, in case they might defect or be overthrown. And to some—notably the increasingly influential George Rendel (1889–1979), head of the Eastern Department of the Foreign Office from 1930 to 1938—it seemed that the obvious way of pleasing these potentates and making them more popular was to jettison the Jewish National Home in Palestine. The potentates confirmed that this was indeed the case.[46]

So in the summer of 1936, three Arab princes, from outside Palestine, became involved in the internal affairs of Mandate Palestine, with the consent and encouragement of the Mandatory.[47] At the same time Arab volunteers, with some aid from these princes, were engaged in trying to overthrow the same Mandatory. It is from this date that the question of Palestine is seen to be internationalized, as it has remained ever since.

Each of the three parties to this important development—the British, the Palestinians who were fighting them, and the princes—had its own particular interests to serve.

The Palestinian interest was the least complicated. Haj Amin had been trying, since 1928, to make Palestine, and Jerusalem in particular, a Pan-Muslim affair. An appeal to the Arab princes, which he made in April, was an obvious step in this direction. It was also seen as a legitimate counter to the nefarious influence of international Jewry. These were the general Palestinian considerations. There was also a personal consideration: the involvement of the Arab princes (with one exception) in the affairs of a Palestine in which religious factors played a predominant part—due largely to Haj Amin's activities—could only increase further the influence and prestige of the Grand Mufti of Jerusalem in the Arab world in general, and consequently in Palestine itself.

The interests of the princes were more complex. The princes concerned were two sovereign kings—Abdul Aziz Ibn Saud, king of what had just entered the League of Nations as Saudi Arabia, and Ghazi, king of Iraq (represented by his Foreign Minister, Nuri Said)—and one vassal emir, Abdullah of Transjordan. The position of the Arab princes in relation to Zionism could be compared to that of the European princes in relation to Jacobinism in the 1790s. In principle, all the princes sincerely detested, on religious and other grounds, the obnoxious and menacing upstart ideological Power. In practice, their approach to the problem was governed by their perception of their dynastic interests, and by their rivalries with other dynasties.

The ablest and most autonomous of the three—and the only one who had won his throne by his own efforts—was the Saudi king, Ibn Saud (1880–1953). Ibn Saud, as a devout Muslim, professed, and no doubt felt, a fierce hatred not merely of Zionism but of Jews and Judaism generally.[48] But as a king, what principally concerned him was to make sure that rival dynasties did not gain some territorial or other advantage out of the turmoil in Palestine, or that if they did, he himself must get some compensating advantage. Thus, when, at a later stage, the partition of Palestine was mooted, the Foreign Office feared that Ibn Saud would react violently, on Pan-Arab and religious grounds. The King's actual reaction was that if Abdullah was to be aggrandized and made independent as a result of partition, he himself would claim Aqaba and Ma'an and a corridor to Syria.[49] Any eighteenth-century Habsburg, Romanoff or Hohenzollern would have completely understood the Saudi dynasty's outlook on international affairs. Ibn Saud's rivals, Abdullah (ruled 1921–1951) and Ghazi (reigned 1933–1939), were princes of the Hashemite line whose family he had driven out of the Hedjaz, and whom the British had installed in Amman and Baghdad, respectively. Presumably to preempt any Hashemite move, Ibn Saud, as early as April, became the first Arab leader to offer Britain his good offices to end the troubles in Palestine.

Abdullah had potentially the most to gain from the situation—a possible accession of contiguous territory, including perhaps Jerusalem—but the least power to bring to bear. His emirate was miserably poor and dependent on British subsidies, and he was hated and feared by Haj Amin. He would have liked, if he could, to make a deal with the Zionists, but in practice he was constrained to subordinate his policies to those of the Arab monarchs, apparently supportive of the Palestinian nationalists, whom he detested.

The main interest of Nuri Said and his master, in turbulent Iraq, was to compensate for the dynasty's unpopular British origins and associations by an apparently independent (and implicitly somewhat anti-British) stance on a popular Muslim issue. Nuri was constrained accordingly to be seen to get in step in terms of Palestinian nationalism, thus irritating official circles in London, and increasing the prestige of Ibn Saud, who could afford to be diplomatic, having no gallery to play to. One of the most sustained consequences of the Palestinian imbroglio has been the rising influence of the politic Saudi princes.

The status of the princes was felt to be enhanced by ambiguous good offices which could be presented in Britain as a service to their ally, and to Arabs—in Arabic—as a service to the suffering Muslims of Palestine. And there was little risk involved; if things went wrong, as was probable, the blame and the consequences would be borne not by the dynasts but by the parties on the ground in Palestine.

What the Palestinians and the dynasts, separately, stood to gain from internationalization was reasonably clear. What the British stood to gain is more nebulous. The theory of the thing was that the authority and prestige of the Arab dynasts would induce the rebels to lay down their arms and trust in the wisdom and benevolence of the Mandatory. But it is not at all clear that the dynasts *had* any authority and prestige in the eyes of the "rebels," who were all pious Muslims, fighting a holy war against Christians and Jews in Palestine. Such Muslims necessarily had more prestige themselves, in their own eyes and those of other Muslims, than had exterior Arab princes whose principalities depended on the goodwill of the infidel Power against whom the holy war was being fought. The Palestinians were unlikely to do anything at the behest of these princes unless they had already decided to do it, for other and much more solid reasons.

The real advantages, from a particular British point of view, which became dominant in the mid-thirties, were rather different. The primary advantage was not, or not necessarily, a national one; it was an institutional one. Internationalization, once accepted, meant that the Foreign Office, not the Colonial Office, would be in charge of the politics of Palestine. This change did not become complete until after the Second World War, but a shift in that direction was already apparent from the mid-thirties on. And this institutional shift combined with and accelerated a major political shift. The Foreign Secretary, Anthony Eden, relied at this time on his Eastern Department, which, under George Rendel, had become a partisan of what we have called "the second option": movement in the direction required by the Arab demands, toward the liquidation of the commitment to the Jewish National Home. The second option had become inherently more attractive in the circumstances of the mid-thirties, and was consistent with the general trend of British policy in the period. But the Foreign Office at this time seems to have greatly exaggerated the "repercussions throughout the Muslim world" argument[50] and to have underestimated the disadvantages, for a major Power, of trying to extricate itself from a long-standing commitment, under the threat of force.

The Government, however, and especially the soldiers, were aware of such disadvantages, and correspondingly reluctant to give very much ground, at least while the fighting went on.

It was on this point that the Arab princes constituted an attractive resource for a Foreign Office bent on major policy change under pressure. The princes could bring decorum—an asset which they possessed in abundance—to a turnaround which might otherwise appear ignominious. The princes' appeals for peace might indeed have little intrinsic effect in bringing the fighting to an end. But when it did come to an end—or even a temporary suspension—the princes would deserve credit, and a hearing, because of the loyalty and statesmanship they demonstrated in a time of crisis. Britain could not concede Arab demands backed by the murderous violence of bands of roaming *fellahin*. But might Britain not, freely and honorably, accept the advice of its proved friends in the Arab world? Surely it might; even though in practice the advice of the princes would coincide exactly with the demands of the *fellahin*. What mattered was the look of the thing, and the princes undoubtedly looked well, in an indigenous sort of way.

So, more or less, the responsible people seem to have reasoned, and the charade went on. From the beginning of July, both the Foreign Office and the Higher Arab Committee—with substantially converging, though ostensibly divergent, intentions—encouraged efforts at mediation by the Arab princes. These efforts, conducted competitively—with Nuri in the lead—led to nothing, as long as it suited the Palestinians to go on fighting. Officially, the Government's policy, throughout this period, was that a Royal Commission—the Peel Commission—was set up to look into "the roots of the Palestine question," but the commission would not set out for Palestine until the troubles were over. Unofficially, the Palestinians were encouraged, through the princely mediators, to expect salvation from the commission, but rebel leaders remained understandably skeptical, no doubt remembering the 1930 White Paper and its fate. As the astringent Simson observes: "So, in spite of the fact that aircraft were sent up to drop brief life-histories of the members of the Royal Commission over the Arab parts of Palestine, the rebellion went on and the Commission stayed at home."[51]

But the autumn of 1937 brought a situation much more unfavorable from the point of view of the rebels. By this time, the British had accumulated a large force in Palestine. The British Government, influenced by the Service chiefs, was not prepared to allow that force to stand there throughout the winter on the basis of what has been aptly called "the non-viable policy of no repression and no capitulation."[52] The Government accordingly decided to introduce martial law. The Higher Arab Committee felt that the rebellion could not stand up to this. The citrus season, which had ended in March, began again in October, and fighters and strikers would alike drift back to work.

Neither the H.A.C. nor the Foreign Office wanted the rebels to look as if they had accepted defeat. The Arab princes were therefore encouraged to issue a joint appeal, which the Higher Arab Committee could accept without loss of face. The mutual suspicions of the Iraqis and the Saudis delayed the appeal until it was almost too late to serve its purpose. As finally published, the appeal ran:

> To our sons, Arabs of Palestine. We have been much distressed by the present situation in Palestine. In agreement with our brothers the Arab Kings and the Emir Abdullah we appeal to you to restore tranquility in order to prevent further bloodshed, relying on the good intentions of our friend the British Government to see that justice is done. Be assured that we shall continue our endeavor to help you.[53]

On the same day (October 10) that the appeal was issued, the Higher Arab Committee published a manifesto urging the people to call off the strike and the disorders. The speed of the response seems indicative of the true nature of the transaction. Shortly after the H.A.C. sent out a secret appeal to end violence "since the British Government have begun to fulfill their promises to us and to carry out the agreements concluded between us and them,"[54] the strikes and disorders ground to a halt. The bands were allowed to disperse without giving up their arms, to the disgust of the military authorities, and to the eventual regret of the civil authorities also.

The way was now open for the arrival in Palestine of the Peel Commission, from which the Arabs had been encouraged to expect so much.

V

In this year, 1936, something snapped in the spiritual bond which had existed between Zionism and official Britain since 1917. The bond had stood many and varied strains, but in 1936, with the entry of the Arab princes, it finally parted. Two observers with somewhat differing points of view—a non-British Jewish Zionist and a British Gentile Zionist—have recorded, in memorable words, their sense of that parting.

To his son, on July 30, 1936, Vladimir Jabotinsky wrote: "The era initiated on November 2, 1917, has ended. What will follow I still do not see clearly." And to a friend at about the same time, he wrote:

> I frankly admit that for the moment I have lost sight of the little trail, which may bring us back to the big main road. It is the first time in my life that such a thing has happened to me. . . . Ever since the Young Turkish revolution thirty years ago, in all the cataclysms we have lived through, I have always had the impression, or the illusion, that I could see quite clearly that particular little track winding its way through bogs and boulders for the special benefit of the Zionist cause. But I cannot boast this now. The main asset in all our Zionist venture, England as we knew her up to yesterday, has disappeared. Sometimes I feel like Sinbad the Sailor . . . must have felt when he established his "national home" on a little island . . . and the island proved to be a whale and *adieu*.

And to the same friend in a letter written a little later in the same year, he put a question about the devalued Balfour Declaration: "A pledge given by Don Quixote—can it be carried out by Sancho Panza?"[55]

Balfour's niece and biographer, Blanche—"Baffy"—Dugdale, wrote, in the following year, her own obituary on the Declaration: "My uncle's document is now a historic piece of paper. It has given us 400,000 Jews and a few friends and that is all. But we must make that enough."[56]

The non-Zionist British historian John Marlowe tells of this same parting of the ways in the chillier mood with which it was contemplated in London:

> Zionism, as a result of its being generally regarded as an actual strategic liability instead of as a potential strategic asset, had lost most of its influence in high places in England, particularly as most of the statesmen who had sponsored it were either dead or in retirement. The idealism, sometimes genuine, sometimes mere dilettantism, which had seen Zionism (like Philhellenism) as part of a new phase of European re-

vival and expansion was so much outmoded and so much at
odds with the actual state of Western Europe as to seem not
merely ridiculous, but perverse. Gone were the days of intimate confabulation between Dr. Weizmann and high officials
of the Foreign Office. . . . Arabism was beginning to be
fashionable among rising young men in the Foreign Service.
Visits to Weizmann's house on Addison Road were no longer
regarded as particularly helpful to official careers in the
making.[57]

Weizmann in his memoirs suggests a link between appeasement
of Hitler and Mussolini and appeasement of the Arabs, and some
Zionist writers tend to follow this lead. Too much should not be made
of such a link. As Marlowe reminds us, by his emphasis on the strategic
factors, the perceived need to conciliate the Arabs was more directly
connected with preparations for the eventuality of war, if appeasement should fail, than with appeasement itself. As Yehuda Bauer has
pointed out, the high point of "appeasing the Arabs"—the White
Paper of May 1939—falls into the historical period when the effort to
appease Hitler had been reluctantly abandoned, and Britain was on
the course that was to lead to war.[58] The conditions in which such a
war would be fought—with the growing importance of Middle Eastern
airfields and other communications, as well as oil—suggested a greater
need to cultivate the friendship of the rulers of the sovereign Arab
states. No corresponding need was any longer felt to cultivate leaders
of Jewish opinion. The Jews had nowhere else to go. If Britain were
to find itself at war with Nazi Germany, Jewish opinion throughout
the world would *have* to support Britain. Nor was there any longer
any tendency to overestimate the importance of that support.

Jewish influence, by the late thirties, lacked the mysterious and
mighty power often attributed to it before 1933. There had been no
state in which the Jews had appeared more prominent and influential
than in the Weimar Republic. Yet the Jews of Germany had altogether
failed to avert the rise to power of Adolf Hitler, and the Jews of the
world had failed to halt either the application of his anti-semitic
policies or his growing ascendancy in Europe.

So there were solid and rational motives for anxiety to cultivate
Arabs, rather than Jews, in this period, without attributing decisive
influence to the policy of appeasement in Europe. Yet it would also
seem unwise to jump to the conclusion that the policy of appeasing
Hitler in Europe, and the policy shift in relation to Palestine, were

entirely disconnected. Both sets of policies were carried out by the same people. Vastly the more important was the appeasement of Germany. In that context, the Jews were a nuisance. A British statesman, trying to improve relations with the Government of Adolf Hitler, had to see both Jewish influence and the existence of sympathy with the sufferings of the Jews as working against him, endangering his work for peace and threatening to plunge his country into an unnecessary war.

As a historian, not unsympathetic to the Conservatives of the period, has written: "Beaverbrook was not the only person who sensed connections between dislike of Continental entanglement, the prospect of war and the feeling that there were 'already too many Jews in London.' "[59]

Such a conjuncture clearly had an inherent tendency to awaken any dormant anti-semitism; and there are always people around in whom anti-semitism is a light sleeper. People who felt that "the Jewish problem" was getting in the way of sensible developments in Europe would be additionally sensitive to the suggestion that, in the Middle East also, a commitment to the Jews was an albatross around Britain's neck.

In the period preceding the Second World War, the troubles in the Middle East tended to blend into a deeper malaise, into which exasperation with foreigners, with ideologies and with Jews all entered. Neville Chamberlain's biographer saw, in the malaise in 1936, ". . . an importation of foreign philosophies into politics domestic; of which Nazi Germany, Fascist Italy and Soviet Russia were the roots, the wrangle over Jew and Arab in Palestine a side-manifestation, the rival prancings and petty brutalities of Communists and Mosley followers a local symptom."[60]

Jews could be seen as coming into, in one way or another, almost every aspect of this general syndrome, or nightmare.

The accessibility to anti-semitism, which was inseparable from a strong commitment to appeasing Hitler, was not the main cause of the policy shift in the Middle East, but it may well have accentuated the shift. Elie Kedourie and others have shown a tendency on the part of policy makers for the Middle East to overestimate the importance of Zionism as a factor in the calculations—as distinct from the rhetoric—of the local dynasts, and to underestimate the importance of dynastic ambitions and fears, and of perceptions of Britain's strength or weakness in the region at any given time.

A further factor which weakened the Zionists was intangible. Among those British politicians who had adopted the commitment of November 1917 were people of romantic inclinations, susceptible to the poetry of Zionism. The men of the late 1930s, on the other hand, prided themselves on being practical men, with no time for airy-fairy sentimentality. The key word of the time, in both Britain and France, is "realism." Georges Bernanos, who was out of step, described the young of this type as *de petits mufles réalistes*: "realistic little skunks." Bernanos was customarily excessive, but the types he had in mind were not likely to be moved by the sort of feelings that could move a man like Arthur Balfour.

The shift in policies and attitudes in Britain necessitated a change in the effective leadership of the Zionist movement. Weizmann's leadership had been indispensable as long as British support was felt to be essential, and seen to be forthcoming, even if sometimes erratically. But now that support was no longer forthcoming. Henceforward, the Yishuv would have to think increasingly in terms of defending its National Home itself against the Arabs certainly, and possibly against the British also. Such a conception, which would have been visionary before 1933, no longer seemed so. The New Yishuv, of 400,000 people, looked as if it might be just capable of standing on its own feet, and it knew it might soon be required to do so. There was, for the moment, no longer adequate scope or purchase for Weizmann's diplomatic talents. The new leader, representing the self-reliance of the Yishuv, had to belong to the Yishuv, living in Eretz Israel, and having the support of a majority in the Yishuv. This could only be David Ben-Gurion.

Weizmann remained as nominal head, and in a sense Foreign Minister, of the movement. Indeed it was Ben-Gurion who had done most to bring him back as president, in 1935. But at the same time Ben-Gurion made it clear to American Jewish leaders that Weizmann's presidency did not mean that Ben-Gurion accepted him as leader: "Weizmann will not be the ruler and leader and he knows it. The Executive will lead. . . ."[61]

Ben-Gurion himself was chairman both of the Zionist Executive and of the Jewish Agency: ruler and leader in Zionism for most practical purposes, from this time on, up to the foundation of the new State and well into its earlier years. Ben-Gurion had very little of the charm, eloquence and international culture that belonged to Herzl and Weizmann, and also to Jabotinsky. But these were not the particular qualities the Yishuv was looking for at this time. Ben-Gurion's biographer describes him as he appeared in 1935–1936: ". . . gruff, tough, lacking refinement and polish. He was a short, stocky man, his face tanned, his expression powerful and energetic. His sense of humour was fairly poor, and his speeches and articles were wearisome and infinitely long. But he stood with both feet firmly planted in the realities of Palestine."[62]

Zionists under Ben-Gurion were able to work and fight alongside the British, for quite long periods—in 1937–1938 and again during the war—under attack from common enemies. But there was no longer any sense of working for a common goal, in the shape of the National Home. The Balfour Declaration had not been formally abrogated, but those in the Yishuv were coming to feel that if they wanted a National Home, as they understood the term, they would probably have to get it for themselves.

VI

The Royal Commission, headed by Lord Peel (1867–1937), a former Secretary of State for India and grandson of Sir Robert Peel, arrived in Palestine in November 1936 with its mandate to look into "the roots of the problem." The commission held sixty-six meetings, most of them dominated by Jewish evidence, since the Arabs boycotted the proceedings until the fifty-sixth meeting (January 12, 1937). The great set piece of the commission's sessions was Weizmann's evidence, given in public session in Jerusalem, on November 25, 1936, as a continuous statement. Weizmann put his whole soul into it. One senses that members of the commission—quite against the trend of the times—fell under Weizmann's spell. Weizmann spoke of the Jews in Europe:

> Everything to the East of the Rhine is today in a position . . . which is neither life nor death. . . . There are in this part of the world six million people for whom the world is divided into places where they cannot live and places into which they cannot enter. . . . What has happened in Germany has been the Writing on the Wall even for the Western communities. . . . That uneasy feeling which used to stop at the Vistula has now reached the Rhine. It infiltrates across the Channel and across the Atlantic. . . . It makes me uneasy to

reflect that one is always the subject of analysis, that one is being dissected and tested. Have we the right to live?

The question must have seemed rhetorical, for this was the period of the "Olympic lull," which set in early in 1936 and lasted into 1938, during which many outside observers assumed that German anti-semitism had reached its peak in 1935—with the Nuremberg Laws—and was now on the wane.

Weizmann continued:

It is a disembodied ghost of a race . . . and therefore it inspires suspicion, and suspicion breeds hatred.

I believe the main cause which has produced the particular state of Jewry in the world is its attachment to Palestine. We are stiff-necked people. We never forget. . . . This steadfastness which has preserved the Jews through the ages and through a career which is almost one long chain of human suffering is primarily due to some physical or pathological attachment to Palestine. . . . In the East End of London, the Jew prays for dew in the summer, and rain in the winter.

Toward the end of his speech, Weizmann spoke of the Arabs, painfully:

I think I can say before the Commission, before God and before the world, that in intention, consciously, nothing has been done to injure their position. . . . On the contrary, indirectly, we have conferred benefits on the population of this country. I should like to be perfectly frank, we have not come for that purpose. We have come for the purpose of building up a National Home for the Jewish people, but we are happy and proud that this upbuilding has been accompanied by a minimum of suffering, by a minimum of servitude and by considerable benefits to the country at large.[63]

Ben-Gurion gave evidence later—January 7—and in a different tone. Weizmann had sought to persuade the commission, and influence its recommendations. Ben-Gurion's basic argument implied that the commission, its recommendations and the whole British Mandate were ephemeral and insignificant things in comparison with the title deeds of the Jews: "I say on behalf of the Jews that the Bible is our Mandate, the Bible which was written by us, in our own language, in Hebrew in this very country. That is our Mandate. It was only the *recognition* of this right which was expressed in the Balfour Declaration."[64]

Haj Amin gave evidence a week later. He too saw the Jewish claim to a National Home in Palestine as fundamentally religious, and he saw it as being in fundamental conflict with Islam: "The Jews' ultimate aim is the reconstruction of the Temple of King Solomon on the ruins of the Haram ash-Sharif, the El-Aqsa Mosque and the Holy Dome of the Rock."[65]

One of the last witnesses before the commission shed further light on the religious dimensions to the conflict. This was an Arab Christian, Monsignor Hajjar, Melkite Archbishop of Galilee, who was introduced to the commission by a member of the Higher Arab Committee. Monsignor Hajjar said: "When the Jews become the majority in the country they will dominate, and when they reach that standing, they will be acting contrary to the Koran which says: 'They have been stricken with misery until the day of Resurrection.' I will now deal with the Christian point of view. Judaism looks to this country as the Land of Promise. According to Christianity, *we* are the new Is-raelites, we are the new people of God."[66] The witness went on to refer to the "spread of immorality and of Communism" and to "women roaming about the streets in bathing costumes."

The commission's report, a lucid and impressive document, was published in July 1937. In its main findings it declared:

> The disease is so deep-rooted that, in our firm conviction, the only hope of a cure lies in a surgical operation. . . . An irrepressible conflict has arisen between two national com-munities within the narrow bounds of one small country. . . . About 1,000,000 Arabs are in strife, open or latent, with some 400,000 Jews[67] . . . But while neither race can justly rule all Palestine, we see no reason why, if it were practicable, each race should not rule part of it. . . . Partition seems to offer at least a chance of ultimate peace. We can see none in any other plan.[68]

Specifically, the commission recommended that the Mandate for Palestine should be terminated and replaced by a Treaty System; a new Mandate for the Holy Places should be instituted: a Treaty of Alliance to be negotiated between the Government of Transjordan and the Arabs of Palestine on the one hand and the Zionist Organiza-tion on the other, setting up two sovereign independent states, an expanded Transjordan and a Jewish State.[69] "If it offers neither party what it wants," concluded the commission, "it offers each what it wants most, namely freedom and security."

In territorial terms, the commission assigned to the Jewish State a coastal strip from south of Jaffa to north of Haifa, together with Galilee from the sea to the Syrian border. Jerusalem, with a corridor to the sea, was to be under the new Mandate; the rest of Palestine was the new Arab State.

VII

The British Government, in a White Paper issued simultaneously with the published report, expressed general agreement with its findings, and stated specifically "that a scheme of partition on the . . . [suggested] lines . . . represents the best and most hopeful solution of the deadlock."[70]

In the face of strong opposition, however, from all spokesmen of the Palestinian Arabs to the whole idea of partition, the British Government began to back away from the proposed "surgical operation." The idea was allowed to die slowly—through the creation of a second Royal Commission, ostensibly to establish a precise partition line, but really to demonstrate that partition was impracticable. But this was a slow process and for more than a year partition remained the nominal goal of British policy, and the main target of attacks for most Arabs, and some Jews.

There were indeed some Arab leaders who would have liked to accept partition. Emir Abdullah had strong reasons for accepting a solution which would have enlarged his dominions and enhanced his status. The clans and factions in Palestine itself which maintained contact with Abdullah, and feared and hated Haj Amin, had reasons for favoring the extension of Abdullah's power, and the probable elimination of Haj Amin from the new Palestinian State. But those who harbored such ambitions ran into a structural difficulty, which has proved remarkably durable. *Any* Arab leader who accepted *any* compromise with the Zionist enterprise was in immediate danger of being outflanked by his rivals, denounced as a traitor, and in proximate danger of being assassinated. That was, in fact, to be Abdullah's fate, even though no real compromise had been reached.

In this particular case, Haj Amin had the strongest possible incentive to fight the scheme to the bitter end. It is true that it might have set his mind at rest on the design he seemed to fear the most. As the Peel proposals retained the Holy Places under the Mandate, it seemed unlikely that the Mandatory would permit the rebuilding of the Temple of Solomon on the ruins of the Dome of the Rock. However, the proposals did not merely mean a Jewish State, something profoundly repugnant, but would have meant the end of Haj Amin's political power in Palestine, and the triumph of his enemies.

In those conditions, the British could perhaps have *imposed* partition, with not much more difficulty than they were to encounter in the course of *not* imposing it. The reaction of Ibn Saud suggests that it might not have been difficult to win the *de facto* acquiescence of the dynasts for territorial changes that included partition. No such attempt was made. For the Foreign Office, the important elements in the situation were that partition was bitterly denounced by almost all articulate Arabs, and that it was acceptable to the Zionist leadership. Thus, partition appeared to be a move in the exact opposite direction to the one in which the Foreign Office, and eventually the Government, wanted to go. Partition, as a British option, died.

The trouble was that—as the Peel Commission had seen—there was now no real alternative policy. The option the Foreign Office would have liked—an independent (or quasi-independent) Palestine, with "guarantees" for the Jews already there—was not a real option. Neither were Jews prepared to accept such guarantees, nor Arabs prepared to offer them. Haj Amin—who would almost certainly have held supreme power in such a Palestine—had conveyed to the Peel Commission, in a cryptic answer, that there would be no place in his Palestine for Jews who had come there in quest of a National Home. Simply to ditch the National Home—which was what was really involved—would have been eminently feasible, at the Palestine end, back in the days of O.E.T.A. It would still have been feasible, though more difficult, a decade or so later, for example, at the time when it was attempted by the Passfield triumvirate. But by 1936, the situation had radically changed. As the Peel Commission put it: "Twelve years ago the National Home was an experiment, today it is a going concern."[71] In the late 1930s, with a Yishuv now standing at 400,000 people, and with Hitler loose in Europe, it was not feasible for Britain to ditch the National Home. It was obvious that the Jews would fight rather than be incorporated in an Arab-majority state. No British Government could force the Jews into such an entity (any more than any British Government could force Ulster Protestants into a Catholic-majority state).

In Palestine, the real possible alternatives were *either* partition *or* the destruction of the Yishuv by the Arabs.

For Britain, the real options were to impose partition, or to pull out and leave the Jews and Arabs to fight it out, or to stay and improvise.

The decision made, for the moment, was to stay and improvise. The improvisation took the form of crushing Arab rebellion in the present, combined with promising the Arabs an independent state in the future. It was a policy that seemed to work reasonably well in the short run. Palestine was to be quiet for most of the duration of the war. The quiet is more likely to have been due to the severity of the immediately preceding repression than to the promises of the 1939 White Paper. Arabs had heard promises before.

There are those who believe that if Britain had grasped the nettle and imposed partition, as Peel recommended, the subsequent bloodshed could have been avoided or lessened. The most that can reasonably be claimed, on that side, I think, is that imposed partition might have extricated *Britain* from Palestine, at a lower cost in blood, treasure and reputation than the course actually pursued. But British-imposed partition could not have averted, or significantly mitigated, the Arab-Jewish conflict. The Arabs would have tried to destroy a British-created Jewish State, just as they did seek to destroy the U.N.-created Jewish State. And the Jews would have tried to make use of that conflict, or some other opportunity, in order to expand the frontiers of their new state.

Weizmann and Ben-Gurion, together, favored the principle of partition, because it carried with it the Jewish State, even in truncated form. Under their guidance, the Twentieth Zionist Congress, meeting in Zurich in August 1937, approved, as has been said, "a course of action which amounted to the acceptance of partition in principle without saying so directly."[72] The Zionist Executive was authorized to negotiate with the Mandatory for the purpose of "ascertaining the precise [British] terms for the proposed establishment of a Jewish state."

The question, in all this, that remains of most interest today is: Were the Zionist leaders prepared to accept a truncated Jewish State permanently, or were they accepting it only as a stepping-stone to Biblical Eretz Israel? On that question statements by the three leading Zionists of the day—Weizmann, Ben-Gurion and Jabotinsky—are of interest.

Jabotinsky, and his Revisionists, were strongly against partition, and Jabotinsky spoke against it before the Peel Commission when he appeared before it in London on February 11, 1937, as one of its last witnesses. "A corner of Palestine, a 'canton'—how can we promise to be satisfied with it? We cannot. We never can. Should we swear to you we would be satisfied it would be a lie."[73]

The commission, already leaning toward partition, and influenced by Weizmann more than any other Zionist leader, clearly did not care for Jabotinsky, his evidence or his manner of implied superiority to other Zionist leaders. One member put to him the question: "You think you have the brains really?"

Jabotinsky replied: "It is a great question whether it requires more 'brains' to be straightforward than not to be straightforward. I do not know. It is a moot point, as I think you call it in English."[74]

I think that Jabotinsky was indeed more straightforward—and less diplomatic—than those Zionists who sought to give the British the impression that the kind of settlement recommended by the Peel Commission could be acceptable to Zionists as final.

As for Weizmann, universally accepted as the most moderate of the Zionist leaders, he wrote to a friend, after the publication of the report, that the boundaries proposed were "skimpy," but: "The Kingdom of David was smaller; under Solomon it became an Empire. Who knows? *C'est le premier pas qui compte.*"[75]

Weizmann was here in the direct line of Herzl, who had hoped to establish some kind of foothold in the area, perhaps in the *vilayet* of Beirut: "Then I would be a serious but friendly neighbour to the sanjak of Jerusalem, which I shall somehow acquire at the first opportunity."

As for the man who mattered most in this context, the leader of the Yishuv, David Ben-Gurion was altogether explicit about his intentions in a letter written to his son at the time of the Peel Commission. Ben-Gurion wrote:

> A . . . Jewish State in part of Palestine is not the end but the beginning. The establishment of such a Jewish State will serve as a means in our historical efforts to redeem the country in its entirety. We shall bring into the country all the Jews it can contain; we shall build a sound Jewish economy. We shall organize a sophisticated defense force—an elite army. I have no doubt that our army will be one of the best in the world. And then I am sure that we shall not be prevented from settling in all the other parts of the country, either through mutual understanding and agreement with our Arab neighbors or by other means.[76]

VIII

The Arab Revolt, suspended during the deliberations of the Peel Commission, broke out again in the autumn of 1937, following meetings of nationalists at Bludan, in Syria, and at Damascus in early September.[77] But this time the British Government's response was different, and harder. The Peel Commission had been severe on the earlier, softer responses: "If one thing stands out clear from the record of the Mandatory administration, it is the leniency with which Arab political agitation, even when carried to the point of violence and murder, has been treated."[78]

This verdict strengthened the hands of the soldiers, as against the Foreign Office. It became Government policy to give their military the necessary political backing to repress the rebellion and then— but only after the rebellion was clearly crushed—let the Foreign Office take over again. It was to be a textbook example of the old Imperial tactic of "coercion followed by conciliation."

On September 26, 1937, Lewis Andrews (1896–1937), Acting District Commissioner of the Galilee, was murdered. As it happened, Andrews had been the Government's liaison officer with the Peel Commission. This was "the first successful assault on the life of a high-ranking British civil servant, and regarded as an outright declaration of rebellion against British rule."[79]

The Government, ignoring the Higher Arab Committee's condemnation of the crime, put out warrants for the arrest of the H.A.C. members, and removed Haj Amin from his key post as head of the Supreme Muslim Council, which he had held for almost sixteen years. Haj Amin, fearing that, in this mood, the British might actually violate his sanctuary on the Haram esh-Sharif, secretly descended the Haram wall, dressed as a Bedouin, and made his way to Lebanon, where the French gave him asylum. He never returned to Palestine, but even in exile he continued to have more influence over its affairs than any other Arab politician.

On the following day (October 13) the Government further signaled the suspension of conciliation by deciding to remove the amiable Sir Arthur Wauchope from the High Commissionership. His place was to be taken in February 1938 by Sir Harold MacMichael (1882–1969), a colonial civil servant, blessed with good Arabic and no Hebrew, and therefore distrusted by the Jews; unjustly, as it turned out.

Widespread violence broke out throughout the country on October 14, 1937. It was the beginning of a full-scale revolt, which lasted, with major fluctuations, up to the end of 1938. Against it, the British Government this time applied severe military repression: military government, military courts, capital punishment of offenders, collective reprisals against villages.[80]

While coercion of the Arabs was still in progress, the first moves toward subsequent conciliation, and the abandonment of partition, were also taken. The Foreign Office fought hard and skillfully to destroy the partition plan and the Jewish State. The Colonial Office resisted, but with waning resolution. The decisive moment came in December 1937, when the Prime Minister, Neville Chamberlain, threw his great authority—within his own Cabinet—behind the Foreign Office approach, approving F.O.-revised terms of reference which left it open to the new Royal Commission to recommend against partition.[81] No change in policy was to be announced immediately, so that no impression might be given of a surrender to force.[82] Although the actual decisions at this time were purely procedural, they had— as often happens—substantive effect. From the time the Prime Minister came down on the side of the Foreign Office, partition was dead in reality, though officially still the policy approved by His Majesty's Government. So for nearly a year thereafter, the Arabs fought on, in order to kill a policy that was already dead, and the British fought them down, so as to be able to replace the dead policy, in a dignified way; with one they hoped would please those who were still trying to kill the dead one.

The Arab Revolt was so formidable and so sustained that the military authorities needed all the help they could get in repressing it. So they decided to enlist the cooperation of the Yishuv, which was of course forthcoming. Against the rebels the Mandatory made use not only of the Jewish elements in the legal constabulary (for general duties) but also of the illegal Hagana (for offensive operations). Hagana volunteers formed Special Night Squads under the command of the unorthodox pro-Zionist Orde Charles Wingate.[83]

There was a suspended double irony in this phase of Anglo-Jewish cooperation. The first irony was at the expense of the Jews. In helping the British with the first stage—coercion—of their currently unfolding policy, the Jews were speeding on the opening of the second stage: the conciliation by the British of the enemies of the Jews, the process which culminated in the White Paper of May 1939.

The second irony, and a sharper one, was at the expense of the British. The military training which they were providing for the Jews during this period would provide much of the stiffening for the Jewish revolt against the British themselves, less than ten years later. As Christopher Sykes observes: "From the circumstances of the second and more terrible phase of the Arab rebellion the Jews discovered that they were soldiers. Though this was a decisive event, its effect showed much later."[84]

The materials for that revolt were already accumulating, even in this phase of close cooperation. A section of the Jewish youth, maturing since the rise of Hitler, was now near desperation. This mood seems to have increased to something like frenzy following the Nazi annexation of Austria in March 1938, and the spectacle, in Vienna, of a public orgy of Jew baiting, such as had been thought to be inconceivable in a great modern center of civilization.

The outside world, while shocked by Nazi atrocities, did little to help the victims. A conference of thirty-one countries, which met at Evian in early July, did no more than confirm the validity of Weizmann's diagnosis, before the Peel Commission, of the condition of the European Jews in the late thirties: ". . . the world is divided into places where they cannot live and places into which they cannot enter." Palestine was excluded from the Evian agenda at the insistence of the British Government. It was hardly surprising, in these conditions, if a section of the Jewish youth in Palestine became fanaticized. (But Britain admitted more Jews to its home territory, in proportion to size and population, than did any other country, including my own, Ireland.) Such youths were drawn into the Revisionist armed units, which had now taken the name of National Military Organization: Irgun Zvai Leumi. They despised the Hagana policy of self-restraint (Havlaga) and believed in indiscriminate retaliation against members of the rival community. At the end of June 1938, the British hanged a Revisionist youth for shooting at an Arab bus. The Irgun retaliated, not against the British—for the moment—but against the Arabs, collectively. In July 1938, the Irgun exploded land mines in the fruit market in Haifa, killing 74 persons and wounding 129.[85] It was the most savage bout of terrorism yet experienced in Palestine.

All the official Zionist and Hagana leaders passionately condemned Irgun, which was repudiated by most of the Yishuv. The majority of the Yishuv stuck to Havlaga, indeed to an extent which impressed a contemporary Gentile observer as even possibly excessive: "The policy of self-restraint now made demands which went beyond human nature and it was inevitable that Havlaga would become modified. Even so it remains a very extraordinary thing that the essential policy not only was retained but was conscientiously adhered to by the Jewish majority. The exceptions, however, were much wider than they had been."[86] In another context, the same observer points out that "the moral price that the Jews paid for this moral feat was the growth of a certain lack of confidence in their ability to fight back. . . ."[87]

What Irgun represented was the refusal of some Jews to pay that moral price. Irgun retained enough support to play an important part in the emergence of the State of Israel, and—as a tradition—in its subsequent history.

IX

In the first phase of the Arab Revolt, the Foreign Office had warned that "a wave of anti-British feeling [was bound to] spread over the Arab and Muslim world if the Arabs and their friends are able to represent that His Majesty's Government are not prepared to give the Arabs a square deal. . . ."[88]

This prediction was put to the test, in the period from the summer of 1937 to the late autumn of 1938, and it was scarcely borne out during that period. Throughout this time partition, as recommended by the Peel Commission, remained the official policy of the British Government. In the early part of the period, it was really the policy; in the later, only ostensibly so; but the policy was officially reaffirmed before the League of Nations as late as September 17, 1938,[89] and it was not explicitly abandoned until November 1938. The Government appeared, throughout the repression of the Arab Revolt, as committed to the creation of a Jewish State. Against that commitment, the Arab Revolt was directed. It was a determined, brave, widespread revolt, and the Government repressed it with a severity never before experienced under the Mandate. In that repression, the Government called on, and received, the aid of Jewish settlers against the Arab patriots, while at the same time other Jewish settlers perpetrated atrocities against Arab civilians. The leaders of the Palestine Arabs were jailed or deported. The most conspicuous, and venerated, of all those leaders, the Grand Mufti of the Third Holiest Muslim City, was forced into exile by the British.

One might think that if there were any possible conditions existing inside Palestine which could have caused the Arab and Muslim world in general to revolt against the British, those conditions were met in 1937–1938. But there was no revolt outside Palestine. The reactions of the Arab dynasts were extremely cautious. The Palestinian leaders had called, from the beginning, on the Arab kings and Governments to come to the rescue. Immediately after the publication of the partition proposal, the Higher Arab Committee had implored the Arab rulers "in the name of the sacred land . . . your Arab chivalry and your religious obligations, to work for rescuing the country from imperialism, Jewish colonization and partition."

The response, at least at the official Arab level, was meager enough. Of the Arab states within the British sphere, only Iraq and later Egypt made any public protest (at the League of Nations).[90] Emir Abdullah of Transjordan, King Ibn Saud of Saudi Arabia and Imam Yahya of Yemen sent evasive replies.[91] Volunteers in significant numbers from Arab countries joined the Palestinians in their fight,[92] but there was no attempt, throughout the period of the revolt, at any kind of concerted action by the Arab Governments against Britain. The principal sufferers, outside Palestine, from the revolt and its repression were not the British, but the Jews of the rest of the Middle East, numbering about a quarter of a million people. An anti-Jewish drive gained momentum in the summer of 1938, especially in Iraq, Syria and Lebanon. The way was prepared for the later exodus of the Jews in question to Israel.

There was a good deal of popular, semiofficial and official—but disavowable—support for the Palestinian rebels. This mostly took the form of fund raising—mainly in Iraq—and propaganda. The Governments—even the Iraqis—did their best to discourage the supply of arms to the Palestinians.[93] There does not seem to have been any question of the use of arms outside Palestine against the British.

Thus the wave of anti-British feeling had proved nothing like as strong as had been feared. Yet there were some good grounds for continued apprehension on this point. One reason for the British success in dealing with the revolt was that the Axis had made remarkably little effort to exploit Britain's difficulties either in Palestine itself or in the region.[94] There was some propaganda effort, more anti-Jewish than anti-British, but apart from that nothing, much to the disappointment of Arab leaders, including the Mufti, of Nazi representatives in Arab capitals and of the German population in Palestine itself, the so-called "Templars." One reason for this restraint in Berlin was the attitude of the German Foreign Office, the head of whose Middle Eastern Division, Otto von Hentig, advised, at the beginning of the second phase of the Palestinian revolt, that it would be "out of the question" to support the Arabs with arms or money, "since the Arab states were at best lukewarm on the issue."[95] But the basic reason for this German restraint was probably Hitler's known high opinion of the British Empire, and his long-held conviction that a deal could eventually be done, on the basis of German respect for the Empire and British respect for German expansion in Europe.

In the event of war between Britain and Germany, Hitler's reasons for restraint would obviously cease to operate. Arab revolts, backed and/or exploited by Germany and Italy, might prove more formidable than anything yet known. And the British were concerned by signs of new and growing interest in Egypt—the most strategically sensitive country in the area—in the Palestine cause. This growing interest culminated in the holding in Cairo, in October 1938, of an Inter-parliamentary Arab Congress which passed resolutions rejecting Zionism and partition and called for the establishment of a parliamentary government in Palestine.[96] This was part of a growing self-assertion, against Britain, of Egyptian nationalism.

In the following month, the British Government, having announced its abandonment of partition and the Jewish State, invited the Governments of Iraq and Egypt to prepare the way for a conference in London over Palestine with the participation of the Arab states. The fact that this decision was made at the height of the Czechoslovak crisis, which was to be temporarily resolved by the Munich agreement, did nothing to lessen a general Jewish conviction that all this was part and parcel of a general system of appeasement.

The arguments on the other side are well summarized by Christopher Sykes:

> The concern of the Arabic-speaking world with Palestine was not a chimera imagined by orientalists and Arabophils. It was a real fact and an extremely dangerous one. It tended to make the Arab world friendly-disposed to Nazi Germany, and a large part of the oil resources of Britain were situated in the Arab world. To have opened a major quarrel with Arab states

when Europe was moving towards war would have been an act of folly by Great Britain without precedent.[97]

X

The London Conference on the future of Palestine was held in St. James's Palace. It was attended by the representatives of five Arab countries—Egypt, Saudi Arabia, Iraq, Yemen and Transjordan—as well as by a Palestinian delegation (which was split between followers of the Mufti and people who were frightened of him),[98] the Zionist Executive and of course the British hosts. It was really more like a demonstration than a conference. Its very composition seemed to demonstrate the strategic and numerical importance of Arabs, as against Jews. Its proceedings and procedures demonstrated the impossibility—already avowed by the Peel Commission—of finding any solution acceptable to both the Arabs and the Jews. The three sets of representatives did not meet together, in one conference, but separately: British with Arabs, and British with Jews. The Palestinian Arabs would not meet the Jews at all, or be in the same room with them.

There were some joint meetings between the Zionists and the leaders of the Arab states (without the Palestinians). At one of these, Aly Maher of Egypt made a courteously worded appeal to the Zionists to stop, or at least limit, immigration to Palestine. Weizmann was interested in the spirit of Maher's appeal, but Ben-Gurion, followed by the rest of the delegation, was adamant in rejecting the appeal altogether. In a striking—and to me convincing—image, Ben-Gurion compared an appeal to the Jews, in 1939, to stop immigration into Palestine to asking a woman in labor to stop birth.[99]

This "conference" could not, and did not, result in any agreement. It broke up on March 17, 1939, two days after Hitler's occupation of Prague, the event that ended the process, and the hope, of appeasement in Europe.

The proceedings at St. James's Palace had no other function except to prepare the way for an "imposed solution," or rather a unilateral statement, from the British Government, which would be much more favorable to the Arabs than any official statement since the beginning of the Mandate. This was the famous White Paper of May 1939.[100]

The main provisions of the White Paper were: no partition; no Jewish State; an independent Palestine State (technically not just an Arab State) within ten years; Jewish immigration, after five years, would not be allowed "unless the Arabs of Palestine were prepared to acquiesce in it."

Those were the "pro-Arab" parts, making up most of the document. But there were also two provisos, highly unwelcome to the Arabs, intended to make the package that much less obnoxious to the Jews. These were that a further 75,000 Jews would be admitted within the five-year period, and that the independence of a Palestinian State depended on adequate safeguards for the Jewish community.

The point about Jewish "safeguards" balanced the one about Arab "acquiescence." As has been well said: "Thus a sort of double veto was established. The Arabs could block the growth of the National Home. The Jews might prevent the attainment of national independence."[101] In theory, the double veto was supposed to promote negotiation between the two parties. As Herbert Samuel put it sardonically, in the House of Lords debate: "Each side is given a veto on the aspirations of the other in order to induce both to become friends."[102] And he added, speaking out of bitter experience: "Both of them will, of course, exercise their veto."

But if that indeed were to happen, there was a contingent benefit, from the point of view of the strategic and Imperial interests of the Mandatory. "This formula [the double veto] could serve as a means to ensure the continuation of British rule in Palestine. After the conclusion of the Anglo-Egyptian Treaty [of 1936] which enabled Britain to keep troops in Egypt for an additional twenty years only, unlimited British presence in Palestine became a necessity in the minds of British military strategists in the late 1930s."[103]

"Divide and rule" is often a fatuous slogan when it is taken to mean that divisions among subject peoples are created by their rulers. But rulers can make use of genuine, and deep, divisions among their subjects in order to justify—and with some weight—their continuing rule. The double veto in the White Paper of 1939 seems a classic example of this phenomenon.[104]

The legality of the White Paper, in terms of the Mandate, was open to question, and was hotly contested by the Jews. The Permanent Mandates Commission, reporting to the Council of the League, found unanimously "that the policy set out in the White Paper was not in accordance with the interpretation which, in agreement with the Mandatory Power and the Council, the Commission had placed upon the Palestine Mandate." The Council's consent was required, under Article 27 of the Mandate, for any change in its terms. But the outbreak of war put an end to the League's active life, and the Council never met to consider the matter.[105] After the war, the Charter of the United Nations (Article 79) provided that the status of the existing Mandates should be decided by the Mandatory, "in conjunction with the states directly concerned." Probably by no coincidence, this proviso favored a continuation, or extension, of the White Paper policy—taking "the states directly concerned" as the participants in the 1939 conference in St. James's Palace.

Obviously, a matter of this kind is not to be determined just by legal argument; obviously also, the relation of the League to the various Mandates—as to much else—had been not much more than window dressing. All the same, the peremptory manner in which the Mandate had been drastically revised by the Mandatory itself did have a practical significance for the future. What it conveyed to most Zionists, and to the Yishuv in particular, was that Britain was openly treating the Mandate, and indeed the League itself, as a superannuated legal fiction, and also treating the Balfour Declaration as an outworn commitment. Britain now appeared almost openly in a role which British policy had hitherto been at pains to camouflage: that of a power which was in Palestine by right of conquest, and whose authority to determine the future of Palestine rested ultimately on force. Those who passionately opposed the new policy were encouraged, by the circumstances of its promulgation, to begin to think of force both as legitimate and as the only means of challenging the White Paper policy effectively, when the time should come.

Up to now the British, when they thought of rebellion in Palestine, had always thought of *Arab* rebellion. But what was now beginning to take shape—though its actual eruption was postponed—was *Jewish* revolt, starting from the conviction that the White Paper was the negation of the National Home. As Jabotinsky wrote from Warsaw: "Even the Jewish sigh 'Next year in Jerusalem' becomes anti-British."[106] A Jewish historian has written: "Had the War not interfered, the revolt in Palestine would have continued, but with one change—the rebels would have been . . . the Hagana and . . . other [Jewish] underground organizations as well, instead of the Arab rebels. The war changed everything for the Jews."[107]

XI

The negotiations which culminated in the White Paper of 1939 have been called, by a historian of the subject, "the high-water mark of Arab diplomacy over Palestine."[108] Yet the Arab response to their own victory was entirely negative, at least in public. The Higher Arab Committee, meeting in Beirut, rejected the White Paper—contrary to the advice of Egypt and Iraq—as "totally inadequate." Then the Arab states,[109] beginning with Egypt, successively rejected a document which they had done so much to shape, and which they privately regarded with some satisfaction. Another durable pattern was emerging. The Arab states, contrary to some British hopes, were not able to exert any moderating influence over the Palestinians. On the contrary, the influence of the Palestinians over the Arab states was sufficient to induce these to fall into line, in their public declarations, with a Palestinian intransigence which the Iraqis and the Egyptians at least privately deplored. The Saudis, for their part, were too prudent to be drawn into any displays of moderation perceptible to the Palestinians. Their diplomacy too has had a remarkable degree of consistency. There was yet another durable factor: political assassination. In the latter period of the Arab Revolt, the Mufti's people had concentrated on murdering Arabs regarded by them as traitors. Advocates of acceptance of the White Paper were now so classified.

It has been claimed that the White Paper "did succeed very imperfectly but in the main, in its primary object":[110] that of eliminating Arab hostility to Britain during the Second World War. As against that, Weizmann argued that Iraq's attempted defection to the Axis in 1941 demonstrated the failure of the White Paper. To that, the obvious—and equally unprovable—counter is to say that the troubles would have been even worse without the White Paper. And so on.

The policies in fact pursued by the Arab states during the war were those of "wait and see"; what Sykes calls, in the case of Ibn Saud, "benevolent neutrality." Is not this precisely the policy one would expect to see pursued, in the circumstances, by prudent Muslim rulers, with no particular reason to trust any of the non-Muslim powers concerned, or any of their promises or declarations? Would they really have rallied to the Allied side if there had been no Balfour Declaration, or to the Axis side if there had been no White Paper? It seems unlikely.

It is true that the rulers in question had to take some account of the attitudes of their subjects, which were anti-Zionist, anti-British, anti-French and pro-Axis. But how could the White Paper work to mollify the attitudes of these subjects, since it was rejected by their own leaders, and scornfully denounced by the Palestinian leader who had by far the greatest following inside and outside Palestine—Haj Amin?

Whatever the effects of the White Paper outside Palestine, its effects inside Palestine were clear. The mixed population of Palestine, always hitherto divided on all political matters, was now agreed on wanting an end of British rule, for which Arabs and Jews each hoped to substitute their own. From now until the end of the Mandate— since the White Paper was never rescinded—[111] the Mandatory ruled in Palestine without the consent of either section of the population.

XII

The main response of the Yishuv leadership, under Ben-Gurion, in the months between the publication of the White Paper and the outbreak of war, was increased illegal immigration, bringing in as many as possible of the Jews trying to get out of Europe, as the area under Nazi domination expanded and Nazi ferocity became increasingly open. The British responded to illegal immigration partly by police efforts, and partly by deducting estimated "illegals" from the already reduced quotas available for legal entries, and also by efforts to induce Balkan states to close their borders to Jewish refugees. The British also brought to an end the phase of military cooperation with Hagana which had marked the later phases of the Arab Revolt. The Hagana leadership prepared to go underground.

The Jewish Agency, despite its officially recognized role within the Mandatory system, repudiated Mandatory policy in the matter of immigration. The Jewish people, it stated, regarded the suspension of immigration "as devoid of any moral justification and based only on the use of force. . . . It is not the Jewish refugees returning to their homeland who are violating the law but those who are endeavouring to deprive them of the supreme right of every human being—the right to live."[112]

When even the official representatives of the Jews,[113] hitherto so cautious, felt obliged to hold to language of that order, it is not surprising that some Revisionists felt entitled to meet force with force.

That summer, High Commissioner MacMichael reported that "the general attitude of the Jews is one of calculated resentment plus periodical acts of violence."[114] Just one month later, on the very eve of the war (August 26), the Irgun committed its first major act of anti-British terrorism, laying a trap mine which killed two British police inspectors.

The Twenty-first Zionist Congress, which was to be the last before the Holocaust, met in Geneva from August 16 to 26, 1939. Officially, the Congress declared its unremitting hostility to the policy of the White Paper, at the same time proclaiming its unwavering support of Britain in her defense of democracy in the Western world.[115]

Of greater significance for the future was Ben-Gurion's statement to the Congress which constitutes a kind of informal Declaration of Independence on behalf of the Yishuv: "The White Paper had created a vacuum which must be filled by the Jews themselves. The Jews should act as though they were the State in Palestine, and should so act until there would be a Jewish state there. In those matters in which there were infringements by the Government, the Jews should act as if they were the State."[116]

The Twenty-first Congress broke up earlier than planned because of the announcement of the Hitler-Stalin Pact (August 23, 1939). There is a photograph of the Congress platform, taken just after the news of the pact broke. In a small group—the copy before me shows twelve heads fully—four, including Weizmann, have a hand over their face or their head. Ben-Gurion, beside Weizmann, has his head bowed over his hands, which are crossed on his chest. They do not look like men who have just heard a piece of political news. They look like people who have heard a death sentence pronounced on members of their family.

The pact meant, of course, that the jaws of a trap were about to close on what an older German enemy, Treitschke, had called "the inexhaustible Polish cradle" of European Jewry.

Winding up the Congress, on the day after the news of the pact, President Weizmann said: "It is my duty at this solemn hour to tell England . . . we have grievances . . . But above our regret and bitterness are higher interests. What the democracies are fighting for is the minimum . . . necessary for Jewish life. Their anxiety is our anxiety. Their war our war."[117]

Ben-Gurion's position was similar in terms of immediate policy, but significantly different, both in tone and in implications: "We shall fight the war as if there were no White Paper, and the White Paper as if there were no war."

Weizmann was speaking as the leader of an international movement; Ben-Gurion, as the *de facto* head of a new and unrecognized state.

XIII

As long as Nazi victory seemed a real possibility, fighting the war remained, for the Yishuv, a matter of far greater urgency and importance than fighting the White Paper. Up to the end of 1941, 10,881 Jewish soldiers were enlisted in all branches of the British forces,[118] and by the end of 1942, some 18,800 were serving—approximately twice the number of Arab recruits, from a much larger population.[119] The Jews pressed for the formation of large Jewish units—indeed a Jewish Army—but the British resisted this pressure, partly because of fear of repercussions in Arab lands, but more because of a reasonable fear that they might find themselves fighting such an army if they tried to implement the White Paper after the war. The British were suspicious of the fact that Hagana—now, in Zionist terminology, "comrades not in uniform"—retained its structure intact, and to a lesser extent, they tended to be wary about armed Jews, even in British uniform.

The White Paper's constitutional provisions remained in suspense for the duration and never of course came into effect. But the immigration restrictions were fully maintained, and as the war went on, and the Jews of Europe became increasingly desperate, it was British rigidity on immigration which gave new life to the idea of fighting the White Paper, and eventually turned that into simply fighting the British.

In 1939–1940, however, almost the whole Yishuv was wholeheartedly in support of the British. The Irgun not only dropped its prewar terrorist tendency, but worked particularly closely with the British during this period. The pro-British spirit, which was a paradoxical and erratic part of the Revisionist heritage from Jabotinsky (who died in 1940), became dominant under David Raziel (1910–1941), who was head of Irgun until his death in action in May 1941. Strangely, in the light of later events, the symbiosis between the Irgun and British intelligence became so close at one time that the language

Opposite top, Revisionist (hard-line Zionist) meeting in Warsaw, 1939. Menachem Begin is at lower left; his mentor, Vladimir Jabotinsky, at lower right. In August of that year, Jabotinsky told Ben-Gurion's mainstream Zionist associate Berl Katznelson: "You have won. You have the rich American Jews. We had only the poor Polish Jews, and they are gone."

Opposite bottom, The Twenty-first Congress of Zionists, Geneva, August 1939: the last before the war and the Holocaust. Participants in this Congress heard the news of the Russian-German pact. "They do not look like men who have just heard a piece of political news. They look like people who have heard a death sentence passed on members of their own family."

Right, Avraham Stern (1907–1942), head of *Lehi,* known to the British as "the Stern Gang." Offered to help the Germans take Palestine from the British "in exchange for a Hebrew State and the transfer of the Jews of Europe to that State." These "monstrous proposals were the only ones that corresponded to the monstrous predicament of the European Jews" (author).

Below, The *Struma,* an unseaworthy cattle boat carrying 769 Jewish refugees, sank in the Black Sea in February 1942, having been cast adrift by the Turks after its passengers had been refused entry visas to Palestine. The loss of the *Struma* is commemorated in the monument to the Holocaust at Yad Vashem.

CENTRAL ZIONIST ARCHIV

Karadenizde Çankaya motörü nasıl battı?

Karadenize çıktıktan sonra, bir infilâk neticesinde batan ve içinde 769 Yahudi bulunan Struma vapurunun limanımızda alınmış bir' res mi

of C.I.D. reports took on the color of Revisionist ideology, with the Irgun appearing as a kind of Jewish Tories (the "national movement" defending Western values) while the Hagana represents "the Left."[120]

Irgun's policy of close cooperation with the British was inherently unstable. A section of Irgun rejected the policy altogether. This section, headed by Avraham Stern (1907–1942), was known in the Yishuv as Lehi and to the British as "the Stern Gang." Lehi's extremism seemed very close to insanity. In January 1941, Lehi made an offer to Hitler, through Beirut and the German Consulate at Ankara. The message of their envoy, Naphtali Lubentchik, was that Lehi was prepared to "assist in the conquest of Palestine, and its delivery from the British to the Germans, in exchange for a Hebrew state and the transfer of the Jews of Europe to that state."[121]

At first sight, this offer seems so bizarre and so repulsive that one might be inclined to dismiss it as a mere freak, of no general significance. This would be unwise for two main reasons.

First, the idea is not so wildly deviant, in a Zionist sense, as it may sound. It is in fact Herzlian, in its scale, in its scope, in its messianic drama, in its disdain for material obstacles and in its willingness to shake hands with the Devil in the cause of the liberation of the Jews. Allowing for the differences between peacetime and wartime, Lubentchik's mission to Beirut was analogous to Herzl's mission to St. Petersburg to meet Plehve in 1903. And the logic of the mission to Plehve had in fact been quietly accepted by the modern Zionists, from 1933 to 1939, in the Ha'avara transactions.

Second, Lehi's monstrous proposals were the only ones that corresponded to the monstrous predicament of the European Jews. The sane and rational policies of Weizmann and Ben-Gurion were geared to something much less than that scarcely imaginable reality. To be the wartime allies of the Power that closed the gates of Palestine to the European Jews made sense—from a Zionist point of view—only on the assumption that most of the European Jews would be still there, after the war, when the gates of Palestine were to be forced open. Weizmann, like Herzl before him, had had a sense of impending disaster, long in advance. But even Weizmann does not seem to have fully imagined the scale of the disaster, once it was directly impending. Avraham Stern was almost alone in realizing that if the Jews of Europe were to be saved at all, they would have to be saved *during the war*. That could be done only by a deal with Hitler. Such a deal was obviously improbable, but it was not altogether inconceivable.

Hitler loved dramatic turnings of the tables—as he showed in 1939 and 1941—and this one would have been extremely embarrassing to Britain, especially in its relations with America.

In the event, nothing came of the idea. Stern's envoy, Lubentchik, was arrested at Acre on his return from Beirut; it has been supposed that the Irgun leadership, then bitterly hostile to Lehi, may have denounced him to the British. Stern himself was tracked down, just over a year later, by the British police, aided by both Hagana and Irgun, and shot dead in his hiding place in the course of capture.[122]

In his lifetime, Avraham Stern was almost universally regarded, in the Yishuv, as a dangerous lunatic. Today, many Israelis, though certainly not all, regard him as a hero and martyr.

In the Yishuv, in the early years of the war, Irgun was on the margin; Lehi, on the margin of a margin. Ben-Gurion was the leader; never an unquestioned leader, but one whose lead was always followed by most of the people. After the events of May 1940 in Europe, when Churchill replaced Chamberlain, Ben-Gurion shifted the emphasis of his policy: more on fighting the war, less on fighting the White Paper. "Victory," he wrote on July 15, 1940: "the participation of the maximum Jewish force in the defense of Palestine and in bringing about Hitler's defeat—that, to my way of thinking, has to be our whole program of activity until the victory."[123]

Churchill was a friend to the Jews, and to Zionism. The Yishuv now hoped—and many assumed—that the White Paper, that product of appeasement, would be automatically discarded, once Churchill had replaced Chamberlain. But the White Paper was not just, or mainly, a product of appeasement. It represented a still-dominant way of thinking, strategically and diplomatically, about the defense of the Empire in the nerve centers of the Middle East. And the same chain of great events—beginning with the German invasion of the Low Countries—which brought Churchill to power on May 10, also brought Italy into the war. This brought the war closer to the Middle East. And that in turn reinforced the arguments in favor of respecting the immigration provisions of the White Paper: that is, keeping Jews out of Palestine in order not to antagonize Arabs.

At the same time the events of the summer of 1940, by greatly widening the area of Nazi rule in Europe, and creating an overall atmosphere of Nazi irresistibility, sent increasing members of Jews in quest of the one remaining possible haven: Palestine.

Thus these events simultaneously strengthened the British barriers around Palestine *and* hurled more Jews against those barriers. It is hardly surprising that the Anglo-Jewish *rapprochement* desired by both Ben-Gurion and Churchill—and especially by Weizmann—never came to much as regards Palestine.

The event which did most to turn many Jews even against Churchill's Britain, even during the most dangerous phase of the war with Hitler, was the affair of the *Struma*. The *Struma* was an unseaworthy cattle boat carrying 769 Jewish refugees from the Romanian Black Sea port of Constanza in the direction of Palestine. From Istanbul, in December 1941, the refugees applied for entry visas. The Colonial Office, under Lord Moyne, rejected the applications. The Turks then had the *Struma* turned back into the Black Sea and cast adrift. She sank on February 24, 1942. There were only two°survivors, who were then admitted to Palestine "as an act of clemency." The grief and indignation of the Jewish people over the fate of the *Struma's* passengers were intense and left a bitter memory. The event is commemorated at Yad Vashem, the memorial to the victims of the Holocaust.

It was in the angry aftermath of the loss of the *Struma*—in April 1942—that the young Menachem Begin (1913–   ), then a soldier in the Polish army-in-exile, first came to Palestine. Begin had been a disciple of Jabotinsky's, whose mantle he was shortly to assume. But even in his master's lifetime, Begin had criticized Jabotinsky for being too pro-British. Begin now threw his personal influence against Irgun's established policy of cooperation with the British. While rejecting Lehi's policy of seeking alliance with Hitler, he sought to draw together the whole underground, including Lehi, in preparation for a Jewish war of liberation against the British.

Begin's ideas were clear-cut, which has always been his strength. But the actual Jewish-British relationship in Palestine during the war went to extremes of ambivalence. Jews were roused to fury by each odious new manifestation of Britain's immigration policy. To Jewish denunciations of these, the British responded with a cold, contemptuous anger at what they regarded as Zionist exploitation of human misery, for political ends, in time of war. And yet the Jews continued to serve in the British forces, and the British knew that if the war reached Palestine, the Jews were the only element in the population on whose support against the Germans they could count. This led the British Army, in times of apparent military danger, to ignore the forebodings of the civilian authorities and to provide special training for Hagana units.

Thus, in the first half of 1941, after the loss of Greece and Crete seemed to leave the Middle East open to attack, the British trained Jewish commando units, the first elements of the famous Palmah—the "strategic reserve of the Hagana"[124]—which took part in the campaigns of Iraq and Syria in the summer of that year. The Irgun commander, David Raziel, was killed in the course of an operation in Iraq.

Strangely, the period in which the foundations of the closest British-Jewish military cooperation were laid was also the period of the greatest wartime Jewish-British confrontation: the *Struma* period, December 1941 to February 1942.

This was a time when Rommel's forces were advancing on Egypt, and when many expected the German forces in Russia to win an outright victory in the following summer. Palestine might be attacked from the west, or from the north—which the British originally thought more probable. The British thought they might be forced to evacuate Palestine, and they wanted to leave behind them a trained Jewish guerrilla force to harry the German occupiers.

In these conditions the British set up a training school at Kibbutz Mishmar Haemek, where Jewish volunteers—members of *kibbutzim* and of the Palmah—received intensive instruction in such subjects as sabotage, demolition and partisan warfare throughout the summer of 1942.[125]

By the autumn of 1942, the perceived danger of a German invasion was over. Rommel's advance was checked at the first battle of El Alamein in July, and Rommel was decisively defeated at Second Alamein in October. In Russia, the German forces prepared for the winter that was to end in Stalingrad. Palestine was never again in danger from the Germans.

The end of the danger ended also the period of "irregular" British-Jewish military cooperation. But that period had lasting results. As Professor Bauer says: "For the first time an independent Jewish force was created. It was to become an appreciable factor in the defense of the country." "The country" here means not British Palestine but the Yishuv and Eretz Israel.

As it worked out, the combination of British civilian and military policies toward Palestine, during the war, resulted in furnishing the Yishuv with both the motivation and the means to fight both the British and the Arabs, at the end of the war, for the freedom of the Jewish State.

If Jabotinsky had lived into the summer of 1942, in Palestine, he might have found himself beginning to make out again, in a disturbing shape, the outlines of that "little track."

XIV

During the period when the war seemed to be going badly for the Allies—up to the autumn of 1942—there were some good grounds for the Foreign Office's fears of an Axis-supported Arab revolt. Haj Amin, in various places of exile, did his considerable best to foment just that, and succeeded, in one instance.

The beginning of the war found the Mufti in Allied territory, Beirut, which he left in October 1939, to take up residence in Baghdad, capital of the sovereign (though treaty-bound) state of Iraq. That the French should be glad to be rid of the Mufti is understandable. What is very odd is that the British should have had no objection to the arrival, in the most sensitive and most unstable area of their sphere of influence, of a person of whose incendiary powers they had recent experience. The Foreign Office seems to have imagined that the Mufti could somehow be made to serve the Allied cause, through the benign influence of Nuri Said Pasha. "If so," as Nuri's biographer observes without overstatement, "a miscalculation would seem to have been made."[126]

The Mufti was feted in Baghdad, as an Arab and Muslim hero, and put himself at the center of a pro-Axis political effort which culminated, in early 1941—with the Germans apparently winning, and approaching the Middle East—in a pro-Axis coup headed (ultimately) by Rashid Ali. On May 9, when hostilities had already broken out between Iraqi and British forces, the Mufti issued a *fatwa*, an "official ruling on a point of Islamic law,"[127] broadcast over Iraqi and Axis radios, declaring *jihad* (holy war) against Britain. The British, according to the *fatwa*, "have profaned the el-Aqsa Mosque and have declared the most unyielding war against Islam, both in deed and in word. The Prime Minister at that time [presumably Neville Chamberlain] told Parliament that the world would never see peace as long as the Koran existed. What hatred against Islam is stronger than that which publicly declares the Sacred Koran an enemy of human kind?"[128]

It was a poor return for so many years of scrupulous respect for

Muslim sensibilities—and of sedulous cultivation of the Mufti. The British intervened, from Amman, and defeated Rashid Ali's forces. The Germans promised support, but it failed to arrive in time.

British forces entered Baghdad. But before they did, the last days of free Baghdad were spent in a pogrom in which several hundred of the city's Jews perished at the hands of the Mufti's followers.

As the Germans had proposed to use Syrian airfields, with Vichy collaboration, to bring help to Rashid Ali, the British and the Free French took Syria from Vichy in the following month. The Mufti escaped—again—from Baghdad, along with Rashid Ali, and took refuge in Teheran. When Soviet and British forces jointly occupied Iran, in September 1941, the Mufti escaped yet again, and eventually made his way to Berlin. This latest exploit of the Mufti's was appropriately greeted by the great *Daily Express* columnist Beachcomber: "Unofficial spokesmen, out of touch with authoritative sources, are saying that the elusive Mufti cheated. We hid our eyes, and counted up to a hundred but the Mufti shouted 'Cuckoo!', and ran away for the fourth time."

This Arab revolt would no doubt have become a more formidable affair if the Germans had given it more encouragement and support. There was widespread Arab sympathy with Rashid Ali and the Mufti, and little spontaneous Arab support for the Allied cause. Brigadier J. B. Glubb—whose well-trained Arab Legion, from Transjordan, took part in Britain's Iraq campaign—noted that except for his own Legion, "every Arab force . . . previously organized by us mutinied and refused to fight for us, or faded away in desertions"[129] at the time of the Iraqi revolt.

The revolt came, from a German point of view, at a very bad time, when German resources were already fully preempted for the invasion of Russia (June 21). But there were also political reasons against wholehearted commitment to the Arab cause. Hitler had to think about Vichy's susceptibilities (and the Arab territories Vichy controlled) and those of Mussolini, to whom he had promised Egypt. Also, the Nazis, as they sometimes showed, did not feel too comfortable about helping people as low down on "the human ladder" as the Arabs were to pull down even enemies whose places were on the upper rungs.

All the same, Hitler was mildly interested in the Mufti, and continued to offer him some vague encouragement. After Hitler had received him in Berlin, on November 21, 1941, and lectured him for ninety minutes, the Mufti recorded in his diary the Fuehrer's message, beginning with the words: "The objectives of my fight are clear. Primarily, I am fighting the Jews without respite, and this fight includes the fight against the so-called Jewish National Home in Palestine."[130]

But Hitler also made it clear that he would do nothing at all for the Arabs for the moment, not even issue the pro-Arab declaration for which the Mufti was begging. After Germany had defeated Russia, there would be time enough for that. When German forces reach the southern Caucasus "then the hour of the liberation of the Arabs will have arrived. Germany has no ambitions in this area but cares only to annihilate the power which produces the Jews."[131]

The Mufti, with his blond hair and blue eyes, made a relatively favorable impression on Hitler: "Despite his sharp physiognomy resembling a mouse, he is a person who has among his ancestors more than one Aryan with probably the best Roman heritage."[132] But probably more revealing of Hitler's real attitude was his social behavior on the occasion of that meeting, as recalled by his interpreter: "Hitler refused either to shake the Mufti's hand, when held out to him, or to offer him coffee."[133]

Haj Amin stayed in Germany for the duration of the war, but in a role of diminishing significance, once the war receded from the Middle East. One witness at Nuremberg claimed that the Mufti played an important part in devising the Final Solution, but the testimony is unsupported and seems improbable. It is certain that he repeatedly exerted himself to prevent Jewish emigration from the territories of Germany's allies.

At the end of the war, the Mufti, once more, "escaped," this time via Berne and Paris to Beirut. In 1948, he was able once again to preach *jihad* against the new State of Israel.

XV

As the war progressed, it became increasingly clear to the Zionist leadership that the key to the future lay in America. Both Weizmann and Ben-Gurion paid several visits to the United States, with partially conflicting purposes. In the summer of 1940, Churchill pressed Weizmann to go to America "in order to stimulate Jewish and general opinion in favor of the anti-Nazi cause."[134] Churchill placed so much value on this idea, at this time, that he even promised Weizmann the integrated Jewish fighting force for which the Zionists were looking.

The hopes which Churchill placed in American Jewry were misplaced at this period. American Jews, like almost all other Jews, wanted an Allied victory. But the very obviousness of this fact made it almost impossible for them to influence general American public opinion about the war. This was forcibly brought home to Ben-Gurion when he visited the United States in late 1940. One prominent Jew, asked for support for the Allies and the Yishuv, sympathized but said he could do nothing "publicly."

> Ben Gurion then asked him, "Which are you first, a Jew or an American?" The answer: "A Jew. We are a minority here. If I stand up and demand American aid for Britain, people will say after the war that dirty Jews got us into it, that it was a Jewish war, that it was for their sakes that our sons died in battle." Ben-Gurion reported that he had found this attitude prevalent in all the Zionist groups with whom he spoke.[135]

But from December 1941 on, after America's entry into the war, the general climate of opinion became much more favorable to Jews and Jewish causes. Only the most rabid anti-semite could blame the Jews for Pearl Harbor. And anti-semitism was now the ideology of America's enemies, an unpatriotic creed. The sort of constraints that had previously affected the Jews were now felt, even more uncomfortably, by the enemies of the Jews.

Zionism had been growing fast in America, since the rise of Hitler, and by 1942, most Jews were Zionists. Sympathy with the victims of Hitlerite persecution had always been general in America, but it became identical with patriotism when Hitler declared war on the United States, in support of the Japanese.

Conditions were therefore favorable, in 1942, for an intensified Zionist effort, and this was made at a special and historic conference of representatives of all American Zionists held in the Biltmore Hotel, in New York City, in May 1942.

Both Weizmann and Ben-Gurion addressed the Biltmore Conference. Although it was Weizmann who seems to have made the more favorable impression on the conference, it was Ben-Gurion who made the resolutions of the conference serve his revolutionary ends in Palestine.

Ben-Gurion and Weizmann were now seriously antagonistic to each other, as Ben-Gurion increasingly claimed the role of active leadership for himself. Part of the antagonism was due to what are called "personality differences," which sometimes turn out to be "personality similarities" deep down. Both were secretive and could be devious. Professor Bauer seems to hit off this aspect very neatly when he writes: "The president [Weizmann] was not always fastidiously candid even with his friends. At times his most intimate friends did not know of business he was carrying on. Of course, similar assertions were uttered by various elements about Ben-Gurion as well, and certainly with no less justification."[136]

Far more important was the divergence between the two great leaders, not on basic policy indeed, but on major strategy, and in spirit. Weizmann still hoped for a peaceful, negotiated solution, involving the British, and possibly some sort of federation with an Arab state or states. Ben-Gurion, while not altogether dismissing such hopes, was braced for some kind of fight, with either the British or the Arabs, or both. And he wanted to approach that danger in a militant posture.

At the Biltmore, the blunt fighter outmaneuvered the master diplomat by a classic display of diplomacy. One reason for Ben-Gurion's triumph may have been that he instinctively envisaged (as Weizmann did not) an international conference in the Diaspora as being a situation which called for diplomacy. Ben-Gurion felt himself to be, and was accepted in the Yishuv as, *de facto* Prime Minister of his country, Eretz Israel, and he was at the Biltmore to carry his country's point, and bring around Diaspora Jewry to it. For Weizmann, on the other hand, Zionism was one entity, geographically dispersed, and it was not a theater for diplomatic negotiations. This honorable conviction had gotten Weizmann into one kind of trouble before, and it got him into another now.

Ironically, the Biltmore Resolution, which Ben-Gurion put to revolutionary use in Palestine, was based on an article by Chaim Weizmann. In an article published in *Foreign Affairs*, in January 1942, Weizmann had said that Jews in Palestine should "control their own emigration" and "have a state of their own." These became the essential principles of the Biltmore Resolution endorsed by the conference. The only substantive difference was that "a state of their own" became "a Jewish Commonwealth integrated in the structure of the new democratic world."

Now, what was one thing in a signed article in a specialized (even if semiofficial) journal is apt to become another when endorsed by a widely representative (even if semiofficial) conference. This was especially the case with a Zionist conference. From the beginning Zionists had always been coy about public and collective proclamations of commitment to a Jewish State. The founder of international Zionism, and author of *The Jewish State,* had refrained from asking the First Zionist Congress for any commitment to a Jewish State. So on the whole it had gone on, and American Zionists had been particularly cautious in their formulations. So the Biltmore Resolution, though it contained no doctrine from which Weizmann could dissent, was nevertheless a long step forward on a path on which he was in no hurry to advance.

The delegates—and even possibly Weizmann himself—may not have fully appreciated the revolutionary implications of the Biltmore Resolution when brought into the context of wartime Palestine and the Mandatory's inflexible—and almost fanatical—hostility to Jewish immigration.

Ben-Gurion's biographer says that "the delegates did not comprehend that the resolution meant turning their backs on the policies of Dr. Weizmann and adopting the perilous path proposed by Ben-Gurion."[137] It is not surprising if they were confused, since the declaration welcomed and exploited by Ben-Gurion seemed identical with policies recently espoused by Weizmann. Ben-Gurion, however, immediately sent up a flare that illuminated that "perilous path," and the zone of future conflict. Basing himself on the declaration's words— "that the gates of Palestine be opened"—Ben-Gurion demanded the admission of two million Jews.

Weizmann was furious at what he regarded as Ben-Gurion's demagogy. The antagonism between the two men flared up openly in informal discussions with American Zionists in the aftermath of the Biltmore. When Weizmann tried to tone down the Biltmore policy, to keep lines open to Britain, Ben-Gurion openly attacked him: "He wants always to seem reasonable, and not only to be reasonable, to an Englishman, he hears more what he would like to hear than what he hears. . . . For this reason I believe it is not in the interest of the movement that Dr. Weizmann act alone."[138]

The Americans were shocked at Ben-Gurion's attack, and Weizmann was mortally offended at what he regarded as attempted "political assassination." In a draft letter to the Executive, he cries out with the pain of a deposed king, calling his *de facto* successor "petty dictator, humourless, thin-lipped, morally stunted, fanatical, stubborn, apparently frustrated in some ambition."[139]

But Weizmann was going back to England; Ben-Gurion, to Pales-

tine. Ben-Gurion's interpretation would be accepted in the Yishuv—
which is where it came from—and the Zionists of the Diaspora, in the
long run, had no alternative but to support the Yishuv, and its leader,
David Ben-Gurion.

XVI

In November 1942, a group of Palestinian citizens were allowed
to leave Poland and return to Palestine. They brought with them to
the Yishuv the news that the Nazi persecution of the Jews had now
turned to a systematic campaign of mass annihilation.[140] The news
was confirmed by the Allied Governments in December.

In a speech at the Berlin Sports Palace, on September 30, 1942,
Hitler had recalled a prophecy he had made in his Reichstag speech
of September 1, 1939, "that if Jewry should plot another world war
in order to exterminate the Aryan peoples of Europe, it would not
be the Aryan peoples who would be exterminated, but Jewry. . . ."
And Hitler added, "At one time the Jews of Germany laughed about
my prophecies. I do not know whether they are still laughing or
whether they have already lost all desire to laugh. But right now I
can only repeat: they will stop laughing everywhere, and I shall be
right also in that prophecy."[141]

By the end of that year, the world knew what Hitler had meant.
The Yishuv had to live now with the knowledge that European Jewry
was perishing. Most of the Yishuv felt that the only effective thing
they could do was to contribute to the Allied war effort, in the hope
that victory would come in time to save considerable numbers of
European Jews.

In the meantime, some Jews were helped to escape. A United
Rescue Committee, representing all factions in the Yishuv, established
contact with the Jewish underground in Europe. Small missions of
specially trained Hagana volunteers were parachuted into the Balkans
in 1943–1944 to collect military intelligence for the Allies, to
strengthen the Jewish resistance and to help get Jews out. In this way
some 10,000 Jews were enabled to escape and settle in Palestine.[142]
But at the same time anger mounted in the Yishuv against what was
seen as the failure of the Allies to make any major specific effort to
help the European Jews, and in particular against Britain's refusal
even in these extreme circumstances to open the gates of Palestine.

An Anglo-American conference at Bermuda in April 1943 considered the question of aid to refugees from Nazi-controlled countries. But the conference was governed by a dual exclusion. At the request of the Americans, it agreed not to discuss U.S. immigration laws, and at the request of the British, it agreed not to consider the entry of additional Jews into Palestine.[143] Word of the almost entirely negative outcome of Bermuda reached the Yishuv at the same time as the news of the crushing by the Germans of the rising of the Warsaw ghetto.

It was in this period, not surprisingly, that "the terrorist societies first took secure root."[144] Lehi (Freedom Fighters) was revived and won recruits among the Revisionist and Oriental youth, and among illegal immigrants. The Irgun now drew close to the Freedom Fighters, and built up its own strength, with help from Jews amongst the Polish military units brought to Palestine in 1942-1943. One of these Polish Jewish soldiers, Menachem Begin, was given leave of absence, in May 1944, to take over the Irgun's supreme command. In a vicious circle which the British had already experienced in Ireland, apprehension about the growing strength of terrorism led to arms raids by the authorities, and the raids then increased the disaffection of the general population, thus helping the terrorists.

The growing strength of the terrorist organizations during 1943, and the actual flare-up of terrorist violence in 1944, had extremely unfortunate political effects from a Zionist point of view. The Churchill Government in 1943-1944 was preparing to repudiate the 1939 White Paper. On December 20, 1943, a Cabinet committee which included Lord Moyne—hated by Zionists for his part in the *Struma* tragedy—had recommended the partition of Palestine on the basis of the 1937 Peel Report. At the beginning of 1944, Churchill told Eden: "Some form of partition is the only solution."[145]

Officially, the Zionist leadership was opposed to partition, but this was a bargaining position only. In fact, the leadership knew that a Jewish State—and control over immigration—could not come into being without the partition of Palestine. To have the British Government drop the White Paper, and return to Peel, in the closing years of the war, would have been the greatest political triumph then possible for the Zionists. Weizmann, during 1944, seems to have come very near to this triumph. It was to be dashed from him by the terrorists.

Although the Prime Minister and most of his colleagues—and even the High Commissioner, Sir Harold MacMichael—had already given up on the White Paper, the White Paper nonetheless remained official policy. The Foreign Office, deeply committed to the White Paper, managed to defer the announcement of its abandonment throughout 1944. In Palestine, the terrorists, with the campaign of violence which broke out in the spring of 1944, in fact rescued the very document against which they thought they were fighting.

Shootings of policemen and explosions in public buildings occurred sporadically throughout 1944, and in August of that year an attempt was made on the life of the High Commissioner, Sir Harold MacMichael. The Zionist leadership and the press of the Yishuv condemned these acts, and Weizmann's negotiations continued. On November 4, Churchill told Weizmann that he was in favor of partition, and believed that he and Roosevelt "together could impose it at the end of the war." But two days later Lord Moyne, then British Minister Resident in Cairo, was murdered there, with his driver, Corporal Fuller, by members of Lehi. Moyne was a friend of Churchill's, and Churchill never again showed any active interest in Zionism. Addressing the Commons on November 17, Churchill said: "If our dreams for Zionism should be dissolved in the smoke of the revolvers of assassins and if our efforts for its future should provoke a new wave of banditry worthy of the Nazi Germans, many persons like myself will have to reconsider the position that we have taken so firmly for such a long time."

The Zionist leadership now put into operation a policy of full cooperation with the British authorities against terrorists. This was the so-called *saison*, when the Hagana helped the British round up members of Irgun.[146] Civil war within the Yishuv was averted only by Begin's policy of nonretaliation against Jews. The Zionist leadership hoped that, through the *saison*, they might hold the British to their (unannounced) support for partition. But nothing came of that. After the Cairo murders, the Foreign Office was fully back in control.

In Palestine, Lord Gort had replaced Sir Harold MacMichael, and in Cairo, Edward Grigg had replaced Lord Moyne. The men replaced, unpopular as they had been with Zionists, were in fact in favor of partition—and a Jewish State. Those who replaced them were hostile to the idea of a Jewish State—especially Grigg, who advised Eden that partition "would very likely bring into existence a Jewish Nazi-state—of a bitterly dissatisfied and therefore aggressive character."[147]

The "Jewish Nazi" idea had been common currency in British official circles in the Middle East since 1941. It was a sinister association of ideas that was to reappear with a strange frequency in the years to come.

As the end of the war approached, Eden reminded the War Cabinet of Britain's interest in Middle East communications and oil. "If we lose Arab goodwill, the Americans and the Russians will be on hand to profit from our mistakes."

The Foreign Office assumption that the decisions of the super-powers in relation to Palestine would be governed by competition for Arab goodwill was now beginning to lead the British into serious miscalculation.

When the war in Europe ended, on May 8, 1945, the British commitment to the White Paper remained intact. To hold to the White Paper in the circumstances of 1945, and so to exclude the survivors of the concentration camps from Palestine, was to invite conflict with a united Yishuv. The *saison* petered out.

XVII

On July 26, 1945, when Clement Attlee became Prime Minister, he found waiting for him a memorandum, addressed to his predecessor by President Truman, expressing "the hope that the British Government may find it possible without delay to take steps to lift the restrictions of the White Paper on Jewish immigration to Palestine."[148]

As applied to the new Government, that seemed a reasonable hope. The victorious Labour Party had opposed the White Paper from its inception, and had reiterated, in 1944 and 1945, its commitment to the National Home and unrestricted Jewish immigration.[149] But Attlee sent a noncommittal interim reply back to Truman. Truman kept up the pressure. In August, he sent to Attlee a report from his representative, Earl G. Harrison, on the conditions of 100,000 Jewish survivors of the extermination camps, now housed in camps— some of them former Nazi concentration-camp premises—in Germany and Austria. "To anyone who has visited the concentration camps and who has talked with the despairing survivors," wrote Harrison, "it is nothing short of calamitous to contemplate that the gates of Palestine should be soon closed." Palestine, according to Harrison, was definitely and preeminently the first choice of the refugees.[150]

Attlee's reply on September 16 was unsympathetic. The Jews, he suggested, had no more to complain about than had a lot of other people:

Above, Harry S. Truman with Chaim Weizmann, after the foundation of the State of Israel. Just as Weizmann's relationship with Balfour had helped open the way for the Balfour Declaration, so his relationship with Truman helped open the way for recognition of the State of Israel. According to Lord Passfield, the whole Arab-Israeli conflict was unfair because "the Jews have Dr. Weizmann, and the Arabs do not."

Below, Prime Minister Clement Attlee opening the Lancaster House Conference in September 1946. Foreign Secretary Ernest Bevin is on Attlee's right, and a Yemeni delegate on Bevin's right. Attlee is appealing to Arabs and Jews to "make concessions necessary for peace."

One must remember that within these camps were people from almost every race in Europe and there appears to have been very little difference in the amount of torture and treatment they had to undergo. Now if our offices had placed the Jews in a special racial category at the head of the queue, my strong view is that the effect of this would have been disastrous for the Jews.[151]

Attlee added the familiar pro–White Paper argument—familiar, but now from a Labour leader—about "setting the Middle East ablaze" and "the ninety million Muslims of India" as well.

By September, the Yishuv and the American Zionists knew that the Labour Party, in office, had changed its tune, and that only a limited immigration—1,500 a month—would be permitted. An emergency session of Jewish leaders at Jerusalem issued a proclamation: ". . . Jewish immigrants will stream to Palestine by all means. . . . The Hebrew Book of Books will by its eternal strength destroy the White Paper . . . the Jewish State will be established."

Already in August, Ben-Gurion had issued a public warning: "I wish to tell the British Labour Party, if for some reason or another, it maintains the White Paper for an unlimited period . . . we in Palestine will not draw back in the face of England's great power and we shall fight against her."

On October 1, Ben-Gurion, acting on that warning, sent a coded telegram to Hagana headquarters instructing the Hagana to institute an armed uprising against Britain.[152] Shortly afterwards, Hagana began daily broadcasts over its mobile, illegal Voice of Israel radio station. At the same time, Hagana re-established cooperation with Irgun and Lehi. And when, on the night of October 31, the Palestine railway system was blown up in 153 places, and many other acts of sabotage took place, the action was defended by most of the Jewish press.

This was a new guerrilla war, vastly more formidable than the old. This postwar guerrilla war engaged mass public support among the world's surviving Jews, both in Palestine and in the United States. And the immediate political objective of the guerrilla war—freeing of Jewish immigration into Palestine—was one that had been publicly endorsed by the President of the United States, and was supported by American public opinion.

This was the kind of fight Britain could not possibly win. As a source in no way friendly to Zionists put it, "The British Government dare not estrange the U.S. by employing the full rigour of military repression against the Jewish Resistance Movement. . . ."[153]

Britain—as the leading Zionists well knew—had had fairly recent experience of a closely comparable situation. In the Irish "troubles" of 1919–1921 the authorities had attempted in 1920 "the full rigour of military repression" but had been unable to go through with it, mainly because of America, and the strength of the Irish in the American system. Since those days, the relative strength of Britain, as compared with America, had generally declined. The American Jews were as strong, in terms of direct political "clout," in the major cities, as the Irish had been, and they were much stronger in the media. They also had—in the fate of the survivors of the Holocaust—an immensely strong humanitarian aspect to their cause, evoking widespread sympathy, far outside the Jewish community. The President's personal commitment on immigration into Palestine both reflected those pressures and intensified them. The Irish cause had had strong congressional support, but no support either from President Wilson or from President Harding.

The leverage which Jews could exert in America in the 1940s was thus much greater than the leverage available to the Irish in the 1920s. On the ground, in the territories concerned, the armed forces at the disposition of the Jews were more numerous and better armed and trained than the I.R.A. Yet the *lesser* American leverage, combined with the lesser potential for local resistance, had been enough, in 1921, to break up the United Kingdom of Great Britain and Ireland.

That precedent was well within the adult memory of the Parliament of 1945.[154] One might think it would have suggested the strong desirability of *not* taking on the Jews of Palestine, backed by the Jews of the United States. One might have expected concessions to Truman on immigration, followed by a cautious evolution away from the White Paper, and in the direction of partition. Such an evolution would have been entirely in line with the Labour Party's declared policies as well as with the realities of Anglo-American relations—the most important of all international considerations in the conditions of 1945.

No such evolution took place. The Attlee Government decided, instead, to put up a fight for a policy which Labour had always opposed, and which its predecessors had been thinking of dropping. No major concession was made on immigration. Instead the Government, hoping to gain time, set up a twelve-man Anglo-American Committee of Inquiry to examine the problem, both in Europe and in Palestine. But in announcing this, the Foreign Secretary, Ernest Bevin, gave a clue to the direction of his thinking, and that of his Government, about immigration and about Jews. He publicly repeated the warning already privately given by Attlee: "Jews must not try to get to the head of the queue."

Inevitably, the Foreign Secretary's statement provoked fury among Jews, both in the United States and in Palestine. In Tel Aviv, crowds rioted for two days and were fired on by British troops. Six Jews were killed. Zionist propaganda exploited these deaths in America, to no less effect than Irish propaganda had exploited similar deaths in the 1920s. The "Irish" cycle was now in full swing. The Attlee Government had another chance to get out of it when the Anglo-American Committee of Inquiry, in its report in March, unanimously recommended the immediate admission of 100,000 Jews, and Truman publicly called on Britain to act on this recommendation. But the Attlee Government refused "until disarmament of the Jews had taken place."

To people placed, as were the Jews of Palestine, in the midst of hostile populations, a call for their disarmament sounded very much like calling on them to accept a fate such as that which had recently been endured by most of the Jews of Europe. So the cycle continued.

XVIII

It is worth looking at the British Government's reasons for persisting in so peculiarly unpromising a course.

Formally, the reasons remained essentially the same as those originally offered for the 1939 White Paper: Unrestricted Jewish immigration, and partition, would set the Arab world, and the Muslim world, ablaze. Foreign powers—in 1939, the Axis; in 1945, the Soviet Union—would take advantage of this conflagration.

But in fact this case was far weaker than it had been in 1939. Fear of a general Arab revolt *because* of Palestine was probably exaggerated even in 1939. But at least the Middle East policies followed by the Chamberlain Government did have a certain rough common sense about them, in terms of preparation for imminent war. It made a kind of sense to crush the rising of the Palestinian Arabs with the help of the Jews—without worrying about whether *that* would set the

Arab world ablaze—and then to announce Palestinian policies which
might have a sedative effect on Arabs—without worrying whether
these might annoy the Jews. The Jews had nowhere else to go. America was not manifesting any concern, at that time, nor were American
Jews particularly active.

But the Holocaust, the almost complete Zionization of American
Jewry and the defeat of Hitler meant that the Yishuv now had
powerful allies—and "somewhere else to go," politically speaking. At
the other end, the Arabs could less plausibly be portrayed as about to
revolt against the victorious Allies (post-1945) than they could be
thought of as potentially about to join an Axis bandwagon during
World War II. True, there was the Soviet Union to be considered, but
that factor surely called for the avoidance, rather than the acceptance,
of British confrontation with the United States over Palestine.

By hindsight we can now see that whether a Power did or did not
support a given course of action in Palestine had very little effect on
its subsequent standing and influence in the region. Saudi Arabia and
the Gulf States have not refused to deal with the United States because of its responsibilities for the creation and support of Israel.
Syria and South Yemen have not spurned the Soviet Union for not
only having voted for the creation of the State of Israel, but having
furnished the arms which made it possible for that infant state to beat
off its Arab enemies. And Arab nationalists, in Egypt and elsewhere,
were not reconciled to their pro-British rulers by any grateful memories of Britain's fidelity to the White Paper, or her principled opposition to Jewish immigration, or even her help to the Arab side in the
first war against Israel.

Realpolitik, then, would seem to suggest that more attention
should have been paid to Jewish susceptibilities, and less to Arab,
than actually happened, in the conditions of 1945. In fact, British
policy makers at this time seemed to be governed much more by their
emotions, and the emotions of their public, than by rational assessment of British interests. A very clear index of this is the major policy
shift that occurred inside the Churchill Cabinet after the murder of
Lord Moyne. If partition had been the best option available to Britain
up to the murder, it remained so after the murder, logically speaking.
Emotionally speaking, not so. It became important to punish the Jews
by depriving them of what they wanted, even if it might be in Britain's
interest to let them have it. So stick to the White Paper, even if the
White Paper is obviously unworkable. This was a general state of

mind which Attlee and Bevin originally shared with their predecessors, but which became more obsessive as the months went on.

Most Jews suspected that this attitude was basically anti-semitic. They found this suspicion confirmed by the Attlee-Bevin language about the head of the queue and by other indices. When General Barker, military commander in Palestine, announced military boycott measures against the Jewish community—in circumstances set out below—he said that these measures "will be punishing the Jews in a way the race dislikes as much as any, by striking at their pockets and showing our contempt for them." Jewish ill-feeling about this was not diminished by the knowledge that General Barker had commanded the unit that liberated Belsen concentration camp.[155] It was suspected that such tactless utterances were only overt expressions of a more widespread hostility, which generally found only discreet or oblique expression. This suspicion was well founded. About the Foreign Office records of the period, Bethell writes: "This feeling [of resentment] is well illustrated by a note written in the Foreign Office by Armine Dew on September 1, 1944: 'In my opinion a disproportionate amount of the time of this office is wasted on dealing with these wailing Jews.' "[156]

Officials don't write that sort of thing on files, if they feel that other officials are likely to think the comment in poor taste. The comment was in fact neither reproved nor exceptional; it represented the dominant official view. That view was, in part, stimulated by the news from Palestine. Dew was writing after the attempt on the life of the High Commissioner. Worse was to happen later. When British officials, soldiers and police were being shot down by Jews in Palestine, it was natural for hostile feelings about Jews to arise, and accompanied by the appropriate negative stereotypes. It is not enough to call that phenomenon "anti-semitism" and leave it at that. At the height of the Irish troubles, plenty of nasty things were said about the Irish. Yet that implied equation would not be right either. No modern British statesman ever became nearly as obsessively anti-Irish as Ernest Bevin became anti-Jewish—without losing the support of the Prime Minister, the Government, Parliament or the people.[157] Lloyd George remained throughout eminently pragmatic and rational—though occasionally brutal by calculation—in every phase of his dealings with the Irish question.

Nor does the notion of feelings-appropriate-toward-the-people-who-are-attacking-you altogether cover the phenomenon. As we have

seen, the British military in Palestine disliked the Jews from the beginning, even when it was the Arabs who were giving the trouble. And
this attitude subsisted right through the Arab Revolt, in which the
Jews helped the British. In the mess of the Palestine Mobile Force in
1945, Richard Crossman was told: " 'All through the Arab revolt, when
our men were being shot in the back and protecting the Jews, most of
them liked the Arabs. . . . The old Arab will take a pot at you in the
night, but he'll offer you coffee next day, when you come to investigate. The Jew doesn't offer you coffee, even when you're protecting
him.' "158

People who disliked the Jews before the Holocaust generally
didn't dislike them any the less because of the Holocaust. On the contrary. The Jews were seen as more pushing, strident and demanding
than ever—and cashing in cunningly on their new asset of enhanced
entitlement to sympathy.

These attitudes were widely current among Gentiles, not just the
British, in this period. In 1946, I represented Ireland at the Conference of the International Refugee Organization in Geneva. As an Irish
representative in those days was supposed to find out what the Vatican thought, I had lunch with the Vatican representative, and found
out. The Vatican representative was a jovial Irish-American Monsignor. The Monsignor was at least not mealymouthed. "I'm not anti-
semitic," he said, "I just hate them." Throughout lunch he talked
about the Jews, and nothing else. They had done very well out of the
war and were now exploiting the real displaced persons in the camps.
Selling razor blades. On the black market.

Dislike of the Jews was existential. If they conformed to the traditional stereotypes—pushy, acquisitive and so on—they were disliked
for that. But if they departed from the stereotype, they were felt to be
cheating. Thus one of the most cherished of the stereotypes was that
the Jew was unwarlike. This had never been regarded as a point in
his favor—Joseph Chamberlain thought they were "cowardly"; Treitschke, "lacking in the martial virtues"—but for the Jew to become
warlike was regarded as a monstrous mutation. It was all right for
"the old Arab" to "take a pot at you," but for the Jew to do so was
contrary to the law of nature.

Thus, in the interval between the Holocaust and the emergence
of the State of Israel, the same ancient forces and dark associations
which had led to the Holocaust, and were leading to the State, still
clung to the Jews and held them to Europe, while at the same time

rejecting them. And this could only deepen and strengthen the Zionist conviction of the necessity for a Jewish State.

XIX

In May 1946, the report of the Anglo-American Committee of Inquiry came out. It recommended a binational Palestinian State for which the way would be prepared by a trusteeship. It also recommended the immediate admission of the 100,000. Truman promptly welcomed the second recommendation. Attlee, in a statement to the House of Commons, made clear that Britain would not implement the recommendation unless "the United States would be prepared to share the . . . additional military and financial responsibilities." In practice, this was a formula for rejecting the committee's report. In the following month, Ernest Bevin explained to the Labour Party Conference in Bournemouth that the reason why the Americans were pressing for so many Jews to be admitted to Palestine was that they "did not want too many of them in New York."[159]

In the same month, the Attlee Government authorized High Commissioner Sir Alan Cunningham (who had replaced the ailing Lord Gort the previous year) to crack down on the Jewish Agency. Intensive searches were carried out in the main centers of Jewish population. Thousands of Jews were arrested, including a number of members of the Agency Executive, and the Yishuv was subjected, for about a fortnight, to a kind of military siege. David Ben-Gurion escaped arrest, being abroad at the time of the searches.

The Government's exasperation with the Agency leaders, especially Ben-Gurion, was understandable. The Agency from time to time condemned terrorist acts, and sometimes took steps to discourage them, but it refused to continue the wartime policy of cooperating with the authorities against Irgun and Lehi. Indeed it cooperated, at least on occasion, with Irgun and Lehi against the British. Ben-Gurion was known to be in control of the main Yishuv armed forces in the Hagana, including Palmah, and these forces engaged in carrying out illegal immigration, and in sabotage, and in general in what Ben-Gurion himself had declared to be "an armed uprising against Britain." Yet the same Ben-Gurion in public professed to know nothing about all this. He had told the Anglo-American Committee of Inquiry that "Hagana is a Hebrew word, meaning defense." His biographer has described Ben-Gurion's dual role in this period:

As he led his people into an armed struggle, Ben-Gurion became a unique personality, changing identities as easily as
others change jackets. In London, he was the chairman of the
Jewish Agency Executive, an official personage, engaged in
regular formal contacts with the British Government. In Paris,
he was the head of the Palestine insurgency movement, mobil-
izing personnel, arms and money and working out stratagems
for striking at the same British Government he had visited the
day before and whose representatives he would meet again
the next day.[160]

The British can hardly be blamed for refusing to go on playing
that particular game. Yet their attempted crackdown, which appears
to have been mainly a result of British military pressure on the
Attlee Government,[161] was unsuccessful; all it did in the end was to
demonstrate the extreme weakness of Britain's political and material
position, in the postwar world, in the presence of the American
factor. By the end of June, the British Government had already decided "to suspend its disciplinary steps, although it had neither disarmed nor impaired Hagana's striking force."[162] The Government was
driven to backtrack in this way because the large postwar loan which
Britain needed was going through Congress (House of Representatives, July 8–13). The leader of the American Zionist activist wing,
Dr. Abba Hillel Silver, had publicly advised that citizens should ask
their congressman "whether . . . the United States can afford to make
a loan to a Government whose pledged word seems to be useless."[163]

It was slowly becoming apparent that the British Government
could no longer afford to pursue policies which offended a large section of American public opinion. By the end of the year, the attempt
to clamp down on the Agency and Hagana had been altogether dis-
continued.

That attempt had not only gone badly wrong in terms of international politics; it was also miscalculated in terms of the fight against
terrorism. The attempt had been directed against Hagana, not against
Irgun and Lehi, and it seems to have had the effect of giving greater
scope to Irgun and Lehi. At the end of July, Irgun blew up Government offices in the King David Hotel, killing about eighty British,
Jewish and Arab civil servants and wounding about seventy others.
The British imposed a four-day curfew on Tel Aviv, and carried out
systematic searches. In America, the publicity given to General Barker's apparently anti-semitic statements, in the wake of the King
David bombing, increased anti-British feeling.

Arab states, possibly with British encouragement, made some effort at this time to offset American pressure on Britain by applying counterpressure of their own to America. American investment in the area had increased enormously—nineteenfold in the case of oil—during the war, and the State Department, like the Foreign Office, feared damaging repercussions as a result of pro-Zionist gestures. In practice, the only significant effort by Arab states in that line came after President Truman, in October 1946, had not only made another public effort to procure the admission of the 100,000 but had also, for the first time, endorsed the establishment of a "viable Jewish State" in Palestine.[164] Iraq declined to discuss air agreements with the Department of State, and Syria refused to grant transit rights to ARAMCO, whose projected pipeline was now to terminate in Lebanon, bypassing Palestine. If these positions had been maintained, and these examples followed, American policy making might have been significantly affected. But in fact the two Governments speedily reversed themselves, when they found that they would damage their own interests. Pan American Airways announced it would overfly Syria and Iraq, and the Trans-Arabian Pipeline Company announced it would shift the terminus back to Palestine; the Arab attempt at sanctions in support of the Palestinian cause collapsed. Ibn Saud was too wise even to threaten sanctions, having far too much to lose. He contented himself with addressing a dignified letter of remonstrance to President Truman, to which he received a polite but noncommittal reply.[165]

The Arab states, while not willing to run the risk of antagonizing American interests, remained anxious to help the Palestinians win an independent state, free from Jews. The Mufti—after yet a further series of "escapes"—had made his way from Europe to Cairo in May. Although he was not admitted to Palestine by the Mandatory, he succeeded in placing the politics of Arab Palestine again under his control, through a Higher Executive Committee of his nominees. The Higher Executive was recognized and supported by the Arab states—which, with British encouragement, had formed the Arab League—and preparations for the final struggle with the Jews were under way. At a conference with the British in London in September, the Arab states had demanded an independent Arab State in Palestine "not later than December 31, 1948." To gain time, the British adjourned the conference's proceedings for three months.

In December 1946, the Twenty-second Zionist Congress—the first since the Holocaust—met in Basel. Since the last meeting, the world Jewish population had been reduced by more than one-third. And the proportion of Jews enrolled as subscribing Zionists had more than tripled, rising from 6.2 percent in 1939 to 19.6 percent in 1946. In absolute terms world Zionist enrollment had more than doubled, from one million in 1939 to well over two million in 1946. The United States had now replaced Poland as the chief Zionist center, with almost half the world membership.

The Basel Congress endorsed the Biltmore Program, with its explicit commitment to a Jewish State. The first Congress after the Holocaust was thus also the first to acknowledge formally the *Endziel*— the ultimate goal—of Zionism.

The highlight of the Twenty-second Congress was Weizmann's address, on December 16, an address described by Abba Eban as "the most remarkable of his oratorical feats at any Congress."[166] Old and almost blind though he now was, Weizmann spoke with a strong voice. He directed his attack against the terrorists in Palestine and, especially, against their American sympathizers. Eban, who was present, writes:

> As he delivered his attack against vicarious "activism" by those who intended to stay away from the gunpowder, a delegate called out "Demagogy." He stopped his discourse, took off his glasses, and stood in stunned silence. Never had this happened to him. His age, infirmity, patient toil and sacrifice had been violated in a moment of dreadful rancour. The Assembly sat in horrified tension as he pondered his reply. The Congress protocol quotes him as follows: "Somebody has called me a demagogue. I do not know who. I hope that I never learn the man's name. I—a demagogue! I who have borne all the ills and travails of this movement (*loud applause*). The person who flung that word in my face ought to know that in every house and stable in Nahalal, in every little workshop in Tel-Aviv or Haifa, there is a drop of my blood. (*Tempestuous applause. The delegates all rise to their feet except the Revisionists and Mizrachi*) . . . If you think of bringing the redemption nearer by un-Jewish methods, if you lose faith in hard work and better days, then you commit idolatry (*avodah zarah*) and endanger what we have built. Would that I had a tongue of flame, the strength of prophets, to warn you against the paths of Babylon and Egypt. 'Zion shall be redeemed in Judgement'—and not by any other means."

Weizmann's peroration came to be quoted often, in later years, as condemning aggressive tendencies, already present in Zionism, and

later seen as dominant in it. The point is valid, but there are some
limits to its validity. Certainly Weizmann sincerely abhorred the
bloody deeds of Irgun and Lehi. But Weizmann was not a pacifist.
He supported the policy of illegal immigration: a policy that could
not be effectively conducted except through the efforts of armed
forces—Hagana, Palmah—in conflict, at least occasionally, with the
armed forces of the Mandatory. And he knew (though he disliked
the knowledge) that, in periods of active conflict—and especially
when the Mandatory tried to clamp down on the Yishuv as a whole—
Hagana and Palmah, and the Agency leaders, cooperated on the
ground with Irgun and Lehi. The Zionist effort, toward the end of the
Mandate, was in fact a continuum, which included both Weizmann
and Begin, however much they disapproved of each other.[167]

Nor was Weizmann altogether as dovish, in terms of *Arab* policies, as some of his language made him appear. For at least ten years
now, he had been working for the partition of Palestine. He had been
prepared to accept even a very small Jewish area, with the *arrière-
pensée* that it could become bigger later. No one, least of all so brilliant an intelligence as Weizmann, can have imagined, at any time
from 1936 on, that the Jewish area could have grown larger as a result
of *voluntary* territorial concessions by the Arabs. Weizmann was a very
great man, but it would be a mistake to sentimentalize him in
retrospect.

Weizmann made a great emotional impact on the Congress, yet
it rejected him politically. He favored Zionist participation in the
resumed London Conference in January. A majority rejected this
idea—and implicitly Weizmann's type of leadership along with it—
as too "pro-British." After that rebuff Weizmann would no longer
allow his name to go forward for the presidency, and that office was
left unfilled, out of respect to Weizmann.

A new type of dual leadership emerged, corresponding to the
contemporary realities of Zionism. Ben-Gurion became Executive
Chairman in relation to Yishuv affairs, and the activist Rabbi Silver
of Cleveland, Executive Chairman in relation to America.

Together, the two leaders represented the points of the American-
Jewish pincers which now held the Mandatory in an agonizing grip.

XX

Early in 1947, political movement began in Britain. For several
months the opposition had been urging the end of the Mandate. After

the failure of the resumed London talks, Churchill pressed this advice: "If we cannot fulfill our promises to the Zionists we should, without delay, place our Mandate for Palestine at the feet of the United Nations, and give due notice of our impending evacuation from that country."

As the Mandate—now rejected, though on contradictory grounds, by virtually the whole population of Palestine—floundered on, in blood and obloquy, the Churchillian argument carried great weight. The Attlee Government gave ground before it, at least in appearance. On February 18, 1947, the Government announced: "His Majesty's Government have of themselves no power under the terms of the Mandate to award the country to the Arabs or the Jews, or even to partition it between them. . . . We have therefore reached the conclusion that the only course open to us is to submit the problem to the judgment of the United Nations."

The United Kingdom requested a special session of the General Assembly of the United Nations to consider the matter. From a Western point of view, the General Assembly was indicated rather than the Security Council, because of the so-called Soviet "veto" situation: that is, the fact that the Security Council could reach no substantive position without the support of all the Permanent Members, including the Soviet Union. The British had also their own specific reason for choosing the General Assembly (see below). The Palestine question was accordingly inscribed on the agenda of a special session of the General Assembly to be held at Flushing Meadows, New York.

This movement proved to be decisive in precipitating the termination of the Mandate, and the creation of the State of Israel, but it was certainly not so intended by the British officials concerned. In this matter, the British Government's advisers relied on what was known as "the blocking third" in the Assembly's procedures. For any substantial decision on the part of the Assembly, a majority of two-thirds of those present and voting was required. The British correctly calculated that most of those voting (the Latin-American bloc and some others) would be strongly influenced by the United States, and that there would therefore be no question of a General Assembly resolution favoring an independent Arab State. The danger—from the Foreign Office's point of view—of a vote in favor of partition and a Jewish State was more significant, but the Foreign Office was confident that a safe "blocking third" would muster against it. This would be made up of the eleven Muslim members, including five Arab states[168] plus the Soviet bloc. A senior British adviser on Middle East affairs, Harold Beeley, wrote: "This was a unanimous view in the Foreign Office, that even if we wanted partition, we would never get the U.N. to approve it."[169]

On Foreign Office assumptions, then, the General Assembly was deadlocked on Palestine. If so, nothing could be lost by submitting the problem to the judgment of the United Nations, since no such judgment (it was thought) could be handed down. On the other hand, some time was gained, which might turn to the advantage of the Mandatory Power, perhaps due to the deepening gravity of the Cold War, and growing awareness among responsible Americans of the danger of setting the Middle East ablaze. If things should not in fact develop in that way, it might indeed become necessary for Britain to abandon the Mandate, an option which it had already been considering. But in referring the matter to the United Nations, which it believed to be deadlocked, the Foreign Office did not see itself as becoming committed to that option, or any other. It saw Britain as keeping all its options open, while gaining time. (These were the Foreign Office calculations. The politicians concerned, by this time, wanted to get rid of the Mandate.[170])

The Foreign Office was assuming that future Soviet moves would be governed by past Soviet rhetoric (in this case anti-Zionist rhetoric) to the exclusion of present political opportunism. One might think that an enormous precedent to the contrary—the Hitler-Stalin Pact of 1939—might have led some at least in the Foreign Office to question that assumption, but apparently not.

Some Zionists seem to have seen the British move as more substantial than it was. Thus Abba Eban, now a negotiator with the Jewish Agency, wrote: "Some British officials may have hoped for the return of the Mandate, without obligations to facilitate Jewish immigration, but they must have realized that there was a risk that the United Nations would vote for a different solution."[171] But in reality British officials did not believe there was any such risk; they believed that the U.N. could not vote for *any* solution, and that Britain would remain free to do whatever it thought best. But there was nothing in the U.N. proceedings, at this stage, that worked to reduce violence in Palestine. Even the best outcome available, from a practical Zionist point of view—partition—would not satisfy Irgun, which demanded all of original Mandate Palestine, including Transjordan. Violence increased throughout the spring and summer of 1947. In

March, an explosion at the Goldsmith Officers' Club, Jerusalem, killed eleven and injured fourteen people. A further cycle of executions and reprisals followed.

The special session of the General Assembly took place from April 28 to May 15. The meeting made no immediate decision in substance but decided to set up an investigating eleven-member body, the United Nations Special Committee on Palestine (UNSCOP), whose report it would consider in the autumn.

But by far the most significant event of the session, and probably of the whole postwar diplomacy around Palestine, was the intervention of the Soviet Deputy Foreign Minister, Andrei Gromyko, toward the end of the debates. Gromyko attacked the "bankruptcy of the mandatory system of Palestine"—a general attack which was not unexpected—but he went on to endorse "the aspirations of the Jews to establish their own State"; a complete innovation in terms of Soviet foreign policy. He would prefer some form of binational solution, he indicated, but if that was not available then it would be necessary to consider ". . . the partition of Palestine into two independent States, one Jewish and one Arab."[172]

It was now clear that there was not likely to be any "blocking third" against partition. A British maneuver intended to gain time was turning into a preliminary to abdication.

The motives of Soviet policies, especially in Stalin's time, are generally a matter for guesswork. The most obvious of the imputable motives, in retrospect, seem two: to weaken the collective Western position, in a critical region of the world, at the start of the Cold War, and to exploit dissension between the Western allies. And the British and Americans assumed all along that the Russians wanted to do precisely those things. But they did not assume—and the British Foreign Office at least ruled out even the possibility—that they would do these things in the way they actually did. The Russians were expected to play the Arab card. Instead, they played the Jewish card, and brought the Mandate down with it. The Bolshevik enemies of Zion, like so many of its other enemies in the past, had come to the rescue of Zion, at a critical moment in its fortunes.

Why did the Russians, contrary to general expectation, treat Arab goodwill as a matter of little weight in the scale? Again, one may guess, from what is known of Stalin's temperament and history. He had little use for intangible phenomena, like the authority of the Pope, or the goodwill of groups of people. By past reversals, he had let down vast numbers of people who trusted him, both in the West and in China. What he liked were concrete advantages—and concrete *dis*advantages to his adversaries. And he liked sudden, rough surprises. The Attlee Government and its advisers had put themselves in Stalin's hands. Their whole Palestinian position at the United Nations was now leaning confidently on the votes of the Soviet bloc. By moving those votes into the wrong column—which he could do with one telephone call—Stalin had the power to make the British collapse. It is not surprising—though it seemed so at the time—that he chose to use that power. It was the kind of tactical coup that suited his humor.

The UNSCOP members went to Palestine in the summer. They could see and hear that the Mandate seemed untenable. On the day the UNSCOP members arrived in Palestine, a British military court sentenced three members of Irgun to death. UNSCOP appealed; its appeals were ignored. Irgun captured two British sergeants, on July 12, and threatened to kill them if the British sentences were carried out. The Irgunists were executed at the end of July 1947, and the hanged bodies of the two sergeants were found two days later. Irgun had planted a mine below the bodies, and members of the British party who cut down the bodies were injured in the resulting explosion.

The murders of the sergeants caused the greatest wave of anti-Zionist fury yet experienced on the British side. In Britain itself there were sporadic anti-semitic riots in several British cities, but these were generally discouraged and died down after a few days. The repercussions among the troops in Palestine were much more serious, as was natural. Troops in Tel Aviv went on the rampage, firing on buses, smashing up cafés and committing various other acts of violence. Five Jews were unlawfully killed by the marauding troops. No one was ever charged. The situation in Palestine was getting more and more like that in Ireland in the summer of 1920, when Black and Tans and Auxiliaries exacted bloody vengeance for the bloody deeds of the I.R.A.

There was one continuing element in the Palestine situation, however, that was unique. This was the refugee element. Between July 1945 and the end of 1946 some thirty ships entered Palestine waters with Jews from Europe, and during 1947 the ships kept coming.[173] Most of the larger ships were intercepted by the Royal Navy, and their passengers were interned, in either Cyprus or Palestine. A few of the smaller ships managed to land their passengers. Where the passengers got through, it was a gain for the Yishuv, in people. Where they were apprehended, it was a gain for the Zionist cause, in propaganda terms.

The most famous case was that of the biggest ship involved. *The President Warfield*, renamed the *Exodus*, was an 1,800-ton four-decker river steamer, carrying 4,500 passengers—concentration-camp survivors, packed very tightly. The *Exodus* sailed for Palestine from the French Mediterranean port of Sète in mid-July. She was shadowed by four British destroyers. On July 18 British boarding parties stormed the *Exodus* and eventually overcame the stiff resistance of the passengers. In the process, three Jews were killed; twenty-eight others needed hospitalization. The wounded were brought ashore at Haifa. UNSCOP delegates were on hand to watch the *Exodus* come in, with her escort of destroyers, and to observe her condition: ". . . gashed open on both sides, her decks black with fuel-oil squirted at the boarders. Railings were ripped off, liferafts lay all askew and cables dangled from the bridge. There were children looking out of the portholes, British sailors with bloodstained clothes and head bandages. The whole scene was filmed and photographed."[174] The scene was the subject of a twenty-thousand-strong rally in New York within a week.

The matter might, as far as world publicity was concerned, have ended there, if the usual procedure had been followed, and the passengers taken to Cyprus for detention. But Ernest Bevin was annoyed that the French had allowed them to leave, and he insisted that the refugees return to France.

On July 29, accordingly, the passengers of the *Exodus*, now distributed among several British ships, were back in a French port, Port-de-Bouc. This happened to be the day the three Irgun men were hanged in Acre prison. The French offered asylum to those passengers who wished it, but the French Government announced—through the then Minister for Ex-Servicemen, François Mitterrand—that no measures would be taken to force or pressure them into landing. Most of the passengers decided to remain aboard. The British ambassador in Paris, aghast at the horrifying publicity both in France and in the world, begged Bevin to withdraw the ships. Bevin mulishly insisted that the French must disembark the passengers, whether they went willingly or not. The French, of course, refused. Bevin was now receiving alarm signals from both the Washington and Paris embassies. Meanwhile, with the ships still in Port-de-Bouc, there occurred the sharp deterioration in Palestine itself, with the discovery of the murdered and booby-trapped sergeants, followed by the rampage of the troops. The first event no doubt hardened Bevin's strange determination not to allow the passengers to go to Cyprus. The second hardened American opinion against the Mandate.

Eventually, the passengers of the *Exodus* were taken by Bevin's decision to a displaced persons' camp at Poppendorf, near Luebeck, in Germany, where they arrived in September. If Whitehall had been working in collusion with the Zionist propaganda machine, it could not have contrived a more telling conclusion to the two-month saga of the passengers of the *Exodus*.

XXI

On August 31, the UNSCOP team completed its report, in Geneva. Unanimously, the group recommended the ending of the British Mandate as soon as possible. A majority report—seven to three, with one abstention—recommended the partition of Palestine into an Arab State and a Jewish State, with an international zone containing the Holy Places. The American Secretary of State, George C. Marshall, promptly announced that the United States "puts great weight" not only on the unanimous conclusion but also on the majority ones.

In essence, though not in detail, UNSCOP's recommendations were the same as those of the Peel Commission ten years before. There was really nothing else that an international body could advise, with any hope of success. The Mandate was obviously in a terminal condition. In theory, the Mandate could be replaced by a Palestinian State, as demanded by all Arabs, under some arrangements similar to the White Paper. In practice, for reasons discussed above, this was no longer a real possibility. In the immediate terms with which UNSCOP was concerned—possible acceptability by the General Assembly—it was a nonstarter, for reasons which all United Nations people well understood. At that time, and for long after,[175] United States influence over other delegations—primarily the Latin-American ones—was such that no propositions seriously opposed by the United States had any chance of attaining a bare majority in the General Assembly, let alone the two-thirds required by the Charter. Neither the White House, nor Congress, nor American public opinion would find a "White Paper" solution acceptable—whatever State Department officials might have liked—so UNSCOP would have been wasting its time in recommending anything of the kind.

Partition, on the other hand, might just make its two-thirds. The statements of the Soviet Deputy Foreign Minister, in advance of the UNSCOP report, and of the American Secretary of State, after the report, suggested that that might be the case.

The British Government and its advisers disliked the UNSCOP report, and the Arab League publicly condemned it. There was still a hope, though a greatly fading one, that a "blocking third" might be mustered against it in the General Assembly.

The real alternatives now available to Britain were the same, whether the General Assembly resolution on partition carried or fell just short of a two-thirds majority, with both superpowers voting in favor. In either case, the Mandate and the White Paper were both untenable. The alternatives were to remain long enough to insure as smooth as possible a transition to partition or simply to pull out and leave the Jews and Arabs to fight it out.

On October 17 the British Government made clear that it had chosen the latter course. On that day, the Colonial Secretary, Arthur Creech-Jones—a onetime Zionist—told the United Nations that his Government "would not accept responsibility for the enforcement, either alone or in concert with other nations, of any settlement antagonistic to either the Jews or Arabs or both, which was likely to necessitate the use of force."

As regards the rationale for this decision, Harold Beeley long afterward told Lord Bethell:

> Maybe we were wrong. Maybe we should have put troops along the partition frontiers and made sure that partition was carried through. I agree that this would have been a more dignified posture. But in the Foreign Office's view, it would have involved a serious injustice to the Arabs. And it would not have been in Britain's national interests. All through 1947, Bevin was negotiating with prime ministers Nokrashi and Saleh Jabr of Egypt and Iraq, for the protection of the Suez Canal and our oil concessions, and to integrate the two countries into the Western alliance. All this would have been ruined if we had played a part in creating the state of Israel.

But of course they *had* played a part, and a very big one. It was too late now to stop the coming to fruition of the Balfour Declaration. But it is possible that Bevin and his colleagues thought that it was *not* too late. It is not clear what they thought would happen when

Britain pulled out. Military opinion on the subject seems to have been divided—Richard Crossman says that General Officer Commander (G.O.C.) Palestine told the Anglo-American Committee that in that event the Jews would hold all their areas.[176] But the British Government's official position always was that partition could not be enforced without heavy British reinforcements. To the extent that they believed that, they must also have believed that without such reinforcements, the Yishuv would be overrun and a Palestinian State come into being.

On November 29, 1947, the crucial vote came in the General Assembly. Thirty-three delegates voted in favor of the UNSCOP report, and partition; thirteen against, including all the eleven Muslim states; ten abstained, including Britain. The Jews of Palestine danced in the streets when they heard on the radio that the two-thirds had been achieved, and that the General Assembly had endorsed the Jewish State.

Weizmann was in New York at this time—as *de facto* Foreign Minister of the undeclared state. Abba Eban depicts him, on the eve of the crucial vote, as throwing himself into "the frenzied pursuit of wavering votes."[177] It is clear that he did, but the most effective pursuing was done by the Government of the United States. When I became a delegate to the United Nations, nine years later, old hands there still often spoke of that traumatic November 29, and of the pressures brought to bear on smaller Governments by the United States—through both official and unofficial channels—resulting in last-minute reversals of instructions, recalls of Permanent Representatives, and in one case a change of Foreign Minister. Once the White House decided in favor of partition, and once the United States delegation was committed to voting in favor of the corresponding resolution, it became important—in terms of American domestic politics—that the resolution should win, thus showing that "world opinion" approved President Truman's policies. As long as the United States was in a position to control a two-thirds vote, the General Assembly was accepted as not merely a faithful register of world opinion but even as "the moral conscience of mankind."

To sit in the Assembly, and be part of the moral conscience of mankind, was sometimes a disconcerting experience. Abba Eban, who was at Weizmann's right hand at the material time, knows all this infinitely better than I do, but as a good diplomat he glosses it over a little, at this point. Joseph Lash, an experienced American U.N. watcher, has succinctly explained how the vote on November 29 was managed, contrary to assurances previously given:

[Undersecretary for Near Eastern and African Affairs] Loy Henderson was authorized by Undersecretary of State Robert A. Lovett to assure Arab representatives that while the U.S. would vote for partition, it would not pressure other U.N. members to do so. At the same time, however, David Niles, an administrative assistant to the President, instructed Ambassador Warren Austin's deputy at the U.N., Herschel V. Johnson, to twist arms if necessary.[178]

Weizmann's diplomatic role remained supremely important, not merely at this moment, but right up to the creation of the State of Israel; but it was in relation to the United States that his diplomacy was chiefly required. He was not so much a sheep dog, rounding up wandering votes, as a watchdog, with an unwavering eye on the State Department. There were key people in the State Department who were much more in sympathy with the British Foreign Office's view of things than with President Truman's policy. This was to emerge very clearly, a little later on.

Early in December, the British Government made it known that, without attempting to carry out the policy recommended by the General Assembly, it would continue its rule in Palestine until May 15, 1948, when it would declare its Mandate at an end. For the five terminal months of the Mandate, the British forces in Palestine would be used only in self-defense. In practice, this meant that the British forces would not intervene in the fighting that now broke out between Palestinian Arabs and Jews, while the Arab states prepared for their own attack in mid-May.

In the Yishuv, David Ben-Gurion led the preparations for the coming war, with a Clemenceau-like concentration of purpose. Speaking at a meeting of his party, Mapai, in January 1948, Ben-Gurion said:

Many important and precious things which comrades are speaking about . . . do not penetrate my ears now, and I no longer know their significance. Just now I heard [X] speak about the state, and it seemed to me that I had forgotten the meaning of the word. I heard him say that the wisdom of Israel is the wisdom of redemption, and neither do these words mean anything to me, for I feel that the wisdom of Israel now is the wisdom of war, this and nothing else, this and this alone. Without this wisdom both the word "state" and the word "redemption" are emptied of their content. . . . So I am not able nor do I wish to see beyond the next seven or eight months, for in my eyes they determine everything, for during them the war will be decided, and nothing exists for me now but this war.[179]

The reasons for refusing to carry out partition have already been discussed and are relatively clear. The reasons for choosing to linger in Palestine for five months, with no avowed policy, have never been satisfactorily explained. But the manner in which this decision affected the balance of forces in and around Palestine is clear. During this period, British forces were in a position to hamper the Yishuv's efforts to increase its armaments[180] while the neighboring Arab states were able to increase their armaments, with British cooperation. It seems hard to escape the inference that, since this was the main material result of the five-month stay, this was also the result intended. If so, it looks as if the British officials hoped that British withdrawal would be followed by Arab victories and the emergence of a friendly Palestinian State.[181]

Sporadic attacks by Arabs against Jews began in November, and were followed by reprisals against Arabs, in which Hagana as well as Irgun took part. In the new circumstances, Havlaga (self-restraint) no longer held. The whole country broke up into mutually hostile security zones. As a whole, the British forces held aloof but "a few British policemen and soldiers, hardened against Jews as a whole by their experience of terrorism, and demoralized by the general disintegration, committed random acts of violence against Jewish civilians."[182] The worst such act was the Ben Yehuda Street explosion (February 22, 1948) in which fifty-two people died, mainly Jews.

The final effort of the Palestinian Arabs to avert the emergence of the Jewish State was itself averted in April 1948—the month before British rule ended—as a result of the most frightful atrocity of the entire Arab-Jewish conflict. On April 9, 1948, in an attack on the Arab village of Deir Yassin, near Jerusalem, Menachem Begin's Irgun killed 250 Arab civilians, including many women and children. In his book *The Revolt*,[183] Begin says that Deir Yassin was "an important link in the chain of Arab positions enclosing Jerusalem from the West" and that its capture was part of a strategy, agreed with Hagana, for keeping open the lines of communication between Jerusalem and the rest of the Yishuv. There seems no reason to doubt those particular statements. As regards the appalling civilian death toll, Begin says that advance warning was given[184] by loudspeakers to civilians to leave, and that many of them did leave; many of those who remained were killed unintentionally in the course of the storming by Irgun of stone houses defended by Arab forces. The Arab account of the matter was that the civilians were deliberately massacred, and this view was widely shared in the Yishuv, outside the ranks of Irgun. The Jewish Agency condemned Irgun. Begin puts it this way: "Arab headquarters at Ramallah broadcast a crude atrocity story alleging a massacre by Irgun troops of women and children in the village. Certain Jewish officials, fearing the Irgun men as political rivals, seized upon this Arab horror propaganda to smear the Irgun." Hardly anyone outside the ranks of Begin's political followers accepts that version.

What actually happened at Deir Yassin may be in dispute, but there is no serious dispute about the effects of what was believed to have happened there. The news of Deir Yassin, as broadcast on the Arab radios, precipitated a flight of the Arab population away from the areas with large Jewish population. As George Kirk puts it: "There can be no question that the publicity which the Arab press gave to the massacre at Deir Yasin, for the purpose of attracting sympathy, greatly accelerated the demoralization and flight of non-combatant Arabs."[185] Kirk is a "White Paper" man, a source unfriendly to Zionists of any stripe, but Begin's own account does not differ materially on this point (if we take "massacre" as replaced by "alleged massacre"): "But out of evil [the "massacre" allegations] good came. This Arab propaganda spread a legend of terror amongst Arabs and Arab troops who were seized with panic at the mention of Irgun soldiers. The legend was worth half a dozen battalions to the forces of Israel."

By mid-May about 300,000 Arabs had already fled their homes, many seeking sanctuary in neighboring countries, whose broadcasts encouraged them to believe that they would soon be returning, in the wake of the conquering armies of the Arab states.

In a reprisal action for Deir Yassin, Arabs ambushed a medical convoy bound for the Hadassah Hospital and the Hebrew University (isolated on Mount Scopus), and seventy-seven doctors, nurses, university teachers and students were killed. This incident occurred within two hundred yards of a British military post that made no attempt to intervene, although the attacks continued over seven hours. Christopher Sykes comments: "This most hideous achievement of the 'crass kind' was perhaps the worst blemish on the tarnished British military record of that time."[186] A further cycle of reprisals and counterreprisals followed.

Jewish authority was now consolidated in the coastal plain and in eastern Galilee, but there was still some doubt both about international recognition of the Jewish State, and about its area. It was in this context that Chaim Weizmann rendered the last of the great series of his diplomatic services to the cause of Zionism; a series which had begun forty-two years before, in a conversation with Arthur Balfour.

On January 23, 1948, Abba Eban, from New York, cabled to Weizmann, in London, to come to the United States "in view worsening situation."[187]

Weizmann had left the United States after the crucial General Assembly vote, assuming that there was now no *diplomatic* danger to the emerging Jewish State. But in December the situation had sharply deteriorated, from a Zionist point of view. The President had soured on Zionism, partly because of attacks on him by Abba Silver and his following among American Zionists, and partly because of pressures within his own Administration—Defense, State, National Security Council and C.I.A.—and from the opposition. The Defense establishment had come around to a view closely resembling that of their British counterparts. Defense Secretary James Forrestal had told the House Armed Services Committee that the "unworkable scheme" (partition) would cost America its Middle East oil supply. Also, Russian support for the scheme laid Truman open to Republican charges that he was gullibly "playing Russia's game in the Middle East." Truman reversed himself, agreeing to postpone partition and to transfer the Mandate to the Trusteeship Council. The new policy was much more congenial to the State Department than the old one had been. American diplomacy in December set out to undo the General Assembly resolution which American diplomacy had done most to secure in November.

When Weizmann returned to the United States, there was a considerable delay before he could see the President, for whom Zionism had become bad news. But Weizmann did not give up easily. He found a Jewish haberdasher from Independence, Missouri, Eddie Jacobson, who had once been a business partner of the President's and remained a personal friend. At Jacobson's entreaty, Truman agreed to see Weizmann. The interview took place on March 18, 1948. Weizmann was a sick man at the time, but his powers were undimmed. Truman concludes a remarkably vague account of the meeting with the words: "When he left my office I felt that he had reached a full understanding of my policy and that I knew what he wanted."[188]

What really happened, after the Weizmann-Truman interview, was that "my policy" was turned around 180 degrees, back to what it had been in November. The President again committed himself to work for the establishment of a Jewish State.

Of course, there were other considerations at work. Nineteen forty-eight was an election year, and a policy entered into the previous December may have begun to look more risky by March, as the Jewish vote loomed up more palpably, and questions of high statecraft about oil and Russians and the future of the Middle East may have come to look more speculative and contingent. In the early months of 1948, Henry Wallace, the left-wing candidate for the Presidency, had been reported as making gains among Jewish voters, and the Republican candidate, Thomas E. Dewey, with his New York base, was bidding for support in the same quarter. Democratic leaders in New York and other states insisted that Truman take dramatic and effective steps on behalf of the Jews. Truman resented these pressures.[189]

It seems to have been Weizmann, once more, who tipped the wavering balance. Personal relations were important with Truman; Rabbi Silver had rubbed him the wrong way, and was told to go to hell. Weizmann rubbed him the right way and established a remarkable empathy, which comes out clearly in Truman's appreciation of Weizmann: "He had known many disappointments and had grown patient and wise in them."[190]

As an enemy of Zionism, Lord Passfield, had observed, more than ten years before, the whole Arab-Jewish controversy was unfair because the Jews had Dr. Weizmann, and the Arabs did not.

As chickens run around for a while after their heads are cut off, so diplomatic maneuvers often continue for a while after their animating political authority has departed. So, on March 19, the day after the fateful—but unannounced—interview, the American ambassador to the United Nations, Warren Austin, told the Security Council that all efforts to implement partition should be suspended. The General Assembly was to be convened in special session to work out a plan for temporary trusteeship.[191]

As Abba Eban said it, the President was "not surprisingly assailed by the formidable armory of invective which Zionism had perforce stored up during the dark, long years of failure. The only absent voice was that of the man who had the most right to feel betrayed."[192]

Weizmann called Eddie Jacobson on March 22 to express his confidence that Truman would still fulfill his promise. "The President," says Eban, "never forgot that act of faith."[193]

As inconclusive debate went on in the General Assembly during

Above, Weizmann addressing the Twenty-second Zionist Congress, December 1946. "Would that I had a tongue of flame, the strength of prophets, to warn you against the paths of Babylon and Egypt. Zion shall be redeemed in Judgment—and not by any other means."

Below, David Ben-Gurion proclaiming the independence of the State of Israel, May 14, 1948. On the wall behind him is a portrait of Theodor Herzl.

April, around the moribund but still procedurally extant "trusteeship" idea, partition was establishing itself through conflict, on the ground in Palestine, with the dividing line roughly approximating that of the Assembly's resolution.

On Passover Eve, April 23, 1948—with less than a month to go to the end of British rule in Palestine—Weizmann received a message through Judge Rosenman, one of Truman's advisers. The President had told Rosenman: "I have Dr. Weizmann on my conscience." The message that now reached Weizmann was: "If the General Assembly session could be surmounted without reversing partition and if a Jewish state was declared, the President would support it."[194] The President stipulated that, on this matter, he would deal with Weizmann, and with him alone.

The Zionist diplomats were no longer worried about the trusteeship proposal in the General Assembly. By May 5, the idea seemed to be dead. Presumably the American delegation, knowing that the idea no longer had presidential favor, did not "twist any arms"—as the U.N. phrase goes—to win support for it. But the State Department still hoped that the Jewish State might be averted, or at least postponed. General Marshall warned Ben-Gurion against proclaiming the State. Meyer Weisgal, from Nice, telephoned Weizmann, in New York, to ask his advice. Weizmann replied: "Proclaim the State, no matter what ensues."[195]

On May 14, in Tel Aviv, Ben-Gurion, as Prime Minister, held the ceremony of the proclamation of the State of Israel. On the following day at 6 P.M. (11 A.M. Washington time) the British Mandate expired, and eleven minutes later Truman announced United States *de facto* recognition of Israel.[196]

"The old Doctor will believe me now," he said.

Ben-Gurion, Weizmann's longtime rival and eventual supplanter, sent Weizmann a message on behalf of his Government: "On the occasion of the establishment of the Jewish State we send our greetings to you who have done more than any other living man towards its creation. Your stand and help have strengthened all of us. We look forward to the day when we shall see you at the head of the State established in peace."

Peace was not yet. On the expiration of the Mandate five Arab states attacked Israel. Egyptian planes bombed Tel Aviv, and Ben-Gurion's first broadcast, as Prime Minister of Israel, was from an air-raid shelter.

BOOK TWO

5

THE YEAR ONE

C'était la même Terre; et les mêmes Hébreux
—CHARLES PÉGUY

IN FEBRUARY 1948, in London, Ernest Bevin received Tewfic Abu al-Huda, the Prime Minister of Transjordan, together with Sir John Glubb, commander of Transjordan's Arab Legion. Huda notified Bevin of King Abdullah's intention to take over, after British withdrawal, in the areas allotted to the Arabs under the General Assembly resolution of November 29, 1947. Bevin indicated his approval, but added: "Don't go and invade the area allotted to the Jews."[1]

Coming from the British Foreign Minister, this advice carried weight. Transjordan had become formally independent in 1946, but it still remained, in substance, a British protectorate. The British Resident in Amman had become British Minister "without," as he said himself, "causing any drastic modifications in my activities."[2] As for the Arab Legion, it was British trained, British financed and led by British officers.

Bevin's advice, pacific though it was in form, in fact helped to precipitate the conflict, for two reasons. First, it freed the Arab Legion to take over *in the areas assigned to the (Palestinian) Arabs*, under the United Nations partition resolution. This aroused the desperate antagonism of the Mufti—whose sway it would end—and the competition of other Arab leaders. Neither Egypt nor Syria, let alone the Mufti, was prepared to let Abdullah inherit Palestine. He might nonetheless have been able to take over in the areas allotted to the Arabs by agreement with the Jews—who, of course, vastly preferred him to the Mufti—had it not been for the second and fatal factor: Jerusalem.

Jerusalem was not among the areas allotted to the Jews under the United Nations resolution. It was to be an international zone. But the manner of Britain's withdrawal, and Bevin's refusal to cooperate in any way with the United Nations in advance of withdrawal, made internationalization in practice impossible.

Now Bevin, by confining his restraining advice to "the area allotted to the Jews," left it open to Abdullah, and Glubb, to move into Jerusalem. That was inherently attractive, because of the prestige that would be acquired by the King, as protector of the mosques. Abdullah would probably have preferred to avoid a war at all, but Arab expectations were pushing him in that direction, and Jerusalem appeared a sanctioned objective. In the end, the King decided to pre-empt his critics.

At a meeting of the Arab League, in Cairo, Abdullah gave notice that the Arab Legion would enter Palestine immediately, once the Mandate had come to an end. This announcement is said to have caused "consternation and confusion" among the delegates.[3] In particular, the Egyptian Premier, Nokrashy Pasha, was unwilling to commit regular forces to Palestine. He was well aware of the unreadiness of his own country's armed forces. Also the generally successful fight Hagana had been putting up against the Palestinian Arabs and the volunteers of the Arab Liberation Army hardly promised a walkover. But once one of Palestine's Arab neighbors decided to commit its regular forces against the Yishuv, the rest could hardly hold back. The most realistic of the Arab leaders might have serious qualms, but the mood of Arabs generally was triumphal. And this mood was infectious. "If war broke out between Jews and Arabs," writes Attlee's latest biographer, "the Foreign Office and the British Chiefs of Staff reported categorically, the Arabs would throw the Jews into the sea."[4]

II

David Ben-Gurion did not rejoice, along with the rest of Tel Aviv, on the day when he proclaimed the establishment of the State of Israel. "I feel no gaiety in me, only deep anxiety, as on the 29th of November [day of the U.N. partition resolution] when I was like a mourner at the feast."[5]

The survival of the new State was seriously in question, in the first phase of the fighting. True, it was not quite such a David-and-Goliath contest as some accounts suggest. The population statistics— 40 million Arabs to 1 million Jews—are not directly relevant to the military situation. Accounts vary, but the numbers actually engaged on the two sides seem to have been about equal. But the Arabs had a huge initial superiority in terms of equipment and firepower, heavy weapons, armor and aircraft. The Jews hoped to compensate for that handicap through superior morale, initiative, dedication and skill. But that hope had yet to be tested against regular armies.

The Arab chiefs of staff, meeting in Damascus in April, had worked out, on paper, a coordinated offensive. Syrian and Lebanese armies were to invade northern Palestine and occupy Tiberias, Safed and Nazareth. The principal effort would be opened by the Iraqi Army and the Arab Legion south of Lake Tiberias, moving west toward the port of Haifa, the main objective of the opening phase of the campaign. The role of the Egyptians was to pin down Jewish forces south of Tel Aviv.

In practice, there was no unified Arab campaign. Nominally Abdullah was commander in chief of the Arab armies, but in reality the armies—other than his own Arab Legion—paid no attention to him, nor he to them. The Damascus strategy might possibly have worked, if the Arab Legion—much the most efficient component of the Arab forces—had been committed to the attack on Haifa. But Abdullah wasn't interested in Haifa, which was in any case out of bounds, in terms of Bevin's advice. Abdullah kept his forces in the West Bank territory designated by the U.N. for the Arab State, and in Jerusalem (theoretically internationalized).

So the Arab armies attacked piecemeal. The Syrians attacked in the Jordan Valley—a zone of heavy Jewish settlement—in brigade strength, with an armored-car battalion, an artillery regiment and a company of tanks. They captured the town of Zemah, and on May 20 attacked the important settlements of Degania, among whose defenders was Moshe Dayan, whose father had helped to found these settlements. Degania was defended by only seventy men—armed with mortars and machine guns, and using Molotov cocktails against the Syrian tanks. The defenders managed to beat off the Syrians, who retreated. By May 23, the Syrians had withdrawn from the Jordan valley. The news of the successful defense of Degania spread rapidly, greatly encouraging the Jews, by proving that settlements could hold out against attack by regular Arab forces.[6]

The Lebanese Army made a limited invasion into Northern Galilee, but then stopped, after an Israeli counterattack into Lebanon. The extent of Lebanon's participation in the war was determined by the mixed Christian-Muslim character of its polity, and the tenuous nature of the purely Arab bond across the religious divide. However, other Arab forces—Fawzi al-Kaukji's Arab Liberation Army of volunteers—were able to penetrate, through the Lebanese-held Gate of Malkya, into Central Galilee, where they were enthusiastically welcomed by the local Palestinian Arabs. At the same time the Syrians returned to the attack, this time capturing the long-established border settlement of Mishmar Hayarden, controlling the strategic Bridge of the Daughters of Jacob, across the Jordan river.

To the south of the Syrian, Lebanese and "Liberation" armies, the Iraqi Army first attacked the settlement of Gesher, but was repulsed as the Syrians had been at Degania. The Iraqis succeeded, however, in capturing the settlement of Geulim, but were driven out of it again by the Israelis, who then counterattacked into Arab territories, capturing Arab villages and laying siege to the town of Jenin. For the Iraqis the offensive phase of their operations was over.

In the extreme south, the Negev desert, Israel was attacked by the largest and potentially most formidable of the Arab forces, the Egyptian Army. Advancing along the coast to threaten Tel Aviv, the Egyptians were halted at the settlement of Yad Mordechai, south of what is now the port and city of Ashdod. Yad Mordechai was named after Mordechai Ancelevitz, leader of the Warsaw Ghetto rising in 1943. Many of the settlers were veterans of either that rebellion or other partisan fighting against the Germans. The defenders of Yad Mordechai numbered little more than one infantry company. The Egyptians, in their attack, used two infantry battalions, one armored battalion and one artillery regiment. Yad Mordechai held out for five days. The settlement was evacuated on May 24.

The five days gained by the defenders of Yad Mordechai were crucial for the survival of Israel. Israel's danger was greatest in the very early days of the fighting, when Israel still depended on the meager store of arms illegally imported or acquired by the Yishuv during the Mandate. Every day now gained was a day in which Israel, a State recognized by the superpowers, could freely import new and greatly superior weapons (from the Soviet bloc, since there was a Western embargo covering the region). Hagana agents had been buying weapons even before the end of the Mandate, and they were now coming in fast. Egypt's Air Force had held command of the skies up to now, bombing Tel Aviv and other Jewish centers, and an Egyptian brigade, with five hundred vehicles, was moving north. But on May 29, the first Israeli fighter planes—four Messerschmitts—attacked the Egyptian column. Although not much material damage was done, the Egyptian advance was halted near what is now Ashdod.

The Egyptian rank and file seem not to have been aware that they were engaged in an invasion. Gamal Abdel Nasser, who was a junior officer in this campaign, later recalled asking a private soldier, after the Army had entered Palestine, why he thought he was there. "We are engaged in maneuvers at Rebeiki, sir," the man replied. Rebeiki was the Army's regular exercise ground in Egypt.[7] Troops unprepared to this degree were naturally shaken by the fierce resistance at Yad Mordechai, and after the appearance of the Israeli fighters, the Egyptian forces simply dug in.

The Egyptian thrust from the south had seemed the greatest threat to the survival of the new State. But it was in the center, in the Jerusalem sector, that the Israelis experienced their greatest rebuffs, and losses, at the hands of the Arab Legion, now the Transjordanian Army, Abdullah's forces, under Glubb's command.

Abdullah's forces didn't really threaten Israel's survival. But the threat they did represent was only barely second to survival in Ben-Gurion's mind. They threatened to cut off Jerusalem from Israel, and to incorporate the city into Abdullah's emirate (Transjordan, later Jordan). For Ben-Gurion, as for most Zionists, a State of Israel shut off from Jerusalem would be almost meaningless.

Jerusalem, at this time, consisted of a New City, largely Jewish, and the Old City, within its sixteenth-century walls, which was largely Arab, but contained a sizeable Jewish Quarter. Transjordanian forces, having crossed the Jordan, by the Allenby Bridge, on May 15, deployed around Jerusalem, and also attacked the New City. When the attack on the New City was repelled—at Notre Dame Monastery on May 24—Glubb's Transjordanians did not continue with direct attacks on the main center of Jewish population, but concentrated on the Jewish Quarter of the Old City, whose inhabitants were mainly pious Jews, of the Old Yishuv, traditionally inimical to secular Zionism. Frantic Israeli efforts to relieve the Jewish Quarter failed after regular Transjordanian forces had entered the Quarter. On the morning of May 28 a delegation of rabbis approached the Transjordanian command. On the same day, the Israeli garrison surrendered, after the Transjordanians had agreed to safeguard prisoners and the civilian population. The Transjordanians carried out their obligations.

The siege of the New City continued. The Transjordanians, with strong forces, held Latrun, in the Valley of Ayalon, on the main road from the coast to Jerusalem. The Israelis attacked this position repeatedly, but were beaten back, with heavy losses. But they just managed to keep a lifeline open to Jewish Jerusalem by working on a rough cross-country trail—known as the Burma Road—which they made usable by motor vehicles, bypassing the Transjordanian positions.

The Security Council had called for a truce on May 29. The truce, agreed to by all combatants, came into force on June 11, for one month. The political and diplomatic background to the truce, and to the fighting, has now to be considered.

III

Internationally, the central fact of the new situation was President Truman's prompt recognition of the new State, *de facto*, on May 15, followed three days later by *de jure* recognition from the Soviet Union.

Truman's recognition of Israel put the Attlee Government in yet another painful dilemma. The logic of the 1939 White Paper—logic which the Foreign Office still doggedly sought to pursue—required Britain to give priority to the views of those Arab regimes which were still, though in varying ways and degrees, Britain's clients. In order of importance that meant Egypt, Iraq and Transjordan. Above all, this logic required Britain to do what it could to safeguard the prestige of these regimes in the eyes of their own subjects. But, once the Arab armies had attacked Israel, there was only one way of safeguarding the prestige of the regimes, and that was to help them to beat the Israelis. Their subjects exuberantly and confidently expected them to win, and wipe out what they called "the Zionist gangs." If they failed to win a war which their subjects assumed they would win easily, Britain's friends would be utterly discredited, and Britain's influence fatally undermined. So the White Paper anti-partition logic pointed in the general direction of support for the Arab side in the war.[8]

On the other hand, Truman's recognition of Israel served notice that support for the Arabs would bring with it renewed friction with the Americans. And Britain was less than ever before in a position to bear such friction. President Truman, in the month before he recognized Israel, had launched the Marshall Plan, on which now depended all hopes for the recovery of Western Europe, including Britain. A Middle Eastern policy which required Britain to defy President Truman—even with some covert sympathy from the State Department—was at variance with the realities of Britain's position in the postwar world.

These realities were now acted out in the rituals and theater of the United Nations. On May 17, the United States introduced in the Security Council a draft resolution, declaring that the situation in Palestine constituted a breach of the peace within the meaning of Article 39 of the Charter—implying the possibility of the use of force by the Great Powers—and calling for a cease-fire within thirty-six hours.[9] Britain offered an amendment deleting the reference to Article 39, and this was carried; something which could not have happened without the cooperation of the State Department, whose sympathy with the Foreign Office position, in this period, had the unfortunate effect of leading Ernest Bevin farther up the garden path.

Britain's little victory, on behalf of its Arab friends, caused the powerful and energetic pro-Israel lobby in the United States to press for the suspension of the American loan to Britain. As this pressure endangered the Marshall Plan, the cornerstone of American policy in the period, the United States brought pressure of its own to bear on Britain, to bring its Middle East policy into line. The Attlee Government backed down, and agreed to stop its arms shipments to the Arab states. The Security Council, on May 29, adopted a resolution ordering a cease-fire, and also prohibiting the importation of arms or military personnel into Palestine or the Arab states. A cease-fire, based on this resolution, came into effect on June 11.

President Truman has been criticized by some pro-Israel writers for supporting an embargo, denying military assistance to Israel in its hour of need. Such criticism misses the whole point of the embargo, which was to stop Britain helping the Arabs. Israel was well organized to beat any United Nations embargo, and continued to import arms from many sources, mainly Czechoslovakia. But Britain was obliged to respect the embargo—obliged by American pressure, not really by a Security Council resolution, which it could have vetoed had it not been for the pressure in question. Britain complied strictly, and even abruptly recalled almost all its regular officers serving with the Arab Legion,[10] thus seriously disrupting that force—"a shattering blow," Glubb called the decision.

Thus at one stroke, Britain's client regimes were deprived of any material support from their patron, and deprived also of their sole traditional source of arms and military training. They were also served notice that they could no longer depend on any major Power while both the United States and—for the moment—the Soviet Union backed their enemy.

The Security Council resolution of May 29—and the realities which dictated Britain's compliance—left Ernest Bevin's Middle East policy in ruins, though Bevin was to go on trying to defend what was left of his policy for another eight months.

IV

To Israel, the truce had come, as one commander said, "like manna from Heaven." It was a breathing space for exhausted people, and also an opportunity to build up resources for the expected next round. But the truce was hardly ten days old when a dispute broke out between Israelis which for a time seemed to threaten the infant State with civil war.

On May 28, Order No. 4 of Ben-Gurion's Provisional Government had created the Israel Defense Forces, and prohibited the establishment or maintenance of any other armed force. But it was impossible to put this order into effect during the fighting with the Arabs, and Irgun maintained a separate existence after the truce came into being. David Ben-Gurion was determined to put Order No. 4 into effect. The episode of the *Altalena* gave him his opportunity.

The *Altalena* was a ship—called after a pen name of Vladimir Jabotinsky—commissioned by the Irgun to bring in arms and volunteers. The arms were apparently a free gift to the Irgun from the French Government, which also promised a further supply of arms, and general support for Irgun.[11] The arms and volunteers of the *Altalena* were badly needed by Israel, but there were two difficulties from the point of view of Ben-Gurion's Government. One was that as the sailing of the *Altalena* from the French Mediterranean port of Port-de-Bouc had been widely publicized, it would be a flagrant breach of the Security Council resolution, in the presence of United Nations observers. The other and more weighty difficulty was that such a large consignment of arms might enable Begin's Irgun to challenge the authority of the Government of Israel. Ben-Gurion's Provisional Government decided to prevent the importation of the arms, by force if necessary. On June 21, Hagana—now Israel Defense Forces—set the *Altalena* on fire on the beach at Tel Aviv. Fifteen men were killed in the fighting, most of them on the Irgun side. One of the Irgun casualties aboard the *Altalena* was Avraham Stavsky, who fourteen years before had been accused, and later acquitted, of the murder of Chaim Arlosoroff, also on the beach at Tel Aviv.

Civil war seemed very near but was averted when Begin—who had been aboard the *Altalena* when it was set on fire—broadcast that evening over the Irgun underground transmitter: "Irgun soldiers will not be a party to fratricidal warfare, but neither will they accept the discipline of Ben-Gurion's army any longer. Within the state area we shall continue our political activities. Our fighting strength we shall conserve for the enemy outside."[12]

What this meant in practice was that Irgun would cease its paramilitary activities in the territories "allotted to the Jews" by the U.N. resolution, but would continue these activities in any other area of Palestine it might choose, including—and especially—the "international zone" of Jerusalem. Ben Gurion accepted this distinction for the time being.[13]

The *Altalena* crisis was safely over, but the vision of that burning ship on the beach at Tel Aviv was to haunt the political life of the new State for decades to come.

V

The truce declared on June 11 lasted until July 8. During this period, the United States exerted itself, through the United Nations, to try to secure a lasting peace in the area. There was an unusually high level of ambiguity in U.S. policy about what *kind* of peace. President Truman's recognition had established that it must be a peace in which the State of Israel would survive, and in any case the Arabs did not seem capable of destroying it. On the other hand, the State Department agreed with the Foreign Office about the need to save as much as possible of the faces of the pro-Western and moderate Arab regimes which had gone to war with Israel. And the saving of these particular faces required that the peace settlement should be as unpleasant for Israel as was compatible with the survival of Israel.

Formally, the peacemaking effort was conducted by a United

Nations mediator, Count Folke Bernadotte (1895–1948), who had been appointed by the Security Council on May 20. The mediator had a deputy, Dr. Ralph Bunche. United Nations realities are almost invariably not what they seem, and in this case the deputy was more important than the mediator.

Count Bernadotte's tragic fate, in the course of his service as mediator, has had the effect of retrospectively distorting his role and stature. He has been depicted as a figure of transcendent wisdom. At the time, pro-Israel propaganda depicted him as a British stooge. Neither view can be sustained. From his memoirs,[14] Count Bernadotte emerges as a ceremonious and rather naïve person, with a strong sense of duty, and slightly Quixotic.[15] Glubb Pasha, who was cast in a similar mold, saw him as Chaucer's "verray parfit gentil knight." Like many persons of courtly background and disposition, Count Bernadotte found Arab aristocrats more congenial than Jews. To Moshe Sharett (1894–1965), Israel's Foreign Minister, he complained about Jewish "arrogance and hostility."[16]

Jewish hostility was caused by the mediator's insistence, from very early on, that he did not regard himself as bound by the General Assembly's resolution of November 29, 1947. Technically he seems to have been right. The mediator was a servant of the Security Council, and recommendations of the General Assembly, unlike Security Council decisions, do not purport to bind member nations—and still less the Security Council itself, or its servants. But Israeli opinion, in the heat of a struggle for survival, could not be expected to take much stock of such technicalities. Israelis generally saw Bernadotte's attitude to the General Assembly resolution as endangering the very existence of their State, perhaps by opening the way to some new version of the "trusteeship" proposal. Inevitably this aroused strong hostility in Israel to Bernadotte. Out on the desperate fringes of Israeli life this hostility was to take homicidal form.

From Bernadotte's memoirs, it appears that he liked to do the talking, and left the drafting to Ralph Bunche. That meant that the real politics of mediation were in Bunche's hands. And here it is highly relevant that Bunche was an American, a black American, but an American.

I don't want to be misunderstood on that point. Ralph Bunche, whom I knew and liked personally, and under whom I served in the United Nations Secretariat,[17] was never less than a conscientious international civil servant. He would never "take his orders from Washington." All the same, a special relationship existed. At this time, and for a long time after, the Secretariat of the United Nations, as a whole, was far more influenced by the United States than by any other country. This was partly because of the sheer power of the United States, which "paid the piper," or most of the piper, but also because of a complicated blend of idealism and *Realpolitik*. The American general public, at this date, cherished high hopes about the United Nations, and tended to identify it with "the moral conscience of mankind." The public proceedings in the General Assembly and the Security Council took place in the United States and presented the international debate to the American public, often in dramatic form.

This situation made the United Nations far more important, at this time, to the United States Government than to any other Government. Putting it bluntly, the United Nations could be used to make any given United States policy look good. It also gave the United States opportunities to influence a particular outcome, without carrying direct public responsibility for that outcome.

Within this context, the position of the senior Americans in the Secretariat was of particular importance. They were in a much better position than "foreign" officials to talk confidentially with officials in the State Department, and (sometimes more important) in the White House. They knew what kind of formula in an official document would be broadly acceptable in Washington and what would not. That was why Bernadotte left the drafting to Dr. Bunche.

The mediator's plan, drafted by Bunche and presented by Bernadotte, was signed on June 27. It represented what could be agreed on between the United States and Britain, with the United States now the dominant partner, but Britain still influential, through the meeting of minds between the Foreign Office and the State Department. The plan had much more to do with this particular Western balance of forces than with the balance of forces in Palestine. It provided for a "union," involving the whole of Mandate Palestine, with a partnership between an enlarged kingdom of Jordan and the Jewish State. Jordan would be confirmed in possession of its West Bank territory (including East Jerusalem). "The Arabs" would acquire the whole of the Negev (which immediately led to conflicts between Egypt and Jordan). Israel was to be compensated with Western Galilee. Unlimited Jewish immigration would be allowed for two years; after that it would be controlled by a United Nations agency. All Arab refugees were to be allowed to return to their homes.

This plan had no attractions for any of the local principals except Abdullah. From an Israeli point of view, it was not as bad as had been feared, since it was more Bunche than Bernadotte. But it was unacceptable for many reasons, the main one being that it set limits to the sovereignty of Israel. For the Arab leaders—other than Abdullah—the plan was doubly infuriating, because of its concessions to the Jews and its bounty to Abdullah.

So both Israel and the Arabs rejected the plan outright. Even Abdullah did not dare to accept a plan that was being comprehensively denounced throughout the Arab world. So there were no local takers at all for the Bernadotte Plan.

The plan was much worse than a mere nonstarter. It actually helped to precipitate a renewed conflict, because it sharply stimulated those rivalries between the Arab leaders which had done so much to precipitate the original conflict. The Arab states were not in fact anxious for renewed conflict, but they competed in belligerent declarations. The Mufti, who stood to lose everything by any compromise remotely resembling Bernadotte's "union," set the pace, and Egypt followed.

Abdullah, for his part, clearly saw the folly of another fight. As he told Sir John Glubb: "If I were to drive into the desert and accost the first goatherd I saw, and consult him on whether to make war on my enemies or not, he would say to me, 'How many have you got, and how many have they?' Yet here are these learned politicians, all of them with university degrees, and when I say to them, 'The Jews are too strong, it is a mistake to make war,' they cannot understand the point. They make long speeches about rights."[18]

But the other Arab leaders, principally King Farouk and his ministers, were under too much pressure to ask sensible, goatherdlike questions. They had whooped up their impending victories and hushed up their actual defeats. Their populations were puzzled by the truce, and infuriated by the news that Palestine was about to be partitioned between the Jews and Abdullah, seen as a stooge of the British and a collaborator with the Jews. The Arab Governments' own rhetoric thrust in the direction of renewed war, by denying that the war was over. The Arabs had a *common* language, but competing states; and consequently competing radio stations, each of which could be heard by the subjects of its rival powers. The competitors boasted, taunted and egged one another on. They operated within a rhetorical tradition which has been described by the Arab sociologist Halim Barakat in the following terms:

Arab society is verbal and expressive, since the Arabs are not a people who speak out only when it serves their aims and plans: they often make proclamations which cause them harm. The Arab voices his views and feelings without caring whether he is furthering his own interests or harming them, while the Westerner only makes statements which are beneficial to his interests. . . . One of the results of free and spontaneous expression in Arab society is release, and purification of the spirit, through catharsis. . . . Hence the Arab saying 'Reproach is the soap of the soul.' . . . The most important factors to be noted are the aggressive and mocking speeches, articles and poems of political leaders and others. These enable the Arab to feel that he has overcome his powerlessness. . . . The communication media have fostered this tendency to self-purification.[19]

On July 9, the truce was due to expire, and the Egyptians, whatever their real intentions, sounded as if it would not be renewed. On the day before, July 8, fighting broke out in the Negev. It is now considered likely that the fighting was initiated by Israel, but those who had insisted that the war was not over were hardly in a position to complain when it was shown that they had inadvertently been telling the truth.

VI

The fighting lasted for ten days. The Arabs gained almost nothing by it, but the Israelis succeeded in widening the Jerusalem corridor, thus establishing themselves securely in the divided city. They also captured large areas of Lower Galilee, including the Arab towns of Lydda and Ramle, whose inhabitants left.

By the time of the second truce, more than 500,000 Arab refugees had left Israeli-held territory. In the long and sterile polemical war that has been conducted over these unfortunate people, the Arab side refers to the refugees as "driven out,"[20] while the Israeli side prefers to say that they "fled." In fact it appears that some—perhaps a majority—fled, while some were driven out. Some, including the Palestinian Arab leadership, left of their own accord as early as January 1947. In the early phase of the fighting—before the intervention of the Arab regular armies—the Hagana had no policy of driving out Arabs and in at least one case, at Haifa, tried hard to persuade them to stay. In this phase, the Arabs fled, mainly in panic caused by the news of the Irgun's massacre at Deir Yassin.

In the last brief phase, after the Arab armies were welcomed with enthusiasm by the Palestinian Arabs, the Israel Defense Forces changed their policy and, as one historian puts it, "encouraged, usually prodded and occasionally coerced"[21] the Arabs to leave the territories coming under Israeli control. Most of the refugees went to what now became Jordan; others went to the Egyptian-held Gaza Strip. Most of the refugees were housed in camps hurriedly organized by the United Nations.

From very early on, Ben-Gurion's Government set its face against the return of the refugees to their homes (unless as part of a possible, but obviously remote, general peace settlement). "I think that one should prevent their return," Ben-Gurion told his Cabinet on June 16. "War is war . . . and those who have declared war on us will have to bear the consequences after they have been defeated."[22]

General hostilities ceased in mid-July, but sporadic truce violations continued through August and September, especially in the divided and disputed city of Jerusalem. After the *Altalena* incident, Irgun and Lehi members had concentrated in Jerusalem, both to escape the jurisdiction of Ben-Gurion's Provisional Government[23] and in the hope of conquering the Old City with the Wall of the Temple. It was in Jerusalem that the mediator, Count Bernadotte, was murdered by three members of Lehi, on September 17, 1948. Just as the murder of Lord Moyne had done, the murder of Bernadotte excited international anger against Israel. Somewhat paradoxically, this helped Ben-Gurion to assert his authority in Jerusalem, where he disbanded Irgun and detained members of Lehi. In the circumstances, the United Nations could hardly object to this particular exercise of authority, even in an area not "allotted to the Jews." Within three days of the murder of Bernadotte, the underground organization had been completely disbanded throughout Israel. The Provisional Government was now in complete control of all Jewish-held territory.

Just before Bernadotte's murder a revised form of the Bernadotte Plan had been completed, and this now came before the General Assembly. The impracticable "union" of Israel and Jordan was now dropped, and the plan, in its new version, was basically a partition of Palestine, between Israel and Jordan, giving Jerusalem and the Negev to Jordan, while Israel was allowed to keep Western Galilee. Being a Bunche draft—a compromise between the United States and Britain—

the new Bernadotte Plan was supported at the United Nations by the United States and Britain. Israel disliked the plan, for giving too much to Jordan, but was ill placed to fight a plan coming forward in the venerated name of the mediator, murdered by Jews in Jerusalem, in the course of his work for peace.

Israel was rescued from its difficulty by the Arabs and the Soviet Union. The Mufti and the Egyptians roused the Arab world against a plan for rewarding the traitor Abdullah. The Russians resisted anything that would increase British influence, through rewarding a British client state. Together, the Arabs, the Russians (plus Ukraine and Byelorussia), a number of Catholic states (wanting an "international" Jerusalem) and Israel were able to muster a "blocking third," preventing the General Assembly from approving the revised Bernadotte Plan.

As before, however, the result of the U.S.-British compromise aimed at peace was to precipitate renewed local conflict. As soon as the new Bernadotte Plan was mooted, and while it looked as if it might be adopted by the General Assembly, Ben-Gurion was moved to make good his claim to the Negev, awarded to Israel by the United Nations in November, occupied by both Egyptian and Transjordanian forces, and now (it seemed) about to be awarded by the United Nations to Transjordan. To try to take the Negev *after* it had been awarded to Jordan would be to fly in the face of the United Nations and the United States: a good reason for moving *before* the Bernadotte Plan could carry, while still being able to claim the authority of the older General Assembly resolution (November 29, 1947).

The boundaries of the Jewish-held area, at the time of the second truce, were unsatisfactory, from the point of view of its Government, in three main ways. Abdullah's forces held the Old City and the Wall. Abdullah's forces also held a large area to the west of the Jordan—Judea and Samaria—bringing the Arab-Israel border dangerously close to Tel Aviv. Finally, Egyptian forces still held a large part of the Negev, and were also dangerously close to Tel Aviv.

Ben-Gurion might have liked both to push Abdullah back, in Judea and Samaria, and to drive the Egyptians out of the Negev. His military advisers told him that it would not be possible to do both of these things. He then decided to concentrate on the Negev, thus preempting the Bernadotte Plan. The choice may seem surprising and—significantly—it was criticized at the time, from the Right. Strategically, the Samarian "bulge" seemed more dangerous; the Jordanians were ten miles from Tel Aviv; the Egyptians, forty. In terms of the Bible—Ben-Gurion's "Mandate"—Judea and Samaria meant far more in Jewish history than did the Negev desert.

But there were good reasons for Ben-Gurion's choice. Abdullah had been a reluctant and rather unambitious enemy. Of all Israel's enemies, he seemed the most likely to make a durable peace. His forces were likely to put up a stiffer resistance, if attacked, than any other Arab army. Also the danger of British intervention was much higher in the case of an attack on Jordan than in any other case.[24]

Egypt, on the other hand, was more vociferously hostile than Jordan, and militarily weaker at that time. Cairo Radio was the most powerful and the most active of the broadcasting stations, whose competition in propaganda had helped to precipitate the two attacks by the Arab states on Israel. Egypt was by far the largest and most important of the Arab states, and potentially the most dangerous of Israel's enemies. If Egypt could be decisively defeated, and brought to an armistice conference, the moral effect on Israel's other enemies would be strong. Also, if Egypt was decisively defeated in the Negev, Abdullah was too realistic to press his claim to the area. Secretly, he would be glad to be rid of the Egyptians, more dangerous neighbors to him than to Israel, because of their support for the Mufti.

The Egyptians, like other parties to local truces, rather often committed minor breaches of the truce agreement. In all such cases, the party to the truce which no longer finds the truce of advantage to it can invoke such minor breaches to justify an all-out attack on the other party. This Israel now did, twice. The first attack, in October, drove the Egyptians out of much of the Negev. In the second attack, in December, the Israelis drove the Egyptians out of the rest of the Negev—and also dislodged small Transjordanian forces which were there to stake the "Bernadotte" claim to the territory. Then the Israelis pushed on into Egyptian territory, Sinai.

Israel's invasion into Sinai brought a quick and strong reaction from Britain. On December 31, Britain offered to invoke, in defense of Egypt, the Anglo-Egyptian Treaty of 1936. However, the Egyptian Government itself refused to allow the treaty to be invoked, preferring instead to seek an armistice with Israel, through acting mediator Ralph Bunche.[25] The British connection had become so unpopular in Egypt that the Egyptian Government, rather than use that connection in its own defense, preferred even an armistice with Israel—necessarily on Israel's terms—to the contamination of being seen to owe anything to Britain's friendship.

It was an almost surrealist *dénouement* to the policy pursued by the Foreign Office for ten years: a policy dominated by the perceived need to be popular in the Arab world, and therefore to treat the Jewish National Home as expendable. This policy had encouraged the Arabs in expectations and competitive ambitions which plunged them into a disaster for which they blamed Britain, with some justice. Britain's "pro-Arab" policies had won for it more *Arab* enemies than the "pro-Israel" policies of the United States and the Soviet Union had won for those countries. It looks as if the Foreign Office, in this period, could have done with the advice of a competent desert goatherd.

In the course of Bevin's unappreciated exertions on behalf of Egypt, R.A.F. planes went on reconnaissance missions over Israeli-held territory on the border between Israel and Egypt.[26] Israeli forces shot down five of these planes on January 7, 1949.

For a short time, it looked as if Britain and Israel might actually find themselves at war. Under pressure from the United States and Britain—and having in any case attained their original objectives, both military and political—the Israelis withdrew from Egyptian territory, and prepared for an armistice with Egypt.

At the same time, the British Government also retreated. Members of the Government, especially the Chancellor of the Exchequer, Sir Stafford Cripps, were understandably worried about a policy line which was so anti-Israel as to strain relations with the United States at a time when the future of Britain's economy depended on these relations. It had been argued that this was a price worth paying, in order to placate the Arabs, but it now appeared that the Arabs, far from being placated, were infuriated. There was therefore no longer any defensible reason for persisting in a policy which annoyed the United States, in addition to everyone else. Even before the reconnaissance debacle, the Conservatives, in opposition, had shifted their hitherto passive attitude over Palestine, to the extent of advising the Government to extend *de facto* recognition to Israel. The ill-fated reconnaissance brought matters to a head, Cripps moved against Bevin inside the Government, and Churchill indicated that the opposition—for the first time—would vote against the Government, over Palestine. As Crossman says: "This was the end."[27]

In the Commons debate on Palestine on January 26, 1949, Bevin's Middle Eastern policy was effectively interred.[28] "The State of Israel is now a fact," said Bevin, "and we have not tried to undo it." He went on to tread heavily, yet once more, on Truman's toes: "I ask the

House to realize that at this point the whole question of who should be elected to certain offices in the United States turned on this problem, and the United Kingdom had very little latitude after that time."[29]

Churchill attacked Bevin for his "astounding mishandling" of the Palestine question, and for his very strong and direct streak of bias and prejudice, and also for miscalculation. The course Bevin had taken, said Churchill, "led inevitably and directly to a trial of strength, and the result was opposite to what I believe he expected it to be."

It was a strong speech, but as Attlee suggested in his reply to the debate, Churchill's strictures might have been more helpful if they had been made "at the time and not now."[30] Attlee indicated, without quite saying, that his Government was about to extend *de facto* recognition to Israel.

Three days later, on January 29, Bevin called in Joseph Linton, Israel's unofficial representative in London. Linton later recalled the historic conversation in which Ernest Bevin informed him of Britain's decision to grant *de facto* recognition to the State of Israel. Bevin was affable and explained that he had been misjudged; he was not anti-Zionist.

Joseph Linton later told a journalist that, at that moment, he felt "no rancour or resentment, only a touch of sympathy," toward Ernest Bevin. "After all, who had done more to bring Lord Balfour's policy to final fruition?"[31]

VII

As Ben-Gurion had calculated, the defeat of the Egyptian forces led not only Egypt but Israel's other Arab neighbors to seek armistice agreements. The negotiations were organized by the acting mediator, Ralph Bunche, with great tact and firmness.

Up to this point the process of United Nations mediation had been—in reality, though not in form—an effort to coordinate the Middle East policies of the United States and Britain. Dr. Bunche had been constrained, by the realities prevailing behind the façade of the United Nations, to concentrate his great talents, as a diplomatist and draftsman, on this particular task. He was successful in producing texts which those two Powers could support at the United Nations: the texts of Bernadotte's Plan, Marks I and II. But plans which did meet that particular Western test were unfit to provide any kind of peace settlement in the region; in fact, they served only to set off new phases of fighting.

By the end of January 1949, however, the "Western context" of United Nations mediation had become much simpler. For one thing the re-election of Truman—regarded up to November 1948 as a lame-duck President—discouraged those who, in both America and Britain, had hoped for a radical change in United States policy toward Israel after November. Israel's defeat of Egypt, immediately followed by Egypt's staggering rebuff to Britain, laid bare the comprehensive failure of Ernest Bevin's Middle Eastern policy. At this point Bevin, in effect, retired hurt from the Middle Eastern scene. At the same time, both Israel and its contiguous Arab states had had enough of fighting, for the time being, and were anxious to move from the highly precarious condition of a non-negotiated truce to the relative stability of negotiated armistice. This new context gave Dr. Bunche a much freer hand. He could now give his full attention to the local realities, without having to take account of Western differences. With these advantages on his side he brought about, in a remarkably short time, armistices between Israel and all its neighbors.

Each of the armistice negotiations was conducted on a strictly bilateral basis, thus insulating the negotiation process from the factor of Arab competition in anti-Israeli gestures. And Bunche also insisted on direct negotiation between Arabs and Israelis in his presence, avoiding the system of two separate parallel negotiations, as favored by the London Conference of 1939. The negotiations resulted in an armistice with Egypt (February 24, 1949), followed by armistices with Lebanon (March 23), Jordan (April 3) and Syria (July 20). Of the states that had attacked Israel, only Iraq, with no common frontier, felt no need to conclude an armistice.

The State of Israel, as Bevin had acknowledged, was now a fact. But in the eyes of all its neighbors, it was a horrifying and a humiliating fact. Arabs, both Muslim and Christian, had always despised Jews. When their armies were repelled by what they had called "the Zionist gangs," their contempt recoiled against themselves. The events of 1948–1949 entered the Arab consciousness as *al-Nakba*, "the disaster." "This colossal failure," writes the Arab historian A. L. Tibawi, "had a profound reaction in all the Arab states."[32]

The first targets of Arab indignation were the regimes, alliances and leaders who had led the Arabs to defeat. In Egypt, Premier

Nokrashy was assassinated at the end of December 1948. King Farouk's reign was ended, by military coup, three and a half years later. In Syria, coup succeeded coup; no less than three of them in 1949 alone. In Jordan, Abdullah, the only Arab leader who had come well out of the war, was destroyed by what he had gained.

In 1950, he merged Transjordan and the Arab-held part of Palestine, including the Old City of Jerusalem, into the Hashemite Kingdom of Jordan. The King was assassinated on July 20, 1951, as he left the Mosque of al-Aqsa, in the Old City, after Friday prayers. The Haram esh-Sharif, where the mosque stands, had been Mufti territory, and it was the Mufti's men who killed the King. But the Hashemite dynasty survived, represented today by Abdullah's grandson, Hussein.

Lebanon and Iraq were less immediately affected. Lebanon had not been enthusiastic about the war, and its forces had barely been involved in the fighting. Iraq, not having a common border with Israel, could represent itself as undefeated. These regimes were to perish— almost ten years later in the case of Iraq, twenty-seven years in the case of Lebanon—not directly because of *al-Nakba*, but because of later events, some of which were set into motion by *al-Nakba* while others were antecedent to it (e.g., the interreligious and intertribal tensions of Lebanon).

Those who led the radical, revolutionary and putschist movements in the Arab world were primarily hostile to the old Arab regimes, and their patrons (Britain, France). The most successful of the new leaders, Gamal Abdel Nasser (1918–1970)—who led the coup against Farouk in 1952, and came to sole power in 1954—was not particularly anxious for a second round, a war of *revanche* against Israel. But the logic of his own rhetoric pointed him in that direction, willy-nilly. If the great sin of the old regimes had been their failure in the war against Israel, then the test of the success of the new regimes had to be their capacity to fight Israel and win. And the Arab states—under new regimes as under old—continued to compete in rhetoric, egging one another on toward a second round, in very much the same way as they had gotten themselves into the first round.

And on the Israeli side, also, there were those who were not averse to the idea of a second round.

6

HOLOCAUST
IN MIND

Honorable judge! Our trial drags on and
  I lose patience
One has to admit I got caught up in an unfortunate
  ambiguity

—ABBA KOVNER

*T*HE FIRST national elections to the Knesset, the parliament of the new State, took place in January 1949. Ben-Gurion's party, Mapai, became the largest one, and was to dominate the politics of Israel for nearly thirty years. Ben-Gurion formed a Government with the support of a number of small parties, almost all religious. The largest opposition party was the left-wing Mapam, whose connections with the Communist states were soon to split it and weaken the Left. The third-largest party—and soon the main opposition—was Menachem Begin's Herut, the continuation of Irgun, in constitutional, civilian form, with an irredentist program, claiming (in theory) all of 1918 Palestine, including Jordan.

On Ben-Gurion's invitation, Weizmann returned to Israel as President. His wife, Vera, noted in her diary: "Chaim ought to be happy but is he? He looks like a man who has climbed the highest mountain, and on reaching the top is more exhausted from his efforts than elated by his achievement."[1]

In addition to general reasons, felt by all Israelis, Weizmann had some personal ground for disappointment. He had hoped to wield some authority in the State he had done so much to bring into being, but it was soon borne home to him that all power in Israel was in the hands of the Prime Minister (and, to a much less extent, his colleagues in Government), and that the President's functions were to be purely ceremonial. The symbolic value of bringing Weizmann to Israel as President was quite similar to that of the transfer to Israel, in the same year, of the remains of Theodor Herzl. In both cases, great precursors were being appropriately honored.

Ben-Gurion treated President Weizmann as such a precursor, a valued friend of Israel, from the outside; but a stranger, in space and time, in the State which the Yishuv had won. Ben-Gurion marked this point, cruelly, by refusing to allow Weizmann to add his name to the list of signatories to Israel's Declaration of Independence. The signatories, Ben-Gurion ruled, had to have been in Eretz Israel on the date of the declaration. No matter that Weizmann, on the date in question, was at the post assigned to him in the service of Israel, close to Truman, holding him to his promise. He still didn't belong among the signatories, members of the Yishuv, real Israelis.

That the greatest of Zionist statesmen should have become, even to that degree, a stranger in the Jewish State was an irony that Leon Pinsker could hardly have foreseen.

Zionism itself, in the hour of its triumph, was itself becoming something of a stranger, an anachronism, in the new State. Those who led in the fight for independence—the children of the *kibbutz*—were heirs to the Zionist tradition, in the fullest sense. All those who wielded power in Israel, or who aspired to wield it, were Zionists. Zionism was the dominant ideology and rhetoric. Yet one easily detects, in modern Israeli literature, a widespread feeling among the young that the high-minded thought and language of the Zionist elders have little meaning in the world the young have had to grow up in.

"If you give me another sandwich," says a young soldier in a play by Yigal Mosenson, "I will explain it all. I want you to know that the boys are complicated, very complicated. It has been impossible for them to express themselves, especially since their parents are all educators and are all members of the Second *Aliyah,* and what not, and of course that becomes more and more complicated. . . . I doubt whether I have explained it. Should I return the sandwich?"[2]

What made things, and people, so complicated was a tension between past language and past and present realities in relations with Arabs. Thus in his autobiographical book, *My Life with Ishmael* (Hebrew, 1968), Moshe Shamir recalls discussions in his youth in

Kibbutz Mishmar Ha-Emek: "In the dining hall the leaders spoke of 'the brotherhood of man.' None of them knew a single word of Arabic. They had never in their lives spoken to an Arab like one man speaking to another. . . . In the excellent modern school on the *kibbutz* no Arabic was taught. But they talked a lot and they talked nicely."[3]

Amos Oz, in his short story "Nomad and Viper," gives an example of "talking nicely." The *kibbutz* secretary, Etkin, is talking with a Bedouin elder (following some Bedouin pilferage from *kibbutz* land). The Bedouin elder apologizes. Then Etkin "opened his remarks with a frank and clear statement about the brotherhood of nations—the cornerstone of our ideology—and about the quality of neighborliness of which the peoples of the East had long been justly proud, and never more so than in these days of bloodshed and groundless hatred."[4]

The gap between such rhetoric and the neighboring realities for Israel, from 1948 on, are so wide that some of the writers, in some moods, seem to treat the whole Zionist enterprise as a ghastly mistake. Thus S. Yizhar writes, in a story published in 1949, about an Arab village destroyed in the 1948 fighting: "We came, we shot, we burnt, we blasted, we repulsed and expelled and exiled . . . what the hell are we doing here?"[5]

A later Israeli writer, Josef Mundi, made the founder of Zionism into a character in a black farce, *It Turns*, produced in Tel Aviv in January 1970. The play, set in a lunatic asylum, has three characters: "a man called Theodor Herzl," "a man called Franz Kafka," and a dressmaker's dummy, in French uniform, called "Dreyfus." "Kafka" is writing his *Penal Colony* and "Herzl" is planning his Jewish State. "Dreyfus" is a convict in the Penal Colony; he is also the raw material for the Jewish State. Herzl explains the virtues of Dreyfus to Kafka:

"He is strong. He endures amazingly. Because he has nothing human about him. He has no veins, no brain, no heart. Only the strength to deliver blows. I have succeeded, Franz, I have succeeded! It's fantastic! I have created the new Jew!"

Kafka has built an instrument of torture, and persuades Herzl to get into it, to test the endurance of the "new Jew." As Kafka increases the pressure:

HERZL: This is unendurable! I need an army to defend me, the French want to destroy me.
KAFKA: It's not the French who want to kill you; the Arabs want to destroy you and you want to destroy them.
HERZL: There are no Arabs in my state! Only a desert, and I haven't built it up yet.

KAFKA: No Arabs? (*turns the wheels of the torture instrument*)

HERZL: My back. They're cutting into my back!

KAFKA: It'll be a fantastic story, completely realistic.[6]

It Turns is an extreme case, but the Zionist idea is challenged and questioned, in many ways, in modern Israeli writing. The question is put most directly by Dafi, the young heroine of A. B. Yehoshua's *The Lover*. Dafi's mother, a teacher, is telling the class about the second *aliyah*. Dafi, with some difficulty, manages to get in a question:

"I don't understand," I said, "why you say that they were right, I mean the people of the Second *Aliyah*, thinking that was the only choice, after so many sufferings how can you say there wasn't another choice and that was the only choice?"

I could see she didn't understand.

"Whose sufferings?"

"Our suffering, all of us."

"In what sense?"

"All this suffering all around us . . . wars . . . people getting killed . . . generally . . . why was that the only choice?"

It seemed nobody understood what I meant. Mommy smiled and dodged the question.

"That is really a philosophical question. We have tried to understand their thinking, but now the bell has rung, and we won't be able to solve that question during recess, I'm afraid."

The others all laughed. I wished I could bury myself. The idiots. What was there to laugh about?

Dafi's unanswered "philosophical question" turns up, in varying forms, in all the serious writing. But some of the writers, at least, imply that there is an answer.

Aharon Applefeld is a survivor of the Holocaust who immigrated to Palestine in 1947. His novella "1946"[7] is set in a camp for displaced persons in Italy. These are the survivors of the camps and the forests. They include dealers, smugglers, mad people, whores. Most of them want to get out of Europe, but not necessarily to Palestine.

As always the camp is full of disturbing rumors, the Australian consulate is making a lot of difficulties. And New Zealand isn't in a hurry to grant entrance visas either. A young woman, Hermina, says "If there's no alternative we'll go to Palestine. Lucy and I will sing 'We've come to the land of our fathers to build and be built in it.' The dealers will repent, the smugglers will exchange their trucks for a cart, their merchandise for a plow. Isn't that how the prophets of Zionism saw us?"

As Hermina and Lucy drift off, apparently to become whores in Naples, Hermina's speech looks like another bitter mockery of the Zionist dream. But that, as it turns out, would be a misreading.

An old-clothes dealer finds "an old wall newspaper from a Hebrew day school with a picture of Menachem Ussishkin in it." He is delighted with this find, which reminds him of the "Zionist town" he had been brought up in. Celebrating, he buys a small bottle of brandy, and sings "Zion, Zion," and other songs of his youth. But then sadness takes hold of him.

He remembered his town, his little house and the modest school founded by his late father, a lover of books and of the Hebrew language. None of them had been left alive, only him. Why him? Without them what need was there for a vision? If there was no one to redeem, what need was there for a redeemer?

Again the dream seems to be repelled, and again this is not really the case.

Two of the characters in "1946" represent the two sides in the old debate of European Jewry. Bleiman is the Zionist; Blumberg, the assimilationist.

Bleiman: "The Jewish assimilationists were always a pampered lot; even now they can't stop pampering themselves. . . ."

Blumberg: "That sentence is beyond my comprehension. Allow me to inform you that I do not consider that title offensive in the least. An assimilationist is what I am—an assimilationist born and bred."

Bleiman: "Your success has been rather limited, if you don't mind my saying so."

Rita, Blumberg's wife, an asthmatic, is tired of the endless argument. Then, oddly, a gift of cosmetics, sent to her by a deported camp inhabitant, tilts her mind Bleiman's way:

"We are not helpless victims, we are not dust and ashes. We are brothers to one another. Look what he sent me, even little pedicure tools. You be quiet, Blumberg. I'm ready to go anywhere, even Palestine. The Jews aren't like all the other nations."

Blumberg's application for an Australian visa is turned down, reinforcing Bleiman's point about limited success. The camp inhabitants disperse for various reasons. Then a small ship arrives, offering passage to Palestine for a few illegal immigrants. The last two pragraphs of the novella run:

> "Hurrah, Bleiman, hurrah! The kingdom of heaven is at hand," said Blumberg nastily. Rita put two coats on. Blumberg took her arm with a dignified, chivalrous air.
>
> The searchlights [of the ship] illuminated the abandoned camp. At the touch of the lights the tin roofs creaked in a dull cacophony of pain. "We're coming, we're coming!" cried the vet. This time there was a clear answer to his call: the boats started out towards them. The searchlights were extinguished and the darkness of the water touched the darkness of the sky. The lights came on again for a moment, but now they were turned inwards. The ship was a small freighter with some barrels and a sagging tarpaulin on its deck. Blumberg said in a voice that sounded no different from usual: "Rita, straighten your back and hold your head up high."

II

In the perspective of the mid-twentieth century, the Zionist tradition, in some of its aspects, seemed mistaken or even, to some young Israeli minds, faintly ludicrous. But in one aspect, and that the most central, the Zionists were vindicated.

They had been wrong in their belief that the Jewish State would be peacefully achieved, wrong in their easy assumption of an instant harmony between the Jewish State and the brotherhood of men and nations. And they had—consequently—been wrong about what the Jewish State would be like. It was not a state like other states; its citizens could not be "just like other men." The State, and its inhabitants, were cursed by virtually all who could claim to speak for the original inhabitants of the region to which they had returned. So the Israelis, from having been individual strangers in the Diaspora, had returned as a sort of collective stranger. Israel had become "The Jew of the Nations, La Juive des Nations";[8] the "pariah people" had become a "pariah nation."[9] As the Israeli critic Nurith Gertz puts it, "In Israel the existential problem is a political one. To be or not to be is not a personal problem, but a national one."[10] The Zionist "promise of normalization" was very far from having been fulfilled.

Yet the Zionists had been right about the thing that mattered most. They had sensed that the Jews of Europe were in deadly danger, when no one else had sensed that. Herzl, when Hitler was only six, had already sensed the need for a mass exodus of the European Jews, soon. Weizmann, just at the end of the First World War, had seen the Jews of Europe as already in danger of extermination. Herzl and Weizmann had played Cassandra; most Jews paid no attention to them. So the Jewish State had come too late to save most Jews. But the Zionists had saved hundreds of thousands of Jews: "the saving remnant." There were more than 700,000 Jews in Israel when the new State was declared. Also, and most important to most Israelis, the existence and survival of the State of Israel meant that the Jews of the post-Holocaust world need never again go defenseless to their deaths. As Manès Sperber puts it, the Israelis of 1948 "meant to let the whole world know that the long hunting season was over for once and for all."[11]

"The long hunting season . . ." The perspective is significant. To most Gentiles (I think), the Holocaust, and the Hitler epoch in general, seem an extraordinary aberration, of a mad Hitler, coming out of the blue. Jews, and Israelis in particular, had to be more aware of patterns of continuity and recurrence behind Hitler and the Holocaust. Anti-semitism was not something that Hitler imposed on unwilling or apathetic Germans. It was not the main theme of Nazi propaganda, as the Nazis rose to power, but it was known to be central to their ideology. The main theme was the recovery of German greatness. But the Nazis always made clear that the Jews were a barrier to that recovery, and would be excluded from it. It was on those terms that the Nazis won their mass support.

I have referred to the "normality" of late-nineteenth-century European anti-semitism. One might also speak of its *versatility*. For many centuries, European anti-semitism took a Christian form, theologically defined and justified. With the spread of Enlightenment values, and the elimination of theological authority over society at large, the formal and traditional justification of anti-semitism disappeared altogether; but anti-semitism itself never disappeared. On the contrary, it became more salient and more articulate, in proportion as Jews themselves became more salient and articulate—as a direct consequence of Enlightenment and emancipation. By the end of the nineteenth century, Jews were prominent in many spheres of German life and culture.[12] The only change that made, in anti-semitism, was that the component of hatred began to exceed the component of contempt.

The defeat of the Central Powers in the First World War raised that preexisting hatred to manic proportions. It had been bad enough for German Jews to be doing well when other Germans were also doing well. But for Jews to continue to do well when Germany was defeated and humiliated was literally intolerable. In the Weimar Republic, Jews attained full legal and political equality, and they rose to the top in the professions, in science and art, and in the media. Anti-semitic resentment, proportionate to Jewish success, spread right across the social and political spectrum, including the Social Democrats,[13] from the beginning. Anti-semitism was in fact a bonding force between the old, damaged hierarchies and the lower middle class and working class.

Adolf Hitler began as one of a number of demagogues employed by the General Staff to spread nationalism and militarism among the masses. He owed much, perhaps most, of his eventual success to the genuine passion of his anti-semitism, which animated his electric oratory. Hitler's vociferous determination to isolate the Jews, stripping them of all influence, and not to be squeamish about how he did it, was approved by millions of Germans; otherwise he could never have become Chancellor. The Holocaust itself was not submitted to any referendum, but its execution required the industrious exertions of hundreds of thousands of willing accessories—both German and non-German—as well as the acquiescence or indifference of millions of others. And the rest of the Gentile world, including even those who became allies against Nazi Germany, maintained barriers—as at Evian before the war and at Bermuda during the war—against any possible mass escape of Jews from Nazis.

Seen in this perspective, the Holocaust is not an aberration. It is a vast paroxysm of a deep-seated and apparently incurable disease: Gentile rejection of Jews.

It is in that perspective that strong Zionists, and most Israelis, see the matter. The Holocaust was the final, absolute confirmation that the Zionist "hunch" had been right. Assimilation had been an illusion. In the Blumberg-Bleiman dialogue, Bleiman had been proved right. The message to the assimilated was indeed: "Your success has been rather limited, if you don't mind my saying so."

A large section of the population of Israel in 1948 had suffered Nazi persecution. Many thousands had arrived before the war; others arrived illegally during the war and after it in the last years of the Mandate; 100,000 survivors of the camps and forests arrived in the first six months of the new State. In addition, almost all the Old

Yishuv came from one or another of the lands in which the Nazis had worked to destroy the Jews. Almost all had relatives murdered by the Nazis. And even those new Israelis who were now arriving in increasing numbers from the Muslim lands—many of whom had never seen Europe—had their own awareness of the European Holocaust. In their host countries, the native population had been sympathetic to the Nazis and hostile to the Jews. They knew that the Grand Mufti of Jerusalem had spent the war in Berlin, and they could easily guess what would have been likely to happen to the Jews—not only in Palestine, but elsewhere in the Muslim world—if the Grand Mufti had been able to return to Jerusalem in the wake of a victorious German Army.

That the new State—founded only three years after the Holocaust ended—should be dominated by the memory of the Holocaust was inevitable. But it was much more than a memory; it was also a fear, and a determination. "What has happened," says Aristotle, "can happen." Most Israelis believe that a second Holocaust is possible, and this belief does not seem to get less as the Nazi Holocaust recedes into history. In a 1974 survey, a large sample of Israeli students was asked the question: *"Do you think that a Holocaust is possible in the future?"* Twenty-two percent replied: "Yes, in all countries." Fifty-eight percent replied: "Yes, but just in some countries." Twenty percent replied: "No, in no country."[14]

Belief in a possible future Holocaust implies the need not merely for a Jewish State but for a strong Jewish State, powerfully armed, capable not only of defending itself but also of rescuing threatened Jews, bringing them in and protecting them. And leaders in Israel— from Ben-Gurion to Begin and Shamir—have fostered the belief in such a need, both because they personally shared that belief and because of its power in nation building. It was for this reason that David Ben-Gurion brought Adolf Eichmann to trial in Jerusalem in the spring of 1961. The moral, to be brought home to the young, was "Never again." If "Never again" is a myth—which is far from certain— it is a unifying myth. Specifically, it tends to unite the Ashkenazic and Oriental communities, whose differences have been a cause for anxiety (see Chapter 7). The 1974 survey shows that 50 percent of the sample "agrees completely with the statement *"Every Jew in the world should see himself as a survivor of the Holocaust."* Eleven percent thought that "only those from Europe" should see themselves in that light; 23 percent thought "only those who themselves suffered." Sixteen percent didn't agree at all. But generally the most significant fact revealed by the survey is that almost as many Orientals (46 percent) as Ashkenazim (53 percent) were in the "agrees completely" category.[15]

Among Gentiles interested in Israel, there is impatience with Israeli Holocaust consciousness—and especially with what is seen as the exploitation of the Holocaust by Israeli leaders, since 1977 especially by Menachem Begin. In particular, the notion of a possible *new* Holocaust seems fantastic, obsessive, paranoid. Ever since the *real* Holocaust, the majority of the world's Jews live in the United States. Can anyone, in their sane senses, imagine a Holocaust of Jews in the United States? Blumberg looks at Bleiman.

For obvious reasons, the idea of a possible Holocaust in the United States is not one likely to be given much of an airing in Israel or elsewhere. But clearly there is a significant minority in Israel that believes it *is* possible, including that 22 percent of students who answered "in all countries." Israeli students are exceptionally mature,[16] serious and well informed. How can so many of them believe in such an outlandish possibility as that?

The reason is, I think, that so many of them are aware of the faith and fate of the Blumbergs. Jews in Imperial Germany could not possibly imagine that modern Germans might take to persecuting Jews. And they were right, as long as Imperial Germany endured, with its pride in itself as a *Rechtstaat*.[17] But when Germany was defeated, humbled and driven in on itself, then the Jews were singled out for blame, and their persecution by the State began, fifteen years after the defeat.

Nobody can believe that persecution of the Jews is possible in contemporary America, a strong, long-established pluralist democracy, where the rule of law is better defended and safeguarded than in any other polity. What those who still answer "in all countries" have to have in mind is the possibility that, at some future time, in some unknown and barely imaginable circumstances, the United States might experience a national disaster comparable in scale and effects to that sustained by Imperial Germany in the second decade of the twentieth century. Under such conditions, might not similar reactions occur: the search for scapegoats, the finding of the Jews?

Science fiction? Yes, but the memory of the Holocaust is the memory of a science-fiction scenario that became part of history. Those who answer "in all countries" believe that the genocidal potential of anti-semitism is latent in the Gentile world generally, ready to manifest itself under conditions of exceptional stress, such as recur in history.

The "in all countries" people are in a minority; but those who believe that a second Holocaust is possible *somewhere* are a large majority in Israel. A minority in Israel rebels against this degree and kind of Holocaust consciousness, and the extent to which politicians encourage it or exploit it. It remains true that Holocaust consciousness has been and remains a large part of the consciousness of Israel. And it plays a large part also in the shaping of Israel's awareness of its neighbors, and attitudes to them.

III

To the outsider, reading modern Israeli literature in translation, it is not always easy to know whether or not a given reference is to the Holocaust. The Israeli writer, writing for his own people, in Hebrew, does not have, and does not wish, to spell everything out. His audience, on the basis of shared, intense experience and heritage, understands him *à demi-mot*. Still, one can make out some things. Much of the system of reference to the Holocaust is oblique, and sometimes antithetical. Thus when Amos Oz refers to the "philosophical Soiree of the Goethe Society" or "the beautiful German town of Baden-Baden," he is really talking about something quite different. Stefa, the "heroine" of *Touch the Water, Touch the Wind*,[18]—set in Poland in the early winter of 1939—is "not in the least apprehensive of the Germans. In the first place she abhorred wars, et cetera, and had no faith in them. Secondly from the racial point of view she was only Jewish up to a point, and in outlook she was a devoted European. Moreover, she was a fully paid-up member of the Goethe Society."

So when Pomeranz, Stefa's fully Jewish husband, takes flight into the forest, Stefa does not go with him. Professor Zaicek, the eminent philosopher, and president of the Goethe Society, stays behind too, and tries to mend the antique Gothic clock in the drawing room.

Just like Pomeranz, then, who had fled to the forests, Professor Zaicek, too, was the son of a watch-maker. Who of them isn't, Stefa asked herself. There was once a little song current in some of the villages which bore popular testimony to the connection between Jews and watches:

> *Good morning, fine morning, my dear Mr. Jew*
> *Let me propose a small deal to you*
> *You have a watch, I have a hatchet*
> *Throw me your watch and see if I catch it.*

One of the economic consequences of the Holocaust was the sudden throwing on the market, in both Germany and Switzerland, of millions of secondhand watches. The "little song" suggests that the Holocaust constituted the logical completion, in modern, rationalized, industrialized, wholesale form, of a myriad, age-old retail transactions. The Holocaust had its roots in traditional Germany, just as much as the Goethe Society had.

Such examples could be multiplied many times, but this would give a wrong idea. It is not that the writers are always consciously trying to emphasize the Holocaust; it is that they find it hard to escape from it. Common words, "smoke," "oven," "ashes," "sparks," "chimney," "wire," "rails," carry it with them. In the following passage, the Israeli critic Nurith Gertz is writing about a particular novel—Amos Kenan's *Holocaust II*, set in a post-nuclear-war camp—but her comments are capable of somewhat wider application:

> . . . Memories of pine forests, blue skies and snow-covered landscapes lead to visions of the transports to the death-camps. It is almost like the Midas myth twisted so that everything turns not to gold, but to blood, war and death. Even the moment of love becomes the moment of execution: a shapely woman opening a door, slipping off a shoe or a silk stocking is transformed into a naked woman taking her last steps towards the extermination chamber.[19]

The anguish often takes metaphysical or antimetaphysical form. The God of the Jews is in question:

> *Our father took his bread, bless God*
> *forty years from one oven, He never imagined*
> *a whole people could rise in the ovens*
> *and the world, with God's help, go on*[20]

Commenting on Kovner's long and complex poem, of which the above lines are part, the critic Edward Alexander wrote:

> The covenant which was given at Sinai has been returned in Europe as the whole Jewish people returns—in smoke—to the God who did them the dubious favor of choosing them as his special people. The feeling at this point in Section 28 (con-

taining the lines quoted) is similar to that in Glatstein's famous poem "Dead Men Don't Praise God": "We received the Torah on Sinai and in Lublin we gave it back."[21]

But Kovner also sees "a retrieval in Sinai." Like Applefeld he sees a meaning in the Return, even after the Holocaust.

Yet for some the Biblical heritage, while remaining inescapable, is still too much:

> *Moses Moses lead the people*
> *You can see, I need more sleep, I'm so tired*
> *I'm still a boy*[22]

God is a trickster who has decamped:

> *Jerusalem,*
> *The former address of God*

And:

> *Still playing*
> *God imprisons me in a wardrobe*
> *And leaves me the key.*
> *I grope in the dark and breathe the scent*
> *Of strange lives. Blindly I must wait*
> *But I know*
> *Even if he lingers*
> *He will not come*[23]

Joel, the hero of Yehuda Amichai's novel *Not of This Time, Not of This Place*, returns after the Second World War from Israel to his native city of Weinburg, in southern Germany, looking for revenge; simultaneously he remains in Jerusalem, leading his ordinary life. Neither the revenge nor the life seems to come to anything. Near the end, Joel says, "Once I awoke with the cry 'My God, why have You forsaken me?' And immediately after I cried, 'My God, my God, why have You not forsaken me? Why didn't you leave me in my peace, without vengeance and without love?'"

At the end of David Shahar's short story "The Death of the Little God," the character known as "the Little God"—because he has a scientific theory about God being little—tells of a dream about a conversation with his father. The dream is set in the father's study:

> A map of Palestine . . . was hanging on the eastern wall.
> Opposite the map, on the western wall, the faces of Herzl
> and Nordau stared down from their golden frames. . . . His

father went to the table and spread out on it an issue of the *Welt,* the Zionist organ, which grew and grew till it covered the whole table. . . . "Now tell me what's going on in the world."

. . . "God is growing smaller, Father, and now already, compared to an ant, God looks like a flea compared to an elephant. He is still alive, wriggling and writhing under the weight of the world He created, but it is only a matter of time before His death agonies cease."

"And how long will it take before He disappears?" . . .

"Two or three weeks, perhaps less."

"Then, this is the end?"

"Yes, this is the end."

On hearing this his father jumped off the table and started to knock his head against the map of Israel. He knocked his head and cried out with pain, knocked and cried, and with each knock his body became smaller, and his son knew that only he could save him but his whole body became stiff and numb and he could not move a limb. He froze with cold and fright and saw how his father was getting smaller and smaller, knocking his head against the wall and vanishing, till nothing remained of him except the reverberation of his knocking.[24]

Here cosmic anguish has also a secular history, a local habitation and a name.

IV

References to landscape, in Israeli literature, very often convey a sense of threat:

> *Mountain landscape like a dissected body*
> *Turned to stone. Deeply they blacken before the*
>   *storm and in their death*
> *The villages are lit in threatening whiteness*[25]

This feeling is particularly strong in the writings of Amos Oz: "The mountains are invisible but their presence broods over the valley. The mountains are there. . . . In total silence they are there. Standing like curved columns, like giants frozen in some obscene act and turned to stone, the mountains are there."[26]

Before we built a city on this spot the sand-dunes stretched right down to the beach. The desert touched the sea. In other words, we came here and forced these two furious elements asunder. As if we poked our heads into the jaws of the sea and the desert. There are moments on hot summer days when I have a sudden feeling that the jaws are trying to snap shut again.[27]

Sometimes the hostile landscape is explicitly associated with hostile human inhabitants.

In the distance were more and more strange mountains and strange villages stretching to the end of the world, minarets of mosques, Shu'afat, Nabi Samwil, the wail of a muezzin borne on the wind in the evening twilight, dark women, deadly sly, guttural youths. And a slight hint of brooding evil, distant, infinitely patient, forever observing you unobserved.[28]

As Ehud Ben-Ezer writes: "The Biblical landscape [here of pre-1967 Jordan] is alien to Israelis as long as its inhabitants hate them and threaten their lives. This is not a moral problem, questioning the justice of one cause over the other. It's a fact of life in 'a besieged country.' "[29]

The threat is a fact of life, indeed. But the "moral problem" is also a fact of life, and troubles the writers in varying degrees. Ben-Ezer himself refers to "self-flagellations"—that is to say, self-reproach at treatment of Arabs—in the writings of Benjamin Tammuz and others, and ascribes these to "perhaps the deep remorse felt by a people traditionally accustomed to making the highest moral demands on itself, and finding that they fall short."

The poet Avner Treinin, in the concluding lines of his poem on the Gates of Jerusalem, evokes memories of slaughter both of Jews by Arabs and of Arabs by Jews:

> That's a Hebron Gate
> remember the slaughter in twenty-nine
> and Dir Yasin and the Via Dolorosa
> the natural religions of Zion that's a gate
> to the Gate of Mercy the blocked gate[30]

In the section "Admission of Guilt" in his long poem "A Canopy in the Desert," Abba Kovner writes:

> *You may attack your brother*
> *(shall murder*
> *shall murder)*

Earlier in the same poem, in the section "Sermon of a Sunstruck Man," Kovner had written:

> *Honorable judge! Our trial drags on and*
> *   I lose patience*
> *One has to admit I got caught up in an unfortunate*
> *   ambiguity*

On this poem, and these lines, the critic Edward Alexander makes the illuminating comment:

> The reason why God and his covenant are said to reside only in darkness and mystery is that the Jewish people, having achieved its difficult return to the promised land, now finds itself "mixed up in an unfortunate ambiguity." Having carried the letters of the covenant back to their source for validation and reconsecration, the Jewish people finds itself caught in a conflict between the covenant and the historical necessity to survive within history, whose overriding commandment is an inversion of the Sinai injunction, saying to the Jews of a beleaguered Israel: "You may attack your brother/shall murder/shall murder." The "unfortunate ambiguity" is in fact a horrible paradox whereby the price of Jewish survival may be the surrender of the very reason why Jewish survival was ever thought important.[31]

But Kovner ends the section "Admission of Guilt" with the words:

> *I admit my guilt*
> *but I do not confess*

Generally, the "moral problem" is overshadowed by the fact of the siege, and by the meaning which the siege takes on, in the light of the history of the Jews. The weight of that history causes the war with the Arabs to be seen "as a battle with the ghosts and phantoms of the national memory, peopled by generations of enemies whose purpose is to destroy the Jewish people."[32]

Between the wars, the Yishuv had seen the behavior of Arab mobs, and the apparent connivance of the authorities, as repeating the pattern of the Russian pogroms.

After the end of the Second World War and the Holocaust—followed, within the same decade, by the attempt of the Arab states to

destroy Israel—another parallel inevitably suggested itself. Mr. Nehamkin, in Amos Oz's *Hill of Evil Counsel,* has a dream: "Hitler was
not dead but had hidden himself away among the murderous Bedouins
in the darkness of the tents of Kedar."

Shraga Unger, the old Zionist lecturer who is the narrator of Oz's
"Late Love,"[33] has a fantasy, while reading *The History of Israeli
Tank Warfare.* He imagines that the victorious Jewish armies of the
middle- and late-twentieth century are there to fight the earlier op-
pressors of the Jewish people in Europe:

> Hundreds of Jewish tanks crossing the length and breadth of
> Poland, brutally trampling our murderers underfoot, inscrib-
> ing a savage Hebrew message across the scorched earth. . . .
> And I can see Moshe Dayan, in his dusty battledress, stand-
> ing awesome and gaunt as he receives in a grim silence the
> surrender of the Governor of Kishinev.
>
> All the church bells ring out. On the plains herds of
> horses rear up on their hind legs. The fury of the Jews sweeps
> on and on. My heart inside me like a wild thing burst into
> savage howls.
>
> But after a while there came a limpness.
>
> I took another look at the photograph and said to my-
> self:
>
> "Tanks, Na! Such clumsy machines. And for the time be-
> ing all we are facing is miserable Arabs."
>
> And can I gain any relief from a book on tank warfare?
> How absurd it all is.

Neither Mr. Nehamkin nor Shraga Unger is altogether in his right
mind. But the tendency to run together Russians, Germans and Arabs
is not confined to the mentally disturbed. Contemporary Arabs are
widely seen as trying, however inefficiently, to finish off the work that
Hitler nearly finished. Those who see things in that way—and that
means most Israelis—feel justified thereby in a posture of implacability
toward Arab claims, and in stifling doubts about the "moral problem"
of the treatment of Arabs by Jews.

Both to Arab writers and to some concerned outsiders, this introduction of the European Holocaust into the modern Jewish-Arab debate seems like a monstrous irrelevance, a monumental piece of bad
faith. Arabs had nothing to do with the European Holocaust, or earlier
European persecution of the Jews. Jews were not persecuted in Arab
lands.[34] Arab writers, like Edward Said and Sami Hadawi,[35] point out

that Arabs are not, and cannot be, anti-semites. They are anti-*Zionist*
for good reasons. They are not trying to exterminate the Jews, or even
drive them out of Palestine. They want to replace the Jewish State—
Said in particular makes much of this—by the "secular and democratic state" of the Palestinian National Covenant. In such a state, the
right of the Jewish minority would be fully protected. The Arab
program has nothing in common with the genocidal policies of Adolf
Hitler, and it is calculated insult to the Arabs to suggest that it has.

Israelis will accept a part, though only a small part, of this argument. They agree generally that Jews have historically been better,
or less badly, treated in Arab and Muslim lands than in Christendom.[36]
But Israelis do not accept that Arabs, and Palestinian Arabs in particular, did not sympathize with Nazi Germany and its policy toward
the Jews. Not only was the Grand Mufti Hitler's guest in Berlin, while
the Holocaust was going on, but he remained the unquestioned leader
of the Palestinian Arabs after the defeat of Nazi Germany. His association with the Nazis evidently did him no damage at all in the eyes of
his followers.[37]

The distinction between being anti-Zionist and being anti-Jewish
is accepted as being a distinction made by Arab intellectuals of
Western formation, addressing Western audiences (and also, no
doubt, in their own minds). Israeli experience does not suggest that
ordinary Arabs recognize any such distinction. In the Mufti-inspired
riots of 1929 in Palestine, for example, most of the victims were pious
Jews, living in the Holy Places. Not merely were these not Zionists, in
the political sense; many of them were strongly *anti*-Zionist. That
made no difference: the rioters were out to kill such Jews as they could
catch, without distinction of opinion. Nor is there any reason to believe
that, say, the rioters who sacked the Jewish quarters of Baghdad, in the
summer of 1941, made any attempt to find out which Jews were Zionists
and which were not. Arab broadcasts and writings addressed to Arabs,
as distinct from Arab publications intended for the outside world, are
hostile not only to Zionists but also to Jews generally.

Against that background, few if any Israelis have any belief in a
future for Jews as a guaranteed minority in a secular democratic state
with an Arab majority. Such a concept is seen as purely tactical and
propagandist, designed to appeal to Western ears, and having no
connection with local reality. The reality, as most Israelis see it, is that
most Arabs yearn not merely to get rid of the Jewish State but also
to get rid of its inhabitants, in one way or another.[38]

In those conditions, Israelis are disposed to believe that the same Gentile propensities which in Europe eventually produced the Holocaust are still all around them among their Arab neighbors. The best guarantees against a second Holocaust are Israeli vigilance and Israeli armed strength.

Westerners point out that a Holocaust of Jews by Arabs is wildly improbable, given the actual balance of forces between the two sides. Basically, the Israeli reply to that is that a second Holocaust *is* improbable, and that Israelis aim to keep it that way.

Beyond doubt, the memory and image of the Holocaust have been among the sources of support in Israel for inflexible policies in dealing with Arabs.

But the Holocaust is now two generations away. Is its memory growing dim, and its influence fading? If this is happening, it seems to be only very slowly; as indeed might be expected, considering the scale and nature of the event. The Israeli psychologist Simon N. Herman, who has carried out two surveys—in 1965 and 1974—of student perceptions in this matter, found as follows, in an article published in 1977:

> The memory of the Holocaust continues to exercise a pervasive influence on the perception of the students of Jewish-Gentile relationships. They do not place much reliance on Gentile good-will, although they have less of a distrust of them than have their parents. Comparing our 1965 and 1974 studies, there is now more of a tendency to see the Gentile world—at least part of it—as anti-Semitic. The students tend to speak of Gentiles in general terms, as a broad universal category, marked off from Jews. . . . The Jewish people regards itself as a nation of survivors, and no study of Israel, of Jewish identity and of the relationships between Jewish and other groups can ignore the profound implications of this background factor.[39]

If the memory is fading at all, it is not fading evenly: note the growing tendency, between 1965 and 1974,[40] to see the Gentile world as anti-semitic. What is perhaps more significant is the consciousness of "Gentiles in general terms as a broad universal category from which [Israelis] are marked off as Jews."

That kind of general consciousness of Gentiles has an important bearing on the Israeli view of relations with Arabs. Arabs are not merely a numerous, though weak, regional population hostile to Jews

and Israel. They are also part of the vast and powerful "universal
category" of Gentiles, which is also seen as (at least in part) potentially—and in some cases actually—hostile to Jews and Israel.

In this perspective, the idea of a possible second Holocaust seems
less implausible than it looks in the light of the contemporary balance
of forces in the region. If some major shift were to happen within the
Gentile world—as a shift happened in Central Europe in the second
decade of the twentieth century—anti-semitism might flare up again
in the world outside the Middle East, and eventually tilt the local
balance against Israel.

The poet Itamar Yaoz-Kest has drawn attention to fluctuations
in Israeli perceptions of, and interest in, the Holocaust. In periods
when Israel is "riding high," as in the six years after the Six Day War
of 1967, native-born Israelis, Sabras, did not want, according to this
writer, "to hear about the tragic Jewish fate. They felt exaggerated
pride in themselves and feelings of superiority towards Diaspora
Jews."[41]

Such a state of mind, of course, would suggest that the Holocaust
is irrelevant to Israel. It was something that happened to other people,
different from Israelis, and inferior to them. It was only after the unnerving near-failure of the first phase of the Yom Kippur War, in 1973,
that these young Israelis (in this view) "realized the falsity of their
own self-image."

> The conclusion is that the Israeli character suffers from a
> lack of proportion, stemming perhaps from the Zionist promise
> of normalization; anything less leads to despair and dreams of
> running away from history—as if there really was a possi-
> bility of a totally secure national, and perhaps even personal,
> existence in some other place, some paradise on earth.[42]

After 1973, the sense of siege returned, with a sense of possible
Holocaust, behind the siege.

V

In trying to understand what the Holocaust, and the prehistory
of the Holocaust, mean to the people of Israel, I have been thinking
about the history of my own people, the Irish Roman Catholics.

Mr. Ken Livingstone, the hard-leftist chairman of the Greater
London Council, said in the summer of 1983 that the sufferings of the

Irish people, over eight hundred years, added up to something as bad as the Holocaust of the European Jews. That is an eccentric opinion. For one thing it leaves out the fact that the oppression of the Jews in history vastly exceeds that of the Irish, in duration, consistency and intensity, *even if no account is taken of the Holocaust at all.* Also the figure of eight hundred years—dating the beginning of suffering from the Norman Conquest of Ireland toward the end of the twelfth century—is a hollow piece of propaganda. The medieval Irish probably suffered no more and no less from the Norman Conquest than the medieval English did. Ireland's real and special troubles began in the late-sixteenth century, when the native Irish began to pay the price of backing the Counter-Reformation—and the deposition of heretic princes—against the Reformation sovereigns of England and Scotland.

The price—paid also by the other local losers in the dynastic-religious wars of the Renaissance period—included frequent episodes of ferocious and indiscriminate military repression. It also included something more special. This was the imposition, after the victory of the Protestant cause at the end of the seventeenth century, of a code—the Penal Laws—which presumed no such person as an Irish Roman Catholic to exist. The Penal Laws were in force during most of the eighteenth century; Irish Catholics were deprived of the right to bear arms, and of the franchise, and debarred from entering the professions. It was during this *relatively* short period that the historic experience of the Irish Catholics came closest to what the experience of the Jews had been, through most of the Christian centuries. Daniel O'Connell (1775–1847), the great Irish leader at the end of the Penal period, was conscious of the parallel, and a warm supporter of Jewish enfranchisement in Britain and Ireland.

The Penal Laws were gone by the end of the eighteenth century, but Irish Catholics remained at a huge social, economic and educational disadvantage as against a Protestant Ascendancy, which owned most of the land. The Irish Catholic rural population of the mid-nineteenth century consisted largely of subsistence farmers and their families, with the potato as their staple crop and food. In several successive years in the late 1840s the potato crop failed. In the resulting famine, a million people died, and a million emigrated, mainly to America.

British Governments of the period made sporadic and parsimonious efforts at famine relief, but they were inhibited by prevailing economic doctrines, and their efforts were obviously inadequate. Many

Catholics, with the bitterness of past experience, saw these failures as deliberate. Particularly in the retrospect of the Irish-American survivors, the Irish Famine was seen as "a man-made famine." Modern Irish historians generally reject this view of the matter, but it is a widely, if hazily, held view of Irish people, at home and abroad.

Even today some Irish people—and some "sympathizers"—refer to the Great Famine as an event comparable to the twentieth-century Holocaust. If we are speaking of the intention and behavior of Governments and people, the comparison is untenable. The worst the British Government of the day can be accused of is callous lethargy; there was nothing remotely resembling a plan for mass murder, or collusion by the British public in the execution of such a policy. But there is something comparable in the *scale* of the events, and in impact on the consciousness of a people. I shall come back to that.

The late-nineteenth and twentieth centuries have been a period of social and economic recovery and advance for Irish Catholics. Independence for most of Catholic Ireland was preceded, in 1919–1921, by a period of attempted military repression, rather closely resembling the attempted repression of the Yishuv in 1945–1948. At the end of this period, Ireland—as later, Palestine—was partitioned.

Northern Ireland, in accordance with the wishes of the Protestant majority of its inhabitants, remained in the United Kingdom. The rest of the country, overwhelmingly Catholic, seceded. Though the actual line of the border was (and is) open to serious question, some form of partition was the only way of taking account of the divided allegiances of the population of Ireland.

The attempt of Mr. Livingstone (and others) to read Irish history as an equivalent to the Holocaust is absurd. Its disproportion does no more, I believe, than reflect the fact that the Irish are "in" for the moment, and the Jews "out," as recipients of the sympathy of the international Left. I don't expect this distribution of that particular sympathy to do the Irish much good, or the Jews much harm.

Thus there is no equivalence, but there is comparability, between the Jewish and the Irish Catholic historical experience. Both are, though in greatly differing degrees, experiences of oppression and stigmatization, and experiences of different ways of handling those phenomena. "Irish history" and "Jewish history" belong to a different order from "English history" or "French history." The Irish and Jewish variety of history has run underground, for long periods, without official existence, beneath quite different versions of history. The Irish and Jewish varieties attained official existence only retrospectively, with the coming of statehood. And then perhaps—and perhaps inevitably—too *much* official existence.

The Irish still have difficulty in coming to reasonable terms with their underground past, even though the worst of the past experiences are more than a hundred years away. Most of us know that the British people of today mean no harm to us, and most of us actually like them (and better than other people). We know that no one among our neighbors wishes to destroy our State. Most of us, in our conscious minds, reject the effort of the I.R.A. to force Northern Ireland out of the United Kingdom, against the will of a majority of its inhabitants. Yet the I.R.A. has power over us, through our common collective memory. It can force us to rerun, somewhere at the back of our minds, the film of our underground history. The death of a hunger striker can do it, or the picture on the screen of a British soldier searching an Irish person; or even an insulting headline in a London popular newspaper. And it is that film playing in Irish minds on both sides of the Atlantic that makes it possible for the I.R.A. to keep going.

Knowing how that matter stands, I feel I am in a position to *begin* to grasp what Jewish history must mean to a modern Israeli. The murder of six million Jewish men, women and children took place much more recently than the (relatively) quite small-scale depredations of the Black and Tans (paramilitary counterinsurgents), still etched on the Irish collective memory. And behind the Holocaust, in time, is a history, not of centuries but millennia, of oppression and persecution at the hands not just of one Power but of the whole Gentile world. And just after the Holocaust, the attainment of a State menaced from its birth by the hatred of the whole surrounding population.

If *we* are still rerunning films in our minds, what films *they* have to rerun!

But there is another Irish parallel—between the Catholics of Northern Ireland and the Palestinian Arabs. A little over 350 years ago, the Catholic natives of large regions of Ulster were displaced from their homelands, by forfeiture or purchase, and replaced by a population differing from them both in religion and in political allegiance, and more advanced in techniques, education and social organization. The natives remained in the area, mainly as tenants on the poorer land, and in unskilled employment. The settlers developed the better land, and built up industry.

Today, although the material position of the Catholics has greatly improved, the relation between Catholic and Protestant, native and settler, has lost almost nothing of its pristine animosity. In the General Elections of 1983, one-third of the Catholic electorate voted for a party which declared its "unambiguous support for the armed struggle." That is to say, they voted for the I.R.A., which has for years been systematically murdering their Protestant neighbors. And those who voted in this way were *not* the older people, clinging to ancient grievances. They were mainly the young, hoping to win—three and a half centuries after their ancestors first lost.

In relation neither to the Jewish side nor to the Arab side do the Irish parallels offer much encouragement to hopes of an early and comprehensive settlement, embracing both Jews and Palestinian Arabs. Such a settlement seems hardly possible, unless both sets are much better at forgetting than are the Irish. Perhaps they are.[43]

7

THE SECOND ISRAEL

I only pray that there be no peace, otherwise we shall
destroy each other.
—*An Israeli-Yemeni policeman,*
after the Black Panther riots of May 18, 1971

T HE POPULATION of the new State doubled within the first four
years of the State's existence. The 684,000 new immigrants were made
up, in about equal parts, of the survivors of the European Holocaust
and of immigrants from the Muslim countries of the Middle East and
North Africa. The Europeans, being of the same stock as the majority
of the 1947 Jewish population of Palestine, could be assimilated with
little difficulty; the Oriental Jews,[1] however, began to transform the
character of the society which received them. They also profoundly
affected that society in relation to the region in which it lives, and
therefore to the rest of the world. These Oriental Jews constitute the
"second Israel."

The origins and movements of the Oriental Jews have been summarized as follows, by Raphael Patai:

> . . . the Oriental Jews are those Jews who have lived in Asia
> and Africa ever since their ancestors were exiled from the
> land of Israel. From 732 BCE[2] on, contingents of the popula-
> tion of Israel and Judah were moved into Assyria, Babylonia
> and Egypt. Subsequently, their children and later exiles went
> from these countries, as well as from Palestine itself, to other
> lands in Asia and Africa, including Turkey, Syria, Persia, the

Arabian Peninsula and the entire North African littoral. The descendants of these exiles remained in the various countries of the Near and Middle East and in contiguous areas of Central Asia for two to two-and-a-half millennia. . . . An off-shoot group of these Oriental Jews moved across the Straits of Gibraltar when the Moors conquered Spain in the early eighth century.[3] A few hundred years later, when the Spaniards and the Portuguese retook the peninsula, the Jews remained in their cities of residence and exchanged their Arabic mother tongue for Spanish. After their expulsion from Spain in 1492 they retained their Ladino [Judeo-Spanish language] in their new places of settlement in North Africa, the Ottoman Empire and elsewhere."[4]

By 1972, there were nearly 600,000 Jews in Israel who had been born in Muslim countries. Including children born to Oriental immigrants in Israel, the Oriental Jews already by the mid-sixties made up just over half the population of Israel. Today, they are about 60 percent; their birthrate, though falling, is still significantly higher than that of Jews of European origin in Israel.

I propose to consider here first the relation of the Oriental Jews to the Muslim world from which they came, and then their relation to the other inhabitants of the State of Israel.

II

According to the Arab writer Sami Hadawi:

> One can leaf through the pages of Middle East history and survey many eras of civilization and still find the same story of mutual respect between Arabs and Jews. In the Holy Land, as elsewhere in Arab lands, they lived together in harmony, a harmony only disrupted when the Zionists began to claim that Palestine was the "rightful possession" of the "Jewish people." . . . Despite what happened in Palestine, the friendly relations between Arabs and Jews in other Arab countries have not been affected.[5]

This view of history is shared by many recent Arab writers and speakers. Ahmed Shugeiri, first Secretary-General of the P.L.O., made it very familiar to his auditors at the United Nations. But it is not a view that can be sustained, within any normal definition of "respect."

"Mutual respect" implies equality. But Muslims and Jews were not on a footing of equality. As long as the Muslim realms were fully autonomous, Muslims were superior; Jews, inferior. The Jews, like the Christians throughout most of the countries of Muslim rule, were *dhimmis,* protected subjects of a Muslim sovereign; tolerated, subject to the observance of certain conditions, including the payment of the Koranic poll tax, the *jizya.* They did not have equality before the law; the testimony of a Jew (or Christian) was not valid against that of a Muslim in a Muslim court. Jews (and Christians) could be required to wear special clothes, or badges; they were forbidden to ride a horse or to bear arms. The combined disadvantages of being disarmed, and without means of legal redress, left them helpless (unless they could find an effective Muslim patron) against any Muslim who might choose to abuse them. In short, Jews were obliged to respect Muslims, at least outwardly. Muslims were in no way obliged to respect Jews.

It is true that in the last century of the Ottoman Empire, and when its decline was already far advanced, *dhimmi* status and the *jizya* were formally abolished. In November 1839, the young Sultan Abd al-Mujid (reigned 1839–1862) signaled his accession by a reform—the *Tanzimat* of Gulhane—which laid down the doctrine of the complete equality of all Ottoman subjects. The reception of this decree has been described by an authoritative British source:

> The feelings of dismay and even ridicule with which this proclamation was received by the Mussulmans in many parts of the country [Turkey] show how great a change it instituted, and how strong was the opposition which it encountered among the ruling racé. The non-Mussulman subjects of the sultan had indeed early been reduced to such a condition of servitude that the idea of their being placed on a condition of equality with their Mussulman rulers seemed unthinkable.[6]

The power of the late Ottoman sultans was not such as to insure that ordinances, resented by their subjects, were universally respected. That the decree remained a dead letter at least in some sections of the Empire is suggested by continuing complaints of ex-*dhimmis* up to the end of the nineteenth century.[7] Yet the abolition of the *dhimmi* status and the *jizya,* under Ottoman law, constituted a great change in the legal status, and a significant consequential change in the social status of the minorities concerned. But it was a change imposed from above, not one willingly conceded by the Muslim majority among whom the Jews and Christians lived.

The formal abolition of *dhimmi* status was generally regarded as a response of Ottoman weakness to the exigencies of the European Powers and the prestige of European conventions. The social promotion of the former *dhimmis*—like the working of the Capitulations system—was part of a pattern of Western encroachment. "For both Christians and Jews this [Western] interference meant that at last they were no longer without champions in their dealings with the Muslim majority."[8] Also, those who were promoted in that way were themselves part of that pattern. As Western encroachment advanced, the placid contempt which had generally marked the Muslim side of the *dhimmi* relationship began to turn to sullen resentment, together with a sense of helplessness. "It began to dawn on Muslim opinion that in future the treatment meted out to non-believers in their midst would have to be guided not merely by traditional practice, but with an eye to the reactions of the Great Powers of the West."[9]

"Mutual respect" as a description of either the *dhimmi* situation or the post-*dhimmi* situation is quite untenable. On the other hand, Muslim writers are on firm ground when they say that, for many centuries after the Muslim conquests, Jews preferred to live under Muslim rather than Christian rule. Jews in Spain, in the eighth century, welcomed as their liberators the Arab conquerors of the Visigothic kings. In the same period of initial Arab expansion, the Jews of Syria (including Palestine) welcomed the Arab conquerors as their liberators from the Byzantine yoke. Jews of the eastern Mediterranean, seven centuries later, welcomed the Ottoman Turks. When Jews were driven out from the Iberian peninsula, by decrees of Christian sovereigns, in the last decade of the fifteenth century, it was in Muslim lands that they took refuge. Many of those who fled from Muslim lands to Israel after 1948 were descended, or partly descended, from people who had turned to Muslim lands as a refuge after 1492.

Dhimmi status was far from ideal, but it was vastly preferable to, say, the attentions of the Spanish Inquisition. And at some times, and in some places, the status of some Jews was much better than what *dhimmi* status seems to imply. At the court of the Umayyad Caliphs at Córdoba, in the tenth century, certain Jews played a notable and influential part in a glorious period of Muslim civilization. So much so indeed that early-medieval Córdoba has furnished an acceptable topic of conversation on the rare and precarious occasions of attempted Arab-Jewish *rapprochement* in the twentieth century: as when Dr. Weizmann met Emir Faisal in June 1918.

There were also times and places in which Muslim treatment of Jews was much the same as the worst Christian treatment of them. Muslim fundamentalists rejected the convention of the *dhimmi*, as incompatible with the purity of Islam. Whenever a wave of fundamentalism spread across the Muslim world—as under the Almoravides[10] in eleventh-century North Africa—Jews and Christians were likely to be offered a choice between conversion and death. Sometimes Jews and Christians were killed, even if willing to accept conversion; sometimes their conversion was followed by a penitential scourging.

But in general, Muslim contempt for Jews was of much lower intensity than Christian hostility to Jews. There was a clear theological basis for this difference. Christians, until quite recently, saw the Jews as an accursed people who had not merely rejected but crucified the Son of God. The offense of the Jews, in the eyes of Muslims, is the serious, but less awesome, one of having rejected the teaching of the Prophet. For that offense it was generally a sufficient penalty that the Jews should submit to Muslim rule, and be humble.

As Bernard Lewis puts it, whether you describe Muslim rule over minorities as "tolerant" or not depends on "whether you understand by tolerance, absence of discrimination or absence of persecution. Discrimination always existed, in a permanent and necessary way, inherent in the system, institutionalized in law and practice. On the other hand persecution was atypical and rare."[11] Professor Lewis goes on: "On the whole—and unlike the anti-semitism of the Christians—Muslims feel neither fear, nor envy, nor hatred towards non-Muslims, but simply contempt . . . the epithets habitually used are monkey for the Jews and pig for the Christians."[12]

The contrast between medieval and Renaissance Christian Europe and the Muslim world in the treatment of Jews is relevant to modern controversies about Zionism, and Arab reaction to Zionism. But this particular contrast has little relevance to the conditions experienced by the generation of Oriental Jews who emigrated to Israel, mainly in the mid-twentieth century.

Up to the modern period, Muslim rule was generally preferable to Christian rule, for Jews. But the enormous changes which took place in Europe, especially from the end of the eighteenth century on, and the impact of those changes on the Muslim world, transformed that situation for a time.

The tremendous success and dynamism of nineteenth-century Western Europe—in contrast with the stagnation of the Muslim world—was the success of a *secular* society, with plenty of room for Jews. Or so it seemed, then. European rule, protection and influence became attractive to Jews. The Jews of Tunis put up the tricolor cockade to celebrate the fall of the Bastille (and, later, of the Most Christian King). The Jews of Egypt welcomed Bonaparte; and later welcomed the British. The Jews of Algeria were given equal rights, and later full citizenship, by the French. The Jews of Tunisia were given equal rights under the *Pacte Fondamental,* dictated by Napoleon III to the Bey (1857).[13] The expansion of Western influence in the declining Ottoman Empire benefited the Jews, both directly and indirectly. Many Jews lived under the protection of a European Power through the Capitulations system. The remainder of the Jews benefited when European influence obliged the Ottoman sultans and other Muslim rulers such as the Dey of Algiers, the Bey of Tunis and the Sultan of Morocco to proclaim the equality of all their subjects before the law.

At the same time, with the decay of the central Ottoman power, conditions throughout the Sultan's realms and former realms grew increasingly insecure except where European power was clearly dominant: as French power was in Algiers and Tunis, and British power was in Cairo during the nineteenth century; and as British and French power became throughout the Muslim world (except the Turkish heartlands) in the present century, between the two world wars. As a result of all these changes, the Jews of the Middle East and North Africa reversed their former preference for the Islamic world, as against Europe. The nature of the change can be symbolized by a contrast of two Purims.

Purim is the feast instituted by Mordecai, according to the Book of Esther, to celebrate the deliverance of the Jews from Haman's plot to kill them. Special Purims have been instituted by Jews in many lands to celebrate the death of a local tyrant or deliverance from some particular danger.[14]

In sixteenth-century Morocco, when the Portuguese Army was defeated by the Muslim commander Abd al-Malik at the Battle of the Three Kings (1578), Moroccan Jewry "commemorated the event by a joyful Purim (*Purim de los Cristianos*)."[15]

More than three centuries later, the Jews of Iraq saw a *European* victory over a *Muslim* power as occasion for a Purim. After the British took Iraq from the Turks (1918), the Jews of Iraq began to commemorate the British occupation as a modern Purim.[16]

Not only did the Jews welcome the expansion of secular European power into the Muslim lands, but they were well placed to help in this process, especially through the knowledge which many members of the trading community had of both European and Oriental languages. Oriental Jews played a significant part in the European administration of North Africa and the Middle East in the nineteenth and twentieth centuries.

From the mid-nineteenth century on, Muslim resentment of Western domination and of Jews tended to go together. Thus in the fourth and fifth decades of the nineteenth century: "The Moroccan people, already fanaticized by the French conquest of Algeria, accused the Jews of being the agents of European influence in Morocco."[17] At an earlier date, the Egyptian historian al-Jabarti had been shocked by the fact that in his day, after the abolition of *dhimmi* status, non-Muslims, "contrary to ancient custom, wear fine clothes and bear arms, wield authority over Muslims and generally behave in a way which inverts the order of things established by divine law."[18]

Resentment of Zionism, about a century later, should be seen not in isolation but as part of a long-established general pattern, and in particular, part of a general resentment against the liberation of the *dhimmis*. Manifestations of anti-Jewish feeling, as part of a general anti-Western feeling, appeared long before the Balfour Declaration, and before there was any general awareness of the Zionist enterprise. In 1882, in the first manifestation of Egyptian nationalism, the revolt of Arabi Pasha against British *de facto* annexation, the Jews of Alexandria came under attack, and many of them fled to Malta. In Morocco, in the first decade of the twentieth century, Muslim indignation against increasing French penetration repeatedly took the form of attacks on Jewish communities: sack of the Jewish Quarter in Casablanca in 1907 with thirty dead; of the Jews of Settat, 1908, forty dead; of Fez, 1912, sixty dead.[19]

The Balfour Declaration was a significant part, but only a part, of a general enterprise resented in all its aspects by Muslims. This was the institution of non-Muslim rule over Muslims throughout the Muslim world (except Turkey). As Siegfried Landshut puts it:

> If the incursion of Western political power and Western liberal ideas during the last century militated against discrimination, it has *pari passu* accentuated existing differences between the two communities. Even before the Zionist issue had burst like a bombshell on the Eastern Mediterranean,

the increased Western orientation of the Jews on the one hand, and the increased xenophobia of the Arabs on the other, were steadily widening the gap between them.[20]

The Zionist enterprise was a conspicuously obnoxious aspect of an unacceptable and incomprehensible general phenomenon.

Islam is a triumphalist creed, *par excellence*. The explosion of Islamic power around the Mediterranean in the period immediately after the death of the Prophet had been a conspicuous manifestation of the Will of God. God's Will was also manifest in the long ascendancy of the Faithful over the *dhimmi* peoples. The end of that ascendancy, the enfranchisement of the *dhimmis,* the encroachment of the European infidels, denizens of the House of War,[21] into the House of Islam, and then the rule of infidels—assisted by the local *dhimmis*—over the Muslim world made up a stupendous reversal of the proper order of the universe. For, as an Arab authority states: "Islam, like communism, insists on assumption of political power, as the will of God has to be worked on earth by a political system."[22]

That the Zionist enterprise should become possible was a peculiarly wounding manifestation of that reversal. It was resented, not just in itself and locally, but as a symbol of a general Muslim humiliation. As an American intelligence agent in Iraq wrote near the end of the Second World War: "Most Jews, in the Arab mind, are miserable, cowardly and unclean. So the idea of a portion of the Arab world being governed by Jews is intolerable. Palestine, therefore, has become more than a remote political problem, it is now a question of personal religion and honour."[23] Or, as an Oriental Jewish writer has put it: "That a land Arabized by *jihad* should have been lost to a *dhimmi* people by the beneficiaries of the *dhimmi* condition during 13 centuries is considered as a catastrophe of cosmic dimensions."[24]

III

Western European dominance over the Muslim world seemed to reach its height—and did reach its greatest extent—in the years immediately after the First World War, and after the final disintegration of the Ottoman Empire. But in reality, Western European dominance over the region was already entering a long and uneven decline, which ended only two generations later with the failure of the last European rearguard action, that of France in Algeria, in 1962.

The slow recession of Western power began in 1929, in Iraq, where a serious tribal revolt drained British resources. Weakened and impoverished by the First World War, and now hit by the Great Depression, Britain shifted the balance of its indirect-rule policies in the direction of greater autonomy for client regimes. Iraq became independent (but treaty-bound) in 1932; Egypt followed suit in 1936. Britain's vulnerability was exposed by Mussolini's Abyssinian success. This suggested a need both to placate client regimes and to try to keep them popular. This gave an unexpected leverage to the regimes. Princes who had originally been expected simply to do as their advisers told them now offered advice of their own, or even found their advice eagerly solicited.

We have seen the bearing of this trend on events in Palestine, in the genesis of the 1939 White Paper. But the trend toward Arab autonomy also had serious implications for Jews in other Arab lands. As soon as Iraq attained limited independence in 1932, it introduced anti-Jewish legislation, and dismissed Jews from official posts, of which they had held a number, under the Mandate.

These measures might be attributed in part to resentment of Zionism, although the measures were taken before the Arab Revolt and the internationalization of the Palestine problem. But the Jews of Iraq would surely have been at risk even if Zionism had never existed. These Jews had welcomed the coming of the British Mandate, had commemorated it as a modern Purim, and had served it faithfully. So Muslims who resented the British Mandate, as most Muslims did, were bound also to resent the Jews of Iraq, for their own sake, and not just as persons suspect of Zionism. No doubt Zionism added more fuel to the flames. But there was plenty of fuel there already, even without the Zionist extra. When the Baghdad mob slaughtered Jews on June 1–2, 1941, they were no doubt inflamed by the preaching of the Grand Mufti on the fate of Palestine. But it seems likely, in the circumstances of the case, that they were more directly and personally inflamed by the certain knowledge that the Jews of Baghdad were pleased by the suppression of the pro-German, popular, Arab-nationalist government of Rashid Ali.

Similar considerations apply more generally throughout the region and the period. As Britain and France disengaged from the Middle East and North Africa, around the middle of this century, and were replaced by Arab nationalist Governments, the Oriental Jews had to be at risk, throughout these vast regions, even if there had never been any Zionism. The Oriental Jews had helped the spread of Western influence, and had benefited from it. They had welcomed the coming of European rule, and had benefited from that. With the withdrawal of the Europeans, and the coming to power of fervid Arab nationalist Governments, the Jews in every "decolonized" country were bound to be unpopular and in some danger—as they had also been in Morocco, for example, while the colonial tide had been advancing.

The situation was perhaps clearest in Algeria, the only Arab country which had to fight a long and bitter armed struggle to win independence—and the last to win it. The revolutionary movement—the F.L.N.—called on the Jews to support the independence struggle, and warned them that if they failed to support it, there could be no future for them in an independent Algeria. The Jews of Algeria had been naturalized as French in 1870. Although they had undergone recent persecution at the hands of a French Government (Vichy), they overwhelmingly preferred a French future to their future in an independent Algeria. They left *en masse* from 1961 on; 140,000, the great majority, went to France.[25] By 1969 only 1,000 Jews were left in Algeria. There seems no good reason to believe that any of this would have happened any differently if there had never been any Zionism or any State of Israel.

The Jews of Algeria were exceptional in that, having been French citizens, putatively living in part of "metropolitan France," they had somewhere to go, even if there had been no State of Israel. For many others—including most of the Jews of Morocco, Iraq and Yemen, main sources of immigration into Israel—there would have been nowhere else to go if there had been no Israel. It is argued, of course, that they would not have had to go if there had been no Israel. Certainly it was the shock of the defeat of the Arab armies by the "Zionist gangs" which precipitated most of the mass migration of these populations. But if Israel had not been there—both to precipitate their departure and to receive them—it seems likely that they would have had to face an increasingly depressed, hazardous and unpopular future in their countries of "origin."

IV

The migrations to Palestine, first of the European Jews, and then of the Oriental Jews, are generally considered either as totally dis-

tinct phenomena or as phenomena connected only through the resentment aroused by the European migration among the host populations
of the countries of origin of the Oriental Jews. The first migration, in
this view, triggered off the second, and that is all that connects the two.

As against that, it seems to me that the two migrations are only
distinct phases in one continuous world-historical process. Both migrations were the products of the same interplay of forces: the forces
that led to the emancipation of the Jews, and the later reaction against
these forces.

The primary force leading to the emancipation of the Jews was
the triumph of liberal and secular Enlightenment values over divinely
sanctioned authority in Western countries by the beginning of the
nineteenth century. The emancipation of the European Jews was a
direct effect of the triumph of those values. The emancipation of the
Oriental Jews was an *indirect* effect of the same phenomenon. The
great success of the liberal and secular Western states in the nineteenth century gave high prestige to their ideology. It also gave them
the financial, cultural and military means, for a time, to extend the
area of their authority, bringing with them some of the habits and
conventions of their ideological tradition—including an aversion to
theocratic and "superstitious" practices. The spread of Western influence, bringing with it a strong—if rather stale—whiff of Western
ideology, brought about the legal emancipation of the Oriental Jews.

The Jews, both European and Oriental, were both beneficiaries
and victims of the ascendancy of Enlightenment values. They became
victims, because they had been beneficiaries; and because they had
been considered to be people who should not benefit. Traditional societies, resenting the encroachment of subversive alien values, inevitably tended to take out their resentment on the local Jews, many
of whom everywhere eagerly welcomed the advent of the values in
question. In that respect, there was no fundamental difference between
the Russian Empire, where most of the European Jews lived, and the
Muslim lands, where the Oriental Jews lived.

The Muslim mobs which attacked Jews in Morocco in the early
years of the twentieth century and the Orthodox mobs which attacked
Jews in the Pale of Settlement in the same period had similar motives
for resentment: both traditional and novel.

Moroccan and Russian Jews did not take to one another much
when they eventually met in Israel, but the reasons why they were
both there were basically the same.[26]

There were these broad similarities in the situation of the Jews, before the First World War, in the whole vast belt in which most of the world's Jews then lived: the belt that stretched from the Baltic down through Eastern Europe and the Middle East, and out along the northern coast of Africa to the Atlantic. All along this belt, whether the local majority population was Muslim or Christian, there was resentment of the West, and of Jews; and a conjuncture of the two resentments.[27]

The First World War, the victory of the Western Allies and the collapse of both the Russian and Ottoman empires had two main effects on the situation of the Jews.

First, Jews benefited from the initial expansion of Western influence and authority, both in Eastern Europe—through the re-creation of Poland, allied to France—and through the Mandate system in the Fertile Crescent (as well as through the overthrow of Holy Russia). It seemed an occasion for a general Purim.

Second, the Allied victory created in the defeated Germanic lands a center of manic, racist nationalism, which identified the Jews as the prime representatives of the evil forces which had defeated Germany. The rise and early successes of the Nazis stimulated already-existing anti-Jewish feeling throughout the whole area. Eventually, many Eastern Europeans willingly helped the Nazis to exterminate the Jews of Europe. From the evidence of Baghdad, in May–June 1941, it can hardly be doubted that the Germans would also have had willing local help, if they had been able to carry out a similar program in the Middle East.

After the Second World War, almost all the Jews of Muslim countries left (for reasons examined). In the whole arc from the Baltic through Eastern Europe and the Middle East to the Atlantic—the arc which had once been the zone of habitation of most of the world's Jews—there was only one significant island of Jewish population left by the mid-twentieth century: the State of Israel.

V

Oriental Jews had been about half the population of the Old Yishuv in 1882, when the first Zionist pioneers began to arrive. By 1947, Oriental Jews were down to 23 percent, although about 70,000 Oriental Jews—mainly Yemeni farm laborers—had come to Palestine

Above, "Operation Magic Carpet": Yemeni Jews arriving in Israel, after 1948.
Below, Oriental Jews in a temporary transit camp (*ma'abara*), after 1948.
Bottom, Ashkenazic instructor teaching Oriental immigrants to dance. The Oriental immigrant "was expected to learn to be an Israeli in terms laid down, and conveyed to the immigrant, by European Jews."

between the wars. The Orientals were poorer and less educated than the European Jews, and they led a sort of ghetto existence within the Yishuv. The eminent Israeli sociologist S. N. Eisenstadt refers to "an undue concentration of Oriental Jews in the lower and lower middle classes, in certain cities (Jerusalem, Tiberias) and in special quarters, sometimes slums."[28]

Most of the Oriental Jews who came to Israel in such large numbers after 1948 were poor and uneducated, like their predecessors. Many of them arrived *en masse*, in airborne operations with glamorous code names: "Operation Magic Carpet" (the Jews of Yemen), "Operation Ezra and Nehemiah" (the Jews of Iraq).

Inevitably the conditions met on arrival were less joyous than such code names. In the beginning, most of the newcomers had to be housed in improvised camps (*ma'abarot*) in considerable discomfort. Many were housed in the habitations of those Arabs who had left Jewish-occupied territory. This accommodation was probably not much worse than what many of the Oriental Jews had left behind in their countries of origin. It was, however, in striking contrast with the housing standards which the European Jews, with the support of the American Diaspora, had been able to achieve for their community during the Mandate years.

Transitional difficulties were to be expected in the reception of such a huge influx. But the difficulties of absorption, in the middle and longer term, were to prove much greater than official Zionist rhetoric found it easy to admit.

There were, to begin with, large elementary economic and linguistic difficulties to be overcome. The Oriental Jews were mainly small traders and craftsmen—as indeed most of the European Jews had been. Israel had little or no need for such skills, geared as they were to the needs of quite different societies. Also, few of the newcomers spoke modern Hebrew (and none Yiddish). Some spoke Judeo-Spanish (Ladino), and some spoke French or English, but most of them habitually conversed in various Jewish dialects of Arabic—a language which was in even less demand than their commercial and industrial skills. The newcomers, in fact, brought almost nothing with them that the receiving population felt it needed: nothing except the fact of their Jewishness.

Both the economic and linguistic deficiencies of the newcomers required a great effort of re-education. The Europeans (Ashkenazim) had to be the teachers and the Orientals their pupils. The newcomers—those of them who were still young enough—had to learn

Hebrew, and to be taught skills which would enable them to become self-supporting in Israel. But this last was not merely a matter of technical training; it required also an ideological training: the inculcation of a new value system. For example, most of the Oriental Jews thought of heavy manual labor as something the Arabs did. They would have to be taught the (European) Zionist conception of the dignity of labor before they would be fit to set up *moshavim* (cooperative farms) for themselves. In fact the Orientals, or at any rate the Oriental children, would have to become Zionists—in the sense that European, and in particular Russian, Jews understood Zionism.

The official aim of the Government and the Histadrut was the *mizzug galuyot:* the integration of the exiles. The economic, linguistic and cultural gap would have made this a difficult aim to achieve in any case. But a greater difficulty lay in the fact that the two sets of migrations were radically different *in kind.* The European migration—in the main and in its dominant sections, the second and third *aliyot*—was the migration of an elite of volunteers. The Oriental migration was a migration of masses. If Herzl's conception of a mass movement of the European Jews could have been fulfilled, the European population which would have arrived in Palestine would not have been so very different from the Oriental population which did in fact arrive. In both cases: mainly a population of simple Judaic faith, with a messianic concept of the meaning of the Return and a population feeling little or no interest in ideas originating in the Gentile world.

If such mass migration had been possible—or if the Jews returning to Israel had consisted of a *representative cross section* of both European and Oriental Jews—then integration might not have been a very difficult proposition, once the initial language difficulty was overcome.

But Herzl's European mass migration never materialized. The Jewish masses of Europe either emigrated to America or stayed in Europe and were murdered. The European Jews who came to Palestine in the first three *aliyot*—those who were to set the tone for the Yishuv—were very exceptional Jews, and much more Europeanized than the Jewish masses.[29] There was certainly a messianic element in their Zionism, but it was so overlaid by secular and rationalist language, and by the terms of the socialist debate in prerevolutionary Russia, as to be virtually unrecognizable to non-European, and non-Europeanized, people. Thus, it was not in practice possible for Zionists of European origin to teach Zionism to Orientals without also trying to Europeanize them. Since the teaching had to emphasize the secular character of Zionism, it could also be felt as an attempt to dejudaize those under instruction. Thus it devalued the *whole* culture of the Oriental immigrants. Simultaneously, it undermined the authority—traditionally greater—of the Oriental parents and elders. In so doing, it directly humiliated the parents, and indirectly humiliated the children.

The whole process was often referred to officially as "the melting pot." And in many ways, it did resemble the American educational melting pot of the nineteenth century, in which also both languages and value systems were changed and parental authority was reduced. But there was an important difference. The American immigrants came to the New World prepared for great changes in their lives in an overwhelmingly foreign environment. The Oriental Jews thought of themselves as coming back to their original home, there to live with other Jews. But how different those other Jews seemed to have become and how much better equipped they were to live in the common National Home, under conditions largely created by themselves!

VI

It is commonly asserted that Zionism had made little or no impact on the Oriental Jews. This view is hotly and eloquently disputed by a writer of Egyptian-Jewish origin, Bat Ye'or. According to Bat Ye'or: "Zionism was in actual fact a greater success among the Oriental Jewish masses than among their Western co-religionists, notwithstanding the absence of theories and ideologies."[30] That is to say that what she—legitimately—here calls Zionism was something quite different from the Zionism known and practiced by the Russian Jews, whose version became dominant in Israel. The Oriental Jewish masses, she says, "brought to their understanding of Zionism a messianic fervor born of national traditions kept alive through religious observance." What she describes here seems very close to the basic Zionism of those European Jews who welcomed Herzl in Sofia and Vilna and elsewhere in the 1890s. At a deep emotional and spiritual level, the Zionism of Europeans and Orientals seems to be essentially the same; but that of the Europeans who actually reached Palestine had been so modified in the terms of its expression, by European Gentile culture, that the kinship between European and Oriental notions of Zionism was obscured, for both sides.

As Bat Ye'or puts it:

The political-atheistic culture of the socialist leaders, which had grown out of the socio-cultural Judeo-Christian symbiosis in Europe, represented, at the cultural and socio-political levels, something entirely alien to the reality of a Jewish minority in an Islamic country under colonial rule. . . . This *dejudaized Zionism* [my italics] ran exactly counter to *fundamental Zionism* [my italics] grounded as it was in national and religious values. . . . For Oriental Jews steeped in Arabic culture what solution could a Zionism steeped in Russian culture bring to their particular preoccupations?

To bridge the gap between the two cultures would have required something like the genius, the style, the imagination and the popular touch of a Theodor Herzl.[31] Jabotinsky, with so many of Herzl's qualities, might also have done much to bridge that gap had he lived (and it was a disciple of Jabotinsky's, Menachem Begin, who was in fact to do most to bridge it). But David Ben-Gurion, and his colleagues in Government and the Histadrut, made the gap even wider, with serious and possibly fatal consequences for the long-term future of Labor in Israel.

The attitude of the Israeli establishment toward the Oriental Jews, in the fifties and sixties, and even later, might be defined as benevolent but pessimistic paternalism, strongly affected by negative racial attitudes and stereotypes, mitigated by the sense of a common Jewish bond. The negative attitudes applied in their full force to the adults, and especially the elderly among the Oriental immigrants. These were "the generation of the desert" and there was no hope for them.

For the children, there was some hope, but how much and how soon was open to question. Some prevailing stereotypes emerge from a newspaper exchange at the beginning of the Oriental mass immigration. The opening comment registers the shock of the initial Oriental arrivals *en masse:*

A serious and threatening question is posed by the immigration from North Africa. This is the immigration of a race the like of which we have not yet known in this country. . . .

Here is a people whose primitiveness reaches the highest peak. Their educational level borders on absolute ignorance. Still more serious is their inability to absorb anything intellectual. . . . There is no hope even with regard to their children: to raise their general level out of the depths of their ethnic existence—this is a matter of generations![32]

What is perhaps most remarkable about this passage is the lightning speed with which the writer reaches his pessimistic conclusion about the learning abilities of these children. This was 1949; the people in question had only just arrived, and their (inevitably) bewildered children were then making their first contacts with the Israeli educational system.

Another writer, of a more amiable disposition, came to the defense of the Orientals, in a way:

> This is exactly the "race" we need. We suffer from an overdose of intelligence, of brain-workers and of brain-work. . . . We need, like air to breathe, sizeable "injections" of naturalness, simplicity, ignorance, coarseness. These simpletons, these childish Jews, with their simple-mindedness and their natural intelligence . . . are a life-elixir against our overintellectual worrisomeness.[33]

Officially, the Israeli establishment deprecated negative stereotyping of the Orientals. Actually, they contributed to it. There was a strong vein of irritability and grumpiness in their genuine but cold paternalism. Among the many and great virtues of the Founding Fathers of Israel, tact never figured—as many British officials would feelingly acknowledge—and the frequent utterances of the Israeli leaders on the subject of their Oriental fellow citizens were relentlessly and crashingly tactless. Thus, as late as the mid-sixties, Ben-Gurion could speak as follows: "Those from Morocco had no education. They love their wives, but they beat them. . . . Maybe in the third generation something will appear from the Oriental Jew that is a little different. But I don't see it yet. The Moroccan Jew took a lot from the Moroccan Arabs. The culture of Morocco I would not like to have here. And I don't see what contribution present Persians have to make."[34]

And much more in similar vein, at various times, over more than two decades, from Ben-Gurion and his colleagues. The word "primitive" was thrown around freely. Golda Meir at one time caused particular offense by saying: "Anyone who doesn't speak Yiddish isn't a complete or perfect Jew." Oriental Jews, who call the Ashkenazim "Yiddishers," took this as a denial of their Jewish existence. "Teach us Yiddish, Golda" was among the cries of the first anti-Ashkenazi Oriental demonstrations in 1971.[35]

Language of this kind, coming from politicians in a working democracy, and reflecting adversely on huge blocs of voters—soon to be a majority in the State—must be highly unusual, and is probably unique. This phenomenon cannot fully be accounted for by European (and Russian) racist attitudes, though these certainly existed. After all, American politicians of "Wasp" origin began to conceal their abundant ethnic prejudices, in public, as soon as Irish, Italian, Jewish and other ethnic voting blocs emerged in the electorate.

I suspect that two main elements (in addition to racism) entered into the felt need to keep on scolding or snubbing the Orientals. The first was patriotic and didactic. The Oriental Jews, after all, *were* backward, in terms of the culture and economy of Israel. It was desirable to get them to overcome their backwardness both for the sake of Israel, to which their backwardness was a heavy financial burden, and for their own sake. To stop them being backward, by constantly reminding them how backward they remained, may have seemed a promising pedagogical approach.

But it seems probable, given the circumstances, that deeper emotional forces were at work: bereavement, and refusal to be comforted. The National Home had been built by European Jews, for European Jews. It had been expected that at the end of the war, large numbers of European Jews, survivors of Nazi persecution and close kin to the Yishuv, would arrive in Palestine. But Nazi persecution, atrocious beyond all precedent, had left only small numbers of European Jews. The places the larger numbers of Europeans would have filled were filled by Orientals. In a sense, the Orientals were substitutes for the European dead. They were Jews, but not quite the right Jews. Their children were not quite the right children. The right ones were dead, murdered in Europe.

In the circumstances, it is hardly surprising that the substitutes, with their strange speech and strange appearance, should have received rather a gruff and grudging welcome. They were treated as, in a family, less-loved children may be treated after the untimely and intolerable death of a specially beloved child. Such children have to be cared for, and admonished frequently, for their own good and that of society.

VII

Inevitably, the immigrants resented the way they were received, and their low status in the Jewish State. Their resentment was often bitter, yet there were well-defined limits to it.

The young immigrant was expected to learn to be an Israeli, in terms laid down, and conveyed to the immigrant, by European Jews. The immigrant's own culture was simply something of which he must divest himself as quickly and thoroughly as possible. He was culturally naked. He had to become aware that there were two hypotheses present in the minds of his instructors. There was a malign hypothesis: that the immigrant was incapable of ever attaining European intellectual standards or—in a "culturalist" variant, which became influential because it evaded the charge of racism[36]—he might attain these standards, but so slowly that even the youngest immigrants, and the first, and perhaps the second, generation of Oriental Jews born in Israel, would never be worth much more than the "hopeless" adults of the mass migrations—"the generation of the desert."

There was also a benign hypothesis, according to which the Orientals could become good Israelis quite quickly if they paid attention and worked hard. Unfortunately, the structure of the classroom situation—and of the home situation behind the classroom— was such as to reinforce the first hypothesis and to discredit the second.

As compared with European pupils, Oriental pupils were at a triple disadvantage, which was literally stupefying. The classroom was about Western-style education, about Zionism and about Israel. The European children were children of Western-educated Zionists, brought up in Israel—*their* Israel, which was also the Israel of the classroom. Of the Oriental parents, many had no education at all, at least in the Western sense, and few had more than a scrappy elementary education. As for Zionism, the Zionism of the classroom— Russian and secular—was a closed book to all the Orientals. There were Oriental Zionists, among the Yemenis in particular, but their branch of Zionism—explicitly religious and literally messianic—was not *à la mode* in Israeli classrooms in the days of David Ben-Gurion. And finally Israel—the Israel of the Ashkenazim—remained *terra incognita* to the Orientals for many years.

Add to that the linguistic disability. Add to that the fact that while everything the Europeans knew was to their credit and advantage, everything the Orientals knew was to their *dis*credit and *dis*advantage—Arab stuff, which anyone would be better without.

Small wonder that the academic performance of the Orientals was disastrous in the beginning, or that subsequent academic progress has been slow, just as the "culturalists" supposed. And the comparative educational results, combined with the comparative cultural factors which led to those results, tended to perpetuate the social stratification of Israel, with Ashkenazim on top and Orientals underneath. Inevitably, some—though not all—Orientals ascribed this situation to prejudice. This is true in a sense, but doesn't quite fit the situation, as other Orientals have seen. The basic prejudice involved, the one which tended to advance the Europeans and depress the Orientals, was one in favor of Zionism. And deep down—despite jarring difficulties in the formulation of Zionist feeling—this prejudice was one the Orientals shared. They had chosen to live in the Jewish State, whose Zionism they found to be European Zionism. The Orientals had no common secular version of Oriental Zionism to oppose to this. In fact, the Orientals had, in the early years, little or no sense of belonging to any kind of Oriental community, other than their own particular one (Yemeni, Iraqi, etc.), although a sense of common Oriental *interest* seemed to emerge later. Certainly, there was no common Oriental heritage to which they wished to cling, as the Europeans clung to their European-plus-Zionist heritage. On the contrary, the Orientals themselves wished to become de-Orientalized and Europeanized. Analyzing the results of a 1968 survey, the sociologist Yochanan Peres observes: "Prejudice against Orientals is, on the average, as strong among Orientals as among Europeans."[37] He suggests that the prejudice is by Orientals of a particular group against Orientals-in-general. The majority of Orientals, according to these findings, want complete assimilation and explicitly cite the Europeans as a favorable model. "If the Europeans hadn't founded this country, we would have had nowhere to come," one woman said. And another: "We need the Europeans: they are the brain."

Both comments refer to the reality of a siege situation. The threatened Oriental Jews took refuge in a fortress built, successfully defended and commanded by Europeans.[38] The fact that they have received a grudging enough welcome in the fortress doesn't mean they don't need it, and the skills of its commanders. Or, as Sammy Smooha puts it: "The centrality of the Arab-Israeli dispute in the integration of the Jewish groups cannot be overemphasized. The common enemy is felt as an immediate and fatal threat to the lives and statehood of all the Jews. . . . As long as the entire Jewish community is mobilized to fight for its survival, nondominant Jews would prefer not to rock the boat."[39] Some of the "nondominant" suggest that it is *only* for this reason that they accept Ashkenazi primacy. Thus Eli Eliachar, head of the Council of the Sephardic Community, is reputed to have said: "If we ever get peace in the Middle East, we will have civil war at home."[40] On that condition, civil war in Israel would appear to be a remote contingency.

VIII

Integration has in fact been happening, though at a very slow rate. The surest index is the rate of intermarriage—between Orientals and Europeans—which has been increasing by 1 percent per annum, and now stands at 23 percent. Another index is the comparative birthrate. The Oriental birthrate is still considerably above the European, but is steadily declining.

The period after the 1967 war was a turning point in the relations between the two communities. Erik Cohen writes:

> Tens of thousands of soldiers of Oriental origin took an active part on the various fronts. It was generally acknowledged that they fought bravely and thereby sealed their full acceptance into Israeli society. It had been asserted in the past that the Orientals did not contribute significantly to national defense: this assertion was proved wrong. Now a "blood covenant" was created between Ashkenazim and Oriental fighters. In those days of national euphoria it seemed as if the Orientals had finally ceased to be second-class citizens.[41]

Yet they had not ceased to be second-class citizens. And the Government of Israel, in this period, took action which underlined their second-class status most provocatively.

The Government of Israel, in the aftermath of the Six Day War, provided special incentives for European immigrants. The new immigrants—arriving after the war was safely won—were provided with large new flats and generous loans, while the Orientals, whose important share in winning the war was widely acknowledged, were left in their slums, and some of them in their original transit camps. The message was crystal-clear. After the war, just as before it, the leaders of Israel considered Europeans much more desirable than Orientals as citizens of Israel. To some extent the Orientals even agreed with that, in acknowledging their need of the European leadership which had created Israel. But it was a different matter to be asked to give place to newcomers, just because these were European, and for no other reason. And this provocation occurred at a time, after the victory, when the siege seemed over, and there was no longer need to be afraid of "rocking the boat."

The first Oriental protest movement in the history of Israel emerged in Jerusalem at the beginning of 1971. This was the group known as the Black Panthers (Panterim Shehorim). They were not really like their rejectionist and separatist American model. They were integrationists; they even wanted Orientals who had been declared "unfit" to be readmitted to the Army. They demanded slum clearance, more jobs, better educational opportunities, an end to all discrimination against Orientals. "It is not by chance," writes Professor Cohen, "that the Panther movement started in the slums of Western Jerusalem opposite the comfortable new Jewish quarters of the 'Eastern city' being rapidly built by the authorities and where many of the new immigrants were housed."[42]

Finding their demands not met, the Black Panthers started a major demonstration in Jerusalem, which turned into a riot. Presumably the object of the Black Panthers was to give the authorities a good fright. If so, they succeeded. What frightened the authorities most, probably, was the fact that Oriental Jews *generally* approved the demands and the protest, if not (explicitly) the rioting. "Respectable" Orientals might have been expected to dissociate themselves from the activities of a bunch of Moroccan slum boys, with a provocative name. But this did not happen. On the contrary, the general feeling of Oriental Jews was that it was "about time" for protest of this kind. Golda Meir's Government responded with major concessions: "Some of the demands were fully acceptable and considerable sums of money were at once appropriated to deal with pressing problems in the urban slums, such as rehabilitation, youth problems, and education."[43] Henceforward there prevailed, in relation to Oriental needs and attitudes, an official sensitivity, which was positively Proustian, at least in comparison to the bluff contempt of David Ben-Gurion.

Apart from the assistance supplied by a frightened Government, the Orientals were also making progress for themselves. They were moving up as the Irish and the Italians moved up in American life, through the sensitivity of ward politicians to the ethnic vote: "The parties in local elections were extremely conscious of the need to balance the ticket." By the early seventies there were Oriental mayors in 30 percent of Jewish municipalities, and where the mayor is European, the deputy mayor is often Oriental. As members of local councils the Orientals "did even better for as early as 1965 they were represented almost in direct accordance with their numbers."[44]

On the national scene, the Oriental impact has been of a different kind, though certainly not less significant. Orientals are not yet proportionately represented in the Knesset. Shlomo Avineri writes: "It will obviously be some time before this [local] shift will be as visible on the national level as well—after all, it took two generations of urban [ethnic] politics to produce an Irish Catholic president of the United States."[45] But the local and the national shifts have manifested themselves in different, though ultimately complementary, ways. At local level, it has been a question of securing an adequate quota on the slates of all parties, through the "balanced ticket." In national politics, the Oriental voters shifted the electoral balance of the State by turning away from Labor and throwing their weight on the side of the parties of the Right. And this occurred in spite of the fact that Labor—by the decisive year, 1977—showed itself far more willing than the right-wing Likud to nominate Oriental candidates.

In the beginning—in the forties and into the fifties—Orientals had voted for the governing party, Ben-Gurion's Mapai. They came, after all, from lands in which the Government was all-powerful, and constitutional opposition a thing unknown. But by the next decade, they had begun to swing away, and the swing was sustained, and eventually decisive: "In 1951 Mapai won 45.9 percent of the votes in immigrant and development towns and [Begin's] Herut only 4.9 percent; in 1965 Mapai was down to 34.4 percent and Herut up to 22.9; and by 1977 Mapai was down to 20 percent and [Begin's] Likud up to 42 percent."[46] This shift was the main reason for the fall of Labor in 1977 after almost thirty years continuously in power. And this happened despite the fact that Labor "made valiant efforts to balance its Knesset lists with Orientals, women, youth, etc., in a manner to gladden the heart of any 'affirmative action' bureaucrat in the United States."[47]

It is sometimes suggested that the partiality of Orientals for Likud is explained by their common hostility to Arabs. That common hostility exists, but it probably played only a secondary part in the swing of the Orientals away from Mapai to Likud. No political party, in any working democracy, could afford to treat an ethnic bloc as Mapai treated the Orientals, from 1948 to 1971, and expect to retain its loyalty. It ought to have been obvious that the Orientals, as soon as they began to understand how democracy worked—it being an

entirely unfamiliar concept in the lands they came from—would turn
to Mapai's opponents. Ben-Gurion and his colleagues often behaved
and spoke as if they thought the Orientals were too dumb ever to find
out how democracy worked. By the time Mapai realized that the
Orientals had found out, all right—and started to woo them—it was
too late.

Likud was attractive because its emphasis on patriotism was
readily comprehensible, and clearly relevant to the immediate environment. Mapai's ideology, a blend of Zionism and European socialism,
was complicated and required, for its understanding, the ingurgitation
of Russian history, in quantities uncongenial to Orientals. Also, in
proportion as Orientals came, perforce, to understand something of
this ideology, they were bound to resent what they understood. The
Mapai's leadership, the children of the second and third *aliyot,* the
people of the *kibbutzim,* had become an aristocracy of merit, a service
elite. Their position at the top of society was conspicuous after the
mass immigration of the mid-twentieth century. The Orientals were
on the whole prepared to accept and respect both the idea of an
elite and the character of this elite. But when the Orientals began
to understand the egalitarian nature of the doctrines which this elite
was commending to *them*—the underdogs of society—the thing was
bound to appear in the light of a bad joke. And the joke appeared in
a much worse light after 1973, when the elite seemed for the first
time to have partially failed in the supreme duty, for whose sake its
preeminence was accepted: the defense of Israel.

Attitudes toward the Irgun also contributed to the shift. Oriental
Jews had made up a large proportion of the membership of the Irgun.
Likud's cult of the Irgun was therefore congenial—as an acknowledg-
ment of a phase in the struggle for the Jewish State in which not only
Ashkenazim but Orientals as well were felt to have played a glorious
part. Mapai, in constantly disparaging the Irgun, were felt to be denying
to the Orientals any glory, any heroes, any role in the creation of the
State.

Both Likud and Mapai were European-led. But Mapai appeared
more emphatically and more exclusively European. And Likud did not
carry any of the blame for the things that had been done, and not
done, under Mapai rule, from the foundation of the State. So it was
natural that Oriental ambivalence toward Ashkenazim should polarize:
projecting the bad feelings onto Mapai and the good feelings onto
Likud.

There was, then, an abundance of weighty reasons for the shift, without attributing decisive weight to the element of "common hatred of Arabs." But, by reason of the shift, the attitude of Oriental Jews toward Arabs becomes a matter of importance for the future conduct of the besieged polity.

IX

"The primitive element," wrote David Ben-Gurion in 1959, "is . . . subjected easily to political and social demagogy. Its hatred for the Arabs is great, and the talk about the conquest of historical borders captures their hearts."[48]

Ben-Gurion was thinking, of course, of the Oriental Jews, and the shift toward Begin, then already perceptible. Understandably, he did not acknowledge that his own attitude toward "the primitive element" might have had at least as much to do with Oriental rejection of Mapai as did hatred of Arabs.

There seems to be no doubt that the expressed attitudes of Oriental Jews toward Arabs are significantly more hostile than those of Ashkenazim. Surveys show a consistently higher level of declared anti-Arab feeling among Orientals than among Ashkenazim. Depending on the nature of the proposition put, the gap varies between around 2 percent and around 25 percent. Thus 91 percent of Europeans and 93 percent of Orientals agreed, in 1968, with the general proposition "It would be better if there were fewer Arabs." But the concrete proposition "Disagree to have an Arab neighbour" found 78 percent of Orientals in its favor, as against only 53 percent of Europeans.[49]

In another survey, in 1969, the question was put: "To what extent would you support an aggressive policy towards the Arab States?" This question revealed a large gap. Fifty-three percent of Orientals, as against only 32 percent of Europeans, answered "To a great extent."[50] "Many Oriental respondents," according to Peres, "sought to explain their negative feelings by referring to previous unpleasant experiences under Arab domination."

There is no doubt that the "unpleasant experiences" had occurred, and in recent times. It happened that the three largest groups of Oriental immigrants to Israel—Yemenis, Iraqis and Moroccans—had particularly negative experiences under Muslim rule. The Yemenis, living under the medieval theocracy of the Imam, had never experienced even formal emancipation; they remained *dhimmis* to the end, with the aggravation that the Shi'i Muslims of Yemen regard *dhimmis* as not merely inferior but unclean, so that constant precautions had to be taken to avoid contaminating their superiors. The Moroccans knew the depth of the hostility of their Muslim neighbors from the repeated pogroms of the last period of Moroccan independence, the pre-1912 period. The Iraqis had known the more recent horrors of the Baghdad massacre of June 1941. And on top of all that, all the immigrants experienced the wave of hostility, in every part of the Muslim world, that followed the defeat of the Arab armies by "the Zionist gangs."

Against that background, the hostility of Oriental Jews seems understandable. Yet sociologists doubt whether the background in fact explains the levels of hostility expressed. Both Smooha and Peres have suggested that this may have more to do with upward social mobility within Israeli society than with brooding on the Arab past. "Lower-class Orientals," says Smooha, "are seemingly disposed to enhance status within the Jewish quasi-caste by taking a harder line than the Ashkenazim against the Arabs."[51] Peres offers a slightly different but compatible explanation, also based on upward movement within Israeli society: "The Orientals feel that they must reject the remaining traces of their Middle Eastern origin to attain the status of the dominant European group. By expressing hostility to Arabs, an Oriental attempts to rid himself of the 'inferior' Arabic elements in his own identity and to adopt a position congenial to the European group which he desires to emulate."[52]

Shlomo Avineri suggests a parallel between the upward movement of the Oriental Jews in Israel and the upward movement of Irish and Italians (and Jews) in nineteenth-century America.[53] The Irish-American ascent was accompanied by the making of very much the same point as Smooha sees the Orientals as making. The Irish-Americans, as is well known, always stressed their extreme antipathy to the British. This has usually been attributed to mere sentimental brooding on the past; thus, for example, Evelyn Waugh spoke of Irish Catholic immigrants to America as bringing with them "their ancient rancours and the melancholy of the bogs." They brought their rancors with them all right, but they also found that these rancors were a resource worth exploiting in the American context. In the American schoolroom, the immigrant children discovered that the great and holy event of history was the American Revolution. And

the American Revolution had been a revolution *against the British!*
And who had a better right to be against the British than the Irish
had? To be loudly anti-British was to be 100 percent American. It was
also a rewarding position in relation to the large pro-British (and
anti-Irish) section of the Wasp establishment. To be pro-British was
to be un-American, the Irish proclaimed, as they moved up. Other
non–Anglo-Saxon immigrant groups tended to agree, and Wasp supremacy started to slip.

The vociferous anti-Arabism of the Orientals in Israel seems to
work in a similar way. Its manifestations, and the dovish responses
they evoke from the side of Mapai, serve to suggest that the Mapai
establishment is "pro-Arab"; therefore not as good as the 100 percent
Israelis, the Orientals.

The anti-Arabism of the Orientals is quite genuine (like the anti-
Britishness of the Irish-Americans). But then anti-Arabism is, for
obvious reasons, very widespread in Israel, among *all* Jews.[54] What
has to be accounted for is the *excess* of Oriental over European anti-
Arabism. And it does seem that that excess can be better accounted
for as an oblique attack on the most disliked section of the European
establishment, rather than as a manifestation of "primitive" resentment
of the former Arab rulers. Groups which feel discriminated against
are more likely to have their *present* rulers on their minds rather than
their former ones. If they stress their animosity toward their former
rulers—as Irish Americans did, and as Oriental Israelis do—they are
likely to be telling their present rulers something, in an Aesopian way.

The attitudes of the Orientals obviously have a significant bearing on the future handling of the siege. If the hypothesis favored here
is correct, it is probably wrong to suggest that Oriental anti-Arabism
is likely to rule out any settlement with the Arabs. Orientals did not
defect from Begin over his settlement with Sadat.[55] Orientals might
well accept a similar settlement with Syria, *negotiated by Likud*. But
if Mapai were to return to power, and attempt a settlement, ceding
substantial areas of the West Bank, there would probably be a popular
explosion, in which Orientals would be likely to play the largest part.
But, for various reasons considered later,[56] that supposition seems
unlikely to be put to the test.

It may be expected that, as Israel becomes more integrated, the
excess of current Oriental anti-Arabism, over the general level, will
decline, and that the politics of Israel, in relation to this matter, will
be considered on a correspondingly cooler and more pragmatic plane.

But the process of integration is still proceeding at a very slow pace. As long as it remains far from completion, the "Oriental factor" will probably continue to operate in favor of Likud, and against Mapai— and also to make a reputation for "dovishness" increasingly a liability in the internal politics of Israel.

8

DIPLOMACY
AND WAR
1948-1967

We have a secret weapon which we can use better than guns and machine guns, and this is time. As long as we do not make peace with the Zionists, the war is not over, and as long as the war is not over, there is neither victor nor vanquished. As soon as we recognize the existence of the state of Israel, we recognize by this act that we are conquered.
—AZZAM PASHA, *Secretary-General of the Arab League*[1]

Justum est bellum . . . quibus necessarium.
—LIVY, ix, i, 10

THE CONDITION of the region, after the Armistice Agreements, was one of neither war nor peace. All Israel's land frontiers, the armistice lines, remained closed. All of Israel's neighbors, and all other Arab countries, boycotted Israel. From the end of 1951 on, the Suez Canal was closed to ships flying the flag of Israel; so were the Straits of Tiran, at the entrance of the Gulf of Aqaba, Israel's eastern access route. These actions were justified by the concept that Israel and its neighbors were still in a state of war: a state which had been suspended, not ended, by the Armistice Agreements.

Efforts were made, under international auspices, to move from armistice to peace. The U.N. General Assembly had set up a Conciliation Commission consisting of the United States, France and Turkey: a composition reflecting an international situation relatively favorable to Israel, in the immediate aftermath of the fighting. A kind of conference was organized by the commission, and met at Lausanne in the first half of 1949. The conference ran rather on the lines of the London Conference of ten years before. The Arab delegates and the Israelis did not meet officially, although there were several private meetings between Israeli and Egyptian and Jordanian representatives. Israelis and Arabs met separately with the mediators; the Arabs met the mediators as a group, and therefore competitively.

The armistice talks, separately conducted between Israel and each individual Arab adversary, had led to practical, if limited, conclusions. The Lausanne Conference led only to a temporary continuation of the state of affairs resulting from the separate negotiations. These results were fairly representative of the average workings, over decades, of what later came to be known as "the peace process."

Israel wanted peace behind recognized and secure frontiers.[2] There was only one Arab State—Abdullah's Transjordan—which was (secretly) prepared to recognize Israel behind some kind of negotiated frontiers, and there was none, as it turned out, prepared to recognize frontiers acceptable to Israel.

Collectively and formally, the Arab states, as often, declared categorical preconditions, without making it clear what exactly they would be prepared to do if their preconditions should be met: this unpromising negotiating position is known as "setting preconditions to negotiation." The preconditions were: return of all the refugees to their homes, and withdrawal of Israel to the frontiers laid down by the General Assembly resolution of November 1947, which meant withdrawal from one-third of Israeli-held territory, including Jerusalem. Israel was not prepared to readmit large numbers of (presumably) hostile refugees, or to withdraw from any place, without correspondingly solid advantages to itself; advantages which were not on offer. (Israel was not prepared to withdraw from Jerusalem in exchange for any conceivable advantage.)

The Arab position sounds unreasonable; and so it was, from an Israeli point of view. From the point of view of the Arab "negotiators," it was quite reasonable. The Egyptians and the Syrians represented tottering Governments, humiliated by the outcome of the war and the acceptance of the armistice. Even an advantageous peace with Israel would be regarded by their populations—or at least the politically

conscious among these—as the crowning enormity and ultimate betrayal. A strategy of "minimum demands"—which the Arab public
would expect to be followed by further demands, and eventually the
liquidation of Israel—met the "negotiating needs" of these very sick
Governments. Lebanon and Jordan—less damaged by the war, politically and militarily—had their reasons for going along, ostensibly,
with Egypt and Syria. The famous Lebanese "compromise" between
Christian and Sunni Muslims required a heavy stress on "the Arab
bond," and nominal subscription to any available Arab consensus.
Jordan's King had his ambitions, but there was no point in divulging
these until separate and secret negotiations would show whether the
ambitions were capable of fulfillment. So Lausanne was a total deadlock.[3]

II

Before, during and after the armistice negotiations and the Lau-
sanne talks, representatives of Israel met repeatedly with Abdullah.
Formally, the conversations led to nothing; no peace was ever signed.
Ben-Gurion thought the British might not let Abdullah sign a peace,
and Abdullah himself stated that "his friend Sir Alec Kirkbride,
Britain's Minister to Transjordan, did not agree that Jordan should
enter into such a treaty with Israel while other Arab states, mainly
Egypt, had not done so."[4]

Today, some Israeli scholars believe that the failure of the negotiations was due exclusively to opposition within Jordan, contrary
to Abdullah's implication. In any case, whatever the source or sources,
the opposition prevailed.

Peace was not possible. What was possible, and achieved within
limits, by Israel and Jordan, was a tacit *modus vivendi*, based on a
recognition of common interests. One common interest (for the time
being) was that the West Bank should belong to the Hashemites,
rather than to any other Arab State—or to the Palestinians, led by
Haj Amin al-Husseini, backed by Egypt. Another such common interest (also for the time being) was the *status quo* in Jerusalem, then
under threat. The United Nations, in its partition resolution of November 1947—the same resolution which Israel originally relied on as
legitimizing its existence—had provided for an internationalized
Jerusalem (*corpus separatum*), as the Peel Commission had also done;

this was something which Herzl and the earlier Zionists had often professed themselves willing to accept. Late in 1949, a powerful lobby—in terms of U.N. votes—declared itself at the General Assembly in favor of reconfirming Jerusalem's international status. The lobby was made up of the Latin-American and other Catholic states (at the urging of the Vatican), the Communist states and the Arab states, with the exception of Jordan. On December 9, 1949, the General Assembly voted in favor of the *corpus separatum,* by 38 to 14, with 7 abstentions. As majorities go, it was a better majority than the original partition resolution had had.

Ben-Gurion now defied the General Assembly, promptly and dramatically. On December 11, the day after Israel learned of the General Assembly vote, the Cabinet of Israel, at Ben-Gurion's insistence, decided to make Jerusalem the seat of government, the capital of Israel. "Jerusalem," Ben-Gurion announced, "is an inseparable part of Israel and her eternal capital. No United Nations vote can alter that historic fact."[5]

In taking this stand, Ben-Gurion was certainly influenced by the fact that in totally rejecting internationalization, he spoke, not merely for the Jews, but for the ruler of the rest of Palestine. The Muslim King, who now controlled most of the Holy Places, could not give them up to some international body without an unbearable loss of prestige, to himself and to his dynasty. It was in Britain's interest to avert that: consequently, it was in the interest of the British Government—though little to its taste—to let Israel get away with it. So in this case, exceptionally, the British Foreign Office would tell the State Department substantially the same thing as the Israeli delegation[6] at the U.N. would tell the U.S. delegation: let the General Assembly resolution of December 9, 1949, quietly wither away, which it duly did.[7]

III

Ben-Gurion then had strong reasons to keep lines open to Abdullah—the sole Arab leader interested in such communications. Ben-Gurion's manner of keeping the lines open was interesting and characteristic. Ben-Gurion was Minister for Defense, as well as Prime Minister, for the first five years of the State.[8] His towering prestige— after leading Israel to statehood, and then leading its successful defense against what seemed overwhelming odds—made him far more than a normal Prime Minister, under conditions of collective Cabinet responsibility.[9] Essentially he controlled any aspect of Government which he wished to control. One such aspect was foreign affairs, the importance of which he regarded as second only to defense in Israel's conditions. Ben-Gurion kept the negotiations with Abdullah, like other important matters, under his own personal control. He involved in these negotiations not only the Ministry of Foreign Affairs, then headed by Moshe Sharett, but also his own ministry, Defense; significantly, he chose to have his ministry represented in the secret negotiations in Amman by young Colonel Moshe Dayan.

Dayan and Sharett were in sharp contrast. They seemed like archetypes of the hawks and doves of Israel, and Ben-Gurion had uses for both. Sharett was seen as being in the tradition of Weizmann. He may well have been more in the tradition of Weizmann than Weizmann would have been if Weizmann had had the reins of a government. Weizmann had respected international opinion, as material on which he worked to bring the Jewish State into being. Sharett respected international opinion as a moral force, whose approval Israel needed at every step. He took the United Nations literally, attributing a high degree of moral authority to the resolutions of its principal organs. He reproached himself bitterly for failing to avert the passage of the United Nations resolution of December 9, 1949, on Jerusalem, and he offered his resignation to Ben-Gurion on this issue.[10] He also advised that Israel should not go directly against the U.N. resolution. Ben-Gurion rejected his resignation and ignored his advice, without even bringing the advice to the attention of their Cabinet colleagues.[11]

In general, Ben-Gurion found Sharett useful, as genuinely and earnestly representative of a certain Israeli idealism, shared or appreciated by many Jews of the Diaspora, and in Israel itself and by some Gentiles. The actual making of foreign policy was firmly in Ben-Gurion's hands, and Ben-Gurion attached little importance to Sharett's advice, and despised his deference to the United Nations: "*Oum, shmoum,*" Ben-Gurion used to say; Anglice, *Uno, shmuno.*[12] Sharett suffered, as had Weizmann, from Ben-Gurion's grumpy and dismissive manners, and his often devious and ruthless behavior, in contrast to his lofty public professions. But the sincerity of Sharett's suffering was also an asset to Ben-Gurion's Israel. The anguish of the Foreign Minister helped to compensate for the ruthlessness of the Prime Minister, as Israel moved away from the limitless benign possibilities of a longed-for ideal into the narrow span of cruel choices open to a besieged nation-state.[13]

Moshe Dayan was already a favorite of Ben-Gurion's among a class in which Ben-Gurion put much hope for the future of Israel: the Maccabees, young officers born in Israel, brought up in *kibbutzim* or *moshavim* (cooperative settlements) and tested in war. Dayan had lost an eye in action against the Vichy French in the invasion of Syria, during the Second World War, and had particularly distinguished himself during Israel's war for survival (1948–1949). Ben-Gurion, who tended to distrust his contemporaries, in both the civil and military establishment of Israel, sought to bring on younger men, and hoped that one of them would succeed him as Prime Minister.[14] Dayan, the epitome of the New Jew, seemed the most likely prospect. Not only his martial record, but the quality and character of his mind, appealed to Ben-Gurion. Dayan was a realist, to the point where realism begins to look, to many, like cynicism; this did not distress Ben-Gurion. Dayan came to have the reputation of a hawk, and perhaps cultivated this, but in reality he was neither hawk nor dove.[15] Like Sharett, he was a passionate Jewish patriot, and a calculator of what might be of advantage to Israel, but unlike Sharett, he did not attach, in his calculations, a very high value to making a favorable impression on the Gentile world. World opinion was a factor in Israel's predicament: something to be cultivated generally speaking, but something also to be flouted, on occasion deliberately and with *éclat*—as Ben-Gurion had done in his response to the resolution of December 9, 1949—if a vital interest of Israel so required.

It seems reasonable to infer that by including the not-very-diplomatic Dayan in such an important negotiation as that with Abdullah, Ben-Gurion meant to get a more reliable assessment of the real possibilities than he could expect from what he saw as the sentimentalists in Sharett's Foreign Office.

Dayan has left a vivid, and characteristically sardonic, picture of Israel's first Foreign Minister in negotiation with Jordan's Hashemite King:

> Towards Moshe Sharett [the King] was well disposed—at first. Sharett spoke a polished Arabic and was meticulously well mannered and appropriately reverent in the presence of royalty. But at one of our meetings—a rather unsuccessful one; it was a hot night, we dripped sweat, and there were many mosquitoes on the wing—Sharett corrected the king

when he mentioned in passing that China had not been a member of the League of Nations. A king never errs, and Abdullah stood by his statement. Sharett, like a demonstratively patient kindergarten teacher with a backward child,[16] kept saying, "But Your Majesty, you are wrong. China *did* belong to the League." That was the end of *that* meeting—and of the royal regard for Sharett. In the car on our drive back, I asked Sharett what the devil it mattered what the king thought about China and the League. Sharett turned on me with some heat: "But China *was* a member of the League of Nations!"[17]

Dayan himself seems to have found courtly protocol burdensome:

We would dine with the king prior to getting down to business, and for an hour or so before the meal there would be political gossip of what was happening in the capitals of the world, an occasional game of chess, and poetry readings. In chess, it was obligatory not only to lose to the king but also to show surprise at his unexpected moves. And when he read his poems, in epigrammic Arabic, one had to express wonder by sighing from the depths of one's soul.

The negotiations did not lead to peace. But they did prove that the State of Israel could conduct negotiations with an Arab leader, with a view to permanent peace, and not just armistice. There seemed good grounds for hope that the siege might actually be raised, just where it pressed closest, inside Jerusalem, and within ten miles of Tel Aviv. That hope was dashed on July 20, 1951, on the Haram esh-Sharif in Jerusalem, when Abdullah was murdered as he left the Mosque of al-Aqsa after Friday prayers. This "execution" was hailed throughout the Arab world as fully justified, since Abdullah was known (or at least rightly believed) to have been in negotiation with Israel.

As interpretation of the motives of the murderers, this is probably inadequate. The murderers were followers of Haj Amin—one of them a Husseini kinsman—and Haj Amin (like his followers) had strong motives, not directly connected with Israel, for hating Abdullah. Their feud was an old one, and the results of the 1948 war were of a nature to intensify enormously Haj Amin's bitterness against the King. For sixteen years, from 1921 to 1937, Haj Amin had himself been something very like a king in Arab Palestine—and a more independent kind of king than Abdullah was—and for another eleven years—1937 to 1948—he had been a kind of rightful king in exile, whose loyal subjects longed for his return. He had undoubtedly expected to return, in the wake of the victorious Egyptian Army, and to be supreme, with Egyptian support, in an entirely Arab Palestine, from the Jordan (or perhaps farther east) to the sea. But as things incredibly and horribly turned out—from his point of view—Haj Amin found himself shut out from all of Palestine: from the Jewish part by his Jewish enemies, and from the Arab part by his Arab enemy, Abdullah. Abdullah held the West Bank and East Jerusalem, including the Muslim Holy Places. Haj Amin's Egyptian friends, humiliatingly defeated and chased back into Sinai, had no say in the affairs of Palestine. The crowning insult was the thought of the odious Abdullah, lording it on Haj Amin's old sacred stronghold, the Haram esh-Sharif, and praying in that great and splendid mosque in which Haj Amin had preached in the glory of his days as Grand Mufti—and from which he was now unceremoniously excluded.

If ever a man had motive for murder, Haj Amin had, even if Abdullah had never negotiated with any Jews. But what mattered politically, in the aftermath of Abdullah's murder, was not what may have motivated the murderers and their chief, but how the murder was seen in the Arab world. The murder itself may have been no more than the terminal incident in a long feud between Arab potentates. It was generally seen, by Arabs, as a satisfactory, and consoling, incident in the unended war with Israel. Seen in that light, Abdullah's murder cast a long shadow. Gamal Abdel Nasser, who joined the ruling junta in Egypt in the year following that murder, and became supreme in Egypt and preeminent throughout the Arab world within a few years of the event, never lost sight of what happened to Abdullah.[18] The murder at the Mosque of al-Aqsa showed that any Arab leader who came to be thought of as negotiating peace with Israel would be in double jeopardy. Obviously he would be in danger from fanatical enemies of Israel, but he would also expose himself to increased danger from those who might hate him for other reasons, but could now justify his "execution," as a traitor, before the Arab world.

Abdullah's grandson Hussein had been with his grandfather at the moment of his murder. It may be assumed that that moment has left its mark on Hussein's policy as king, a policy which has shown a consistent reluctance to break the limits of Arab consensus. As there was no Arab consensus on anything except on the need to squeeze Israel, and eventually eliminate it, this meant subscribing to that policy, at least in appearance.

Israel's hopes of achieving even one open land border were

dashed. It was clear, from the early fifties on, that Israel was in for a long siege. As Moshe Dayan wrote: "The Jews had conquered the Arab armies but not their hatred."[19]

IV

Arab hostility, suspended and waiting for its chance, had to be accepted as a fact, over which Israel had no direct control. The attention of Israel's policy makers now concentrated on relations with major Powers outside the region, principally the United States, the Soviet Union and Britain.

The major question to be determined was whether Israel should align its policies (avowed or unavowed) with those of the United States or whether it should try to stay neutral—or "nonidentified" to use the Israeli term—both in the Cold War and in any future clash between the superpowers. From its origins, and in its first declarations, as an independent State, Israel was pledged to "nonidentification": in Hebrew, *ee-hizdahut*. "Israel," Foreign Minister Moshe Sharett informed the Knesset on June 15, 1949, "will in no case become identified with one of the great blocs of the world as against the other."[20] But in making this ringing declaration, Sharett was, as often, out of tune with the more powerful, and less fastidious, mind of his master, David Ben-Gurion.

Ben-Gurion had indeed, in the period immediately before independence and for a short time thereafter, often proclaimed his adherence to the principle of *ee-hizdahut*. But there were very good reasons for doing so, in that period. Israel absolutely needed the support of both the superpowers in order to win "world recognition" for the Jewish State. *Oum, shmoum* might be absurd, but its blessing for the new State was a greatly prized asset. But within a month of winning that recognition, Ben-Gurion showed that his commitment to *ee-hizdahut* was less than total. "If necessary we will change it," he told the Central Committee of his party, Mapai, on December 3, 1947.[21]

Ben-Gurion didn't change it immediately: *ee-hizdahut* was still a valuable card during Israel's fight for existence in 1948–1949, when the United States put an embargo on arms for the region, and the flow of Soviet-bloc weaponry was Israel's lifeline. But very soon after Israel's independence was consolidated, Ben-Gurion had to make a choice, and he unhesitatingly chose the United States.

The precipitating factor was the renewed flow of British arms to replenish the depleted arsenals of its Arab clients, Jordan, Iraq and Egypt. These arms were intended not for use against Israel, but to restore British prestige and influence; despite the intention, the most likely use for the arms was against Israel. In theory, and in pursuit of *ee-hizdahut,* Ben-Gurion could have tried to enlist both superpowers on his side, against Britain, but this was not practical. The relations between the superpowers were much worse than they had been in 1947, when they had voted together in favor of the Jewish State. Any attempt by Israel, in the political climate of 1949–1950, to bring Soviet influence to bear against Britain, an ally of the United States, would have been likely to hurt Israel, both with the White House and with the Jewish community in the United States, and to increase what Ben-Gurion regarded as the inveterate hostility of the State Department. Ben-Gurion made his choice and addressed his appeal for arms to the United States, backing that appeal with pressure from the pro-Israel lobby. The result was the Tripartite Declaration of May 25, 1950, under which the United States, Britain and France bound themselves to regulate the supply of arms to the Arab states and to Israel and to guarantee the armistice borders against any attempt to alter them by force.

Events in the region, within five years, were to make nonsense of the Tripartite Declaration, but for the moment it gave some reassurance to Israel. It was interpreted, reasonably enough, as meaning that the United States would keep Israel supplied with arms, matching the flow of British arms to Arabs. But also, since Israel was relying on America for military supplies, within the framework of an agreement which assumed the exclusion of Soviet influence from the region, Israel's role in relation to the Tripartite Declaration meant the beginning of the end of the policy of *ee-hizdahut.*[22]

A month later, with the outbreak of the Korean War, *ee-hizdahut* finally expired, though its demise was denied. In giving the loyal diplomatic (though not military) support of the Government of Israel to every major American initiative throughout the war, Moshe Sharett denied that any departure from nonidentification had taken place. The Korean War was a *United Nations* action[23] and how could support for the United Nations be equated to identification with a bloc? A good Sharett point, with an appeal also to the Ben-Gurion mind. *Oum, shmoum* was good for something after all. The Soviet leaders were not fooled. They saw Israel as having thrown in its lot with the United

States, and the Soviet Union took up an anti-Israel and pro-Arab position which it has never since abandoned, although it has always stopped short of opposing Israel's right to exist.[24]

V

The timing of Israel's abandonment of nonidentification was determined by the immediate politico-military situation around 1950. But the *nature* of Israel's choice was determined by long-term factors, both emotional and material.

It is often suggested that the bond between Israel and the United States consists in their common commitment to democratic values. In a sense that is true, but I think not quite in the same sense that the orators intend. Israel is magnetically attracted to the United States, not by a doctrinaire attachment to democratic theory, but by a down-to-earth feeling for the results and workings of democracy in the United States. And it is repelled by the Soviet Union by an equally down-to-earth feeling for the results and workings of the Soviet system.

One factor that had to be taken into account by Israel was the comparative position of the Jews in the Soviet Union and in the United States. Once that factor is considered, the choice of the United States is seen as imperative.

In the Soviet Union, the Jews, like most other people, have no political power or influence. Their apparent influence, in the early years of the Revolution, vanished with the rise of Stalin and the fall of Trotsky. They remain a helpless people, at the mercy of the authorities, as they were in the days of the tsars. The authorities have not behaved as outrageously toward them as Alexander III and Nicholas II used to do, but they show their disfavor, and can go to whatever lengths seem appropriate to them. Russian people remain anti-semitic—as the Israeli leaders born in Russia well knew. Official policy is against anti-semitism, but is anti-Zionist. Anti-Zionism can be a good way of manifesting anti-semitism in practice, while remaining anti-anti-semitic in theory. There were extremely ugly anti-semitic manifestations in the last years of Stalin, during the Prague Trials of Slansky and others (November–December 1952) and the Doctors' Plot (January 1953). The manic phase of anti-Zionist anti-semitism ended with Stalin's death (March 1953), but anti-Zionism continued, growling or strident. Soviet backing for the Jewish State (1947–1949) had been an exceptional, opportunist episode, apparently motivated by a desire to embarrass the British (and, no doubt, trouble the Anglo-American alliance).

Despite all this there were Israelis, heirs to the "Russian revolutionary" tendencies of the second and third *aliyot*, who preferred a link with "the socialist countries" to any link with the capitalist U.S.A. These were mainly concentrated in Mapam, the labor grouping to the left of Ben-Gurion. But Mapam was split and discredited—as a result of the Prague Trials and the Doctors' Plot. Not merely did these show "the socialist countries" in a most sinister light, but Mapam itself—precisely because of its courting of the Soviet Union—was a principal target of denunciation by the prosecution. Mapam, it seemed, was a nest of imperialist spies, working for the United States; one of its members was arrested and tried in Prague. Mapam's advice—that the Soviet Union could be trusted—now recoiled against itself, ludicrously. If the Soviet Union could be trusted, Mapam itself was a nest of spies. And if Mapam was not a nest of spies, the Soviet Union could not be trusted. Impaled on this fork, by the object of its own affections, Mapam suffered a decline. The beneficiaries of its decline were the hard liners, on Ben-Gurion's right. Begin's Herut now emerged as second in importance among Israel's political parties.

VI

Even if the Soviet Union had chosen to cultivate Israel—or at least its own sympathizers there—the appeal of the United States was inherently far greater. The Jewish community in the United States is the largest, the richest and the most powerful in the world and it is devoted to Israel. There was a time when many American Jews hesitated to identify themselves with the Zionist cause, feeling that the appearance of a "double loyalty" could serve as a pretext for anti-semitism. But that period had ended around the time of the Biltmore Conference (1942), with America's entry into the war against Hitler, and with the first news of the Holocaust.

The memory of the Holocaust itself creates a bond of an emotional intensity unparalleled in any other international relation. It is no sentimental trope, but the literal truth, to say that the Jews of America and the Yishuv, at the time of the fight for Israel's independence, were children of a common bereavement: still recoiling from the news of the massacre of the common stock from which they both sprang. The events of 1945–1948—with the British attempts to keep the Holocaust survivors out of Palestine, and the subsequent Arab attempts to destroy Israel—were of a nature to raise the pro-Israel commitment of American Jews to a high pitch of passion. But, passionate as it was, it was also skillful, and decisively effective.

The term "pro-Israel lobby" seems too weak to cover a phenomenon which is unique in its combination of size, emotional motivation, intensity and diversity of activity, and ingenuity and efficiency of operation. Other ethnic lobbies—I think of the Irish one, naturally[25]—seem puny in comparison. The basic strength of this phenomenon lies in the unique sense of solidarity which exists between the children of the Holocaust. As an American academic authority—not particularly sympathetic to the pro-Israel lobby—puts it:

> The core of Israel's constituency in the United States . . . is the American Jewish community with its powerful bonds of loyalty and affection for the Jewish state. . . . Just as the Jewish State of Israel is "unique and unprecedented," so too is the Israeli lobby in the United States. . . . The root strength of this most formidable of domestic political lobbies—a fact imperfectly understood by Arabs—lies not in its skill in public relations, access to the media or ample financing, although all these are impressive, but in the solid, consistent and usually unified support of the Jewish communities of the United States. The resources thus made available to the Israel lobby heavily outweigh the lobbying power of Arab Americans or of the Arab governments, even, in the cases of some of the latter, with the assets of costly, sophisticated public relations campaigns.[26]

One might think that so formidable a lobby, devoted to the interests of a foreign country, would become a focus for the most virulent anti-semitism. This has not happened, at least at the mass level. Opinion surveys show that anti-semitism actually reached its peak right at the end of the Second World War—when Jews seemed at their most helpless, ever—went on declining through the fifties and sixties—when Jews began to look distinctly less helpless—and is still in decline.[27] Surveys also show widespread and steady support for Israel.

This combination—of a decline in anti-semitism combined with a conspicuous rise in Jewish political power—suggests conclusions gratifying to Zionists, especially of the Jabotinsky tradition. It suggests that sadism—excited by the proximity of defenseless individuals—may be a significant component in anti-semitism, and that, when the individuals cease to appear defenseless, some potential anti-semites tend to lose interest.

That, however, is speculation. A more measurable, and mundane, explanation may be found in the nature of the contemporary American political system; a system in which, as Seth Tillman puts it, Congress has become close "to a brokerage for the special interests represented by its members."[28]

These special interests avoid confrontation, and seek alliances with other special interests. Collusion, rather than collision, marks the operation of ethnic lobbies. Such lobbies have themselves acquired a legitimacy which they lacked in the years of Wasp hegemony. The reproach of "divided loyalty" is no longer aimed at Poles or Greeks or Irish—*provided* their activities are not seen as hostile, or potentially hostile, to the United States. The proviso is vital. If Israel had, for example, taken a neutralist position during the Korean War, that position would not merely have made Israel itself unpopular in the United States, but would have made American Jews suspect of divided loyalty. This could have posed a serious threat to Israel's survival. As a result of this consideration, successive Governments of Israel have been careful to align their foreign policy with that of the United States—except where Israel's own vital regional interests are seen to be involved. The counterpart of Israeli leverage over the foreign policy of the United States is American leverage over the general foreign policy of Israel, though not where Israel's own security is felt to be at stake.[29]

VII

The emergence of the State of Israel had an epoch-making significance for American Jews. The Jews now had an "old country" in a sense that Poles, Greeks, Irish, etc. could understand. It may have seemed odd that the "old country" of the Jews should be this extremely new State, and that the Jews should have acquired it only after coming to America, instead of leaving their old country to *come* to America, like everyone else.[30] Still, there it was, an old country of the Jews' very own, with a visible place on the map: a rather special old country indeed, in that it had come into being with the blessing and backing of the United States. It had also the blessing of the Soviet Union, but that rather curious fact could be forgotten, once—from the early fifties on—Moscow began its long and loud denunciations of Israel: denunciations which unintentionally fortified the position of American Jews, and therefore served the interests of Israel. Yet another manifestation of a pattern which recurs throughout the history of Zionism and of Israel.

From the point of view of the Jews, the "old country," and their attachment to it, were more ancient than any other nationality. But to Gentiles, that attachment seemed incomprehensible until they could see with their own eyes the mark of it on the map. The Jews then became more "like other people," more "human," less weird and magical and menacing.

What American Jews have done for Israel is well known. What Israel has done for American Jews is perhaps less obvious, but hardly less important. The need to create Israel, and the need to sustain it, obliged the Jews of America—from the Biltmore Conference of 1942 on—*to seek, find and wield political power* at national level, for an international purpose. Although Jews, from the 1880s on, had been one of a number of significant ethnic groups cultivated by party machines, and although they had occasionally influenced American foreign policy—in relation to Russia—their political activity, as a distinct group, had been limited. But as European anti-semitism reached its genocidal paroxysm, American Jews were driven to sustained and energetic political activity, as a unique political force: making up (along with Gentile sympathizers and allies) the Zionist lobby, later the pro-Israel lobby. Around that lobby Jews made themselves into a notable political power in the land.

It was, of course, something of a paradox that Zionism should lead to the emergence of a concentration of Jewish power in the Diaspora; Theodor Herzl would have been surprised. But the subtlest of Zionist thinkers, Ahad Ha'am, would not have been surprised. He had never believed that most of the Jews of the world would move to the Land of Israel. He had hoped that some Jews could establish there a home, of which most Jews in the Diaspora could be proud, and therefore hold their heads higher. And his hopes were, in that respect, fulfilled.

A number of foreign Governments—notably those of Britain and the Arab countries—thought it reprehensible, even scandalous, that the pro-Israel lobby, with its principal power base in the Jewish voting blocs of a number of great American cities, should be able to inflect American foreign policy to a significant degree. This view is shared by a certain number of eminent Americans, especially among State Department officials and academics responsive to State Department assessments. On this view, American national interests—seen as requiring a sustained effort to win and hold the goodwill of Arab states— have often been sacrificed in favor of the special interests of an ethnic lobby. How far this may be the case in fact is considered elsewhere. In the context of the lobby and its effectiveness, the significant point is that the "State Department" view remains a minority view. Most Americans regard lobbying as a legitimate aspect of democracy; they often belong to one or more lobbies themselves, and tend to admire efficient and determined lobbies, of which the pro-Israel lobby is the archetype. Being pro- or anti-lobbying in itself is a sort of Gentlemen *vs.* Players game. And in American history, it's a long time since the Gentlemen won a match.[31]

The most remarkable aspect of the lobbying factor is the relative absence, or impotence, of a *counter* lobby. Granted the tremendous importance of Arab oil to the economies of America and its allies, and granted the no less tremendous financial interests involved, one might have expected a great *anti*-Israel lobby to emerge. But this has not happened.

Countering the notion that the pressure of the pro-Israel lobby on foreign policy is illegitimate, Abba Eban wrote: "An ambassador need be no more ashamed of invoking his country's assets in sympathetic opinion than of drawing attention to resources of oil, if it has any."[32] Eban could have added, out of intimate experience, that sympathetic opinion can be a stronger resource, politically speaking, than oil or money. Sympathetic opinion, if strong, commands votes, the only indispensable resource in democratic politics. The oil interests, for all their colossal *economic* resources, have nothing that can compare with the *political* force represented by the Jewish vote, in association with the intensity of Jewish feeling for Israel, and the sophisticated, disciplined use of this power base to win support from other groups.

Any group in America, with anything to lose, would shrink from confrontation with the pro-Israel lobby, and the oil interests are no exception. As Seth Tillman writes: "Outside the realm of energy costs, uses and taxation, the oil companies have in fact been chary of taking public positions on Middle East issues, much less of pressing these on Congress."[33] In this reserve, the oil companies show their accustomed good sense where their own interests are concerned. Taking "public positions on [the] Middle East"—and above all, "pressing these on Congress," God forbid!—would mean bringing down on the oil companies the full fury of the pro-Israel lobby: a sturdy and determined adversary and well capable of hurting the oil companies where it hurts most: in that vulnerable "realm of energy costs, uses and taxation." So if the oil companies are chary, they have something to be chary about.

Also the oil companies know, none better, that the masters of most Middle Eastern oil are unlikely to sever, or seriously weaken, their ties with the West just because of American friendship for Israel. The hatred of these astute princes for Israel is sincere, but their devotion to their own economic interests is no less sincere, and takes precedence.

VIII

Great though the influence was later to become, the pro-Israel lobby had little influence over America's Middle Eastern policies in the early years of the State of Israel.

America, influenced by the Zionist lobby, had helped Israel to win its independence, which America was the first to recognize. American Jews were steadfast—contributing, for example, the huge sums required for the absorption of the postindependence refugees—but official America was increasingly aloof. True, the Tripartite Declaration of May 1950 was to some extent reassuring; but the declaration and what it stood for were soon undermined by events inside and outside the region.

After the outbreak of the Korean War, in the month following the Tripartite Declaration, American policy makers became almost exclusively preoccupied, naturally enough, with the Soviet Union, its ambitions and the need to counter these. In this perspective, the Middle East—with its oil, its communications, its "strategic space" and its proximity to the Soviet Union—appeared as the region in which the vital interests of the West were most exposed. The decay of European dominance in the area was seen as leaving a "power vacuum," which Soviet ambition might be tempted to fill. France had gone from the area altogether, ousted not by the Arabs, but by Britain, mainly in an effort to win Arab goodwill, with the usual negative result. Britain's authority over its Hashemite protégés, in Jordan and Iraq, remained intact, but its authority over Egypt—by far the most populous and strategically important country of the region—was in continuing and terminal decline. One stage in that decline had been marked by Egypt's rejection of Britain's offered help, against Israel, under the 1936 Treaty. A more dramatic event signaled a new stage: the coup of the night of July 23–24, 1952, when a group nominally led by Mohammed Nagib and in reality by Gamal Abdel Nasser, with some American encouragement, ousted Britain's client king, the unpopular and profligate Farouk. The "power vacuum" was beginning, near a great nerve center of world marine communications. And in 1954, after Nasser personally assumed supreme power (February), Britain formally agreed (July) to evacuate its forces from its vast base in the Canal Zone.

The period from 1952 to 1956 was the most anxious and dangerous in the history of Israel, to date. Of the two superpowers which had originally backed Israel, one was almost completely alienated; the other seemed to be increasingly perfunctory in its expression of friendship; no other Power at all had yet appeared as a backer of Israel.

From the point of view of the policy makers in the State Department and the Pentagon, Israel appeared at best as a nuisance, at worst as a heavy liability to the interests of the United States. To people in map rooms, poring over the current state of the Great Game, Israel had to appear as an excrescence, a miserable sliver of land, painfully nicked out of the majestic and populous expanse of the Arab and Muslim lands. The "mark on the map"—however it may have impressed the general public—looked to such policy makers like a blot. The influence of such officials was under restraint as long as Truman was President, with his strong personal commitment to Israel and to President Weizmann. But the Truman-Weizmann epoch, for Israel, ended in November 1952, when Weizmann died, and when Dwight D. Eisenhower was elected President of the United States.

President Eisenhower, with his military background, saw politics in world-strategic terms. He was not much interested in lobbies; he had had no difficulty in being elected, and need expect no difficulty in being re-elected. In any case, most Jews voted for the Democrats, anyway. The Republican platform included, of course, a commitment to the survival of Israel, but it was clear from the general policy statements of Eisenhower himself, and especially of his Secretary of State, John Foster Dulles, that Israel would be expected to subordinate its security to the general defense needs of the Free World. As these needs might be interpreted as requiring the goodwill of Israel's hostile neighbors, the international situation became more unfavorable than ever before, from Israel's point of view. Furthermore, British policy makers, who had endured so much at the hands of Truman, now thought they might be able to restore something of their former influence in the Middle East, under cover of the defensive concepts of the Eisenhower-Dulles Administration, in order, as Patrick Seale puts it, to "perpetuate the British presence in the Arab world behind the screen of a military association."[34]

The ill-conceived efforts of an apparently infatuated Foreign Office to attain this improbable objective, and the even more ill-conceived response of a British Government to its failure to achieve what it set out to do, were to lead—before the end of Eisenhower's first term—to a disaster even more comprehensive than that which like-minded efforts had precipitated in Palestine—and at the same time to a conclusion wildly and maniacally at variance with what was supposed to be the policy behind the whole effort. The first long bout of seeking Arab goodwill (1939–1949) had led to the crushing humiliation of the Arabs: a humiliation which the Arabs then, not altogether without reason, blamed on Britain. The second effort (1953–1956) was to end, even more dottily, in the Anglo-French invasion of Egypt (in falsely denied collusion with Israel), in the humiliation of Britain and France, and in the destruction of British influence, even where it had lingered, in Jordan and Iraq.

Arab goodwill is an elusive and volatile political substance. The trouble is that the regimes whose goodwill is sought often have no goodwill toward one another. So if you win the goodwill of one, you are liable to incur the hostility of another. From the ensuing imbroglio you may emerge with much less goodwill than you would have had if you had never started looking for the stuff. As in this case.

Britain was not actively looking for Arab goodwill for itself. It was encouraging the Americans to seek the goodwill of Britain's own client states, thereby propping up Britain's own positions in the region. American officials in this period were agreed about the importance of seeking Arab goodwill but were in two minds about how to do this, as was to be seen from Dulles's subsequent dithering. According to one school of thought, Arab nationalism was the horse to back. That meant wooing Nasser, and treating Britain's client regimes as expendable (as the American Embassy in Cairo had done in 1952). Another school favored reliance on Britain's alleged expertise about the area. You might think that confidence in that commodity might have been weakened by the course and outcome of Britain's policy in Palestine. But some American officials seem to have felt that Britain's Palestinian debacle did not detract from its regional expertise, since it was at least partly due to a nonregional factor: the power of American Jews in American domestic politics. Such officials also shared the vaguely sporting approach of their Foreign Office equivalents. It was *unfair* that domestic pressures should influence foreign policy—just as Lord Passfield thought it unfair that the Jews should have Dr. Weizmann and the Arabs not—so the unhappy and predictable results of that unfairness somehow did not count.

A desire to compensate for perceived cosmic injustice may be an amiable personal trait, but it doesn't seem to make for realistic formulation of foreign policy.

IX

Israel's own policy making, during this loneliest and most perilous period of the State's existence, was not at its highly competent best. Ben-Gurion—perhaps in the grip of some kind of nervous breakdown—retired, or ostensibly retired, in December 1953, to Sdeh Boker, in the northern Negev desert, to the south of Beersheba, after concocting, to succeed him, a weirdly unworkable Government. Moshe Sharett became Prime Minister, which gave the new Government an appearance of moderation. The appearance was misleading, since Sharett was not in control. The Minister for Defense was Pinchas Lavon, an ex-dove turned hawk, who did not consult or inform his Prime Minister about defense matters. The Chief of Staff was Moshe Dayan, who may or may not have kept his minister informed, and may or may not have been kept informed himself about what his subordinates were doing. The one thing certain about the Government which the unhappy Moshe Sharett presided over was that there was no possibility of coordinating foreign policy and defense policy: a most alarming condition for a country in Israel's predicament. Members of the Government tried to make up for this by traveling into the desert to consult Ben-Gurion in his retirement. This did not work very well either.

Even if the Government of Israel at this time had been organized on less eccentric lines, there were inherent difficulties. The most persistent one concerned the question of raids and retaliations. Ever since the Jewish State came into existence, Arab infiltrators—*fedayeen*—had been carrying out hit-and-run raids into Israel. Israeli casualties rose steadily through the first half of the fifties:

1951	137
1952	147
1953	162
1954	180
1955	238[35]

Arab Governments generally disclaimed responsibility for these raids, but it became Israeli policy to retaliate in such a way as to hurt the Arab Governments, in the hope of forcing them to bring the *fedayeen* under control. As Moshe Dayan put it, in an address to officers of the Israel Defense Forces: "It is in our power to set a high price on our blood, a price too high for the Arab community, the Arab armies, and the Arab governments to think it worth paying."[36]

The *fedayeen* raids were frequent, but on a small scale; the Israeli retaliations—like one at Kibya in October 1953—were less frequent, but on a much larger scale, and aroused much more international attention. As Abba Eban sardonically put it: "The idea that Arabs could kill Israelis without any subsequent Israeli reaction was close to becoming an international doctrine."[37]

It was not a doctrine that Israel could accept, then or later. But Israel's refusal to accept it, in the circumstances of the early fifties, necessarily put a heavy strain on relations with the United States. The folly of certain Israelis now increased that strain.

In the summer of 1954, Britain was preparing to leave the Suez Canal Zone—thus withdrawing what Israelis regarded as a buffer between them and Nasser's Egypt. In a wild attempt to get Britain to stay, Israeli officials sent agents to burn British and American premises in Egypt, in the hope that these attacks would be blamed on the Egyptians. This demented operation—a revealing one, as regards the state of near-desperation pervading Israel at the time—was bungled: the agents were caught, some were hanged, and others received prison sentences.[38] This disaster precipitated the return of Ben-Gurion to the Government.

X

The prestige of Gamal Abdel Nasser stood very high at the beginning of 1955. After the departure of the British from the Canal

Zone, Nasser stood out as the first genuinely independent ruler of modern Egypt: a status which automatically ensured his preeminence in the Arab world. Through great personal magnetism, electrifying oratory and the powerful radio at his disposal, he soon consolidated that position.

Nasser does not seem to have consciously intended confrontation either with Israel or with Western countries, but his style, his ambitions and his circumstances speedily led to both types of confrontation. Nasser felt himself to be, and presented himself as, the proud new Arab, in radical contrast with the corrupt regimes of the past. As the most shameful feature of those old regimes, in the eyes of Arabs, was their defeat at the hands of "the Zionist gangs" in 1948–1949, Nasser's posture necessarily carried an implicit promise to reverse that verdict. One of Nasser's close associates, and a member of his Government, made that explicit on January 9, 1955: "Egypt will strive to erase the shame of the Palestine War even if Israel should fulfill all U.N. resolutions. It will not sign a peace with her. Even if Israel should consist only of Tel Aviv, we should never put up with that."[39] As an authority on the region has put it: "The policy of the Arabs over the years . . . became the prisoner of their verbal threats to destroy their enemy."[40]

Near the end of February 1955, David Ben-Gurion returned to power—at first as Minister for Defense, nominally "under" Moshe Sharett (whom he was to replace as Prime Minister in the following November). Ben-Gurion had once hoped that Nasser could be the leader under whom peace between Egypt and Israel could be achieved, but he now saw Nasser as Israel's most dangerous enemy. The unremitting verbal hostilities of Cairo Radio were being increasingly accompanied by violent acts. *Fedayeen* raids were now coming from Egypt, a "front" hitherto quiet. Ben-Gurion saw a guerrilla war of attrition building up on all Israel's frontiers, posing a long-term threat to Israel's survival.

He struck back hard, on February 28, with a massive raid, led by Ariel Sharon, against Egyptian military installations in Gaza: thirty-six Egyptian soldiers and two civilians were killed. The Gaza raid was a military humiliation for Nasser; it followed hard on a diplomatic humiliation: the signing, on February 24, of a defense treaty between Iraq and Turkey, giving rise to what soon became known as the Baghdad Pact.

The significance of this event was that, for the first time, an Arab country was included in the system of defensive alliances which Western diplomacy was building up around the frontiers of the Soviet Union. Dulles had built up his "northern tier" of allies: Greece, Turkey and Iran. To add Iraq to this was not an American idea, but a British one, and the Americans were initially cool to it, as well they might be, given its fairly predictable repercussions. But the Americans went along with the British idea, and armed Iraq in 1954.

From the viewpoint of Israel, the Baghdad Pact appeared most menacing, especially if Jordan were to be included in it, as seemed likely at first, granted Britain's continuing authority there. It looked as if Israel's Arab enemies were about to be armed by Israel's cooling friend, while Israel itself was locked in growing isolation. The arms were intended by the donors for defense against Russians, but Israel feared that they were much more likely to be used for new attacks against Israel.

Israel was now rescued—yet once more—from a desperate predicament by a determined enemy. Nasser bitterly resented and denounced the Baghdad Pact. No doubt there was an element of personal pique—at being upstaged by an Arab rival—in this reaction, but there was clearly a genuine feeling of outraged Arab nationalism. Nasser, it is believed, was not unwilling to enter some kind of defense agreement with the West, but certainly not one in which priority was given to Britain's Hashemite clients in Baghdad. Britain seemed to be making a bid to restore its former preeminence in the Arab world, under cover of American fears of Russia.

Cairo Radio, on Nasser's direction, now went into an orgy of attacks on Western imperialism. The primary objective was to keep Syria and Jordan out of the Baghdad Pact, and bring them within the fold of Nasser's Arab nationalism. But the attacks ranged very widely, including support for the F.L.N. in Algeria and the Mau Mau in Kenya. The rhetoric—especially Nasser's own—was incandescent, and the response of the Arab masses overwhelmingly favorable. Arab resentment of European rule, and Muslim resentment of Christian rule, were powerful forces working in Nasser's favor.

Nasser, after the events in Gaza and Baghdad, felt a need for arms, to fortify Egypt both against Israel and against Arab competitors. Nasser's tirades against Western imperialism tended to cut off supply from that quarter, but opened up to him another source of supply. On September 27, 1955, Nasser announced the conclusion of an arms deal with Czechoslovakia—acting for the Soviet Union. The

Baghdad Pact, aimed at excluding Soviet influence from the Middle East, had resulted in bringing it in.

From a military point of view, the Czech arms deal—under which Egypt was to receive some three hundred medium and heavy tanks of the latest Soviet type, two hundred MiG-15 jet fighters, etc.—was exceedingly menacing. Moshe Dayan wrote, about these arms: "In quantity alone, they tipped the arms balance drastically against Israel; in quality, the tilt was even more drastic."[41]

Israel now had a clear interest in a preemptive attack on Egypt, before Egypt could "absorb and digest" most of the new weapons. Moshe Dayan reckoned that would take six to eight months; others reckoned as much as two years.

Diplomatically, the reverberations of the Baghdad Pact had altered the situation greatly—and quite unintentionally—to Israel's advantage. Politically, the pact had been a disaster: not a single other Arab State was to follow Iraq's example. On the contrary, Britain's other client in the area deserted, under the Nasserite pressure. In March 1956, King Hussein dismissed the British commander of the Arab Legion, John Bagot Glubb, thus ending thirty-four years of British hegemony in Amman.

But if the planners of the Baghdad Pact had miscalculated, so also had Nasser. The violence of his attacks on Britain and France had unintentionally rescued Israel from the potentially lethal isolation in which it had found itself in the 1953–1954 period. Nasser had made Britain and France into potential allies of Israel, since he provided all three with a common interest: the political destruction of Nasser himself.

Nasser was also stirring up trouble for himself in the United States. To Israel's benefit, the two "pro-Arab" tendencies in American official thinking—roughly, the pro-British-pro-Hashemite school and the pro-Arab-nationalist-pro-Nasser school—were now at loggerheads, and in different kinds and degrees of discredit. The pro-Hashemites were necessarily discredited when the Hashemites themselves split, under the impact of Arab nationalism. It became painfully obvious that those British officials on whom certain State Department officials had relied as their guides to the region were now themselves hopelessly lost amid the region's contemporary realities. At the same time, Nasser had gone too far, from the point of view of his American friends, by the violence of his attacks on "Western imperialism," followed by the Czech arms deal.

Nasser now made an excellent target for the attentions of the pro-Israel lobby in the United States. That lobby, like Israel itself, had been in difficulty in 1953–1955. It was in danger of looking as if it might be undermining the security and defense needs of the United States. But the Czech arms deal brought that dangerous period to an end. It was the Arab world—in the person of its most prominent and popular leader—which now looked like a threat to the West. In taking on what was left of pro-Nasser influence in Washington, the pro-Israel lobby need feel no inhibitions.

Egypt had been looking for a loan from the World Bank to finance a huge engineering project: the Aswan High Dam. Both the United States and Britain had earlier favored this policy, but Britain was now, understandably, cooling. The pro-Israel lobby now set itself the objective of blocking American support for the project. Abba Eban, then Israel's ambassador in Washington (and Permanent Representative at the United Nations), writes: "On instructions from Jerusalem we joined in helping to frustrate Egypt's ambitions for American aid in the Aswan Dam project. . . . Israel's friends in the Congress joined their colleagues who, for other reasons, opposed the idea of giving Nasser a windfall without any reciprocal gesture on his part."[42]

Eban records the successful outcome of the lobby's activities, at a moment when he crossed the path of his Egyptian colleague:

> The Egyptian ambassador in Washington, Ahmed Hussein, had apparently not been following these tendencies [in Congress] when he arrived blithely from Cairo to see Dulles in the expectation of receiving American confirmation of the Aswan Dam project. He crossed me in the lobby of Dulles's office as I went out and he went in.
>
> To his consternation, Dulles brutally informed him of the American refusal to finance the Aswan Dam project.[43]

In those lines you can detect the distinctive note of a diplomatic cat who has been at the political cream.

Nasser's reaction to this diplomatic rebuff was swift and spectacular, as his style required. On July 26, before a huge cheering crowd at Alexandria, Nasser announced the nationalization of the Suez Canal Company. Two days later, the British Prime Minister, Sir Anthony Eden, wrote to President Eisenhower: "My colleagues and I are convinced that we must be ready in the last resort to use force to bring Nasser to his senses. For our part we are prepared to do so. I have this morning instructed our Chiefs of Staff to prepare a military plan accordingly."

XI

The bizarre pattern of politico-military activity which became known to the world as "Suez"—significantly, Israelis always refer to "Sinai," their own part in it, only—was shaped mainly by a peculiar British predicament. Eden and his colleagues wanted to "topple Nasser," *but without forfeiting Arab goodwill.* This objective was inherently unattainable, since Nasser was overwhelmingly popular in the Arab world, and a British attempt to topple him could only have the effect of making him even more popular (living or dead) and bringing down further waves of execration on Britain. British policy makers of the period, however, thought they had found a way around this difficulty. Not Britain, but *Israel,* would attack Egypt, and Britain and France would then intervene "to separate the combatants" in order to protect the Canal, and in the interests of international order; toppling Nasser in the process, without the Arabs noticing.

France and Israel had reasons of their own for going along with this improbable scenario. The French attributed all their Algerian troubles to Nasser's propaganda, money and arms.[44] They needed Britain as a partner in the hazardous enterprise of destroying Nasser, and were prepared to acquiesce, in a perfunctory sort of way, in Britain's scenario. French cynicism seemed to enjoy taking part in a charade put on by British hypocrisy: Foreign Minister Christian Pineau, in particular, used to seem almost to wink at the United Nations audience when he alluded to such matters as "separating the combatants"; *et autres questions anglaises,* as Michelet used to say.

Israel's reasons were of greater weight. The *rapprochement* with France took Israel out of its isolation. After the Czech arms deal, Ben-Gurion and his colleagues had considered war with Nasser's Egypt inevitable, and wanted it fought before Egypt's new weapons could be "absorbed and digested." The tacit alliance with France, and the flow of French arms to Israel, made victory likely. The decision to go to war in 1956 seems to have been made by Ben-Gurion in June of that year. In that month, Chief of Staff Moshe Dayan and Shimon Peres, Director-General of the Defense Ministry, reached, in Paris, "a firm agreement on the purchase of arms which would enable us to

AP/WIDE WORLD

On the road to Suez: British Prime Minister Sir Anthony Eden (right) with Foreign Minister Selwyn Lloyd, January 1956. Eden is threatening "British air action against any Israeli or Arab major aggression." This foreshadowed the "separating the combatants" ploy of October–November 1956.

meet the quality, if not the scale, of Egypt's Soviet weaponry."[45] In the same month Ben-Gurion forced the resignation of his Foreign Minister, thus brusquely ending Moshe Sharett's eight increasingly painful years of governmental association with a leader who treated him with increasingly manifest disdain. Ben-Gurion chose, as Sharett's successor, Golda Meir, on whom he knew he could count to back him up in what he was about to do. He also knew that Golda Meir, brought up in Milwaukee, knew how to talk to the great American public, and that this might be the most important qualification a Foreign Minister could have in the perilous diplomatic aftermath of the impending operations.

Ben-Gurion, naturally, disliked the British-inspired scenario which called on Israel, as he put it, "to mount the rostrum of shame so that Britain and France could lave their hands in the waters of purity."

Moshe Dayan, however—by his own account—showed Ben-Gurion that it was only by being prepared "to mount the rostrum of shame" that Israel could win access to what it needed. Britain and France could defeat Egypt without Israel's help. "The sole quality we possessed, relevant to this context, and they lacked was the ability to supply the necessary pretext. This alone could provide us with a ticket to the Suez Campaign 'Club.' "[46]

Reluctantly, Ben-Gurion agreed to pay for that ticket, and to play the unattractive role written for him in London. But he was worried about the Americans; less worried, perhaps, than he ought to have been, but worried. He thought the Americans should be told in advance. In discussions with the French—at Sèvres on October 22–24, 1956—Ben-Gurion "tried several times to persuade them to put off the campaign until after the American elections," impending in the following month. But one of the great beauties of the Suez plan, in the minds of its begetters, was that it would take the Americans by surprise on the eve of their elections, and that they would then be restrained from negative reaction, for fear of the pro-Israel lobby. The fact that the Prime Minister of Israel clearly did not share their confidence in the omnipotence of the pro-Israel lobby, in such a case, seems to have made no impression on these infatuated minds.

Ben-Gurion overcame those misgivings also. He wanted to end the *fedayeen* raids, to act before Egypt felt the military benefit of the arms deal, and to end the Egyptian closure of the Gulf of Aqaba to Israel's shipping and to cargoes for Israel. In the Knesset, on October 15, Ben-Gurion hinted at Israel's growing military strength, due to its secret agreement with France. He quoted some verses by the Israeli poet Natan Alterman, which included the line: " 'Good that Israel's day should know that from the night it draws the power of life, the power of fire.' "[47]

A fortnight later, in the late afternoon of October 29, Israel's attack opened with a paratroop drop deep inside Sinai, and about thirty miles from the Suez Canal. Israel's military operations in Sinai, under the command of Moshe Dayan, were brilliantly successful, resulting, within eight days, in the expulsion of the Egyptian forces from all of Sinai, including Sharm al-Sheik, on the Straits of Tiran, where Egyptian artillery for years had closed the Gulf of Aqaba to Israeli shipping.

Politically, the operations went wrong from the start, due mainly to the miscalculation about American reaction. Eisenhower sent Ben-Gurion a message (through Rabbi Abba Hillel Silver), asking him to withdraw his forces, after liquidating the *fedayeen* bases, and "return immediately to your own borders. . . . The President emphasizes that, despite the temporary convergence of Israel's interests with those of France and Britain, you shall not forget that Israel's strength is principally dependent on the United States."[48]

Faithful to the scenario agreed on with his European allies, Ben-Gurion decided to ignore, for the moment, the President's polite but ominous request. It soon began to look as if Israel had escaped from its isolation and encirclement of the 1953–1955 period only to plunge into a potentially far more perilous predicament: that of simultaneous defiance of both superpowers.

When there was no positive reply from Ben-Gurion to the President's message, the United States went to the Security Council (October 30) with a proposal for "immediate cease-fire and withdrawal of Israeli forces behind the armistice lines." Britain and France then vetoed the United States resolution, having just announced their own joint ultimatum, ostensibly addressed to both Israel and Egypt. This device fooled no one. It was immediately apparent that the stage was being set—by some remarkably clumsy stagehands—for an Anglo-French assault on one of the countries addressed, in planned collusion with the other.

Eisenhower was understandably infuriated because of the failure of Britain and France to consult with the United States before embarking on a spectacular and hazardous enterprise which might well result in a large increase in Soviet influence in the Middle East. He was no less incensed at the personal insult involved in springing this bright little trick on him on the eve of his elections. The veto was a further piece of impudence, and also a futile one. The veto in the Security Council has no material significance, any more than the rest of the United Nations. The U.N. is essentially a spiritual institution which can give, or refuse, a blessing or a curse. If the blessing or curse cannot be had from the Security Council altar, it can be sought from the other altar: the General Assembly.

The United States now brought the matter before a special Emergency Session of the Assembly, for a ritual cursing of the participants in the Suez adventure. That the curses would be forthcoming, in impressive volume, was a foregone conclusion. The United States could control a two-thirds majority there, if it needed, but in this case no "arm twisting" was required. The smaller countries, especially the ex-colonial ones, regarded the Anglo-French intervention with lively and spontaneous abhorrence. The Soviet Union had also a particular interest just then in denouncing a Western act of aggression, since it was engaged in an aggression of its own at the time against Hungary. Suez made an excellent distraction, from a Soviet point of view.

So the curses rained down from many quarters, and were summed up in a minatory resolution. Such resolutions are the modern counterpart of medieval excommunication. If you are strong enough, you can safely ignore such verbal thunder. But if you are already exposed in some way, the institutionalized curse may increase your danger by legitimizing possible measures against you. In this case, the Suez partners were threatened with attack by the Soviets—if they failed to withdraw in compliance with the resolution—and could feel no assurance of even contingent support from the other superpower. And the partner which was most at risk, as we shall see, was Israel.

XII

I was sitting as a very new delegate[49] to the General Assembly for that Emergency Session and I heard Abba Eban, Israel's Permanent Representative, make a speech, on November 1, 1956, which became famous in the annals—and in a sense, the literature—of Israel:

> Surrounded by hostile armies on all its land frontiers, subjected to savage and relentless hostility, exposed to penetration raids and assaults by day and by night, suffering constant toll of life among its citizens, bombarded by threats of neighbouring governments to accomplish its extinction by armed force . . . embattled, blockaded, besieged, Israel alone among the nations faces a battle for its security anew with every approaching nightfall and every rising dawn.

In my ignorance at the time—both about the nature of the United Nations and about Israel's requirements—I didn't think much of that speech, nor was I as much impressed by Eban himself as I see in retrospect I ought to have been. He was at that time portly in appearance, and rather plummy in public discourse; he looked like Beach the Butler, and sounded like an archbishop. Many people underestimated him; a great mistake. I thought his speech was addressed not to the General Assembly but to the American television audience, and this was indeed the case. I also thought the speech was histrionics, and so it was. But it was not empty histrionics; it was histrionics with a political purpose, of vital importance to Israel. Abba Eban was using the stage and pulpit of the United Nations to maximum effect to dramatize the siege of Israel before the American public.

It is a good stage for this purpose, both because of the intrinsically histrionic character of the institution itself and because the reality of the siege is reflected in the rhetoric of United Nations proceedings. Israel's enemies, especially Arabs and Communists, enthusiastically cooperated with Eban, to his country's advantage, not theirs, in mounting the dramatized version of the siege of Israel on the stage beside the East River. Abba Eban was a master of using this spectacle to galvanize and mobilize, in an emergency, Israel's friends in America. He was also, as we shall see, a master in the use of the political force so mobilized.

Israelis who disparage *Oum, shmoum* should reflect that if the United Nations headquarters were ever removed from New York—at the very nerve center of American communications—Israel would be deprived of its most powerful and inspiring means of reaching, in any time of crisis, the friends of Israel in America, and the American public in general.

XIII

Israel was now exposed to strong and conflicting pressure from its Suez partners and from the superpowers. On November 4, an Israeli representative told the General Assembly that Israel would agree to a cease-fire, as demanded by Britain and France, "provided a similar answer is forthcoming from Egypt." At this, according to Moshe Dayan, "The British and French representatives almost jumped out of their skins, for if both combatants ceased fire, there was no justification for Anglo-French intervention."[50] (The British and French had not yet gotten around to invading Egypt; they landed in the Canal Zone two days later.) The Powers which had ordered a cease-fire now insisted on continuation of fire, in order to justify joining in the firing themselves, on the pretext that it was continuing.

It was now becoming clear that the Anglo-French end of Suez was doomed. Britain's friends now made an effort to get Britain off the hook. Lester Pearson, Canadian Minister for External Affairs, proposed, on November 2, the creation of an international force, and the proposal was carried on November 5. In its original essence, the idea was to set up a token force to go to Egypt and there mime the execution of the purpose for which Britain and France pretended that they had to intervene in Egypt: the "separation of the combatants." Britain and France could then honorably withdraw, having "accomplished their mission." And such was, shortly afterwards, to be the preposterous conclusion of the preposterous Anglo-French enterprise.

Fighting did not end until November 6, and in the meantime all the Suez partners, but most particularly Israel, appeared in danger of bringing down some kind of Soviet intervention against them. Premier Bulganin was brandishing the Soviet Union's newly acquired missiles. On November 5, he sent Israel a note saying that Israel's action "places in question the very existence of Israel as a State." On November 6, in Paris, the U.S. ambassador informed Premier Guy Mollet that a (threatened) Soviet attack on Britain and France would lead to U.S. retaliation. "The conspicuous omission of Israel," according to Michael Brecher, "was not unknown to her decision makers."[51] On November 7, the C.I.A. leaked a report—attributed to U.S. Ambassador Bohlen in Moscow—that the Kremlin intended to "flatten" Israel on the following day.[52]

For the first time, Israel seemed to be threatened with destruction by a Power which actually had the present capacity to destroy Israel. It is worth reflecting on what might have happened if Joseph Stalin had lived another four years. If he had lived into the missile age, and still retained the paranoid "anti-Zionism" of 1952–1953, November 1956 might have seen the end of the history of Israel.

Israeli "decision makers," according to Brecher, took the Soviet threats seriously. But this did not seem to be true, at first, of the chief decision maker, David Ben-Gurion. Ben-Gurion, even two days after Bulganin's note, seemed more affected by the triumph of Israel's arms over the Egyptian forces than by Israel's worsening international predicament. On November 7 he delivered what became known as his "victory speech": an extraordinarily truculent statement, in the unpromising circumstances. The Armistice Agreement with Egypt, Ben-Gurion declared, was "dead and buried"; "the Armistice Lines have no more validity." As for the United Nations force—the basis of the painfully achieved international compromise—he dismissed this out of hand: "On no account will Israel agree to the stationing of a foreign force, no matter how called, on her territory *or in any of the territories occupied by her* [my italics]."[53] Ben-Gurion seemed to be talking as if he had defeated not just Egypt but both superpowers as well. Retribution for this brief bout of hubris came swiftly.

On the same day as the "victory speech," Israel received a chilling reminder of the actual state of its current international relations, when the General Assembly voted for "immediate withdrawal," by 65 votes to 1; the one being Israel.

Israel's international isolation was now complete, and much worse than it had been before Israel had fallen in with its two imaginative, erratic and ill-starred allies, on the road to Suez.

The United Nations vote was, as ever, symbolic and symptomatic only, but unprecedented material pressure quickly followed, this time from the United States. President Eisenhower immediately conveyed to Ben-Gurion an expression of his "very deep concern" at the victory speech. Undersecretary of State Herbert C. Hoover, Jr., then spelled out what the President's "very deep concern" would mean for Israel, if Israel chose to ignore it: "Israel's attitude will inevitably lead to most serious measures, such as the termination of all [U.S.] governmental and private aid, United Nations sanctions, and eventual expulsion from the U.N." Hoover also warned that if Israel's nonwithdrawal led to Soviet penetration of the Middle East, "Israel would be the first to be swallowed up."[54]

As if that grimly explicit message was not enough, the president of the World Zionist Organization, Nahum Goldmann, warned that the pro-Israel lobby in America could not live with the victory speech: "It will be impossible to mobilize an American-Jewish front to support this posture. . . . If this should lead to cessation of the Jewish Appeal and Bonds, I foresee great difficulty in renewing these enterprises, even if the American authorities would again give their agreement."[55]

Ben-Gurion later told an interviewer that he must have been "drunk with victory" at the time of the victory speech. If so, he sobered up very quickly. The Israeli Government, meeting on the evening of November 8—the day after the victory speech—approved a formula proposed by Abba Eban: "The Government of Israel declares her willingness to withdraw her forces from Sinai when satisfactory arrangements are made with the international force that is about to enter the Canal Zone."

All Israel's diplomatic efforts now hinged on that same international force that Ben-Gurion had treated with contumely the day before.

While agreeing to Eban's formula for conditional withdrawal, the Government also agreed that, if that failed, unconditional withdrawal would have to be accepted. It was now up to Eban, in his dual capacity as Permanent Representative at the United Nations and Ambassador in Washington, to see if he could make his own formula stick. The

Government's acceptance that the only alternative was unconditional withdrawal gave Eban ample scope in the interpretation of his own formula.

XIV

In retrospect, Ben-Gurion's victory speech seems salutary, a *felix error*. It forced Israel to look into the gulfs that open before a small country which simultaneously gives serious offense to both superpowers. Ben-Gurion—once forced to recognize the need, in the last resort, to withdraw unconditionally—now left to his Foreign Office the matter of how best Israel might extricate itself from the desert it had conquered. Israel's Foreign Office was now in a much stronger position than before. It had, for the first time, in Golda Meir, a Foreign Minister who had the confidence of the Prime Minister. And Golda Meir knew that nothing better than Eban's formula was available, and that only Eban could get his formula to work.

Between November 1956 and March 1957, Abba Eban conducted a classic diplomatic rearguard action, withdrawing slowly, but not too slowly, and winning small but important concessions for each phase of withdrawal. There were factors working for him in the aftermath of the crisis. The particular situation—Israel slowly yielding, under American official pressure, the fruits of its victory against heavy odds—was propitious for the revival and remobilization of the pro-Israel lobby, whose activities were ably coordinated by Eban and his colleagues. The general context was also getting more favorable. Once the shock of the crisis was over, there was a widespread feeling that the West generally, and not merely Britain and France, had suffered a humiliating defeat, and that the Soviet Union had increased its prestige, at no cost to itself, by its missile rattling. The United States Government, on the other hand, was felt—not only by Democrats but by right-wing Republicans—to have let down its allies, and truckled to the Russians.[56] In these conditions, the pro-Israel lobby could recover from its disarray, and gain a hearing and an increasing purchase on public opinion. So Eban could afford, to some extent, to take his time, and look for conditions.

What Eban wanted was to insure, as far as possible, that the international force should be used to guarantee that the *fedayeen* raids should not be renewed, and that the Straits of Tiran should henceforward be open to Israeli shipping, as to all others.

Eban knew that the international force would be a token one, and would probably be unable to prevent *fedayeen* raids if Nasser chose to start them up again.[57] But if Nasser agreed to the stationing of an international force on Egyptian soil, with the implicit or explicit condition that the force would prevent *fedayeen* raids, then the renewal of such raids would be a matter of major international concern. This had never been the case in the past; Israel had been told, in effect, to ignore such incidents. Once the raids were prohibited, by international convention (even a tacit one), Israel's right of retaliation, in the last resort, would, to that extent, be established as legitimate.

The whole operation was about legitimacy. This applied especially to Israel's second (and perhaps principal) objective: the reopening of the Straits of Tiran. Outside observers have sometimes been puzzled by the tremendous importance Israel attaches to this matter. The straits are of some economic importance, as Israel was to prove when they were reopened and the port of Eilat was developed.[58] But that is not the main point. The point is that by closing the straits to Israel, Egypt *had successfully challenged Israel's legitimacy, with the passive acquiescence of the international community*. The straits giving access to the international waters of the Gulf of Aqaba are in international law open to the ships of all nations. By closing the straits to Israel, and proclaiming the gulf an Arab lake, Egypt asserted that Israel is not a nation, like other nations; by acquiescing in the closure, the international community tacitly assented to that proposition. But the proposition is a potentially lethal one, as far as Israel is concerned. Hence the importance of the straits: legally, politically and symbolically, over and above their economic importance.[59]

In these negotiations—the principles of which, and not the details, are what concern us here—Eban had to deal primarily with the United Nations Secretary-General, Dag Hammarskjold. Hammarskjold, whose star was still rising over the world of international politics, had of course regarded the whole louche and lurid Suez adventure with fastidious abhorrence. I think he didn't like Israel very much, and Israelis distrusted him. But he had sound international reasons for letting Eban have what he wanted. Eban's demands were reasonable in themselves, by the criterion of international peace, law and order. Also the idea of giving the force a real role in peace preservation in the Middle East— instead of merely serving as a face-saver and consolation prize for Anthony Eden—deeply appealed to Hammarskjold. It fitted in his dream of gradually enhancing the influence and prestige of the United

Nations until it came eventually to approximate the role of a world government.

Nasser never explicitly agreed to the role of the force which Eban and Hammarskjold worked out between them, but he acquiesced in it, both at the time, and for ten years thereafter. He badly wanted, in 1957, to get the Israelis out of Sinai; he had no means of getting them out himself and he would have been aware—through his able and well-informed Foreign Minister, Mahmud Fawzi—that the Americans were no longer in a mood to force them out unconditionally. And he had no immediate desire, after Sinai, for another round with Israel.

Dulles privately endorsed the Eban-Hammarskjold conception of the role of the force. As a lawyer, he saw these arrangements—particularly the reopening of the straits—as right and proper. As a politician, he could see that the arrangements took him off an increasingly nasty political hook, by getting the pro-Israel lobby off his back.

Thus a consensus, partly explicit, partly tacit, was established between the four parties principally concerned: Israel, the United Nations, the United States and Egypt. On the basis of this consensus, the Foreign Minister of Israel, Golda Meir, made a statement to the General Assembly on March 1, 1957. The statement had been jointly drafted by Eban and State Department officials, and had been personally approved by Dulles.[60] In this statement, Mrs. Meir told the Assembly that Israel would complete its withdrawal, on certain "assumptions"—i.e., that *fedayeen* raids would stop and the straits be reopened. The statement also included warnings, of which the following was the most significant:

"Interference by armed force, with ships of Israel flag exercising free and innocent passage in the Gulf of Aqaba and through the Straits of Tiran will be regarded by Israel as an attack entitling it to exercise its inherent right of self-defense. . . ."

The Permanent Representative of the United States, Henry Cabot Lodge, then publicly acknowledged that these "assumptions" were "not unreasonable." It was the least he might say, since his own colleagues had helped to draft the statement.

XV

Ten years later, after Nasser had expelled the international force, it became the custom in Israel to disparage the international arrangements consummated in March 1957. Remarkably, the woman who as Foreign Minister had announced that consummation was among those keenest to disparage it. "A compromise of sorts," she calls it in her memoirs. "It wasn't much, and it certainly wasn't what we had been fighting for, but it was the best we could get—and it was better than nothing."[61]

Such disparagement is altogether out of place. These arrangements gave Israel ten years of peace with Egypt, and thus improved its position vis-à-vis its other Arab neighbors. They gave Israel time in which to absorb its immigrants and strengthen its vitally important relations with the United States. Above all, these arrangements enhanced Israel's legitimacy, especially by legitimizing its right of resistance. Specifically, they insured that the United States would not impede or inhibit Israel's right to armed retaliation if Egypt attempted to return to the pre-Suez situation by closing the straits. The arrangements thus included an insurance policy against their own breakdown. In four months, Eban's diplomatic achievement—when one considers the terrifying nadir of isolation in which Israel found itself in November 1956—is comparable to Talleyrand's in 1814–1815. There are differences: France had suffered military defeat; Israel had gained a brilliant local military victory, the results of which seemed to be turning into a major international disaster, threatening Israel's very existence. Allowing for these differences, the achievements of the two diplomatists are of the same type and order.[62]

If the people of Israel had realized the full extent of their isolation in November 1956, and the full significance of the "assumptions" of March 1957—in making it possible to avert such isolation in the future—they would have had cause for a special Purim. As it was they seem to have been impressed only by the fact that they had been obliged by international pressure to give up the fruits of victory.

XVI

The ten years from the early summer of 1957 to the early summer of 1967 were years of growth, progress and relative tranquillity for Israel. There was an upsurge in immigration—55,000 in 1956 and 70,000 in 1957—mainly from Egypt and North Africa, in consequence of the crisis that had led to Suez, and of the Suez War itself. Large numbers of immigrants also came from Eastern Europe (and the differ-

A World Health Organization worker counseling an immigrant from Western Europe.

ential treatment of the two sets caused social stresses). By 1965 Israel's GNP had increased two and a half times since 1952; between 1950 and 1969 industrial production quintupled, and agricultural production also greatly expanded.[63] A major irrigation project—the National Water Carrier—based on the Jordan waters brought water from Lake Galilee to the Negev desert. This project had been planned in the early fifties but had been postponed due to Arab objections and American pressure.

In the regional context, Israel's overall position had significantly improved. Egypt, in those years, remained effectively neutralized.

Jordan, which had become something like a tributary of Egypt in the period before Suez, now became dependent on America, after Hussein had dismissed his pro-Nasser Government in the spring of 1957. This implied some mitigation to manifestations of hostility to Israel, although Hussein, with the fate of his grandfather always in mind, was careful never to depart publicly from the Arab consensus. Of all Israel's Arab neighbors, only Syria posed a significant direct threat to Israel during this period. As long as Egypt remained neutral, Syria was helpless, militarily speaking. When the Syrians reacted to the Israeli irrigation development by an attempt to divert the headwaters of the Jordan (1964–1965), repeated attacks by the Israeli Air Force obliged Syria to abandon this particular project.

Politically, however, the Syrian threat was serious. Under increasingly leftist-nationalist Governments from 1962 on, Damascus and its radio set an extremely high standard in militancy for the Arab consensus. Hussein was obliged to try to keep up; Nasser was kept under pressure to resume the struggle. The Syrians also—and under their pressure, the Jordanians and Egyptians—encouraged the Palestinian exiles to set up their own political and paramilitary organization. In 1964 an assembly of Palestinian Arabs, meeting in Hashemite East Jerusalem, set up the Palestine Liberation Organization,[64] which in turn was to establish a Palestine Liberation Army, in order "to attain the objective of liquidating Israel." In practice, and for the moment, this meant the resumption and extension of *fedayeen* raids, as demanded by Syria.

The power of Damascus in this period came from the fact that it was saying what Arabs generally wanted to hear, and encouraging the Palestinians to do what Arabs wanted done. What Dayan had said after 1948 applied at least as strongly after 1956: "The Jews had conquered the Arab armies but not their hatred."

XVII

The improvement in Israel's regional context in this period was significant, but limited and precarious. The improvement in the wider international context was large, and proved durable.

The main factor in this improvement was a *rapprochement* with the United States, steadily growing toward an implicit but firm alliance. This process was helped on by important developments inside the Arab world. On July 14, 1958, Iraq, the last large bastion of British authority in the Middle East, collapsed, when militant nationalist officers under Brigadier Karim Qassem overthrew the Hashemite regime, and a Baghdad mob massacred the young King Faisal, along with the former regent Abdul Ilah, members of their families and Prime Minister Nuri Pasha, Britain's best friend in the Arab world, and an architect of the Baghdad Pact. That pact itself, Nasser's denunciation of it and Britain's subsequent attack on Nasser had all combined to cast Nuri in the deadly role of a traitor to the Arab cause; and the *failure* of the Suez attack seemed to show that Britain was no longer able—as it had been in 1941—to protect its clients in Baghdad.

As the Baghdad Pact was part of the Western system of alliance, Qassem's coup was seen as anti-American and pro-Russian, as well as anti-British. There was a swift, and somewhat ludicrous, Anglo-American reaction. British forces went into Jordan, at the solicited invitation of Hussein. American forces went into Lebanon, at the solicited invitation of President Camille Chamoun. The proclaimed objective was to save the regimes in question from being overthrown by pro-Russian elements; there was also, originally, an idea of carrying out some kind of Hashemite restoration in Baghdad, but that idea had to be abandoned, since there were no Iraqi Hashemites left alive. It soon became clear that the Anglo-American military expeditions in Lebanon and Jordan were serving no good purpose at all. The regimes in question were not in any immediate danger, and any *long-term* danger they were in could only be increased by the presence of foreign troops with the proclaimed objective of propping up the regimes. Having tried and failed to get some kind of U.N. blessing for their enterprise, the United States and Britain withdrew their forces, having achieved nothing in particular.

The net effect of the Baghdad coup and its sequel was to strengthen Israel. The pro-Arab influences in and around the State Department were in disarray, and in some degree of discredit. Both their main options seemed to have broken down. The "Baghdad Pact" option had been exploded, in Baghdad itself: no Arab State would contemplate alliance with the West. The "Arab nationalist" option was hardly in better shape. The main theme of the populist leaders who appealed to the Arab masses was "the fight against Western imperialism," which included the United States. The United States got little or no thanks for the decisive, but inconspicuous, help it had given to Nasser at the time of Suez. As Arabs saw it, Britain, France and Israel had been forced out of Egypt by the Soviet threats; and it was also due to fear of war with the Soviet Union that the United States had asked the invaders to withdraw.

British influence, which had been very strong in Washington, in relation to the Arab Middle East, especially in the period from 1952 to 1955, was now on the wane. There were still those—up to the end of the Eisenhower Administration, at least—who deferred to British expertise about the region, but there were others who were more impressed by the failure of that expertise to foresee or avert a series of disasters, from Palestine to Suez and Baghdad.

Since British influence in America had always been used in senses unfavorable to Israel, the relative decline of that influence strengthened Israel. And Israel itself began to look more attractive, from an American point of view, against the dark background of the Arab world, after Suez and Baghdad. Iraq had changed, in the space of a few hours, from a devoted friend of the West into a bitter enemy. The same, it was felt, could happen at any moment in any other Arab country with a (currently) friendly regime. In Israel, however, and in Israel alone, it was a question of the friendship not just of a regime but of a *people*. The people of Israel had approved the policy of alignment with the West. The people were bound to the United States by very strong ties of blood, interest, affection and similarity of institutions. Here was a country which could not turn into an enemy overnight. Here was a country which could be depended on in an emergency—as Israel showed in the post-Baghdad period when it allowed its airspace to be used to fly in British troops for the support of Israel's enemy, the Hashemite regime in Jordan. And this stable, democratic country happened also to be the strongest military power in the region, as it had convincingly demonstrated in the Sinai campaign.

Another development, favorable to Israel in its relations with the United States, which took place at this time was a decisive (though little noted) shift in relations between the United States and the United Nations. The General Assembly of the United Nations, meeting in New York in Emergency Session in August 1958, refused the United States the blessing it sought for the Anglo-American landings in Lebanon and Jordan. Instead, it passed a resolution—drafted by India and accepted by the Arab states—which constituted a polite "go home." This was the first time the General Assembly had rejected any proposition strongly recommended to it by the United States.

Up to this point, the American public had been officially and semi-officially encouraged to see the United Nations as a body with two faces. One face was distorted; this was the Security Council, "crippled by the Soviet veto." The other face was noble and wise; this was the General Assembly, reflecting "world opinion" and expressing "the moral conscience of mankind."

All that was fine, as long as the United States was assured of a safe two-thirds majority in the Assembly on any important matter. But when that ceased to be the case, from the summer of 1958 on, it was only prudent policy on the part of the United States to deflate the moral authority previously imputed to the General Assembly. It was discovered that the Assembly, far from representing "world opinion," was made up of Governments, most of which, being undemocratic and otherwise unsavory, didn't even represent the opinion of their own people. From the point of view of Israel, this was a fortunate discovery. The General Assembly—with the growing influence within it of the Arab group and the wider Muslim bloc, together with the influence of the oil-rich Arab countries over the poor states of black Africa—had become a setting in which Israel had become increasingly isolated, moving toward the pariah status later thrust on it. If the United States had continued to be able to get—and therefore feel it needed—majorities at the Assembly, Israel would have been increasingly felt as a liability to the United States, in terms of "world opinion," since to influence is also to be influenced by what you can influence. As it was, with the progressive downgrading of the Assembly and its views, in the aftermath of August 1958, the pro-Israel lobby could work in growing harmony with United States official agencies to the general tune of *Oum, shmoum.* So Israel, whose independence owed much to the moral authority imputed to the United Nations in 1947, also benefited from the spreading eclipse of that notion, which began eleven years later.

XVIII

In the post-Baghdad conditions, Israel began to be seen no longer as a *minus* for America—as had been the case in the days when the Baghdad Pact had been incubating—but as a distinct *plus*. These were more favorable conditions than had ever before obtained for the work of the pro-Israel lobby. And there was a self-reinforcing mechanism at work here. The favorable conditions led to a larger, richer and more powerful pro-Israel lobby. And the stronger the lobby became, the harder it would be to reverse the tendency toward closer association with Israel.

It was in this period—the late summer and autumn of 1958—that the relationship between Israel and America settled into the pattern of close and friendly association which has prevailed continuously— though not without occasional clouds—since that time. There were, and are, those, both in Israel and in the United States, who think the relationship *too* close. Michael Brecher, noting the "greater depen- dence" of Israel on the United States in this period, says that Israel was "not a vassal" but "on the way to becoming a client state."[65]

I don't think that "client state" fits at all well. Far from being a docile "client," Israel has probably come to exert more influence over American policy in relation to the Middle East than America can exert over the policies of Israel, on matters which are of vital interest to Israel. Surely no "client state" has possessed such influence within the polity of its "patron state" as Israel possesses within the American political system. I can see why some *Americans* might object to the character of this relationship, but from the point of view of Israel I should have thought it a highly satisfactory outcome, after the cruel years of isolation, and after that hair-raising November of 1956, under simultaneous threat from both superpowers.

XIX

By the end of the 1950s, Israel was stronger and less isolated than ever before. Yet the Prime Minister, David Ben-Gurion, was uneasy. He feared complacency, a tendency to rely upon others, a loss of touch with the terrible past of the Jews, a lessened awareness of the dangers in which the Jews of Israel still stood, as long as they were surrounded by the hatred of their neighbors.

An opportunity now presented itself, as Ben-Gurion saw it, to cor- rect these tendencies. Israeli agents in Argentina located Adolf Eich- mann, one of the principal agents of Hitler's Final Solution. On Ben- Gurion's instructions, Eichmann was kidnapped, in May 1960, and taken to Jerusalem, interrogated there and then put on trial. The trial lasted for 114 sessions, over a period of four months (April–August 1961). On December 15, 1961, Eichmann was sentenced to death. On May 31, 1962, after an unsuccessful appeal, Eichmann was hanged in Ramla prison.

In a speech on Israel's thirteenth Independence Day, Ben-Gurion spelled out the lesson of the Eichmann trial:

> Here, for the first time in Jewish history, historical justice is being done by the sovereign Jewish people. For many generations it was we who suffered, who were tortured, were killed—and were judged. . . . For the first time Israel is judging the murderers of the Jewish people. . . . And let us bear in mind that only the independence of Israel could create the conditions for this historic act of justice.[66]

The young in Israel, asked by sociologists what lessons they drew from the trial and evocation of the Holocaust, replied by stressing the dangers inherent in the position of a Jewish minority living among non-Jewish majorities. This was precisely the message that Ben-Gurion intended to convey, together with the message that a new Holocaust could only be surely averted by a strong and self-reliant Israel.

The ghosts that Ben-Gurion had made to walk in Jerusalem made Germans shudder too. Coldly, Ben-Gurion used that effect in order to consolidate relations with Germany. "There is no Nazi Germany anymore," he said. Germans were relieved, and grateful, as Ben-Gurion intended them to be.

In his dealings with postwar Germany, Ben-Gurion had combined strong emotion with cool calculation: a combination highly characteristic of the central tradition in Zionism. Initially, Moshe Sharett, back in the days of *ee-hizdahut*, had laid down a strong anti-German line, on moral grounds. "The people of Israel and Jews throughout the world," Sharett had told the General Assembly on September 27, 1950, "view with consternation and distress the progressive readmission of Germany to the family of nations, with her revolting record intact, her guilt unexpiated, and her heart unchanged."[67]

From the sequel, one can imagine Ben-Gurion letting Sharett say that, and then waiting for a call from Bonn, or Washington. The conjuncture was dangerous, both for Germany and for Israel. The pro-Israel lobby could make the German comeback difficult and painful. But it would also be dangerous for the pro-Israel lobby to be seen to obstruct the Government of the United States with regard to a European objective which was seen as a vital American national interest. If it acted in that way, the lobby might be discredited and Israel itself cut off. The situation was one that called for a deal—an implicit one, of course—and the deal duly took shape. West Germany offered Israel reparations for the Holocaust. Ben-Gurion accepted, and the pro-Israel lobby was inhibited from anti-German agitation. In terms of the Sharett Doctrine, the reparations showed that Germany was now ready to expiate at least some of her guilt.

The acceptance of reparations from Germany touched off a political furor in Israel. Begin and his Herut denounced the deal with the same vehemence that Jabotinsky and his Revisionists had used to denounce the financial dealings with the Nazis before the war. There were violent scenes in the Knesset, and a riot outside it. But Ben-Gurion held firm, under the effective slogan, "Let not the murderers of our people be their inheritors as well." The German reparations—almost $5 billion to the end of 1965—did strengthen Israel, in military, technology and otherwise. Ben-Gurion was determined both that the trial of Eichmann should take place, and that it should not be allowed to damage, but be made to strengthen—as it did—Israel's relations with contemporary Germany.

As it happened, Ben-Gurion and Chancellor Konrad Adenauer met in America, by arrangement, shortly before Eichmann's capture. As a historian of Israel puts it, "Adenauer in his way needed a meeting as badly as the Israeli prime minister. A photographed handshake with Ben-Gurion could make all the difference in the chancellor's reception in the United States. . . ."[68] Ben-Gurion asked for another series of large loans, and Adenauer, in that context, readily agreed: "We will help you for moral reasons and for reasons of practical politics," he told Ben-Gurion.

That a German Chancellor should feel an urgent need to be photographed with the Prime Minister of the Jewish State was a singular vindication of the dream of Theodor Herzl.

XX

By the mid-sixties, danger started getting closer again to Israel. The reasons for this were partly internal, partly external. The main internal event was the final departure from office of David Ben-Gurion, after a break with his own party (over the Lavon Affair). Ben-Gurion's principal protégés in the politico-military establishment, Moshe Dayan and Shimon Peres, followed their leader into the political wilderness. The new Prime Minister was Levi Eshkol, who was also his own Minister for Defense. The Foreign Minister was Abba Eban.

The new Prime Minister was what the jargon of a slightly later period would call a "low-profile" man. He was kind, patient, shrewdly humorous; unusually well liked, for an Israeli politician. His policy was one of strengthening Israel's defenses, but at the same time emphasizing Israel's anxiety for peace. Abba Eban, because of his previous roles as ambassador and Permanent Representative, was associated in the public mind—somewhat misleadingly—with the primacy of the effort to propitiate international public opinion. It was possible, therefore, looking at the new Government, to imagine that the policies of Moshe Sharett had begun to prevail, with the departure of Ben-Gurion.

This was hardly the case. There had been a change of style, not of the substance of policy. The Israeli establishment of the period— Mapai—were mortally tired of the Ben-Gurion style: paternalist, populist, volcanic, unpredictable, overbearing and endlessly demanding. Ben-Gurion was the father of his people, all right, but many of his children found him impossible to live with. Under Levi Eshkol, people were looking for something more like "normalcy." The sequel would suggest that when a country in Israel's position looks for normalcy, it is in danger of finding something quite different.

The change in the Government, carrying with it the impression that the new Government might be easier to deal with than Ben-Gurion had been, happened at an unfortunate time. Changes had been occurring inside what has been called "the inter-Arab system,"[69] which made renewed war a likelier option. The implication that Israel might now be more anxious to avoid war increased that likelihood.

The main factor making for war was the decline in Nasser's prestige, and his need to recover from that decline. Nasser's prestige in the Arab world stood very high indeed immediately after Suez. Backed by the Russian allies whom he himself had had the courage to win, he was felt to have humiliated Britain and France, the alien lords of the Arab world. For a while after that, his prestige advanced still higher. The 1958 coup in Baghdad was originally generally ascribed to the rising tide of Nasserism. And in 1958 also, Syria, on its own initiative, merged its sovereignty with that of Egypt, in the United Arab Republic. This seemed like the beginning of the political unification of the Arab world. Nasser was at the zenith.

After that, things went badly wrong. In Iraq, Qassem, having made his own revolution, felt no need of Nasser's leadership; he would find his own way to Arab unity. Baghdad Radio treated Nasser with disrespect. Then the United Arab Republic got into trouble; Syrians resented being treated as vassals of Egypt. Syria seceded from the U.A.R. in September 1961; Nasser was left with the empty title of the State, and the memory of a failure. Damascus, and its radio, were hostile. Then, in September 1962, a military revolt, of "modernizing" type, broke out in Yemen, overthrowing the medieval-theocratic regime of the Imam. Yet the Imam held out in the feudal north of the country, with the support of Saudi Arabia. Nasser sent troops, eventually in large numbers, to help the modernizing officers against the Imam. The Egyptian military effort failed, and the troops bogged down, among an increasingly hostile native population.

By the mid 1960s, Nasser was almost completely isolated in the Arab world. The hostility of the conservative states, which he had earned in the mid-fifties, had hardened in the sixties, mainly because of the threat which his effort to bring modernization to the Arabian Peninsula posed to Saudi Arabia, a resourceful and elusive adversary. He had also against him two revolutionary and militant-nationalist Arab states: Syria and Iraq.

Syria, in particular, was now stealing the thunder that had been Nasser's in the fifties. Syria was the only one of Israel's neighbors in this period which was willing to run serious risks of confrontation with Israel. Damascus Radio taunted Nasser with cowardice, and in particular—a most sensitive point—with "hiding behind the skirts of the United Nations." Amman, Baghdad, Riyad joined in the jeers: Nasser was being deluged in abuse and mockery, scrubbed with "reproach . . . the soap of the soul." This flow of hostile propaganda, all to much the same tune, coming from so many and from such different Arab sources, hurt Nasser among his own countrymen as well as outside. He was under the heaviest kind of rhetorical pressure to make at least some gesture of defiance in the direction of Israel.

The pressure was now greatly increased, in May 1967, by a move of the Soviet Union. The Soviet Union, in this period, had been concentrating its attention in the region on Syria. Both Nasser's regime and Qassem's had clamped down, for their own internal reasons, on their local Communist parties. The Soviets had in fact first alienated Nasser by their support of Qassem—who went on a left-wing tack initially—and then found themselves left in the lurch by Qassem, when he too locked up his Communists. The Soviets, like the West, were finding the quest for Arab goodwill a tricky kind of dance. But Syria, especially after a left-wing Ba'athist coup in February 1966, had moved into the Soviet orbit.

This presented the Soviets with an acute problem. The Syrians had turned to the Soviets because they needed backing in their dangerous confrontation policy toward Israel. The Soviets didn't want to be seen to let Syria down, as against Israel. The loss of Syria, after those other losses, would be bad for Soviet prestige; and no doubt bad also for the hierarchical standing of the various high officials who had made the decisions leading to so humiliating an outcome.[70] But neither did the Soviets wish to let matters proceed to a confrontation between Israel, backed by the United States, and Syria, backed by the Soviet Union. That would be dangerous in itself, and particularly dangerous for the Soviets, since Israel was much the stronger of the local "proxies."

In these conditions the Soviets apparently decided that it was urgently necessary to try to involve Egypt, as a deterrent to an Israeli initiative against Syria. On May 13, the Soviet ambassador informed Nasser that the Israelis were planning to attack Syria on May 17, and that they had already concentrated eleven to thirteen brigades on the Syrian frontier for this purpose.[71]

This was untrue, to the extent that no such concentration existed. But it was true that some kind of retaliation against Syria had been considered in Israel, and the Soviets may have gotten hold of a contingency plan. In any case, the Soviet communication, true or false, presented Nasser with a threat, and also an opportunity.

The threat was that if Israel did indeed crush Syria, and Nasser was seen to stand idly by while the heroes of Arab nationalism were destroyed, Nasser would be discredited, and perhaps overthrown. The opportunity was that if he made a gesture threatening to Israel, and if then Israel refrained from attacking Syria (whether because of the threat or not), Nasser would be seen, once again, as the savior and protector of the Arabs.

On May 15, Nasser put his armed forces in a state of maximum alert, and combat troops began to pour into Sinai, toward the border with Israel. This was the first of a series of overt acts which were to lead within less than three weeks to the Six Day War.

The deployment in Sinai need not, by itself, have led to war. Nasser had carried out a similar deployment in 1957, to "relieve pressure" on Syria, and later withdrew his forces, claiming to have averted a Turkish threat. But this time Nasser went fatally further. The earnest efforts of the Eshkol Government to "reassure" Nasser that Israel had no aggressive intentions against Syria seem to have suggested to Nasser that Israel was so anxious to avoid war that further risks could be taken.

On May 18 the Egyptian Government notified Secretary-General

U Thant of its decision "to terminate the existence of U.N.E.F. [United Nations Expeditionary Force] on the soil of the U.A.R. and in the Gaza Strip." The Secretary-General immediately signified compliance. The international force on whose presence Israel had predicated the "assumptions" of its withdrawal was now no more.

U Thant has been roundly abused by a number of Israeli and pro-Israeli writers for this quick compliance.[72] In fact, he had no substantive alternative. U.N.E.F. was a token force only. Once the Egyptian Government had withdrawn its permission for the force to be there, the Government was in a position to ignore the force, and immediately did so. The key countries contributing to the force—India and Yugoslavia—immediately announced their own compliance with the Egyptian Government's decision, and the other contributing countries soon followed suit. It has been said that Thant should have taken the matter to the General Assembly. In strict propriety of protocol—and in accordance with an assurance apparently given by his predecessor, Hammarskjold—no doubt he should have done so. But in practice, what use would that have been—especially to Israel? The General Assembly by this date had an automatic majority in favor of any such militant nationalist stance as Nasser was now taking. The General Assembly would have turned into a Nasser propaganda benefit, with a resolution and vote to match.

It is argued that at least in that way, or some other way, Thant could have "gained time." Gained time for what? If Nasser had intended to invade Israel, he could have gone right ahead in any case, ignoring the U.N. force—just as Israel was to do in 1982, in Lebanon. But Nasser didn't want to invade Israel. He just wanted to be seen to *defy* Israel. And he wanted to get rid of U.N.E.F., not because U.N.E.F. stood in his way in any material sense, but because it had become insufferable to him as a symbol. It had once been useful to him, but the taunts of his Arab brothers had turned it into a symbol of his humiliation: a symbol he thought he could now, perhaps, get away with breaking.

The symbolic force had been washed away, by the soap of the soul.

For Israel, the force had gained two things: time, and when time ran out, an enhanced degree of legitimacy for a riposte.

It was clear that Israel had now to prepare for an announcement of the closure of the Straits of Tiran: a *casus belli*, from Israel's point of view, as declared in March 1957. It is possible that a stiff warning at this point might have averted war, but the Eshkol trumpet still gave an uncertain sound, and Nasser took heart. On May 22, Eshkol disclaimed any aggressive intentions on the part of Israel and called for the withdrawal of Egyptian and Israeli forces to their previous positions. On the same day, Nasser, speaking at an air base in Sinai, announced the closing of the Gulf of Aqaba to Israeli shipping, and to all ships carrying strategic material to Israel. For good measure, Nasser added: "They, the Jews, threaten war; we tell them: welcome. We are ready for war."[73]

Eshkol's responses remained very mild, to the fury and disgust of many Israelis. But there were reasons for the mildness, quite apart from Eshkol's own hope that war could still be avoided. Israel's armed forces, consisting mostly of its normally civilian population, needed time to prepare for war, in a crisis which had taken Israel entirely by surprise.

There were also diplomatic reasons for moderation and the gaining of time. Eban wanted no noises at all resembling Ben-Gurion's near-disastrous "victory speech" of November 1956. Eban wanted time to remind the Western Powers—most especially the United States—of their commitments of early 1957, and to elicit, if possible, reaffirmation of those pledges, especially reaffirmation of the international character of the Straits of Tiran and the Gulf of Aqaba. That reaffirmation would have the effect of legitimizing Israel's *casus belli*. As Israel's military chiefs saw the matter, Nasser's blockade announcement "was not to be viewed merely as the specific act of blocking movement to and from Israel . . . but was to be considered above all as a challenge to Israel's deterrent power. Unless Israel *itself* nullified Nasser's action . . . it would be the signal for further encroachments that would sooner or later lead to war, but under more unfavorable conditions."[74]

On Eban's recommendation, however, the Government decided to make an intensive diplomatic effort—in order to secure American understanding and avoid the isolation of Sinai—before resort to war. The military chiefs did not oppose the idea of such an effort. Eban had two arguments which carried weight with them: "(1) To ensure arms aid when war came; (2) To retain the fruits of victory."[75] At a governmental meeting on May 23, it was decided:

"1. The blockade is an act of aggression against Israel.

2. Any decision on action is postponed for 48 hours, during which time the Foreign Minister will explore the position of the United States."[76]

Eban now set out for Washington, via Paris and London. It was in appearance a rather lame and dismal negotiation—as Eban's detractors have not failed to point out—but Eban got the substance of what he wanted, though not what he was ostensibly looking for.

The mission began inauspiciously, with a majestic snub from General de Gaulle. De Gaulle waved aside any commitments "France" might have entered into in 1957 on the question of the right of passage through the straits. De Gaulle had not been in power then—as he reminded Eban—so these were not really commitments of France. He warned Israel not to shoot first.

In London, Harold Wilson was much more sympathetic, though noncommittal in substance. But at least Eban could proceed to Washington with the knowledge that Britain would not now be trying to drive a wedge between the United States and Israel, as so often in the past.

The reception in Washington was good, in some ways almost too good. President Johnson, in his Capitol Hill days, had been a good friend to Israel—he never saw anything illegitimate about lobbies—and he was still friendly. On May 23 he had publicly renewed Dulles's private commitment of 1957. "The right of free, innocent passage of the international waterway is a vital interest of the international community." That declaration, after Nasser's closure of the straits, was in itself a major breakthrough. But Eban was obliged to follow it through. Before it could take unilateral action—and in order to avoid isolation in the wake of the action—Israel had first to ascertain whether "the international community" was itself prepared to do anything to uphold its own "vital interests" in the straits and the gulf.

The answer, in reality, was no, and it would have suited Israel better—and might have saved some bloodshed—if that answer had been promptly forthcoming. Instead Johnson talked of an "international naval escort," to be set up by the maritime Powers, which would reopen the straits, and there were even some halfhearted efforts toward the formation of such a force. Eban's policy—of isolation avoidance—required time to be given for the international naval escort either to materialize or to be acknowledged to have failed to do so. This meant that the original "48 hours" would have to be considerably extended. The President warned that "it was vital that Israel should not take pre-emptive action" (May 25) and that "Israel will not be alone unless it decides to go alone" (May 26).[77] Grave reasons for delay. This delay, whose reasons could not be appreciated by a wide public, had strong effects, both inside Israel and among Israel's Arab neighbors.

In Israel, by May 29, pressures for immediate war were mounting; the military chiefs were ready for action. The popular mood was rising to fury at the apparent feebleness and prevarication of Ben-Gurion's unworthy successor.

On Israel's borders, there was joy. It seemed that Nasser had prevailed, and the Jews were afraid to fight. The end of Israel seemed to be around the corner. Nasser himself seemed to be as drunk with his imagined victory as Ben-Gurion had been with his real one, ten and a half years before. On May 29, Nasser told his National Assembly: "The issue today is not the Gulf of Aqaba or the Strait of Tiran or U.N.E.F. The issue is the rights of the people of Palestine, the aggression against Palestine that took place in 1948, with the help of Britain and the United States. . . . They want to confine it to the Straits of Tiran, U.N.E.F. and the rights of passage. We want the rights of the people of Palestine—complete."

Meaning the end of Israel.

A great bandwagon formed. Hussein came to Cairo and placed his armed forces under Egyptian command. The radios of the Arab world dropped their attacks on one another and concentrated their attention on Israel in a paroxysm of triumphant hate.

In this time—which is known in the history of Israel as the Hamtana, the "waiting period," from May 23 to June 4—the mood of the people of Israel came as near to despair as it had ever come. Visions of the Holocaust were more vivid than they had ever been. Nasser was in fact nothing like Hitler, but he managed to *sound* very like Hitler, in his broadcast speeches. The responsive roars of the crowd sounded like Nuremberg rallies. Eshkol's pacific, almost apologetic style, in response to the Arab threats and encroachments, evoked the most terrible memory of all: that of the *helplessness* of the European Jews in the face of the rising Nazi threat.

The contrast between Eshkol and Nasser was profoundly distressing for Israelis. Nasser was one of the most charismatic leaders who ever lived; perhaps *the* most charismatic, in proportion to his actual achievements and failures. Levi Eshkol was surely the *least* charismatic leader who has ever paved the way for,[78] and presided over, a spectacular military victory. On May 28 Eshkol went on radio, in response to the thunders from Cairo. It wasn't much of a speech in any case, but Eshkol fumbled his delivery, mumbled his lines, lost his place, misread and corrected himself. It was a Charlie Chaplin performance. It is said that Israeli soldiers, listening to that speech, broke their transistors and burst into tears.

Pressure mounted to get rid of Eshkol, at least as Minister for Defense, and replace him with Moshe Dayan: not merely a brilliant general, but a powerful symbol, the archetype of the New Jew, while Eshkol was sounding like a very old one. But Dayan in the Cabinet meant early war, and then perhaps isolation. Grimly, Eshkol and his Government sweated it out.

On May 31, relief came. On that day, Dean Rusk, Johnson's Secretary of State, told a congressional committee: "The United States is not at this time planning any separate military activity in the Middle East, but only within the framework of the United Nations. . . ."

The phantom multinational naval escort, fading into the blue, need no longer be waited for. Then, in answer to a—possibly planted—journalist's question, Rusk added: "I don't think it is our business to restrain anyone."[79]

The light had turned green. The pro-Israel lobby had not been wasting its time. The Hamtana was drawing to an end.

On the same day, by no coincidence, Abba Eban informed the Chief of Staff, Yitzhak Rabin, "that he withdrew his political inhibitions to a military riposte: the waiting period had achieved its purpose—Israel would not be isolated as in 1956."[80]

On the following day, Moshe Dayan replaced Levi Eshkol as Minister for Defense, and the Government (with Eshkol still as Prime Minister) was widened into a Government of National Unity, including Menachem Begin. After nearly twenty years of ostracism, the former commander of Irgun was now at last accepted as part of the legitimate politics of Israel. In Cabinet, Begin quoted the Bible at length, while the secular and humorous Eshkol gently punctuated his discourse with "Amen, Amen!"

With Dayan as Minister for Defense, and Begin in the Cabinet, Israel was now clearly headed for war. But it was too late for Nasser to draw back. Not for the first time, he was the prisoner of his own rhetoric. To avert war, he would have had to announce the reopening of the Straits of Tiran to the shipping of Israel, and this he could not do. Yet war, when it actually came, seemed to take him completely by surprise.

On the morning of June 5, the Israeli Air Force, flying in low from the sea, destroyed the Egyptian Air Force on the ground.[81] Jerusalem, wishing to avoid early pressure for a cease-fire, issued no communiqué about this decisive action. Cairo Radio announced a string of Egyptian victories. Jordan and Syria entered the war on

Above, Egypt's closure of the Straits of Tiran to Israeli shipping was Israel's *casus belli* for the Six Day War in June 1967.
Below, Chief of Staff Yitzhak Rabin (left) and Defense Minister Moshe Dayan at the taking of the Golan Heights on the last day of the Six Day War, June 10, 1967.

Egypt's side, without knowing that Egypt was already defeated. Cairo had told Hussein that 75 percent of the *Israeli* Air Force had been destroyed, and that Egyptian forces had advanced deep into Israel. The Israeli Air Force then destroyed the Jordanian and Syrian Air Forces. Israeli ground forces—with Brigadier Ariel Sharon conspicuous in the most critical action—broke through the heavily fortified Egyptian positions in Sinai and advanced to the Suez Canal. Israeli forces also occupied the Egyptian-held Gaza Strip, from which Palestinians had been raiding into Israel.

Having defeated the main enemy, the Israel Defense Forces now turned, first against Jordan, and then against Syria. Hussein's forces were driven back behind the Jordan. Israel began its occupation of the West Bank: Judea and Samaria. Israel also now held all Jerusalem, with the most sacred place in Judaism, the Western Wall of Herod's Temple, to which Jews had been denied access during the Jerusalem occupation. Emotionally the capture, or recovery, of the Old City was the high point of the war, and of Israel's history to date. A popular ballad, "Jerusalem the Golden," was speedily altered to meet the occasion, and had a huge success. The new version ran:

> We have come back to the deep well
> To the marketplace again.
> The trumpet sounds on the Mount of the Temple
> In the Old City.
> In the caverns of the cliff
>   a thousand suns.
> We shall go down to the Dead Sea again
> By the road to Jericho.

In the north, a final campaign against the Syrians ended in the capture of the Golan Heights, from which Syrian artillery had shelled the settlements of Galilee. On June 10 all parties accepted a Security Council cease-fire order.[82]

XXI

Israel's military victory was complete, and stunning. But ten and a half years before, a comparable victory had been followed by total isolation, threats from both superpowers and enforced withdrawal. What remained to be seen was how strong the pressure would be, this time, and from what quarter it would come.

This matter was put to the test when the Soviet Union requested the Secretary-General to convene an Emergency Session of the General Assembly "to consider the situation and liquidate the consequences of aggression and secure the immediate withdrawal of Israel forces behind the Armistice Lines." Ninety-eight Member States endorsed the request for an Emergency Session, but three "did not concur." Two of the three were Israel and the United States.[83] Israel was no longer isolated.

The changed role of the General Assembly was reflected in the venue, and the objection. Because of the change in voting patterns, the General Assembly had (for the moment) become "the moral conscience of mankind" for the Soviet Union, while no longer possessing any such authority for the United States. But the United States had still enough influence in the General Assembly to muster a "blocking third" against any proposition to which it objected. By no coincidence, all the resolutions calling on Israel to withdraw from all the occupied territories failed to win the necessary two-thirds.[84] Anyone who knew the Assembly realized that these resolutions could not have failed, in the circumstances, without active support for Israel from the United States.

The matter came back to the Security Council, now a more congenial theater for the United States—and consequently for Israel—than the Assembly.[85] In the Council, to general surprise, a compromise resolution—proposed by Harold Wilson's Britain, but accepted in advance by the United States and Israel—was passed unanimously. This was the now famous Resolution 242, of November 22, 1967, which has been central ever since to the public debate on "the future of the West Bank." In its main operative part, Resolution 242 calls for:

(i) Withdrawal of Israeli armed forces from territories occupied in the recent conflict.

(ii) Termination of all claims or states of belligerency and respect for and acknowledgement of the sovereignty, territorial integrity and political independence of every State in the area, and their right to live in peace within secure and recognized boundaries.

Israel could live with this by adhering consistently to a linkage between the two paragraphs. In expressing Israel's acceptance of the principles of the resolution, Israel's representative told the Council how Israel understood the resolution: "There was a clear understanding that it was only within the establishment of permanent peace with secure and recognized boundaries, that the other principles could be given effect."

Addressing the Council on behalf of the Arab countries, the representative of Syria perhaps inadvertently made clear that he understood the resolution in precisely the same sense.[86] He objected to it because "the central issue of withdrawal was made subject to conditions to be imposed on the Arab countries." (Subsequently Arab spokesmen were to maintain that this was not the meaning of the resolution at all.)

The Soviet Union accepted the resolution—thus making it unanimous—because it wanted paragraph one, and there was no way of getting one without two; the United States had, as well as a veto, a majority of supporters in the Council.

A fine point concerned the word "territories"; not "the territories" in the English text of the resolution. This was to be the basis of Israel's claim that the resolution required it—contingently—to evacuate *some* but not *all* the territories in question. Russian does not have a definite article, so "territories" in the Russian text would not have the exclusive significance it has in English. The French delegate pointed out that the French text—*des territoires occupés*—contained the definite article. The representative of Israel indicated that it was not the French translation, but the original English text, that Israel was accepting.

All in all, in the circumstances, this outcome represented something of a political triumph for Israel. Not only did Israel now have a text it could live with—instead of a peremptory order to get out, as in 1956—but it had something far more important: the political alliance and support of a superpower.

Patiently, in the long progress from the rearguard action of 1956 to the Hamtana of 1967, the diplomacy of Israel had achieved a breakthrough. It did not, however, advertise its satisfaction.

9

THE SHIRT
OF UTHMAN

Visually, our situation can be seen as a pincer of sorts,
with the weaker jaw the Arab minority in the country,
and the strong menacing jaw the mostly hostile Arab
majority of the countries of the region, with the Jews of
the State of Israel located in the middle.

—*An Israeli*

We are . . . Uthman's Shirt.

—*A Palestinian*[1]

AFTER THE 1967 WAR, there were three distinct bodies of Palestinian Arabs.[2] These were: the Arab inhabitants of Israel proper; the Arab inhabitants of territories occupied by Israel in 1967—the West Bank and Gaza; and the Palestinian diaspora in the Arab states, mainly Jordan and Lebanon.

There has been considerable interaction between these three groups since 1967, but their conditions of existence are so widely different that I shall consider each group separately.

A. THE ARABS OF ISRAEL

The minority of Palestinian Arabs who remained in Israeli-held territory in 1948 became citizens of Israel, and are the only section of the original Arab population of Palestine which has that status. These

Israeli Arabs make up (in 1984) one-sixth of the total population of Israel.

Israel has no written constitution,[3] but its Declaration of Independence guarantees social and political equality to all the citizens.

That guarantee has been honored in certain important respects, but in others it has not: at least in substance, whatever the judicial forms.

Both the ways in which the guarantee was honored and the ways in which it was not have helped to build up a community which is an increasingly formidable enemy to the Jewish State[4] within the boundaries of the State of Israel and among its citizenry.

From the beginning, in the early Ben-Gurion years, when Moshe Sharett was Foreign Minister, there was an ambivalence among the Israeli authorities, as well as the Jewish citizens, about these Arab fellow citizens.

On the one hand, there was a sincere wish to honor the guarantee, and—especially on the part of Sharett and his allies—to prove that those who accused Zionists of being anti-Arab were wrong.

Working against that, and in favor of a highly restrictive interpretation of the concept of equality of citizens, were two basic factors: the nature of Zionism, and the security of the State.

Zionism was about a Jewish State. It was not about a binational State. Zionism had been a European idea, born of the problems and longing of the Jews of Europe. Its models were the European nation-states, and especially the most successful nation-states: Britain, France and (Wilhelmine) Germany. Weizmann had explained that he wanted the National Home to be as Jewish as England was English; France, French; etc. This didn't mean that non-Jews could not be citizens: quite the contrary. They could be citizens, without being part of the national mainstream. They could in fact have the kind of status that assimilationist Jews had accepted in Western Europe, and that Zionists had refused.

There is a sufficient irony there, and Arab spokesmen have sufficiently stressed it; and sometimes grossly overstress it, as when they suggest that Zionists aimed at treating Arabs not as the British had treated Jews, but as the Nazis treated them. There was a further irony which seems to have escaped attention. The status which Arab citizens could have, as citizens of this State of Israel, was very similar in substance (though not at all in judicial expression) to the old *dhimmi* status of Christians and Jews under Muslim rule: the status of tolerated outsiders. Arab spokesmen have celebrated that status, applied to Jews under Muslim rule, as ideal. As applied to Arabs under Jewish rule, they see the imperfections of the new *dhimmi*. The circle of ironies is complete.

Some Zionists argue that Arabs are indeed full citizens of the *State* of Israel, and that all they are excluded from, and legitimately so, is the Jewish *sector* within the State of Israel. There are Zionist institutions—such as the Jewish Agency and the Keren Hayesod—financed by Jews of the Diaspora, for the development of the Jewish sector within the State of Israel, and of Jewish education, etc. Arabs outside Israel—notably the oil-rich princes—could have financed a similar development in the Arab sector within Israel. This did not happen, because of the Arab world's boycott of Israel, and because the Arab world generally—and up to recently—saw the Arabs who had stayed behind in Israel as suspect.

The Palestinian Arabs' feeling of being "stepchildren"—as they often put it—was deepened by the contrast between the large resources flowing to the Jewish sector, from the Zionist institutions, and the relatively meager funds—though significant in absolute terms[5]—allocated by the State of Israel to development of the Arab sector.

II

The inherent character of the Zionist enterprise put Palestinian Arabs at a disadvantage. But the disadvantage became compounded once Israel's Arab citizens were seen as a serious internal threat, being natural allies of its besiegers, whose arrival they had welcomed in 1948 in Galilee.

From the time of the State's foundation, Israeli leaders, especially Ben-Gurion, viewed the Arab remnant in Israel as a potential fifth column. It was not a serious immediate threat in the first ten years of the State, when it was a small minority, poor, weak, ignorant and leaderless. But the Arab citizens were concentrated in border areas, especially in the north, and were presumed to be in sympathy with the Arabs beyond the border: with those states still at "war" with Israel, and with Palestinian exiles whose best—or only—hope of returning to their homes lay in the destruction of Israel.

Ben-Gurion's distrust of the Arab remnant was implacable, and seems in retrospect clairvoyant. Although most Israeli Arabs, in the

early years, supported Ben-Gurion's party, Mapai, with their votes—
and indeed gave it twice as much electoral support as Jewish electors
did[6]—no display of loyalty could disarm Ben-Gurion. "We cannot,"
he told colleagues, "be guided by subversion which the Arab minority
has *not* engaged in. We must be guided by what they *might* have done
if they had been given the chance."[7]

Ben-Gurion continued in that attitude throughout his seventeen-
year tenure as Prime Minister. Near the end of that tenure (1965) he
spoke at length on the matter, calling the Arab districts "hotbeds of
hate and conspiracy." But at the end of that speech, he showed his
bleakly lucid capacity to see the situation from the point of view of a
member of Israel's Arab minority:

> Many members of the minority here do not look upon them-
> selves *as* a minority but rather consider us a minority—a for-
> eign, usurping minority. This is the difference between the
> Arab minority here and minorities elsewhere. In our case the
> facts make it possible to think it is not the minority but
> the majority who constitute a minority, since the minority is
> surrounded by tens of millions of its fellow-countrymen be-
> yond the borders.[8]

From the beginning, the new State treated its Arab minority
largely—but never entirely—in accordance with its founder's vision of
them, as presumed enemies within the walls. The areas in which 90
percent of Arabs lived were immediately placed, from 1948 on, under
Military Government, with three regional councils: Northern Command, Central Command, Southern Command. Military Government
was something with which the inhabitants of Palestine were already
familiar. It had been introduced by the British, under the Mandate, in
the thirties, in order to crush the Arab Revolt, in which it succeeded,
and afterwards used, without success, in the forties, in the effort to
crush the Jewish revolt. The Jews now simply took it over, for the
control of Arab-populated territory.

In the chaotic conditions of 1948–1949, Military Government was
a strict necessity of war, although it did not assume full legal form
until 1949–1950. Optimistic Israelis—not including the Prime Minister—thought it would soon disappear, with the coming of peace. In
fact it lasted for eighteen years, and when it was abolished, in 1966,
much of its essence was retained, though in mitigated form.

The most salient feature of Military Government was restriction
of movement. Article 125 of the Emergency (Security Zones) Regula-

tions of 1949 gave military governors the power "to proclaim any area or place a forbidden (closed) area . . . which no one can enter or leave without . . . a written permit . . . failing which he is considered to have committed a crime." Under these provisions, 93 out of 104 Arab villages in Israel were constituted as closed areas, out of which no one could move without a military permit; movements of eighteen tribes of Bedouins in the Negev were also subject to military control.

Military governors also had powers to banish, to restrict residence, to detain without trial and to impose curfew. The most used power, however, was the power to restrict residence. The justification for the existence of this power was military security, but in practice the power was also used for purposes of political control. Under siege conditions, it is difficult to maintain the distinction between the military and the political sphere.[9]

Officers of the military administration told a news conference, after ten years' experience, that: "It is a principle of the military authorities not to tolerate nationalistic organizing within the area under its control."[10] Thus local sports were permitted, but countrywide associations of sport were not. A fortiori, countrywide political demonstrations were prevented. Purely political manifestations of Arab nationalist, or anti-Zionist, feeling could also be punished by the military authorities. In one case, seven Arab villagers were ordered "to report to Acre police station twice a day for three months because they had 'made fun' of a portrait of Theodor Herzl when it appeared during a film in a Nahariyah cinema."[11]

III

These were, of course, emergency provisions. They could be justified in principle, as one justifies the suspension of *habeas corpus*, and the use of detention without trial, by a democracy, during a war. The trouble was that the emergency was an exceptionally long one, and that the emergency regulations applied to only one out of two main categories of citizens, and to that category collectively and almost universally. The nearest parallel seems to be the treatment of Japanese-Americans during the Second World War. Japanese-Americans were treated worse than Israeli Arabs, as long as their emergency lasted. But theirs was a limited emergency. The Japanese external enemy was decisively defeated, and accepted defeat. The Arab external enemy, on the other hand, was repeatedly defeated, but never wholly accepted defeat.

It would be difficult to reconcile the conditions described above with the principle of equality of citizenship, but an attempt can be made to do so on both temporal and spatial grounds. The emergency is defined as temporary. Also, the regulations apply not to categories of citizens—Arabs, Jews—but to *areas,* and their inhabitants. But the emergency has become a chronic condition, and the point about areas is no more than a quibble. The areas were defined in such a way as to include the Arabs, and to restrict and control them. Although the Military Government has gone—inside Israel's "recognized" boundaries—the restrictions and control remain.

Israel's Arab inhabitants are citizens of Israel—and their citizenship confers certain important advantages on them. But they are *unequal* citizens, both because they are non-Jews in what is basically (though not totally) a Jewish State, and because they have been seen consistently, and with reason, as a security risk.

There are two great questions. Can the Arabs remain as unequal citizens? And if not, which will go: their inequality or their citizenship? We shall come back to that.

The generation of Arabs which was already grown up when suddenly it found itself part of Israel probably did not worry very much about that contradiction, or about equality of citizenship. They had never known equality, democracy or responsible government: not under the Ottoman Empire, not under the Mandate. They knew the Jews had won, and the Arabs had lost, and nothing in their experience could have suggested to them that equality would result from that; it would not have resulted had the boot been on the other foot—as Haj Amin made clear.

That first generation of Arab Israelis accommodated itself to the fact of subject status. But their children grew up with the knowledge of their proclaimed right to equality, and of the denial of this right in practice.

The loss the first generation experienced as a result of the departure of the British, and the victory of the Jews, was a loss not of equality but of land and of power. Both went together, in the great and sweeping expropriations of Arab and Muslim land and property which accompanied and followed the defeat of the Arab armies and their Palestinian allies.

The course of the actual fighting had involved the seizure of much Arab land by Jews, and especially by the *kibbutzim*. These seizures were retroactively legalized by the Knesset, under the Land Acquisition (Validation of Acts and Compensation) Law, 1953. Arab lands were also seized by the military authorities, on security grounds, and used for Jewish settlement (also seen as an aspect of security, in border areas). In these cases, and in general where the Arab owners remained within the boundaries of Israel, compensation was payable; the authorities were anxious to pay it, but the owners often refused, hoping to recover the land. Most of the land and housing seized belonged to the majority of Palestinian Arabs who had left what became Israel during the fighting. This was confiscated under one of the earliest measures of the new State, the Absentees' Property Law, 1950. The land and houses went to Israel's new immigrants, many themselves refugees from Arab countries. In these cases, the original owners in practice received no compensation, although in theory, compensation would be payable as part of an eventual overall negotiated settlement. According to the Arab writer Sabri Jiryis: "374 Arab towns and villages, or 45 percent of all Arab settlements in Palestine, disappeared after the creation of Israel. They were demolished and their land given to Jewish settlers."[12]

Dispossessed Arabs found it hard to understand, and impossible to accept, that land titles, inherited from Ottoman times, and respected under the British Mandate, could now have lost their validity. An Arab peasant is said to have asked an official at the Israel Lands Administration: "How do you deny my right to this land? It is my property, I inherited it from my parents and grandparents, I have the *kushan tabo* [deed of ownership]."

The Israeli official is said to have replied: "Ours is a more impressive *kushan tabo*. We have the *kushan* of the land from Dan to Elat."[13]

IV

The revolution in land ownership involved also a revolution in communal power. Arabs as individuals had had no political power under either the Ottoman Empire or the Mandate. But Arabs *as Muslims*—which most of them were—had had the highest social status, since the days of Caliph Omar, had collective wealth associated with that status, and had been able, under the Mandate, to convert that status and that wealth into an important source of collective political power. The British—mindful of the ninety million Muslims of India— had been deferential toward Islam and its institutions. Under Haj Amin, as Chief Mufti and chairman, the Supreme Muslim Council had become one of the three main power centers of Palestine, rivaling the power both of the Jewish Executive and of the Mandatory itself.

The main source of the council's power—apart from the Muslim faith itself—had been the *waqf:* the religious endowment to which the faithful could (and many did) donate their wealth for the benefit of the Muslim community. By the time of the Mandate, the *waqf* represented a great accumulation of wealth, by the standards of the region. Through the *waqf*, the Supreme Muslim Council (and its chairman, the Chief Mufti) wielded great powers of patronage, and exerted community influence, from the Haram esh-Sharif in Jerusalem through every mosque in Palestine, over the Muslim population. The *waqf*, as used by Haj Amin, had become the nervous system of the resistance to the Zionist enterprise.

After Israel's victory over its immediate armed enemies—with the repulse of the Egyptians into Sinai in 1949—David Ben-Gurion, altogether consistently, moved decisively against the spiritual enemies of Zion. In 1950, his Government imposed the Law of Abandoned Property upon the *Wagf*. Thus at one stroke, many thousands of acres of agricultural land,[14] large tracts of urban real estate, and thousands of houses, businesses and shops came under the control of the Custodian of Absentee Property, to be used for the benefit of the new Jewish immigrants. And by that act, collective Muslim wealth and the influence associated with it were nullified, as far as territory controlled by Israel was concerned. The long Muslim ascendancy, encroached on only under the Mandate, was here overthrown. The Nazareth writer Atallah Mansour has summed up the effect of this measure: "What had been the Palestinian Arabs' focus of political and economic power under the Mandate was neutralized and the Moslem community, which comprises the vast majority of the Arabs in Israel, lacks even a loose national organization."[15]

Ben-Gurion's imposition of the Law of Abandoned Property on the assets of the *waqf* was a politico-religious revolutionary act, comparable in scope and range to Henry VIII's Dissolution of the Monasteries. The point needs to be stressed, since the nature of this momentous transition has sometimes been glossed over. Thus the Israeli historian Jacob M. Landau, having expounded the "system of autonomous religious institutions" and "tradition of community organization" which prevailed under the Ottoman Empire, and was respected by the Mandatory Power, goes on: "This structure remained unchanged despite changes of government in Palestine. It was confirmed anew at the end of the British Mandate; then it became an integral part of Israel's institutional framework."[16]

Anyone who can believe that judgment has to be capable of believing also that Henry VIII of England "confirmed anew" the status of the monasteries when he dissolved every one of them.

It is true that the *forms* of institutional continuity were respected as far as possible, but the *spirit* of officially tolerated Islam in the new State of Israel had to be radically different from what had been the case under the Mandate. Indeed in certain important respects—though not in all—the conditions of the acknowledged institutions of Islam, within Israel, resembled conditions under the Ottoman Empire more than they did conditions under the Mandate. The sultans had seen to it that their authority over the mosques of their Empire was respected. The British, conscious of their infidel status, in relation to these matters, were far less exigent. From 1922 to 1936, the British had behaved as if what was said in the mosques was no concern of theirs: all that belonged to the sphere of religion, not of politics.

But Islam acknowledges no such separation of spheres: that notion belongs to the history and philosophy of the West; to the House of War, not to the House of Islam. Haj Amin had realized from very early on that the attitude of the Mandatory left him much more freedom than he would have had under a Muslim sovereign. Using to the full the resources of the *waqf,* Haj Amin and his supporters turned the mosques of Palestine—absolutely legitimately, from their point of view—into centers of agitation against the Jewish National Home (in any form). The Mandatory had acquiesced in that, even though the Jewish National Home was an integral part of the Mandate itself.

The State of Israel, from the beginning, asserted its authority—not formally but substantively—over the mosques within its jurisdiction. By its seizure of the *waqf,* and in other ways, it insured that the *qadis* (Muslim religious judges) would be persons dependent on the State, and responsive to its will. Suitable *qadis* were readily found.[17] The Koran would not be (publicly) interpreted in a manner inconvenient to the new State. The mosques *outside,* beyond Israel's borders, might—and did—resound to the *jihad* against the Zionist usurpers, but the *jihad* would not be preached on the soil of Israel itself.

Like many other matters in the relationship of Israel to its Arab citizens, this system worked well, from Israel's point of view, in the early years of the State; less well thereafter.

V

For about the first ten years of the new State, the Arabs of Israel were remarkably docile and tractable. The reasons for this are clear. This was a leaderless population: "a flock without a shepherd," according to an Arab writer; "a body without a head," according to an Israeli official.

It was a small flock, or body, in those days. Out of an estimated 900,000 Arab inhabitants in 1947 in the territories which came to be included within Israel's armistice borders, 700,000 had gone before the end of 1948.[18] Those who had gone included all the Arab elites. The top leadership of the Palestinian Arabs, the religious-cum-political elite centered on the Supreme Muslim Council, was now in exile, along with Haj Amin. But the much wider commercial and social elites had also gone, together with almost the whole urban population. The figures for the non-Jewish population of the main urban centers, before and after 1948, are very striking:

	BEFORE	AFTER
West Jerusalem	75,000	3,500
Jaffa	70,000	3,600
Haifa	71,000	2,900[19]

As Ben-Gurion's first adviser on Arab affairs, Yehoshua Palmon, put it: "The center had fled, all that was left was the periphery."[20]

Through the Military Government system, described above, the new State exercised a high degree of physical control over the movements of Arab villagers outside their villages. But it also wanted—as the Mandatory had done—to have some control over what went on inside the villages, as potential foci of hostility to the State. This was achieved, with a high degree of success in the early years, through the only active Arab institution that remained: the *hamula*, or extended family.

The population of the villages was made up of *hamulas*, clans of people bearing the same name; each *hamula* was in varying degrees of contention with the others. The British, in their dealings with the villages, had operated on the "take me to your leader" principle, as they usually did throughout their Empire. They had found out which was the most powerful *hamula*, and who was the most powerful man in that *hamula*, and they had made that man *mukhtar* (headman), subject to good behavior, from a British point of view.

The new State had no use for the old *mukhtars*, knowing how they had cooperated with the British in the effort to quell the insurrection of the Yishuv. But the Israelis did not just replace the old nominated *mukhtars* with new ones. They did something much more interesting: they introduced, for the first time, democracy at village level, using the Israeli system of proportional representation for the election of local councils.

This local democracy was quite genuine, and in no way rigged, but its effects—whether intended or not—were very gratifying from an Israeli point of view. Those *hamulas* which had been the "outs" under the old system took to the new democracy like ducks to water. These found—or were shown—that, under the new system, *hamulas* formerly subordinate could, by combining forces, take over authority at village level from a formerly dominant *hamula*. The new councils, mostly elected on this basis, had every incentive to cooperate with the State authorities, winning the cooperation of those authorities in return, and getting results, in terms of services and patronage, which would benefit the village in general, and the newly dominant *hamulas* in particular. The new councils were "vitally important sources of remuneration, influence and prestige."[21]

Through these democratic mini-revolutions at village level, a new Arab elected establishment was created, with a definite interest in cooperation with the new State. In the nature of the situation, there were also villagers who resented these great changes in the village polity. One study of a village records "some villagers" as blaming "the so-called Israeli democracy for bringing dissension."[22] It is not stated whether the villagers who saw matters in that light were members of formerly dominant *hamulas*, but it seems improbable that they were among the beneficiaries of the new system.

In terms of the Military Government system, Arab inhabitants of Israel were cast in the role of *subjects* only. But in terms of the local government system, the elected councils and their electors were *participants*, operating their part of the system and deriving limited but real benefits from it. They were also acquiring, for the first time, experience of the workings of democracy; something which they might later, when more numerous, be able to use at national level.

The local councils, based on the inter-*hamula* revolution, have proved the most solid political achievement of Israel in relation to its Arab citizens. Because of their democratic character, the councils provide *a majority* of Israel's Arab citizens with solid material incentives to cooperate with the State. The rise of an educated Arab elite was slow to undermine the system of "*hamula*ism." Writing at the end of the seventies, Lustick recorded a "notable lack of success" in the struggle of "reformists" to break the *hamula* system, and a "sharp decline" in the anti-*hamula* lists."[23] But writing only a few years later, Eli Rekhess notes a change: "The proportion of young educated Arabs on local councils has gradually and steadily increased and the older generation is being pushed out of power positions."[24]

For a shorter time, Arab cooperation at national level seemed to work as effectively as it did at local level. In the early years of the State, the Arab representation in the Knesset—about five members— was elected on lists associated with Ben-Gurion's Mapai, voted invariably with the Government and appeared to be as soundly Zionist as any Jew in the Knesset. These M.K.s were, of course, drawn from the newly dominant *hamulas* in the local council system, and had a vested interest in supporting Mapai and the Government. An Arab nationalist view of such M.K.s is provided by Sabri Jiryis, whom they reminded of "the fictional 'Fashid,' the Arab as Herzl imagined him in the future Zionist state, accepting his fate and behaving exactly as the Zionist society expects him to behave."[25]

The P.L.O. poet R. Husain wrote of such people:

> *Give me a rope, a hammer, a steel bar,*
> *For I shall build gallows,*
> *Among my people a group still lingers*
> *That feeds my shame and walks with downcast heads.*
> *Let's stretch their necks!*
> *How can we keep in our midst*
> *One who licks every palm he meets?*[26]

Poor Fashid! There will need to be a lot of gallows, since it seems that an actual majority of Arabs in Israel have actively (though decreasingly) cooperated with the Israeli system, through the *hamulas* and the local councils in particular.

VI

It was only after the Suez/Sinai war—which was seen by Arabs as a victory for Egypt—that there came the first clear signs of unrest among the Arabs of Israel. Since then, growing numbers of Arabs—especially in the larger towns and among the young—have been emerging as Arab nationalists, rejecting cooperation with the Zionists and manifesting solidarity with the militant West Bank Palestinians. There are many reasons for this change of mood, but two of these are probably basic, and both are due to implicitly contradictory policies pursued by Israel.

1. Resentment at the Military Government system, the land confiscations and the markedly superior relative status of the Jewish population, under the "Jewish State" aspects of Israel.
2. Strengthening of the position of the Arab community *in absolute terms,* due to improvements in public health, standards of education and—in some respects—economic opportunities.

The resentment was inherent in the situation from the beginning; growing confidence, and knowledge, made it possible to begin to give political expression to the resentment.

The Arab population was growing rapidly in numbers—both absolutely, and relative to the Jews—and, as it grew, it developed a new, educated leadership, replacing the elites who had gone, and challenging the elites fostered by Israel under the democratized *hamula* system.

The health of the Arabs of Palestine, wretched under the Ottoman Empire, had improved dramatically under the Mandate, partly because of the efforts of the Mandatory itself, and partly because of the efforts of Hadassah. Under the efficient public-health services of the new State, the improvement continued, for Arabs remaining within Israel's borders, with results disquieting to Israel's political analysts. The life expectancy of Arabs in Israel became only very slightly inferior to that of the Jewish population, and was in fact that of an advanced country. But the birth rate among the Arabs continued at "Third World" levels into the sixties, and though it fell off thereafter, it still greatly exceeded that of the Jews. As a result of this combination, the rate of natural increase of the Arab population became more than twice that of the Jews: in 1976, 38.4 percent per thousand among Arabs, as compared to 18.0 percent among Jews.[27] By 1979, the rates in *both* communities had slowed down: 35 percent among Arabs, 15.1 percent among Jews.[28]

In the early years, that formidable differential in natural increase was offset by the very large Jewish immigration of the fifties and part of the sixties. As a result of the conflicting effects of natural increase, on the one hand, and immigration, on the other, the Arab proportion of the population remained approximately stable until quite recently, but is now rising sharply.[29] It is reckoned that by 1993 the Arabs, at one million, will make up 20 percent of the total population.

A very reliable sourcebook on this subject is the Van Leer Foundation's 1983 Symposium, *Every Sixth Israeli*.[30] If an equivalent symposium is held, and the results published, ten years later, the title will probably have to read *Every Fifth Israeli*. As every Arab born in Israel is an Israeli citizen, these demographic data and projections constitute an implicit long-term challenge to the Jewish State.

VII

The proportion of *educated* Arabs is also rising, quite steeply, and faster than the rise in the proportion of educated Jews. In 1954–1955, only 1.9 percent of Arabs held matriculation certificates, while 15.8 percent of Jews did. By 1972–1973, 12.5 percent of Arabs held such certificates, 43.6 percent of Jews. The Arab proportion had increased more than sixfold; the Jewish, less than threefold.[31] In 1948–1949 there were no Arabs attending universities; by 1968–1969, there were about 600; by 1978–1979, 1,300. The rise in Arab pupils attending high schools is even more dramatic: from 14 in 1948–1949 to 17,207 in 1978–1979.[32]

Early Zionists held that the Arabs would benefit from the Zionist enterprise, and that therefore they would come to accept it. In certain ways, the Arabs who stayed in Israel *did* benefit from the Zionist enterprise. In terms of health and of earnings, and in education, they are better off than the Palestinian Arabs were under the Ottoman Empire and the Mandate, and than are the populations of Israel's Arab neighbors.

Of the economic progress made by the Arabs of Israel between 1948 and the early 1980s, Eli Rekhess has written: "The development of infrastructure services in the Arab village, the 'green revolution' in Arab agriculture, which has become mechanized and modern, the absorption of Arab manpower in the services and industry—all led to a substantial rise in income levels and standards of living."[33]

The Zionist enterprise brought these real benefits to the Arabs of Israel, but the Arabs of Israel were *not* reconciled to the Zionist enterprise. On the contrary, those who have received most benefits—the best educated among the Arabs—are those who are least reconciled to the State of Israel.

There are many reasons for the failure of this particular Zionist hope. One reason lies in the basis of comparison. A young Arab, growing up in Israel, does not contrast his or her position with what it would have been under the Ottomans or the British, or in Egypt, etc. Those are abstract and academic topics. The contrast actually visible, all the time, in daily life, is the contrast between the condition of the Jews and the condition of the Arabs. That contrast is bound to excite at least some degree of resentment in any Arab consciousness. The Arab schools, for example, may be good in comparison with those of Egypt, etc., but as compared with the Jewish schools—which have the exclusive benefit of the flow of funds from the Diaspora—the Arab schools are poorly equipped.

Another reason concerns the curriculum. The Hebrew curriculum for both Jews and Arabs was strong in the history and literature of Zionism. The Arabic curriculum was strong in the classics of the Arab middle ages. Fouzi el-Asmar, an ex-pupil, has recorded the effect of that contrast on a class of young Arabs: "We felt deprived because of the total absence of national poems, patriotic poems, especially since the Hebrew curriculum was full of these."[34]

The State Education Law of 1953 laid down one educational goal for all pupils in Israel, whether Jewish or non-Jewish. The object was "to base elementary education in the State of Israel on the values of Jewish culture and the achievements of science, on love of the homeland and loyalty to the State and the Jewish people, on practice in agricultural work and handicraft, on *chalutzic* [pioneer] training and on the striving for a society built on freedom, equality, tolerance, mutual assistance and love of mankind."

The idea of teaching Judaism and Zionism to Arabs was not a very good idea, as the Israeli educational authorities were to recognize after a generation of experience. Those who taught Zionism were impressing on their pupils the supreme importance of national identity and national commitment. In the minds of young Arabs, that could only mean *Arab* national identity and commitment. Teaching Zionism to Arabs speeded up the growth of Arab nationalism in Israel. Some pupils even took over the vocabulary of Zionism, turning it against the Zionists. "If we do not help ourselves," writes Muhammad Wattad, "by taking the initiative so as to arrive at the greatest possible auto-emancipation, we will be ground down—we will not be like every man, but like the dust of man."[35]

Autoemancipation! The spark that burned in the mind of Leon Pinsker, a hundred years before in Russia, wafted through the air of a classroom of the Jewish State, into the mind of a young Arab, there to burn with a flame of a different color! This is not the least of the many marvelous peregrinations of the Zionist idea.

By 1972, the Israeli educational authorities had realized that teaching Zionism to young Muhammad was not working out very well. In that year, the notion of "one educational goal for all Israelis" was dropped, and "basic orientations for Arab education" were introduced. The first two basic orientations were:

1. Education in the values of peace.
2. Education for loyalty to the State of Israel, by stressing the common interests of all its citizens, while promoting what is distinctive about the Arabs of Israel.[36]

But by that time Arab nationalism, fed by Zionism, among other forces, had acquired momentum, and it now seems irreversible. It was stimulated both by contacts with Jews and by contact—through the airwaves—with Arabs beyond Israel's borders. The more contact, and especially the more intellectual contact, there is between Jew and Arab, the more nationalistic the Arab seems to become. A writer in the *Journal of Palestine Studies* says: "Those who are most vehement and obstinate in their defense of the Palestinian identity are the young men who went to Jewish schools—not only the high schools but also the secondary schools."[37] Even the preoccupation of the Jews with their own terrible past in Europe stirs only a cold resentment in the mind of an Arab interlocutor. The Druze poet Samih Qasim economically evokes the spirit of an Arab-Jewish dialogue:

> *My grandparents were burnt in*
> *Auschwitz*

*My heart is with them, but remove
the chains from my body*[38]

The very national anthem of Israel, "Hatikvah," has been a powerful daily reminder to Arabs that the State of which they are citizens is not their State. As Saad Sarsour pertinently asks: "What can Arab pupils think when they sing 'So long as still within our breasts, the Jewish heart beats true. . . . So long as our hopes are not yet lost—Two thousand years we cherished them'?"[39]

But the Arabs in Israel are not living only in Israel; they are also living in the Arab world. Every day they listen to the radios of Cairo, Damascus, Amman, Beirut and Baghdad. They can watch television originating in Jordan and Lebanon. These broadcasts abundantly fill in the gap in the Arabic school curriculum of which Fouzi el-Asmar complained. As an Arab official of the Israeli Department of Education has pointed out: "The avoidance of the mention of the current national awakening by the curricula and the formal educational framework consigns the national education of the Arab child in Israel to the mass media of the Arab countries."[40]

It is hard to imagine that Arab nationalism will ever be included in the curricula of the Israeli schools. In any case, it clearly doesn't need to be. But it is interesting that an (Arab) official of the Israeli Ministry of Education and Culture, writing about "Arab Education in a Jewish State," can refer to "the current national awakening"—meaning the *Arab* national awakening. The raising of levels of consciousness and expectation as a result of education, the contrast between Jewish and Arab standards of education, the nature of the curriculum, the consequences of the past inculcation of Zionism, the effects of exposure to Arab broadcasting—all these have been conducive to the growth of Arab nationalism. But there is a further factor which makes the educated Arab elite particularly resentful and nationalistic. This is the difficulty experienced by highly qualified Arabs in getting jobs appropriate to their talents. Two stories may suffice to show the nature of the difficulty.

A young Israeli Arab told an inquirer: "My brother is an architect. But no Jew employs him to build anything. Once when a motion-picture theater was to be built near Haifa my brother submitted a bid which was better and lower than [those] submitted by five Jewish architects. . . . But he was turned down by the Jewish owner: How can we be sure you won't build the cinema so that it would fall down on our heads one day and kill all the Jews inside?' "[41]

An Arab educator, Hana Abu-Hana, tells of an Arab schoolboy, Said, who wants to be a pilot: "Said is attentive to the frequent calls on television to the youth in Israel to enlist in programs that prepare them to be pilots or naval officers or electronic engineers. If he imagines that the call is also directed to him—he too is an Israeli youngster—it must be explained to him that the Israeli suit has different sizes, depending on who is wearing it. Said is an Israeli but—apparently—not all *that* Israeli."[42]

In such cases, what blocks the bright young Arab is Jewish distrust of Arabs in general. The distrust is not irrational, in the circumstances. But it tends to increase the potential hostility which it seeks to counter.

VIII

The first ten years of the new State passed off without overt signs of Arab militancy inside Israel. Then, in the summer of 1958, came the first major rioting in Nazareth and later (and on a smaller scale) at the Arab village of Umm al-Fahm. In the fighting at Nazareth, which lasted all day, twenty-six police and many civilians were injured. There were more than 350 arrests.

The Nazareth riots were precipitated by the attempted postponing of a Communist Party–organized demonstration. They seem to have been caused mainly by resentment at the prolonged continuation in peacetime of the policies of Military Government and land expropriation, policies to which the Arabs had originally submitted, as part of the price of their defeat in war. Israel had seemed, for a time, invulnerable. But after Suez, and especially the aftermath of Suez, with Israel's isolation and enforced retreat from Sinai, Israel seemed vulnerable again. Clearly, the outside world had power over Israel; with protests, demonstrations, riots, you could reach the outside world. The Communist Party understood that, and got its message across.

Resentment against Israel, always inherent in the situation of the Arabs, had been greatly heightened by a frightful incident which took place on the eve of the invasion of Sinai: the shooting to death, by the Israeli Frontier Guard, at the Arab village of Kfar Kassim, of more than forty unarmed villagers.[43]

The period was one of stretched nerves in Israel, and of intense suspicion of Arabs, because of the intensifying *fedayeen* raids and the suspicion that Arab villagers in the border areas were cooperating with them or—at best—failing to cooperate with the authorities against them.

On the eve of the attack in Sinai—October 29, 1956—the commander of the Central Area, Major General Zvi Tsur, ordered "that the area conterminous with Jordan be kept absolutely quiet." In pursuit of this policy, a night curfew—from 5 P.M. to 6 A.M.—was imposed in a number of villages in the area. It is significant of the atmosphere at the time that one of the purposes of the curfew was to "prevent the population being exposed to injury by the reserve troops." The order given to the unit enforcing the curfew was: "No inhabitant shall be allowed to leave his home during the curfew. Anyone leaving his home shall be shot; there shall be no arrests."[44]

At Kfar Kassim, the *mukhtar* (headman) was informed of the curfew at 4:30, only half an hour before the curfew was to begin. Villagers out in the fields who did not hear about the curfew in time were shot down by the Frontier Guard as they returned from their work to their homes, between the hours of 5 and 6 P.M. The officer in charge of this operation, Lieutenant Dahan, informed the command over the radio of what was going on, in chillingly cryptic language: "one less" . . . "fifteen less" and "many less; it is difficult to count them." At the "fifteen less," the command realized that things were badly out of hand, and gave orders for the operation to be stopped. But the order was not transmitted in time to stop the "many less." The dead included young boys and girls.

The Government would have liked to hush up the news of Kfar Kassim, but this was not possible. The Hebrew press is not subject to military censorship, and not inclined to exercise self-censorship. When the news broke, it aroused widespread indignation in Israel, among many Jews, and all Arabs.

Subsequently, eleven of the officers and men concerned were put on trial. The most senior officers concerned, Major General Tsur, and his superior, Chief of Staff Moshe Dayan, were neither put on trial nor called as witnesses, and the most senior officer tried—the battalion commander, Brigadier Shadmi—escaped with a fine of one piaster. "Shadmi's piaster" became proverbial in the vocabulary of the Arabs of Israel. Of the junior officers and men involved, eight initially received fairly stiff sentences, of from eight to seventeen years, but the sentences were later reduced on appeal and after review. The longest sentence actually served was three and a half years.

Kfar Kassim, and the subsequent trials, provide an early example of what was to become a deep and settled division among the Jews of Israel over "Arab policy" and its consequences. Jewish opinion was divided—it is not clear in what proportions—between those indignant at the leniency of the treatment of the accused, and the impunity of the senior officers, and those who were indignant that brave men fighting for their country should be put on trial at all, for acts committed on the orders of their military superiors—as was indeed the case.

Kfar Kassim is now part, along with the Irgun massacre at Deir Yassin in 1948, of the language and historiography of Arab nationalism, and of Palestinian nationalism in particular. It is a story to be told to the children, keeping the flame alive. The story is meaningful for Arabs everywhere, but it has come to have a special meaning for the Palestinian Arabs of Israel itself. Mahmoud Darwish, considered the national poet of the Palestinian Arabs, ends his poem about Kfar Kassim, "Death for Nothing," saying "we shall remain," the tombstones on the graves of the victims being "the hand that holds us."

Kfar Kassim was very fresh in Arab minds in the aftermath of the Suez War. It must have contributed significantly to the new militancy that declared itself in this period, first in the rioting at Nazareth, and then in the rise of a new type of Arab politics.

IX

In 1959, in the aftermath of the Nazareth riots, Arab militants set up their own Arab nationalist party, al-Ard. Al-Ard was soon suppressed by the Israeli authorities. Militant support then switched to the Communist Party—now known as Rakah—which has provided, for more than twenty years now, the main political outlet for Arab discontent. Communists, faithful to the Moscow line, are not hostile in principle to the existence of Israel, but neither are they Zionists. The Israeli authorities, conscious of a need for a minimum of good relations with the other superpower, and of the position of the Soviet Jews, have not wished to suppress the Communist Party: it is accepted as a legitimate, if not exactly a legal, opposition. Furthermore the Israeli authorities allow young Arabs to take up scholarships in the Soviet Union, thus increasing Rakah's appeal to ambitious young Arabs.

Arab support for Rakah had steadily increased since 1959—with an initial leap in 1961—while Arab support for the traditional system, at least at national level, has declined roughly *pari passu*. In the beginning, the mass of the Arab electorate was prepared to support Zionist—and specifically Mapai—candidates for the Knesset. This has ceased to be the case. There is no better index to the pace and extent of Arab politicization in Israel than the following table:

ARAB VOTING IN KNESSET ELECTIONS, 1949–1977

Knesset Elections	Communist Party Percentage	Ruling Party Percentage
First Knesset, 1949	22.2	61.3
Second Knesset, 1951	16.3	66.5
Third Knesset, 1955	15.6	62.4
Fourth Knesset, 1959	10.0	52.0
Fifth Knesset, 1961	22.9	50.8
Sixth Knesset, 1965	22.6	50.1
Seventh Knesset, 1969	28.9	56.9
Eighth Knesset, 1973	38.7	41.7
Ninth Knesset, 1977	50.6	27.0

The Communists have now, though only barely, a majority of the Arab electorate, and nearly twice as much support as their traditionalist Arab rivals.

No one supposes that Arab support for the Communists is primarily ideological. It has to do with the banning of avowedly Arab-nationalist parties, and with Israeli acceptance of the Communist Party as, essentially, the only legitimate non-Zionist party. It has also to do with intersuperpower antagonism. Since the United States is seen as the patron of the Jewish State, it is natural for Israel's Arabs to place themselves—in a sense—under the patronage of the other superpower.

Each of Israel's wars has had the effect of speeding up the politicization of the Arabs of Israel. Suez, and the sinister overture to Suez at Kfar Kassim, helped to provide the initial momentum for the whole process. The results of the 1967 war, bringing large numbers of additional Arabs under Israeli rule, combined with the rise of a fiercely militant Palestinian leadership in exile, awoke a quasi-revolutionary mood in a section of the Arab youth. Many Israelis, including Ben-Gurion, had always believed that some of Israel's Arabs would help the *fedayeen*. There were much stronger reasons for that belief after 1967. The number of Israeli Arabs arrested for helping guerrilla operations inside Israel, and on related charges, rose from 48 in 1968 to 320 in 1972.[45]

Those reactions came in the wake of an unqualified and spectacular Israeli *victory*. But the Yom Kippur War of 1973 suggested to Arabs that Israel might actually be defeated. That thought is expressed, with considerable tact, in a contribution of an Arab local councillor to a symposium (of Jews and Arabs) in Jerusalem: "The Yom Kippur war, in which the Arab countries surprised the Israeli army, inspired a new feeling among the Arabs of Israel, about the potential capability of the Arab countries, upsetting the delicate balance to which they had learned to adjust."[46]

In 1976, disturbances broke out throughout Israeli-held territory, with Israeli Arabs and West Bank Palestinians manifesting solidarity. Young Israeli Arabs increasingly spoke of themselves as Palestinians, flew the Palestinian flag and looked to the P.L.O. for leadership. To some, Rakah began to appear not extreme enough, and in the 1977 elections about 8 percent of the Arab electorate boycotted the polls; yet Rakah increased its vote, at the expense of the traditionalists. Israel's Arab population was shifting its weight, against the State itself. As an Israeli political scientist puts it: "It is evident that the long-term goal is an overthrow of the Zionist state and reunion with other Palestinians."[47]

There are different views on this matter among Israeli scholars. One Israeli sociologist takes a remarkably sanguine view. Arabs, according to him, "feel that their fate is tied more to Israel than to that of their brothers on the other side of the 'green line' [i.e., in the West Bank and Gaza]. The 'Palestinian' solution of the conflict, which they favour, is meant for the Palestinians and not for them. They have no intention of moving to a Palestinian state once such a state is established."[48]

Perhaps not; but a growing number of them seem to feel that they will not *have* to move: that the Palestinian State will eventually encompass all Palestine.

Professor Smooha also says that the Arab minority "looks for the solution of its problems within Israel, not outside of it."

Again this may be true in a sense, but not necessarily in the reassuring sense that seems to be intended.

X

After the Suez War—and the Nazareth riots—the Israeli authorities began to be considerably more sensitive to the demands and concerns of their Arab citizens. A major development was the decision of the Histadrut, in 1959, to admit Arabs as full members with equal rights and obligations. This was a notable expansion of what has been called "the civic realm,"[49] the area within which the notion of a common citizenship, shared by Arabs and Israelis, has meaning. By the end of 1971, 42,000 Arab workers—about 40 percent of the total—were members of the Histadrut. Working conditions improved. Sabri Jiryis, a fairly severe critic, concedes, though a bit backhandedly, "The circumstances of the workers are acceptable and even advanced when compared to other aspects of life in Israel."[50]

By the mid-sixties, after the retirement of David Ben-Gurion, the Eshkol Government, under the influence of its liberal adviser on Arab affairs, Shmuel Toledano, moved toward integration of Arabs into Israeli society. Military Government was abolished in 1966. Strict security regulations were retained, but were applied much more flexibly than before. One of Ben-Gurion's favorite projects—"the Judaicization of the Galilee," which required continuing expropriation of Arab land—was tacitly shelved. The Eshkol-Toledano policy was analogous to policies pursued by Tory Governments in Ireland at the end of the nineteenth century: "killing Home Rule by kindness." Not a bad idea, in either case; and in both cases, it might perhaps have worked better if it had been applied earlier.

The growing "Palestinization" of Israeli Arabs, and the cooperation of some of these with P.L.O. *fedayeen,* might have been expected to lead to a sharp and early collapse of the Toledano policies, but this did not happen. The Government accepted Toledano's advice "to treat the Arab according to his deeds." This meant punishing individual subversives, while refraining from clamping down on the Arab community collectively. Toledano tacitly rejected Ben-Gurion's maxim: "We must be guided by what they *might* have done."

It is clear that many Arabs responded favorably, for a time, to the spirit of Toledano's approach. Sabri Jiryis notes a "maturing" of "both the Israeli government and the Arab population"[51] in their attitudes to each other. Arabs in general, in the 1967–1973 period, "adopted a quiet and cautious attitude and kept the door open between themselves and all government bodies."

While there has not been a return to the draconian policies of the first eight years, the "integrationist" momentum of the Toledano period was not maintained either. The obvious satisfaction of Israel's Arab citizens at what they saw as Israel's near-defeat in the 1973 war must have made integration seem a rather unlikely goal. The slippage in Jewish immigration after 1973 made Israel's Arabs begin to look like a more formidable demographic rival. And the spectacle of coordinated demonstrations involving both Israeli Arabs and West Bank Palestinians—who that year, in local elections, elected a number of pro-P.L.O. candidates—gave no encouragement to those in Israel who hoped to see the Arabs of Israel integrated with their Jewish fellow citizens. The journalist and broadcaster Rafik Halabi, who, as a member of the relatively privileged Druze community, was brought up to think of himself as an Israeli Arab, says of the mood of the Arabs of Israel by the end of the seventies: "Today it is hard to find an Arab in Israel who does not define himself as a Palestinian in one way or another; when the P.L.O. is mentioned at mass rallies, the crowd moans with delight."[52]

There are, however, still those who believe in integration, and indeed those who hold that it is already far advanced, in a number of ways. Thus Professor Sammy Smooha tells of "an increasing incorporation of Arabs in Israeli society, or what can be called Israeliness. Most of the Arabs are bilingual. They have daily contacts with Jews. Their way of life is becoming Western. They are exposed to the same communications media as the Jews. They purchase the same consumer goods as the Israelis."[53]

One can accept most of that, with a significant reservation on one point. The Arabs are indeed "exposed to the same communications media as the Jews," but they are also exposed to, and pay attention to, quite different media, carrying a message distinctly unfavorable to integration, the broadcasting systems of the Arab states.

I am familiar with a situation in which a minority is "incorporated" into the majority culture, according to all the Smooha criteria—and *more* incorporated than Israeli Arabs are—and yet is not politically integrated at all. The Catholics of Northern Ireland are physically indistinguishable from the Protestants; they speak one common language with the Protestants, and generally no other language; they live in the same sorts of houses and watch the same television shows. A stranger could walk through any working-class area of Belfast without having any idea of whether he was in Protestant or Catholic territory—until he looked at slogans on walls, testifying to the abiding politico-sectarian mutual hostility of the two look-alike communities.

So a high degree of cultural integration is no guarantee at all of political integration. But Professor Smooha also discerns among Israeli Arabs signs of acceptance of Israel. Some of the figures he cites from the 1976 survey—based on a sample of 722 Arabs—seem, at first sight, to confirm that view: "As for Israel's right to exist at all, 50 percent acknowledged that right without reservation, 29 percent acknowledged that right with reservation, and 21 percent denied that right."[54] But it appears that the "Israel" whose right to exist is accepted by a large majority of Arab respondents is not the same as the Israel that does actually exist. For Smooha goes on, "It is possible to generalize, on the basis of the survey findings and of Arab pronouncements, that the majority of the Arabs (a) accept Israel as a state, but (b) repudiate its Jewish-Zionist character and (c) wish to transform it into a bi-national state." As he says elsewhere: "It is clear that, in the eyes of the Arabs, Israel does not have the right to exist as a Jewish-Zionist state."

Professor Smooha ends his essay with the words: "These findings are quite encouraging, for they clearly attest that Jewish-Arab relations are in fact susceptible to intervention and change, and that better arrangements can be reached, provided there is willingness to compromise and to take the other side into consideration."[55] Pangloss—Voltaire's eternal optimist—concurs.

The findings in question can be "quite encouraging" only if we think it likely that the Jews of Israel are about to de-Zionize their State: that is to say, to repudiate and reverse the whole enterprise, emotional drive and system of thought which brought their State into being. People simply don't do that sort of thing. For the great majority of the Jews of Israel—whether they support Likud or the Labor Alignment—the Jewish State is the expression of their identity, and the guarantee of their security. It is not conceivable that they would melt it down into a binational state. And what these findings show is that Israel's Arab citizens reject the State in which they live, unless it turns into something it refuses to turn into.

XI

Where Palestinian Arabs are concerned, international attention—and to a lesser degree attention in Israel itself—has focused mainly on the population of the West Bank, and on political and paramilitary activities among Palestinian exiles. Relatively little attention has been paid to the Arabs of Israel itself. On current indices, it looks as if more attention is likely to be paid to these people in the years to come.

As we have seen, the Arabs of Israel make up a steeply rising proportion of the total population of the State. They also contain a rising proportion of educated people and of Arab nationalists. This combination suggests that the Arabs of Israel are likely to mount an increasingly effective political challenge to the Jewish State. And as the Jews of Israel are unlikely to abandon, or greatly attenuate, the "Jewish State" aspects of Israel, tensions inside the State are likely to mount.

On this topic, Professor Yehoshua Porath introduces a highly significant comparison. Of the Arabs of Israel he says, "With their numbers they have the power to operate within Israel's democratic political system, to influence its moves, perhaps even disrupt it. (Does anyone recall the tremendous influence that Parnell and Redmond's Irish national party had on parliamentary life in Great Britain in the thirty years prior to World War I?)"[56] Professor Porath does not spell out what that comparison implies, so let me do so.

C. S. Parnell, when he was first elected to the Parliament of the United Kingdom, found Irish representation in that Parliament in a weak and fragmented condition: just as Arab representation in the Knesset has been. By conspicuous, carefully calculated and well-publicized defiance of Britain, in the British Parliament and outside it, Parnell succeeded in raising his popularity in Catholic Ireland to such heights that no candidate could be elected without his personal endorsement. In this way, Parnell was able to build up a tightly disciplined Irish party in the British House of Commons.[57] In appropriate conditions—of "tight" electoral finishes in Britain itself—this Irish party, controlling the balance of power, could determine who would be Prime Minister of the United Kingdom, and could extort commitments to Home Rule for Ireland. There was, of course, resentment among wide sectors of the British public at the idea that persons hostile to the United Kingdom could determine who governed the United Kingdom. In the mid-eighties, Parnell's command of the balance of power and Gladstone's consequent Home Rule Bill convulsed the political life of Britain. In 1912–1914, John Redmond's use of a similarly commanding position, to extort Home Rule for Ireland from the Imperial Parliament, brought the United Kingdom, as well as Ireland, to the verge of civil war—a calamity that was only averted, in the opinion of some observers, by the outbreak of a still greater calamity, the First World War.

As Porath and others see, conditions seem in some ways favorable to the emergence in Israel of some kind of Arab Parnell. But such a phenomenon would necessarily have an even far greater explosive impact on Israel than Parnell and Redmond had on Britain. Britain was not surrounded by Irish people, in overwhelming numbers, hoping not merely for the secession of Ireland but for the destruction of the entire British polity and society. To most Jews in Israel, the idea of a pro-P.L.O. Arab bloc in the Knesset, a bloc which could in certain conditions dominate the political life of Israel, and determine the character of its Government, would be seen as an intolerable threat. If such a development ever does seem imminent, there will certainly be a demand for measures to avert it.

Clearly some Israeli Jews are already thinking along these lines. For Professor Rafi Israeli—a Jerusalem scholar who seems to inhabit a different country from that of his Haifa colleague, Professor Smooha—"the Arabs in Israel, whose national loyalty to their people is now beyond doubt, stand in the front line of the all-Arab effort to overwhelm the Zionist polity."[58] Facing that front line, Israeli frankly advocates disenfranchisement of most Arabs in Israel: "The Arabs who are ready to receive Israeli-Hebrew education, to serve in the military and swear allegiance to the state, should be wholeheartedly and unreservedly welcomed into the Israeli establishment, while those who refuse to do so (and one can understand their reluctance) should remain devoid of such civil rights as voting."[59]

Professor Israeli's point of view is clearly not an isolated or uninfluential one. Moshe Arens—Minister for Defense at the time of writing—has hinted at similar and even apparently more drastic possibilities.[60]

One of those who spoke after Professor Israeli in the Jerusalem symposium was Professor Porath, one of the most eminent Israeli specialists in Arab questions, and one who belongs at the "dovish" end of the Israeli spectrum. Professor Porath clearly agreed with a large part of his more "hawkish" colleague's analysis. "A day will come," said Porath, "when it will be difficult to maintain the character of Israel as a Jewish State by democratic means."[61] And what will happen then? Which is to give: the Jewish State or the "democratic means," based on the present bicommunal franchise? Porath does not

clearly answer these questions. He does explicitly disagree with Israeli's proposal about military service for Arabs, and he says that those
who put forward such proposals "are actually looking for a way to
deprive the Arabs of Israel of their Israeli citizenship." But just at this
point, where the reader is hoping to see an alternative presented,
Porath's normally lucid prose becomes clouded, and seems to verge on
despair: "On the other hand, I say most frankly that it is necessary
to arrive at that [i.e., deprivation of citizenship] but at the end of the
process; if everything comes apart then, that will be proof that we
have achieved nothing and had set out on the wrong course from the
beginning."[62]

Disenfranchisement would not be easy. Many Israelis would regard it, as Porath clearly does, as a horrifyingly illiberal and retrograde
step. Many friends of Israel abroad would share that view; Israel's
hostile critics would be proportionately encouraged. Israel's disen-
franchised Arabs would be discouraged, and many driven to the conclusion that "violence is the only way." The first victims would be
likely to be among those Arabs who kept their voting rights, on Israel's terms. If there is, as appears, an emerging conflict between Arab
voting rights and the Jewish State, it is overwhelmingly probable that
the Jewish State will be preserved, and Arab voting rights abandoned.
The Jewish State was the objective of all those long journeys in time
and space: the essential objective—though not always avowed—since
the days of Pinsker and Lilienblum, of Herzl and Weizmann. And
to the Jews of Israel, since Hitler and the Holocaust, control of a State
seems indispensable for mere survival.

To allow Arab hands to have access to the levers of power in the
State would look like suicidal folly to most of the Jews of Israel. In
practical terms—and quite early on in the process—the power of an
Arab bloc in the Knesset could be used to reduce the military budget:
the Arabs—even of a putatively "binational" Israel—could have no
interest in maintaining Israel's power to defeat the Arab armies. To
abandon the Jewish State, in the circumstances in which the Jews of
Israel are placed, would mean leaving the Jews once more in the
hands of their enemies: just the fate they came to Israel to avoid.

The day of choice between the Jewish State and the Arab franchise is still some way off, but the nature of the choice can hardly be
in doubt. How far off that may be depends on the speed and forms of
the politicization of the Arabs of Israel.[63]

An Israeli lawyer, David Glass, in the sentence quoted at the head of this chapter, refers to Israel's Arab minority as "the weaker jaw" of the pincers. Numerically, this is true. In other ways—in their geographical location, in their rate of increase, in their citizenship, in the size of their educated elite, and above all in their intimate knowledge of the language, the media, the strengths, the weaknesses and the divisions of the Jewish community—they will be the more dangerous of the two jaws of the pincers. The Arabs of Israel itself are also the only Arabs who are capable of mounting a political—as distinct from a military or paramilitary—challenge to the Jewish State.

A bleak prospect, but so is the alternative, from a Zionist point of view. The crunch could come when the Jewish State began to be threatened by the emergence of an Arab Parnell. How curious, in this context, that the author of *The Jewish State* should have seen himself as the Jewish Parnell.

The Jewish State has its logic, and the siege of that State has its logic. The Arab population of Israel constitutes (by now) that part of the besieging forces which is actually installed inside the citadel. It seems unlikely that the besieged will ever allow the resident section of the besiegers a decisive say in the conduct of the defense of Israel.

B. West Bank and Gaza

At the end of the Six Day War, Israel found itself in control, for the first time, of large territories densely populated by Arabs, and only by Arabs.

There was only one part of the newly acquired territory whose future was not in doubt, from an Israeli point of view. This was East Jerusalem, with the Old City and the Wall. Immediately after the war, East Jerusalem was annexed to the State of Israel, and reunited with the rest of Israel's capital city. Its Arab inhabitants—67,000 in number after the war—became citizens of Israel, with the same rights as other Israeli Arabs.

Israel's annexation of East Jerusalem has never been internationally recognized, but then neither Israel's possession of West Jerusalem nor Jordan's possession of East Jerusalem had ever been internationally recognized either. Both Jordan and Israel had successfully defied international opinion—as expressed through the United Nations—as regards Jerusalem, and Israel proposed to go on doing so. The strength of the Israeli consensus on this matter has been memorably expressed

by Meron Benvenisti, a former deputy mayor of Jerusalem, and probably the most "dovish" personality who has ever played a significant
part in the mainstream politics of Israel: "Every Israeli concedes
that the united city, at least the borders established in 1967, should
remain under Israel's sole sovereignty 'forever,' and that there can be
no compromise according to which any other state would receive
sovereign status in the city."[64]

There could be no doubt in Israeli minds about the future of
united Jerusalem, but about the remainder of the occupied territories
there were varying doubts, misgivings, hopes and ambitions.

The end of the war left Israel in possession of the whole of
former Mandate Palestine (post-1921) up to the Jordan river (as well
as Syria's Golan Heights, and Egypt's Sinai). The newly occupied
areas of Palestine consisted of the West Bank, formerly held by
Jordan, and the Gaza Strip, formerly held by Egypt. Unlike 1948,
1967 saw the exodus of only a minority of Arabs from Jewish-occupied
territory.[65] A census conducted by Israel in September 1967 showed
nearly a million Arabs living in the occupied territories: 595,900 in
the West Bank and 389,700 in Gaza.[66]

The populations of the two areas were very different in composition and status. The population of the West Bank was made up of a
settled population plus a refugee population from the Israeli-held
coastal strip. But the refugees, as well as the settled population, were
Jordanian citizens free to work in Jordan, when they could find work.
Most of them lived in camps supported by the international community—through the United Nations Relief and Works Agency—but
there was no legal barrier to their integration into Jordanian society,
and the more enterprising among them both worked outside the
camps—which took on increasingly the character of poor residential
suburbs to the larger population centers—and also drew their
U.N.R.W.A. relief, as U.N. officials knew.

In Gaza, on the other hand, between 1948 and 1967, the refugee
population remained refugees in the fullest sense of the word, entirely
dependent on U.N.R.W.A. and unable to work outside. They were
cut off, in this period, by the Armistice Line, from the contiguous
populated territory, which was part of the State of Israel. They were
under Egyptian rule, but they were not accepted as Egyptian citizens,
or allowed to travel to Egypt proper, from which they were in any
case separated by the Sinai Desert. The importance of Gaza to Nasser's Egypt was as a "springboard" for the putatively imminent libera-

tion of Palestine; its population was valued as a reservoir of *fedayeen*—1954–1956—and of potential *fedayeen* thereafter; and as cards at Nasser's political disposal within the inter-Arab system of rivalries. In Gaza, a population of nearly 400,000 people was cooped up in a closed coastal strip of land twenty-five miles long and eight wide. This was the most miserable and frustrated of all the Palestinian refugee populations.

II

In the first few years after June 1967, the occupying authorities faced a relatively serious security threat, both in the West Bank and in Gaza. This was the period when the Palestine Liberation Organization, supported by all the Arab states—though reluctantly by some of these—was coming forward as the spearhead of the Arab war against Israel. The P.L.O. now planned a war of liberation, like that in Vietnam, based on the native population of the occupied territories. The P.L.O. acknowledged that the terrain—being very small and very bare—was much less suitable than Vietnam for guerrilla operations. But it was expected that the Arab population would form a "human forest" under cover of which the *fedayeen* could conduct their war of liberation.

In this period, Yasser Arafat, then unknown to the Israelis, crisscrossed the West Bank on his motor bicycle, recruiting young people for the resistance. What he hoped to do was to implant a resident resistance in the occupied territories, as distinct from a resistance by raiders from across armistice lines.

In the event, although Israel had to cope with serious guerrilla activity in the first few years of the occupation, no implantation occurred, and nothing like any "new Vietnam." The area on which the hopes and efforts of the P.L.O. were mainly concentrated—the West Bank—was particularly disappointing. There were many people—most of the settled population—with quite a lot to lose, and with examples before their eyes of kindred people who had lost everything. There was verbal popular support for the *fedayeen;* there was also widespread willingness to inform. The Israelis were able to pick up the potential guerrillas and transplant them beyond the borders.

Among the desperate and embittered population of Gaza, the resistance was more serious. By 1970, P.L.O. fighters, armed with

UPI/BETTMANN NEWSPHOTOS

Israeli roundup of Arabs in the Gaza Strip, August 1969, following Arab guerrilla attacks in the area.

Kalachnikov rifles, grenades and other weapons, virtually controlled the Strip, killing off suspect Palestinians as well as attacking Israelis: fourteen Palestinians and twelve Israelis were killed by P.L.O. fighters in this period, according to the Druze journalist Rafik Halabi.[67]

As a member of the Israel Defense Forces—into which Druze, unlike other Arabs, are conscripted—Halabi took part, with repugnance, in the clearance of the Strip in the following year. He describes a routine search of one of the refugee camps:

> Then we entered Mugazi and systematically searched house after house, following a standard formula. The soldiers would kick in the rickety door and burst into the hut. All the men were frisked and interrogated; closets were thoroughly searched; any place that could possibly serve as a hideaway got close scrutiny. In one house we were met by an old woman who kept muttering, "May Allah have vengeance on you." The commander of my squad asked me to translate. "Allah have pity," I told him, afraid that if he knew what she was saying he would harm her. Instead he just chuckled, and I could feel the revulsion rising in me over what we had to do.[68]

Through such systematic searches, and the demolition of parts of the camps, followed by many detentions and expulsions, P.L.O. rule in Gaza was ended, and the phase of internal armed resistance was brought to an end, by 1972, throughout the territory—though *fedayeen* activity across the borders took quite a heavy toll. In defeating the P.L.O. armed effort in the West Bank and Gaza, Israel was greatly aided by the defeat of the P.L.O. forces in the East Bank, by Hussein, following Black September, 1970. About a hundred of the P.L.O. crossed the Jordan and flung themselves on the mercy of the Israel Defense Forces rather than fall into the hands of the Bedouin soldiers of the Hashemite King.

III

Moshe Dayan, as Minister for Defense and, as hero of the hour, the most authoritative figure in the Eshkol Government, was in effective control of the occupied territories under Military Government in the early and—in terms of policy—the formative years. In the immediate aftermath of the victory, Dayan had lived in expectation of a telephone call from Amman, leading to a comprehensive peace settlement, based on the return of part of the occupied territories to Jordan, and an agreed and stable frontier between Israel and Jordan.

The expected telephone call never came. King Hussein—even after he had been forced to crush the P.L.O. as an organized and quasi-autonomous force on his own territory—preferred to remain (as far as possible) within the Arab consensus, and therefore in a state of war with Israel. But it became a very strange state of war: perhaps the strangest that ever existed.

Dayan's policy was to leave the political and social arrangements of the Arab population in the territories as far as possible under Hashemite or pro-Hashemite control, subject only to Israel's requirements as regards security, including defensive settlements.

Dayan refused to introduce Israeli civil administration into the area, or to allow the Military Government to interfere in Arab affairs any more than was thought to be required by Israel's security. There was not to be in the territories anything like the revolution from above imposed by David Ben-Gurion on the communal life of the Arabs of Israel: the *waqf*, for example, remained in the hands of local Muslim dignitaries (appointed by Hussein), hostile though these proclaimed themselves to be to Israel. The policy was to leave the Arabs of the West Bank to conduct their affairs as much as possible as they had conducted them under Jordanian rule. The currency on the West Bank remained the Jordanian dinar. The law, for West Bank Arabs, remained Jordanian law, interpreted by courts in Amman. The schools were Jordanian schools teaching a "revised Jordanian" curriculum: the revision being the required elimination of the "hate Israel" passages in the regular Jordanian curriculum.

In every way, West Bank Arabs were encouraged to look at Amman as still their capital. Many of them, especially the educated young, resented the Hashemite monarchy, and would have been glad to see it overthrown by the P.L.O. But Hussein won in 1970-1971, and Hussein's Amman, controlling communication with the rest of the Arab world, remained the effective capital of the West Bank for purposes of practical business, though not of rhetoric.

The nerve centers of the whole system were the bridges across the Jordan—including the Allenby Bridge, near Jericho, and the Damiya Bridge, twenty kilometers to the north—kept open at the end of the war by order of Moshe Dayan. The Open Bridges proved an extremely successful and durable institution, and perhaps the only one that has been popular with Jews and Arabs alike. In one aspect, the bridges kept alive the social and commercial realities of the old Hashemite Kingdom, on both sides of the Jordan. Arabs from either side were free (subject to security searches) to travel and to move their goods to the other side. And goods were free to move from Israel itself, as well as the West Bank, to the East Bank, and from there to any part of the Middle East.

In terms of the siege, then, the results of the 1967 war brought both a kind of tightening and a kind of loosening. The tightening was the bringing of a large number of potentially hostile people into Israeli-ruled territory—within the walls, as it were, though not (like the Israeli Arabs) within the inner citadel itself. The loosening consisted in the partial piercing of what had been, before 1967, a hermetically closed barrier between Israeli-controlled territory and that of Israel's neighbors. Now the barrier was permeable, both ways, except to passage by Israeli Jews.

IV

The relation which established itself between Israel and Jordan over the West Bank, after 1967, has been described by various scholars as "a tacit alliance," a "pattern of tacit alliances," a "virtual condominium" and "an informal dual rule." I should like to adopt Ian Lustick's felicitous coinage: "adversarial partnership."

As might be expected, the adversarial partnership has fluctuated between its components. In the first few years, when Hussein was trying to work with the P.L.O., ensconced in the East Bank, the rhetorical stress, at least, remained wholly adversarial. After Black September, 1970, and up to 1973, the partnership verged on the overt, and West Bankers openly upheld it. In September 1972, an Egyptian proposal, in the Arab League, to close the bridges was strongly opposed by the West Bank mayors, as well as by Jordan, and came to nothing.

In 1973, Hussein was constrained by the logic of his "Arab consensus" policy to join with Egypt and Syria in the Yom Kippur War against Israel. But even this daunting problem in Israel-Jordan relations was handled in the spirit of adversarial partnership. The King sent a brigade to fight the Israelis *on the Syrian front,* but secretly asked the Israelis not to retaliate along the Jordanian front. Israel had its own excellent reasons for agreeing, so the bridges remained open throughout the war. The adversarial part of the relationship was fought out in Syria, while in Palestine the pragmatic partnership stood the strain.

Further strains followed the Yom Kippur War. Arabs everywhere, including both banks of the Jordan, were elated by that war, seen as proving Israel's vulnerability. Pro-P.L.O. enthusiasm reached its highest pitch. Hussein's Jordan was isolated and under a cloud; those open bridges, in the Arab nations' hour of need, had not escaped notice. The Arab Summit at Rabat in 1974 recognized the P.L.O. as sole legitimate representative of the Palestinians.[69] Hussein, in order to keep within the Arab consensus, was obliged to subscribe to this declaration.

Rabat, taken in conjunction with the P.L.O.'s ferociously anti-Israel stance, seemed to rule out, for the future, any form of "partnership," even "adversarial," between Israel and any Arab country. Not so, in reality.

In January 1975, only a few months after Rabat, representatives of Jordan, Egypt, Syria and the P.L.O. met in Cairo. There they agreed that the Palestinians "would maintain their Jordanian citizenship and the rights deriving therefrom."[70] In the following month, the Jordanian Premier, Zayd al-Rifai, referred publicly to "the reality which has been created by the merger of the East and West Banks." "The two peoples," he declared, "are completely merged in one entity and common institutions."[71] This declaration would be hard to reconcile, literally, with what Jordan had declared at Rabat, in the previous year, but the two declarations were reconcilable politically, and were reconciled, at Cairo.

Hussein was now involved not just in one "adversarial partnership" but in two; the second being with the P.L.O. By democratic indices, the P.L.O. seemed to be gaining in the West Bank, and Hussein losing. West Bankers accepted Rabat as speaking for them, and experienced a sense of exultation when they watched Yasser Arafat, on television, addressing the United Nations, on November 13, 1974. The municipal elections of April 1976 gave the West Bankers an opportunity to demonstrate solidarity with the P.L.O. The traditional, pro-Hashemite representatives were voted out, in the larger centers, and replaced by candidates declaring support for the P.L.O. To some observers, the eclipse of Hussein in the West Bank seemed complete. The relevant chapter in Rafik Halabi's *West Bank Story* has the title "Exit Hussein, Enter the PLO." David Hirst, in *The Gun and the Olive Branch*, wrote that at Rabat Hussein "gave away half his kingdom."

The P.L.O. had entered, in a way, but Hussein did not exit, and had not given anything away, except rhetorically. The P.L.O. now controlled most of the rhetoric of West Bank politics, but Hussein still had authority, quietly exercised, over many of the pragmatic aspects. The bridges stayed open, and many of the newly elected "pro-P.L.O." representatives went over them, in 1976 and after, to audiences in Amman with the Hashemite King. The salaries of West Bank officials were paid by Jordan, and subsidies from the oil-rich states reached the West Bank through the banking channels of Amman. These last are known as the "steadfastness funds."

Sumud—steadfastness—has become a key word in the West Bank. One who is steadfast is a *samid*. To West Bankers, picking their way through their triple political environment—Israeli, Jordanian and P.L.O.—*sumud* had become a useful and versatile concept. It evokes and expresses the approval of the Arab world for West Bankers staying where they are. This approval was not something to be taken for granted; in the period between 1948 and 1967, the Arabs of Israel itself were regarded as traitors for having stayed on; now they too can be regarded as *samid*.

The acceptance of what *sumud* stands for also reflects the acceptance by the P.L.O. of its own failure to "implant" itself, in an armed, revolutionary role, and its falling back on an electoral and rhetorical role, which Israel has tolerated in practice. *Sumud* then gives West Bankers who adhere to it common ground with both the P.L.O. and Jordan, without, generally speaking, incurring the active hostility of Israel. It is a word people can go on living with, and with a sense of dignity. The jacket of *The Third Way: A Journal of Life on the West Bank,* by the young West Bank lawyer and writer Raja Shehadeh, carries the words: "Between mute submission and blind hate—I choose the third way. I am Samid."[72]

V

The population of the West Bank and Gaza has been rising, under Israeli rule, but at considerably lower rates than that of the Arab population of Israel itself. The average annual growth rate of the West Bank population between 1968 and 1980 was 1.4 percent; for Gaza in the same period, 2.3 percent. Both were less than the growth rate of Israel's Jewish population (2.53 percent) and much less than that of Israel's non-Jewish population (almost entirely Arab).[73] There is a very high fertility rate, but its effects are mostly canceled by a high rate of emigration (particularly affecting educated people) to Jordan and the principalities of the Gulf. The growth rate, though low, is higher than it was under Jordan.

The West Bank economy, under Israeli rule, has been severely characterized by Meron Benvenisti. He calls it "undeveloped, non-viable, stagnant and dependent"; also "unbalanced, subservient and distorted."[74]

No doubt several of these adjectives can be justified—though one feels like asking "In comparison with what?"—but "stagnant" is a curious description on Mr. Benvenisti's own showing. Between 1968 and 1980, the Gross National Product of the West Bank increased at an average rate of 12 percent per annum; the per capita GNP also increased by 10 percent.[75] That rate of increase, over a twelve-year period, cannot be matched by many countries, and is not compatible with the picture of a stagnant economy.

"Dependent" seems more applicable, but it is rather a loaded word, which can be used to make a positive development sound negative. Thus Mr. Benvenisti writes, "West Bank agriculture is dependent on Israel for techniques, machinery and fertilizers."[76] In fact, West Bank agriculture has benefited greatly from this dependency. The total value of West Bank agricultural production rose from 114 million Israeli pounds in 1968 to 350 million in 1972.[77] But the effects of this boom can be seen as increasing dependency. As everywhere, improvements in agricultural techniques and productivity have meant fewer people working on the land. Those displaced in this way have found work in Israel, at lower wages than those accepted by Israelis (the gap is said to be decreasing). The parts of the West Bank contiguous to Israel have become, in effect, dormitory suburbs. The number of West Bankers now commuting for work in Israel is variously reckoned at 29 percent (official figure) and 49 percent (Benvenisti's figure).

The profit-conscious attitude of modern Israelis is often contrasted with the austere idealism of the pioneers of the second *aliyah*, with their insistence that Jews should do all their own manual labor. It seems worth noting, however, that the austere idealism worked out more harshly for the Arabs affected than the profit-conscious attitude does.

The tendency of West Bankers to work in Israel is generally discussed in unfavorable terminology ("Bantustans," etc.). There is some reason, however, to believe that this phenomenon may be less resented by those who are actually involved in it than by those who contemplate it from afar.

The Arab writer Salim Tamari asks the pertinent question: "Why do [the workers he has been talking to, in the Ramallah district] prefer to work in Israel, and face a daily routine of national humiliation, than to work for an Arab employer in the West Bank when such work is available for equal wages?"[78]

A significant part of the answer is supplied by one of Mr. Tamari's local interlocutors, Hasam: " 'With Arab contractors,' says Hasam, 'I have to remind them four or five times to pay me, and by the time they do, I lose a good part of my money, because of inflation. The Jew can't afford to cheat you, since he [usually] has four or five sites to finish, and he wants his work done.' " The workers concerned, according to Mr. Tamari, "are aware of the resentment against their work in Israel among nationalist circles in the West Bank and abroad, but they view this disdainfully."

In both the West Bank and Gaza, inhabitants of refugee camps have been fully employed in Israel, while retaining their refugee status and benefits. This was implicitly acknowledged, in measured official language, by the Commissioner General of the United Nations Relief and Works Agency for Palestine Refugees in the Near East in his report for the period July 1978 to June 1979: "If it were possible for the Agency to investigate need properly, it seems reasonable to suppose that many refugee families in East Jordan, the West Bank and the Gaza Strip where full or virtually full employment prevails . . . would be transferred from R category [eligible for all services] to N category [not eligible]."

Access to work in Israel has made a dramatic difference to life in Gaza, in particular. Rafik Halabi, who had been horrified by the conditions he had found in Gaza during his military service there in 1971, found the scene transformed into "a new Gaza" on his return to the area in the mid-seventies. The mayor of Gaza took Halabi and his television crew on a tour of Gaza City at 5 A.M. Halabi writes:

> I led my crew to Palestine Square at dawn, and the scene that unfolded before us was incredible. Thousands of laborers crowded into the square had created a true carnival atmosphere as they busied themselves preparing their breakfasts— soft doughnut-shaped rolls sprinkled with sesame seeds, hollow pita overflowing with a paste of chickpeas known as *humous,* spicy fried calf's liver, steaming coffee, and glasses of the aromatic drink called *sahlab,* made of ground almonds, milk, and mastic, an evergreen resin. It was the labor market run by the *ra'isin* (local Arab contractors), who supplied hands for Israeli farms and other enterprises.
>
> Such a scene would have been inconceivable five years earlier. But once the grenades stopped wreaking their destruction and Israeli troops no longer stalked the Gaza Strip with bayonets drawn, the laws of economics began to exert their influence on the fabric of relations between the State of Israel and the occupied region.[79]

But Halabi does not draw any optimistic *political* inferences from the relatively benign economic development he records. On the contrary, he ends his chapter—only a few lines below that "carnival" scene—with the words: "There is ample cause to fear that the next outburst is only a question of time."

To the Arabs of the West Bank and Gaza, as to the Arabs of Israel proper, Jewish rule brought a significant degree of economic progress, better material conditions—including a 15 percent annual increase in wages—and benefits in the spheres of public health and education. The settled Arabs of the West Bank, who had had something to lose when the Israelis arrived, had more and more to lose as the occupation went on. The refugees in Gaza, who had had nothing to lose in 1967, had something to lose by 1975. These conditions had probably much to do with the P.L.O.'s failure to "implant" itself as an armed resistance. "There seemed to be little doubt," writes Professor Bard O'Neill, "that the improved standard of living, the rise in consumption, and the increased trade were partially responsible for the tranquilization of the West Bank and the undermining of *fedayeen* attempts to set up a clandestine base there."[80]

But the "tranquilization" was relative, and essentially confined to the refusal of a *fedayeen* base. The rising prosperity was accompanied by a continuing rejection of Jewish rule, with the rejection most manifest among those who might appear to have benefited most: the educated classes. The appearance was partly deceptive, because the Israeli economy, overstocked with educated Jews, had very little use for educated Arabs. *Un*educated West Bank Arabs were in demand in Israel; educated West Bank Arabs were in demand in Jordan and the Gulf States.

The eastward emigration of educated Arabs from the West Bank and Gaza has been a safety valve, as far as Israel is concerned, but the student population has led the protest movement against Israeli rule. Bir Zeit University, in the West Bank, in particular has been the main focus of the protest movement. Apart from basic resentment of Israeli rule, and apart from the general propensity of students to protest, the particular situation of this student population puts a special premium on protest. In the regions where these students have their best hope of finding jobs, a record as an anti-Israeli militant is likely to be favorably viewed, provided it is understood that the proclivity to protest is confined to conditions in territory under Israeli rule, and will not make trouble for Arab rulers. Those educated Arabs who do remain in the West Bank—through either a *samid* commitment or a failure to find work outside—are generally resolutely hostile to Israeli rule. H. A. Kampf writes: "In spite of the general prosperity prevailing in the West Bank, the relative condition of the white-collar workers, civil servants, school-teachers, and newly graduated college students has generally declined, thus providing these groups that usually play a key role in the opposition to an alien ruling power with an additional reason for opposing Israeli authority."[81]

Mr. Kampf, in 1973, conducted a study of West Bank Arab attitudes to Israeli rule. His study is based mainly on "seventy-eight in-depth interviews of West Bank Arabs." Asked to compare the actual occupation with their expectation of it in 1967, four respondents out of five said it had turned out better than they had expected. Asked to compare Israeli to Jordanian rule, a majority said that Israeli rule was either better, less brutal, more efficient or less corrupt than Jordanian rule. Most of those interviewed felt that "they had not been treated badly and most had, in fact, received material benefits." All the same, a large majority utterly rejected Israeli rule: "Asked the basic question whether they would want to see an Israeli withdrawal from the West Bank even if this meant a collapse of the economy, seventy-eight percent said yes, regardless of the consequences." As one respondent put it, "Arabs are not 'like cows' which only ask to be fed, but independence and national dignity are as important to them as economic prosperity."[82]

VI

As the years of occupation lengthened, controversy over the West Bank came to be increasingly dominated by the question of the Jewish settlements. Arab opinion was of course strongly opposed to *any* Jewish settlements in the occupied territories, and was generally supported by international opinion. It was widely held that all such settlements were contrary to international law and the Geneva Convention, concerning the military government of territory occupied in war. Israeli jurists replied that this was not equivalent to military occupation of a part of the territory of a sovereign state, since Jordanian sovereignty in the territory in question had never been internationally recognized. Jewish opinion in Israel was divided both about whether there should be such settlements at all, and—among those who thought there should—about what the purpose, character and situation of such settlements should be.

I shall be concerned in this section with settlement policy, and pressures on policy, under the predominance of the Labor Alignment, from 1967 to 1977. The policies of the Likud Government, from 1977 on, will be considered in Chapter 12.

The basic idea, during the years of Labor predominance over the West Bank, was one of limited but quite large-scale settlement, for strategic purposes. Yigal Allon, Deputy Premier in the Eshkol Government, drew up a complex plan, of which he presented the first version to the Government as early as July 26, 1967. The widely discussed Allon Plan was never officially adopted, but "it gradually became the territorial and ideological base for large-scale official settlement programs in the occupied territories. . . ."

Allon had been a senior commander in the 1948–1949 conflicts, and the central strategic concept was one which he had pressed—unsuccessfully at the time—on Ben-Gurion, in March 1949: ". . . not possible to know a border more sound than the line of the Jordan for the full length of the land. The advantages of the Jordan line rest not just on its waters, which are not a decisive obstacle against a modern army, but on the Jordan Rift for its full length, including the steep and continuous mountain slopes."[83]

In line with this concept, the Allon Plan proposed the incorporation into Israel of a strip twelve to fifteen kilometers wide along the western bank of the Jordan river and the western shores of the Dead Sea. (In this whole zone, the Arab population was quite small—about 20,000 at the end of the 1967 war.) In the zone to be incorporated, Allon called for "the early erection of rural and urban settlement bases according to security necessities."[84] He further called for new Jewish urban estates in East Jerusalem—also on security grounds—new towns to overlook "the heavily Arab-populated centers" of Jericho and Hebron.

The other main aspect of the Allon Plan consisted of an effort to avoid the permanent acquisition by Israel of large blocks of land densely populated by Arabs. Most of the occupied area north of Jerusalem—Samaria—was to have "autonomy"—not precisely defined—possibly in some kind of confederation with Jordan, in which case there could be a corridor, through the Israeli security zone, linking Samaria to Jordan. As for Gaza, it was hoped that the population would accept transfer to the autonomous (or Jordan-confederated) West Bank and that the Strip itself could then be incorporated into Israel.

The autonomy aspect of the Allon Plan had a rather ghostly look from the start. It seemed inconceivable that Hussein would run the huge risks involved in signing *any* peace agreement with Israel for the sake of an agreement which deprived him of any say in Jerusalem, as well as of 40 percent of his former territories west of the Jordan.

The autonomy aspect may have been intended mainly to reconcile moderate Jewish opinion to the more dynamic, or annexationist, aspects of the Allon Plan. In any case, the Governments of Levi Eshkol, and later of Golda Meir and Yitzhak Rabin, took no formal decisions about either incorporation or autonomy. But they did press ahead with the settlement plans for the Jordan valley and the East Jerusalem area, recommended by Allon. *In those parts of it which were implemented*, the Allon Plan was a document of annexationist tendency. But the questions it raised, or expressed, over the future of the densely populated Arab areas did have the effect, during most of the period between 1967 to 1977, of closing these areas to Jewish settlement.

There were already pressures for the annexation and settlement of all the territories. Begin and his Herut (later part of Likud) opposed withdrawal from *any* of the territories of Palestine conquered in the 1967 war. Begin and his colleagues remained in the Government of National Unity (formed in 1967) for three years, but withdrew from it in August 1970, after Golda Meir—who had succeeded to the premiership when Levi Eshkol succumbed to a heart attack—publicly stated that Israel accepted Resolution 242 "in all its parts" with the object of achieving among other things "withdrawal of Israeli forces from territories occupied in the 1967 conflict."[85]

Begin and his followers passionately believed that Zionists had no right to give up any part of Eretz Israel, and certainly not Judea and Samaria. Many agreed with him, especially those in the religious parties and in the more messianic strand of secular Zionism. Public opinion was moving Begin's way, and after the Yom Kippur War of 1973, it moved faster.

To many Israelis, the circumstances of the Yom Kippur War strongly suggested that Israel had a vital need to hold on to the territories. In that war, the Arab armies—to general astonishment—had achieved strategic surprise. The occupied territories had given Israel room for maneuver, and allowed it time to recover from the surprise. But what if the Arabs had achieved surprise against an Israel fighting from within the 1967 frontiers? Hussein had kept effectively out of the Yom Kippur War, when faced with Israel's strong positions along the Jordan. But would he have kept out if his own forces were still within ten kilometers of the sea, and strong Egyptian forces moving out of Sinai had taken the Israel Defense Forces by surprise in the Negev instead of on the Suez Canal?

To many Israelis it seemed as if the occupation of the territories might have been the factor that saved Israel, in 1973, from military defeat, followed by the extermination of the Jewish population.

In reality, the Labor Government could not fairly be faulted for a neglect of security in their policy for the occupied territories; they had consistently put security first. Only after that had they been concerned to avoid what Abba Eban, in a characteristic phrase, called "superfluous domination." But after the Yom Kippur War, many Israelis were not inclined to listen to anything the Labor politicians said. The Labor leaders were collectively held responsible for the

failure of intelligence, the surprise and the near defeat. With them—
in the eyes of Oriental Jews—the Ashkenazic establishment and the
officer class drawn from the *kibbutzim* were also discredited. Only
Begin and his friends—having withdrawn from government three
years before, on grounds that began to look good in retrospect—
escaped discredit. They now had the public ear, and with them were
all those who, for one reason or another, resisted the return of any
part of the occupied territories.

This mood was intensified by developments in the immediate
aftermath of the Yom Kippur War. Three events of 1974 deepened
the sense of siege. In May, *fedayeen* kidnapped ninety Israeli schoolchildren at Ma'alot. In the subsequent rescue operation by Israeli
forces, twenty of the children were killed. The horror felt by all Israel
took a particular political turn when it was found that the organizers
of the *fedayeen* operation in Ma'alot were well-known Palestinian
"moderates" who had been in dialogue with Israeli "doves." In October, the Arab Summit at Rabat recognized the P.L.O.—the confederation of *fedayeen* groupings—as sole legitimate representative of the
Palestinian people. And on November 13, Yasser Arafat, head of the
P.L.O., addressed the General Assembly of the United Nations, where
he received a standing ovation. The fury with which Jews watched
that was redoubled by the knowledge of the jubilation with which
Palestinian Arabs were watching the same spectacle.

Favored by this general mood, a movement now came to the
fore—favored by Herut and by some in the religious parties, and even
in Labor—for the *unofficial* settlement of Jews in the occupied territories, without regard to Arab sensibilities, population densities or
international public opinion.

VII

Gush Emunim—Block of the Faithful—was founded on February 7, 1974, at Gush Etzion, near Jerusalem, by several hundred young
activists belonging to the National Religious Party. It is basically a
religious group, but the issues of religion and land are here inseparable. Members of Gush Emunim hold that both the Jewish nation and
the Jewish land are holy, since they were both chosen by God. "The
Gush see themselves as a spiritual elite forced into politics by the
urgency of the hour in which the Israeli Government strayed from
Zionism."[86] The Gush feel they are both fulfilling a religious mission

and also reviving the spirit of the pioneers and the first *kibbutzim.*

Although few in number, the Gush have a disproportionate strength, drawn from their sincerity and determination, combined with the continuity between the spirit of their movement and an important part of the traditions of Judaism and Zionism. The Labor Alignment seems to have found them correspondingly awkward, and even unnerving, to deal with, in the last years of its unbroken period of ascendancy, 1974–1977.

The Gush established themselves as a force in the politics of Israel through the pertinacity with which they followed their policy of *hitnahalut. Hitnahalut* is translated as "colonization," but as applied by the Gush in practice, what it really meant was squatting illegally in Arab-populated territory—and then, when evicted, squatting again; and so on if necessary. This technique forced an already unpopular Government to become still more unpopular by being seen to get tough with religious, Zionist Jews, out of concern for the sensibilities of the Arab enemies of the Jewish State. This threw a heavy strain on the Labor Government, and the strain became heavier after the results of the municipal elections of April 1976 seemed to show that most West Bank Arabs were supporters of Yasser Arafat.

By the end of 1976, Labor resistance to *hitnahalut* cracked. In December, Shimon Peres, Labor Minister for Defense—and later leader of his party, and Prime Minister (1984)—allowed Gush settlers in Sebastia, near the Arab town of Nablus, to remain in a nearby army camp "until the Government had decided on a suitable alternative location."[87]

To a significant extent the Gush had succeeded in breaching established policies on settlement limitation, even before the victory of their own friends and allies in Likud in the Knesset elections of May 1977. However, the overall results of settlement policy in the ten years of Labor Government in the territories consisted of settlements regarded as defensive in character, within the general framework of the Allon Plan. By 1977, there were thirty-two such settlements on the West Bank, mainly initiated and manned by members of the *kibbutz* and *moshav* movements.

VIII

Israeli public opinion, as represented in the Knesset, steadily hardened on policy for the occupied territories during the first ten years of occupation. The hardening process has been monitored, stage by stage, in a valuable study of attitudes of members of the Knessets of the period, carried out by two political scientists: Avner Yaniv, of Haifa University, and Fabian Pascal, of Northwestern University, Illinois.[88]

Yaniv and Pascal set out by making the old Dove/Hawk antithesis much more meaningful than it usually is. They distinguish, initially, three categories of Hawks and three categories of Doves, each category being defined by its attitude toward policy for the occupied territories. The categories run as follows:

1. *Unconditional Hawks:* would object to the return of any of the territories.
2. *Militant Hawks:* would agree to return part or parts of the territories occupied *outside Palestine* (Sinai, Golan) but would retain all the West Bank and Gaza and make the River Jordan Israel's political as well as strategic frontier.[89]
3. *Moderate Hawks:* essentially Allon Plan people, taking the River Jordan as the strategic border but not necessarily the political border.
4. *Moderate Doves:* also Allon Plan people, but with more emphasis on avoiding "superfluous domination" (Eban) and consequently on autonomy, confederation, or whatever, for Samaria and other areas of dense Arab population.
5. *Militant Doves:* would support the return of *all* territories occupied in 1967 as well as the establishment of a sovereign Palestinian State in the West Bank and Gaza even if such a state were to be governed by the P.L.O. However, they would not support any of that unless it is implemented on a reciprocal basis.
6. *Unconditional Doves:* This category consists of supporters of everything which is supported by category (5). But they argue that Israel should agree to make all these conditions *unilaterally*, without expecting any immediate quid-pro-quos from the Arabs, save for recognition and a peace treaty.

For practical purposes, the authors regroup their six categories into three operative ones:

Hawks: first two categories

Moderates: categories (3) and (4)

Doves: last two categories.

In the Sixth Knesset, which represented the people at the time of the 1967 war, Moderates were securely predominant. The proportions (in the 120-seat Knesset) were:

Moderates	73
Hawks	37
Doves	10

Thereafter, while Doves—partly based on the Arab vote—remained fairly stable, always much the smallest of the three factions, Moderates steadily declined, and Hawks rose, sharply in the last phase:

Seventh Knesset (1969):

Moderates	67
Hawks	42

Eighth Knesset (1973):

Moderates	61
Hawks	43

Ninth Knesset (1977):

Hawks	62
Moderates	49
(*Doves*	9)

It should also be noted that within the Moderate group, by 1977, Moderate Hawks outnumbered Moderate Doves. True Hawks—Militant and Unconditional combined—outnumbered all others; just as Moderates had outnumbered all others ten years before.

While Moderates retained their relative strength within the Labor Alignment, the Alignment was now in minority opposition. Within Begin's Likud, there was an internal shift toward even greater hawkishness. In 1967, the percentage breakdown inside Begin's group was 68 percent Hawks, 32 percent Moderates. In 1977—out of a total Likud membership expanded from twenty-eight to fifty—the proportion was 86 percent Hawks, 14 percent Doves.

(There can be no doubt about the general validity of these findings, though they are not based on an analysis of voting patterns, which would be impossible, since the Knesset does not take roll-call votes. The assessments represent the agreed findings of a panel of four experienced judges, consisting of two parliamentarians—one hawkish, one dovish—and two political correspondents—also one hawkish, one dovish.)

Very properly, the authors warn the reader against drawing too large conclusions from the rather dramatic attitudinal shift, in relation to the future of the territories, which their figures disclose. Their paper ends with the words:

> The semblance of a greater inflexibility may be functional to the extent that it leads others, friends and foes alike, to act on the basis of an anticipated inflexibility. But the actual policy-outputs would be quite similar to those which could be expected from any center-to-left combination of forces. One cannot speak of an end to ideology in Israel's foreign policy since substantial pockets of ideologically inclined members can be isolated, especially in the ranks of the center-to-right blocs. *But ultimately a similarly apprehensive yet pragmatic policy-orientation is likely to prevail whoever is in power* [my italics].

There is much wisdom in those words, especially in the last sentence: "apprehensive yet pragmatic" is penetrating, and worth retaining. Yet a word of qualification may be in order. To people living, as most of us do, in societies and polities whose right to exist is neither contested nor menaced, "apprehensive yet pragmatic" may have a somewhat sedative ring, suggestive of the personality (and probable pattern of conduct) of a suburban bank manager.

But Israeli apprehensiveness is not of this order. Israeli apprehensiveness is elemental and existential: the apprehensiveness of a people menaced throughout recorded history; and almost destroyed, in the Old World, in the fourth decade of the twentieth century; and still threatened by the deep hostility of its new-old environment. The pragmatism of the Jewish State, linked to an apprehensiveness of that order, is liable to manifest itself at times in ways that hardly look pragmatic to those who have less to apprehend.

In the minds of increasing numbers of Israelis, the near-miss of the Yom Kippur War linked the retention of military control over the West Bank, in particular, to the needs of Israel's survival. On that point, at least, pragmatists and mystics were as one.

For West Bank Arabs, this shift inside the spectrum of Jewish opinion, in relation to the territories, had chilling implications. What it amounted to was that a "compromise"—the Allon Plan—which all Arab leaders rejected with contempt, was simply no longer on offer.

The dominant forces in the Knesset and in Israel—by 1977 consisting of Unconditional Hawks and Militant Hawks—were agreed in opposing *any* concession of Palestinian territory. On this dominant view, all the territories conquered in the Six Day War—consisting, together with pre-1967 Israel, of the whole of post-1921 Mandate Palestine, up to the line of the Jordan river—were to continue to be controlled by Israel, whether formally annexed or not.

The hawkish ascendancy might or might not prove lasting. The strength of the Moderates, while recessive in this period, was still very considerable, and dominant within the Alignment, Israel's alternative Government. More ominous—in terms of a possible peace settlement— was the nature of the debate itself, within Israel, as contrasted with the debate among Arabs. The two debates did not overlap at any point. The two communities, or nations, were talking among themselves about quite different things, and discussing contingencies with which the other side was quite unlikely to present them.

Inside Israel, what divided moderates from hawks was the question of what to do if Arab leaders were prepared to accept an Allon Plan–type settlement, recognizing Israel, within expanded boundaries, subject to conditional cession of a part of the occupied territories. But there were no signs that any Arab leaders would even consider any West Bank settlement along those lines.

On the Arab side, what divided hawks from moderates was the question of what to do if Israel were prepared to hand over *all* the territories, including East Jerusalem, with the Old City and the Wall, to a Palestinian State, to be run by the P.L.O. In exchange for such a transfer—which its opponents called "the mini-State"—Arabs asked themselves whether they should be prepared to extend some form of recognition to Israel, within its pre-1967 boundaries.

Again the debate lacked a basis in reality. The Knesset would be no more likely to take serious cognizance of such a proposition than would the agenda of an Arab Summit be likely to include discussion of the Allon Plan.[90]

IX

It was rather clear that the Arabs of the West Bank and Gaza faced a prolonged period of Israeli occupation. But the occupation, as well as prolonging itself, was beginning to take on new and disquieting aspects. The first Jewish settlements—mainly in the thinly populated Jordan Valley—had had a limited, secular defensive purpose. The new settlers of Gush Emunim type were messianic fundamentalists, bent on the redemption of the whole Land, and determined that all who opposed their mission should be swept out of the way.

A dovish former Knesset member, David Glass, records the shock of a visit to a fundamentalist settlement on the West Bank. "I was struck dumb by the first question put to me in that place: 'What would you do if you were Joshua and were commanded to destroy the seven peoples?' . . . It was clear to all those present that the question alluded to practical applications in the present; the settlement is in fact surrounded by Arab villages."

David Glass asked the questioner what *he* would do:

He replied that in the first stage he would ask the Arabs to leave the country willingly. I asked what he would do if they chose not to leave willingly. He replied: "In that case I would force them to leave." I thought that was one man's view, but to my astonishment I saw that many of those present supported it. There are many people in Israel who think likewise, but do not give public expression to their views. As I said, I don't know which is more dangerous, those shouting at the gate or those poisoning the wells clandestinely.[91]

Among the Arabs the *samid* response to such settlers is to refuse to leave willingly, but also to refrain from providing the settlers, and their backers, with a major excuse—in the form of *fedayeen* implantation—for massive repression, forcing Arabs in large numbers out of the territories.

Sumud, throughout the first ten years of the occupation, had been a relatively easy course, even convenient, as well as dignified. But in the late seventies, fading hopes (of Israeli withdrawal) combined with the advent of a new and alarming type of settler made *sumud* more difficult. If, in spite of that, *sumud* remained tenable, that seemed to be because the alternative meant a high risk of losing everything. And the Arabs of the territories, by 1977, unlike the Gaza population of 1970, had a lot to lose.

C. PALESTINIANS IN EXILE: RISE OF THE P.L.O.

After the Six Day War, the number of Palestinians not under Israeli rule was very slightly less than the number under Israeli rule:

just over 1.5 million as against just over 1.6 million. The distribution of the Palestinians among the Arab states was as follows:

States Bordering on Israel

Jordan (East Bank)	644,200
Lebanon	288,000
Syria	183,000
Egypt	39,000

Other Arab States

Kuwait	194,000
Saudi Arabia	59,000
Iraq	35,000
Elsewhere	67,000
	1,509,200[92]

The Palestinian population of the Arab states was made up of those who had left Jewish-controlled territories in 1948 plus those who had left the West Bank and Gaza during, or just after, the Six Day War. Relations between the Palestinians and the populations and governments of their host countries had been strained from the beginning—especially in the two countries which had taken in by far the greatest numbers of Palestinians: Jordan and Lebanon. In Jordan, by the early seventies, Palestinians made up about 50 percent of the total population and about 85 percent of the population of the capital, Amman. Many of the more politically minded of the Palestinians belonged in the Haj Amin tradition, hostile to the Hashemite dynasty and hoping for its overthrow.

In Lebanon, Palestinians made up a smaller proportion of the total population, but presented an even greater potential threat to the national polity. The political life of Lebanon revolved around a "national understanding" for a sharing of power between the Maronite Christians, Sunni Muslims and Shi'i Muslims—very much in that order. The intake of more than a quarter of a million outsiders, almost all Sunni Muslims, was resented as a possible threat to this balance.

Throughout the fifties, and up to the mid-sixties, however, any political threat from the direction of the Palestinians must have appeared remote and contingent. The Palestinians, in the early years, were (in the main) a demoralized and distressed population, supported by an international agency, U.N.R.W.A., and generally looked down on by the host populations.

Fawaz Turki, who left Haifa, as a boy, for Lebanon, has written about his experiences: "I was a Palestinian. And that meant I was an

outsider, an alien, a refugee and a burden."[93] Turki remembers, as a
youth in Beirut, walking along the famous Corniche and joining "a
crowd of onlookers, watching a street entertainer with his performing
monkey. The entertainer proceeded to tell his animal to 'show us how
a Palestinian picks up his food rations.' I was a rough boy of fourteen,
hardened to street life, but I could not suppress an outburst of tears."[94]

Turki writes of hating Arabs more than Jews, and says: "The
Egyptians ruled over us in Gaza, and the Arabs in the Levant, as
badly as the Zionists ruled over our brothers and sisters in Israel."[95]
In general, for Turki: "The whole Middle East is a sick lie. An
abominable comedy. A repulsive quagmire. The area I saw from the
outside when I lifted a stone, and looked."[96]

Fawaz Turki's bitter experience of contacts with the Arab hosts
of the Palestinian refugees was not exceptional. Rosemary Sayigh,
who carried out a number of interviews with Palestinians in camps in
Lebanon as late as the 1975–1978 period, found a general experience
of hostile and contemptuous treatment by the host population. The
Palestinians were regarded as "a reminder of national humiliation,"[97]
which they had brought on the Arabs generally. They were thought of
as people who had first "sold their land" and then "fled." The notion
of Arab solidarity had been of little practical use to the Palestinians,
among the mass of the local Arab population, since "Arabism is the
ideology of the cities and the urban intelligentsia." But those who
adhered to that ideology were not interested in the people of the
camps either, seeing them as simply peasants. The local peasants
thought the Palestinians, being unlucky themselves, might be the bear-
ers of bad luck—in which the local peasants were not far wrong—
and taunted them with questions like "Where are your tails?"[98] (Apparently a joke about cowardice, "turning tail.")

Material conditions improved somewhat for the Palestinians toward the end of the sixties. Many families were receiving money from
members who had work in the Gulf States; many had jobs, as well as
U.N.R.W.A. support. The children went to school; educational levels
were considerably higher among the Palestinians than among their
host populations. But the stigma of having run away remained with
them.

Interestingly, Rosemary Sayigh connects that stigma with the rise
of militancy in the camps, around 1960: "Like loss of land and property, their loss of respect had revolutionary implications, making them
determined to recapture esteem through militant action."[99]

II

The first group to have some success in recapturing esteem in this way was Fatah, founded in Kuwait in 1958–1959 by a group of Palestinian students, including Yasser Arafat, who may not have been the original leader, but was the principal spokesman as soon as the group moved to Beirut and began to attract the attention of a wide public.

Arafat has become quite literally a legendary figure. Even his place of birth (circa 1928) is a matter of controversy. He says himself he was born in Jerusalem, in one of the houses since pulled down by the Israelis, after the conquest of East Jerusalem in 1967, to clear the large open space that is now in front of the Western Wall. Others say he was born in Gaza. His biographer, Thomas Kiernan, believes he was born in Cairo. That biography has itself a legendary Arabian Nights quality.[100] It is based exclusively on reminiscences about Arafat, by relatives and friends, or former friends. One of the few things that can be inferred from these reminiscences, with a reasonable degree of certainty, is that many people who know Arafat don't like him. (In making use of this biography, I have drawn on the interviews for what they seem to show of the political context in which Arafat worked, without accepting various damaging anecdotes, whose reliability is unascertainable.)

Wherever Arafat may have been born, he was brought up in Gaza. His name, at birth, is said to have been Rahman Abdul Rauf Arafat al-Qudna al-Husayni. He belonged to a well-to-do trading family, with excellent social and political connections. His mother, Hamida, belonged to the great Husseini *hamula*, dominant in the religious and political life of Palestine under the Mandate. Haj Amin was a distant cousin of Arafat's. Arafat's father, Abdul Rauf al-Qudna, was a prominent member of the Ikhwan—the Muslim Brotherhood. The Ikhwan and the Husseinis were sometimes allies, sometimes enemies; it was another of those "adversarial partnerships." From his earliest boyhood, in the last years of Mandate Palestine, Arafat grew up among the interfactional politics of Arab nationalism, with its shifting alliances, its feuds, betrayals and frequent violence. It was good training for what was to come.

Those who reminisce about Arafat often talk about those large, prominent eyes of his, which he could use to convey affection or menace, shifting at will from one expression to the other, with a somewhat hypnotic effect. As well as being an accomplished actor himself, he has shown a remarkable flair for the theatrical element in politics, for getting and holding the attention of an audience. Not that his talents should be reduced to that. To survive as long as he has done, in the near-desperate type of politics in which he has been engaged, must take a great deal of cool intelligence, as well as courage, and extraordinary powers of resilience. Still, his histrionic capacity is a particularly important part of his political repertoire. Under defeat after defeat, betrayal after betrayal—betrayed in turn by Jordan, by Syria in Lebanon, by Egypt, and by Syria in Lebanon again, and then yet a third time—he has acted out his role in such a way as to hold the sympathy and admiration of a large audience; and even to create the impression that in some ultimate sense, it is he who is winning.

A rather impressive aspect of Arafat's political debut is that he made no attempt to trade on his family's political connections—quite the contrary. Entering politics, he dropped his father's name, as well as the name of his mother's family. He met Haj Amin, but was not impressed. That whole generation of leadership was discredited by *al-Nakba*, the disaster; especially in the eyes of a generation which had yet to experience disasters of its own making. Retaining the Koranic "Arafat"—after the sacred mountain, near Mecca—out of his own name, he took "Yasser" from Yasser al-Bira, successor to Sheikh Qassam in the guerrilla war of the thirties. (It was Yasser al-Bira who was responsible for the assassination of Lewis Andrews, Acting District Commissioner of the Galilee, on September 26, 1937.) Arafat was setting out to make himself the symbol of the Muslim *fedayeen*.

Fatah, the political and—ultimately—paramilitary group founded by Arafat and his associates, was marked from the beginning by a shrewd, pragmatic political intelligence. Confining itself to one purpose only—the liberation of Palestine—Fatah aimed at eventually securing support, and funding, from as much as possible of the Arab world. Its very name—and the name of Arafat—carried a message of quiet reassurance to Saudi Arabia and the principalities of the Gulf. As well as being an acronym in reverse of the Arabic initials for Palestinian National Liberation Movement, *fatah* means literally "opening," but has a specific Islamic connotation. It has come to mean opening by conquest of a land for Islam. Thus Fatah Misr, for example, means the early Islamic conquest of Egypt.[101]

The name Fatah implied that this group was not interested in Westernizing, secularizing or spreading Marxist ideas; in short, that it contained nothing incompatible with orthodox Islam. At the same time, Fatah, having touched that Muslim note subliminally, left it at that: there were no Muslim fundamentalist appeals, as with the Ikhwan. Fatah wanted to close no important Arab doors; it wanted to attract the support of the secular, modernizing Arab states—chiefly Egypt and Syria—as well as the orthodox and oil-rich ones. Fatah was Muslim, but not *too* Muslim, which was about right, for the region and the time.

The ideological minimalism of Fatah was in sharp contrast with the ambitious ideologies of some of Fatah's later *fedayeen*-sponsoring competitors, notably George Habash's Popular Front for the Liberation of Palestine. The P.F.L.P. is a Marxist organization of "new Left" type, with anarchist connections. It aims at revolution throughout the Arab world. In this way, the P.F.L.P. automatically cut itself off from support or funding by all but a few eccentric Arab states. But the P.F.L.P. was also exotic in other ways. Several of its leaders, including Habash, are Christians. As has been pointed out, few Arabs would follow a leader whose first name was George, whether he was a Marxist or not.

In the early sixties, Fatah was beginning to attract attention by the fiery journalism of its organ, *Our Palestine,* and by its emphasis on Palestinian self-reliance, as distinct from dependence on the Arab states. At the end of 1962, the newly victorious F.L.N. in Algeria hoped that Fatah might become the nucleus of a Palestinian version of the Algerian revolution. In December 1962, representatives of Fatah, including Arafat, were invited to Algiers and later—through the Algerian connection—to Peking. Neither the Algerian nor Chinese contacts had any notable consequence, other than that of getting Fatah and Arafat talked about; rather like Herzl's meetings with princes.

Fatah, in this period, was a purely propagandist and journalistic enterprise; its militarism, though bloodcurdling, remained rhetorical only. But toward the mid-sixties, its rhetoric, Palestinian salience and international activity caught the attention, and happened to meet a need, of a much more serious revolutionary group: officers of Syrian military intelligence, then beginning to be controlled by the left wing of Syria's Ba'athist Party, which seized power at government level in February 1966.

What the Syrians needed was a Palestinian front organization to take responsibility for *fedayeen* attacks, out of Lebanon and Jordan, against targets in Israel. The Syrians were not primarily concerned with the effects of these operations on Israel itself. What they were interested in, primarily, was the effects of these operations on the internal balance of the inter-Arab system, tilting it in favor of Syria. They knew that Israel, by its established doctrine, would respond to all such attacks by retaliation on a much larger scale. That was the point of organizing the attacks out of Lebanon and Jordan, not Syria. Israeli retaliation would put the "reactionary regimes" of Lebanon and Jordan at risk. If they acted against the *fedayeen*, they would put themselves outside the Arab consensus, reveal their "true character" and increase their unpopularity with their own people. If they failed to control the *fedayeen*, they would incur further Israeli retaliation, and be in danger of collapse. Either way, Syria, and Ba'athist influence in the Arab world, stood to gain.

But the main psychological and political target of the raids was to be neither Lebanon nor Jordan, but Nasser's Egypt. This was the period when Syria was bent on applying "reproach . . . the soap of the soul," to Nasser, to make him come out from behind the United Nations and confront Israel. Again, either way, the Ba'athist leaders stood to gain, in terms of political standing and influence within the Arab world. If Nasser "stood idly by," while Lebanon and Jordan were attacked by Israel, and Syria threatened, Nasser's pretensions to the leadership of the Arab world would crumble. If on the other hand, Nasser was forced to confront Israel, this would be seen as a major political victory for Syria, the pacesetter of Arab nationalism.

Considered purely in terms of its results within the inter-Arab competition for preeminence, Syrian policy in this period was shrewdly calculated and brilliantly successful. The Hashemite and Maronite regimes were shaken; Nasser was obliged to toe the Syrian line; the rival Ba'athists of Baghdad were outmaneuvered and outshone.

Machiavelli has had disciples in many lands during the last five hundred years, but surely none more thorough-paced, crafty and consistently ruthless than the school of young radical nationalist political officers who emerged in Damascus in the sixth decade of the present century. Among these was Hafez al-Assad, who was to become Minister for Defense after the 1966 coup, and autocrat of Syria, through another coup, in November 1970.

Syria's policy was one of calculated high risks. Syria was pushing

Lebanon and Jordan over the brink, and dragging Egypt in the same direction. Obviously there was a risk that Syria would go over the brink. But the politic Syrians seem to have believed that war with Israel was acceptable, even desirable, once Egypt too was involved. What was intended was a war of attrition, inherently much more damaging to Israel than to the Arabs, with their vastly more numerous populations. This miscalculation of the immediate military realities was not peculiar to the Syrians at this time, but was shared by many military experts, including the defense correspondent of *The New York Times,* Hanson Baldwin.

Syria was setting the pace in the Arab race to the Six Day War.

The Machiavellians of Damascus were about to bring great additional misfortunes on the Palestinian people, but in the process of doing so, they made the political future of Yasser Arafat.

III

Broadly, the nature of the deal between Damascus and Fatah was as follows:

The Syrians recruited *fedayeen* mainly in Lebanon. Syria would arm the volunteers, and give them some rudimentary training. Then they were to go into Israel, to kill Jews and blow up installations. Damascus Radio would then broadcast magnified accounts of these exploits, ascribing them to Fatah, and so making Fatah famous in the Arab world, building up pressure on other Arab leaders to rally behind the Palestinian freedom fighters in an all-Arab revolutionary war of liberation. Fatah's well-established insistence on the need for Palestinian independence of the Arab states made it particularly suitable as a front organization for the Syrians, in this period.

The combined operations of Syrian intelligence and Fatah did not get going until 1965, but already in the previous year, Nasser and Hussein were sufficiently alarmed by the implications of the growing cult of the *fedayeen* to try to bring the movement under control. The agency through which it was hoped to inhibit guerrilla activity was none other than the Palestine Liberation Organization, founded in Jerusalem in May 1964, under the auspices of the Arab League, which is to say, Nasser's Egypt. As David Gilmour writes: "At that time the P.L.O. was not designed to do much about liberating Palestine. Its role was to shout a bit about solidarity and so on, but not to do any actual fighting. Its purpose was to contain rather than express Palestinian nationalism, to act as an outlet for Palestinian frustration—not to be an effective military organization which might drag the Arab states into a war with Israel."[102]

To lead this rhetorical enterprise, Nasser chose an entirely appropriate person: Ahmed Shugeiri. I knew Shugeiri as a delegate to the United Nations in the late fifties. All delegates are constrained in the General Assembly to become connoisseurs of windbags, and Shugeiri was, by common assent, the windbag's windbag. He used to begin his oratorical set piece each year with the words: "I am honored to address the members of the United Nations"—pause for effect—"all [x] of them." X always represented whatever the real current membership was, minus one. Israel was a non-nation. And so on.

Nasser's P.L.O. did not work out well for him; in fact it helped to precipitate what he most wanted to avoid. Shugeiri's P.L.O. was loudly denounced by Arafat's Fatah, so that Fatah looked to the Syrians like a designated instrument for puncturing Egypt's Palestinian windbag. The P.L.O. policy of vehement inactivity was now to be shown up, through Fatah, with "the propaganda of the deed," in the territory of Israel. Cooperation between Fatah and Syrian intelligence was finally agreed in December 1964. Arafat himself is said to have sharply quelled the objections of those who argued that Fatah should stick to its policy of "no alliances" with Arab Governments. The tacit alliance was formed, and the first armed operation conducted under its umbrella was announced on New Year's Eve, 1965, in Fatah's famous Military Communiqué No. 1.[103]

In fact, the operation announced in Military Communiqué No. 1— an attack on Israel's National Water Carrier—never actually took place, since the members of the first secret demolition team were all arrested by the Lebanese before they could cross the border. This failure was of relatively little importance. Military Communiqué No. 1 made its point, irrespective of the substance behind it. The Governments of Egypt, Lebanon and Jordan condemned the action. As Kiernan says: "Only Syria praised the action; but then, of course, Syria had engineered it."[104] This operation, and then later ones, with more substance to them, were trumpeted by Radio Damascus, together with the name of Fatah; other sections of the Arab press and radio followed suit. Fatah became an object of identification and hero worship; recruits poured in, building Fatah into a paramilitary organization with some potential of its own.

Pressure on Nasser and the P.L.O. increased throughout 1965 and 1966. Eventually—toward the end of 1966—the P.L.O. was turned right around, and converted from a *fedayeen*-repressing institution into one that launched and claimed *fedayeen* attacks of its own out of Gaza. Syria's strategy was working.

There seems to be no doubt that Fatah played a significant part, though a subordinate one, in the process that led to the Six Day War, and thus to the occupation of the West Bank and Gaza. And that disaster proved to be the second major stage in the rise of Fatah.

IV

One might think that consideration of the part which the encouragement of *fedayeen* had played in the process that had led to a comprehensive and spectacular defeat might have suggested a need to *dis*courage such activities in the aftermath of the defeat. But it didn't work like that, or not immediately. The defeated Arab regimes thought it best to adopt a defiant posture. The Arab Summit at Khartoum, in August 1967, adopted the famous "three noes": "no peace with Israel, no recognition of Israel, no negotiations with Israel. . . ."[105] The mood of Khartoum was propitious for the *fedayeen* organizations, or at least to those of them who were prepared to cooperate with the principal Arab regimes. As Rosemary Sayigh says: "For the regimes, the Resistance Movement (which they had tried to suppress before 1967) now had a specific usefulness, in diverting public opinion from the defeat, and giving it new hope."[106] Fatah and Arafat were popular, thanks mainly to Radio Damascus, and the regimes badly needed association with accepted Arab heroes. The heroes also needed the backing of the regimes.

This political context presented Arafat with a valuable opportunity, which he took, showing a notable flair for diplomacy, as well as publicity. In the period before the Six Day War, he had begun to find his dependence on Syria alone increasingly irksome; he had even earned a spell in a Damascus jail. On the eve of the war he had been seeking agreement with Nasser's P.L.O. After the war, he moved in the same direction, with more confidence. Syria and Egypt now cooperated in a major reorganization of the P.L.O., around Arafat. In 1968, the P.L.O. became a federation of *fedayeen* organizations, of which Fatah was by far the largest component. On February 4, 1969,

Arafat, while remaining leader of Fatah, became chairman of the executive committee of the Palestine National Council—effectively, chairman of the P.L.O., and symbol of the Arab fight for freedom. The P.L.O. was now supported—at least through one or more of its component organizations—by all the Arab states.

From very small beginnings—first as spokesman for a student propagandist group and then as little more than a cover and cat's-paw for Syrian intelligence—Arafat had managed to bring himself to center stage within the inter-Arab system. His Fatah did not become the purely autonomous Palestinian force it had set out to be. But it had acquired more than one patron—Egypt and Saudi Arabia, as well as Syria—and so a certain freedom of maneuver. In addition, Arafat's status as symbol of the Arab struggle gave him significant leverage in his dealings with his patrons and with other Arab regimes.

Arafat at this time was an extremely lucky politician, as well as a clever one. The very magnitude of the disaster in which he had helped to involve the Arabs, and the Palestinians in particular, resulted in a huge access of prestige and influence to him personally, and to the movement under his control. But the condition of this prestige and influence was continuation on the old hair-raising course, of which they constituted the reward.

V

In the aftermath of the Six Day War, the Arab world, with the politic encouragement of the Arab regimes, expected a great increase in *fedayeen* activity. (For the regimes, the *fedayeen* provided a means of palliating the humiliation of their defeat, while escaping at least some of the consequences of direct military action, by the regimes, against Israel.) Still more recruits and money poured into the reinstituted P.L.O., and especially into Fatah. Yet the basic problem remained, after the war, as before the war. *Fedayeen* activity would bring large-scale Israeli retaliation, with which the Arab states were not capable of coping. Syria had handled that problem before the war by insuring that the *fedayeen* raids should be launched from Jordan and Lebanon, so that those states would receive the retaliation. Nasser, who had opposed that strategy before the war, now fell in with it. Damascus was calling the tune.

Egypt and Syria, the strongest of the Arab states, were easily able to control the limited number of Palestinians admitted to their territories. Israel's two other Arab neighbors, Jordan and Lebanon, were much weaker in relation to far larger Palestinian populations on their territory. The regimes of both countries were unpopular in the Arab world; the *fedayeen* were popular, at least in the abstract, and at a distance. There was general support, outside Jordan and Lebanon, for the idea of the liberation of Palestine by the *fedayeen*, based in Jordan and Lebanon only.

Arafat moved his headquarters, with Syria's approval and Hussein's acquiescence, from Damascus to Amman. In Lebanon, the Government at first tried to resist being drawn in. But Palestinian leaders in Lebanon, backed by the Arab regimes—and by the "outs" within the Lebanese system—demanded the right to organize as *fedayeen*. There were violent clashes between the Palestinians and Lebanese forces, and it became clear that the Lebanese Army—made up of Muslim enlisted men, under Maronite officers—could not be relied on in such a situation. The Lebanese President, Charles Hélou, appealed for Nasser to mediate. Nasser agreed. There were negotiations at Cairo involving Yasser Arafat (representing the P.L.O.), Emil al-Bustani (Lebanese Chief of Staff) and Mahmud Riyad (Egyptian Foreign Minister). The negotiations resulted in the (secret) Cairo Agreement of November 3, 1969. In exchange for a meaningless recognition by the P.L.O. of "Lebanon's sovereignty and the authority of its Government," the Lebanese side recognized the P.L.O.'s right to act from Lebanon against Israel, thus scrapping the Israel-Lebanon Armistice Agreement of twenty years before.[107]

VI

In Jordan, in the immediate aftermath of the Six Day War, relations between the P.L.O.—or Fatah at least—and the host Government seemed reasonably good. In March 1968, at Karameh, Fatah and Jordanian forces together inflicted relatively high casualties—twenty-three dead—on an Israeli armored column. This exploit was hailed with enthusiasm throughout the Arab world, where it was seen as a major defeat for Israel. For a short time, Hussein even spoke of himself as a *fedayeen*.

The entente between Hussein and Arafat, in this period, could probably only have survived if the *fedayeen* had succeeded in implanting themselves—as was originally hoped—as an underground resistance based on the population of the West Bank. Arafat tried that, and failed. That failure left the East Bank as the *fedayeen*'s logical base for their operations against Israel. This was bound to set them on a collision course with Jordan.[108]

All the same, the collision might have been deferred, or even avoided—by concentrating *fedayeen* activity in a Lebanon base—if things had been left to Arafat and Hussein: two politic and pragmatic leaders (if we allow for their particular circumstances, and the requirements of their general context). But neither Arafat nor anyone else was in control of the P.L.O. The P.L.O., despite its name, was not an organization at all. It was a name, and a forum, for a miscellaneous collection of paramilitary factions, some of them backed by individual Arab countries, for reasons which might have little enough to do with liberating Palestine. Such a collection of factions was vulnerable, as the Arab states themselves were vulnerable, to the self-destructive urge to overbid—the obsession with pacesetting.

In the case of the P.L.O. in Jordan, the pace was set, in the late sixties, by George Habash's small but hyperactive Popular Front for the Liberation of Palestine, closely followed by its breakaway organization, the Popular Democratic Front for the Liberation of Palestine, led by Nayif Hawatmeh. The P.F.L.P. was backed by Iraq, not averse to causing trouble both for Jordan and for Fatah and its Syrian backers.

Proclaiming that "the road to Tel Aviv lies through Amman," the P.F.L.P. and the P.D.F.L.P. competed in an attempt to bring about a revolution in Jordan, which they hoped would be followed by other revolutions in the Arab world. They also competed in spectacular acts of international terrorism, culminating, in early September 1970, in the hijacking of four international civil airliners, three of which were brought to a desert airstrip in northern Jordan, where passengers were held hostage, after the planes themselves were blown up.

Hussein was now faced with the stark choice of acting against the *fedayeen* organizations or risking the loss of the rest of his kingdom, either to the P.L.O. revolutionaries or to an Israeli invasion, backed by the United States, which had been deeply angered by the hijackings: one of the planes was a Pan American 747.

Hussein decided to move against the P.L.O.; interestingly, he made no distinction between the "extremists" and the others; he wanted to get rid of the lot. Unlike the Lebanese Government, Hussein had an army willing to undertake this task. Jordan's fighting troops were mostly Bedouins, who hated the Palestinians. But the main question was: What help would the Arab states, all of which nominally supported the P.L.O., now give to the P.L.O. forces in Jordan in their hour of need?

In the event, only one Arab State gave any material help. Palestinians believed that Hussein had Nasser's "tacit approval." Iraq, whose support for the P.F.L.P. had done most to put the whole P.L.O. at risk, did nothing, although it had troops in Jordan—theoretically on their way to Israel—and had threatened to intervene.

Only Syria intervened on the side of the P.L.O.; or to be more precise, one faction in Syria's ruling group intervened. The Government sent in more than a hundred tanks to fight the Jordanians. But the Minister for Defense, Hafez al-Assad, was also head of the Syrian Air Force, and refused air support for his country's tanks. The Syrian armored force was badly defeated by Jordanian ground and air forces and withdrew, leaving a large number of vehicles captured or destroyed.

It has been variously suggested that Assad feared war with Israel, or that he was influenced by Soviet disapproval of Syrian intervention.[109] It seems worth noting that the domestic effects of Assad's course—the destruction of the armored force that accepted a rival faction's order, and the preservation of the Air Force that accepted Assad's order—altered the internal balance of forces in Syria in Assad's favor. That that would be the probable effect of the grounding of the Air Force was hardly a circumstance likely to escape the attention of the most successful of the Machiavellians of Damascus. In any case, two months later, Assad seized supreme power in Syria, and became one of the dominant figures in the Middle East.

After the repulse of the Syrians, and toward the end of Black September—as the Palestinians called it—Nasser convened a meeting of Arab leaders in Cairo, to which Hussein and Arafat were summoned. On September 27, a cease-fire was signed, with the P.L.O. forces on the defensive. On the following day, Nasser died, and was succeeded by Anwar Sadat. In the following year Hussein, unopposed by any Arab State, completed the eviction of all P.L.O. forces from Jordanian territory. It was now only in crippled, crumbling Lebanon that the P.L.O. forces could find bases for autonomous activities.

These activities, in the period 1971–1973, mainly took the form of spectacular acts of international terrorism, as practiced by the P.F.L.P. and P.D.F.L.P. in the run-up to Black September. Fatah, which had hitherto followed a relatively restrained policy in these matters, now relieved the frustration of its members by setting up a "cover" organization, nominally independent but in fact an arm of Fatah: the Black September Organization,[110] for the purpose of international terror. It was Black September which assassinated the Jordanian Prime Minister, Wasfi al-Tal, on the steps of the Sheraton Hotel in Cairo, on November 28, 1971. It was also Black September which, in September 1972, carried out what remains the most publicity-effective of all terrorist coups: the disruption of the Munich Olympics by the kidnapping of nine Israeli athletes, all of whom were killed, along with some of their captors, in the course of a rescue attempt. Munich was generally condoned, if not admired, in the Arab world. "The only forthright condemnation," says David Hirst, "came from King Hussein. . . ."[111] It was otherwise with the next major exploit of Black September. On March 1, 1973, armed men of Black September took over the Saudi Embassy in Khartoum and murdered three of the ambassador's diplomatic guests: in Arab terms, a far more atrocious act than the killing of Israeli athletes in Germany.

Khartoum was all the more embarrassing in that the Black September cover blew, and the Arab world could see that Fatah was responsible. The killers had demanded the release, among others, of Abu Daud, a Fatah leader imprisoned in Jordan. Abu Daud now declared, over Jordanian television: "There is no such thing as Black September." He identified the controllers of Black September operations as three leading Fatah men, including Arafat's deputy, Abu Iyad.

Fatah, under the impact of its defeat in Jordan, had gotten very far from the principles of its foundation. If it continued along these lines, it risked becoming as isolated as the P.F.L.P.—and as cut off from Saudi funds. Arafat pulled back, in a characteristic blaze of publicity, denouncing hijackers, "renegades" and "mercenaries," and promising the punishment of those responsible.

Fatah's fortunes were at a low ebb in the first half of 1973, at the end of its Black September phase. But Fatah was floated off again, on the flowing tide of Arab optimism following the Yom Kippur War.

VII

Fatah had helped to precipitate the Six Day War, but neither Fatah nor the P.L.O. had much to do with the calculations which led

Above, Yasser Arafat at the seventh Arab Summit Conference at Rabat, October 1974. It was this conference which declared Arafat's P.L.O. to be "the sole legitimate representative of the Palestinian people." Arafat was here awarded head-of-state status, and the nameplate in front of him says "Palestine."

Below, King Hussein of Jordan at the 1974 Rabat Conference. Rabat, with its endorsement of the P.L.O., was widely considered a setback for Hussein, whose forces had driven the P.L.O. out of Jordan three years before. But Hussein voted with the others for recognition of the P.L.O. as "sole legitimate representative of the Palestinian people."

Bottom, President Anwar Sadat of Egypt at the 1974 Rabat Conference. Sadat also voted for the P.L.O. as "sole legitimate representative." Three years later, however, Sadat declared that the P.L.O. itself had "annulled" the Rabat recognition.

THREE PHOTOS: UPI/BETTMANN NEWSPHOTOS

to the Yom Kippur War of 1973. But the political conjuncture which followed the Yom Kippur War lifted the P.L.O. and Fatah to new heights, in the ostensible esteem of the Arab regimes, and then of all other regimes, with two exceptions.

The Arab ex-belligerents—principally Egypt and Syria—were in an equivocal position vis-à-vis the Arab world in the aftermath of the 1973 war. On the one hand, they were admired for having taken Israel by surprise and—as was thought—almost defeating the Israel Defense Forces; on the other hand, they had inexplicably agreed to a cease-fire, letting Israel live. Egypt and Syria both needed the cease-fire. But they also needed to claim that, despite the cease-fire, the struggle against Israel continued. These needs could hardly be reconciled, except by leading the Arab states in a solemn ceremony of rededication to the P.L.O. This ceremony was duly observed at the seventh Arab Summit Conference at Rabat, October 26–29, 1974.

All summit conferences have their hypocritical side, but surely the H-content at Rabat must have been one of the highest ever. There they all were, solemnly pledging their support to the P.L.O. as "sole legitimate representative of the Palestinian people." There was Hussein, who had crushed the P.L.O. forces on his own territory and driven them out. There was Assad, who, at the moment of truth, had come to the rescue of Hussein, dooming the P.L.O. in Jordan. There was Sadat, already on course to his separate peace, ditching the P.L.O. And there were the lesser actors: the representative of ruined Lebanon, in whose accelerating disintegration the P.L.O. was a principal agent; the representative of Iraq, which had egged on its friends in the P.L.O. in the activities which led to their ruin and had left them in the lurch; there were the Saudis and Sudan, humiliated and frightened at Khartoum; and there were all the rest of them, prodigal in verbal devotion to the P.L.O., and entirely passive when the object of that devotion was driven by an Arab King to its last refuge, in Lebanon. Tacitus writes of the *graves amicitiae principum:* the heavy friendships of princes. Heavy indeed, for the Palestinians, were the friendships of the princes of the Arab world.

With his Rabat laurels still fresh, Yasser Arafat went on to New York, and the General Assembly of the United Nations, where his hundred-minute "gun and olive branch" speech earned him a standing ovation from almost the entire membership on November 13, 1974. Almost: the delegation of Israel was absent, and the delegation of the United States remained seated. The delegates of the Western European countries, sworn foes to international terrorism, joined in the standing ovation for the head of Fatah and the P.L.O.

I happened to be a member, at the time, of one of the European Governments in question, the Republic of Ireland, and I asked our Foreign Minister, Garret FitzGerald, whether it was altogether wise for Ireland to be so fulsome about the P.L.O.: might there not be a precedent in relation to the I.R.A.? Garret thought not; there were indeed some terrorists in the splinter groups under the P.L.O. umbrella, but Arafat and his Fatah were the moderates. That was the general European tune at the time. I did not know then, and I am sure Garret did not, that it was Fatah, under its Black September flag of convenience, which had perpetrated the Munich kidnappings, culminating in the massacre of the hostages.

As General Alexander Haig has so well said, there is often "subterranean policy" as well as "stated policy." Stated policy is on the record; subterranean policy has to be guessed at. My own guess is that a Western European official would have talked more or less like this to a trusted colleague at this time:

"This fellow Arafat has his head well screwed on. He knows he needs the Saudis, for their money. So do we of course, especially now. So we and Arafat have *that* much in common. The Saudis think it would be a good idea for us to butter him up a bit. Help to build up his influence, as against the wild men. He won't want to hurt the Saudis, if he can help it. And the Saudis will do their best to discourage him and his friends from attacking European targets. Provided we give them a hand, build up the fellow's image and so on. Worth trying, and doesn't cost us anything. On the other hand, it *might* cost us something not to go along with the Saudis."

VIII

Certainly, that appearance at the U.N. must have done a great deal for Arafat's image and influence among ordinary Palestinians. To people who had so long suffered humiliation, both from Israelis and from Arabs, so great a demonstration of *respect,* from such an international gathering, must have brought much-needed balm. And Arafat played his part well, and dressed well for it. That *keffiyeh* and that soiled windbreaker, standing out amid the bourgeois dapperness of the General Assembly, made precisely the required point: Arafat was taking a bow, not for himself, but on behalf of the ordinary Palestinian, and in particular the rank-and-file *fedayeen*.

There must also have been a sense of expectation: a feeling that it all *meant* something. After all, the General Assembly's resolution of November 29, 1947, had legitimized the creation of the State of Israel, which came into being less than six months afterwards. Did not the proceedings of the General Assembly in 1974—which included the passage of an impeccably pro-P.L.O. resolution—reverse the earlier verdict of world opinion, and *de*legitimize the State of Israel? And should not consequences follow from that?

In fact, no practical consequences followed. The reasons why the General Assembly vote of 1947 was important have already been considered. But by 1974, General Assembly proceedings had become devalued. The superpowers were no longer interested in trying to influence those proceedings. The General Assembly had become a place for Third World countries to let off steam, and for Western Europeans to pay lip service to causes ostensibly favored by the Saudis. (If there was any serious international business to be done, requiring the use of the United Nations theater, it was now conducted in the Security Council, not the Assembly.)

The sympathy of the world's governments with the Palestinian cause was sham, like the sympathy of the Arab regimes.

But the P.L.O. had, all the same, attained a genuine, though limited, degree of international power and influence, as a result of two factors:

a. Its value to the more astute and effective Arab regimes, as an instrument for substitute action and deflection. The constant pressures for action against Israel could be met by "support for the P.L.O." And the dangerous consequences of action against Israel, and even of "support for the P.L.O.," could be deflected by insuring that the P.L.O. operated out of someone else's territory: Jordan, say, or Lebanon.

b. The proved capacity of the P.L.O.'s components to conduct major international terrorist operations, combined with a somewhat less certain capacity, on the part of the P.L.O. leadership, to check such operations. The concept of "deflection" is important here too.

IX

After Rabat and New York, Arafat was to go on to many more journeys, and more international glory, of the same kind. But the *fedayeen* of the P.L.O. remained stuck among the rocks of southern Lebanon, and were now drawn into the incipient civil war which their presence there had helped to set in motion. The Lebanese Civil War broke out at Beirut in March 1975. By the following year, the P.L.O. was openly involved in the fighting, on the side of the anti-Maronite forces. The P.L.O., which had earlier announced that the road to Tel Aviv passes through Amman, now found that it passed also through the Christian towns of Lebanon. As Abu Iyad, Arafat's deputy—and the reputed head of Black September—declared in May 1976, at Beirut: "The way to Palestine passes through Lebanon . . . it passes through Ain Tura and Ayun al-Siman [Christian strongholds] and it must reach Junya [the Christian capital]."[112]

Hafez al-Assad had, however, no intention of letting the P.L.O. take that route to Palestine. Syrians had always considered that Lebanon is part of Syria, and Assad had now the opportunity of intervening in Lebanon, in the Syrian-approved role of arbiter of Lebanon's destinies. In April 1976, Syrian regular forces intervened directly, initially supporting Christians and attacking Syria's natural allies in the P.L.O., Muslims and "Leftists" (who were really mostly Druze). But it was not Assad's policy at this time to evict the P.L.O. from Lebanon, as Hussein had done from Jordan. He simply aimed to cut them down to size, and confine them to a buffer zone[113] in southern Lebanon, between Israel and that part of Lebanon controlled by Syria. In that zone, the P.L.O. was free to try to liberate Palestine, and free to take the consequences of that attempt, on its own.

By 1977, there were an estimated 222,000 Syrian troops in Lebanon, and much of Lebanon was controlled by Syria, directly or indirectly.

The Arab summits at Riyadh (October 18, 1976) and Cairo (October 26, 1976) in effect ratified what Syria had done. The role of Syrian forces in Lebanon was recognized under the elegant title of La Force Arabe de Dissuasion. It was the P.L.O., primarily, which had been "dissuaded," with the tacit approval of all those who had paid homage to it at Rabat.

X

Fuad Jabber, of the Institute for Palestine Studies, in Beirut, concludes his very illuminating study, "The Palestinian Resistance and Inter-Arab Politics,"[114] with the sagacious and pregnant words: "While the valuable asset of popular support has permitted the Resistance to counteract in many ways the weakening effects of dependence, the Palestinian national movement is likely to remain at the mercy of the dynamics of inter-Arab politics—as it has been since its inception—so long as it lacks a substantial degree of structural unity and ideological cohesion."

Ordinary Palestinians, it seems, have their own way of expressing what it feels like to be "at the mercy of the dynamics of inter-Arab politics." Nels Johnson, traveling in Palestine after the events narrated in this section, found "several different individuals who referred to themselves . . . as *qamis uthman*. . . . One man explained it this way:

" 'We are only Uthman's Shirt. After the Caliph Uthman was murdered, leaders would say, "I do this in the name of Uthman," when they wanted people to believe them. But they only used his name. They waved his bloody shirt. Today we Palestinians are Uthman's Shirt.' "[115]

10

DOING WITHOUT
DIPLOMACY
1967-1973

Israel has no foreign policy, only a defense policy.
—MOSHE DAYAN

HUBRIS AND EUPHORIA had had their orgy in the second half of May and the first days of June 1967 in Cairo and Damascus and other Arab cities.

After the Six Day War, Hubris and Euphoria shook off the dust of the Arab cities and took up residence, in a quieter and more insidious style, in Jerusalem.

The influence of the twin scourges was not felt at once in the shaping and conduct of Government policy. In the immediate aftermath of the dazzling victory, Levi Eshkol's Government of National Unity was prepared to surrender large quantities—though never all—of the occupied territories, in exchange for peace. On June 19, 1967, the Cabinet adopted a four-point resolution, which it communicated to the Government of the United States on June 22, but did not make public.

According to this resolution, Israel was prepared, in exchange for a full peace treaty, to withdraw to the international border with Egypt, with the provisos that Sinai was to be demilitarized, and Israel's freedom of movement guaranteed in the Straits of Tiran and the Suez Canal. Israel was also prepared to withdraw to the inter-

national border with Syria, with the Golan Heights to be demilitarized. About the West Bank and the Gaza Strip, the resolution was
unforthcoming, telling the Americans only that these matters "would
be considered separately, as would the problem of the Palestine
refugees."[1]

In fact the Government, as then constituted, was not in a position
to negotiate about the West Bank at all. The Labor members might
have been prepared to negotiate on the basis of some version of the
Allon Plan, if they could have found any Arab, or even American,
takers for that one. But for Begin and his followers—who remained
part of the Government for three years after the Six Day War—
"Judea and Samaria" were utterly nonnegotiable: an integral part of
Eretz Israel. This division of opinion within the Government remained amicable, because it remained entirely academic. For Hussein—the indicated partner for Israel under the plan—to say "Allon
Plan" was the same as to say "nonnegotiable."

What seems remarkable, in retrospect, about the resolution of
June 19 is that Begin and his colleagues should have been prepared,
at that early stage, to surrender Sinai, albeit conditionally. It seems
probable that Begin, and other Cabinet members, at this point expected great American pressure, of the kind that had forced Israel to
withdraw from Sinai in 1957, and that they were prepared to sacrifice
Sinai and the Golan in order to hold on to Judea and Samaria.

Abba Eban knew that no pressure of anything like the intensity
of which he had borne most of the brunt in 1957 was to be expected
in 1967. Partly this was because he himself had maneuvered so patiently and skillfully, in both 1957 and 1967, precisely in order to
insure that no such pressure would be applied again. Perhaps he had
maneuvered all too well, for Israel's good, and for his own usefulness
as Foreign Minister. Unlike the Sinai victory of 1956, which was part
of a wider operation condemned and then wrecked by the United
States, 1967 was a victory in a war to which the United States had
given its informal assent; a victory too in whose reflected glory
neither the Johnson Administration nor a wide section of the American
public were disinclined to bask. This was a time when the fact that
the war in Vietnam was unwinnable was beginning to sink in. A win
for "our side," using our arms, over adversaries armed and backed
by the Communists, was a much-needed piece of good news. So
there was no serious pressure on Israel during the remaining nineteen
months of the Johnson Administration.

II

No pressure, and also no present willingness on the part of the Arabs to negotiate anything at all with Israel. The first meeting of the Arab states after the war—the Khartoum Conference, August 19 to September 1, 1967—issued its famous "three noes": no peace with Israel; no recognition of Israel; no negotiations with Israel concerning any Palestinian territory.

Actually, the proceedings at Khartoum were much more pragmatic, and more interesting, than might be inferred from the bravado of the "three noes." Khartoum was preeminently a case where Kissinger's Law applies: appearance and reality seldom meet in the Middle East.

The real business at Khartoum was a deal between Nasser and the oil-rich states. In exchange for a direly needed annual subsidy of $225 million to Egypt, Nasser undertook to cease his propaganda attacks against the monarchical and otherwise "reactionary" regimes, to begin the withdrawal of his troops from Yemen and generally to cease his old revolutionary carryings-on.[2]

The Nasser who survived the Six Day War—which he called "the setback"—was unlike the old Nasser in some important ways. By his deal with the Saudis and their like, Nasser implicitly abandoned his great Pan-Arab dream. Arab states, and their leaders, were henceforward to be treated with respect, not scorned, as tiresome and ephemeral obstacles to the fulfillment of Arab unity, under Egyptian leadership.

The deal, and the abandonment of the dream, had two important and closely related corollaries. The first was that if Egypt could no longer aim at leading the Arab world into unity, there was no longer much point in Egypt's courting popularity in the Arab world. Even the main *means* of courting popularity—radio attacks on unpopular Arab regimes—had been abjured. And if popularity was no longer essential, or altogether feasible, there was a liberating converse: *un*-popularity could be acceptable, if the interests of Egypt required it. Nasser never drew the full consequences of those propositions, but his successor, Anwar Sadat, was to do so.

The second corollary was that Egypt was no longer the slave of its own propaganda, and of its image in the Arab world. Since Nasser and his successor no longer cared much about the crowds of Damascus or Baghdad—whatever about those of Cairo—they could afford to take their own time, in the light of their own national interests, without being precipitated into spectacular but imprudent initiatives. All this made Egypt a potentially more formidable adversary for Israel, but it also made Egypt a potential treaty partner.

Functionally, the importance of Israel as a subject for discussion and—in one respect—initiative at Khartoum was that it served to disguise the essentially Thermidorian nature of what really happened at Khartoum. The Arab revolution had been quietly put on the shelf, but the tone and style of the Arab revolution could be sustained when confined to the subject of Israel. Cairo Radio could no longer rant about the Arab kings, but about Israel it could go on ranting to its heart's content, for some years to come.

Khartoum's support for the *fedayeen* served a similar purpose. Who could say the Arab revolution was over, when the revolutionary war was actually being waged by the *fedayeen?* After Khartoum, Israel became the sole objective of all that was left of the Arab revolution.

According to the Lebanese thinker Fouad Ajami: "The Arab-Israeli conflict itself, on which the radicals depended as a catalyst of revolutionary upheaval, was in reality a conservatizing force."[3] It is an interesting thought, and directly contrary to what had long been the received wisdom of the British Foreign Office and the U.S. State Department. For the Khartoum and post-Khartoum period at least, it is the Ajami thesis which seems to hold. Saudi support for the *fedayeen* deflected attention from the close Saudi association with Israel's great backer, the United States. And Egypt, also supporting the *fedayeen*, had now debarred itself from exposing the equivocal nature of the Saudi support, and indeed from attacking *any* Arab State for alleged or real subservience to the West.

In these conditions, Israel's existence seemed quite compatible with other American interests in the region. The existence of Israel may have even been helpful to those interests by lending a certain distant charisma of *jihad* to otherwise prosaic oil sheikhs. Israel's *existence* was not a threat, but Israel's continued occupation of certain territories involved high risks.

III

The equivocal, or perfidious, nature of the support of the Arab states for the Palestinians has been discussed in the last chapter. But there was another form of Arab hostility to Israel at this time: a form which had nothing to do with Palestinians, and which was sincere and serious. This was the resentment of the defeated Arab states at the continued presence of Israeli forces in their own territories. This resentment was most powerful in the strongest Arab state: Egypt. The Golan Heights were of relatively little significance to Syria; in Jordan, Hussein, however deeply he resented the loss of the West Bank, knew that there was little he could do about it. About all he could hope to do for the moment was to hold on to what was left of his little kingdom, against the pressure of the *fedayeen*.

For Egypt, however, the continued presence of Israeli troops all along the east bank of the Suez Canal, closing the Canal to shipping, was intolerable. The Canal was of immense importance to Egypt, in terms both of revenue and of prestige. Nasser had to be seen making some attempt to get it back. After leading the ringing negations of Khartoum, he could hardly travel the path of negotiation with Israel; at least, not for the moment. Nasser felt himself forced into the apparently hopeless expedient of renewed hostilities against the victors of the Six Day War, immediately after their victory.

During 1968, the Egyptian artillery carried out sporadic bombardments against Israeli positions on the other side of the Canal. In February 1969, Nasser announced a policy of "constant military activity" along the Canal. The so-called War of Attrition began in March. It lasted until August 1970.

IV

For Israel's military planners, the idea of a war of attrition was anathema. In a long war of attrition between Israel and Egypt, with approximately equal casualty rates on both sides, Israel would slowly bleed to death. So it was necessary to deter attrition by the use of "asymmetrical response," retaliation on a scale far exceeding any individual provocation, as in the case of *fedayeen* raids.

That is a principle of general application, understandable in Israel's peculiar predicament. But in this case, the Government of Israel was led, for a time, to push "deterrence" to extreme and dangerous lengths.

The Soviet Union was already fairly heavily involved in Egypt, re-equipping the Egyptian forces, though not, at this time, with the most modern equipment. Nasser's war of attrition, Israel's retaliations and Soviet reactions to Israel's retaliations began to carry a growing risk of direct Soviet intervention, with a proportionate risk of superpower confrontation.

The situation was complicated, and its risks greatly increased, by the fact that, from the autumn of 1969 on, Golda Meir's Government— formed after the death of Levi Eshkol—was receiving conflicting signals from Richard Nixon's Byzantine Administration. The Secretary of State, William Rogers, was pressing for a cease-fire, and a negotiated peace. The President's National Security Adviser, Henry Kissinger, seems at this time to have been encouraging escalation. Israel's ambassador to Washington, Yitzhak Rabin, who was close to Kissinger, cabled Jerusalem on September 19, 1969: "The National Security Council is considering the impact of Israeli military operations against Egypt. . . . Nasser's standing would be undermined, and that would in turn weaken the Soviet position in the region. . . . *The willingness to supply us with arms depends more on stepping up our military activity than on reducing it* [my italics]."[4]

Golda Meir seems to have found this advice congenial. On her visit to Washington in September 1969, she established a system of "direct communication," through Rabin and Kissinger, bypassing her own Foreign Office and ignoring the State Department. Rabin describes this peculiar system with some complacency:

> Kissinger, acting on behalf of the President, would approach me, and I would transmit his messages directly to Golda's personal assistant, Simcha Dinitz, in Jerusalem. The premier would do the same in reverse. At the President's request, Golda approved the suggestion. If this proposal reflected a distressing lack of confidence in Eban and Rogers, I certainly was not to blame for it. . . . This now became the principal mode of contact between the two countries on the most important issues.[5]

The fruits of this "mode of contact" were quite speedily evident, in escalating conflict, and rejection of diplomatic efforts.

On October 25, 1969, Ambassador Rabin (a former Chief of

Staff) recommended "deep penetration" bombing of Egyptian targets. In the context of the "principal mode of contact," Golda Meir had to understand this unusual piece of ambassadorial advice as coming ultimately from the President of the United States, through Kissinger.

Abba Eban has recalled that, in this period, the Israeli Cabinet was "divided between those willing to take the risks of a deep penetration of Egypt's air space for massive attacks on Cairo, and those who feared that this would bring the Soviet Union to Egypt's defense, with a consequent disturbance of the strategic balance."[6]

Eban, obviously, was among the latter group. But Israel's Foreign Minister, during this period, was effectively outranked and overruled by his own ambassador. Eban acknowledges that the "decisive element" in the Cabinet discussion was Rabin's advice. "Rabin bombarded us with cables urging escalation against Egypt and other Arab states. He clearly believed that there were some people in Washington who were sympathetic to such a course."[7] Golda Meir believed the same thing. And it is impossible that she could have relied on Rabin's version of Kissinger's approach, if it had not accorded with her own impression, when she met Kissinger herself.

The debate about escalation was now interrupted by a diplomatic initiative. On October 29, 1969, Secretary of State William Rogers offered an interpretation of Security Council Resolution 242, as affecting Egypt and Israel. He proposed "the international frontier between Egypt and Israel" as "the secure and recognized border between the two countries." There would be "a formal state of peace" between the two, negotiations on Gaza and Sharm al-Sheik, and demilitarized zones.

In laying these proposals before Egypt and the Soviet Union, as it did, the State Department had some reason to believe that they might be acceptable to Israel. They were fully in line with the four-point resolution adopted by the Israeli Cabinet on June 19, 1967, and communicated to the Americans on June 22. But the Government of Israel no longer regarded the 1967 resolution as binding. Dayan told Rabin that the Government had gone back on these resolutions in 1968. If so, they seem to have done so without specifically notifying the Americans, which seems odd since it was obviously for the Americans—only—that the document was prepared, and it had been handed to Dean Rusk by Abba Eban.[8]

In any case, for Golda Meir, relying on "the principal mode of contact," Rogers and his initiative were of secondary account. The real message—coming indirectly, as she believed, from the President himself—was not Negotiate. It was Escalate.

On November 17, the Government of Israel delivered its negative answer. In accordance with the courtesies of the new "mode of contact" system, the answer was delivered not to the Secretary of State himself, but to Henry Kissinger, by Ambassador Rabin.

The Israelis had good reason to distrust the State Department, and to be ready to bypass it, when absolutely necessary. But to treat this great institution so unceremoniously seems imprudent. "Respect, but suspect" had been the sensible motto of David Ben-Gurion about any American initiative. Golda Meir applied this maxim distributively, confining the respect to the White House, and the suspicion to the State Department. This seems a mistake, on both counts.

On January 7, 1970, the Israeli Air Force made its first "deep penetration" strike into Egypt. "The Rogers Plan," noted a triumphant Rabin, "was in its death-throes."[9]

Rabin, in his memoirs, implies that the escalation of the war— taken on his advice, apparently at the prompting of Henry Kissinger (who was to succeed Rogers as Secretary of State in September 1973)—was not followed by any untoward consequences for Israel. The reality is rather different.

V

On January 22, 1970, a fortnight after the start of Israel's "deep penetration" bombing, Nasser flew to Moscow. The object of his mission was to get effective air-defense, surface-to-air missiles— SAM-3s—with Russian crews to operate them. His Russian hosts tried to stall. Brezhnev feared "serious international implications . . . the making of a crisis between the Soviet Union and the United States." Then Nasser put his cards on the table. If Moscow was not prepared to help him, " 'in the same way that America helps Israel,' " then Nasser would step down, announcing that, since the Russians had failed him, he had decided to " 'hand over to a pro-American President.' " At this, according to Mohamed Heikal, Brezhnev got to his feet, protesting: " 'Comrade Nasser, don't talk like this. You are the leader . . .' " Nasser interrupted him: " 'I am a leader who is bombed every day in his own country, whose army is exposed and whose people are naked. I have the courage to tell our people the unfortunate truth—that, whether they like it or not, the Americans are masters of the world.' "[10]

After a meeting of the whole Politburo—attended, for the first time, in peacetime, by twelve Soviet marshals (according to Heikal)—the Kremlin decided to give Nasser everything he asked for, and much more. The Soviet Union was now fully committed to the modernization and retraining of Egypt's defense forces. Israel's "deep penetration" raids into Egypt had succeeded in causing a major shift in the military balance of the region, in favor of Egypt, and against Israel.

The Government of Israel had, of course, expected an adverse reaction from the Soviets, though hardly as effective an adverse reaction as they got. But the Government—or at least Mrs. Meir and her ambassador in Washington—were fully confident of the unquestioning support of the other, and superior, superpower. They believed that they had established unprecedentedly close relations with the President of the United States. They also believed that, in turning down the Rogers Plan, and comprehensively snubbing the whole State Department, and then sharply escalating the war with Egypt, they were doing just what President Nixon expected of them. Perhaps they had been, but if so the President changed his mind, no doubt because of the increased risk of superpower confrontation.

Quite the contrary to the euphoric expectations of Rabin and Mrs. Meir, the United States Government now began to apply quiet, sustained, and eventually effective, pressure on Israel to stop escalating, accept a cease-fire and start negotiating, on the basis of some version of 242, and the Rogers proposals.

Gideon Rafael, the extremely astute Director-General of Israel's Foreign Office at the time, provides a subtle, understated and convincing analysis of Mrs. Meir's position in the first half of 1970. In Golda Meir's visit to Washington in September 1969, she had tried to avoid the topic of peace negotiations—since her Government was now "fundamentally divided" on that matter—and to concentrate on arms procurement: "what Golda used to call with housewifely joviality 'her shopping list.' "[11] She believed that, since the President said nothing about negotiations, the State Department's insistence on the need for them could safely be ignored. "She was strengthened in her belief by Ambassador Rabin's general aversion to institutions entrusted with the conduct of foreign affairs"—a lovely touch that, from the career head of the institution of which the ambassador was nominally a servant—"and [by] Dr. Kissinger's advice to pay attention only to what the President said."

Rafael goes on: "But the presidential security adviser failed to enlighten her that Presidents in meetings with foreign heads of government prefer sometimes to leave certain controversial matters untouched, relying on their Foreign Secretaries to fulfill the less pleasant duties."

In Rafael's opinion—and it is a weighty one—the Prime Minister, relying on inexpert advice, had missed the significance of the Rogers initiative. The Rogers Plan should have been seen as "a warning sign, pointing to Washington's resolve to terminate the escalation of the fighting and the widening of the Russian involvement."

Golda Meir was now about to get into some trouble with her shopping. She had received from Nixon promises of new aircraft and electronic warfare equipment. On returning to Israel she boasted that "her shopping bag was heavier than when she had left." But it was not in fact heavier. Delivery had indeed been promised. But delivery was delayed.

Rafael explains the technique of the "subtle squeeze":

> The United States had its own idiom, which was more of a sign language. Certain things which were expected to happen, just did not happen. Rarely would the administration inform Israel that it had taken countermeasures because of a certain action or policy disapproved by it. American diplomacy preferred the silent treatment, and it was often rather late in the day before its meaning dawned on Israel's policymakers. Suddenly certain delivery schedules would be delayed. Financial aid, previously promised on the highest level, encountered unexpected obstacles and the whole matter had to go through new processing.

As Rafael hints, this was far too subtle a message for Golda Meir. By March 1970—a little more than a month after Nasser's successful shopping spree in Moscow—the message had still not gotten through to Israel's policy makers. Washington decided to drop the silent treatment. The despised State Department notified the Israeli Embassy in Washington of its intention of making a public statement about holding Israel's arms request in abeyance for an undetermined period. Stunned, but still hopeful, the Embassy turned to the White House, but got no response. The famous "back channel" was blocked. Contrary to Ambassador Rabin's interpretation of the realities of power in Washington, the State Department was speaking for the President. Mrs. Meir's Government was now advised to make a vehement public protest, followed by "an appeal to public opinion": mobilization of the pro-Israel lobby in America with the object of making the Nixon Administration make a U-turn.

While the Government was still contemplating these heroic measures, Gideon Rafael, that wily tactician, decided it was time to take a hand. Up to now, Ambassador Rabin had had it all his own way, and the professionals in the Israeli Foreign Office had been ruthlessly pushed to one side. But now the State Department had put the boot in, which had been thought to be impossible, and the Government of Israel was suffering. Rafael seems to have sensed—he is of course discreet about it—that the cries from Washington of the terrible ambassadorial cuckoo in the Israeli Foreign Office nest could no longer sound quite so beguiling as they did of yore, in the ears of her whom they had most beguiled. Golda Meir might now, at last, feel the need for the advice of a professional.

Rafael had served under Mrs. Meir when she had been Foreign Minister, and he sounds as if he liked her personally, though he was not inclined to overrate her flair for foreign affairs. He now rang her up. She asked him around at once and offered him, as she usually did to her visitors, "a cup of strong and tasty American coffee, brewed by herself in her own special way which was her best-guarded secret." Over this brew, he dissuaded her.

Gideon—whom I knew quite well at the United Nations—is good at every diplomatic exercise, but perhaps particularly strong in dissuasion. With his modest, faintly rueful manner, he manages to convey to the dissuadee that both are engaged in a joint exercise in exploration, as a result of which the outlines of that from which it is advisable to be dissuaded become clear, to both parties. In this case, he had a clinching *argumentum ad feminam* in reserve, which I am sure he allowed to loom, barely discernible, in the mist. This was "the fact that, after she had pointed to her bulging shopping bag upon her return from her meeting with the President, it would be politically unwise and diplomatically harmful to divulge that its size had dwindled."

Golda Meir backed quickly away from her contemplated public confrontation with Nixon. It took much longer to persuade her to agree to what Washington wanted, beginning with a cease-fire. It is, on the face of it, peculiar that her Government should have been so unwilling for a cease-fire. The justification for escalation had been that it was required to deter attrition: a rational proposition in itself, but hardly compatible with unwillingness to agree to a cease-fire, even if Egypt was willing to agree to one.

It seems that the Meir Government was still, even at this late date, in the grip of the vision prompted by all those Rabin telegrams. The Government hoped to destroy Nasser politically by bombing Egyptian cities. In the matter of "toppling Nasser," Golda Meir's mind seemed perilously close to the obsessive condition of Anthony Eden's in 1956.

Golda Meir had another, and more singular, reason for rejecting a cease-fire. This was that if she accepted a cease-fire, on the American terms, Israel would be accepting Security Council Resolution 242. It seems to have slipped her mind that Israel had *already*, in 1968, publicly and solemnly declared its acceptance of 242, which was much to Israel's advantage at the time.[12] Levi Eshkol, the then Prime Minister, had approved the acceptance of 242 and maintained his acceptance in the teeth of objection from Moshe Dayan.[13] Yet Eshkol's successor had by now convinced herself—and several of her colleagues were even more convinced—that what had publicly happened, on a matter of vital importance to Israel, had never happened at all.

This wishful amnesia is symptomatic of a somewhat unhealthy mental condition to which a number of important public figures in Israel were subject in the period between June 1967 and October 1973.

Meanwhile the American pressure was kept up, tactfully, but firmly: Rogers made his public "holding in abeyance" speech on March 23. The very able American ambassador in Tel Aviv, Walworth Barbour, presenting the Rogers text to Golda Meir, threw in some sweeteners; not quite everything would be "held in abeyance," just yet. He also threw in a silky word of reassurance, with a faint aftertaste of menace. "The ambassador assured the Prime Minister that the relations between the United States and Israel were to remain as steadfast and firm as they had been during all the years of Israel's nationhood."[14] No Prime Minister of Israel could take exception to that one; but, after the door had closed behind the ambassador, even the intrepid Golda Meir might well have shivered a little as she took in the significance of three words in the ambassador's assurance: "all the years."

The relations could be as "steadfast and firm" as they had been, for example, in the mid-fifties, in the days of John Foster Dulles and the Baghdad Pact. . . . Or they could be as "steadfast and firm,"

God forbid, as they had been in the dreadful days of early November, 1956, when Israel had been simultaneously threatened by both superpowers: with annihilation by the Soviet Union; and, by the United States, with abandonment in the face of the Soviet threat.

With admirably controlled finesse, the ambassador had put the Prime Minister under notice that the idyllic period of relations immediately after the Six Day War, under L.B.J. and then in the early months of Nixon, was not to be taken as having established a permanent norm. The relationship had had its ups and downs before, and was likely to have them again. Right now, it was a bit down. The down would continue until Mrs. Meir's Government stopped bombing Egypt, and stopped pretending that it had never accepted Resolution 242.

In the following month, the Israelis noticed for the first time that the Soviet Union was moving into Egypt to a far greater extent than ever before. Israel was now faced with a modified, or incipient, form of the great fork of November 1956. It was running the risk of confrontation with one superpower, without being able to count on full support by the other, if it continued on its present course.

The temerarious Prime Minister, nonetheless, persisted in that now hair-raising course throughout the spring and early summer of 1970. The risk she was running was nothing less than the total extinction of Israel. Henry Kissinger, for reasons of his own, once asked the Soviet ambassador in Washington, Anatoly Dobrynin, how the Soviet Union would react if its troops in Egypt were captured by Israelis. Dobrynin replied, "If the Israelis threaten us, we will wipe them out within two days. I can assure you our plans are made for this eventuality."

Finally, on July 30, Israeli fighters shot down four Soviet planes, with their *Russian* pilots, about thirty kilometers west of the Canal. On the following day, the Government of Israel accepted a cease-fire, and the application of Resolution 242, "in all its parts": Rogers' wording.

Golda Meir had at last jammed on the brakes, very near to the edge of the cliff.

VI

At the beginning of August 1970, Secretary of State William Rogers could work toward a negotiated peace between Egypt and

Israel—the most urgent priority for the United States in the Middle East—with reasonably good hopes of success.

As far as the Egyptian side was concerned, the State Department knew—through the Saudis—that Nasser, at Khartoum, had thrown in the sponge, as far as Pan-Arab leadership was concerned. Nasser's objectives now were limited Egyptian objectives, and the overriding one was to get the Israelis away from the Canal and out of Sinai. If there was no other way of bringing that about, Nasser might well go to war again, once the Soviet military buildup of Egypt had reached a sufficiently advanced stage. But if the same objective could be attained by peaceful means, "the new Nasser" would not be too worried about what the Palestinians, or any other Arabs, might think about such a transaction.

There was more than one Rogers Plan. Shortly after the proposals for withdrawal from Sinai, Rogers put forward, separately, proposals for withdrawals from the West Bank. The separation of the two sets of proposals—rather than wrapping up everything in a general "242" plan—is significant (though not unprecedented). It is also clear that the two sets of proposals were not equally important or urgent. Rogers knew that it was inconceivable that an Israeli Government, containing Menachem Begin, would hand over Judea and Samaria—or any part thereof—to the Hashemites, or anyone else. He also knew that no Israeli Government—even without Begin—was likely to offer Hussein anything that Hussein could take the risk of accepting (especially at a time when he was in deep trouble with the P.L.O.). In any case, the West Bank was of slight consequence, internationally speaking, compared with Sinai and the Canal. It was the dispute between Israel and Egypt, not the dispute between Israel and Jordan (or the Palestinians, or the Arab world), that threatened to bring about a confrontation between the superpowers.

It seems that what the Americans were really looking for was what was achieved nine years later, after the Yom Kippur War: a separate peace between Israel and Egypt. In the circumstances, the proposals for the West Bank can hardly have been much more than window dressing: a contrivance for soothing the Saudis, with a distant prospect of the Haram esh-Sharif restored to the House of Islam.

On the Israeli side, it seemed reasonable to hope that Golda Meir's Government, having looked into the abyss, and agreed to a cease-fire, would remain sufficiently alarmed by the implications of the Soviet buildup in Egypt to see the need to engage in serious negotiations leading to peace between Israel and Egypt, through evacuation of all Egyptian territory. Unfortunately, this did not work out, partly as a result of certain consequences, domestic and international, of the cease-fire agreement.

The domestic consequences came first. On August 4, 1970, Menachem Begin and his five colleagues resigned in protest against Golda Meir's acceptance of Resolution 242. The Government to which they had belonged had itself not merely accepted 242, but interpreted it liberally (as far as Egypt was concerned) in the immediate aftermath of the Six Day War. But that was then, and this was now. The national mood had clearly hardened.

Begin's resignation was carried out in his characteristic apocalyptic style, invoking the memories of Auschwitz and of Masada. The latter was particularly ominous, in the context.

Masada is the symbol of besieged Israel. This Herodian fortress was the last outpost of the Zealots during the Jewish War against Rome (A.D./C.E. 66–70/73). It was defended by a Zealot garrison, under Eleazar, the son of Jair, against the Roman Tenth Legion, commanded by Flavius Silva. When a breach was made in the wall, at the end of a prolonged siege, Eleazar persuaded his followers to kill themselves, or one another, rather than be captured and enslaved. There followed the mass suicide of 960 men, women and children.

In modern Israel, Masada has come to have a special significance for the training of the young in general, and for the elite formations of the Israel Defense Forces in particular. On the spectacular site where Herod's fortress once stood, on the summit of a steep, conical rock, towering thirteen hundred feet over the Dead Sea shore, the new officers of the Israeli Armored Corps annually take their oath: "Masada shall not fall again."

By conjuring up the ghosts of Masada, in the context of Golda Meir's acceptance (or rather reacceptance) of Security Council Resolution 242, Begin was implying that to seek to attain peace by relinquishing occupied territory—*any* occupied territory—was a breach of security such as had, in the past, precipitated the mass suicide of Israel's heroes.

Any politician willing to try to negotiate peace, even with Egypt alone, in the Israel of the early seventies, would have to fight not Hubris and Euphoria only, but Hysteria as well.

Golda Meir seemed in a precarious political position, caught between serious American pressure and Begin's appeal to a widespread and growing chauvinist mood. But the American pressure was shortly to be eased as a result of some of the consequences of the cease-fire within the inter-Arab system.

The P.L.O. denounced the cease-fire as treason to the Palestinian and Arab cause. Nasser was no longer in a mood to put up with this sort of thing, or to be swayed by it. He closed down the Fatah radio station in Cairo. Hussein then—feeling that he had Nasser's tacit approval—moved against Fatah and the rest of the P.L.O., in the circumstances described in the last chapter.

Syria—or rather a part of the Syrian armed forces—then invaded Jordan.

The Nixon Administration was extremely alarmed. The annexation of any American client state by any Soviet client state was not at all what it needed. At a meeting in Washington on September 20, Kissinger discussed with Rabin contingency arrangements for a possible Israeli intervention in Jordan. Israeli forces massed along the line of the Jordan river. The Syrians retreated; their own internal divisions, Hussein's spirited resistance, and Russian advice, as well as the threat from Israel, may all have influenced the Syrian decision. But the Americans were particularly impressed by the effectiveness of the threat from Israel.

Israel's credit in Washington was greatly enhanced, and that in itself would have tended to ease the pressure. But there was a more specific and functional reason for easing it. It was not possible to apply pressure to Israel without weakening Israel relatively, through "holding in abeyance" weapons or finance. But after the Jordan crisis, it rather looked as if weakening Israel might be the same as weakening the influence of the United States itself in the Middle East. The Nixon Administration did not again apply to Israel—until the closing stages of the Yom Kippur War—the degree of pressure that had been applied during the War of Attrition.

For the rest of 1970, Golda Meir had no inducement to serious negotiation. The War of Attrition was over, but there was no apparent willingness to negotiate on the part of the Arabs. The "three noes" of Khartoum still held. But in February 1971, that situation changed radically. On February 4, Nasser's successor, Anwar Sadat, addressed the Egyptian Parliament. He told the Parliament "that if Israel withdrew her forces in Sinai to the Passes, I would be willing to reopen the Suez Canal; to have my forces cross to the East Bank . . . to make a solemn official declaration of a cease-fire; to restore diplomatic relations with the United States; and to sign a peace agreement with Israel through the efforts of Dr. Jarring, the representative of the Secretary-General of the United Nations."[15] He confirmed the message in a note to the United Nations, February 14.

After that great, historic initiative, things went on exactly as before, until the Yom Kippur War; and the reason for the Yom Kippur War was that they did go on exactly as before.

After February 1971, as before, Gunnar Jarring, the Swedish diplomat whom the Secretary-General had designated as his special representative, under Section 3 of Security Council Resolution 242, continued his efforts as required by that section, "to maintain contacts with the States concerned in order to promote agreement." And after February 1971, his efforts and contacts met with the same degree of success as before, which was none whatever.

Gunnar Jarring does not seem to have been a particularly inspired negotiator. His main intellectual interest was linguistics, and Gideon Rafael comments: "It was far easier for him to understand the fine nuances of Turkomanish dialects than the subtleties of oriental politics. He understood what the contenders said but not always what they meant."[16] But even the most gifted negotiator in the world could not have made progress in this case, because there was no willingness on the Israeli side to take up the Egyptian initiative in a serious way.

This is remarkable in itself. David Ben-Gurion, from the days in which the State of Israel came into existence, had always hoped that one day there would be an overture from Cairo, leading to a negotiated peace between Israel and Egypt. He was ill and in retirement when that overture came—in a startlingly explicit form—and his successors just let it lie there.

VII

The apathetic immobility of Golda Meir's Government, in relation to the prospect of peace with Egypt, in the two years and eight months between Sadat's diplomatic initiative of February 1971 and his military initiative on Yom Kippur of 1973, can hardly be explained except by reference to the internal problems of that Government. It is true that there were external problems also. After the departure of Begin and his colleagues, Golda Meir's Government—like most Governments in Israel—had a narrow majority. Begin, in opposition, was sure to scream "Masada" as soon as the Government moved toward a negotiated peace. But the Government disposed of an effective reply to that. The authorized diplomatic representatives of the Government of National Unity under Levi Eshkol had publicly and solemnly agreed to Security Council Resolution 242. Begin and his colleagues were members of that Government, and they had not fallen on their swords in the breach of the beleaguered fortress. They had carried on with business as usual. The opposition was not a very serious problem. The real problems—and they were crippling—were inside the Government itself.

Consider the position of Golda Meir's Foreign Minister, Abba Eban. Never was so brilliant a light hidden under so comprehensive and impenetrable a bushel as was the case with Abba Eban's mind in the years between the Six Day War and the Yom Kippur War. Eban came to be so boxed in by three more powerful colleagues— Golda Meir, Yitzhak Rabin and Moshe Dayan—as to have virtually no influence over major foreign-policy decisions in the Government of which he was Foreign Minister.

It had not been so bad as long as Levi Eshkol lived. Eshkol knew himself to have no experience or skill in foreign affairs, and he rightly trusted Eban. But even under Eshkol, Eban was overruled in the matter of the most important appointment within his department: the post of ambassador in Washington. The appointment, by Eshkol, of Yitzhak Rabin to that post, in February 1968, took the most vital aspect of Israel's foreign relations—the relation with the United States— almost entirely out of the control of the Foreign Minister, and of his department.

Rabin's biographer, Robert Slater, asserts that Rabin's appointment to Washington had Eban's "enthusiastic backing."[17] When I read that, I wrote in the margin: "A likely story!" Rabin's own memoirs—published later than his biography—tell a different story. Eban, he said, had "some reservations" about his appointment, and he goes on: "Even then Abba Eban was not one of my greatest admirers, and in all fairness I should add that the feeling was mutual."[18]

As long as Levi Eshkol lived, the Foreign Minister could hope to exert some control over his imperious and disdainful envoy. But when Golda Meir succeeded as Prime Minister, the ambassador in Washington became—as we have seen—a more important official than his nominal superior.

The new Prime Minister had herself been Foreign Minister and so was not inclined, as Eshkol had been, to defer to Abba Eban's expertise. Also, having been brought up in Milwaukee, she had some reason to feel that she understood Israel's most important foreign affair—America—better than her English-bred Foreign Minister could do. There were personality differences as well. Abba Eban is rather grand; by Israeli standards, almost impossibly grand. Golda Meir prided herself on being down-to-earth, grandmotherly. When she visited the United States, the crowds adored her. But in the salons of Washington, and the dining rooms of the United Nations, it was the ambassador who shone, not his Foreign Minister. Golda Meir would not have been human if she had not resented that a bit, and she was human. We have seen how reductively she deals in her autobiography with the most substantial achievement of her period as Foreign Minister: the conditional retreat from Sinai, the work of her ambassador. The "mode of contact" established with the White House in 1969 must have been congenial, as bypassing both her Foreign Minister and those State Department officials among whom he moved with such ease.

Boxed in as he then was, between his Prime Minister and his ambassador in Washington, who were shaping foreign policy over his head, Abba Eban was in an almost intolerable position. But the Golda-to-Yitzhak "mode of contact" was only a part of the Foreign Minister's effacement in this period. He was also eclipsed, in the shaping of foreign policy, by the Minister for Defense, Moshe Dayan.

Israel's predicament has always been such that in any Israeli Cabinet the Minister for Defense is the most important member, next to the Prime Minister, and sometimes—as in this case—overshadowing the Prime Minister. And Moshe Dayan, even irrespective of his office, had a unique and towering personal prestige in this period. The prestige he already had as conqueror of Sinai in 1956 had been so great as to force his inclusion, by popular acclaim, in Eshkol's Government of National Unity. And after that, he had immediately appeared in the role of the avenging angel of the Six-Day War. Golda Meir's Government was not in a position to take—or even to respond to—any major initiative in the field of foreign policy without the consent of the government's hero-in-residence, the Minister for Defense.

According to Dayan's view of the matter, foreign affairs were part of his ministry's remit. His repeated aphorism (perhaps inherited from Ben-Gurion), "Israel has no foreign policy, only a defense policy," was hard doctrine for Dayan's annihilated colleague, the Foreign Minister of Israel. Rightly or wrongly, Abba Eban decided to continue, though thus grievously hemmed in. According to Rafael: "Eban sometimes rebelled but generally felt that he had to accept this situation unless he should decide to resign, a step he used to contemplate with more frequency than consequence."[19] It might have been better if he had resigned, and told the public why.

If Moshe Dayan inspired awe and admiration among the people of Israel in general, the feeling he inspired among his colleagues was one of fascinated fear. As Gideon Rafael puts it, his colleagues were "reluctant to cross Dayan's path, fearful of being run over at a dimly-lit political street-crossing."[20]

On foreign policy, Dayan's utterances were unpredictable, enigmatic and sometimes at variance with one another. He was dove and hawk by turns. Up to August 1970—the cease-fire and the end of the War of Attrition—the dove often, though not always, seemed to predominate. He had been against advancing to the Suez Canal. He had favored "a long leap into the icy water" of the Jarring talks. He flew kites about limited withdrawals from the Canal bank, but then allowed the kites to drop. In August 1970, he raised difficulties about the cease-fire, seeking to delay the departure from the Government of Menachem Begin. For a time his colleagues even feared that he might resign along with Begin, thus "running them over." He stayed on, but increasingly made noises congenial to Begin and his colleagues. By August 1971, as the Minister responsible for the occupied territories, he was talking about "creating facts" in these territories. "If the Arabs refuse to make peace"—this was six months after Sadat's peace offer—"we cannot stand still. If we are denied their cooperation, let us act on our own."[21]

One of the facts Dayan decided to create was a settlement, for Begin's followers, on occupied Egyptian territory, at Yamit, near the Gaza Strip. The decision to establish the settlement at Yamit was one of Sadat's reasons for going to war in 1973.[22] By the spring of that year, Dayan was outranting Menachem Begin. In April 1973, in a ceremony on the peak of Masada, he proclaimed his vision of "a new State of Israel with broad frontiers, strong and solid, with the authority of the Israeli Government extending from the Jordan to the Suez Canal."[23]

Hubris there had made his masterpiece.

Many of Dayan's words and actions in the period between August 1970 and October 1973 could be accounted for on the hypothesis that he was aiming at heading, after the next elections, a new Government of National Unity, including Begin and his followers. Unfortunately, the Yom Kippur War was to come before the elections.

VIII

In the spring of 1971, when the Government of Israel had to make up its mind on the form of its response to the Sadat initiative, Dayan was still far from having evolved into the superhawk he was to be by 1973, but he was already concerned about keeping lines open to Begin.

Abba Eban prepared the draft of Israel's response. Even Eban's draft revealed the constricted character of Israel's diplomacy under the Government of Golda Meir. The draft had to reflect, at least in some way, the Prime Minister's oft-repeated insistence that the Arabs must be prepared to sit down at the negotiating tables with Israel *before* Israel would indicate what it might be prepared to negotiate. Eban's draft ran:

a. Israel welcomes Egypt's readiness to conclude a peace agreement.
b. It proposes to discuss with Egypt all points contained in her reply to Ambassador Jarring, as well as all topics mentioned in Israel's memorandum "Essentials of Peace" and any additional questions mutually agreed upon.
c. In these negotiations, to be held on the level of Foreign Ministers and under the auspices of Dr. Jarring, both sides will present their detailed positions on the territorial, demographic, military and other outstanding issues.[24]

The element of "give" in this document was contained in the second paragraph, in the reference to the memorandum "Essentials of Peace." This was an Israeli Foreign Office document communicated to Ambassador Jarring on his visit to Israel on January 8, 1971. In it "Israel explicitly endorsed the withdrawal as well as all the other provisions of Resolution 242."[25] It may have been this draft—though it annoyed the Egyptian Foreign Office—that prompted Sadat to make his peace initiative of February.

The Israeli Foreign Office, however, had been going too fast for the Prime Minister. On the day after Jarring's departure Golda Meir took into her own hands the control of "all activities connected with the Jarring mission."[26] The Foreign Office, which had already lost control over relations with America, now lost control over the indirect negotiations with the Arabs, through Jarring. There was nothing therefore of major importance to Israel that the Foreign Office did control in this period.

The Government could not withdraw the "Essentials of Peace" memorandum—since this had already been communicated to Jarring, and by him to Sadat. But the Government could add to the Eban draft something so unpalatable to Sadat as to deter him from taking up "Essentials for Peace." This the Government duly did. A "short but highly significant"[27] amendment to the Eban draft was moved. Supported by the immense authority of the Minister for Defense, the amendment carried. It ran, simply: "Israel will not withdraw to the pre–June 5, 1967, lines."

Sadat was being put under notice that even if he took the immense risk—for any Arab leader—of attempting to negotiate a peace treaty with Israel, that treaty would still leave Israel in possession of Egyptian territory, to an unknown extent. The "peace process" was now hopelessly jammed.

Ten years later, Moshe Dayan wrote a book called *Breakthrough* to celebrate his own contribution to the attainment of a peace treaty between Egypt and Israel in 1979. But the "breakthrough" was just as possible in 1971 as it was in 1979, if the Government of Israel had been interested. Sadat's offer of February 1971 was the core of what became the peace treaty, eight years later, after a destructive war, deeply damaging to Israel.

The Yom Kippur War could have been avoided if the Government of Golda Meir, under the ascendancy of Moshe Dayan, had not acted on the assumption that Israel needed no foreign policy, only a defense policy. But of course that assumption reflected a general public mood which had established itself after the Six Day War, no doubt inevitably. This was a mood of confidence in Israel's quasi-omnipotence, and in the permanent impotence of all the Arabs. Certain public men—notably Dayan and Rabin—both shared that mood and seem to have fitted to it their own political expectations and ambitions.

The Minister for Defense, in ultimate control of foreign policy, as well as of defense policy, and being also—as Military Governor—

overlord of the occupied territories, believed the Arabs to be of such little account that neither Egypt's peace overture nor its preparations for war need be taken seriously. Dayan's assumptions were widely shared, both in the Government and in the defense establishment.

These assumptions in Israel were fortified when, on July 18, 1972, Anwar Sadat announced the expulsion from Egypt of the bulk of his Soviet military advisers. This dramatic move was almost universally interpreted by Israeli policy makers as causing "irreparable harm to Egypt's military strength, virtually incapacitating its army to fight, let alone to launch another war in the foreseeable future."[28]

There was only one dissenter from this view, one Cassandra. This was Gideon Rafael. As Abba Eban recalls, Rafael "raised the possibility that Sadat's expulsion of Soviet forces might herald his desire to make the war option more concrete. The Soviet Union might have been regarded by Sadat as an inhibiting factor rather than as a potential supporter of military action."[29]

Rafael's analysis, communicated to his Minister within two days of Sadat's announcement, is a remarkable piece of political clairvoyance:

> Israel should be alert to the possibility that in due time Egypt might renew the hostilities with limited extension. It would act under the assumption that the United States would restrain Israel from using its full strength in a lengthy campaign to defeat Egypt decisively. Sadat possibly supposed that after a short and violent conflagration, where he had proved his readiness to fight, the United States would put its full weight behind a political solution.[30]

Rafael's masterly analysis failed to convince even Eban. And Eban, had he been convinced, would have been quite unlikely to convince his colleagues. The attribution of such sophisticated political reasoning to the Egyptian leader would have appeared implausible. Sadat had been generally underestimated internationally, and the current rulers of Israel were not inclined to lag behind in the matter of underestimating adversaries.

Sadat's "break with the Russians" was more demonstrative than substantial. He sent most of the advisers packing, but he did not withdraw his permission for the Soviet use of Egyptian air and naval facilities, much the most important part of the Soviet-Egyptian relation, for the deployment of Soviet power in the Mediterranean. The flow of Soviet military aid to Egypt continued. Sadat had managed to impress the Americans by "breaking with the Russians" without actually breaking with the Russians.

After Dayan's Masada speech of April 1973, revealing that the Government of Israel now regarded the Suez Canal as one of the "strong and solid" frontiers of the State of Israel, the Egyptian leader knew that he had just two options. He could resign himself to the permanent loss of all Egyptian territory occupied by Israel, and to the humiliation of the permanent presence of Israeli forces along the Canal, and also to the growing political threats to his leadership that would go with prolonged acquiescence in occupation and humiliation. Or he could go to war, and accept the huge risks that would go with an Egyptian military challenge to the victors of the Six Day War.

Sadat made his decision to go to war. The decision was taken after a number of contacts, through a number of channels, with Henry Kissinger, in Washington. The relation between those contacts and Sadat's decision to go to war is a matter which deserves examination, which it will receive, in the next two sections.

IX

Did Henry Kissinger, during 1973, encourage Anwar Sadat to launch an attack on Israel?

Testimony strongly suggesting that Kissinger did just that is contained in a recent book by a prominent Egyptian personality, Mohamed Heikal. Heikal had been Nasser's closest confidant, and after Nasser's death in 1970, he became a close adviser to Sadat. The testimony in question is contained in Heikal's book *Autumn of Fury: The Assassination of Sadat*.

According to Heikal, Sadat, in the early months of 1973, "began to get an increasing number of messages through his most consistent channel of information—Kamal Adhem and the C.I.A."

Kamal Adhem was the head of Saudi intelligence at this time. Heikal goes on: "These were to the effect that Kissinger . . . would not want the administration to get more involved in the Middle East's problems as long as these were more or less dormant."

Kissinger at this time was still National Security Adviser to the President, and responsible for the C.I.A. He did not become Secretary of State until September 1973, on the eve of the Yom Kippur War. "The administration," in the passage quoted, has to refer to the

White House, as distinct from the State Department, which was involved in the Middle East, willy-nilly.

Heikal adds:

But if the area began to show signs of hotting up, that would be a different matter [my italics]. When I was in London many years later [March 1982] Kamal Adhem confirmed this to me, saying he had spoken to the C.I.A. man in charge of military affairs and that now, with the Israelis showing signs of increasing obstinacy, it might be that the Americans were willing to do a little heating up themselves. As late as September 23, when David Rockefeller met Sadat at Bourg el-Arab, he passed on the same message . . . a little heating up would be in order.[31]

A little later, Heikal records his opinion that these advices helped to make up Sadat's mind on the side of war: "The messages he began to receive from Washington that some hotting up of the situation would not be unacceptable reinforced pressure from the army and mounting public dissatisfaction to draw him into the battle."[32]

Neither of the principals—Sadat and Kissinger—mentions any "heating up" advice, but Sadat clearly did draw from Kissinger's responses the *conclusion* indicated by Heikal. Sadat, in his memoirs, mentions a meeting in Paris between his representative, Hafiz Ismail, and Kissinger:

Hafiz Ismail's meeting with Kissinger in Paris February 1973 failed to produce any results. It was impossible, as I have always said, for the United States (or, indeed, any other power) to make a move if we ourselves didn't take military action to break the deadlock. The drift of what Kissinger said to Ismail was that the United States regrettably could do nothing to help so long as we were the defeated party and Israel maintained her superiority.[33]

Elsewhere in his book, Sadat gives a somewhat fuller version of the same meeting. Kissinger is said to have told Ismail:

You may be capable of changing existing realities—and consequently our approach to the "solution"—or you may not. If not, certain solutions have to be found which *follow from your position*, and these will be different from the solutions you suggest. I hope my meaning is clear; I am not calling on Sadat to change the military situation for, if he tries to do

that, Israel will again defeat you. She will score an even
greater victory than she did in 1967, which will make it difficult for us to do anything at all.[34]

Whatever message Kissinger intended to convey, the inference
which Sadat actually drew from what he said was that it was only by
going to war that he could induce the United States to put enough
pressure on Israel to secure the return of his territories. And this does
seem a fair inference from the first sentence quoted—"You may be
capable [etc.]"—even though the hint in that sentence is formally
cancelled by the "don't get me wrong" stuff that closely follows. I
shall return to that crucial sentence, *in the context of its international
setting*, later in this analysis.

Henry Kissinger, in his own memoirs, does speak of "heating up,"
in the sense Heikal reports. But he speaks of it as something occurring
to Sadat quite spontaneously, part of "an extraordinary tactic that no
one fathomed."[35] Kissinger reports a Security Council assessment of
December 20, 1972, according to which: "Though . . . Sadat was
capable of a limited attack, there seemed no rational military purpose
for it. It too would be defeated; hence its sole function would be to
heat up international concern and pressure for negotiation. Its failure
would only deepen the diplomatic stalemate."[36]

It is possible to read that last sentence as an attempt to throw
the reader off the scent, which is otherwise fairly strong. It was immediately after that assessment, in early 1973, that—according to
Heikal—the messages began to flow in, through the intelligence channels, from Kissinger to Sadat, to the effect that "some hotting up of
the situation" would be in order.

Kissinger's account of his meeting with Hafiz Ismail in Washington, in February 1973, is much less informative than Sadat's account
(from Ismail) of the same meeting. Kissinger doesn't even mention
his advice to Sadat *not* to go to war, let alone the oblique hint with a
contrary tendency that appears to have accompanied that impec-
cable-sounding advice. Instead of information, Kissinger here throws
in generalities about the nature of negotiation, plus one of his fairly
rare and altogether deplorable purple patches. He found Ismail an
impressive-looking chap, a finding which precipitates the following
gusher:

". . . an archetypical Egyptian has survived, his face etched on
the statues and temples that are the closest any nation has come to
achieving eternity—an expression at once gentle and transcendent; a
posture at once humble and enduring; a look both human and yet

gazing into an infinity beyond the limitations of the human scale."[37]

As an attentive Kissinger reader, I have formed the impression that when his prose goes all soulful, as in the above unappetizing sample, he is probably skating over some transaction about which he doesn't want his readers to be precisely informed.

Kissinger had one more meeting with Hafiz Ismail, in France, in May 1973. The account of what was said is in itself unilluminating, but at least there can be no doubt about the impression left, by Kissinger's conversation, on the mind of his interlocutor. As Kissinger tells it:

> The American official who had found the meeting place reported to me that after I left, Ismail, visibly dispirited and glum, had sat alone in the garden for a long time contemplating the waterfall behind the house, head cupped in hands. His staff had left him alone, but finally his young daughter joined him and appeared to cheer him up. He told the American later that he hoped to maintain contact with me whatever the vicissitudes of the peace effort. Our relationship would be important even in case of an armed clash, he said.
>
> For Ismail knew that Sadat was determined on war. Only an American guarantee that we would fulfill the entire Arab program in a brief time could have dissuaded him. That was patently impossible. And Ismail, though a military man, was enough imbued with the extraordinary humanity of the Egyptian to dread what reason told him was now inevitable. The Middle East was heading toward war. We did not know it. But he did.[38]

This confirms Sadat's own account of the conclusion he drew from what Kissinger had to say. It is consistent with Sadat's account of Kissinger's advice. And it is far from incompatible with Heikal's account of the secret messages coming in to Sadat, from Kissinger, through the C.I.A. and Saudi intelligence.

X

Having considered the memoirs of the principals, let us take another look at Heikal's allegations, which are of course more specific and more startling than anything explicitly set out in the main memoirs.

One reason for questioning Heikal's allegations is that there's nothing in Heikal's earlier book[39] on the origins of the Yom Kippur

War (to the Arabs, the Ramadan War) about any Kissingerial advice to "heat up." The earlier book does say that from September 1971 on, Sadat's dealings with Washington were through Kissinger, not the State Department.[40] But he is not specific, in the earlier book, about what Kissinger may have said, or conveyed, through intelligence channels.

When Heikal wrote *The Road to Ramadan*, Sadat was still alive, and Heikal had his confidence. But when Heikal came to write *Autumn of Fury*, Sadat was dead. In his last years Sadat had dismissed and imprisoned Heikal for opposing the separate peace between Egypt and Israel.

There are alternative principal hypotheses, both fairly plausible, about the discrepancy between the two books. These alternatives are:

Hypothesis A: In the earlier book, Heikal was not free to discuss the transactions revealed in the later book. Had he done so he would have incurred the anger of both Kissinger and Sadat, and risked grave penalties. In the later book, on the other hand, he is free to tell the truth, without fear or favor, and does so.

Hypothesis B: The earlier book is the one to be taken seriously. In the later one, Heikal is seeking revenge, by trying to depict his former master as an American stooge. To this end, he invents promptings from Kissinger, which have no existence, except in his imagination.

Perplexed by these conflicting possibilities, I consulted an eminent authority on the politics of modern Egypt. In his (private) reply, my authority advises that the account in *Autumn of Fury* should be taken with a grain, or more, of salt. "Heikal is a slippery customer. He may have been a witness to many things, but he is not always reliable in his reporting. . . . Undoubtedly in *Autumn of Fury* Heikal had every reason to show up Sadat as a willing tool of American policy."

Clearly, this advice points in the direction of Hypothesis B. I lay this advice before the reader, who should not underestimate the weight of authority behind it. At the same time, perhaps presumptuously, I still find Hypothesis A—that the allegations in *Autumn of Fury* are credible—more convincing than the alternative.

My reasons are partly connected with *Autumn of Fury* itself; partly with the international conjuncture in the period with which the allegations are concerned.

As regards *Autumn of Fury*, it is true that this book generally tries to depreciate Sadat (though not vehemently), while the author's earlier books generally tended to flatter him (though not grossly). But the passages in *Autumn* containing the allegations do not appear to be polemical, either in tone or in tendency. Sadat is not portrayed as simply doing the bidding of the Americans. He is shown as reaching a rational decision, on the basis of a number of factors, one of which was Kissinger's advice. Would it be worth any writer's while to *invent data*, only to come up with a picture like that?

More generally Hypothesis B—falsification—seems to me to strain belief, more than the alternative. Mohamed Heikal is a distinguished personality, with an international reputation, both within the Arab world and outside it; he is also the most eminent journalist and publicist produced by his country in the twentieth century.

None of this means that what he—or any other distinguished personality—says in a memoir has to be taken as gospel.[41] Memoirs should always be scrutinized with possibilities of *suppressio veri* and *suggestio falsi* in mind. But flat lies are quite unlikely, on the part of people with reputations to lose, except in cases where the memoirist has some strong motive to lie: as, for example, the need to conceal, or distort, some discreditable transaction in which the writer was personally involved. There seems no reason to believe that any such factor could be involved here, in the nature of the case. So Heikal's allegations—about matters within his knowledge—cannot just be brushed aside.

Perhaps the strongest reason for treating the allegations seriously is that they fit perfectly, without any forcing, into the international conjuncture in the context of which they occur.

If Kissinger did indeed suggest—indirectly and/or implicitly—to Sadat the need for a military initiative ("heating up"), this was sound advice in terms of *realpolitik*, from a statesman in Kissinger's position, to one in Sadat's position.

Consider, first, Sadat's precarious position as of mid-1973. Israel was treating both his peace overtures and his threats of war with open contempt. Dayan had answered him with Masada and Yamit: Israel's frontier along the Suez Canal, and Jewish settlement of Egyptian territory. Sadat had said that 1971 would be the Year of Decision; that was two years ago, and he had gotten nothing. Humiliation was undermining him; there were riots in Egyptian cities. His senior officers were asking him what he was waiting for. Another year, or even less, of immobility and apparent impotence could well have finished him.

From the point of view of Kissinger, and his colleagues in the

American intelligence and defense communities, the fall of Sadat
would have been a disaster. At least since May 1971, when he dismissed, and later arrested, the powerful pro-Soviet elements in the
old Nasser establishment, Sadat had been signaling that he wished
to mend his fences with the United States. That signal was strongly
reinforced in the following year, when Sadat expelled the bulk of
Egypt's Soviet advisers.

In Washington, the visible weakening of Sadat, in 1973, had to
be seen as a weakening of American influence and prestige in the
region. Even before Sadat had made his openly "anti-Soviet moves,"
Kissinger had strongly urged the Israelis—through Ambassador
Rabin—to respond favorably to Sadat's initiative of February 1971.[42]
Israel's response had been negative from the beginning and became—
by 1973—triumphalist and defiant.

Nor was the Nixon Administration, at any time from 1971 to
1973, in a position to shift Israel's position by the usual kinds of pressure. In the spring of 1971—less than six months after Black September, when Israel's massing of forces had "rescued" America's Arab
client Hussein—serious pressure on Israel seemed unthinkable. The
only mode of pressure normally available to Washington, on Israel,
is the delay of supply. But the delay of supply necessarily weakens
Israel vis-à-vis its Soviet-armed Arab neighbors. And in the aftermath
of Black September, the weakening of Israel seemed the very reverse
of what American interests required.

During 1972, the Middle Eastern context shifted. After July—
with the expulsion of the Soviet advisers from Egypt—a negotiated
peace between Egypt and Israel, helped on by the United States,
necessarily had great attraction for American foreign-policy makers.
Such a peace could mean that the two most important states in the
region would be America's clients. But there were counterarguments
in terms of domestic policy: 1972 was a presidential election year,
not a good time to apply pressure to Israel.

And by the spring of 1973, Nixon was not in a position to apply
pressure to anyone who enjoyed political influence in America.
Nixon was now in the throes of Watergate. The last thing he needed,
at this time, was to bring down on himself, in addition to his other
troubles, the wrath of the pro-Israel lobby, in Congress and in the
country. The Government of Israel, of course, fully understood this.
It is against that background that, for example, Dayan's Masada
speech (April 1973) has to be seen.

DOING WITHOUT DIPLOMACY   519

Henry Kissinger and his colleagues, in 1973, were reduced to two options. One was to write off Sadat: to leave him, as the phrase went, "slowly twisting in the wind"—a chilling spectacle to any other Arab leader who might be tempted to look to America for support. The other option was to convey to Sadat, in one way or another, that the United States could come effectively to his assistance only if he himself could first change the balance of forces by military action.

In whatever form, or forms, this message may have come through, it is certainly the message that Sadat—who was no fool—thought he was getting from Kissinger: "The drift of what Kissinger said to Ismail was that the United States regrettably could do nothing to help so long as we were the defeated party and Israel maintained her superiority."

It is clear that for Sadat, the "drift"—Kissinger's real message, as distinct from the accompanying "flannel"—is in the following sentence of Kissinger's statement to Ismail: "You may be capable of changing existing realities—and consequently our approach to the 'solution'—or you may not."

The key words here are *and consequently our approach,*" and these have far-reaching implications. What Sadat had to understand from these words was that if he could attack Israel with some degree of success, the reactions of the United States would not be unfavorable in terms of his own position.

That was really all that Sadat needed to know.

As Gideon Rafael had read Sadat's mind in the summer of 1972: "Sadat possibly supposed that after a short but violent conflagration, where he had proved his readiness to fight, the United States would put its full weight behind a political solution."[43]

Rafael had read the trend of Sadat's mind correctly. Sadat had now tried out his supposition on Kissinger, and read Kissinger's response as positive. Or possibly Kissinger himself had already encouraged the supposition indirectly, leading to Ismail's mission, and the confirmation, from the horse's mouth, in "and consequently our approach . . ." The explicit—but indirect—advices alleged by Heikal are fully in line with Kissinger's "drift," as interpreted by Sadat.

In a conversation after the Yom Kippur War, Kissinger is said to have discussed with Golda Meir his (pre–Yom Kippur) talks with Hafiz Ismail. As Kissinger then recalled it—according to the Israeli journalist Matti Golan—he, Kissinger, had regarded the idea of Sadat's going to war as altogether laughable. "Who is Sadat? We all thought he was a fool, a clown. . . . A war, Egypt? I regarded it as empty talk, a boast empty of content."[44]

None of that rings true. Sadat seems to have been looked down on as some kind of "caretaker" when he succeeded Nasser in September 1970. But less than a year later, when he dismissed and jailed his pro-Soviet rivals, he had clearly established himself as someone to be reckoned with. And by July 1972, with the expulsions of the Soviet advisers, and the adroit management of those expulsions, he had become a person of high international consequence: not least to the United States.

Nor was war so preposterous as an option for Egypt. Egypt could not, indeed, win such a war. But if Egypt could start one and avoid crushing humiliation (through a cease-fire backed by both superpowers), that would do, from Sadat's point of view—as Rafael had foreseen. And the military-technological balance had shifted in Egypt's favor, through the introduction of the Soviet surface-to-air missiles close to the Canal. Israel could no longer achieve such a devastating air strike as that with which the Six Day War opened.

At the same time that Henry Kissinger seems to have been giving one kind of encouragement to Sadat, he was giving another kind to Golda Meir. What encouraged her about Kissinger, in 1973, was what she believed to be his "passivity." In rejecting the warnings of her Foreign Office about the "dangers of a diplomatic deadlock," she invoked (*inter alia*) the superior international prestige, and apparent attitude, of Henry Kissinger. As Gideon Rafael recalls: "She did not share our apprehensions. She preferred the assessment of the defense establishment, which dismissed the existence of a military threat for the next two or three years. Why should Kissinger remain so passive if he believed that a diplomatic vacuum was militarily dangerous? Apparently he saw nothing wrong in a stalemate and certainly did not expect the collapse of the cease-fire, adjudged Golda."[45]

From the other evidence quoted, it seems more than just possible that Kissinger remained "so passive" in this period precisely *because* he understood "that a diplomatic vacuum was militarily dangerous"; and because he believed, not without reason, that a peace between Israel and Egypt—a peace which was an important policy objective of the United States—would not be attainable until the then rulers of Israel had been jolted out of their overweening complacency by unexpected military danger, followed by enhanced awareness of Israel's dependence on the United States.

The behavior of the American intelligence community, during this period, seems to have been consistent with this hypothesis. Even after the evacuation of Soviet citizens from Egypt on October 4, American intelligence could see "no clear signs of impending hostilities."[46]

William B. Quandt, who was a staffer for Kissinger's National Security Council at the material time, asks some pertinent questions: "Why was the American intelligence community wrong? Why was Kissinger caught by surprise? Where were all the Middle East 'experts?' "[47]

Quandt's answers to these questions are not particularly illuminating, being to the general effect that it was thought that the Arabs were too weak to start a war, and in any case the Israelis themselves weren't worried. But there is a rather startling footnote to this anodyne text: "*Some analysts at CIA deliberately played down evidence of preparation for hostilities* [my italics], fearing that each side might overreact to the moves of the other."[48]

There is a fine ring of impartiality in the "each side" and "the other" explanation. But, in the nature of the situation, the "evidence of preparation for hostilities" was evidence of Arab preparations for an attack on Israel; not the other way around, since Israel was making no such preparations. Notice also the inherent assumption that these analyses would be read by the parties concerned (who otherwise could not possibly "overreact" to them; or indeed "underreact," which may be more to the point).

Now these doctored reports—"deliberately played down"—could not possibly fool the Egyptians and the Syrians, who knew what they themselves were up to. The only people they could fool, or even be intended to fool, were the rulers of Israel, who would read them as confirming their own overconfident assumptions. And that does seem to fit, with other details, into a suggestive pattern.

XI

At 1400 hours on the afternoon of Yom Kippur, October 6, 1973, the Egyptians and Syrians launched their simultaneous attack, achieving, as Israel's best-known military historian acknowledges, "strategic and tactical surprise."[49]

The Egyptian offensive opened with an air attack, accompanied by a devastating artillery barrage against Israel's famous fortified Bar-Lev Line, on the west bank of the Canal. Herzog writes:

> . . . 2,000 guns opened up along the entire front: field artillery, medium and heavy artillery and medium and heavy mortars. In the first minute of the attack, 10,500 shells fell on Israeli positions at the rate of 175 shells per second. A brigade of FROG surface-to-surface missiles launched its weapons, and tanks moved up to the ramps prepared on the sand ramparts, depressed their guns and fired point-blank at the Israeli strongpoints. Over 3,000 tons of concentrated destruction were launched against a handful of Israeli fortifications in a barrage that turned the entire east bank of the Suez Canal into an inferno for 53 minutes.[50]

After fifteen minutes of this, the first wave of 8,000 Egyptian assault infantrymen crossed the Canal, in an extremely well-rehearsed action. Further waves followed, and the Bar-Lev Line was overrun; the evacuation of the fortification was ordered on October 7, at about 11:00 A.M. The Israeli fortifications were undermanned and unready, to an extraordinary degree. Herzog writes:

> The full impact of the Egyptian crossing along the 110 miles of the Suez Canal fell upon a total of 436 Israeli soldiers in a series of fortifications seven to eight miles apart, and three tanks actually on the waterfront. They were men of the Jerusalem Brigade, serving their annual reserve duty, and constituted a typical cross-section of average Jerusalemites. Because Jerusalem had absorbed a large proportion of new immigrants of late, many of the men serving in the fortifications were inexperienced soldiers with little or no battle experience.[51]

There could be no starker measure of the extent of Israel's overconfidence in this period than the contrast between the scale of that initial Egyptian attack and the scale of the resources immediately available to resist it.

Similarly, on the northern front, two Israeli brigades came under attack from more than three Syrian divisions: 1,100 Syrian tanks against 157 Israeli tanks. By midday on Sunday—after twenty-two hours of fighting—90 percent of the officers of the Israeli brigades, and most of the men, were either killed or wounded. On Sunday, twenty-four hours after the first blow, Syrian forces were within ten minutes of the River Jordan and the Sea of Galilee. On the southern front, by midday on October 7, the Egyptian 7th Division had crossed the Canal with all its forces.

The first twenty-four hours were necessarily the worst for an Israel taken by surprise. Israel's enemies had large standing armies—that of Egypt being one of the largest and best-equipped in the world—whereas Israel had to depend mainly on a citizen army of reservists, most of whom were at home or in the synagogues on Yom Kippur of 1973. The holy day, however, made easier the calling up of the reservists because their whereabouts were known, and the roads were clear.

On October 8, Israel launched a counterattack on the great Egyptian bridgehead on the west bank of the Canal. But the attack failed, with heavy casualties. In three days, Israel had lost fifty aircraft and hundreds of tanks.

The following five days—October 9 to October 14—were the time of deepest anxiety and depression for the Government of Israel. On October 9, Golda Meir prevented Moshe Dayan from broadcasting, because she was afraid of the effect which the Minister for Defense might have on the morale of the troops.[52]

Three days later her own Government notified its Foreign Minister, then in New York, of its willingness to accept a cease-fire "in place."[53] That is to say that the Government would, at that time, have been prepared to accept the reconquest by Egypt of territory about whose future Israel had earlier refused to negotiate.

Yet, by that time, Israel's military recovery was already under way. The Israeli General Staff had decided to concentrate its offensive activities on the northern front. By October 10, the Syrians had been driven out of all the territories reconquered by them in the opening days of the war. On October 11, Israeli forces advanced into Syria proper, seeming to threaten Damascus.

The Israeli defeat of Syrian forces and the incursion into Syria form the pivotal event of the Yom Kippur War, in terms both of the international political context and of the course of the war itself.

The threat to Damascus alarmed the Soviet Union, which began a massive airlift of armaments to Cairo and Damascus. The Soviet airlift alarmed the Nixon Administration, which—contrary to its previous cautious policy—responded with a no less massive airlift to Israel, in American Air Force transports. The potential for superpower confrontation was in place in the region.

The threat to Damascus also drew the Egyptians forward, from their strong positions on the Canal, to relieve the pressure on their Syrian allies. This move was strongly opposed by the able Egyptian Chief of Staff, General Saad el-Din Shazli. Shazli thought that Egypt's best policy was to remain on the Canal, beneath the umbrella of the surface-to-air missiles, and fight defensive actions, as it had done successfully on October 8. But Sadat—under pressure from both Syria and the Soviet Union—overruled Shazli, by direct order.

On Sunday morning, October 14, the Egyptian armored forces began their offensive into Sinai. The resulting engagement is said to have been "one of the largest tank battles in history (apart from the battle of Kursk in the Second World War), with some 2,000 tanks locked in battle along the entire front."[54]

This tank battle was the turning point of the war; it ended that evening with a complete victory for Israel. Two hundred sixty-four knocked-out Egyptian tanks were counted on the battlefield; Israel had lost only about ten tanks. Egyptian forces fell back to the Canal. Israel decided to follow up its victory quickly by a (long-planned) crossing of the Canal. On the day after the tank battle, the first of the forces under the command of General Ariel Sharon crossed the Canal; "into Africa" as he said. By October 19, the Israelis were across the Canal in force, destroying Egyptian missile bases and threatening to cut off the Egyptian Third Army.

The Soviet Premier, Alexei Kosygin, had been in Cairo since October 16, to mark how seriously the Soviet Union was taking both its own airlift and that of the Americans. Sadat was now—as Golda Meir had been a week before—in favor of a cease-fire "in place." He now asked the Soviet Union to throw its weight behind a cease-fire, which of course it had resisted in the earlier phase of the war.

On October 16, the Gulf States announced a 70 percent increase in the posted price of crude oil. On October 17, the ten oil-producing Arab states, meeting in Kuwait, announced a decision "to reduce production of petroleum by at least 5 percent progressively each month until Israel withdraws completely from territories occupied by Israel in the 1967 war and the legal rights of the Palestinians are restored." This was followed by an embargo on oil sales to the United States and the Netherlands. (Both the production cutbacks and the embargoes were dropped early in 1974.)

On October 20, Henry Kissinger was in Moscow, at the invitation of the Soviet Union, to discuss the terms of a cease-fire agreement to be "recommended" by the two superpowers to the Security Council.

XII

In the matter of embattled Israel's lifeline to the United States, Golda Meir put her trust implicitly in Henry Kissinger, from the beginning of the war, as before it.

Yitzhak Rabin had retired from the Embassy in Washington, in March 1973, in order to prepare to run for the Knesset, in the General Election then expected for October 1973. True to her policy of ignoring and bypassing Israel's Foreign Office, Golda Meir appointed her own personal assistant, Simcha Dinitz, to succeed Rabin as ambassador in Washington. Dinitz's previous experience of a diplomatic character seems to have been limited to taking down, for the benefit of Golda Meir, Rabin's telephoned accounts of Kissinger's views.

Granted this rather specialized introduction to his new career, it is not surprising that the new ambassador should have stood somewhat in awe of Henry Kissinger, and this he seems to have done. As Matti Golan describes the relation established between the Secretary of State and Israel's ambassador in 1973: "Kissinger, supreme artist of personal diplomacy, sensed what Dinitz was like from the moment the ambassador arrived in Washington. He started massaging his ego. . . . Without desiring it, without even being conscious of it, Dinitz turned into Kissinger's man."[55]

Kissinger's policy, in the early—and for Israel by far the most dangerous—phase of the war, was to stall on the supply of arms to Israel. On this point, we do not have to rely on Golan, an Israeli journalistic source severely critical of Kissinger, for what I think are sound Israeli reasons. There is independent confirmation from a loyal Kissinger staffman. William Quandt reports "mounting pressure" by Israel for arms, from October 8 on—the day of Israel's repulse by the Egyptians on the east bank of the Canal. The American response was cautious; "in principle," Israeli losses would be replaced, but not by an American airlift. El Al planes, with effaced markings, could pick up "modest quantities" (Quandt) of supplies. "When Dinitz complained about the slow American response, Kissinger blamed it on the Defense Department, a ploy he used repeatedly over the next few days."[56]

According to Golan, Kissinger was able, during the first week of the war, to use his "special relation" with the bemused Dinitz to insure that the Embassy did not "give the signal" which would unleash the pro-Israel lobby in Congress and the press, bringing pressure on Nixon "to come out of his Watergate cocoon" and insure massive aid to Israel. Kissinger headed this off by working on Dinitz: "He never left Dinitz alone. He spoke to him at least six or seven times a day. Each time he promised that the arms were coming, the arms were coming. And Dinitz, with his trust in Kissinger unshaken, agreed to wait."[57]

Kissinger's diplomatic tactics, subtly matched to his political strategy, worked like a charm, as far as Israel was concerned, up to October 12. On that day: "Prime Minister Meir, under pressure from the United States to accept a cease-fire in place, apparently appalled by the mounting casualties, and recognizing that American arms might not be readily forthcoming if she refused, finally agreed to accept a cease-fire in place."[58]

But what exactly was Kissinger's political strategy at this point?

On that matter, I see no reason to doubt (in this instance) Kissinger's own account, as given to a press conference, on October 12, 1973: "After hostilities broke out, the United States set itself two principal objectives. One, to end the hostilities as quickly as possible. Secondly, to end the hostilities in such a manner that they [sic] would contribute to the promotion of a more permanent, more lasting solution in the Middle East."[59]

The sic interpolated into that passage is not mine, but William Quandt's. But I find it interesting that Quandt—a sober official and not given to spattering sics over the prose of his superiors—feels the need for a sic just there. What Kissinger's choice of words reveals is that he is thinking of the local hostilities as something which, rightly used, can contribute to an objective important to the United States. That is how he shows himself to be thinking, while the hostilities are actually on. But was he already thinking that way even before the hostilities began?

I don't know the answer to that one, but Quandt's sic seems to be relevant to the consideration of the hypotheses discussed earlier in this chapter.

XIII

But already, by the time of that press conference (October 12), Kissinger's tactical achievement—though not, ultimately, his strategy—

had begun to come unstuck. On October 10, the Soviet Government had responded to the Israeli defeat of Syria by its own airlift to Cairo and Damascus. On October 11, Golda Meir, as well as expressing willingness for a cease-fire in place, had sent an urgent personal appeal (for an airlift to Israel) to Nixon.[60] For the first time since 1969, the Government of Israel felt a need to bypass Henry Kissinger.

On the morning of October 13, Sadat made his first major mistake, by his refusal of a cease-fire in place. Later on the same day— having taken stock of the Soviet challenge, Golda Meir's personal appeal and Sadat's refusal—President Nixon ordered the great airlift to Israel, in giant American transport aircraft.[61]

Although the airlift was something which Kissinger had done his formidable best to defer, it could be made to fit very well into his general strategy. Both the airlift itself and the agonizing delay which had preceded it had to bring home to Israel the extent of its dependence on the United States. And as for Sadat; well, Sadat had ignored Kissinger's repeated pleas for a cease-fire in place, combined with a warning (October 9): "All right; you've made your point. But where do we go from here? We can't expect the situation to hold for long, and when it changes it's going to change against you."[62]

Sadat had chosen to ignore Kissinger's advice and warning. Sadat could now see exactly what he had gotten himself into by ignoring Kissinger.

After the war, both parties, mutually chastened and sobered, would be likely to listen carefully to what they would hear from the Secretary of State.

In this late phase of the war, as after the initial Arab victories, Kissinger's immediate objective was still a cease-fire in place. That became a very popular objective with the American and Western publics, after the imposition of the Arab oil embargo, news of whose coming into force reached Kissinger during his flight to Moscow to meet Brezhnev (October 20).[63]

Despite the embargo, Kissinger in Moscow was in an extraordinarily strong negotiating position. His immediate objective was a cease-fire in place. But his negotiating adversaries had a far more urgent interest in such a cease-fire, because the Israelis were now beating the Egyptians as well as the Syrians, and seemed on the verge of decisive victory. In these conditions, Kissinger could virtually write his own ticket, and he clearly did so. Within four hours, he had reached the agreement with the Soviets to which Security Council Resolution 338 later gave solemn expression in terms of international law. That resolution, adopted by the Security Council on October 22, called for a cease-fire in place within twelve hours, for the implementation of Resolution 242 and for "negotiations between the parties concerned under appropriate auspices aimed at establishing a just and durable peace in the Middle East."

"Negotiations between the parties" was the new element, and was designed to help secure Golda Meir's agreement. Just at the time the Security Council was agreeing on 338, Kissinger was in Tel Aviv, on his way home from Moscow. Reluctantly, and perhaps with reservations, Golda Meir and her colleagues agreed to the resolution and the cease-fire, which (from a military point of view) robbed them of the fruits of a most hard-won victory.

Just after Kissinger had returned to Washington (October 23) the Soviets informed him that Israel had violated the cease-fire. Whoever may have violated it, the renewed fighting was to Israel's advantage, militarily speaking. The Egyptian Third Army was now surrounded, and the Israelis threatened to destroy it, or failing that, to starve it out. The Soviet Union made clear that it would not accept the liquidation of the Third Army. Brezhnev, in a letter to Nixon, threatened, if necessary, to take "appropriate steps unilaterally." American forces were immediately placed on a relatively high state of alert, known as Def Con 3.

The superpowers seemed nearer the brink than at any time since the Cuban missile crisis of 1962.

Kissinger now leaned hard on Israel. It is not clear whether he threatened them with sending United States forces to relieve the Third Army, or, as seems more probable, with "an implied threat not to help them if they found themselves in confrontation with the Soviets. . . ."[64] In any case, Kissinger left the Israelis in no doubt as to where they stood. "You will be forced if it reaches that point," he told Dinitz.[65]

The Government of Israel now knew that if its armed forces went on with their victorious offensive, Israel would be faced with a renewal of the awesome predicament which had followed its military victory of 1956 (and had loomed again in 1970): the simultaneous threat of annihilation from one superpower and of abandonment from the other.

On the afternoon of October 25, the cease-fire came into effect, and this time held. The Yom Kippur War was over, in stalemate.

XIV

In its combined military and diplomatic aspects, the Yom Kippur War was the most traumatic ordeal that Israel had ever undergone. Israel now knew that its Arab enemies had grown more formidable than had been believed to be possible, and that its relations with the United States were of a more cryptic and conditional character than had been confidently assumed since the Six Day War.

In October 1973, Hubris and Euphoria spread their wings once more and deserted Jerusalem, not necessarily forever.

11

STEP BY STEP
1973-1977

Israel has no foreign policy, only a domestic political
system.

— HENRY KISSINGER

YOU CAN'T WIN!

However expressed, that was the feeling that pervaded Israel
in the immediate aftermath of the Yom Kippur War. It was also the
unequivocal message Israel had just received from both superpowers.
With the cutting off of the Egyptian Third Army, total military victory
had been within Israel's grasp, and then snatched from it. Victory had
been vetoed by the superpowers, one of which was Israel's only
friend.

Though more smoothly delivered—in the tones of Henry Kissinger—the message had been basically the same as that received from
the Eisenhower Administration seventeen years before: "If you want
to fight the Russians, on this one, you'll be on your own."

More generally, Israel at this time was made conscious of its
extreme isolation, not merely in the region, but in the hemisphere.
During the war, the Western European countries—except for Portugal—had denied U.S. aircraft headed for Israel the right to land
and refuel on their territories.[1] In the circumstances, that was a transaction that had to remind Israelis of certain earlier closings of doors,
in the thirties and forties. As if to emphasize that point, the Soviet
Union, in 1974, cut back the level of Jewish emigration to Israel. At
the same time, nearly all African countries—previously courted by

UPI/BETTMANN NEWSPHOTOS

Prime Minister Golda Meir, President Nixon and National Security Adviser Henry Kissinger, January 1973. Meir's Government at this time believed itself to have unprecedentedly close access to the President through Kissinger. Kissinger's role at this period is discussed in the text.

Israel, not without success—had broken off relations, most of them after Ariel Sharon's forces had crossed the Canal "into Africa."[2]

In the wake of the Yom Kippur War, the countries of the Old World—from the British Isles to Japan—took pains, in varying ways and degrees, and at varying paces, to mark their disapproval of Israel and their sympathy with the Arabs. If Israel had a friend at all, in all the Old World, the character and reputation of that friend were such as actively to increase the malaise of many thoughtful Israelis. For the friend was the Republic of South Africa, the other pariah nation of the Old World. This was not only a burdensome friendship, in terms of relationships with the indigenous governments of the non-white majority of the world's people; it was also burdensome in terms of Jewish history, and Zionist tradition.

When the extent of Israel's enhanced isolation came gradually to be realized, in the postwar period, it led inevitably to the further growth among Israelis of what one Israeli scholar has called "their old, holocaust-inspired siege syndrome."[3]

Yet of course, Israel's enhanced isolation in this period did not derive from any recrudescence of anti-semitism (though it may, in some cases, have stimulated such a recrudescence). It derived from the perceived self-interest of the Western European countries and Japan, the great consumers of Arab oil, and beneficiaries from Arab investment of petrodollars. After the fourfold rise in oil prices, it was felt necessary by the consumers to do everything possible to attract the investment of the vast additional Arab wealth. So it seemed politic to distance oneself carefully from Israel, and to express and exhibit sympathy with the Arab, and Palestinian, cause.

All this was, and is, not without an element of comedy. You could make pro-Arab statements, or cast pro-Arab votes, while at the same time winking in the direction of the United States, to signify that your statements and votes should not be taken too literally. The Japanese seem to be particularly good at this. Henry Kissinger records a pertinent conversation, of November 1973, with Kakuei Tanaka, then Prime Minister of Japan: "Some sort of declaration of sympathy for the Arab cause was necessary, according to Tanaka, even granting that it would not change American policy. Nor, he emphasized, was it really Japan's purpose to influence American policy."[4]

Understandably, Israelis resented the less-than-disinterested lectures on international morality that they now increasingly received from the great consumers of Arab oil. They also resented the general lack of interest in the question—rather easily answered—of who had started the war that had just ended. In the past, Israel had been blamed for planning an aggressive war—Suez/Sinai, 1956—and for striking the first blow—Six Day War. Now it was only too apparent that it was Egypt, not Israel, which had planned the Yom Kippur War, and struck the first, devastating blow. Yet it was Israel, not Egypt, that got all the blame from the international community. That seemed another case of You can't win.

But in this particular case, the international community, though perhaps fortuitously, had more justice on its side than most Israelis would admit. Sadat had indeed planned the war, and started it. But he had done so only after making a serious peace initiative and finding it treated with contempt.

Israelis legitimately blamed Golda Meir's Government for the errors of judgment which led to Israel's military unpreparedness for the Yom Kippur War. But they could have condemned it, with no less justice, on a more fundamental count: that of bringing about the war for which it was unprepared and yet for which it had allowed its adversary no alternative, compatible with his own survival.

The question of peace in exchange for territory had now to be explored seriously after more than two thousand Israeli deaths in war, and in circumstances much less propitious for Israel than those which had prevailed almost three years before, when Sadat had first made his historic offer. Yet it seems that it was a precondition for a serious exploration of the question that the circumstances should become less propitious for Israel.

II

For nearly two years after the Yom Kippur War, the dominant presence in the diplomacy of the Middle East was that of the American Secretary of State, Henry Kissinger. The war—whatever part Kissinger may or may not have played in its origins—gave him his great opportunity for personal diplomacy, and he took that opportunity with immense skill, verve and devious energy.

In global terms, Kissinger's main aim was to get the Soviet Union out of the region, as far as possible, while pretending to welcome it in, as part of a superpower consensus, under the general principles of supposedly prevalent détente.

For the "pretending to welcome" part of this program, Kissinger's main instrument was the so-called Geneva (Peace) Conference which opened on December 21, 1973; this was not really a conference at all—it had neither agenda, nor terms of reference, nor rules of procedure—but an ambiguous rite of legitimation, with an aspect of suspended menace.

The participants at Geneva were the United States, the Soviet Union, Egypt, Israel and Jordan. The proceedings were presided over by the Secretary-General of the United Nations, Kurt Waldheim, a man with considerable experience both of the theatrical side of international diplomacy and of some of the realities behind the scenes.

What the Soviets seemed to think was legitimized at Geneva was their own role as active partners in the peacemaking process in the region. What was actually legitimized was the role of Henry Kissinger, as sole mediator. And the Soviets themselves had helped to confer this legitimacy, thus unwittingly consenting to their own exclusion, so happy were they with the dignified and deferential nature of the ceremony in which their exclusion was legitimized.

Formally, what the conference did was to approve an American proposal for the establishment of joint committees to work out disengagement agreements.[5] But in fact every detail of such agreements had to be sanctioned by the Governments concerned. And the two principal Governments concerned—those of Egypt and Israel—both wanted to advance, or to protect, their separate and opposing interests under American mediation, and without active Soviet involvement.

Kissinger appears to have convinced Sadat, even before the war, that only the United States, through the influence over Israel which Israel's dependence on the United States conferred, could help Egypt to recover its lost territory. The Soviet Union could not do this, having no influence over Israel, and it was therefore in Egypt's interests to cooperate with the United States, and shut out the Soviet Union.

Previous Secretaries of State had always tended to see Israel merely as a domestically imposed burden and handicap for American foreign policy in the Middle East. Kissinger's more unorthodox and penetrating mind saw how Israel, and America's not-quite-unconditional commitment to Israel, could be made an asset to the United States in its dealings with Israel's Arab neighbors. The implicit, and sometimes fairly explicit, message from America to those neighbors was: "If you want anything out of, or back from, that awkward and formidable neighbor of yours, you've got to come to us."

Sadat had gotten that message. America's support for Israel, during its war with Egypt, actually helped to bring Egypt within America's sphere of influence: a phenomenon quite contrary to the conventional wisdom of the State Department and the British Foreign Office.

The great American airlift to Israel actually became a political asset to Sadat, after the war. It explained why the victory which Sadat had claimed had been followed not by the overthrow of the Jewish State but by a cease-fire along the Suez Canal. As Sadat explains in his memoirs, Egypt had indeed defeated the Jews, but it could not be expected to take on a superpower. On October 19, the day he decided to accept the cease-fire, Sadat cabled to his reproachful ally, Assad: "I am willing to fight Israel, no matter how long, but never the U.S.A."[6] Hence not only the cease-fire, but the need for negotiation.

As an account of the Yom Kippur War, Sadat's version left out a few matters, but it was sound politics, whatever the history. Both in Egypt itself and in the Arab world generally, the need to believe in the victory over the Jews was so strong as to make Sadat's explanation credible, at least for a time.

III

In his extension of American influence in the region, Henry Kissinger not only needed to be able to exert pressure on Israel, he also needed to be seen, in the Arab world, as the exerter of the indispensable pressure, without which Israel would never move. Spontaneous concessions by Israel were unhelpful to the United States, and sharply discouraged.

In the immediate aftermath of the war, direct military contact had been established between Egyptian and Israeli forces. General Aharon Yariv, of the I.D.F., met regularly with General Abd al-Ghani al-Gamassi, of Egypt, at Kilometer 101, on the Cairo-Suez road, to arrange such urgent matters as the stabilizing of the cease-fire, and supply arrangements to Egypt's surrounded Third Army. The generals got on well together, all too well from Kissinger's point of view, since they were moving toward early disengagement too fast, and with an appearance of Israeli spontaneity. Kissinger now warned the Israelis, in effect, not to move until he pushed them. As William Quandt says:

> Kissinger did want to demonstrate that a sustained United States role was essential for sustained diplomatic progress.
> . . . If the oil boycott was to be lifted, it would also be in return for American success in promoting agreement. And if Soviet prestige was to remain low, the United States must remain in charge of the negotiations. Kissinger therefore advised the Israelis to slow down at Kilometer 101, and to reserve their position on disengagement "until Geneva." To some observers this seemed cynical, but it fitted into Kissinger's broader diplomatic scheme.[7]

I don't know why the "but."

"Israeli intransigence" had now become an American asset, not to be squandered without advance American approval. As Kissinger himself puts it: "Israel's obstinacy, maddening as it can be, serves the purpose of both our countries best. . . . Our strategy depended on our being the only country capable of eliciting Israeli concessions but also on our doing it within a context where this was perceived to be a stiff task."[8]

As will be seen, Kissinger did not at all care for Israeli obstinacy when he actually experienced it. What he really wanted was the appearance of obstinacy, with the reality of compliance. But this combination was not always available.

IV

Israel's General Election—due in October, but deferred owing to the war—took place on December 31, 1973. The governing Labor Alignment lost five seats, mostly to Likud, but the shift was much less than had been feared, or hoped, and Labor was able to form the Government again. Yitzhak Rabin writes: "Considering that they were exhausted, mourning their dead, and having difficulty in digesting recent events, or comprehending their significance, the voters were merciful towards the Labour Party."[9]

Perhaps if the voters had had more time to digest and comprehend, they might have been less merciful. As it was, the Government was rescued from many of the consequences of its own overconfidence by the errors of its opponents. Labor—ironically in terms of its own past conduct—ran on a "peace" ticket; peace was mentioned seventeen times in the Labor platform. Likud, in attacking Labor, sounded like a war party, to many members of a war-weary electorate. Labor ran on "Geneva," and the nebulous but attractive hopes associated with Geneva. Kissinger's staging of the Geneva Conference was intended to fit—among other requirements—the needs of Israel's Labor Government (since the alternative was the even more difficult Likud). That the conference should meet was regarded as helpful; that it should adjourn, without substantive discussion, was also helpful. Likud was drawn to attack Geneva, without Geneva's having done anything that could possibly merit attack. In this way, Likud seemed to be attacking the mere idea of peace itself. Looking back, after the elections, Labor leaders believed that Geneva had saved them.[10] Golda Meir re-formed her Government, with Moshe Dayan still as Minister for Defense.

With the Israeli elections more or less out of the way, Kissinger could now start on the first round of what was to become famous as his "shuttle diplomacy" between Jerusalem and the Arab capitals. By

January 18, 1974, Kissinger had agreed with Sadat and Dayan on a plan (known in retrospect as First Sinai) for the disengagement and thinning out of forces in the Canal area and the re-creation of a U.N. buffer zone. The published plan was accompanied by private (but leaked) assurances from the United States to Israel that Egypt would not interfere with Israeli freedom of navigation in the Red Sea, and that U.N. forces would not be withdrawn without the consent of both sides—this last being, from an Israeli point of view, an "improvement" over the pre-1967 situation.

After First Sinai, Israeli forces still held the strategic Giddi and Mitla passes in the Western Sinai Desert, but were separated from the Suez Canal by the United Nations buffer force.

In terms of the real interests of all parties, First Sinai was a sensible agreement. But in terms of prestige, it redounded to the credit of Sadat—and of Kissinger—much more than to that of the Government of Israel. Yet the Government of Golda Meir could easily have survived the signature of First Sinai. What brought the Government down was the demobilization of large numbers of reservists, released by the disengagement of First Sinai. The country in general had been stunned and confused, in late 1973, by the Yom Kippur War. But the young people who came home from the southern front, early in 1974, were vengefully angry, and communicated their feelings—and their experiences—to their families and friends.

Most of the fury of the citizen soldiers concentrated on the Minister for Defense, Moshe Dayan. The popular wrath exploded uncontrollably when the Agranat Commission of Inquiry report, in April 1974, cleared both the Minister for Defense and the Prime Minister of what it called "immediate responsibility" for Israel's unpreparedness: "Scenes, reminiscent of the street rallies of 1967, which had forced Dayan, with the support of hysterical party bodies, upon Levi Eshkol, were now reversed against him."[11] Under this pressure, Golda Meir's support rapidly crumbled. On April 11, 1974, she announced her resignation. Moshe Dayan followed her into the wilderness.

Labor had now to find a new leader, and—after a lapse of time— a Prime Minister. Labor's choice fell (April 22) on Yitzhak Rabin. Rabin had much to recommend him. As former Chief of Staff—for a period that included the Six Day War—and former ambassador in Washington, Rabin must have seemed ideally qualified to look after Israel's two most vital concerns: military preparedness and relations with the United States. Also, Rabin's youth was in his favor, at a time when people were looking for a fresh start. Born in Israel, a *sabra*, he was to be the first Prime Minister of Israel who did not belong to the generation of the Founders. But probably Rabin's decisive qualification, in the eyes of the public, was that he was the only prominent Labor person who had not belonged to the Government of Golda Meir. More than one writer confers on Rabin, in this context, the adjective "untainted."[12]

Rabin's exemption from the "taint" of Golda Meir's Administration is another of those ironies which stud this story. As we have seen, Rabin, as ambassador in Washington, had enjoyed more influence over Israel's foreign and defense policies than any member of that Government, under Golda Meir, with the single exception of Moshe Dayan. With Golda Meir's approval, Rabin had assumed control of Israel's relations with the United States. In this, the decisively important area, Rabin had become Israel's real Foreign Minister. Eban— probably unwisely, in the circumstances—continued to carry the responsibility, but Rabin had the power. And although Rabin's public reputation was that of a "moderate dove," his influence on Golda Meir's Government had come down on the side of hawkishness and hubris, especially in the period of the War of Attrition.

When Rabin formed his Government, he dropped Eban as Foreign Minister, offering him instead the post of Minister for Information. The offer was expressive of a sort of curse which had rested on Eban since Ben-Gurion's day: the curse of being regarded by his fellow countrymen as a voice, not as a mind. Eban turned down the offer, and was not included in the new Government. Yigal Allon— author of the Allon Plan—became Foreign Minister.

In his memoirs, Rabin explains the sacking of Eban in the following words: "During his many years as Foreign Minister he had essentially explained policies formulated by others, rather than generate his own political thinking. I had a chance to observe this while serving in Washington."[13] The ambassador himself, as we have seen, had done much to create the phenomenon which he observed.

But Rabin had another, stronger reason for dropping Eban. Eban was the principal supporter—understandably—of Rabin's chief political rival, Shimon Peres. Peres, chiefly known hitherto, in Israeli domestic politics, as the most loyal follower of Moshe Dayan, had challenged Rabin for the leadership of the party. Rabin had won, but by an uncomfortably narrow margin: 298–254. The margin was so narrow that Rabin was constrained to accept his challenger as the holder of by far the most important portfolio in the Government, that of Minister for Defense. The Rabin Government was thus, from its inception, an extremely uncomfortable and unpredictable dyarchy. It was not so much a Government as a stage for an agon, an unremitting contention between two inveterate enemies.

This was an enmity that went back at least fifteen years, to Ben-Gurion's time. Peres had been one of Ben-Gurion's bright young men, and his Deputy Defense Minister, and Rabin believed that Peres had used his influence with Ben-Gurion to thwart Rabin's military career. About this early phase in that ill-starred relationship, Rabin writes, in his memoirs: "It never occurred to me to mix considerations of personal prestige into such fateful matters. But Peres let personal conflicts foment [sic] and seemed to take advantage of human foibles to place his adversaries under pressure."[14] (Those words were published in 1979, by which time Peres was already leader of the Labor Party, and Rabin his deputy, and Labor was in opposition.)

On appointing Peres to his Government in 1974, Rabin writes retrospectively: "I accepted Peres as Defense Minister—albeit with a heavy heart. It was an error I would regret and whose price I would pay in full."[15] In fact—as Rabin himself makes clear—he could not have formed a Government if he had not made that "error" and paid that price. Peres supporters were strong enough to exact the Defense portfolio for their leader.

Whatever the personal merits in the Rabin-Peres vendetta, a Government with that vendetta at its heart was clearly unsuitable for a country in Israel's predicament. Such a Government tended to make that predicament even graver than it need otherwise have been. (At the same time, the great weakness of the Government conferred on it a certain kind of desperate sluggish strength. No one is better placed to resist pressure than the person who knows he *can't* give in to it.)

V

Israel's frequent wars, and high standards of military efficiency, have caused the State to be labeled, quite often, in the international press, as "the Prussia of the Middle East." The comparison necessarily suggests the image of a highly disciplined, hierarchical, authoritarian society. That image is almost ludicrously remote from the realities of the social and political life of Israel.

In the daily life of Israel, as any visitor can observe, deference is in short supply. This is a land of energetic, jumpy, argumentative individuals, each of whom thinks his and her own opinion is at least as good as that of anyone else, however highly placed. The same spirit pervades the country's politics. The Jewish State, in the conduct of its own internal affairs,[16] is intensely and jealously democratic: so democratic as to be almost unworkable.

In the days of David Ben-Gurion, the unique personal authority of the Founder was such as to impose—though even then not without difficulty—a certain unity, and to give a central direction to decision making and, above all, to the formation of policy for the middle and long term.

Since Ben-Gurion's day, however, Governments have tended to be weak aggregates, containing strong personalities, with strongly conflicting views and/or ambitions. This makes it difficult to summon the collective will to take decisions unpopular with any large section of the population. Shlomo Aronson defines "the nature of the post–Ben-Gurion political regime": "It was a multi-party parliamentary system with a collegial cabinet in which the prime minister was *primus inter pares*. The other ministers were his equals, representing and drawing support from many factions—from outside the government and, in most cases, from outside the parliamentary factions as well."[17]

Within this cramping system, Rabin's Government was even weaker than Golda Meir's had been, especially in relation to foreign policy, interlinked with defense policy. Rabin was much less popular than Golda Meir had been, and the support for his Government was even more divided, factionally. Golda Meir's relations with her Minister for Defense, Moshe Dayan, had been tense and fraught, but the Rabin-Peres relationship was very much worse than that. Rabin was so beset that he "could not sponsor any initiatives of his own; he could only react to the initiatives of others, particularly to those of the American secretary of state."[18]

VI

Although Golda Meir had announced her Government's resignation in April, Israeli practice did not allow the resignation to come into effect until the beginning of June. In the interim, Henry Kissinger pressed ahead with his step-by-step diplomacy. The next step aimed at was a disengagement agreement between Syria and Israel, to match First Sinai, between Egypt and Israel.

As he shuttled to and fro—thirteen times in a month—between Damascus and Jerusalem, Kissinger knew that both sides needed some kind of agreement. Assad needed to show that, like Sadat, he could recover some of the territory lost in 1967; this made him, too, able to claim "victory." Israel had an immediate incentive to concede some territory, in exchange for the recovery of prisoners in Syrian hands, and for the return home of reservists from the northern front, to be released by disengagement, as those on the southern front had already been. Yet the Government of Israel was desperately anxious to yield no more than the bare minimum of territory necessary to secure those objectives. The border with Syria, so close to areas of Jewish settlement, is a much more sensitive matter than the desert of Western Sinai.

Kissinger was anxious to get a settlement before the new Government took office in Israel; hence the grueling urgency of this phase of his negotiations. He was very familiar with the personnel of Golda Meir's (now lame-duck) Government. He soon established good relations with the ruler of Syria. William Quandt seems to have found this surprising: "An improbable but genuine personal relationship was beginning to develop between these two very different men."[19]

Yet they were not very different, but very much alike, in everything that was pertinent to their negotiation. "Politics in our present age is not a matter of sentiment, on the contrary it is the facts of power."[20] So Kissinger had told Mohamed Heikal, in Cairo, the previous November. Assad's opinion about the relative importance of sentiment and facts of power was identical with Kissinger's, as had often been demonstrated. The Machiavellian of Damascus and the Machiavellian of Washington were well made to understand each other, once they could identify the ground of common interest.

After much late-night haggling, accompanied by sardonic banter in Damascus and lamentation in Jerusalem, the common ground was identified. Israel agreed to a limited withdrawal from its forward positions on the Golan Heights. The zone evacuated was very narrow, but it included Quneitra: a ruined and deserted town, but a town, and marked on maps, and so important for Assad's prestige. The evacuated zone was to be demilitarized, and monitored by a United Nations Disengagement Observer Force.

The disengagement agreement was signed by military representatives of Israel and Syria, at Geneva, on May 31, 1974.

VII

For Henry Kissinger, the summer of 1974 was the peak. His diplomatic achievement in the Middle East, in the six months following the Yom Kippur War, had been astonishing by any standards, and he had managed to make it look even more astonishing than it actually was, and different from what it actually was.

To the Western public, following Kissinger's airborne diplomacy through the jet-lagged and mesmerized eyes of his press entourage, Kissinger seemed to be making peace virtually single-handedly. As he flitted between the Oriental capitals, hectoring, cajoling, dazzling, conjuring up pieces-of paper with amazing properties of reconciliation, the Secretary of State came to seem the benevolent Superman of the peace process. *Newsweek* and *Time* depicted him as such, and Kissinger agreed.[21]

Kissinger's real achievement in this period was significantly different, and more solid. His achievement lay not in bringing about disengagement but in *managing* disengagement to the advantage of the United States.

Disengagement virtually achieved itself, in this phase, because the regional parties to the conflict wanted it. Indeed, they needed it so much that, at at least one point, as we have seen, the Secretary of State held them back from disengaging too promptly, too spontaneously and too autonomously. Like every good magician, Kissinger wanted his trick to look impossible.

In this phase, Kissinger didn't need to apply pressure in the direction of disengagement; all he needed was to control the working of the pressure. As Nadav Safran says: "The real pressures were implicit in the situation [Kissinger] had helped to shape."[22]

Safran is referring here to Kissinger's handling of affairs during the Yom Kippur War, especially in the closing phase, when Israel was denied victory. But it also seems that, even before the Yom Kippur War, Kissinger may have "helped to shape" the situation which he was to put so brilliantly to use.

Israel needed to disengage, and had strong incentives to do so at a pace and in a manner devised by the United States: the only friend. Urgently needed supplies, as well as future prospects, depended on this. Israel's needs, in relation to its only friend, made the fulcrum of Kissinger's lever with the Arab states. They too needed disengagement—Sadat had needed it desperately—and Kissinger convinced them that only by working through him could they achieve disengagement in such a way as to recover at least some, and perhaps eventually all, of the national territories lost in 1967.

By June 1974, Kissinger's management of disengagement had paid rich dividends in terms of the influence and prestige of the United States in the region. Diplomatic relations between the United States and Egypt, and between the United States and Syria—both broken off in 1967—were now restored, and cordial. At Sadat's entreaty—and to their own advantage—the oil-rich states had promised to end their embargo against the United States. Best of all, the Soviet Union was largely eclipsed in the region. It was entirely excluded from the disengagement process at the wish not only of Israel but of the very states the Soviet Union had backed and armed: Egypt and Syria. Geneva, where the Soviet Union had appeared as equal partners with the United States in December 1973, had become in 1974 no more than an address, and a set of premises, for the registration of agreements reached exclusively under American auspices. And the Soviet Union could not even publicly complain about this, without advertising its decline in influence over its own clients, and in the region generally.

Kissinger's achievement was all the more splendidly conspicuous in that it reached its climax in the middle of the most dismal year, domestically and internationally, in the modern political history of the United States. At the end of April 1975, the total failure of the long American effort in Vietnam had been demonstrated for the world, when Saigon fell to the Communists, and the American ambassador escaped by helicopter. Domestically, by the early summer of 1974, Watergate had entered its terminal stage. President Nixon was bleeding to death, politically, from multiple self-inflicted wounds.

In quest of a cure, through the reflections of Kissinger's glory, Nixon toured the Middle East in June. As the President noted in his diary, the tour tended "to focus attention on other subjects"—other than that of impeachment.[23]

The trip did Nixon no good, but it crowned the apotheosis of Henry Kissinger, seen touring the region of his triumphs with, in his train, an ailing President of the United States.

VIII

In June 1974, Henry Kissinger had still two and a half years to run as virtually sovereign Secretary of State. When Nixon resigned, on August 9, his successor, Gerald Ford, was happy not only to retain Kissinger as Secretary of State but to leave to him the conduct of international affairs, as Nixon had done, with such happy results in that domain, since December 1973.

But the next two and a half years were not so splendid a period for Kissinger as the previous six months had been. True, what was regarded as his main achievement held. Egypt continued to move out of the Soviet, and into the American, sphere. But in consolidating relations with Egypt, Kissinger was led to strain relations first with Israel and then with Syria.

In this period, as in others, Israelis were prepared to "trade territory for peace": provided the territory was not too much, or in the wrong place, and provided the signs of peace were adequate. By late 1974, the signs of peace, on the Arab side, were far from adequate, from an Israeli point of view.

For Israelis, the Arab Summit at Rabat, in October 1974, was a disquieting and infuriating spectacle. Here were Sadat and Assad backing the P.L.O.—*after* Israel's territorial concessions to Egypt and Syria—even more strongly than they had done *before* there were any such concessions. The P.L.O.—now recognized by all the Arab states as "sole legitimate representative of the Palestinian people"—was thereby encouraged to step up its terrorist activities against Israeli people. At the same time, Egypt and Syria, having pocketed their territorial gains, now appeared to close the door against recognition of Israel, or negotiations with it. Both states had accepted Security Council Resolution 242 (eventual recognition of Israel) and 338 (direct negotiations), yet both states were now hinging their recognition on satisfaction of the P.L.O., which refused either to recognize or to negotiate with Israel.[24] Naturally, the mood in Israel hardened against further concessions to any of the Rabat partners. And the mood hardened still further the following month when Yasser Arafat, with the apparent enthusiastic backing of all the Arab states, made his triumphal appearance on the stage of the United Nations General Assembly.

Henry Kissinger was anxious—as it seems, overanxious—to get on with the next step in his diplomacy: Second Sinai, requiring Israeli withdrawal beyond the strategic Sinai passes. He seems to have failed to take adequate account of the hardening mood in Israel, and of the strong emotional grounds for it. He pressed hard for Second Sinai, and met with unexpectedly clear and prolonged resistance.

The Government of Israel, by early 1975, was no longer under any kind of *internal* pressure to reach some agreements, as it had been during the actual disengagement period (because of prisoners and reservists). The internal pressure, once disengagement was complete, all went the other way: against any further concessions to Arabs, except in exchange for visible and solid advantages to Israel. Sadat at this point was not even willing to offer Israel a minimal declaration of "nonbelligerency," as demanded by Israel.

Rabin, deeply conscious of the need for the American lifeline, might have been willing to agree to Second Sinai at this stage had he been in control of his Cabinet, but he was not. On matters such as this, he absolutely needed the assent of his Minister for Defense— and near-equal—Shimon Peres. This assent was denied him.

The Sinai passes may or may not be indispensable in terms of Israel's military defenses. But in terms of Israel's domestic politics, the passes were an excellent terrain for a Minister for Defense wishing to make an effective political stand against his Prime Minister. Peres's hard line prevailed. Rabin, having no choice, resisted Kissinger.

After ten days of fruitless shuttling between Egypt and Israel in March 1975, Kissinger lost patience with Israel. On March 22—having spent the day on a tour of Masada—Kissinger told the Israeli Government: "Step-by-step has been throttled . . . the United States is losing control of events."[25]

Kissinger then immediately returned to Washington, "going public" on the way, against Israel. He told reporters on the plane that Rabin was "a small man whose only concern was what Peres might say of him." Israel was stuck with leaders whose main concern was with "their petty personal rivalries."[26]

A touch of hubris there too perhaps: in that "small" and that "petty."

Once back in Washington, Kissinger forcefully expressed his displeasure by directing the disconnection of the special line, which had been installed during the Yom Kippur War, between his office and that of the Israeli ambassador, Simcha Dinitz.[27] President Ford, no doubt on Kissinger's advice, also made known his displeasure with

Israel—something he was to regret in the following year—and omi-
nously announced a "reassessment" of America's whole policy in the
Middle East.

By "going public" in this way, and at this time—when he might
instead have simply applied the "subtle squeeze"—Kissinger seemed
to show something less than his usual sureness of touch. A significant
part of the Secretary's success so far had been due to his skill in keeping the pro-Israel lobby off his back. That was what that special line
had been for. By cutting it off, snubbing the ambassador and his
Government, and implicitly threatening Israel itself, Kissinger was
now inviting the attentions of the lobby in question, and in favorable
conditions for the lobby's operations.

In conditions of military emergency—including not only wartime,
but the subsequent periods of unstable cease-fires—the pro-Israel
lobby cannot be brought effectively into play, for counterpressure
against American pressure. In these conditions, Israel's needs are of
great urgency, while the lobby takes time to mobilize and make its
weight felt. But in conditions of no military emergency—as in March
1975—there is time for the lobby to mobilize, which it now began
to do.

IX

Meanwhile in Washington, throughout April, the reassessment
promised by President Ford went ahead. Kissinger solemnly conferred—on April 1, perhaps not unsuitably—with the best and bright-
est of the foreign-policy establishment: Dean Rusk, McGeorge Bundy,
George Ball, Cyrus Vance, George Shultz, Robert McNamara and
others. Over the next several weeks, Kissinger sat at the feet of various
academic and ambassadorial pundits, in his new role as a humbled
practitioner anxious to learn from the wise how to conduct international affairs. The general drift of the advice received from the consensus of these sages has been summed up as follows: "The time for
step-by-step diplomacy was past. A more ambitious strategy was
needed. The Palestinians could no longer be ignored. The Soviets
would have to be brought into the negotiations."[28]

It seems likely that what Kissinger was interested in at this point
was scaring the Israelis, by reminding them that there were nastier
options than Second Sinai, and more dangerous men in Washington
than Henry Kissinger. The threat, essentially—and Kissinger was to

use it a little later explicitly to Rabin[29]—was that of re-establishing the Geneva Conference, not just for show this time, but for business. The "Geneva" stick, in Kissinger's dealings with Israel, was a variant of the "nice cop/tough cop" ploy: "If you won't listen to me, you'll have to listen to Gromyko."

Kissinger's tactics of the spring and early summer of 1975 are now a matter of historical interest only. But the consensus of "thinking people," which these tactics were designed to discover and exhibit, has become a lasting and somewhat influential aspect of the international scene. It is a consensus that has influenced policy, to a limited extent, and the appearances of policy, to a greater extent. And it is a consensus that has provided the *leitmotiv* of a huge amount of "informed comment" on the Middle East over the past ten years.

The central idea is that a comprehensive settlement, embracing both the P.L.O. and Israel, both must and can be attained. This idea has been encouraged, since the summer of 1974, obliquely but persistently, by the more pragmatic elements in the P.L.O. itself, headed by Yasser Arafat. Arafat's thinking on this point was stimulated by Henry Kissinger's successes in the early "disengagement" phases of his post–Yom Kippur diplomacy. If Israel was being forced to surrender occupied territory first to Egypt, and then to Syria, could not Israel also be forced to surrender territory to the P.L.O. on which a Palestinian State would be established?

The P.L.O.'s Palestinian National Council, meeting in Cairo in June 1974, "called for the establishment of the people's national independent and fighting authority on any part of Palestinian land to be liberated." This was seen as a victory for the P.L.O. moderates. As one observer noted in the aftermath of that meeting, the decision "seems to clear the way for the leadership to explore the possibility of the more restricted goal with the powers concerned."[30]

To many moderate and benevolent minds in the West, the idea of such a compromise, bringing peace to the region, became, and has remained, profoundly attractive.

Yet there were certain difficult questions, and these have not gone away, or been satisfactorily answered.

First of all, would the Palestinian State be based on compromise with Israel, or would it be a springboard for the overthrow of Israel? "Compromise," said the Arab advocates of the Palestinian State in their dialogue with the West, generally conducted in private; "springboard," said the same people in inter-Arab discussions.

Western well-wishers to the P.L.O. moderates think that the private assurances, and public hints, made in the Western context should be taken seriously, and that the public declarations in the inter-Arab context may safely be ignored. Skeptics—including myself—think that the statements made to Arabs are more likely to reflect the realities of the region, and also that these statements—solidly based as they are on the movement's fundamental charter, the Palestinian National Covenant—would be difficult and dangerous to go back on. In any case it seems clear that P.L.O. moderation and the Jewish State are incompatible. An Arab scholar who has made a study of "moderates" and "rejectionists" in the P.L.O.—and appears to support the "moderate" tendency—has the following to say in "The Moderate Group: The View from Fatah." "The relationship between . . . armed struggle and liberation is organic. . . . The step that follows liberation is the dismantling of the 'racist' political and economic structure of Israel as a state and the establishment of a democratic non-sectarian, secular Palestine in which Jews, Muslims and Christians would live together as Palestinian citizens with equal rights and duties."[31]

If that is so, it seems to follow that the Palestinian State, which these moderates seek to establish "on any part of Palestinian land to be liberated," would be dedicated to the destruction of the Jewish State. At the very least, it is not hard to understand why Israelis believe that that would be the case.

The second set of difficult questions concerns Israel. Is the cession of territory to the P.L.O. for a Palestinian State something which Israel is expected to accept voluntarily; or will it have to be imposed on Israel; and if so, how?

The voluntary option, being the more agreeable, has often been recommended, as something which Israel should see the need to accept, in its own best interests. That argument was well presented in an article by Stanley Hoffman which appeared in *Foreign Affairs* during the "reassessment" period.[32] The argument for a comprehensive Israeli peace initiative, taking in the Palestinians, has, as William Quandt points out, a "major flaw . . . such a policy would require a strong Israeli government backed by a broad public consensus. That apparently was lacking."[33]

Tougher-minded peacemakers involved in the reassessment—George Ball apparently among them—could see that Israel would never *voluntarily* hand over the West Bank and East Jerusalem to the P.L.O. So that solution would have to be imposed, by the fiat of the superpowers, reunited at Geneva.

But for many Israelis—and not just Begin's Likud—such an "imposed solution" would be indeed the *casus Masadae*. Would American public opinion really support the joint overpowering of Israel by the United States and the Soviet Union together?

The reassessors seem to have been wandering rather far from certain realities of the regional situation they were discussing, and from certain realities of the political context in which they themselves were—in varying degrees—involved. The politicians concerned, at least, were now to be brought sharply back to a sense of reality.

X

On May 21, seventy-six United States senators sent a letter to President Ford urging him to be "responsive to Israel's economic and military needs."[34] It was evident that the pro-Israel lobby had lost none of its political clout. And the following year was a presidential and congressional election year. Kissinger's publicized reassessment had put his master's political future—and his own—at high risk.

That summer, in Washington, reassessment wilted. Kissinger, after a little more huffing and puffing with Rabin, got back to his step-by-step peacemaking, and to the modest problem of how much he would need to sweeten Second Sinai to get the Israelis to agree. In July, he was closeted with Ambassador Simcha Dinitz—in the Virgin Islands—to work out the details. Both sides had by now received enough of a mutual fright to show respect for each other's positions. The "sweeteners" for Israel were in proportion to its demonstrated stubbornness and political clout. In addition to a promise of $2 billion in aid, the United States agreed to drop the idea of an interim withdrawal in the West Bank, and to accept that only "cosmetic" changes could be expected in any Second Golan. On these understandings Israel agreed, at last, to withdraw from the Sinai passes, leaving them as a demilitarized zone, monitored by American technicians, as well as by U.N.E.F.[35]

Second Sinai, embodying the withdrawal provisions, was signed at Geneva on September 4, 1975. Also, Israel received, in a special secret memorandum in Geneva, significant assurances in relation to the United States and the P.L.O. The secret memorandum—which was, of course, promptly leaked to the press—contained the statement: "The U.S. will continue to adhere to its present policy with respect to the P.L.O., as long as the P.L.O. does not recognize Israel's right to exist and does not accept SC Resolution 242."[36]

The net effect of all that reassessment, and of the responses to it, was to narrow, not widen, the bounds of America's "step-by-step" peacemaking. American peacemaking was now reducing itself—without acknowledging the fact—to a single objective: a separate peace between Egypt and Israel.

The awkward team of Rabin and Peres had achieved, by reason of their very awkwardness, an awkward kind of diplomatic victory. Israel had succeeded in shutting out of the "peace process" two of Israel's neighbor states: Syria and Jordan (as well as the P.L.O.). The exclusion of the neighbor states was hardly in accordance with any sober assessment of Israel's diplomatic needs. But it was very much in accordance with the internal and external constraints of Israel's Government in 1975.

In any case, as the presidential election year, 1976, loomed near, it was clear that there was going to be no further pressure on the Government of Israel—and therefore no further progress even toward peace with Egypt—until 1977.

Second Sinai was the last achievement of Henry Kissinger's peacemaking efforts in the Middle East. The total achievement was considerably less magical than it was made to appear in the summer of 1974. But there was achievement in it that has now stood the test of ten years: in the bringing of Egypt into the Western camp, and in the laying of foundations for eventual peace between Egypt and Israel. Peace had been made possible by war. That was certainly Sadat's idea. How much of that idea came from Henry Kissinger remains open to question.

XI

In the Middle East, a peaceful settlement in one area is liable to precipitate violence in another. So it was in September 1970, when the cease-fire agreement between Egypt and Israel helped to precipitate the conflict in Jordan between the P.L.O. and Hussein's forces. So it now was with Second Sinai, which helped to set in motion the train of events leading to the Lebanese Civil War of 1975–1976, and then to the occupation by Syria of most of Lebanon, and Syrian hegemony over what remained of the Lebanese polity.

The P.L.O. leaders were bitterly disappointed and incensed by Second Sinai. They had been encouraged by their Western sympathizers, and by the open reassessment in April, to hope that they were about to be included in a comprehensive peace process, and to acquire, with Western support, a territorial base in Palestine.

Second Sinai dashed those hopes. The P.L.O. felt betrayed, by both the United States and Egypt. The P.L.O. now sought to demonstrate its own indispensability by a take-over bid in its remaining "host country"—Lebanon—joining with various Muslim and Druze factions (usually designated as "Left") to overthrow the long-established hegemony of the Christian Maronites.

Five years before, P.L.O. spokesmen had proclaimed that the road to Tel Aviv lay through Amman. The same spokesmen now proclaimed that the road to Tel Aviv lay through the Lebanese Christian stronghold of Junieh.

As the Lebanese Civil War developed, with P.L.O. participation, in early 1976, both Israel and Syria contemplated intervention: Israel for obvious reasons, and Syria both because it has always regarded Lebanon as properly part of Syria, and because Assad knew that a take-over in Lebanon by forces that included the P.L.O. would be likely to end in Israeli occupation of the country.

In the first months of 1976 the United States warned both Syria and Israel strongly against intervention. The Administration very much did not want a new international crisis in the Middle East— especially one involving Israeli-Arab conflict—in an election year. But as the conflict developed, it began to appear that intervention of some kind could not be avoided. Israel could not allow an alliance that included the P.L.O. to crush the Christians and dominate Lebanon.

From Washington, in 1976, the idea of Israeli intervention in Lebanon looked exceedingly unattractive. It would both detract from and endanger Kissinger's peacemaking achievement: one of the very few appealing items in the Republican Administration's electoral show window. By contrast, Syrian intervention—an inter-Arab affair, and so of relatively little interest to a Western public—seemed much the lesser evil.[37] So in May 1976, Damascus got the green light from Washington for a move in the direction of its permanent objective— Greater Syria. With the implicit assent of both the United States and Israel, Syria moved its forces into Lebanon in June.

On the face of it, there is a striking contrast between the U.S.-Israeli response to Syrian intervention in Lebanon in 1976 and their previous response to Syrian intervention in Jordan in 1970. Over

Syrian President Hafez al-Assad in conference with Yasser Arafat in October 1976, in the early stages of the Lebanese Civil War.

Jordan, Israel—egged on by the United States—had been prepared to go to the verge of war, and perhaps over it, rather than assent to a Syrian take-over. In Lebanon, the U.S. and Israel agreed with, and even prompted, Syrian intervention. But the basic difference is between the nature not so much of the U.S.-Israeli response as of the two Syrian interventions.

The earlier intervention, in Jordan, had been the work of a militant radical—pre-Assad—Government, and it aimed at rescuing the P.L.O. and overthrowing a pro-Western regime. Assad had helped to sabotage that intervention, and to sacrifice the Palestinians. Now Assad's intervention in Lebanon, in tacit concert with the Americans and Israelis, sacrificed the Palestinians again, by denying them and their allies victory and rule in Lebanon. Syrian forces clashed repeatedly with those of the P.L.O. and eventually, though not easily, brought them under control, thus "freezing" the civil war.

The "new Lebanon" took shape, in that particular form which became familiar over the next six years. Over most of the country, the hegemony of Damascus, the Pax Syriaca, prevailed. There were three main durable exceptions, of interest to Israel.

1. In the extreme south of Lebanon, between the Litani river and the border with Israel, was a buffer zone, controlled by Israel, through a local Christian-officered militia.

2. Just to the north of that was "Fatahland," the district around the port of Sidon, controlled by Arafat's forces, and their "left-wing" Muslim allies.

3. In East Beirut, and on Mount Lebanon to the north, and around the port of Junieh was the main Maronite enclave, with very close relations with Israel.

These were arrangements that Israel could live with; at any rate, for the time being.

XII

Assad was loudly denounced, for a remarkably short time, by the media of the Arab world, for his unceremonious dealings with "the sole legitimate representative of the Palestinian people." Not only did the extremist or "rejectionist" Arab states—Iraq especially, and Libya—denounce him, but also Egypt. Sadat even sent a Palestinian unit of the Egyptian Army off to fight the Syrians in Lebanon.

In October 1976, Assad came in from the cold, at a mini-Summit, of Egypt, Saudi Arabia and Syria, meeting at Riyadh. (The composition and the venue suggest American approval, if not encouragement.) Recent events in Lebanon were forgotten, as the parties agreed on a P.L.O.-Palestinian State in the West Bank and Gaza. Subsequently, a general Arab Summit at Cairo in effect[38] ratified the accord attained at Riyadh by the two most powerful, and the richest, of the Arab states.[39] The Syrian occupation of Lebanon became, in retrospect, a Pan-Arab enterprise, "invited" by Lebanon. The Syrian occupying forces acquired a new Pan-Arab name. They became known, to Francophone Lebanese, as La Force Arabe de Dissuasion.

In November, Assad, fortified by Riyadh and by Cairo, moved his Force Arabe de Dissuasion into Beirut itself, and made the Government of Lebanon his puppet. If Assad's forces had not been invited into Lebanon before, they were now.

Assad's stature was not diminished, but greatly enhanced, by his intervention in Lebanon, and his correction of the P.L.O. He now stood at the very center of the inter-Arab system, and of Middle Eastern affairs, internationally speaking. He was regarded by the Soviet Union as their most reliable ally in the region, or at least their nearest thing to a reliable ally. At the same time, the United States knew him as a rational ruler, with whom business could always be done, if any mutual advantage could be discerned. The *rapport* established between Kissinger and Assad, in those sardonic Damascus evenings of early 1974, served both statesmen well—but especially Assad—in the Lebanese crisis of 1976.

Within the inter-Arab system, Assad was beginning to upstage Sadat in the role of champion of the Arab cause. Sadat had already compromised himself somewhat by accepting Second Sinai: a purely Egyptian deal, with no trace of that "comprehensive" aspect which had been hoped for. In contrast, Assad, accepting no Second Golan, seemed disinterested and incorruptible. As we have seen, no real Second Golan had been on offer, but the Arab public did not know this. At the same time, Assad had lost no face by "refusing" territory. He had acquired "compensation"—as the princes of the *ancien régime* used to put it—for Sadat's territorial gains by his own gains in Lebanon. And Assad's gains, unlike Sadat's, had been acquired without any sordid deals with the United States or Israel. Or so it seemed.

By the end of 1976, Hafez al-Assad was emerging as the principal champion not only of the Arab cause in general but of the Palestinian cause in particular. The mainstream P.L.O. leaders, chastened and in the shadow of Syria, in their now-constricted base in Lebanon, had no wish to remind the Arab world of past transactions. Amnesia was in their political interest; and they attained it, and accepted their frightening champion.

The ruler of Damascus, and now of most of Greater Syria, had the Shirt of Uthman firmly in his grip.

XIII

On December 21, 1976, the Government of Rabin and Peres resigned. Its resignation was not directly connected with the defeat of Gerald Ford by Jimmy Carter in the previous month's U.S. presidential elections. But the two events were to mean that from early in 1977, new teams were to be in charge in both countries, involving new tests for the relationship most crucial to Israel.

Rabin was anxious to show that that relationship was in excellent condition. Indeed it was his anxiety to show this that precipitated the elections, and in a most inauspicious manner. Rabin was particularly proud of his Government's achievements in building up the Israel Defense Forces and in obtaining a lavish flow of American military aid, and this in spite of having successfully resisted American pressure in the "reassessment" period. He says in his memoirs that during his period of office (June 1974 to June 1977) "the IDF doubled its over-all strength. The number of planes had risen by 30 percent (including fighter bombers of the highest quality in the world—the F-15's); our tank force had grown by more than 50 percent; mobile artillery had increased over 100 percent; and in armoured troop carriers the increase was 700 percent!"[40]

To mark this achievement, a public ceremony was arranged for the arrival of the F-15s. By what seems a remarkable lack of sensitivity on someone's part, the arrival of the planes was scheduled for a Friday afternoon, just before the onset of the Sabbath.[41] The religious parties took umbrage at this, not surprisingly, since taking umbrage on such points is a large part of the *raison d'être* of these parties. The opposition introduced a Sabbath-related no-confidence motion. The motion failed, but Rabin's coalition colleagues belonging to the National Religious Party abstained. Rabin then resigned on the ground that his Government's cohesion had been impaired.

Rabin's resignation brought forward the Israeli General Election, which had been scheduled for the autumn of 1977, to May of that year. The earlier date seemed advantageous, from the Government's point of view, in terms of Israel's relations with the United States, and the bearing of those relations on the election campaign. There is a certain kind of international trade unionism between democratic Governments. An Israeli Government in the throes of an election campaign—as Israel's Government would now be when the new U.S. President took office in January—is to a certain extent insured against United States pressure. And such insurance is highly desirable when there is a new broom in Washington. Israel's relations with the Carter Administration might be fairly good or fairly bad, but it was not likely that they could be quite as good, for three more years, as Israel's relations had been with the Ford Administration during 1976.

Rabin's Government was on strong electoral ground in terms of Israel's external relations and the state of the national defenses. True, some occupied territory had been given up, without any definite Arab commitment to peace: Likud could hammer on that. But Israel now had freedom of navigation in both the Straits of Tiran and the Red Sea; Israeli nonmilitary cargoes could pass through the Suez Canal; the United States itself was involved in the guaranteed demilitarization of Sinai. Above all, the lifeline to the United States had been preserved and enhanced, without Israel's having made any concessions in the West Bank or Gaza and without any kind of advantage to the P.L.O. Indeed, Israel's territorial concessions to Egypt had—however inadvertently—damaged the P.L.O. by provoking it into its take-over bid in Lebanon, and consequent humiliation at the hands of Syria.

The achievements of Rabin's Government may have been as much the results of that Government's internal divisions—and consequent enhanced obstinacy—as of any particular skill, but the results were of a nature to leave, on the whole, a favorable impression on the electorate. Peres, by making it so very difficult for Rabin to yield to pressure, had, altogether inadvertently, raised Rabin's reputation with the general public. Israel was, at any rate, in a much stronger position than had appeared to be the case in the immediate aftermath of the Yom Kippur War, before Rabin succeeded Golda Meir.

Also a touch of glory had been added to the record by the brilliantly planned and executed I.D.F. rescue of the Israeli captives hijacked by the P.L.O. at Entebbe, Uganda, in July 1976. The glory in question was only slightly dimmed by a semipublic argument as to who was entitled to it, Rabin or Peres.

It was on domestic issues, far more than on foreign, that the Government was vulnerable. There was what seemed at that time an extremely high inflation rate—38 percent—and many strikes. Also, there were widely believed charges of corruption, both in the Labor establishment generally and in the Government itself. This scandalous aspect of the Rabin Government suddenly protruded, in a most ghastly and spectacular fashion, in the very opening phase of preelectoral maneuvering just after the resignation of Rabin's Government. On the night of January 3, 1977, Rabin's Housing Minister, Avraham Ofer, committed suicide on a beach north of Tel Aviv. He had been under police investigation for two months for alleged abuses during his time as director-general of the Histadrut's housing company.

Almost at the same time, the deep division within the Labor Party opened again before the public. Shimon Peres—to Rabin's fury—renewed his challenge for the leadership, and an internal contest had to be held in the run-off for the General Election: an unusual aggravation of democratic process. This time the contest took place at a full delegate convention of the party on February 22. Rabin won again—and once more by a painfully narrow margin, 1,445 votes to 1,404.

On the same day, Asher Yadlin, governor of the Bank of Israel—and nominated by Rabin to that post—was sentenced by a judge in Tel Aviv to a five-year term for taking bribes and evading taxes. During his trial, Yadlin had admitted taking the equivalent of $30,000 in bribery but had alleged that $20,000 of this had been handed over to the Labor Party. As Rabin's biographer notes: "The party which had preached stern socialist morality was now stigmatized as the party of Asher Yadlin and Avraham Ofer. . . ."[42]

It was natural for the Prime Minister, in the later stages of this astonishingly ill-starred campaign of his, to wish to shift attention from the stricken domestic scene, and to try to convince the voters of the primacy of Israel's international relations, and the indispensability of his own talents in that domain. Rabin decided to go to Washington to confer—and be seen conferring—with President Carter.

This was quite a risky decision, in terms of foreign affairs, but it was to prove fatal, for reasons which had nothing to do with foreign affairs.

It was risky because there was a danger of provoking damaging reaction from the new Administration. There were already signs of danger. The new Secretary of State, Cyrus Vance, had been among the sages ostentatiously consulted by Henry Kissinger on April 1, 1975. His appointment should have signaled that reassessment might be in the air (as it was), and that it might be unwise to stir it up before the elections. Rabin, if he received any such signal, chose to ignore it. In early March, Rabin had several talks with the new President in Washington. In these talks, Jimmy Carter made it unmistakably clear that he was indeed thinking along "reassessment" lines. What was far worse, from Rabin's point of view, was that the President now "went public" on this. Immediately after his third talk with Rabin—on March 8—the President made it known that he expected Israel to withdraw to its 1967 frontiers, with only minor alterations. As Rabin himself says: "No President before [Carter] had ever publicly committed the United States to such a position."[43] And ten days later Carter spoke publicly of the need for a Palestinian homeland: for Rabin "a further dramatic change in traditional U.S. policy."

In his memoirs, Rabin complains about how useful the President's remarks were to Likud in its electoral campaign. It didn't seem to occur to him that if he had had the sense to find out (indirectly) how Carter was thinking, and to stay out of Washington until after the elections, Likud might never have received its present from Washington.[44]

But it was a private transaction, on the same day as Rabin's third talk with the President, that was to end Rabin's leadership. On that day, Rabin's wife, Leah, deposited money in a joint account which the Rabins had kept in Washington, in breach of Israeli law. News of the transaction reached the Washington correspondent of an Israeli newspaper, who then secured proof of the existence of the account, and published the news, on March 15, 1977.

At first, this caused little stir. According to Rabin: "The $2,000 in our account represented the balance of our savings from the period we had lived in Washington."[45] That seemed acceptable. But at this point, Peres's biographer helpfully supplies material missing from Rabin's own retrospective account. The Attorney General called for Rabin's bank statements. "And when he did so, it turned out that [Rabin] had lied; not one bank account existed in Washington, but two. And not $2,000 was deposited in these accounts but about $23,000."[46]

On April 7—with a little more than a month to go before the elections—Rabin, in a televised address to the nation, announced his resignation both from the premiership and from the chairmanship of the party. But in fact he was not allowed, under Israeli law, to resign the premiership, in these conditions. Rabin had to remain on, as Prime Minister, in name. Peres was merely "chairman of the Cabinet meetings." Rabin was Prime Minister, "on leave." Labor had no chance of distancing itself from any part of the Rabin record, even the final blots.

In these grisly conditions, Labor could hardly hope to win, unless Likud made some staggering blunder of its own. Likud failed to oblige. Likud's campaign, for the elections of May 1977, was managed by Ezer Weizman, an Air Force war hero, and nephew of Chaim Weizmann. Ezer Weizman was far from being heir to Chaim Weizmann's political mantle, but he does seem to have had a touch of his uncle's political flair. "Look for what is not there," he told reporters, after launching a Likud election manifesto.[47]

What was not there essentially was Masada: heroics, saber

rattling, the territories, the stuff that had frightened off the voters in 1973. What was there instead was the issue of corruption in Government. Begin's modest life-style, and strict personal honesty—universally attributed to him, even by his opponents—were quietly and effectively evoked. "He is an honest man," said Weizman sweetly, "no small thing in these days."[48]

After the General Election of May 17, 1977, Likud, with forty-three seats (four more than in 1973), became the largest party in the Knesset. Labor dropped to thirty-two, down by nineteen from the 1973 figure. Part of the Labor loss was due to the defection of middle-class supporters, alienated by the series of scandals. But part was due to what seemed a more fundamental shift: a mass defection of Oriental Jews. Silver writes:

> In development towns, villages and big-city neighborhoods where the population is overwhelmingly oriental (Jews who originated in Arabic-speaking countries), the Likud won twice as many votes as Labour, with the religious parties registering small gains. In towns which are almost exclusively oriental, such as Ofakim and Netivot in the south and Kiryat Shmona and Beit Shean in the north, the Likud increased its vote by eleven percent, while Labour's share dropped by seventeen percent (the religious parties picked up the other six percent). The trend was similar in towns of mixed eastern and western Jewish population, but with the swing to the Likud in inverse proportion to the number of westerners. The more Jews of American or European origin, the smaller the swing.[49]

Silver comments that this time, unlike previous occasions, Oriental Jews "voted with their hearts instead of their pockets."[50] But it seems likely that their heads came into it as well. In the past, Orientals had voted for Labor as the party of Government. The idea that governing parties might be ousted by elections was novel to the Orientals when they first arrived, and nothing in their experience in Israel, in the first twenty years and more, could suggest to them that major political change, as a result of elections, was a real fact of life. But the 1973 elections had shown that Government could lose support, and the opposition could gain. And by May 1977, the Labor Government, under its Prime Minister on leave, could no longer seem sure winners. To put them out now seemed a feasible objective, and to many Orientals, that was a sweet prospect. "My parents came from

North Africa," said a young man in a development town to the novelist Amos Oz. "All right, from Morocco. So what? Didn't they have their self-respect? No. Their values? Their faith? I am not a religious person. I travel on Saturday. But my parents, why did they make fun of their faith? Why were they scrubbed with Lysol in Haifa port? Why?"[51]

In June, Begin formed his Cabinet, with Ezer Weizman as Minister for Defense, and—a surprise—Moshe Dayan, defecting from the Labor Alignment, as Minister for Foreign Affairs.[52]

Presenting his Cabinet to the Knesset on June 20, Begin delivered a speech, familiar in its emotional content and appeal to history, but significantly new in emphasis. Israel would not, he said, ask any nation to recognize its right to exist:

> We were granted our right to exist by the God of our fathers at the glimmer of the dawn of human civilization nearly four thousand years ago. For that right, which has been sanctified in Jewish blood from generation to generation, we have paid a price unexampled in the annals of the nations. Certainly, this fact does not diminish or enfeeble our right. On the contrary. Therefore, I re-emphasize that we do not expect anyone to request, on our behalf, that our right to exist in the land of our fathers be recognized. It is a different recognition which is required between ourselves and our neighbors: recognition of sovereignty and of the common need for a life of peace and understanding. It is this mutual recognition that we look forward to. For it we shall make every possible effort.[53]

12

PEACE AND WAR
1977-1982

War is Peace.
—GEORGE ORWELL
Nineteen Eighty-Four

THE CARTER ADMINISTRATION's main effort in international affairs during most of its first year in office went into preparing the way for a comprehensive settlement in the Middle East, involving Israel, all Israel's Arab neighbors and representatives of the Palestinians (P.L.O.).

The result of the attempt to achieve a comprehensive settlement was the precipitation, within two years, of a separate peace between Egypt and Israel; a peace comprehensively denounced by the Arab states—with the single exception of Morocco—and by Palestinians of all shades of opinion.

President Carter's principal advisers were his Secretary of State, Cyrus Vance, and his National Security Adviser, Zbigniew Brzezinski. The two differed on many things, but were agreed on the broad lines of a Middle Eastern settlement. Both were comprehensivists, critical of Henry Kissinger's step-by-step policy as lacking in vision, and as ignoring what comprehensivists considered to be the central Middle Eastern problem: the Palestinians. Vance had been one of the wise men consulted by Henry Kissinger on April 1, 1975, as part of the famous "reassessment": the test run of comprehensivism. Brzezinski had been a coauthor of the comprehensivist Bible: the Brookings Institution's Report of 1975. In its first nine months in office—and also sporadically thereafter—the Carter Administration accepted as its guidelines the principles laid down in the Brookings Report.

In the chapter "Not Geneva but Jerusalem" of his book *Power and Principle,* Brzezinski cites the five principles whose pursuit took him and his associates to some unexpected places (as that chapter title obliquely acknowledges). The principles are worth quoting here since—although they have never been consistently applied—they have had an abiding influence over theoretical discourse on the subject. Even today, much editorial writing on the Middle East, in the quality press of Western Europe and America, consists largely of recycled Brookings. The five principles are:

1. *U.S. interests.* The United States has a strong moral, political, and economic interest in a stable peace in the Middle East. It is concerned for the security, independence, and well-being of Israel and the Arab states of the area and for the friendship of both. Renewed hostilities would have far-reaching and perilous consequences which would threaten those interests.

2. *Urgency.* Whatever the merits of the interim agreement on Sinai, it still leaves the basic elements of the Arab-Israeli dispute substantially untouched. Unless these elements are soon addressed, rising tensions in the area will generate increased risk of violence. We believe that the best way to address these issues is by the pursuit of a comprehensive settlement.

3. *Process.* We believe that the time has come to begin the process of negotiating such a settlement among the parties, either at a general conference or at more informal multilateral meetings. While no useful interim step toward settlement should be overlooked or ignored, none seems promising at the present time and most have inherent disadvantages.

4. *Settlement.* A fair and enduring settlement should contain at least these elements as an integrated package:

(a) *Security.* All parties to the settlement commit themselves to respect the sovereignty and territorial integrity of the others and to refrain from the threat or use of force against them.

(b) *Stages.* Withdrawal to agreed boundaries and the establishment of peaceful relations carried out in stages over a period of years, each stage being undertaken only when the agreed provisions of the previous stage have been faithfully implemented.

(c) *Peaceful relations.* The Arab parties undertake not only to end such hostile actions against Israel as armed incursions, blockades, boycotts, and propaganda attacks, but also to give evidence of progress toward the development of normal international and regional political and economic relations.

(d) *Boundaries.* Israel undertakes to withdraw by agreed stages to the June 5, 1967, lines with only such modifications as are mutually accepted. Boundaries will probably need to be safeguarded by demilitarized zones supervised by U.N. forces.

(e) *Palestine.* There should be provision for Palestinian self-determination, subject to Palestinian acceptance of the sovereignty and integrity of Israel within agreed boundaries. This might take the form either of an independent Palestine state accepting the obligations and commitments of the peace agreements or of a Palestine entity voluntarily federated with Jordan but exercising extensive political autonomy.

(f) *Jerusalem.* The report suggests no specific solution for the particularly difficult problem of Jerusalem but recommends that, whatever the solution may be, it meet as a minimum the following criteria:

—there should be unimpeded access to all of the holy places and each should be under the custodianship of its own faith;

—there should be no barriers dividing the city which would prevent free circulation throughout it; and

—each national group within the city should, if it so desires, have substantial political autonomy within the area where it predominates.

(g) *Guarantees.* It would be desirable that the U.N. Security Council endorse the peace agreements and take whatever actions to support them the agreements provide. In addition, there will be need for unilateral or multilateral guarantees to some or all of the parties, substantial economic aid, and military assistance pending the adoption of agreed arms control measures.

5. *U.S. role.* The governments directly concerned bear the responsibility of negotiation and agreement, but they are unlikely to be able to reach agreement alone. Initiative, impetus, and inducement may well have to come from outside. The United States, because it enjoys a measure of confidence of parties on both sides and has the means to assist

them economically and militarily, remains the great power best fitted to work actively with them in bringing about a settlement. Over and above helping to provide a framework for negotiation and submitting concrete proposals from time to time, the United States must be prepared to take other constructive steps, such as offering aid and providing guarantees where desired and needed. In all of this, the United States should work with the U.S.S.R. to the degree that Soviet willingness to play a constructive role will permit.[1]

The authors of the report, and their followers, believed that their principles were not only fair and reasonable in themselves—as they are generally—but also applicable on the ground. Belief in applicability rested largely on an assumption, stated as follows:

The assumption is that the "key Arab states" (Egypt, Syria and Saudi Arabia) are basically interested in a conflict resolution. These "moderate" Arab countries are involved in economic development, having a clear-cut interest in cooperation with the West. They fear Arab Radicalism and are aware of their inability to destroy Israel militarily because of the U.S. commitment to Israel and because of Israel's own conventional (and unconventional) might. Yet the same Arab countries will not accept any conflict resolution short of Israeli withdrawals from occupied Arab lands and some kind of a solution to the Palestinian question. At the same time, if no solution is quickly pursued (to be implemented later), Arab "moderate" regimes will face severe domestic and inter-Arab radical pressures. These "moderate" regimes might thus be endangered, toppled, or would resolve to cooperate with the Soviet Union again or to pursue a radical foreign policy.[2]

There appear to be at least two weaknesses in the Brookings assumption:

1. The confident categorization of Arab states according to primarily Western criteria ("radical," "moderate") with the unwarranted inference that states placed by Westerners in the same category (Syria, Egypt) necessarily want to move in the same direction.

2. The undistributed use of the words "occupied Arab lands," with the unwarranted inference that "key Arab states" are no more interested in Israeli withdrawal from their own territories than in Israeli withdrawal from territory of a third party (West Bank). The most important of the "key Arab states" soon demonstrated that it

was more interested in Israeli withdrawal from occupied Egyptian territory—Sinai—than in Israeli withdrawal from the West Bank.

II

From very early on, and before the change of Government in Israel, the Carter Administration was signaling its strong interest in achieving a comprehensive settlement in the Middle East. "There is no issue, insofar as the United States is concerned, which has higher priority [than the Middle East]," declared Secretary of State Vance on February 8.[3] The Secretary of State toured the region that month, and shortly afterwards (March through May) Washington received Middle Eastern leaders: Sadat, Hussein, Crown Prince Fahd of Saudi Arabia, and Rabin. On May 9, Carter met Assad in Geneva and told the press, in Assad's presence: "There must be a resolution of the Palestinian problem and a homeland for the Palestinians."[4] In speaking of the Palestinians, the Administration was thinking increasingly of the P.L.O. Carter was indirectly in touch that summer with the P.L.O.—through his wife, Rosalynn, and an American academic.[5] The President's objective was to obtain P.L.O. acceptance of Security Council Resolution 242, and some kind of acceptance of Israel's existence within its pre–June 1967 frontiers. These acceptances would free the President from the conditional obligation, inherited from his predecessor, not to talk to the P.L.O.

Yet once more, the Arabs let Israel off the hook. The P.L.O. failed to make it possible for the President to talk with them, as he was eager to do. Partly, no doubt, the P.L.O.'s failure was due to the amorphous character of the P.L.O. itself, a discrepant collection of factions, with no other bond than that of hostility to Israel. The P.L.O., as such, could hardly have met the President halfway. But Yasser Arafat, as leader of Fatah, could have done so, if he had the backing of the "key Arab states," and most particularly of Syria, the P.L.O.'s protector, without whose permission no important P.L.O. initiative was then possible. It appears that that permission was not forthcoming.

Hafez al-Assad, quite reasonably, saw himself as being in a strong political position at this time. Comprehensivism suited him nicely. If the Palestinians were the key to the problem, as was the prevailing doctrine in Washington, it was Assad who controlled access to the key. He was master of the P.L.O.'s habitat, Lebanon; he had direct control of a large section of the P.L.O. armed forces—al-Saiqa, "the Thunderbolt"—and had predominant influence over the P.L.O. as a whole. He did not favor an independent Palestinian state. For him, Palestine was southern Syria, a part of Greater Syria, under construction, as a rival to Egypt. To a sympathetic British journalist, in the spring of 1977, Assad unveiled his ambitions. He had, it seems, a "two-pronged policy." One prong was directed against Egypt. The other prong "aimed to forge a regional power-bloc, consisting of Syria, Lebanon, Jordan and the West Bank."[6]

That was Damascus's version of a comprehensive settlement. Obviously, it left no room for the P.L.O. as an independent policy-forming and negotiating entity. The function of the P.L.O., within the Syrian scheme, was one of propaganda and agitation: with the United Nations General Assembly a most suitable theater for Palestinian exertions. Serious negotiation would have to be left to Damascus. Any Palestinian who might think differently could be brought to order by reference to the uncompromising terms of the Palestinian National Covenant of 1968, and a whole series of resolutions ruling out any idea of negotiations or peace with the "Zionist entity."

Rebuffed by the P.L.O. leader, Carter would have to turn to Assad to secure some kind of Palestinian involvement in his comprehensive settlement. Assad's three and a half hours with Carter, in Geneva in May, have been described as "the zenith of Assad's foreign policy."[7]

III

The Carter comprehensivists, in the summer of 1977, were daunted neither by their failure, to date, with the P.L.O., nor by the unexpected emergence in Israel of a Government pledged to hold on, forever, to all of Palestine, from the Mediterranean to the Jordan.[8]

The President and his advisers at this time seem to have been quite sanguine about the comprehensive prospects, as far as the Arabs were concerned. Carter liked Sadat very much and was convinced— quite correctly, as it happened—of Sadat's genuine desire for peace. He had also found Assad, as he noted in his diary, "very constructive . . . and somewhat flexible . . . in dealing with peace, the Palestinians, [etc.]."[9] Fahd, the Saudi Crown Prince, was "very frank and spoke freely . . . [and] agreed to help in every way he could."[10] On the Arab side, all seemed sweetness, light and Brookings. As Carter wrote: "After meeting with these key Arab leaders, I was convinced that all of them were ready for a strong move on our part to find solutions to the long-standing disputes and that with such solutions would come their recognition of Israel and the right of Israelis to live in peace."[11]

Begin, on the other hand, clearly meant trouble. As Carter noted in his diary for May 23, 1977: "I had them replay [a televised American] interview with Menachem Begin, Chairman of the Likud party and the prospective Prime Minister of Israel. It was frightening to watch his adamant position on issues that must be resolved if a Middle Eastern peace settlement is going to be realized."[12]

Carter realized that it would require considerable pressure from the United States to induce Menachem Begin to take part in a comprehensive settlement which was intended also to involve, ultimately, the P.L.O. He also realized that putting heavy pressure on Israel was a high-risk enterprise, in terms of American domestic politics. But he was a courageous as well as a high-minded politician, genuinely attached to his Grand Design, and willing to accept risks for it. And he knew, as a practical politician, that, if such risks had to be run, the time to run them was now, in the President's first year of office. So the heat was on, for Israel.

IV

Menachem Begin had read the signs and prepared for a tough struggle with a U.S. Administration which appeared—from a Likud point of view—to be the most dangerous to have held power in Washington since Eisenhower's in 1956–1957.

Begin prepared his ground for the struggle with a coolness, shrewdness and pragmatism not widely attributed to him, either inside or outside Israel. "Adamant" he appeared to Jimmy Carter, and adamant indeed he was on what mattered supremely to him: Judea, Samaria, Jerusalem. But he realized it would be folly to try to be adamant about everything. He was willing to "trade territory for peace": certain territory for a certain kind of peace. Addressing the conference of his own Herut Party—the core party of the Likud coalition—before the election, Begin said:

Should the Likud be called upon to form a government, our
first concern will be to prevent war. The Likud government
will undertake peace initiatives. We shall request a friendly
state, which maintains regular diplomatic relations with Israel
and with our Arab neighbors, to convey our proposal to
initiate negotiations for the signing of a peace treaty. These
negotiations must be direct, without any preconditions, and
free from peace formulas produced from outside.[13]

The international border, he indicated, would run across the
Sinai and the Golan Heights. The man who had once cried "Masada!"
and resigned rather than have any contact with that unclean thing,
Security Council Resolution 242, now accepted 242, subject to his
own highly restrictive interpretation of the term "territories."

Likud, as we saw, fought its election campaign with no "Masada"
note. The composition of the new Government reflected the same
pragmatic approach. The key posts, in relation to peace or war, went
to two men from outside the ranks of the Irgun veterans. The most
important post, Defense, went to the organizer of the successful
"Masadaless" campaign, Ezer Weizman. In office, Weizman was to
show himself the Begin Government's most consistent and determined
dove. The Foreign Minister was Moshe Dayan, who, despite the
shadow of Yom Kippur, brought to that office a greater weight of
personal authority than had belonged to any previous incumbent. The
appointment of Dayan as Foreign Minister was part of Begin's preparations for a struggle with the Carter Administration.

These choices were significant in two other respects. First, they
signaled a marked revival in the authority of the Prime Minister's
office. Here was a Prime Minister of Israel who could ignore the
claims. of veteran party activists, and appoint outsiders, chosen by
himself personally, to the key offices. And if he appointed them, he
could remove them—or let them go, as he later did—without political
repercussions. The contrast with previous post–Ben-Gurion Administrations was most marked in the relationship of Prime Minister to Minister for Defense. Levi Eshkol had been forced to give up Defense, and
hand that post over to the people's choice, Moshe Dayan. Golda
Meir's Government had lived in fear of the possible resignation of
Minister for Defense Dayan. Yitzhak Rabin had been forced to accept as Minister for Defense his most detested rival, Shimon Peres,
with a power base within the party almost equal to his own.

But in Begin's Government, neither Minister for Defense Weizman nor Foreign Minister Dayan had any power base other than the confidence of their Prime Minister.

The authoritarian party structure inherited by Begin's party from *Rosh Betar,* Vladimir Jabotinsky, now enabled Begin to emerge as the strongest Prime Minister of Israel since David Ben-Gurion.

The choices reflected Begin's strength; they also symbolized his hard-won centrality. Dayan had been Ben-Gurion's aide and—perhaps—intended heir. Weizman was the nephew of Israel's first President. Together, their names recalled the dominant traditions in Zionism and Israel, which had excluded and condemned Jabotinsky and the Irgun. The inclusion of these Ministers, by Begin's favor, in Begin's Government, symbolized a degree of willingness, even within the old establishment, to accept the former outsider on his own terms.

In terms of negotiations, this was a Government which could decide, and deliver. That much was quickly grasped by President Carter. During Begin's first visit to Washington as Prime Minister, the President noted in his diary (July 19, 1977): "My own guess is that if we give Begin support, he will prove to be a strong leader, quite different from Rabin."

Personally, Carter found Begin "quite congenial, dedicated, sincere, deeply religious . . . a very good man." Begin, for his part, praised Carter to the skies, even comparing him to Jabotinsky, and appeared to approve the comprehensivist approach.[14] Carter was correspondingly disappointed and amazed when Begin, on his return to Israel, publicly proclaimed the permanence of Jewish settlements in the West Bank, thus dealing a deliberate and heavy blow to the credibility of the attempt to find a comprehensive solution embracing the occupied territories in Palestine.

Carter now moved toward a reconvened Geneva Conference, seen as a means toward ending Israeli intransigence by confronting it with the unified approach of the two superpowers. Like Henry Kissinger, he no doubt fancied the idea of the "nice cop" having to give way to the "tough cop": Gromyko. And at the new Geneva, unlike the old, Palestinian representatives were to be present. On September 12, 1977, the State Department issued the most peremptory public statement, affecting Israel, that had been heard since the days of Eisenhower and Suez/Sinai:

The status of the Palestinians must be settled in a comprehensive Arab-Israeli agreement. This issue cannot be ignored if the others are to be solved. Moreover, to be lasting, a peace agreement must be positively supported by all of the parties to the conflict, including the Palestinians. This means that the Palestinians must be involved in the peace-making process. Their representatives will have to be at Geneva for the Palestinian question to be solved.[15]

A lot of "musts."

A week later, Dayan arrived in Washington to prepare for Israel's participation in the resumed Geneva Conference. Dayan was subjected to heavy pressure, both by the President personally and—apparently especially—by the Vice President, Walter Mondale. Dayan had also his own way of conveying his displeasure: "I just let [Mondale] say his piece and make his allegations, and when he wound down I remained silent. They both stared at me, but I said nothing."[16]

In Israel, Moshe Dayan had had the capacity to make his interlocutors "fearful of being run over at a dimly-lit political street-crossing," according to Gideon Rafael. Apparently this capacity had not deserted Dayan, as Israel's Foreign Minister, in Washington. As he himself tells the story:

It was soon apparent that the Americans had sensed my discontent over the President's approach to the nature of an Arab-Israel peace, and my resentment at his complaints against Israel. The very next morning, White House Chief of Staff Hamilton Jordan telephoned the Israeli Ambassador in Washington to say that the President was very pleased with his meeting with me and thought the talks were good and helpful. The Ambassador told him I was back in New York and he would pass the message on to me there. A few hours later Hamilton Jordan again telephoned the embassy to ask what I thought of my talk with the President. He had received news from New York that I was not happy with the White House meeting; and the story on it which appeared in the *Washington Post* was also pessimistic. A few days later Hamilton Jordan rang our Ambassador and asked to see him urgently. He had heard that I was about to address a number of gatherings of various Jewish communities in the United States where I would no doubt speak of the differences between us and the American Government.

This was not guesswork on the part of the White House official. In my meetings with correspondents and Jewish leaders, I had seen no reason to conceal my disappointment. It was also true that I was scheduled to address Jewish meetings in several cities. There were to be fund-raising meetings for the United Jewish Appeal and the State of Israel Bonds; but there was no doubt that in my speeches I would criticize the American position on peace in the Middle East.[17]

Hamilton Jordan might be worried, but the President's foreign-policy advisers were not, yet. The State Department had prepared a draft of a Joint Statement to be issued by the United States and the Soviet Union on October 1. The superpowers committed themselves to a comprehensive settlement incorporating all parties concerned and all questions.[18] "All parties" had to be understood as including the P.L.O., and "all questions" as including the West Bank and Jerusalem. Specifically, the Joint Statement spoke of "ensuring the legitimate rights of the Palestinian people" through "negotiations within the framework of the Geneva Peace Conference . . . with the participation in its work of all the parties in the conflict, including those of the Palestinian people."[19] Vance showed the Joint Statement to Dayan a day or so before it was due to be issued. As Brzezinski notes, in rueful retrospect: "Dayan refrained from reacting—perhaps deliberately."[20]

The experienced eye of the Israeli veteran of war and political ambush had seen something that had (almost inexplicably) escaped the attention of Carter and his foreign-policy advisers: the ground chosen by the Carter Administration for its confrontation with Israel was exceptionally well suited for operations against the Administration by the pro-Israel lobby in the United States. The lobby is more or less helpless—as it found in the days of Eisenhower—if it is seen as running counter to the national interests of the United States. But in the case of the Joint Statement, the lobby would be seen by many Americans as *defending* the true interests of the United States. Almost all Republicans would see the Joint Statement as Carter bringing back the Soviets into a vital region from which a Republican Administration had managed to exclude them. Many Democrats would agree. In this context, "sacrificing Israel to appease the Soviet Union" was a theme to warm the hearts, and vocal chords, of all Carter's opponents, whether normally pro-Israel or not.

Brzezinski, having duly misinterpreted Dayan's silence, forwarded the draft Joint Statement to the President, with Vance's recommendation. The Joint Statement was published on October 1, and was immediately subjected to combined attack from all those Americans who liked Israel and all those Americans who strongly disliked the Soviet

Union. Speaking for both these sections, Senator Henry ("Scoop") Jackson said: "The fox is back in the chicken coop. Why bring the Russians in at a time when the Egyptians have been throwing them out?"

It was a dimly lit political crossing. Carter, in this predicament, showed his first signs of political disarray. Addressing a meeting of Jewish congressmen on October 6 at the White House, he said: "I'd rather commit political suicide than hurt Israel."[21] It was a quaint formulation, since hurting Israel and committing political suicide are entirely compatible activities, as those congressmen were there to remind him.

The administration now mended its fences, providing Dayan with such assurances as were necessary to induce him to call off his lobby. A complicated Working Paper for Geneva was worked out between Carter, Vance and Dayan. Privately, the real message was confirmation that Israel's veto over P.L.O. participation at Geneva still stood, or rather stood again.[22]

This was a significant victory for Israel, secured toward the end of the dangerous first year of the new Administration. It was also a severe setback for the comprehensivist effort.

The Joint Statement of October 1, 1977, in preparation for the resumed Geneva Conference, was to remain the high-water mark of Carter comprehensivism. And the Geneva Conference never did, in fact, resume. It was to remain one of the mirages of the comprehensivist enterprise.

V

Israeli resistance had dented and deflected Carter comprehensivism. But it was from the Arab side that Carter comprehensivism received its deathblow, though the death was a lingering one.

Carter and his associates seem not to have noticed the fact that that Joint Statement of theirs had been very nearly as obnoxious to Cairo as to Jerusalem. The Joint Statement "was received in Egypt with open disappointment and some anxiety; it seemed to accord the USSR that active role in regional affairs which Egypt had been trying to deny it since 1972."[23] Sadat dropped a hint, in a letter to Carter, but it failed to register. On October 4, Carter noted in his diary: ". . . a letter from Sadat . . . urging that nothing be done to prevent Israel and Egypt from negotiating directly, with our serving as an

intermediary before or after the Geneva Conference is convened. . . .
I found Egypt to be the most forthcoming . . . nation in the Middle
East in working toward a peace settlement."[24]

Like Gunnar Jarring (as perceived by Gideon Rafael), Jimmy
Carter "understood what the contending parties were saying but not
what they meant."

The fact was that, from Egypt's point of view, the "pre-Geneva"
setup was turning into a Syrian benefit, to Egypt's detriment. Bringing back the Soviet Union into the politics of the region enhanced the
prestige of the Soviets' friend, Assad, as against that of their ex-friend,
Sadat. The heavy pre-Geneva emphasis on the Palestinians worked
in the same direction, in an even worse way. "The Palestinians" were
Assad's special subject, his forte, his cup of tea. Egypt, having acquiesced in Assad's coup in Lebanon, and in his taming of the P.L.O.,
had lost any real say in Palestinian matters. So these energetic Americans, busily "bringing the Palestinians into the peace process," would
have to court Assad, defer to his expertise, rely on his goodwill, while
Sadat, in the nature of this particular case, would have to play second
fiddle. Not a congenial prospect, personally or politically. And all this
time the odious Assad, under the cloak of zeal for peace and Palestinians, would be adroitly wielding those two prongs of his, jabbing
away at Egypt, and probing for Greater Syrian opportunities.

"All this time" was relevant too. Sadat's prestige urgently needed
enhancement. The credit of Yom Kippur was largely used up. There
had been serious rioting in Egypt—the so-called "uprising of
thieves"—at the beginning of the year. Sadat needed new achievement, for Egypt, and soon. Specifically he needed to answer those
Egyptians who talked of him as Nasser's unworthy successor, with the
words made good: "Nasser lost Sinai to Israel, Sadat got it back."

"Comprehensive settlement," complete with Palestinians, adjourned the recovery of Sinai indefinitely. Sadat was not disposed to
wait for Sinai until the conversion of the Jews, as symbolized by
Menachem Begin's delivery of Judea, Samaria and East Jerusalem
to Yasser Arafat.

VI

"With one bound our hero was free." The fiction formula springs
unbidden to the mind when one contemplates the move by which
Sadat, in November 1977, extricated himself from his predicament,

by transforming the international environment, both regionally and to some extent globally.

On November 9, 1977, Sadat addressed the annual opening of the Egyptian Parliament. Yasser Arafat, described by Sadat as "a dear and wonderful colleague in our struggle," was in the audience. Sadat said he was ready to go "to the ends of the earth for peace. Israel will be astonished to hear me say now, before you, that I am prepared to go to their own house, to the Knesset itself, to talk to them."

This statement, like many others in the speech, was greeted with applause, in which Arafat joined. There has been speculation as to why the P.L.O. leader applauded the announcement of a move which the P.L.O. was soon to condemn as treason to the Arab nation and the Palestinian cause. The most parsimonious explanation seems to be simply that he was in Cairo at the time. Arafat's most consistent characteristic is a propensity to agree with his hosts, wherever he finds himself. He is the ideal houseguest.

Sadat, when he made his announcement, knew that a favorable response might reasonably be expected from Jerusalem. The basis of a deal existed. Sadat knew—through the Romanian leader, Nicolae Ceausescu, and through hints dropped by Dayan on a visit to Morocco in September 1977—that Begin was ready to make territorial concessions, outside Palestine, in exchange for peace. He also knew Begin to be, unlike Rabin, a "strong" leader who could deliver, if agreement was reached.[25]

Yet at first it seemed as if the Government of Israel was about to fumble this historic offer, as an earlier Government had fumbled Sadat's first peace offer, more than six years before. Begin's first public reaction was pettifogging, petulant and perverse: "Sadat could go to the Geneva Conference and present his views there, just as we could."[26] So here was Israel clinging to Geneva, and that obnoxious Joint Statement, while Egypt was already trying to get away from all that.

But four days later, on November 14, Begin did a double take, and rose to the towering height of the occasion. He told a visiting French delegation that he "extends, on behalf of the Israeli Government, an official invitation to the President of Egypt, Anwar Sadat, to come to Jerusalem to conduct talks for a permanent peace between Israel and Egypt." The following day, the official invitation went to Cairo, through American diplomatic channels, proposing that Sadat come to Jerusalem the following week. Sadat agreed.

The decision to invite Sadat seems to have been very much Begin's own. Both Dayan and Weizman were, as they record, suspicious (Dayan) or disdainful (Weizman) of Sadat's initiative.[27] Suspicion was intensified by Radio Cairo's interpretation of the purpose of the visit: "To unmask the true face of Israel, who presents herself as a lover of peace."[28] Begin had the sense to believe Sadat, not his broadcasters. In Dayan's account of Begin's stance at that time, there is discernible an undercurrent of respect, quite unusual in this author: "Pondering over Sadat's true intentions in the days following his Cairo declaration, Begin finally shed all doubt and skepticism, and wholeheartedly favored the visit. He realized its value as a first step in the march to peace, and as an act of historic importance."[29]

Begin had often in the past behaved—and often would again behave—in petty and niggling ways, unworthy of the visionary leader to whose mantle he laid claim. But never did Begin more truly show himself the heir of Vladimir Jabotinsky than by taking firm hold of Sadat's offer, when more sophisticated and pragmatic people failed to see what it meant.

VII

Between the announcement of his wish to go to Jerusalem and the journey itself, Sadat permitted himself the pleasure of a visit to Syria to "consult" with Assad. He found Assad "incredulous," and left him so. Assad, the P.L.O. and some other Arab leaders were bitterly and publicly reproachful, claiming that Sadat's Jerusalem initiative "had torpedoed the united front the Arabs had hoped to present at the Geneva Conference."[30]

Which is exactly what Sadat had set out to do, and succeeded in doing.

Sadat arrived at Ben-Gurion airport at eight-thirty on the evening of Saturday, November 19, shortly after the end of the Jewish Sabbath (showing concerted timing).

If Sadat's announcement of intent left many Israelis cold, his actual arrival had an enormous emotional impact. Half of Israel seemed to be at the airport; the other half was glued to television screens, held there by that unimagined epiphany. There were the due solemnities—red carpet, searchlights, national anthems, guard of honor, twenty-one-gun salute—but it was the man himself who mat-

Left and above, The arrival of Sadat in Israel. He is welcomed by the President of Israel and Prime Minister Begin. "Several observers noted that he was *blacker* than had been expected, and that seems somehow to have added to the potency of the magic the President of Egypt was making at Ben-Gurion airport that November night."

Below, President Sadat begins his first day in Israel with a prayer at the Al Aqsa mosque, fulfilling a wish of the late King Faisal, who had dreamt of praying in Jerusalem before dying.

tered: a tall, strong, stately figure, beautifully dressed; a figure on a scale and in a style appropriate to the hour. Several observers noted that he was *blacker* than had been expected, and that seems somehow to have added to the potency of the magic the President of Egypt was making at Ben-Gurion airport that November night.

On the following morning, the President prayed at the al-Aqsa Mosque; he later visited the Church of the Holy Sepulchre, and the Holocaust memorial, Yad Vashem. On the afternoon of the same day, he addressed the Knesset, as promised. He reminded his audience that his offer of peace was no sudden whim, but a matter of long-settled intent: "I have shouldered the prerequisites of the historic responsibility and therefore I declared a few years ago—on February 4, 1971, to be precise—that I was willing to sign a peace treaty with Israel."[31]

He struck a religious note, with a deeper resonance than is usually heard when politicians touch that chord:

It is fated that my trip to you, the trip of peace, should coincide with the Islam feast, the holy feast of Al-Adha, the feast of Sacrifice, when Abraham, peace be upon him, the great-grandfather of the Arabs and Jews, submitted to God. I say when God Almighty ordered him, Abraham went, with dedicated sentiments, not out of weakness but through a giant spiritual force and a free will to sacrifice his very own son, prompted by a firm and unshakeable belief in ideals that lend life a profound significance.[32]

Sadat the visionary was no less real than Sadat the calculator. The calculator controlled the political specifics of the Knesset address. At first sight, these specifics seemed at variance with the meaning of the journey and the setting. This part of the speech was straight comprehensivist doctrine. "I have not," so said Sadat, "come here for a separate agreement between Egypt and Israel." He went on to call for a peace agreement "ending the Israeli occupation of the Arab territories occupied in 1967," and achieving "the fundamental rights of the Palestinian people and their right to self-determination, including their right to establish their own state." The Palestine cause, according to Sadat, was "the crux of the entire problem." He also asserted, though in less plain language, the Arab claim to Jerusalem. Sadat hardly expected all that to be music in the ears of the Knesset, and it was not. By putting the comprehensivist case strongly and cogently in Jerusalem, Sadat was keeping his lines open to Jimmy Carter and his associates in Washington (as well as the "pro-Western" Arab leaders). Verbally, he had not departed by one hairsbreadth from the comprehensivist approach. For the rest, he could leave his journey and his setting to deliver their distinct nonverbal message, whose import would not be comprehensivist.

Begin, in his reply, refrained from both umbrage and quibble. He and other Israelis were pleased not only by Sadat's presence but by the novelty of some of his language, notably the phrase "we accept living with you in peace and justice." Having taken up Sadat's reference to Abraham—"our common forefather"—Begin wisely left Sadat's political specifics to one side, and concentrated on the reality of the nonverbal message.

> I greet and welcome the President of Egypt for coming to our country and on his participating in the Knesset session. The flight time between Cairo and Jerusalem is short, but the distance between Cairo and Jerusalem was until last night almost endless. President al-Sadat crossed this distance courageously. We, the Jews, know how to appreciate such courage, and we know how to appreciate it in our guest, because it is with courage that we are here, and this is how we continue to exist, and we shall continue to exist.

Begin and Sadat probably understood each other better than Jimmy Carter could have understood either. Yet, as it happened, they both needed Jimmy Carter, and could probably never have reached their separate agreement without the dedicated aid of the great comprehensivist.

VIII

The initial American reaction to Sadat's initiatives was one of "surprise and apprehension."[33] The Brookings approach, as favored by Carter, had one thing in common with the discarded step-by-step approach of Kissinger. Both approaches assumed that the peace process would be managed, throughout, by the United States. Kissinger had succeeded in insuring that, and in checking unauthorized peace moves. But Sadat's offer, Begin's invitation, and then Sadat in the Knesset—all that left Carter and his associates gasping.

Yet when they had recovered from their initial surprise, they had really no political option but to go along. They were already vulnerable, domestically, on Geneva and "bringing the Russians back in." They could hardly now instruct the President of Egypt that he ought to have waited for Geneva—and the Russians—instead of going to Jerusalem. Sadat's great move had captured the imagination of millions of Americans, as well as of people in other lands. It had made splendid television. It was overwhelmingly in Carter's political interest to be seen to be on Sadat's side: helping him, not cramping him.

And Sadat, with consummate political astuteness, made it easy for the President to help him, without any loss of face. It might be, as cynics suspected, that what Sadat was actually doing was scuttling Geneva, and heading toward a separate peace between Egypt and Israel. But he was not *talking* as if he was doing anything of the kind. His speech to the Knesset—as distinct from his presence there—had been full of the purest comprehensivism. And then, on November 26, Sadat announced that the next step would be a preparatory conference—for Geneva. Sadat was making it look as if everything, including his flight to Jerusalem, had somehow all been part of Carter's great plan. And why should the President contradict him? He welcomed Sadat's initiative, while stressing the need for including the Palestinians in the peace process. As Sadat himself had also done.

Zbigniew Brzezinski now showed himself to be the inspired revisionist of comprehensivism. He produced the theory of "concentric circles" of the peace process:[34] "In public, I started speaking of a 'concentric circles' approach, building on the Egyptian-Israeli accord, then expanding the circle by including the Palestinians in the West Bank and Gaza as well as the Jordanians, and finally moving to a still wider circle by engaging the Syrians and perhaps even the Soviets in a comprehensive settlement."[35]

This theory met both the political and intellectual needs of the comprehensivists in the White House, as they prepared to follow in Sadat's wake, toward a separate peace between Egypt and Israel.

IX

Sadat's initiative, once approved by the United States, altered the whole internal balance of the inter-Arab system. Syria, with the P.L.O., was abruptly bundled from the center to the periphery. By bitterly denouncing the U.S.-supported peace process between Egypt and Israel, Syria and the P.L.O. put themselves out of the reckoning, for the time being, as far as the United States was concerned. Before November 1977, Damascus had been seen as holding the key to a comprehensive solution. After November, Damascus was no more than an element in Brzezinski's "third circle," way down the comprehensivist agenda. The politic Assad had been totally outmaneuvered by a bigger politician with a bigger country, and a clearer and more feasible objective.

Assad, by his reactions to his defeat, succeeded only in emphasizing his isolation. He formed a Front of Steadfastness [*Sumud*] and Opposition to Egypt. When the Front met, at Tripoli (December 2–5, 1977), only Algeria and South Yemen participated, along with Syria and the P.L.O., and their host Colonel Qaddafi; "the mad boy," as Sadat called him. The Saudis and Kuwaitis and Jordanians stayed away; Iraq came, but walked out. The Front denounced "the great betrayal" and decided to "freeze" political and diplomatic relations with Egypt. What "freezing" meant was not clear, but Sadat himself clarified it by breaking off all relations with all the participants, plus Iraq. Sadat also declared that the P.L.O., by participating in the Front, had "annulled" Rabat's recognition of its right to represent the Palestinian people.

Sadat's own position within the Arab world was even more isolated than that of Syria, but it was neither peripheral nor extraneous to the peace process. Sadat even emphasized his isolation at this time by his attempt at a "pre-Geneva" conference in Cairo (December 14–22, 1977). Sadat had invited the United States, the Soviet Union, Israel, Syria, Lebanon, Jordan, the P.L.O. and the United Nations. Only Israel and the United States (an Assistant Secretary at the State Department) and a representative of the U.N. Secretary-General (presumably prompted by the United States) attended.

In appearance, Cairo was an even bigger flop than Tripoli. Moshe Dayan, who was not there, rates it "a total failure."[36] The verdict may be too strong. From Sadat's point of view, those empty Arab chairs had a message for the American public: only Egypt was seriously interested in peace with Israel.

There was also a significant symbolic development at Cairo. Although the P.L.O. was not there, its flag was. When Israel objected, this symbol was removed.

Sadat and Begin met again, this time on Egyptian soil, at Ismailia (December 25–26, 1977). They agreed to set up military and political committees for continuing negotiations. There was no agreed communiqué, but Sadat made a laconic concluding statement on the position of the parties concerning Palestine: "The position of Egypt is that in the West Bank and Gaza a Palestinian State should be established. The position of Israel is that Palestinian Arabs in Judea and Samaria (namely, the West Bank of the Jordan) and the Gaza Strip should enjoy self-rule."[37]

X

The Israeli Government's perception of Sadat's approach to a comprehensive settlement (including the West Bank) was outlined that December by the Minister for Defense, Ezer Weizman, to Likud members of the Knesset. "The Egyptians," said Weizman, "are fed up. They would be willing to go for a separate agreement with Israel if only a formula was found that would enable them to delay the question of the comprehensive settlement to a later date."[38]

In quest of such a formula, Begin put forward his plan for autonomy for the Palestinian Arabs of Judea, Samaria and Gaza. The main principles of the Begin Plan were "administrative autonomy" and the selection of an administrative council; security and public order to continue to be the responsibility of the Israeli authorities; residents to be free to choose either Israeli or Jordanian citizenship; residents of Israel to be free to acquire land and settle in Judea and Samaria (and vice versa). On sovereignty, Begin offered a delaying clause: "Israel stands by its rights and its claim of sovereignty to Judea, Samaria and the Gaza district. In the knowledge that other claims exist, it proposes for the sake of the agreement and the peace that the question of sovereignty in the areas be left open."[39]

On Sinai—the really material issue, in the Weizman interpretation—Begin made it clear that he envisaged eventual complete withdrawal to the old international border.

In the Knesset, Yitzhak Rabin attacked the Begin Plan for conceding too much to the Arabs: "He [Begin] will sooner or later bring us back to the lines we had before the 1967 war." The Knesset, however, overwhelmingly approved the Begin Plan. The Likud members knew—through Weizman, and no doubt also through Begin himself—what the plan was about.

On January 4, Carter and Sadat, meeting in Aswan, agreed to

"recognize the legitimate rights of the Palestinian people and enable the Palestinians to participate in the determination of their own future."[40] As in the case of Sadat's Knesset speech, the significance of the Aswan Declaration lay much more in the place where the statement was made than in the actual wording of the statement.

Just a fortnight after the Aswan Declaration, the peace process between Egypt and Israel suddenly stalled. The Political Committee established by the Ismailia Summit met in Jerusalem on January 17, 1978, but on the following day Sadat brusquely withdrew his representatives from the committee, and from Jerusalem. For most of the rest of 1978—until September—the peace process was bogged down.

Sadat and Carter, at Aswan, had just stressed the need for a comprehensive settlement including the Palestinians, so it might be thought that it was on this question that the peace process broke down: that the gap between the Aswan concept and the Begin Plan was simply too wide. Sadat himself encouraged this interpretation, by statements following the breakdown, re-emphasizing comprehensiveness, and calling for "self-determination" for the Palestinians (a notch or two above the Aswan position).

But, as Henry Kissinger has said, appearances and reality are often at variance in the Middle East. The reason for the breakdown had nothing to do with comprehensiveness and Palestinians, and everything to do with Egypt's national objective: the recovery of all of Sinai.

Early in January, Sadat discovered that on this question, vital to Egyptian interests and Sadat's prestige, Begin was prevaricating with him. Begin had promised that, when agreement was finally reached, Egypt would recover full sovereignty over all of Sinai. Begin's course of action, at the beginning of 1978, contradicted this promise. On January 3—the day before Aswan—the Israeli Government secretly decided to "bolster" existing settlements in Sinai, and to break ground for six new settlements in eastern Sinai. After this project had leaked to the press, and in the face of strong protests from Cairo and Washington, the Israeli Government dropped the new settlements, but continued with its "bolstering" project. A majority of the Government clearly thought that Sadat could somehow be induced to conclude a peace treaty under a version of Egyptian sovereignty that allowed for Israeli settlements on Egyptian territory.

This policy of creating new facts in the Sinai, while negotiating with Egypt, was sponsored by the Minister for Agriculture (with responsibility for settlements), Ariel Sharon. Sharon was supported by the Minister for Foreign Affairs, Moshe Dayan, architect of the most important settlement, at Yamit, Sadat's resentment of which had been among the causes of the Yom Kippur War. Begin, at this stage, backed Sharon and Dayan.

There was only one dissentient, in the Cabinet, to the eccentric line of policy which blocked the peace process. The dissentient was the Minister for Defense, Ezer Weizman. Weizman—who had established, and managed to maintain, an excellent rapport with Sadat— was well aware of the strength of Sadat's feelings about Sinai. At the Ismailia Summit, in December, Sadat had told Weizman: "I am ready to conclude a contractual peace treaty, with ambassadors, with freedom of navigation, everything. But you are getting out of the Sinai! That includes all the settlements. They've got to go!"[41]

Weizman declared his opposition to the Sharon-Dayan policy in strong terms: "The Egyptian president was talking 'big business'—and we were engaging in trivialities. Moreover, they were pernicious trivialities, capable of foiling the whole peace process. This was worse than shortsightedness: I considered it a monstrous bid to outwit the peace process and deliberate blindness toward the new relationship emerging between Israel and Egypt."[42]

In retrospect, it seems hard to fault that verdict. For the time, however, the Sharon-Dayan line held. The peace process not merely stopped, but actually seemed to go into reverse. Sadat's fury over the Sinai settlements reverberated in the Egyptian press in language and cartoons which were not merely anti-Begin and anti-Israel but anti-semitic as well. Those in Israel who had always advised against trusting Sadat could fancy themselves vindicated.

Weizman, during this phase, thought he noticed "a strange glint in the eyes of certain of my countrymen":[43] a glint of satisfaction at the failure of the peace process.

XI

As Carter—especially at Aswan—had tied his prestige to the success of Sadat and his initiative, Israel's jamming of the peace process was deeply resented in Washington. Editorials in the United States press in February and March described Begin as a liability to Israel and to U.S. Jewry and argued that it was America's task to bring the debate in Israel over Begin's policies to a head.[44] It was in this period that the Peace Now movement emerged in Israel, in protest against the Begin Government's jamming of the peace process.

Israel's relations with the White House got still worse at this time as a result of American arms sales to Egypt and Saudi Arabia, and of a campaign in Congress mounted against these sales by the pro-Israel lobby.

Sadat visited the United States in February 1978, to a hero's welcome. Weizman, visiting the United States in the following month—in early March—reported "an icy headwind," where Israel was concerned, "funneled through the communications media" and "chilling the hearts of the American public."[45] And while Weizman was actually in the United States, U.S.-Israeli relations got several degrees worse again—as a result this time of a recurring phenomenon, always conducive to friction between the two countries: a serious *fedayeen* raid, followed by Israel's traditional "asymmetrical response."

On March 11, a party of Fatah *fedayeen*, arriving by boat from Lebanon, hijacked two buses along the Haifa–Tel Aviv road and massacred thirty-seven people, passengers and other civilians, wounding eighty-two others. In retaliation, in an effort to eliminate the P.L.O.'s presence in southern Lebanon, Israel, on March 14, launched Operation Litani, a massive military offensive which resulted in the Israeli occupation of southern Lebanon up to the Litani river. Syria did not intervene.

In its response to this crisis, the Carter Administration refrained from directly condemning Israel. But it did press for a Security Council resolution, which it obtained. Security Council Resolution 425, of March 19, 1978, called "upon Israel immediately to cease its military action against Lebanese territorial integrity and withdraw forthwith its forces from all Lebanese territory." The resolution also called for the establishment of a United Nations force (U.N.I.F.I.L.) for duty in southern Lebanon.

The American action in bringing about Resolution 425 was greatly resented in Israel, as was the resolution itself, especially since it ignored the original *fedayeen* attack, and the *fedayeen* presence in Lebanon, and treated "Lebanese territorial integrity" as a fact, instead of the fiction it had become. But Israel gave way, though slowly. (By June, its forces were out of Lebanon, and were replaced by U.N.I.F.I.L.)

In the hope of mending fences, Begin came to Washington a few days after Resolution 425 for talks with Carter. Carter received him icily, and the talks were officially described by both sides as "difficult." Carter kept on pressing, and Begin kept on refusing to budge.[46]

XII

Periods of heavy United States pressure on Israel are worrisome and exhausting, for both Governments. Such periods are apt to be followed by periods of discreet mutual adjustment, with some degree of climbing down, or backing away, either on one side or on both. Such a period now set in.

The new period was quietly inaugurated in talks between Moshe Dayan and Secretary of State Vance in the U.S. (April 26–28). What Dayan now proposed was that instead of negotiating in terms of basic principles, a process that was leading only to sterile reiterations, the parties should try to agree on a framework, within which practical measures could be devised toward bringing about autonomy for the Arab inhabitants of the West Bank and Gaza. And he suggested that the parties, without necessarily endorsing the Begin Plan, adopt that plan as the basis for their discussions.[47]

As these proposals of Dayan's, favorably received by Vance and later Carter, were to lead, within a few months, to the unjamming of the peace process, they deserve a little scrutiny here. The Dayan proposals were remarkable in two main ways.

First, the concept of *framework*—later basic to Camp David— had a touch of genius about it, so neatly did it fit its international context, and the needs of the protagonists. A framework is something on whose general shape people might agree, while leaving for later the decisions on how to fill it in. Then people might fill in part of it, leaving the rest of it to be filled in later. Or not filled in at all, as the case might be.

Israel was offering what its Government assumed Egypt really wanted: in Weizman's words, "a formula that would enable them to delay the question of the comprehensive settlement to a later date," after the conclusion of the separate agreement, which was really Egypt's objective.

The second interesting, and odd, thing about the Dayan proposals was their exclusive concentration on the West Bank and Gaza. As we have seen, it was not on the West Bank, but on Sinai settlements, that the negotiations had broken down. Yet the two problems were linked conceptually, in the minds of the Israeli Government, by a strong desire that they should *not* be linked, practically and politically. What Begin and his colleagues most feared about the removal of the settlements from Sinai was that that would set a precedent, leading to the removal of settlements from Judea and Samaria. That fear would be substantially allayed if the Carter Administration accepted the Begin Plan, even as a basis for discussion. That plan, if ever implemented (even amended, in any form that the Begin Government would accept), would leave Israel in full control of Judea and Samaria, and leave the settlements there intact. If the plan were *never* implemented—as was probable, given its rejection by all representatives of the Palestinian Arabs, whether Hashemite or P.L.O.—American approval of it would be an asset for the future, and a barrier against pressure. So acceptance of "framework" and Begin Plan as "basis" would make the removal of settlements from Sinai a less fearsome prospect, because less precedent-setting, than it had seemed in January. Dayan himself, although he had favored "bolstering" the settlements in January, also favored their removal, provided it was clear that that was a precondition for peace with Egypt. By his course of action from January 18 on, Sadat had made it rather clear that it *was* a precondition.

By his comprehensivist proposals of April, Moshe Dayan was moving, in his own devious and formidably efficient way, toward the conclusion of a separate peace with Egypt.

Jimmy Carter, as spring gave way to the summer of 1978, had strong reasons of his own for coming to terms with comprehensivism à la Moshe Dayan. Sponsoring that Security Council resolution in March had been a very high political risk to run in a mid-term congressional election year, as some of the President's advisers, such as Hamilton Jordan, were acutely aware. Whether that March exercise would be forgiven and forgotten, come November, was something that would depend very largely on the attitude of the Government of Israel.

Also Carter, having pinned his prestige, at the outset of his Presidency, on the idea of "a solution for the Middle East," needed some kind of success in that domain before November. He needed a success, but one that the Begin Government could live with. That kind of success could not readily be reconciled with the Brookings approach, to which the President was publicly committed. But Dayan's proposals— "autonomy" and "framework"—offered an *appearance* of continuity, and a way out, which the President took.

Keeping Faith is the title of Jimmy Carter's White House memoirs. Well, he did try, and he kept as much faith as he could, given the realities of the situation and his own electoral necessities, which is as much as can reasonably be expected of a democratic (small *d*) politician. And it may be that Brookings comprehensivism is something with which it is not possible to keep faith in practice, since Brookings comprehensivism does not seem to be compatible with the realities of the situation to which it is conceptually addressed.

XIII

At the end of July 1978, President Carter dispatched his Secretary of State, Cyrus Vance, to the Middle East, with invitations to Begin and Sadat to meet with him at Camp David, a secluded setting in the Maryland mountains, where they and their advisers would be inaccessible to the press. Begin and Sadat agreed immediately; Sadat with the condition that the United States become a full partner in the negotiations. The Camp David talks began on September 5 and lasted until September 18.

Carter had hoped that the simple, rural setting, and a common dining room, might lead to a growth of informal relations, and so to better understanding, between the Israelis and the Egyptians. In general, that did not happen. There was one exception. Ezer Weizman sought out Egyptian company, and maintained an excellent personal relationship with Sadat. Weizman has a cheerful, outgoing personality, in helpful contrast to the gloomy fervor of Menachem Begin and the inscrutable intensity of Moshe Dayan. Relations between Dayan and Sadat were particularly "difficult." A passage in Dayan's *Breakthrough* unconsciously reveals the enormity of the communication gap between the two. Dayan tells of a conversation between himself and Sadat on September 14. Before their meeting, for tea, Carter had suggested that Dayan avoid controversial topics, and Dayan had promised to speak only of camels and date palms. As Dayan tells it:

> Sadat received me with a polite smile; his manservant brought us small cups of the sweet and fragrant tea he is fond of; and when he left, Sadat plunged straight into the

problems of the conference. It was about to end without an agreement. The main reason, he said, was our stubbornness over retaining our settlements in Sinai. "The concept of building the city of Yamit in the north-eastern corner of Sinai was yours, was it not?" he asked rhetorically. "What did you think, that we would resign ourselves to its existence?"

The camels and the date-palms vanished. "The idea of creating Yamit was mine," I said.

"But before going ahead with its construction we approached you and offered to hand back to you the whole of Sinai within the framework of a peace treaty—and that idea too, was mine. What was your reply? No peace, no negotiations, no recognition of Israel. What was taken by force, you said, would be recovered by force. That was the resolution adopted by the Khartoum Conference at the initiative of Nasser. What did you think we would do, sit with folded arms, while you announced that you were not prepared to reconcile yourselves to Israel's existence, and that you wanted to take Sinai back not peacefully but only through war?"[48]

Hubris and Euphoria may have deserted Israel on Yom Kippur, 1973, but Amnesia clearly had not. Dayan's brain had retained the memory of the three noes of Khartoum (August–September 1967), but had lost all traces of Sadat's offer of a peace treaty less than four years later (February 1971). And this although Sadat, in the course of what had so often been hailed as a memorable guest address, had reminded the Knesset of that peace treaty, proffered by Egypt, more than six years before, and effectively turned down by a Government of which Dayan had been the key member.

On the Egyptian side, Sadat's entourage, more hard-line than he, and not anxious for a treaty, did not wish to associate with Israelis, while the Israelis, with the exception of Weizman, had no craving for Egyptian company. Granted the state of relations, and communications, between the Egyptians and the Israelis, it seems improbable that they would ever have been able to reach agreement without the constant presence and assiduous energy of President Carter.

Much of the verbal discussion at Camp David was about the West Bank, Gaza and Palestinians, but the real negotiating crux was Sinai, and Carter knew this, from Sadat. About a discussion with Sadat at Camp David the previous February, Carter writes: "I tried to persuade him to permit some of the Israelis to stay in the Sinai settlements under United Nations protection. He was quite flexible on all other points, but adamantly opposed to this one."[49]

Above, Begin and Sadat at the press conference in Jerusalem.
Below, Begin, Sadat and President Carter at Camp David.
Bottom, The handshake.

The real problem at Camp David was to get Israel to move on the Sinai settlements. Carter achieved this in discussions with Begin on Day Twelve of the Camp David talks (Saturday, September 16, 1978). Carter writes:

> I thought the discussion would never end. It was obviously very painful for Prime Minister Begin, who was shouting words like "ultimatum," "excessive demands," and "political suicide." However, he finally promised to submit to the Knesset within two weeks the question: "If agreement is reached on all other Sinai issues, will the settlers be withdrawn?"
>
> I believed this concession would be enough for Sadat. Breakthrough![50]

After that, the rest was relatively plain sailing. Taking Dayan's hint and expanding on it, Camp David adopted two "frameworks": a Framework for Peace (mainly about the West Bank and Gaza) and a Framework for a Peace Treaty between Egypt and Israel. As Carter records, Sadat "was not particularly interested in the detailed language of the Framework for Peace."[51]

The Framework for Peace was hazy and really did no more than refer to future (and highly problematic) negotiations. Egypt, Israel and—it was hoped—Jordan and "the representatives of the Palestinian people" were to participate in negotiations about the future of the West Bank and Gaza. A five-year period of "transitional autonomy" was envisaged, "in order to ensure a peaceful and orderly transit of authority," etc.

This language was fully compatible—on Begin's interpretation of what he had agreed to—with the Begin Plan. On Sadat's interpretation, Camp David's Framework for Peace meant something very different from the Begin Plan. Both Begin and Sadat were aware of the wide difference of interpretation, but they were content to leave it like that, and so had Carter to be, for the present.

The Framework for Peace also paid its tribute to the comprehensivist ideal. It aimed, so it said, "to constitute a basis for peace not only between Egypt and Israel but also between Israel and each of its other neighbors which is prepared to negotiate peace with Israel on this basis."

The language of the Framework for a Peace Treaty was more businesslike. It provided for "the full exercise of Egyptian sovereignty up to the internationally recognized border," as well as for

Israeli right of free passage through the Straits of Tiran and the Suez Canal.

The Frameworks were accompanied by letters. A letter from Begin to Carter promised that the question of the removal of the settlers from Sinai would be put to the Knesset, on a free vote. A letter from Sadat to Carter declared that if the settlers were *not* withdrawn from Sinai, there would be no peace treaty between Egypt and Israel. A further letter from Sadat to Carter reiterated the Arab position on Jerusalem. But the Jerusalem letter—unlike the Sinai letter—refrained from linking its subject matter with the conclusion of the peace treaty.

It was also understood, though not included in the Camp David Accords, that both Egypt and Israel were to receive substantially increased American aid.

XIV

Whatever the past shortcomings of Menachem Begin in the matter of the Sinai settlers, once he had made up his own mind on the matter, he set about cutting the Gordian Knot—of Knesset approval—with the assurance of a political master.

At Camp David, Begin had committed himself to do nothing more than put the question to the Knesset. So negative had he sounded, indeed, that at one point Jimmy Carter even besought Begin to be "neutral" in his presentation to the Knesset. But once back in Israel, having signed the Camp David Accords, Menachem Begin threw the full weight of his authority behind a commitment to the evacuation of the settlers, and the conclusion of a peace treaty with Egypt.

Begin went to his Cabinet, looking for authority to put to the Knesset not a question but a definite proposal for the approval of the following resolution:

> The Knesset approves the Camp David Accords that were signed by the Prime Minister at the White House on September 17, 1978. If, in the negotiations between Egypt and Israel towards the signing of a peace treaty, agreement is reached . . . [and] finds expression in a written document, the Knesset authorizes the Government . . . to evacuate the Israeli settlers from Sinai and resettle them anew.[52]

The decisive Cabinet meeting took place on September 24, and lasted for seven hours. As Moshe Dayan recalls:

The Prime Minister was authoritative and single-minded in his defense of the agreement, emphasizing its positive qualities, and mercilessly attacking those ministers who were doubtful or opposed. As a highly experienced parliamentarian, and every inch a political party man, he used skillful debating tactics and procedural techniques. He arranged for the Knesset debate to be held the following day, so there was no time to convene the parliamentary Foreign Affairs and Defense Committee. He also refused to hold discussions within his own party before the debate, customary when major policy decisions are to be taken.[53]

The Cabinet, by a large majority, approved Begin's proposal. In the Knesset itself, on the following day, disturbances came from the right wing of Begin's own party and were led by the extremely bellicose Geulah Cohen, who insisted on proposing a (disorderly) resolution calling for the resignation of the Prime Minister. After Geulah Cohen's expulsion from the chamber, Begin could begin his speech, which he did with the words: "I bring to the Knesset and through the Knesset to the nation, news of the establishment of peace between Israel and the strongest and largest of the Arab States, and also, eventually and inevitably, with all our neighbors."[54]

Shimon Peres, as leader of the opposition, followed. He began—unexpectedly, according to Dayan—by congratulating the Prime Minister and the Government on "the difficult, awesome, but vital decision they had taken to secure peace at a price which had been thought impossible for this Government."[55]

In a passage of great emotional power, Peres quoted "the mother of the sons":

. . . a lady, no longer young, dressed in black, went up to the rostrum. She is one of the great women in the history of reborn Israel, a woman who has lost two sons in Israel's wars, a pioneer in all spheres in which she is active. She is Rebecca Guber, known in Israel as "the mother of the sons." At the rostrum, speaking without notes, she had said to our Labour Party members: "Dear Friends, it is difficult for me to speak, nor had I intended to, for I have just risen from the seven days of mourning following the death of my dear husband. But I had no one to send in my place, for my sons left me no grandchildren. I therefore came myself to say to you that, astonishingly, peace beckons, the peace we have all yearned for. Can we allow this moment to slip away?"[56]

It might have been better if Peres had sat down at that point, but he went on, speedily sinking to the level of the contribution of his rival, Rabin, on the Begin Plan. The Camp David Accords were nothing at all as good as what the Labor Alignment could have gotten. The evacuation of the Sinai settlements could have been avoided, Peres thought. As to the Framework for Peace, it would lead to the establishment of a Palestinian State. All the same, he was going to vote for the Government's resolution.

Peres's performance was remarkably illogical and inconsequential, even as parliamentary speeches go, but on the whole it was helpful to the Government, and to the treaty. Labor support outweighed Likud defections. Moshe Dayan records the final vote:

> All 120 members of the Knesset voted. The result was 84 in favour of the Government's action, 19 against, and 17 abstentions. One of those who abstained was Yehuda Ben Meir, head of the religious party faction in the Knesset. I could not help sending him a note with a one-word change in an old Talmudic quotation: "By abstention shall the righteous live."[57]

XV

In America, the Camp David Accords were a huge success for President Carter, politically. In the wake of the Accords, Gallup recorded a 17 percent leap in the President's popularity rating. But in the Arab world, the reaction to Camp David was overwhelmingly and—outside Egypt—unanimously negative. The conservative states—principally Jordan and Saudi Arabia—which had been noncommittal in the earlier phases of Sadat's peace process now joined with the Front of Steadfastness in condemning it. This made possible the ninth Arab Summit, at Baghdad (November 2–5, 1978), which was attended by every Arab State except Egypt (which was not invited), and resoundingly condemned, with one voice, the Camp David Accords.

Brzezinski's theory of three "concentric circles" of the peace process was now in some difficulty. His two "outer circles" were now as one in denouncing his inmost circle: a phenomenon which his theory had not foreseen. There was no sign at all of a peace process catching on, or rippling out, among the other Arab states. Hussein—according to White House thinking, Sadat's designated successor in the peace relay—coldly declined any such role. On the day the news of Camp David broke—with the envisaged role for Jordan—Hussein declared that Jordan was "neither legally nor morally bound" by anything agreed at Camp David.[58]

Curiously, the feature of Camp David which most aroused the wrath of the assembled and united Arabs at Baghdad was the feature which was intended to placate them: The Framework for Peace, with "autonomy" and "transit of authority." On that matter the noises coming from Baghdad were music in the ears of Begin and his colleagues. Sadat, backed by Carter, had been pressing Israel for speedy implementation of the autonomy provisions, in order to convince the Arab world of the value of Camp David. But at Baghdad, the Arab world made it only too clear that it rejected any implementation of autonomy provisions. As Daniel Dishon puts it, the Arab world (outside Egypt) "did not want autonomy *quickly:* rather it wanted autonomy *scrapped* altogether, along with the rest of the Camp David Accords."[59]

It seems that Sadat would have been less unpopular with his Arab brothers—certainly the conservative ones—if he had forgone his comprehensivist exertions and gone straight for a separate peace with Israel. But Sadat, in emphasizing comprehensivism, was probably less interested in impressing his Arab brothers than in bringing his policy, or at least his rhetoric, into line with prevalent thinking in the White House.

The force and unanimity of Arab opposition did not deflect Sadat from his purpose. The Treaty of Peace between Egypt and Israel, provided for in the second Camp David Framework, was signed in the White House on March 26, 1979. The process of the evacuation of Sinai, under the treaty, began immediately, and on April 30, Israelis could watch on television the first Israeli ship going through the Suez Canal.

XVI

For a time after the treaty, the Carter Administration continued its efforts to widen the peace process. In particular, it sought to bring the P.L.O. into the peace process. It hoped to achieve this by expanding and enhancing the relevant Security Council resolutions in such a way as to make them acceptable to the P.L.O. The history of this effort, and of the paradoxes on which it foundered, is particularly instructive in relation to the unexpected pitfalls which beset the comprehensivist approach.

Thinkers of the Brookings school believed—reasonably, up to a point—that there could be no comprehensive or stable settlement of the Arab-Israeli conflict until the P.L.O. could be brought into the peace process. But there was a preliminary difficulty. At the time of Second Sinai, in September 1975, Henry Kissinger had given Israel a written assurance that there would be "no recognition of and no negotiation with the P.L.O. [by the United States] until the P.L.O. recognizes Israel's right to exist and accepts Resolutions 242 and 338."

Now certain statements of P.L.O. spokesmen, in Western contexts, could be taken as implying recognition of Israel's right to exist. But there was no ambiguity about the P.L.O.'s relation to those Security Council resolutions. The P.L.O. quite clearly rejected them, and had often reaffirmed its rejection of 242 in particular. The stated grounds for rejection were the failure of 242 to recognize the legitimate rights of the Palestinians, and its failure to advert to the existence of Palestinians at all, except in their capacity as refugees.

A way around this difficulty suggested itself. This was to amend 242 (and 338) in such a way as to take account of the P.L.O.'s objections. If the United States supported such a proposal, Soviet opposition was not to be expected, and safe passage through the Security Council could be assumed. The P.L.O., presumably, would accept the amended resolutions, once their stated objections had been met. In doing so, they would also be deemed to be accepting Israel's right to exist, since the old 242 and 338 clearly did that, and the amended versions would also do it. Thus the conditions set by the Kissinger guarantee would have been met, and United States representatives would be free to talk with the P.L.O. Israel would be furious, but it could be hoped that it would eventually adjust itself to the *fait accompli*.

The proposal that the resolutions should be amended was put forward by Kuwait, in the summer of 1979; presumably with the encouragement of some circles in the P.L.O.

The White House took up the idea, and on August 18, 1979, the President's personal representative, Robert Strauss, broached it with Sadat, expecting his support. "Sadat complained genially that the Resolution idea was 'stupid.' "[60] He had no interest in bringing in the

P.L.O. from the cold, thereby possibly endangering his treaty, and his recovery of Sinai.

Stranger still, Assad agreed with Sadat on this one. That same month, Syria sharply opposed the Kuwaiti proposal. Assad did not want the P.L.O. as independent participants in any peace process.

Egypt didn't want it. Syria didn't want it. Did the P.L.O. want it? At first they seemed to want it very much, but then—no doubt under both Syrian and internal pressure—they changed their ground. In March 1980, a P.L.O. spokesman laid down that "an addition or amendment to 242 would be unacceptable." What the P.L.O. demanded was an altogether new resolution "totally separate from 242." This, of course, ran counter to the whole original rationale of the exercise, which was to free the U.S. to talk to the P.L.O., by meeting the Kissinger preconditions.

For good measure, Arafat added that the new resolution should *not* provide for "secure and recognized frontiers" for Israel.

"Expanded 242" was now dead, but not quite ready to lie down. In the early summer of 1980, Britain, on behalf of the European countries—originally encouraged in that direction by Carter—offered to introduce at the Security Council the desirable amending resolution.

On May 30, 1980, President Carter pledged himself publicly "to veto any European move in the Security Council to amend Resolution 242 to provide for Palestinian participation in a comprehensive Middle Eastern settlement."[61] The Europeans withdrew the proposal.

Thus ended the Carter Administration's long effort to apply the philosophy of the Brookings Institution to the politics of the Middle East.

XVII

By that time, however, the shape of the Middle East, as seen from the West, had radically changed. Up to late 1978, Westerners—and Washington in particular—had been in the habit of seeing and discussing the Middle East almost exclusively in terms of the Arab-Israeli conflict. For more than thirty years, an influential school of thought among Western policy makers had seen that conflict as the main source of unrest in the region. Those who had sought for a "solution" to that had seen themselves as trying to bring peace to "the Middle East." And President Carter, unfortunately for himself, had persistently presented himself in that light.

The revolution in Iran, at the beginning of 1979, changed that whole perspective, since this was a major event which had very little to do with the Arab-Israeli conflict. And as the Iranian Revolution took on an increasingly anti-American character—partly due to ill-judged American reactions—the Arab-Israeli conflict became at best a secondary preoccupation for Washington policy makers.

For the United States (which had ignored the oppressive aspects of the Shah's regime) to denounce the oppressive acts of the Shah's then overwhelmingly popular successors was looking for trouble. It was the Senate, rather than the President, which precipitated the anti-American paroxysm in Iran, but it was the President who paid the political penalty for the consequences of that paroxysm.

In the summer of 1979, a U.S. Senate resolution condemning the executions of the Shah's associates (and others) was followed by large anti-American demonstrations throughout Iran. In late October, the Shah's admission to the United States (for medical treatment) sent Khomeini's supporters into the frenzy which culminated, on November 4, 1979, in the seizure of the American Embassy in Teheran, and the taking of the American hostages, creating the issue that was to dominate all Carter's remaining months in the White House and to destroy his hopes of re-election.

As we have seen—in relation to the death pangs of comprehensivism—Carter did not cease, even among his growing Iranian preoccupations, to give attention to Arab-Israeli questions. But the nature of his attention changed as November 1980 drew nearer. In late 1978 and early 1979, Carter had been greatly concerned with Begin's post–Camp David policy of stepping up Jewish settlements in the West Bank and Gaza—as part of Begin's effort to prove that removal of Sinai settlements was *not* a precedent for Judea and Samaria. In this period, Carter told Vance: "I would be willing to lose my election because I will alienate the Jewish community but . . . if necessary be harder on the Israelis."[62]

Carter's domestic advisers were proportionately alarmed: "Ham Jordan—always mindful of the influence of the Jewish community in U.S. domestic politics—cheerfully quipped that perhaps one of us might want to be the first Ambassador to the West Bank, because in two years we would all be unemployed."[63]

Cyrus Vance seems to have assumed that this Kamikaze mood on the part of his master still held good in the election year itself.[64] On March 1, 1980, the United States delegation voted for an extremely tough resolution in the Security Council. The resolution deplored the

Israeli Government's decision to support settlements in occupied territories, declared that these measures "have no legal validity," and
called for the rescinding of the decision and the dismantling of the
settlements.[65]

In the ensuing uproar from Israel and its friends, Carter back-
tracked and disavowed the U.S. vote, saying it was "not deliberate."
As the Security Council Resolution still stood, with all its force in
international law, the Begin Government, and its friends in America,
were not much mollified by Carter's disavowal. The Democratic Party
seemed in some danger, at this point, of losing the pro-Israel vote, most
of which it normally gets. Carter's chances of getting re-elected were
getting thinner all through 1980; if he lost the pro-Israel vote, he stood
no chance at all. It was against that forbidding political background
that Carter, at the end of May, took his irony-studded decision to
veto, if necessary, the European initiative for a comprehensive settlement of the Arab-Israeli dispute.

Willingness to lose an election is found in direct proportion to the
distance to election day. The shorter the distance, the smaller the
willingness.

Comprehensivism, jilted by the United States, and barred from
the Security Council, found a refuge in Europe. At the end of their
Venice Summit meeting, on June 13, 1980, the E.E.C. heads of government issued a statement reaffirming the necessity to associate the
P.L.O. in future negotiations and reiterating E.E.C. support for Israel's "right to a secure existence."

The Venice Declaration got a remarkably poor press in the area
for whose benefit it was ostensibly intended. Israel described the
declaration as "a Munich-like capitulation to totalitarian blackmail."
The P.L.O. might have been expected to respond favorably to a
declaration which enraged Israel to that degree, but not so. Meeting
in Damascus, the P.L.O. representatives described the declaration as
"very weak and very poor." They also advised the European heads of
government "to free themselves of the pressure-blackmail of United
States policy."

Arafat and his close associates had worked hard to get that declaration, with its recognition of "the necessity to associate the P.L.O. in
future negotiations." But the response of "the P.L.O." to the European
initiative depended much more on Assad than on Arafat. And Assad,
suspicious of independent diplomatic endeavors by P.L.O. officials,
discouraged them by causing the fruits of their endeavors to be dis-

paraged, however appetizing they might look in the eyes of those who had produced them.

As a contribution to a comprehensive settlement, the Venice Declaration was no more effective than "expanded 242." But if the Venice Declaration went down reasonably well in Riyadh and the Gulf capitals—as seems to have been the case—the European architects of the declaration will not have been disappointed with the results of their efforts.

XVIII

Rhetorically, and on the subject of Israel, the Arab states, other than Egypt, maintained an appearance of unity after the conclusion of the peace treaty between Egypt and Israel. The Second Baghdad Summit, on March 31, 1979, condemned the treaty, as First Baghdad had condemned Camp David, and called for sanctions against Egypt. A later summit, at Tunis in November of the same year, reaffirmed these positions and maintained the isolation of Egypt.

A feature of the period was an effort by conservative Arab leaders—Crown Prince Fahd and King Hussein—to mobilize the Muslim world for some kind of alleged *jihad* against Israel. A conference of Muslim Foreign Ministers adopted a resolution on the theme: "The Islamic countries declare their commitment to the *jihad* because of what it embodies in its broad human dimensions on the ground that it constitutes steadfastness and confrontation against the Zionist enemy on all fronts: military, political, economic, informative and cultural."[66] A rather figurative kind of *jihad*.

But by that time even the core of anti-Zionist Arabs was already split again, and on the verge of a worse split. On January 14, 1980, the General Assembly of the United Nations met in Emergency Session to consider the Soviet invasion of Afghanistan: a Muslim country. The Arab states voted condemnation, with the exception of the five members of the Steadfastness Front, most of which, including Syria, abstained. The P.L.O. representative—who, having "observer" status, had the right to speak but not to vote—made a strong pro-Soviet speech, presumably with Syrian approval. Syria and its associates had broken a Muslim and Arab consensus, and Syria's dependence on the Soviet Union was sharply lit up.

As Syria—"the leading confrontation State"—was the most hostile of Israel's neighbors, this development was naturally a welcome one, from Israel's point of view. Even better, from the same point of view, was to follow.

In September 1980, war broke out between Iraq and Iran. As the Saudi press put it, it was "a war between an Arab and a stranger," and so most Arabs were expected to back Iraq. Syria, however, apparently influenced by the old hostility between the divergent Ba'athist parties of Syria and Iraq, and the personal antagonism of Assad and Iraq's Saddam Hussein, decided to support Iran against its Arab brothers. Syria's position was a strange and vulnerable one for a country which had loved to present itself as the heart of Arabism. Jordan's King Hussein, long taunted by Syria as a traitor to the Arabs, saw his opportunity to turn the tables on his old accusers, and took it with a will. Hussein now emerged as the champion of the Arab nation against the stranger. Hussein gave active aid to Iraq, and his radio denounced Syria, which replied in kind. Between Iraq and Jordan on the one side, and Syria and Libya on the other, "reproach . . . the soap of the soul" was being applied with an abandon not experienced since the mid-sixties.

Saudi Arabia, while holding to its sagacious policy of not vilifying other Arabs, or even Persians, threw its discreet but weighty support to Iraq and Jordan.

These conditions made life uncomfortable for the P.L.O. Its principal patron and "protector," Syria, was being undermined by its principal paymaster, Saudi Arabia. The P.L.O.'s Syrian patron also seemed driven to extreme and exotic positions—pro-Russian, pro-Persian—damaging to the P.L.O. generally, and especially to Arafat's cherished hopes of an opening to the West. Arafat briefly attempted to mediate between Iraq and Iran, but got snubbed by both sides.

XIX

From Menachem Begin's point of view, the state of Israel's external relations was exceptionally propitious, and increasingly so, during 1980. No serious pressure was to be expected from the United States during a presidential election year, and with American attention concentrated on the plight of the Teheran hostages, almost to the exclusion of any other external topic.

Peace with Egypt could be expected to last, under whatever

stresses, at least until April 1982, when, under the provisions of the treaty, Egypt was due to have recovered the whole of Sinai.

As for the rest of the Arab world—constituting "the Arab consensus" from which Egypt was held to be excluded—that was in a worse state of disarray and internecine conflict than anything experienced since the Khartoum agreements of 1967.

In these conditions, Begin felt free to press ahead, energetically and without inhibitions, with his program for "Judea and Samaria." That program differed from the programs of Begin's Labor predecessors in two main respects.

First, Labor had generally tried to insure that Jewish settlements should be concentrated in areas away from centers of dense Arab population. The Begin Government dropped that limitation, taking the view that the location of Jewish settlements in Jewish—Biblical—land was a matter for Jews, not Arabs, to determine.

Second, Labor's policy—originally laid down by Moshe Dayan after June 1967—required a minimum of interference by Israel with the Arab inhabitants. The Arabs were generally left to run their own affairs, subject only to security controls. Quite a sophisticated political system had grown up (in symbiosis with Jordan) within which the Arabs of the West Bank could conduct their lives with a minimum of contact with the Israeli authorities.

That was a limited but real form of autonomy, never so called, and designed to accommodate local realities with as little friction as possible. This system (call it Autonomy One), which had proved its usefulness over a period of more than ten years, was now threatened by a new version: Autonomy Two.

Autonomy Two—Begin's autonomy—had grown up in quite a different way from the earlier version. The new version was a response not at all to any local realities but to international pressures, and in particular to the demand for a final and comprehensive settlement involving the West Bank. Autonomy One was no use as a response to that demand; for one thing the Arabs—whether "pro-Hashemite" or "pro-P.L.O."—who assiduously worked that system, as a matter of daily routine, would all agree in refusing to it the character of any kind of settlement.

(The word "settlement" is tricky in this context because of its two meanings: "settlement/colony" and "settlement/solution." However, the word cannot be avoided.) Something more pretentious than Autonomy One, in terms of finality and comprehensiveness, was required, and it had emerged in the rather vague shape of Camp David (Autonomy Two). In the West Bank, it was Camp David, as interpreted by Begin. Now, all representative figures in the West Bank— "pro-Hashemite" and "pro-P.L.O." alike—rejected Camp David Autonomy, whether as interpreted by Begin or by anybody else.

So that Begin, if he was to convince the world that his version of Autonomy Two was the true, final and comprehensive settlement— and thus gain international legitimacy for his holding of Judea and Samaria—had to find, or create, new Arab elites, which would accept that version. So Begin was drawn—like the French in Algeria *circa* 1960—into the quest for *interlocuteurs valables:* valid interlocutors who would say, on behalf of the Arabs, whatever Begin might want them to say.

This quest for an alternative elite—soon to emerge, or half emerge, in the form of the Rural Associations or Village Leagues, under Israeli patronage—was inherently alarming to all the old elites of the West Bank, which had accommodated themselves well to Autonomy One, and the kind of veiled coexistence with Israel which that represented.

The attempt to replace a tacit, working accommodation with an internationally recognizable "settlement" was dangerously disruptive even by itself. When the attempt to manipulate Arab leadership was seen in conjunction with the introduction of unrestricted Jewish settlement, and with acts of provocation by some of the new settlers, the result was the greatest wave of unrest that the West Bank had known in thirteen years of Israeli occupation.

The effects of benevolent insistence, from a long way off, on the need for a settlement are not always readily recognizable in the untoward forms they are liable to assume on the spot, in unpredictable interaction with local forces.

XX

The Government had established a yeshiva (Talmudic school) in the Arab-populated town of Hebron, in the West Bank. Hebron, the reputed burial place of Abraham, is today an Arab center with a particularly violent and anti-Jewish tradition; it was the scene of the worst massacre of Jews in 1929. Hebron was also the object of a special redemptive effort by Gush Emunim and other religious and right-wing groups.

On May 2, 1980, six students of the Hebron yeshiva were murdered and seventeen wounded by Arab gunfire as Jewish worshipers were returning from Friday prayers at the Tomb of the Patriarchs. The Government took various repressive steps, including the destruction of a number of houses and shops in Hebron, and the closing of the Jordan bridges to Hebron residents. The Government also expelled three leaders of the Hebron Arabs, including the mayor. The expelled persons went to New York, where they addressed the Security Council. Israel's repressive actions were duly censured.

Although the Government's reactions to the Hebron murders seemed excessive, to international opinion, these reactions seemed quite insufficient to a growing section of Jewish opinion in Israel. On June 2, 1980, the mayors of Ramallah and Nablus were maimed and crippled by car-bomb attacks. One mayor lost a foot; the other, both legs. As these attacks took place shortly after the end of the prescribed mourning period for the yeshiva students, the attacks were generally seen as the actions of Jewish settlers taking the law into their own hands, in retaliation for the murders of the students.

Ezer Weizman, who had been under pressure for his supposed "underreaction" to the Hebron murders, resigned in May, and Begin himself, as Prime Minister, took over also the Defense portfolio. For some months there was a lull, and the Government began to congratulate itself on the success of its firmness, while the Jewish activists ascribed the calm to the salutary effects of "counterterror."

Then, in November 1980, following the closure of Bir Zeit University (because of pro-P.L.O. demonstrations there), serious rioting spread throughout the West Bank, continuing into December. Roads were blocked, Israeli vehicles were stoned and rioters were injured by I.D.F. fire. The West Bankers were preparing for the return of the injured mayors of Nablus and Ramallah, after six months of medical treatment abroad, where they had been fitted with artificial limbs. The first to return, on December 25, 1980, was Karim Khalaf, mayor of Ramallah. Khalaf was welcomed by huge crowds, as a hero and martyr. He declared: "I am going to continue the struggle until we achieve a Palestinian State." The crowd responded with the song: "With guns we shall liberate the land, our whole nation waves the guns, for our liberty we sacrifice ourselves." Mayor Bassam Shaka returned to his native Nablus, and a similar welcome, on January 4, 1981.

Begin's policies of unrestricted settlement and manipulative autonomy had resulted in the reverse of what he had wanted to demonstrate. It was now clear beyond doubt that the Arab population of the

West Bank rejected Begin's version of autonomy. But this did not deter Begin from pressing ahead with his policies, since these did not in any case, in his view of the matter, require Arab consent. This was land that God had given to the Jews. Nor was that just some far-out notion of Begin and his friends, as much international commentary suggested. It was essentially the same claim—the Bible as title deed— that David Ben-Gurion had put forward before the Peel Commission, forty-four years earlier.

There was much talk, and much public evidence, in the winter of 1980–1981, of a dramatic radicalization of the West Bank. It might have been thought, and was sometimes assumed—as had often been the case during the previous six years—that the "conservative" Hashemite influence was giving way before the "radicalism" of the P.L.O. There was a tendency in that direction, but it was offset by other tendencies. In particular, Arafat's Fatah, the main body of the P.L.O., appears to have cooperated during this period with the Hashemites in curbing the growth in influence of the leftist P.L.O. factions (Habash's P.F.L.P., etc.).[67] With Fatah's cooperation, Amman used its control over the flow of money, issue of passports, etc., to cramp and hamper the radical leaders. Hashemite influence, and the authority of the older elites, managed to survive both Begin's autonomy and the populist reaction to it. And the threatened mass revolt remained, during this period, at the level of the theater of the street.

XXI

A presidential election year in the United States is one in which a Government of Israel does not expect to find itself under pressure; though there had been a memorable exception, in 1956. The first year of a new President, on the other hand, is traditionally expected to be "difficult." But when Ronald Reagan became President in January 1981, and when he appointed General Alexander Haig as his Secretary of State, the Begin Government had some grounds for optimism about its relations with the new American Administration. It was not only that the new President had shown himself militantly pro-Israel, during his campaign; that was to be expected. The really reassuring thing was that Reagan's world outlook, as expounded in his speeches, seemed such as to make him see Israel's worst enemies—Syria and the P.L.O.— as the enemies of the United States also: not in function of their hostility to Israel, but in function of their relation to the Soviet Union. Syria was a client of the Soviet Union; the P.L.O., a client of the Soviets' Syrian client. Both were enemies in Reagan's apparently clear-cut book, and their villainy had been seen in their perfidious posture at the United Nations, in January 1980, over the Soviet invasion of Afghanistan.

The Government of Israel could expect that, under Reagan, there would be none of the old Carter hankering after a comprehensive solution, involving Arafat, Assad, and Gromyko as well, according to "the spirit of Geneva." The spirit of the Reagan White House would aim, surely, at the reduction of Soviet influence, and the curbing of Soviet clients.

The "new" American world view had particularly interesting implications, for Israel, in relation to Lebanon. In terms of the general world view now apparently dominant in Washington, Lebanon was a sovereign State, traditionally moderate and pro-Western, but now partly occupied by two Soviet clients: Syria and the P.L.O. (The fact that Syria had installed itself in Lebanon with the acquiescence and even encouragement of Washington might not have been known to Reagan. In any case, Syria had moved closer to the Kremlin since those days, and signed a Treaty of Friendship and Cooperation with the Soviet Union in October 1980.)

For ten years now—since the eviction of the P.L.O. from Jordan—"Lebanon" had been the principal thorn in Israel's side: Lebanon not as a State, but as the remaining political and military habitat for the P.L.O., on Israel's borders.

The question of what, if anything, to do about Lebanon, in any given circumstances, was permanently on the agenda of the Government of Israel. The belief that the *status quo* in Lebanon was now objectionable on both ideological and world-strategic grounds to the President of the United States was a major factor to be taken into account in any future answer to that question, however it might be posed.

XXII

The political and military leadership of the Maronite Christians of Lebanon saw the new conjuncture as highly propitious to the pursuit of its interests. The possibility of an alliance between the Maronites and Israel had been mooted since before the foundation of the State of Israel, and had taken practical forms since the outbreak of the Lebanese Civil War. The Rabin Government is said to have invested $150 million in the equipment and training of the Maronite militia (Kataeb, Phalanges[68]). The connection was well established when Menachem Begin came to power, and it was warmly favored by some senior Israeli officers and politicians—notably Ariel Sharon—and distrusted and disparaged by others.

Begin, when he came to power, threw his weight on the side of developing the Maronite connection. To judge from some of Begin's public remarks, the idea of Jews protecting Middle Eastern Christians, who had been abandoned by the Christian world, appealed to the romantic and Quixotic aspect of his character: "the Polish aristocrat in him."

Bashir Gemayel, the leader of the Maronite militia, was encouraged to make a bid for national power in Lebanon. He had the support of the Begin Government, and the special favor of Ariel Sharon. Bashir was a charismatic and bombastic figure, who liked to talk about the "new Lebanese"—heroic martial Christians who were to be (or already were) to the "old Lebanese," of wheeling-and-dealing fame, as the "new Jews" of Israel were to the "old Jews" of the European ghettos. The flattery implicit in this concept seems to have gone down well with some Israelis—notably Sharon—though not with all. In any case, Bashir was taken seriously among the Maronites, and was an object of hero worship to the Maronite youth.

Bashir could hope that, as the "pro-Western" champion in Lebanese politics, he would have the support of the United States. The Syrians would be against him, but the Syrians, by 1981, seemed to be a weakened force, isolated in the Arab world, damaged by internal discontent and constrained to contract their area of occupation in Lebanon.

By the spring of 1981, Bashir, having ruthlessly—indeed barbarically—disposed of his chief Maronite rivals, was the virtually unchallenged leader of the Maronite community. He now aimed at establishing his claim to lead the Christians of Lebanon as a whole, and so to emerge as the Pan-Christian candidate in the Lebanese presidential elections, due for 1982.

Partly as a move in that direction, and partly with the related objective of challenging Syria, Bashir Gemayel, in late 1980 and early 1981, had extended the protection of his Maronite militia to the Greek Orthodox inhabitants of Zahla, in eastern Lebanon.

The protection of Zahla was an extremely bold move. Zahla is a city of 250,000 inhabitants in the Bekaa Valley, near the Beirut-Damascus road, in the area which Syria regards as vital for its defense. Syria bided its time for a while—possibly to work out contingency arrangements under its new Treaty of Friendship and Cooperation with the Soviet Union—and then, at the beginning of April 1981, struck hard at Zahla, and at Christian positions in the nearby mountains. The Christians of Zahla, bombarded and besieged, paid dearly for Bashir's "protection." Bashir's militia was in no condition to fight the Syrian Army, and by late April, the Maronites had not only lost as far as the Bekaa was concerned, but were at risk in their own Christian heartland. Bashir seems to have assumed that Israel would come to his rescue, and indeed it has been suggested that senior Israeli officers had encouraged him in this belief.[69] Syria had also prepared against that contingency.

In the event, Israel went to the brink, but not over it. On April 28, 1981, Israel's jet fighters, by way of "warning" to the Syrians, destroyed two Syrian helicopters. On the following day, the Syrian Army moved Soviet surface-to-air missiles, SAM-2s and SAM-6s, into Lebanon.

Israel wished to destroy the Syrian missiles, but was held back by the United States. The United States undertook to get the missiles out of Lebanon by negotiation. The State Department's Philip Habib went to Damascus and negotiated, the missiles stayed where they were and Bashir went back to his base.

From this, its first test run, it seemed that Reagan's policy was less resolute in practice than speeches had made it sound. In a statement in early April, Haig had strongly attacked Syria. But on April 17—at the height of the Zahla crisis—Reagan sent a warm congratulatory message to Assad on the occasion of Syria's national day. The message included a phrase mentioning "the role the Syrian leadership could play in strengthening the security and stability of the States of the region."

United States policy during this crisis seems to have been less affected by any new Reagan factors than by traditional pre-Reagan factors: a desire not to be so closely aligned with Israel as to alarm moderate Arabs, such as the Saudis; and also a need to avoid provoking Soviet intervention, and therefore a need to mollify an outraged Soviet client. The particular circumstances of the case suggested a need for extra caution on the part of United States policy makers. Bashir's adventure in the Bekaa assumed—with what degree of encouragement, at what level, on the Israeli side?—that Israel would be drawn in against Syria. Those in Israel who had encouraged that assumption also had to assume that Israel would be supported by the United States, against the Soviet Union, when Syria appealed to the Kremlin, and invoked the treaty. Adventures and assumptions of that kind might have been encouraged by past Reaganite rhetoric, but they had to be discouraged as a matter of practical policy.

As a sheer matter of interest in survival, neither superpower can willingly allow one of its clients to try to determine—by its assumptions and initiatives—a superpower's future course of action in relation to the other superpower. But the superpower-and-client relationship is not symmetrical. No client of the Soviet Union has anything like the influence over its patron that Israel has regularly shown itself to have over the United States, since 1967. And Israel, feeling its own existence to be permanently at risk, is more likely to run high preemptive risks than other client states are. But on this occasion Israel felt obliged to draw back, for the time being.

For Israel, Zahla was a humiliating and somewhat alarming experience. The affair strengthened Israel's chief enemy, both materially and in prestige. Israel's Christian allies were humbled, and resentful at Israel's "betrayal." Their friends, still influential in the Israel Defense Forces, shared their feelings. The memory of Zahla probably goes some way to account for the mood of total self-reliance and "no half measures" which prevailed among Israel's decision makers a little more than a year later, in May–June 1982.

The fiasco at Zahla stands in a similar relation to the Lebanon War of 1982 as the Jameson Raid did to the Boer War. It left unfinished business, and frustrated activists.

XXIII

Nineteen eighty-one was an election year in Israel. In the early part of the year, it looked as if Begin and his colleagues would lose. The main achievement of this Begin Government (1977–1981) had been the peace treaty with Egypt. Notable achievement though it was, this was no election winner. Most Israelis approved the treaty, but it aroused nothing like the enthusiasm which had greeted the original breakthrough, Sadat's arrival in Jerusalem. The handing back of tracts of Sinai with their oilfields and their airfields—and the prospect of the eviction of the settlers—produced at least as much resentment as the peace itself produced relief and satisfaction. The peace itself was felt to be "a cold peace," without 'any friendship in it. Egyptian criticism of Israeli policies in the West Bank and in Lebanon was also resented, and there was a widespread feeling that Egypt might double-cross Israel, and return to the ranks of Israel's foes, once the evacuation of Sinai was completed in April 1982.

Nor was there anything else in the conduct of Israel's relations with Arabs or the United States—always the two main areas of Israel's external concern—which looked cheering or attractive to voters. True, most Israelis—between 62 percent and 74 percent, according to a number of polls taken in the early months of 1981—did support continued settlement activity on the West Bank. But the Government's claims (of mid-1980) to have restored "calm" to the West Bank had been reduced to nonsense at the beginning of 1981 by the rapturous and militant welcome accorded to the crippled and defiant mayors of Ramallah and Nablus.

In and around Lebanon, the picture was even more depressing. Israel had been humiliated, and its Syrian enemy exalted, by the events around Zahla in April. Syria, with impunity, had installed Soviet missiles in Lebanon. Israel's "special relationship" with the Reagan Administration—a relationship from which much had been expected, especially in regard to Syria and the P.L.O.—seemed to have worked out, in this instance, as more beneficial to Syria than to Israel.

In short, there was nothing in Israel's external relations, at the end of May 1980, which could compensate electorally for unpopular developments on the domestic front. As Aaron Klieman puts it: "Israel's international position remained as contentious, isolated and unguaranteed as at any time in the past."[70]

On the domestic front, Likud's mismanagement of the economy was almost universally deplored. Inflation, which stood at around 40 percent when Likud first took office, had reached around 130 percent by the end of 1980. In a no-confidence vote on the economy, in November 1980, Dayan and Weizman—the main pillars of Begin's original 1977 Government—had voted with the opposition.

At the end of May 1981—with the election due on June 30—there seemed little hope for Likud. But by the second week of June, the balance had changed radically, because of a spectacular, and brilliantly executed, military operation ordered by the Government.

On June 7, 1981, Israel's Air Force destroyed Iraq's nuclear reactor, Osirak, located in Tuwaitha, near Baghdad. As an American news report dramatically describes the action, code named Operation Babylon:

> Like a bolt out of the Old Testament, they hurtled at Baghdad out of the setting sun. Nearing their target, six F-15 interceptors camouflaged with the desert mottle of the Israeli air force peeled off to keep guard overhead. Eight F-16 fighter-bombers roared down on the concrete dome of the Osirak nuclear reactor. In a single series of lightning passes, the little fighters dropped their payload of 2,000 bombs. Within two minutes they disappeared cleanly into the gathering darkness, leaving behind a few puffs of flak and a fearsome new turn in a dangerous nuclear game.[71]

Israel had been concerned about the obvious possible implications of the Tuwaitha Nuclear Center since its construction (by the Soviets) in 1963, and especially since the conclusion in 1975 of a nuclear cooperation agreement between Iraq and France (based on guaranteed oil supplies, in exchange for nuclear aid). Whether the Iraqi nuclear project was in fact intended to produce nuclear weapons, or was designed for peaceful purposes only (as officially claimed by Iraq), was an unresolved question. But neither the Government of Israel nor the Israeli public was at all disposed to take any chances on that matter.

International reaction to Operation Babylon was mostly indignant, but the indignation died down rather rapidly. The United States condemned the Israeli raid and its "unprecedented character." Other international reactions—from the Arab world, the Soviet Union and Western Europe—were sharper, but in keeping with already well-established positions. Iraq, still mainly concerned with its war with Iran, took advantage of the situation to mend some fences with the United States (yet another example of the surprise side effects of Israeli military strength). At the United Nations, the Iraqi and United States delegations worked out a "compromise," which was soon enshrined in Security Council Resolution 487 of June 19, 1981. The resolution strongly condemned Israel's action, but without providing for sanctions of any kind, thus relieving the United States of the need to cast an embarrassing veto.

The resolution, embodying a deal between Iraq and the United States, was generally interpreted as a setback for the Soviet Union. The United States had benefited marginally from the Israeli action which it had condemned. In any case, the "international crisis" over Operation Babylon was over.

In Israel itself the news of the operation "was greeted with exhilaration and euphoria among all segments of the Israeli public and across party lines. . . ."[72] Menachem Begin had a theme appropriate to his abiding passion. "There won't be another Holocaust in History," he announced at a press conference. "Never again, never again. We shall defend our people with all the means at our disposal."[73]

As against that stark, clear theme, Labor's position seemed hesitant and confused. Shimon Peres complained about the electorally inspired timing of the action, and suggested that Labor, through its good relations with France's new Socialist President, François Mitterrand, might have been able to have the Iraqi reactor removed peacefully. Neither point impressed the public. A poll taken just before the election showed that 82.9 percent of the sample approved of the decision to launch Operation Babylon, and that 75.9 percent thought that Labor criticism of the decision was unjustified.[74]

Begin's campaign was one of "thunder and lightning," Old Testament, Masada and Holocaust: very different from Likud's low-key campaign of 1977. Emotions were raised and there were a number of violent incidents, most of them involving attacks by members of Begin's Oriental following against Peres and his supporters. Labor's resentment spilled over, ethnically. At Labor's final rally in Tel Aviv, a popular entertainer, in the presence of Peres and his colleagues, referred to the Oriental Jews collectively as "riffraff," thus managing, with one word, to insult more than half the electorate of Israel.

Labor was also dogged, as before, by the "high level of personal animosity and vindictiveness" which had so long characterized the relationship between Peres and Rabin. Early in the campaign, Peres had said he would not give the Defense portfolio to Rabin. Then, at a midnight press conference, very near polling day, Peres said he was prepared to accept Rabin as Defense Minister, in place of his earlier choice. He seemed to be offering a deadlocked Government, since Rabin, in his *Memoirs,* had declared his lack of confidence in the man in whose Government he would occupy the key post.

XXIV

Although Labor, nonetheless, recovered much ground, getting forty-seven seats, as compared with the 1977 catastrophe level of thirty-two, it fell far short of its expectations at the beginning of the campaign, and just drew level with Likud. Likud was able to form a

Government with the assistance of two religious parties (N.R.P. and Agudat) and one ethnic (Oriental) party, Tami.

The elections showed that the ethnic polarization, in the electoral politics of Israel, was even more marked than it had been in 1977. It now seemed clear that there had been a long-term cumulative shift over sixteen years. In the new—and largely Oriental—cities and towns, Alignment votes decreased by 50 percent between 1965 and 1981, while the percentage of Likud votes more than doubled.[75] Two Tel Aviv sociologists found that demographic change appeared to be working in Likud's favor at a rate of about 2 percent per election campaign. As they put it, Likud is "swimming with the current" while the Alignment is "swimming upstream."[76]

In the 1981 elections, Likud received more than 70 percent of the votes of (Israeli-born) Orientals. Among young people from families of North African origin, Likud support approached 90 percent. More than half of the Ashkenazim born in Europe and North America voted for the Alignment, as opposed to less than a quarter who supported Likud.[77]

XXV

The Government formed by Begin after the June election of 1981 was a radically different proposition from the Begin Government of 1977. In 1977, Likud—knowing that its saber rattling had frightened off voters in 1973—had set itself to reassure the public. But in 1981, Begin and his colleagues had not merely engaged in saber *rattling*. Their entire electoral campaign in its last three weeks had hinged on the exploitation of a spectacular and successful *use* of the saber: the destruction of Osirak. Presumably the idea of Israel's using the saber was less alarming to voters in 1981 than it had been in 1977 because, in the meantime, Egypt, by far the most formidable of Israel's potential adversaries, had been neutralized—so at least it was universally hoped, and widely believed—by the peace treaty. In the new conditions, the Begin posture of "taking no more nonsense" from remaining hostile Arab forces on or near Israel's frontiers seems to have been generally acceptable.

The determination of the new Government was both symbolized and drastically reinforced by Begin's appointment of Ariel Sharon as Minister for Defense. From force of personality and of prestige, Sharon was one of the most powerful members of the Government, whatever portfolio he might hold. His record in the 1956, 1967 and 1973 wars—and as commander of the famous Unit 101—had made him, after Yom Kippur and the eclipse of Moshe Dayan, the most illustrious of Israel's soldiers. His prestige from 1973 to the autumn of 1982 was comparable to that of Moshe Dayan between the Six Day War, 1967, and Yom Kippur, 1973.

Yet Sharon, like Dayan, but even more than Dayan, also inspired a deep distrust among colleagues, both military and civilian. Ben-Gurion's feelings toward him had been rather like those of Lenin toward the young Stalin: admiration blended with uneasiness. Sharon was lacking, Ben-Gurion thought, in respect for the truth; also Sharon was too much given to something Ben-Gurion called "gossip," perhaps a less harmless trait than the word makes it sound. In a book published in 1982—before the war in Lebanon—Chaim Herzog, later President of Israel, gives the following portrait of Sharon:

> A very independently-minded and assertive character, Sharon was later in his political career to be accused of dictatorial tendencies by his opponents. He was to be accused, both in this [Sinai, 1956] and later campaigns, of insubordination and dishonesty. He can best be described as a Patton-like, swashbuckling general, who rose in the ranks of the Israel Defense Forces, proved himself to have an uncanny feel for battle, but at the same time to be a most difficult person to command. Few, if any, of his superior officers over the years had a good word to say for him as far as human relations and integrity were concerned, although none would deny his innate ability as a field soldier. Probably because of this, he never achieved his great ambition, to be Chief of Staff of the armed forces.[78]

The appointment of Sharon as Minister for Defense in 1981 had a significance similar to that of the appointment of Moshe Dayan as Minister for Defense in June 1967. It meant that the initiative, and the choice of war or peace, would no longer be left to the Arabs. It also meant that the Prime Minister and the Government were no longer in full control.

It has generally been difficult in Israel for a Government to have full control over its Minister for Defense. That difficulty was magnified many times by the appointment of Sharon to that portfolio. That appointment was like the appointment of a dictator in the old Roman

UPI/BETTMANN NEWSPHOTOS

Ariel Sharon (right), Israel's new Defense Minister, shaking hands with Prime Minister Begin, August 6, 1981, after the Knesset had approved Begin's new coalition Government. Sharon's appointment "was like the appointment of a dictator in the old Roman sense: the conferring of unlimited powers on a soldier for the duration of a perceived emergency."

sense: the conferring of unlimited powers on a soldier for the duration of a perceived emergency.

XXVI

Yet by the time Sharon took over as Minister for Defense—in August 1981—Israel's frontiers were quiet. A period of conflict in July, between the I.D.F. and the Lebanon-based P.L.O., had ended, on July 24, with a cease-fire sponsored (and strongly urged on Israel) by the United States and monitored by a United Nations force (U.N.I.F.I.L.). The cease-fire held, as far as the Israel-Lebanon border was concerned, for almost a year. From Israel's point of view, it was a seriously defective cease-fire. The P.L.O. maintained that it had not ceased to wage war, and that the cease-fire applied only to one particular front. *Fedayeen* attacks directed against Israel, or Israelis, were not breaches of the cease-fire, according to the P.L.O., provided the attacks did not take place across the Israel-Lebanon border. Israel, on the other hand, regarded any *fedayeen* attack, from any quarter, as a breach of the cease-fire by the P.L.O. It followed that if *fedayeen* activities continued—as they did—Israel could at any time treat a particular *fedayeen* action as a breach of the cease-fire and an occasion for the resumption of hostilities, on whatever scale Israel might consider appropriate. The P.L.O.'s theory of a "one-front" cease-fire was too convenient for the P.L.O., and too inconvenient for Israel, to be tolerated indefinitely.

For the remainder of 1981, however, the cease-fire held along Israel's northern border. At this time, the attention of the new Minister for Defense appeared to be concentrated mainly on the problems of the West Bank. Ariel Sharon sought for a time—and with some success, where Israeli opinion was concerned—to acquire a more liberal image: something not known to have preoccupied him ever before. As Eli Rekhess writes:

> Israeli and Arab observers predicted that following the appointment in August 1981 of Ariel Sharon as Minister for Defense in the new Begin Government, the hardline policy in the territories would be taken a step further. These predictions were soon proved wrong. On August 12 Defense Ministry Officials announced that Sharon intended to implement a liberal policy in the West Bank and Gaza Strip. The new policy was to be based on "receptiveness, openness and liberalization," and was aimed at creating an atmosphere conducive to a dialogue between Israel and West Bank Palestinians.[79]

The main feature of the "new" Sharon approach was the institution, in November 1981, of a West Bank Civil Administration, headed by an Israeli Arabist, Professor Menachem Milson. A Civil Administrator might sound more liberal than a Military Government, even though the Civil Administrator was in fact subordinate to the Minister for Defense. But Civil Administration, as practiced by Milson/Sharon, was in fact a lot less liberal than the form of Military Government which had been instituted by Moshe Dayan, and practiced for most of the first ten years of Israeli occupation of the territories. Dayan's "leave them alone whenever possible" system had provided about as benign a regimen as was possible in the circumstances. The new Civil Administration, on the other hand, offered a continuation and intensification of the Begin version of autonomy, requiring sustained intervention in Arab affairs, and a persistent quest for the elusive valid interlocutors.

The result, as might have been predicted, was a sharp increase in unrest in the West Bank. Following two days of campus demonstrations against the Civil Administration, Bir Zeit University was closed indefinitely, on November 4, 1981. Strikes and other disturbances followed; a prominent member of one of the Rural Associations was murdered; curfews were imposed by Israel; and houses were blown up.

Menachem Milson tried, in vain, to woo the more moderate West Bank mayors, and the Jordanians. In December 1981, all the West Bank mayors united in condemning the Civil Administration. In March 1982, the Jordanian Government outlawed the Rural Associations—the principal instrument of the Civil Administration policy—accused their members of "collaboration" with "the occupying authorities," and threatened prosecutions for treason.

This Jordanian intervention was particularly unwelcome and embarrassing to the Begin Government. The efforts of the Civil Administration had been justified by the supposed need to protect West Bank Arabs against P.L.O. extremists. King Hussein was not noted for friendship toward P.L.O. extremists. And Hussein also—unlike the P.L.O.—had influence with the Reagan Administration. The Begin Government's claim to be fulfilling the autonomy provisions of the Camp David Framework for Peace was becoming harder and harder to sustain.

Sharon's reaction was to threaten, and press on. He warned, on March 15, that if the Jordanian ultimatum were implemented—which it was not—Israel "would treat Jordan in the same way as it had treated the terrorist organizations."[80] On March 25, he had the two most prominent and popular of the West Bank mayors—the bomb victims Karim Khalaf of Ramallah and Bassam Shaka of Nablus—removed and arrested. There were no local candidates to succeed them, and they were eventually replaced by former Israeli military governors.

On March 30, all West Bank towns took part in a general strike. There followed an intensifying cycle of riots and repression. The repression was growing harsher. In the disturbances of March to May 1982, thirteen Arab civilians were killed by Israeli fire.

There was severe criticism in the Israeli press of the harder line in the West Bank. But majority opinion continued to support the Government. A poll in mid-May showed 75 percent in support.[81]

XXVII

Israel's decision to attack the P.L.O. in Lebanon, in June 1982, is often ascribed to the desire of Begin and Sharon to strengthen their hold on the West Bank. That there was a connection between the war and the West Bank situation can hardly be doubted. The Government saw its troubles in the West Bank as being "caused" by the P.L.O.— though they seem in reality to have been the results, in a far greater degree, of the Government's own increasingly interventionist policies. Still, for the youth of the West Bank, the presence of the P.L.O. in nearby Lebanon, and the idea—or illusion—of a "liberating army" at hand, presumably did have some inflammatory effect.

Also, by the beginning of 1982, Israel had special reasons, connected with both the West Bank and the United States, for wishing to deal the P.L.O. a hard blow, and soon. In August 1981, Crown Prince Fahd made proposals for the West Bank which called for the setting up of "an independent Palestinian state . . . with Jerusalem as its capital."[82] Prince Fahd did not say that the "Palestinian state" should be run by the P.L.O., but he quoted Yasser Arafat with approval, in his interview, and he clearly hoped for P.L.O. support.

The Fahd Plan—as it soon became known—failed to win endorsement at the Fez Summit, in November 1981, because it contained a clause, "that all states in the region should be able to live in peace," which was widely taken as implying some kind of recognition of Israel's right to exist. However, partly because of that clause, so interpreted, the Fahd Plan was favorably received in the West, including the United States.

This was a period when the Government of Israel was greatly concerned by an apparent rise in Saudi influence in Washington. President Reagan was known to be extremely anxious that Saudi Arabia should not become "a second Iran." This seemed to give the Saudis increased leverage. In the autumn of 1981, the pro-Israel lobby failed in its effort to prevent the sale of highly advanced equipment—including the AWACS surveillance plane and communications system—to the Saudis. Although the House of Representatives voted against the sale by 301 votes to 111, the Senate approved it, on Reagan's strong recommendation, by 52 to 48. The Senate vote may have been influenced by the assassination, on October 6, 1981, of Anwar Sadat. This was felt to show the need for support to America's Arab allies.

For Israel's policy makers, the Fahd Plan together with the evidence of increased Saudi political clout in Washington had ominous implications. It suggested a possible rehabilitation of the P.L.O. and its introduction into the "peace process," under cover of Saudi influence. This gave greater urgency to the idea, already present, of eliminating the P.L.O., as far as it could be eliminated, from its military and political base in Lebanon.

Peace initiatives, in connection with the Arab-Israeli conflict, are liable to have some peculiar side effects. So it was with the Fahd Plan.

XXVIII

But even if there had been no Begin autonomy, no Fahd Plan, and even no Sharon as Minister for Defense, it seems hardly likely that any Israeli Government would have long tolerated the continued presence in Lebanon of the P.L.O. and its armed forces. No state, surely, could willingly tolerate the presence within a neighboring state of a radically hostile political entity, in control of its own armed forces within the same state, and claiming the right to levy war at times and places of its own choosing.

Once Egypt, the most powerful partner, had withdrawn from the hostile Arab coalition, the Government of Israel could reasonably calculate that an action against the P.L.O. in Lebanon would be unlikely to precipitate intervention by other Arab states. The leading remaining "confrontation State"—Syria—was now isolated, not only from Egypt, but from most of the other Arab states as well, and was on especially bad terms with its immediate neighbors, Iraq and Jordan. The Assad regime was also in serious internal trouble. Both as a secular regime and as one which was run in practice by members of the highly deviant Alawi sect, dominant in the Army, Assad's regime was unpopular with many of the Sunni Muslims (who make up the majority of Syria's population) and especially with Muslim fundamentalists, whose influence had been rising, among Muslims generally, since the Iranian Revolution. The assassination of Sadat, at the hands of a well-educated and efficient group of Muslim fundamentalists, suggested the vulnerability of secular rulers governing Muslim populations. The killers appear to have been mainly motivated by revulsion at "existing Westernism in Egyptian society" and the non-Koranic character of the regime.[83] The treaty with Israel was only a secondary charge in the indictment against Sadat, in the view of the conspirators. Assad, as the Alawi leader of a Ba'athist secular State, was equally detestable on both grounds in the eyes of Sunni fundamentalists in Syria, and his "confrontationist" posture in relation to Israel seems to have done little to redeem him in their eyes.

Assad managed to survive, but at high cost, mainly to the population under his rule. At the beginning of February 1982, his forces besieged Syria's fourth city, Hama, then held by Muslim fundamentalists; and in the second half of February, the Government's forces stormed the city. Foreign journalists were not allowed into Hama during the fighting, but afterwards Patrick Seale—a well-informed correspondent, and not unsympathetic toward the Syrian regime—wrote that "at least 25,000 people were slaughtered and whole neighborhoods devastated by the regime's Defense Brigades."[84]

The sheer ferocity of the repression at Hama seems to have deterred other potential rebels, as was no doubt intended—and as Machiavelli recommends. But the internal troubles of the Syrian regime in the winter of 1981–1982, and partly also thereafter, were such (along with other factors) as to suggest to Israeli policy makers that the times were propitious for moves which Syria in happier circumstances would have tried to resist. In December 1981, the Knesset, on Begin's motion, extended the application of the laws of Israel to cover the territory in the formerly Syrian area of the Golan Heights, held by Israel since 1967.

As there was no immediate, practical need for this measure, it was widely seen as an act of defiance, not only of Syria and the rest of the Arab world, but also of the restraining hand of the United States. The Begin Government was undoubtedly smarting under its failure to dissuade the United States from its AWACS deal with the Saudis. It may also have been relatively encouraged by the narrowness of the defeat of the opposition to the deal in the Senate. Traditionally, it is harder for the pro-Israel lobby to avert the provision of American assistance to a third party than it is to deflect pressure from Israel itself. Against that background, the size of the opposition vote in the Senate (together with the overwhelming but inconclusive victory of the opposition in the House) could be read as a warning light to the Reagan Administration, and an encouraging index of Israel's capacity to resist and deflect American pressure, which might be generated by contemplated actions or decisions on the part of Israel.

In any case, and for whatever balance of motives—whether of ideology, opportunity or personalities—Begin's second Government was more disposed to take risks involving the vital American relationship than any previous Government of Israel had been, certainly since Golda Meir and the War of Attrition, and probably since David Ben-Gurion and the planning of Suez.

XXIX

By early 1982, the Governments in both Damascus and Washington knew that major Israeli intervention in Lebanon was under consideration. The response from Damascus was a signal of willingness to sacrifice the P.L.O. provided Israel, when finished with the P.L.O., got out of Lebanon. On February 13, 1982, Louis Fares, a Radio Monaco correspondent in Damascus, whom the Assad regime often used to convey unofficial intimations of its views, quoted a Syrian "high-ranking diplomat":

> If the Israeli intervention takes the form of strikes against Palestinian positions and camps in Lebanon, Syria's intervention will remain limited . . . but if it is a matter of occupation, Syria will certainly give the Palestinians and the Lebanese patriotic forces all the means necessary for checking the occupation and turning the occupier's life into an unbearable hell, and this in addition to conducting the battles that will be called for in a time of need. It is no secret that Israel's military force is now larger than Syria's; therefore, the possibility of Syria's turning to a full-scale war at a time and a place determined by Israel should be excluded. . . . The activity will be limited to resistance to the occupation and to the attrition of the occupying forces . . . but might develop into all-out war if circumstances so determine.[85]

That was a remarkably perceptive statement, and one whose full implications both Israel and—later—the United States would have done well to ponder. At the time, however, it seems to have been of interest mainly as showing that Syria was prepared—not for the first or last time—to leave the Palestinians to their fate, or hurry them to it.

In the same month, Israel sent its director of military intelligence, General Saguy, to Washington to confirm an earlier warning "of Israel's determination to effect a radical change in the *status quo* in Lebanon."[86] At this time, officials of the Reagan Administration tried to dissuade the Israelis from making such an attempt, or at least persuade them to defer it. These officials were afraid that a war in Lebanon might delay Israel's withdrawel from Sinai, and so endanger the still friendly regime of Sadat's successor, Hosni Mubarak. Possibly as a result of these arguments, the Government of Israel decided to defer its action in Lebanon until after the completion of Israel's withdrawal from Sinai (April 25, 1982).

In May, after the completion of withdrawal from Sinai—including the eviction of Israeli settlers by Israeli soldiers—American opposition to Israel's plans for Lebanon and the P.L.O. appears to have weakened. These plans—not at once publicly announced—have been summed up under four headings:

(a) destroying the PLO military infrastructure in southern Lebanon and the creating of a security zone of some forty kilometers, the effective range of the PLO's artillery and rocket launchers; (b) destroying the PLO's position in the rest of Lebanon, particularly in Beirut, to eliminate its hold on the Lebanese political system and to diminish its role in the Arab-Israeli conflict; (c) defeating the Syrian army in Lebanon to effect its full or partial withdrawal from that country and to preempt the possibility of a Syrian-Israeli war; (d) thereby facilitating the reconstruction of the Lebanese state and political system under the hegemony of Israel's allies—Bashir [Gemayel] and the Lebanese Front.[87]

Reagan's Secretary of State, Alexander Haig, seems to have been particularly attracted by the fourth, and far the most ambitious, item in the quadruple package. On May 26, 1982—shortly after a meeting with Ariel Sharon in Washington—the Secretary of State told the Chicago Council on Foreign Relations:

Lebanon today is a focal point of danger . . . and the stability of the region hangs in the balance. . . . The Arab deterrent force, now consisting entirely of Syrian troops . . . has not stabilized the situation. . . . The time has come to take concerted action in support of both Lebanon's territorial integrity within its internationally recognized borders and a strong central government capable of promoting a free, open, democratic, and traditionally pluralistic society.[88]

By the time that statement was made, it was widely known, not only by the Reagan Administration, but by the American public, that a major Israeli attack in Lebanon was to be expected shortly. On April 8, John Chancellor of N.B.C. had discussed the invasion plans on the evening news, showing that the attack would be on a great scale and might reach as far as Beirut.

On May 28, Haig sent a letter to Begin, urging "absolute restraint." But it was a letter couched in mild and vague language which did nothing to offset the impression of Sharon and Begin that they had received from the Secretary of State a slightly camouflaged green light.[89]

The Secretary of State had given a measure of agreement to Israel's contention that a P.L.O. attack on Israel, even if not carried out over Israel's northern frontier, would constitute a breach of the cease-fire.[90]

By the beginning of June, it was clear that the next spectacular *fedayeen* attack would provide the occasion for a large-scale and well-prepared Israeli intervention in Lebanon.

XXX

On June 3, 1982, the occasion came, in the form of a murderous attack by Arab gunmen on Israel's ambassador in London, Shlomo Argov.

As it happened, the P.L.O. was not responsible for this particular attack. Responsibility was claimed by the Abu Nidal group, a terrorist organization which has carried out attacks on P.L.O. "moderates" as well as on synagogues and Jewish establishments in Europe. It has even been suggested that the Abu Nidal group is working for Israeli intelligence. Noam Chomsky writes: "The P.L.O. has charged that [Abu Nidal] is an Israeli agent, noting that his operations 'frequently serve Israeli interests indirectly,' a charge that is 'one of the assumptions (*sic*) you bear in mind' according to a French secret service specialist."[91]

This "assumption" would require me to believe that Israeli intelligence organized, among other things, a murderous attack on a synagogue in Vienna (at the end of August 1981) as well as the attempted murder of Ambassador Argov. If anyone is to believe that charge, those who insinuate its credibility should be prepared to produce some kind of evidence for it, other than statements by P.L.O. spokesmen. Abu Nidal's supposed "Israeli connection" is an unsubstantiated theory of the P.L.O. and its admirers. But Abu Nidal's complex connections with Arab leaders are a matter of record.

Abu Nidal has been a determined enemy of Yasser Arafat since 1974, and he has been harbored and used against Arafat (as well as

Israel), at various times, by two Arab leaders. From the fall of 1974 to that of 1978, Abu Nidal was in Baghdad, where the Iraqi regime made use of him for attacks on Syrian targets, as well as Palestinian and Israeli ones.

In October 1978, at a time of temporary reconciliation between Syria and Iraq, Saddam Hussein "entrusted" Abu Nidal to Assad. Thus, according to *Le Monde*, "Abu Nidal became Syria's instrument in its struggle with its adversaries, including the P.L.O."[92]

In March 1982, another of these temporary inter-Arab reconciliations occurred, this time between Assad and Arafat, and Abu Nidal had to leave Damascus. Where Abu Nidal was at the time of the attack on Argov is not clear, but his presence has been reported in Baghdad.

At the time of the attack on Argov, it was generally known that any *fedayeen* attack on an important Israeli target would be likely to precipitate the long-planned Israeli attack on the P.L.O. in Lebanon. Presumably Abu Nidal and his friends had no objection to that outcome.[93]

Israel chose to assume that the P.L.O.—the main organizer and propagandist of *fedayeen* "war" against Israel—was responsible for the attack on Argov, even if it wasn't.[94]

On the afternoon of June 4 the Israeli Air Force bombed a sports stadium in Beirut, said to be used for ammunition storage by the P.L.O. The P.L.O. in southern Lebanon responded by shelling Jewish centers of population in Galilee. On June 5, the Government of Israel formally accused the P.L.O. of breaking the cease-fire. At 11:00 A.M. on June 6, Israeli ground forces crossed the border into Lebanon. At about the same time the Government of Israel issued the following communiqué:

The Prime Minister reported on the situation on the northern border. The Cabinet took the following decision:
1. To instruct the IDF to place all the civilian population of the Galilee beyond the range of the terrorist fire from Lebanon, where they, their bases and their headquarters are concentrated.
2. The name of the operation is Peace for Galilee.
3. During the operation, the Syrian army will not be attacked unless it attacks our forces.
4. Israel continues to aspire to the signing of a peace treaty with independent Lebanon, its territorial integrity preserved.[95]

The third paragraph was deceptive; the fourth contained a discreet hint at the wider political purposes of Operation Peace for Galilee. As regards the first paragraph, Prime Minister Begin, in a letter to President Reagan, interpreted the protection of the Galilee as requiring Israel "to push back the terrorists to a distance of 40 km [25 miles] to the north. . . ." But Israel's other objectives—hinted at in that fourth paragraph—required Israel's forces to go farther than that.

In the opening phase of the fighting (June 6–7), the I.D.F. destroyed the P.L.O. bases in southern Lebanon, and occupied the coastal towns of Tyre and Sidon. On June 8, Sharon obtained Cabinet permission to attack the missile bases which Syria had set up in the Bekaa Valley a year before. This was obviously an extremely high-risk course. The Government was assuming *either* that the Soviet Union would not react *or* that the United States would back Israel if the Soviet Union did react. On this occasion, the gamble was successful. The Soviet Union did not react—other than verbally—perhaps assuming that the Israeli move was approved by the U.S. Government. Since the Soviets did not react, U.S. intervention was not required. On June 9, the Israel Air Force attacked the Syrian air-defense system and, within hours, destroyed seventeen SAM-6, SAM-3 and SAM-2 batteries, without any Israeli losses. Sharon described this as "one of the most brilliant, complicated and intricate operations ever carried out." In a big air battle, with more than a hundred aircraft taking part on each side, the I.A.F. shot down twenty-five Syrian planes, again without loss to Israel. Israel achieved unchallenged mastery of Lebanese airspace. The Syrians retreated, and the Israelis advanced to Beirut. By mid-June, Israeli forces had entered East Beirut, welcomed there with "Shalom!" by the Maronite militia and population.

In West Beirut, the Syrian and P.L.O. forces were now completely cut off by land. The sea approaches to Beirut were patrolled by Israeli naval units and the airport was within range of I.D.F. fire.[96]

XXXI

The Israelis wished to remain in Beirut until they could achieve two political objectives: the expulsion of the P.L.O. from its "capital" in Beirut and the replacement of Syrian hegemony over the Lebanese

State—or semblance of a Lebanese State—by the hegemony of Israel. The second objective was to be achieved through the election, by the Lebanese Parliament, of Israel's ally, Bashir Gemayel. The Lebanese Parliament was expected, since 1976, to elect whichever candidate was favored by the occupying power (whether Syria or another), rather as medieval territorial magnates could often dictate the election of a pope.

The Lebanese presidential elections were not, however, due until August. Israel's immediate objective was the expulsion of the P.L.O. There was internal debate as to how this should be done. Sharon had expected it to be done by the Maronite militia (Phalanges, Kataeb). The Maronites, however, refused the task, perhaps from fear of heavy casualties, perhaps from fear of compromising Bashir's presidential "campaign," perhaps both. In default of the Maronites, Sharon and Chief of Staff Rafael Eytan favored a direct assault by the I.D.F. on the P.L.O. and Syrian positions in West Beirut. This idea is said to have been opposed by most Israeli commanders—because of concern for probable heavy casualties, both among their own men and in the civilian population—and it was rejected by the Israeli Cabinet, partly with an eye to American reactions.

Israel opted for "a negotiated solution through the good offices of U.S. Ambassador-at-large Philip Habib, while keeping up military pressure against West Beirut."[97] Habib had the almost indefatigable patience of a Kissinger but neither Kissinger's authority nor his luck. His failure after Zahla had contributed to the creation of the situation in Beirut, with which he was not much luckier. This military-diplomatic compromise resulted in a bloody siege, lasting nine weeks.

The P.L.O. leadership had strong incentives to spin out the Habib negotiations (which were in any case indirect as far as it was concerned). Always conscious of "world opinion"—and perennially disposed to exaggerate the importance of that factor—the P.L.O. leaders knew that this war, the most televised war in history, had caused immense harm to Israel's international image. They knew that the more Israel pounded at West Beirut, the worse Israel would look, both internationally and to a significant minority of its own population. The P.L.O. leaders could hope that with the general turning of public opinion against Israel and in favor of the P.L.O., the Reagan Administration might bring more pressure to bear on Israel, and might relax the Kissinger restrictions on dealings with the P.L.O.

The P.L.O. expectations were correct, as far as the effects on world opinion were concerned, but proved excessive as regards the political consequences of world opinion. Reagan did exert some pressure on Israel, but not enough to induce Israel to relax its siege, or do more than halt the shelling and bombings from time to time. By August, the P.L.O. leadership—as well as Syria—was ready to give up. Between August 21 and September 1, the evacuation of Beirut by the P.L.O. and Syrian forces was completed. Over ten thousand men belonging to the various P.L.O. military and paramilitary units left, as did nearly four thousand Syrian troops. Not a single one of the states which had recognized the P.L.O. as "the sole legitimate representative of the Palestinian people" came to the aid of the P.L.O. The Syrians, as we have seen, not merely stood aside (until they were directly attacked themselves) but had actually given notice of their intention to stand aside. Egypt strongly condemned Israel's action, but did not renounce its peace treaty with Israel. As Gabriel Ben-Dor puts it: "What stands out perhaps as the most significant fact in the interplay of old and new in the turmoil of ME politics in 1982 was a 'non-event'; the peace between Egypt and Israel did not collapse."[98]

During the siege of Beirut, the Arab states gave themselves over to a particularly bitter bout of mutual recrimination. Syria blamed the disaster on Egypt's defection. Mubarak spoke of Syria's "secret deal with Israel." The Jordanian press wrote of Syria and its partners as "the Steadfastness Pretenders." Syria retorted by calling Hussein "the spy King," and with oblique threats against the Saudis—silent, but believed to be in league with Cairo and Amman. The general recourse to "the soap of the soul" was so vigorous, throughout August, as to preclude even the holding of an emergency Arab Summit. The meeting was convened, at Fez, in September; "after the funeral," as a P.L.O. spokesman put it. Another spokesman said sardonically that at last the Arabs had achieved unity: "a unity of silence and of betrayal."[99]

Once Egypt had withdrawn, no combination of Arab states was in a position actually to fight Israel, by choice, in 1982. But the relevant Arab states also rejected P.L.O. appeals in June to apply economic sanctions: to break off or suspend relations with the United States, to use the oil weapon. In 1982, there was a glut of oil, not a seller's market, as there had been in 1973. No state was willing to impair its own economic interests for the sake of the Palestinians.

The Soviet Union also decided not to run any risks, either in that cause, or in the cause of its Syrian clients, as far as their Lebanese

Scenes in Beirut, August 1972, before the evacuation of the P.L.O. (and Syrian) forces.

imbroglio was concerned. The Soviets made use of a classical ploy open to a superpower which finds it inconvenient to come to the aid of a party it has encouraged, when the encouraged party gets into difficulty. It was a ploy which had been used by the United States in 1956 in relation to Hungary, as the Soviets no doubt remembered. The ploy is to throw the whole inconvenient mess into the lap of the United Nations. When the United Nations, being intrinsically incapable of resolving any such problem, duly fails to resolve it, the superpower resorting to the ploy can blame "the failure of the United Nations" on the machinations of the other superpower—and display the immaculate cleanness of its own hands. In this case, there were also some supplementary benefits. As Robert Freedman puts it: "By going to the UN Moscow avoided the necessity of direct action, although it was to try to obtain propaganda value from the vetoes cast by the U.S. to protect Israel, while also using the Security Council debates to split the U.S. from its NATO allies, who were far more critical of Israel."[100]

The Arab states, the Soviet Union and the bulk of the membership of the United Nations had encouraged the P.L.O. to persist in its "war" against Israel. But when Israel finally judged it expedient to take that "war" seriously, and fight it, the P.L.O. was entirely on its own.

The support of world opinion can be fatal, if you get to believe in it.

XXXII

On August 23, 1982, while the P.L.O. evacuation of West Beirut was in progress, Bashir Gemayel was elected President of Lebanon by a bare quorum of the Parliament (sixty-two members attending, out of ninety-two). The Israeli elimination of the Syrian factor from Beirut had left the field free to the Maronites. In tune with Syria, many prominent Lebanese politicians—belonging to the Sunni, Shi'i and Druze communities—denounced the holding of such an election, in time of occupation. Syria's own denunciation was particularly ferocious; the Damascus newspaper *al-Ba'ath* had earlier accused Bashir of treason and threatened that "the day of judgment is near."[101]

Damascus had warned, four months before the Israeli invasion, that while it would accept the elimination of the P.L.O. from Lebanon, it would resist any attempt by Israel to assert a hegemony over Lebanon, to the exclusion of Syria. It was precisely in that light that Assad saw Bashir's election. Assad was now serving notice of his intention to do his formidable best to fulfill his threat and turn Lebanon into "an unbearable hell" for Israel's friends.

The election of Bashir to the Presidency was the high point of the Sharon Grand Design for Lebanon. But after the election—and even during the brief remaining span of Bashir's life—it was becoming apparent that the Grand Design was a folly: just as some of the Cassandras in the Israeli Foreign Office and some senior officers in the I.D.F. had always said it was.

Far from aligning himself with Israel and then imposing his will on Lebanon, Bashir tried to distance himself at least to some extent from Israel, and remained isolated and impotent in Lebanon, outside his home base. He tried to recover from his hereditary enemies, the Druze, mountain villages in the Shouf, formerly belonging to the Christians. The Druze drove back his forces without much difficulty.

At a later stage, the Druze captured other Christian villages, and massacred their inhabitants, in accordance with the customary practice of the feuding clans.

Bashir Gemayel, even though nominally President of Lebanon, remained in practice little more than the leader of one of Lebanon's warring clans, and not necessarily the strongest of those clans. He could not possibly prevail against a coalition of other clans, backed by Syria.

On September 14, 1982, a bomb completely demolished a party headquarters building in East Beirut, at which Bashir was speaking. Twenty-six people were killed, including Bashir. In Damascus, *al-Ba'ath* acclaimed the deed, without identifying the perpetrators. In East Beirut, the man arrested and charged was Habib Shartouni, a member of the Syrian Social Nationalist Party.

XXXIII

The immediate response of the Israelis, on September 15, was to occupy West Beirut, which had to be seen as the center of terrorism in general, since Damascus, under Soviet protection, remained out of bounds. A Cabinet communiqué, on September 15, stated that Israel's entry into West Beirut was intended "to prevent any possible incident and to secure quiet."[102]

Within a few days, this kind of explanation was to make it impossible for the Begin Government to shake off responsibility for the massacre by Maronite forces of hundreds of Palestinian civilians, including women and children, in the refugee camps at Sabra and Chatila. Begin himself—according to his own evidence, later, before the Kahan Commission—had told the Chief of Staff on the night of September 14–15 that the move into West Beirut was "in order to protect the Muslims from the revenge of the Phalangists."[103]

In fact what the I.D.F. did in West Beirut, under Minister for Defense Ariel Sharon and Chief of Staff Rafael Eytan, was to introduce the said Phalangists into the Palestinian camps, with the mission of clearing out suspected nests of *fedayeen* combatants. What the Christian soldiers then did, in accordance with the general practice of the Lebanese civil wars, was to take indiscriminate vengeance on the whole population perceived as hostile. This course was predictable in any circumstances; it could be regarded as certain in the immediate aftermath of the murder of the most popular of Maronite leaders. Apparently, the motive of Sharon and Eytan was to spare Israeli casualties, in a war that had already cost more than four hundred Israeli lives. Sharon and Eytan chose to disregard the direct threat to the lives of Palestinian noncombatants, which followed from the use of the armed Maronites.

The massacre which followed was, in one sense, an "ordinary" massacre by Lebanese standards: one of a series of vendetta butcheries which had been going on sporadically since the outbreak of the Civil War in the mid-seventies. Where it was far from ordinary was that those who carried it out had been unleashed at the command of senior Israeli officers, in an area which Israeli forces had entered in order "to prevent any possible incident and to secure quiet," in the wake of the assassination of Bashir Gemayel.

The massacre of several hundred people in the camps continued for almost two days, without attracting the intervention of the I.D.F. But the truth began to come out, mainly through the investigations of Israeli journalists and the eyewitness accounts of individual members of the I.D.F. At first, the Government denied everything. On September 20, a Government statement declared that "all the direct or implicit accusations" of I.D.F. responsibility are "entirely baseless and without any foundation" and are "rejected with the contempt they deserve." Begin at this time rejected a judicial inquiry. In an interview with an American journalist, Begin made a characteristic statement: *"Goyim* kill *goyim,* and they immediately come to hang the Jews."[104]

Revelations continued, however, and the storm grew. On September 25, several hundred thousand citizens, led by the Labor Alignment and its allies, took part in "the largest protest demonstration ever held in the country's history."[105] The deep disquiet of many Israelis was shared by some members of Begin's coalition Government, one of whom (Yitzhak Berman) resigned in protest. The pressure was increased when Israel's greatly respected President, Yitzhak Navon, called for an inquiry by "reliable and independent men," and threatened to resign if the inquiry was not initiated.

On September 28, Begin reversed his position of little more than a week before, and agreed to set up a full and independent inquiry: the Kahan Commission, headed by the president of the Supreme Court of Israel. The commission reported on February 8, 1983. While acquitting Israel of direct responsibility, it charged the Minister for Defense, the Chief of Staff and two other senior officers with indirect responsibility for the killings and it called for the resignation or dismissal of Sharon. After several days of emergency sessions, the Cabinet decided to adopt the Kahan report and recommendations in full. But Sharon refused to resign, and Begin did not want to dismiss him. A vote was taken in Cabinet. Sixteen Ministers insisted that Sharon give up the Defense Ministry, and he himself cast the only dissenting vote. Eventually a compromise was agreed whereby Sharon left the Defense Ministry, but remained in the Government as Minister without Portfolio.

During the Government crisis of February 1983, the opposing public passions reached a pitch of intensity never known before in Israel in wartime. During a Peace Now demonstration outside the Prime Minister's offices in Jerusalem, a grenade was thrown into the demonstrating crowd, killing one demonstrator, Emil Grunsweig, and wounding several others.

In all previous wars, Israelis had closed ranks in the face of a common enemy. The war in Lebanon was the first in which the deep divisions of peacetime Israeli life emerged even more dramatically as a consequence of war. The protest movement against the war was very largely a movement of Ashkenazim, reflecting both their own personal feeling and a widespread—but not universal—revulsion against the war among their relations abroad, members of the Jewish population of Europe and North America. For a large part of Begin's following, and especially his Oriental following, the protest movement was (at best) playing into the hands of Israel's enemies and (at worst) a deliberate treachery to the nation. Thus the war greatly increased the bitterness of an antagonism which had already been bitter enough, in times of peace.

Menachem Begin was, in a sense, a victim of the war he had started, and especially a victim of his own appointment of Ariel Sharon as Minister for Defense. After the Israeli pullback from Beirut, Begin went into a kind of seclusion, soon followed by retirement (September 15, 1983). This was attributed to his grief at the illness and death of his beloved wife. But that grief seems to have been compounded by shock over the massacre at Sabra and Chatila—just a year before his retirement—and its consequences in and for Israel. At the end of Begin's political career, he allowed it to be known that he felt betrayed by Sharon. During the election campaign of July 1984—in which Sharon played a conspicuous part[106]—Begin refused to make even one short broadcast on behalf of Likud, to the deep disappointment of Likud's followers.

UPI/BETTMANN NEWSPHOTOS

Counting of votes as Knesset endorses (61–56) removal of Ariel Sharon (center) as Minister for Defense, February 14, 1983. At left, Prime Minister Begin raises his hand. This followed the findings of the Kahan Commission on the massacres at Sabra and Chatila.

If Begin had been betrayed by Sharon, his betrayal was the direct consequence of his own bad judgment in appointing a notoriously uncontrollable personality to the never-easily-controllable post of Minister for Defense of Israel. In accepting the findings of the Kahan Commission, Begin was accepting what was implicitly a negative verdict on his own judgment. By that acceptance he swallowed his own defiant words—"*Goyim* kill *goyim* . . ."—and implicitly recognized his own ultimate responsibility for bringing about actions which not only dismayed Israel's friends throughout the world, but also divided the people of Israel, internally, as they had never before been divided in time of war.

It was as sad an end as might well be conceived to a long political career, which had been entirely devoted to the selfless service of Israel.

XXXIV

The war in Lebanon was a war which aroused international horror and indignation—even before Sabra and Chatila—in a way that none of Israel's previous wars had done.[107] There are a number of different reasons for this, and it is necessary to distinguish between them. The main reason—and one which some Israelis are rather too quick to discount—is that this was, intrinsically, an especially terrifying war. Israel's armed enemies, whom the I.D.F. was trying to destroy or drive out, were ensconced in built-up areas in the midst of civilian populations, so that civilians, including women and children, got killed or wounded. The I.D.F. did what it could to minimize civilian casualties—by dropping warning leaflets in advance of bombing, for example—but these measures were only partly effective (though more effective than was sometimes realized).[108]

The second reason, less important than the first, was that this, unlike other terrifying wars, in the region and elsewhere, could be seen on television. Those who saw it—civilians in their own homes, among their families—identified with the civilian victims of the war. A friend who is a Gaelic poet wrote a poem after watching an episode of that televised war. He remembers going upstairs, just after viewing that, to look at his children asleep: "my two little Palestinians, withering in the central heating."

Those were primary, human reactions of people with no particular views on the Arab-Israeli conflict. Those reactions of sympathy with the Palestinians—usually envisaged *just* as civilians—inevitably produced hostile feelings toward Israel. There were other reasons, of a more complex kind, which worked to turn those feelings into total, unqualified condemnation of Israel, with an equally unqualified rejection of the idea that Israel had any solid reasons whatever for going into Lebanon to get rid of the P.L.O.

Among unsophisticated people, with little interest in international politics, but under the shock of televised violence, there was, I believe, little realization that the P.L.O. was what this was all about, or awareness even of what the P.L.O. *was* in relation to Israel. Without such realization or awareness, the war seemed just a brutal and unprovoked attack by a powerful state on a harmless and defenseless neighbor, Lebanon. This impression of wanton barbarity on the part of Israel was reinforced by the frequent references to Israeli attacks on "refugee camps." There was very little realization, among the general public, that these refugee camps—in fact, urban areas inhabited by Palestinians—were also military and paramilitary bases, containing people dedicated to the eventual destruction of Israel, and the present destruction of individual Israelis, wherever possible.[109] If you didn't realize that, then a country that kept on attacking "refugee camps" sounded like a monster of a country.

Among sophisticated people—formers of opinion, in particular—reactions were necessarily different, but hardly less hostile. These knew all about the P.L.O., but generally held that the P.L.O., being so inferior to the I.D.F. in present military equipment and efficiency, posed no real threat to Israel. John Le Carré, in an article in *The Observer*, produced an analogy with Ireland. For Israel to attack in Lebanon, because of the P.L.O., was as if Britain should attack in the Republic of Ireland, because of the I.R.A., Le Carré thought. That false analogy is interesting, because it betrays an eagerness, widely prevalent at the time, to underestimate the nature of the sustained provocation against which Israel was reacting.[110]

The Republic of Ireland had not broken down into anarchy, as Lebanon had done, and the I.R.A. had not achieved territorial control over a part of the territory of Ireland, close to Britain, in which it paraded forces armed with Russian tanks and artillery. Had those corresponding conditions prevailed in Ireland, Britain would most certainly have intervened, to clear the I.R.A. out of its territorial base. And Mrs. Thatcher would not have been deterred by the thought that the I.R.A. is a lot less strong than the British Army, for orthodox combat. On the contrary, Mrs. Thatcher would have contemplated that circumstance with some satisfaction.

But Israel is different.[111] Much of the criticism of Israel's action was reasonable, and qualified. But there was quite often an edge, a tendency to excess, evident in Le Carré's analogy, but sometimes taking more sinister forms. The old "Jewish Nazi" syndrome reappeared. Nicholas Von Hoffman wrote in *The Spectator* that "Americans are coming to see the Israeli Government as pounding the Star of David into a swastika."[112] One acquaintance of mine thought that what Israel had done might lead to the justification of what the swastika stood for. This gentleman is a member of an Anglo-Irish landed family, and with some reputation as a writer of light prose. He wrote to tell me that "a terrible thought" had occurred to him. The terrible thought was that if Israel went on like this, "some day people might start saying: *Those chimneys stopped smoking too soon.*"

Please note that this communication was *anti*-anti-semitic in form. The writer regarded that last sentence as a terrible thought, which the Jews were about to make people think.

As suggested earlier, it is sometimes hard to tell *fear* of anti-semitism from that which it is supposed to be afraid of.

Israel's bad press was certainly not "caused" by anti-semitism, but it seemed to me during the summer of 1982 that anti-semitism had been aroused by that press—and television—and was going around in humanitarian garb (as—I think—in the letter from which I have just quoted). I was writing a regular column at that time in *The Observer* (London), so I wrote about this phenomenon on several occasions. My comments were not militantly "pro-Israel": a typical one was headed "Israel is not like Nazi Germany"—hardly a ringing commendation of Begin's Israel. But the tide of public opinion was running so strongly against Israel then that my mild contributions appeared outrageous to a good many readers, almost all of them Gentiles. Also my comments, which would have been anodyne in other circumstances, were welcomed by many Jewish (and some other) readers, conscious of anti-semitism in the air.

I don't want to exaggerate that, either. There were some well-informed commentators on the spot who were very angry indeed against Israel, for reasons which had nothing to do with anti-semitism. These were people who believed that Israel's drive against the P.L.O. in Lebanon was a wantonly destructive act, perpetrated by people who could readily have achieved peace with the Arab world by giving up the West Bank, but who chose instead to attack the Palestinian exiles in order the more easily to hold down the Palestinians of the West Bank. Anyone who sincerely holds that view has a right to be angry, and ought not to be accused of anti-semitism.

In my view, the argument set out above is half true and half false. It is quite true that a part of the objective of Operation Peace for Galilee was peace in Judea and Samaria, through the elimination of dangerous and disturbing neighbors. But it is *not* true—in my opinion—that Israel can win peace by trading territory in the West Bank. I shall not discuss at this stage the reasons for holding that view. Those reasons are set out in the concluding section of this book.[113] Here, it is enough to say that if you believe the option "territory for peace" is not really there—as far as the West Bank is concerned—your view of the operation in Lebanon will be significantly different from what it will be if you hold the contrary view about the West Bank.

If the "territory for peace" option is ruled out for the West Bank, then what is meant by "Israel" today is a Jewish State holding—and incapable of *not* holding—the whole territory between the Jordan and the sea. The entity besieged is *that* Jewish State: not the by-now-imaginary entity within the pre–June 1967 boundaries, which is the subject of so much international discourse.

If we accept that that is the entity which is under siege, it is obvious that the siege—whatever form it takes—will be a long one. It is also obvious that Israel's position is more precarious—with its large and growing Arab population—than would be the case if the "territory for peace" option were really there. The P.L.O. is correspondingly more dangerous. True, it presents no major threat to Israel in the short term. But this is not a short-term situation, as both sides are only too well aware.

Under these conditions, the P.L.O. in Lebanon—as focus for continuous political, as well as occasional physical, assault on Israel—was genuinely perceived as a long-term threat to the Israel that now exists. The decision to get rid of the P.L.O. in Lebanon was not in itself wanton or irrational. There were irrational aspects to the intervention—notably the web of fantasies around Bashir Gemayel—and there were Israeli acts of wanton callousness, or worse, at Sabra and Chatila. But the basic decision to intervene—a decision backed initially by the Labor opposition—was rational, and motivated by what were perceived as the necessities of survival.

So far in this section I have been concerned with international reactions to the war in Lebanon up to but not including the massacres at Sabra and Chatila. As regards these massacres, it cannot be held that Israel got a worse press than the course pursued by Sharon and Eytan had earned for Israel.

In fact, what was surprising was how quickly international indignation began to subside in the aftermath of those particular events. There were reasons for that. Journalists were aware that it was their colleagues in Israel who had exposed the great scandal. The informed public, which had expected a cover-up—as predicted by the celebrated and disillusioned Israeli Jacobo Timerman—found that there was an honest inquiry, whose findings the Government of Israel accepted.[114] And the size and intensity of the public outrage in Israel against what had happened were also visible to outsiders.

In these conditions, I think there was some reaction against the notion of the monster state, created by some of the earlier commentary. In particular the malicious absurdity of the "Nazi Israel" equation stood out for all to see. Here was a "Nazi State" whose press exposed the misdeeds of its own Government and Army, whose people held huge indignation meetings on the subject, and whose honest and fearless judges, by their findings, forced their Marshal Goering to relinquish his military responsibilities.

It was perhaps true that Sharon was a little like the swaggering

Goering, but with that vague similarity of personality,[115] the resemblance of Israel to Nazi Germany ended. And that lack of resemblance had become rather hard to ignore.

XXXV

After Sabra and Chatila, on September 21, Israel agreed to withdraw its forces from Beirut—mainly as a result of American pressure—and the I.D.F. was "replaced" by a token multinational force, mainly symbolic of American goodwill and desire to help the emergence of "a strong and independent Lebanon." On September 21—in conditions very different from those prevailing at the election of Bashir a month before—Bashir's brother, Amin, was elected President, by an almost unanimous Chamber of Deputies, on the same day that Israel agreed to withdraw from Beirut.

Amin Gemayel was not regarded as "Israel's man," as Bashir had been, at the time of his election. He had indeed been regarded as the Gemayel family's interlocutor with the Syrians, and Syria did not oppose his election.

Once elected, however, Amin showed himself less interested in either Syria or Israel than in the United States. He was anxious, in all things, to show himself America's faithful friend, and to be guided by American advice. This policy of his got both himself and his American protectors and advisers into deep trouble.

At the time of Sabra and Chatila, Reagan had warned the Israelis against walking into "a quagmire." But now, with the Israelis beginning to walk away from the quagmire, the Americans walked into it.

Under George Shultz—who had replaced the more "pro-Israel" Alexander Haig as Secretary of State in July—the State Department had ambitious plans for strengthening the moderates in the Arab world, and widening the Pax Americana. In Lebanon, they hoped to bring about the evacuation of both Syrian and Israeli forces, followed by the reunification and reconstruction of the Lebanese State, under its pro-American President. For Palestine they had in mind—under the Reagan Plan announced on September 1, 1982—"self-government by the Palestinians of the West Bank and Gaza in association with Jordan." This was presented as "the next step" in the Camp David peace process, and did represent a certain revival of Carter comprehensivism.

The Begin Government, pledged to hold Judea and Samaria eternally, summarily dismissed the Reagan Plan. As regards Lebanon, Israel would withdraw—after the Syrians had done so.

Damascus objected strongly both to the American plans for Lebanon and to the Reagan Plan for the West Bank. As regards Lebanon, Reagan had said that he aimed to keep the Syrians "on the outside looking in." But Reagan did not really have the means to do this. The Syrians, though chastened militarily by Israel, had their ground forces still mainly intact inside Lebanon. And Syria's hand was greatly strengthened by a Soviet decision, in the autumn of 1982, to send both new ground-to-air missiles and Soviet personnel to Syria. To attempt to force Syria out of Lebanon altogether would now mean running exceptionally high risks. Post-Sabra-and-Chatila Israel, with Sharon no longer in control, was in no mood to run such risks. Nor was post-Vietnam America.

Syria, with its unique experience of, and access to, the jungle of the politics of the eighty or more armed factions of Lebanon, was in a good position, whenever it wanted, to create the "unbearable hell" of which it had warned in February 1982. But President Gemayel, and his American advisers, ignored the warning signs. In May 1983, the Lebanese Parliament authorized President Gemayel to sign an agreement with Israel.[116] The agreement—even if signed—could be of no more than symbolic value, since it would become operative only in the event of Syrian withdrawal. As a symbol, it was no doubt designed to placate Israel and—perhaps especially—the pro-Israel lobby in the United States, suspicious both of the Reagan Plan and of what was happening in Lebanon. But the symbol was also of a nature to precipitate the formation of a hostile coalition of Lebanese factions under Syrian inspiration: the National Salvation Front, embracing Druze, Sunni, Shi'i and a Maronite faction long at feud with the Gemayel family. The N.S.F., attacking the treaty and the regime which had signed it, and their backers, mobilized increasing support throughout the second half of 1983.

The Government of Israel—with Moshe Arens as Minister for Defense in place of Sharon—showed no practical interest in propping up Gemayel, saving its treaty, furthering the American plans for Lebanon or frustrating the Syrians. In August 1983, Israel—resisting American pressure to stay—withdrew its forces from the Shouf mountains, and retreated to the line of the Awali river, in southern Lebanon, cutting its losses after reaching an understanding with the Druze that the P.L.O. would not be allowed to return to the area. This marked the definitive abandonment of the Sharon Grand Design.

Israel's withdrawal from the mountains was followed, as expected, by renewed hostilities between Druze and Christians. The Druze won decisively and massacred an estimated seventeen thousand Christian villagers. The Druze victory was generally seen as a victory for the National Salvation Front, and a major defeat for the Gemayel regime and its American backers.

XXXVI

Encouraged by these internal developments in Lebanon, Assad also set himself to frustrate the Reagan Plan for the West Bank. Indeed the main tangible effect of the Reagan Plan—as of some other peace initiatives,[117] and even peace settlements—was to precipitate a new conflict: this time between the Syrians and Yasser Arafat, and his supporters in the P.L.O.

Neither Arafat nor any other Arabs had actually endorsed the Reagan Plan, but both Hussein and Arafat had been interested in exploring its possibilities, and had explored them together. Hussein needed the help of the "sole legitimate representative," if he was to make any progress toward recovery of the West Bank. Arafat seemed to be interested in a possible breakthrough to the Americans, possibly with some kind of "Sadat" role for himself.

Assad would have none of any of this. He disliked independent initiatives by Arafat; he disliked aggrandizement for Hussein; and he disliked all American attempts to find "solutions" that bypassed Damascus. He decided to break Arafat in Lebanon, and to allow no P.L.O. there except for "P.L.O." elements taking their orders from Damascus. He encouraged a rebellion against Arafat, within Fatah, first in the Bekaa Valley, and then in Tripoli, in northern Lebanon. The anti-Arafat forces had the support of the Syrian Army. By the end of 1983, the Arafat supporters had been forced by the Syrians out of all those parts of Lebanon out of which they had not already been forced by the Israelis in the previous year. The only Lebanese who gave any help to Arafat and his forces were the Maronites, in the face of a common Arab enemy.

By early 1984 the Syrians had also carried their point, against

Gemayel and the Americans. After suicide bomb attacks—attributed to Shi'i militia[118]—resulting in the deaths of hundreds of American Marines, Reagan began the withdrawal of American Marines from Lebanon in February 1984. At about the same time President Gemayel unilaterally canceled his treaty with Israel, and settled down to negotiations with the Syrians and their Lebanese allies.

After a nearly shattering military defeat in 1982, Syria had gone on, in 1983, to achieve astonishing political successes. The results as far as Israel was concerned looked like the reverse of that.

Yet Israel, though at great cost, had achieved half of its original objectives. The two last had failed altogether: Sharon's Grand Design had collapsed in a welter of horrors; the attempt to remove Syrian influence had resulted in a great increase in Syrian influence.

But, as far as the P.L.O. presence in Lebanon was concerned, Israel had achieved its objectives (with some aid from Syria). There was no longer an autonomous P.L.O. with a territorial base of its own anywhere on Israel's frontiers.

The cost of that limited but not insignificant achievement was impossible to estimate. Many Israelis believed that the cost—especially in terms of the greatly deepened division in Israeli society—far exceeded any benefits derived from the war. But most Israelis don't seem to have felt that. There were no signs that Likud had suffered any dramatic decline in popularity or that Labor had greatly gained as a result of the Lebanon war.[119] The division in fact was between a broadly pro-war majority and a minority, which made it all the more alarming to the shocked minority.

In the period of these two Begin Governments, the achievement of peace with Egypt and the results of the war in Lebanon had drastically changed the shape of Israel's relations with its Arab neighbors.

So drastic, indeed, was the change that some outside commentators decided that Israel was not really under siege at all. It became the practice in this period for some journalists to put the word "security" in relation to Israel in quotations. Yet in Israel, the sense of siege, of an abiding threat to security, remains strong. Israelis felt, and with reason, that such acceptance as Israel had won—even from Egypt— was "constrained acceptance." Any serious weakening in Israel's military strength—whether due to domestic dissension, economic collapse, changes in military technology or the weakening of the tie with America—is thought of as likely to draw the whole Arab world in against Israel, and this time for Israel's destruction.

A phase of the siege was over, but Israelis did not feel that the siege itself was over. And it seems likely that their feelings on that point were not so irrational or unwarranted as commentators at a distance, whose own fate was not at stake, often tended to assume.

But can Israel itself end the siege, by timely concessions—as so many statesmen and commentators believe and urge? That question is considered in "Epilogue: Territory for Peace?"

EPILOGUE:
Territory for Peace?

THE ISRAELI GENERAL ELECTIONS of July 23, 1984, resulted in a kind of "hung" Knesset. The Likud lost some ground, and Labor became again the largest party. The balance was such that it would be very difficult for either of the main parties, without the other, to form a workable coalition. Consequently, the formation of a Government of National Unity, embracing both Labor and Likud—as in 1967 to 1970—was being considered.

Commenting on this situation, a spokesman in Washington said that the results were regrettable, because they did not show good prospects for the kind of "bold steps" that would be necessary to advance "the peace process." As far as it goes, the comment is correct. The Government of National Unity, which eventually came into being, with Shimon Peres as Prime Minister and Yitzhak Shamir (Begin's successor as Likud's leader) as Deputy Prime Minister and Foreign Minister, is inherently incapable of taking the kind of "bold steps" the spokesman had in mind, and it would disintegrate if its head seriously tried to take such steps. But what is questionable is the implicit assumption that there are *any* results at all likely in any General Election in Israel, ever, that would lead to the taking of the desired "bold steps": that is, to Israel's withdrawal from all or almost all of the West Bank, and the creation of some kind of Palestinian political entity there, perhaps in association with Jordan, linked to Israel by treaty.

Consider the most favorable of all electoral results (that are at all likely) in terms of the "territory for peace" idea. The most favorable result would be one that would lead to a coalition Government formed by the Labor Alignment with the two dovish parties to the left of it— Shinui and the Citizens' Rights Movement—as its partners.

What kind of "bold steps" could a Government of that kind take? It could offer to Jordan *some* of the West Bank in exchange for a peace treaty. That is Labor's famous—and by now somewhat decrepit—Jordanian option. But it is a heavily hedged option, as Labor has explained it in successive elections, including that of 1984. Jordan would not get back East Jerusalem: Jerusalem would remain united, and the capital of Israel. Israel would also retain its defensive line, and line of Jewish settlements, all along the western bank of the River Jordan, with all the concomitant rights of military access across the general territory of the West Bank.

Labor's Jordanian option is in fact no more than the old Allon Plan, and the Allon Plan, in all versions and aspects, and under all labels, has been consistently and scornfully rejected by Jordan, over more than fifteen years (and it has also been rejected by the United States). Hussein (or any successor of Hussein's) would be running very serious risks if he concluded *any* peace treaty with Israel, even one that gave him back all of Jordan's lost territory. But if he were to sign a treaty that left Israel in possession of all Jerusalem, and of the line along the western bank of the river, he would probably be committing suicide for himself and his dynasty. Which he is unlikely to do.

It seems to be assumed, however, that a Labor coalition could be persuaded, or pressured, by the United States, to "raise the ante" on its Jordanian option, to such an extent as to make it attractive to the Jordanians, as well as to most of the Arab population of the West Bank.[1]

This, again, seems to me exceedingly unlikely. A Labor coalition would immediately be in dire trouble if its Jordanian option—even in its traditional form—were to enter the domain of practical politics, and the actual handing over of parts of the West Bank to Arab control had to come to be debated in the Knesset and in the country. Likud, and its allies of the farther nationalist Right, and of the religious Right, would immediately raise the flag of Masada. Labor and its allies would be branded as traitors, for their willingness to abandon any part of the sacred soil of Judea and Samaria. The debate would become superheated and envenomed, with at least some of the overtones of incipient civil war, and with incidents of violence.

Facing this tremendous emotional assault from the Right, the

Labor Alignment—whatever its allies did—would not be able to count on unity within its own ranks. Recent polls show that 30 percent *of Labor supporters* are now against giving up any part of Judea and Samaria. So the effort to implement the Jordanian option would precipitate not only a major political crisis in Israel generally but also an agonizing crisis within the Labor Alignment.

In those conditions, can it be seriously imagined that any Labor-led coalition would take the "bold step" of *improving* on its Jordanian option—from an Arab point of view? Would Labor and its allies offer to dismantle the defense line along the River Jordan, contrary to Labor's own repeated pledges, thus bringing down against the Labor coalition the weight of the I.D.F. establishment? Or would they offer to abandon East Jerusalem, with the Wall? Or to widen the Jordanian option so as to include the P.L.O.?

It is rather clear that if Labor attempted any of those things, it too would be committing political suicide. The Jordanian option is really safe, for Labor, only as long as the Jordanians refuse to touch it. So the practical and cautious politicians who make up the Labor leadership are likely to continue, as in the past, to emphasize precisely these aspects of their Jordanian option which are most unpalatable to the Jordanians—thus prolonging an *impasse* which is vastly preferable for Labor, in terms of the internal politics of Israel, to the agonizing attempt at a negotiated solution.

It is true that future Governments of Israel—of whatever completion, but especially Labor—are likely to come under pressure, whether real or ostensible, from the United States to take those "bold steps" necessary for the pursuit of the peace process and the Reagan Plan (or some future avatar of the same). No Government with Likud in it could give in to that pressure without making nonsense of Likud's whole tradition and deepest commitment. But even a Labor Government is likely to prefer resistance to such American pressure—resistance with the backing of a great majority in Israel—to the grisly internal consequences likely to follow on the taking of those "bold steps."

Unless there is some very serious flaw in the above analysis, neither the Jordanian option nor the (closely related) Reagan Plan, nor any variant of these, has the capacity of coming to fruition.

II

But suppose—*per impossibile*, as I think—that some variant of the Reagan Plan did come to pass. Let us take one of the rosiest possible hypotheses where the peace process is concerned. Let us suppose that the rather flickering *rapprochement* of 1983 between Hussein and Arafat—the one which cost Arafat his last base in Lebanon—consolidates itself, as appeared to be happening in the spring and summer of 1985. On February 23, the text of an agreement between Hussein and Arafat was released in Amman. The agreement itself could not be the basis for an agreement between the parties and Israel. It demands (among other things) "termination of Israeli occupation of the occupied Arab territories, including Jerusalem" and "total withdrawal from the territories occupied in 1967 for comprehensive peace as established in United Nations and Security Council resolutions." It contains no reference to recognition of Israel, within its pre–June 1967 boundaries, and uses language which seems incompatible with such recognition: "Palestinians will exercise their inalienable right of self-determination. . . ." The document also calls for the inclusion in the peace conference (along with "the five permanent members of the Security Council and all the parties to the conflict") of "the Palestine Liberation Organization, the sole legitimate representative of the Palestine people." (For full text of agreement, see Note 2.)

On the face of it, this is not a very promising peace overture, from an Israeli point of view. However, President Mubarak's follow-up call for direct negotiations, in the United States, between Israel and a "joint Jordanian-Palestinian delegation" (without naming the P.L.O.), was distinctly more interesting to Israel, and met with a cautiously positive response from Shimon Peres. In the summer of 1985, as this Epilogue is being completed, Secretary of State Shultz appeared cautiously hopeful about the possibilities for negotiations, especially in the light of various positive statements from Hussein.

Let us suppose, then, that the Hussein-Arafat *rapprochement*, as followed up by Mubarak, leads to the most favorable possible results: Arafat publicly and explicitly announces his willingness to recognize Israel within its pre–June 1967 limits (subject to a few small variations) and Israel then accepts Arafat's P.L.O. as a partner with Jordan in direct negotiations. Hussein and Arafat are ready to cooperate on the basis of the Reagan Plan, which thus has the backing of the present leader of "the sole legitimate representative of the Palestine people." Israel is ready to withdraw to its pre–June 1967 frontiers (with minor variations) in exchange for recognition, within these frontiers, by the P.L.O. and Jordan.

We are piling improbability on staggering improbability there, but not more so than certain respected editorial writers are doing all the time.

On this basis, Israel hands over almost the whole of the West Bank to some kind of Hashemite-Arafat federation or confederation (the alternative of a full-fledged Palestinian State is considered later).

By this time Israel has given up a lot of territory in exchange for peace. How much peace would Israel actually have gotten in exchange for that territory?

Peace, presumably, with Arafat and Hussein. But how much peace would Arafat and Hussein get, or have in their gift? Can anyone suppose that all, or almost all, of the P.L.O. would go along with that deal, or any deal? The deal would be likely to be denounced, with the usual vehemence, both by the left-wing factions of the P.L.O. and by the Syrian-controlled factions, and all those factions might well gain new adherents, through further defections from Arafat's Fatah. Syria, orchestrating the P.L.O. factions, with its usual ruthless skill, would be likely to make life very hot—"an unbearable hell," as in Lebanon—in the West Bank, and perhaps also in Jordan, for Arafat, Hussein and their friends—even if their combined friends were in a majority in the territory, as they might well be. ("Majorities" and "minorities" are not as important concepts, in this context, as some Western commentators tend to assume.) In these conditions, the territories formerly occupied by Israel—and evacuated in exchange for peace—would be likely to become a happy hunting-ground for various kinds of *fedayeen* activity, directed against all the parties to the detested treaty. The chief Arab parties might well not survive, and the treaty might perish with them. Nor would the actual ensuing conditions be at all preferable, from the point of view of the lives of West Bank Arabs, to conditions under Israeli rule.

It is true that the moderate Arab states—Egypt, the Saudis— would be likely to approve the "territory for peace" arrangements described, but on one condition: that the territories transferred by Israel to Arab rule must include East Jerusalem. Failing that, the deal would be denounced by virtually the whole Arab and Muslim world.

And it is as certain as anything can be that the State of Israel will not give up any part of its capital, Jerusalem, in exchange for anything at all, even peace.

The option of a Palestinian State on the West Bank has also to be considered. It is true that—since this option is firmly rejected by *both* main parties in Israel, as well as by most of the smaller parties, and by the great majority of the population of Israel—the Palestinian State is even less likely to come to fruition than the Jordanian option, if that is possible.

Still, the idea of the Palestinian State has to be considered, since it has the backing, or apparent backing, of the Arab states, even the most moderate ones.[3] It is central to the revised Fahd Plan, as endorsed by the Second Fez Summit, in September 1982—"after the funeral"—and by many resolutions of the General Assembly.

III

The Palestinian State is expected—by both its advocates and its opponents—to be under some form of control by the P.L.O.: "the sole legitimate representative of the Palestine people." Almost all Israelis regard such a State as an immediate threat to the security of their own State, and a longer-term threat to its existence. They believe that the P.L.O. would accept the "mini-State" in the West Bank as an installment of their real objective, which remains all of Palestine. They also believe that the P.L.O. would use that installment as a base for the destabilization both of Israel and of Jordan, with Jordan first on the list. On that last point, King Hussein is known to be in agreement; it is not probable that his idea of a "confederation" would leave the P.L.O. in control of the West Bank. On the other hand, a number of distinguished and influential outside observers believe that Israeli fears on this point are illusory, and that a Palestinian State could peacefully and happily coexist with an Israel withdrawn to its pre–June 1967 frontiers. They point—as Noam Chomsky does repeatedly in *The Fateful Triangle*—to a number of statements permitting that inference, put out by Arafat and some of his associates, generally in Western contexts. As against all that, Israelis point to at least an equal number of P.L.O. statements to a contrary effect—usually in Arabic and some also by Arafat—and to the P.L.O.'s constitution, the Palestinian National Covenant, which is clearly incompatible with the existence of the Jewish State (see Glossary).

It is probably unnecessary to pay too much attention to either set of statements. It is fairly obvious that in the highly unlikely event of a "deal" between Israel and the P.L.O. over the West Bank, the P.L.O. would be hopelessly split. It is indeed split already. The left-wing factions and the Syrian-controlled factions would launch murderous attacks on "the traitors" (as in the Hussein/Arafat scenario). The Palestinian State, long before it could destabilize others, would be likely to lose all stability itself. The Palestinian State, if ever founded, would be likely to collapse almost immediately. But it is altogether unlikely ever to get founded.

IV

It seems to follow that exchanging territory for peace—attractive as that concept is—is not a feasible option for the West Bank.

It looks as if Israel will remain in control of the West Bank for a long time. Many Israelis—and others—view that prospect with deep misgivings, and they are quite right. But whether viewed with misgivings or not, that seems to be the prospect that is actually there.

The really pressing questions now concern not the future of the territories but the future of their Arab inhabitants.

In the first ten years, from June 1967, a kind of working arrangement grew up in the West Bank, whereby the Arab inhabitants were left as far as possible to their own devices, and allowed to continue to feel part of the Arab world, through the Open Bridges policy and the "adversarial partnership" with Jordan. This arrangement—inspired mainly by Moshe Dayan—allowed the Arab population to develop peacefully, and attain a considerable degree of prosperity.

In the following years, and especially from 1980 on, the Likud pressure for increasing Jewish settlements (often close to densely populated Arab areas) combined with the manipulations of Begin-style autonomy made for greatly increased Arab unrest, and some violence. The old working arrangement, with and through Jordan, was strained by these developments, but did not collapse.

There was, however, an evident and apparently growing tendency on the far Right of the Israeli political spectrum to engage in deliberate provocation of the Arabs, in the apparent hope of inflaming violence, which would have to be met by increased Israeli repression, in a cycle which could lead eventually to the forcing out of the Arab population.

Currently, the living symbol of this tendency is the right-wing fanatic Rabbi Meir Kahane, whose election to the Knesset in July 1984 horrified many Israelis (including some rabbis), and alarmed the Arabs, both of the West Bank and of Israel itself. Rabbi Kahane is the author of a work called *They Must Go*, and he avowedly intends to go on making trouble until they do. While Rabbi Kahane was the only member of his group, Kach, to be elected, support for his approach is almost certainly wider than the twenty thousand or so citizens whose votes are needed to elect a member of the Knesset. Both among the ultranationalist Right and the religious Right, and on the right wing of Likud itself, there is at least some approval of his aims, if not of his style and all his methods. And voting results in July 1984 seemed to show that there is more support for such ideas among serving Israeli soldiers than among the population at large.[4]

President Herzog's personal ostracism of Kahane, and his appeals for toleration, and against racism, have the support of most of the press, and of that part of the political spectrum which runs from the Left through the Center to what have been called the Moderate Hawks, well represented, in relation to this matter, by the leader of Likud, Yitzhak Shamir. That is a majority of Israeli society. But the minority that remains—to the right of the right of center—is both significant in numbers and formidable in its determination and dynamism. If that minority cannot be adequately controlled by the State, there is a serious danger that it may make progress in the direction it desires. The interaction of Jewish and Arab extremists could endanger the continuing presence in the West Bank of its Arab population.

By a kind of paradoxical effect often noted in these pages, the main result of the unremitting international efforts to bring about the withdrawal of Israel from the West Bank is probably to speed up that sinister interaction and to increase the danger to the territory's Arab population. Israel's extremists are long conditioned to respond to such pressure by the creation of new facts; while Arab resistance to any such new facts is likely to be encouraged by the thought that, after all, on this matter, the Arabs have "world opinion" on their side. In the event of a catastrophe, the sympathy of world opinion—though it will be copious—is hardly likely to be of much more use to the losers than it has been at any time before in the long series of Palestinian disasters.

Those in the West who urge that the effort to rule over large numbers of Arabs may eventually destroy Israel itself might do well to note that Meir Kahane is making the same point, while drawing from it an inference radically different from what the Western critics have in mind.

V

"Unease in Zion"[5] seems, from the perspective of 1985, destined to be the condition of Israelis for some considerable time to come. The idea of Israel withdrawing to its pre–June 1967 territory, and living there behind secure and recognized frontiers, in peace with all its neighbors, is an agreeable international pipe dream. The reality is that Israel will stay in the West Bank, where its presence will continue to be challenged from within and from without. And Israel's contested presence and the various forms of challenge to it, and responses to the challenges, are likely to increase, at least for a time, the deep divisions already obvious inside Israeli society.[6] (The 1984 elections are ominous in that regard. Labor had hoped to capture disillusioned Likud voters, but failed. There *were* disillusioned Likud voters, but they went everywhere except to Labor and its allies. And the aversion of Oriental voters for Labor now seems a quasi-permanent feature.)

There are those who will agree with much of my analysis as to what is likely to happen, but who will want me to add some kind of condemnation of Israel, for its perversity and folly, in failing to take the necessary "bold steps" in pursuit of the peace process.

I can't do that, because I don't see how I can condemn people for failing to do things which I think they actually *can't* do.

The reasons for Israel's incapacity to abandon all the territory acquired in the 1967 war are bound up with the two great *raisons d'être* of Zionism: the Jewish State and the Return.

Basic to the idea of the Jewish State was the need for Jews to assure the security of Jews, Gentiles having proved, at so many times and in so many places, that they could not be trusted in that matter. So "secure frontiers" are a basic requirement of the Jewish State. The pre–June 1967 frontier—coming to within a few miles of the coast and Tel Aviv—was felt by almost all Israelis to be highly insecure. On the other hand, the line of the Jordan, with the escarpment to the west of it, was judged ideal for defensive purposes by the planners of the I.D.F.

Outsiders advised that Israel did not need such strong defenses against a weak Arab threat, and that in any case Israel would do better to trust to Arab goodwill, to be acquired by the surrender of all the occupied territories. Israelis generally preferred the advice of their own soldiers, on such a matter, to that of outsiders. This followed from the whole ideology of the Jewish State, of Zionism and of the history of Israel, and was an inescapable preference, in the light of those antecedents. And Israelis knew that Arab goodwill was not procurable, by any limited territorial concessions, for the Jewish State. In their more conciliatory utterances—especially to Western audiences—Arab spokesmen rejected the idea of driving the Jews into the sea, and allowed them (ostensibly at least) some kind of role in a future "secular and democratic Palestine". But the Jewish State, that "racist" entity, was anathema, whatever its boundaries. So those responsible for the security of the Jewish State were governed by considerations of military security alone, and not by the vain pursuit of unattainable goodwill.

As for the Return, the idea of a Jewish State elsewhere than in Palestine was considered many times in the earlier history of Zionism. It was attractive to some Westernized, secular Jews. But it was decisively rejected, in 1903–1905, by Zionists of the Russian Empire, who—though mostly of secular consciousness—were deeply influenced by the Jewish religious tradition. For them—and for Zionists generally henceforward—the only goal was Palestine. The Bible was the Mandate—as the "secular" Ben-Gurion told the Peel Commission in January 1937—and Jerusalem was the magnet. If that was so, in a complex and deep-down way, for the secular and partly Westernized Russians, it was so in a quite simple and down-to-earth way for most of the non-secularized and non-Western immigrants from the Muslim lands. For them, this land was their inheritance, by right of Revelation, and Jerusalem was its predestined capital.

The Jews had recovered Jerusalem, after nearly two thousand years, through a train of efforts and events so strange and unprecedented as to appear to some almost miraculous and to others literally miraculous. To expect the Jews, having thus again come into possession of Jerusalem, to hand over the Old City, with the Wall of the Temple, to an Arab Power, or to an international authority, is to expect what cannot be. To ask Israel to give up all or most of Judea and Samaria is to ask for the unlikely; to ask Israel to hand over the heart of Jerusalem is to ask for the impossible.

So the felt needs of the Jewish State, and the animating concept of the Return, oppose what seem to be impenetrable barriers to the voluntary acceptance by Israel of the kind of settlement which international opinion, almost universally, calls for in the West Bank.

VI

That those things are so, as a matter of fact, would be hard to deny, though no doubt the thing can be done. But some, who accept that these things are so—or more or less so—still passionately urge that *they ought not to be so*. The Jewish State and the Return may dominate the situation in the West Bank—and in Gaza and in Israel itself—for today and, perhaps, tomorrow. But they have no right (it is argued) to dominate it. Both are illegitimate concepts. The Jewish State is a racist concept. The Return is a mystical concept; that is to say, superstitious and false. These concepts, being illegitimate, have no right to prevail over a legitimate, rational and humane *principle:* that of the Consent of the Governed.

I should like here to take a brief look at that argument, in terms of the three principles it embraces and opposes.

"The Jewish State is a racist concept." Yes, in a way. It is racist to the extent that all nationalism is racist, and that is a large extent. Simone Weil held that racism and nationalism were essentially the same thing, racism being simply "a more romantic form of nationalism." The Jewish State is the embodiment and creation of Jewish nationalism. And modern Jewish nationalism was very largely a response to European nationalisms, which increasingly rejected Jews—and increasingly on racist principles—as part of the nations concerned. The founders of Zionism were almost all rejected assimilationists. Their logic was clear-cut: "Since the existing states say we don't belong to them, very well, we must have a State of our own."

All nationalism is exclusive; quietly so, or noisily. Most nation-states preserve their national character by stringent immigration controls, according to criteria the most important of which (being of a nationalist/racist character) generally remain implicit. The Jewish State is like other states in its determination to preserve its own national character, as determined by itself, through exclusive processes. Where the Jewish State is unusual, and in part unique, is through the following elements:

(a) The Jewish State did not come into being as the European states did, through a long and gradual process, on the same territory, involving slow exclusions, inclusions and accretions. The Jewish State was created through an unprecedented convergence of scattered people on a *former* national territory, and crystallized at an amazing speed: from a political dream to a State in less than seventy years.

(b) The criterion of nationality, since the creation of the Jewish State, has become a specifically religious one. Now, insofar as racial characteristics are important to racism—and I think they are important—this criterion actually operates *against* racism. There were those in Israel's pre-1948 predominantly Ashkenazic population who would have liked to keep out the Oriental Jews, primarily on racial grounds. But as the criterion of admission was in fact a religious one, the Oriental Jews qualified.

(c) All nationalisms exclude, but the persons whom it was most important for the Jewish State to exclude—for the sake of its own survival—were its fated enemies, the bulk of the previous settled population in the Land of Israel. The present State of Israel, for example, could not admit to citizenship the Arabs of the West Bank without preparing the destruction of—at least—the Jewish State. Which Israel, being—in all essentials—the Jewish State, is not likely to do.

I don't think you can reasonably say that the idea of the Jewish State is *inherently* racist and therefore illegitimate unless you also condemn all other nationalisms—including Arab nationalism—for their exclusivities: quite a reasonable proposition, but one which would stigmatize all states, and most of the population of the globe.

The relation of the Jewish State to Palestine, and to its Arab population, I shall consider in relation to the two other branches of the tripartite indictment: those which concern the Return, and the principle of Consent of the Governed.

VII

The idea of the right of the Jews to return to Palestine, as transcending the will of the majority of the settled population of the area, is certainly basically a religious one (or a religious-national one), whatever secular forms it may from time to time assume.

Does the fact that the Right of Return is basically a religious idea make it *ipso facto* illegitimate?

Probably only the tougher-minded within the secularist tradition would answer that question with an unhesitating "Yes." But *some* kind of yes is implicit in the whole tradition of Western Europe and North America since the eighteenth-century Enlightenment. The post-Enlightenment tradition assumes the separation of religion from the political process. The notion of a *religious* attachment as justifying a *political* claim is inherently repugnant to what has been the dominant intellectual tradition in the West for nearly a quarter of a millennium. The question is, however, whether the dominant intellectual tradition in the West also applies to the Middle East.

On the surface, it might seem to. The rhetoric of the Arab-Israeli debate has been almost entirely the rhetoric of the Western Enlightenment tradition. It is a rhetoric which has extremely high international prestige—as rhetoric—largely due to the phenomenal success of the three great Western revolutions inspired by it—English, American and French—and through the mimicry of much of it by the Soviet Union (as in Stalin's 1936 Constitution). The United Nations Charter is full of Enlightenment language, and United Nations debates are generally conducted in terms of an assumed consensus of commitment to these ideas.

The Arab case against Israel is most effectively expressed in terms of that tradition. For example, the Palestinian State which Palestinian spokesman present to Western audiences as their goal will be—in theory—"a secular and democratic state." In terms of the governing code of debate, based on the Western Enlightenment value system, this puts the Arab states—and the cause of Government by Consent—permanently in the right, and Israel—with its archaic Right of Return and Jewish State—permanently in the wrong.

But this is a domain where rhetoric and reality are far apart. Political practice based on Enlightenment values—the rule of law, freedom of expression and political democracy—exceeds the boundaries of the West in only a few exceptional cases, none of them in the Middle East; with the ironic exception of Israel itself, in its internal political arrangements among Jews. If there were today a Palestinian State, and if it were indeed a democratic State, it would be unique in the Arab world (and unusual in the world as a whole, outside the West). The rulers of the region, in practice, assume and enforce the consent of those they govern, as the rulers of the region have done from time immemorial, without curiosity as to the wishes of the governed. The rule of law and freedom of expression are unknown, as in the past.[7] Secularity is a matter for small elites—some of these, as religious minorities, justifying their own dominance, as the Alawis of Syria do, in terms of secular and progressive ideas. In any case, even the secular elites seem to be increasingly challenged throughout the Islamic world, since 1980, by the rise of Muslim fundamentalism.

Islam, even more than any other of the great religions, denies the existence of the dichotomy, posited by the Western Enlightenment, between religious and political life. Those who, representing—or at any rate speaking on behalf of—Muslim populations, appeal to Enlightenment ideas are engaging in double-talk, masking the realities of what is fundamentally, on both sides, a religious-nationalist culture conflict. A conflict, moreover, which is unlikely to be resolved by appeal to an umpire from the world of the Enlightenment.

The presiding symbol is that of Jerusalem. The claim of the Jews to Jerusalem is not a matter of rational argument; nor is the claim of the Muslims; nor will the two claims be reconciled, or either of them appeased, by arbitration; nor will either accept the counting of heads as decisive, unless it works in their own favor.

The Jews today rule in Jerusalem for the same *material* reason as the British ruled before them, and the Ottoman Turks before them, and all the others before them, back to Caliph Omar and beyond— because they conquered the place. But the *attachment* of the Jews to the city is older and deeper than that of any of its other conquerors.

It is argued that conquest, as a claim to rule, though acceptable in earlier times, and very widely up to 1914–1918, is no longer acceptable since the Fourteen Points, the Atlantic Charter and the Charter of the United Nations. But both the Jewish and the Muslim claims to Jerusalem are anterior to those documents, by many centuries, and will not be resolved by reference to the modern documents, vastly inferior as these are in authority and in emotional power, and in other ways, to the Bible and the Koran.

The Right of Return is based on the Bible, and contested (by implication) in the Koran. But when the Koran is defeated—for the time being at least—the appeal goes out to the post-Christian world, in terms of the post-Christian ideology of the Enlightenment, under the slogan of Consent of the Governed.[8] But any realities pertaining to that slogan belong to the world appealed to, not the world which appeals.

I know well that the above line of thought will be uncongenial to many Westerners—both friendly and unfriendly to Israel—and also to many in Israel itself. The Jews of the Diaspora played a large part in the development and diffusion of Enlightenment ideas,[9] gloried in them, and benefited from them, for a time. Israelis of European origin inherit a value system largely drawn from the European Enlightenment. Indeed this inheritance is one of the sources of the great internal *malaise* of Israel. Most of the Oriental Jews have no such inheritance, and generally tend to find it more or less incomprehensible, and either irrelevant or even noxious to Israel's needs in its actual besieged condition.

I'm afraid—and there are grounds for being afraid—that the Orientals have a point. The Western Enlightenment and the idea of the Return don't fit together; they only rub together uneasily. The idea of the Return comes out of that older world the *philosophes* rejected, and the Return took form under unimaginably harsher necessities than any that had ever impinged on the *philosophes*.

VIII

I wrote at the end of the Prologue that Israel "cannot be other than what it is."

I believe that is so, in the basic sense that Israel is not free to be other than the Jewish State in Palestine, and that the Jewish State, once in possession of Jerusalem, is not capable of relinquishing that city.

The Muslim world is also not free to be other than what it is, and is certainly incapable of acquiescing openly, fully and voluntarily in a Jewish State in Palestine, with Arab subjects, and its capital in Jerusalem.

It seems to follow that the siege will continue, in some form, into an indefinite future.

That is not necessarily or immediately as tragic a statement as it may sound. In certain conditions, the siege could become—for a period at least—a largely latent and almost metaphorical affair. Israel could find itself at peace, in one way or another, with all its neighbors. The peace with Egypt held during the 1982 war in Lebanon. There has been a *de facto* peace, with no *fedayeen*, between Jordan and Israel since 1973; and that also held in 1982. Israel's greatest problem among its Arab neighbors is Syria, with its Soviet backing and its presence, and proliferating influence, in Lebanon.

Yet a *tacit* accommodation, even with Syria, is possible, as was proved in 1976, over Lebanon. That that arrangement broke down later was partly due to the overweening and baroque ambition of Ariel Sharon. But it was also due, and perhaps in larger part, to a stipulation introduced by Israel itself into the tacit agreement of 1976 between Syria and Israel. This was the stipulation that Syrian authority should not extend to Lebanon's far south and the border with Israel. This stipulation led to the development of "Fatahland" in southern Lebanon, beyond Syria's control—and so to the conditions which provided the occasion, if not all the reasons, for Israel's intervention in 1982.

It appears that there was one school of thought in Israel in 1976 which opposed the stipulated restriction over the extent of Syria's authority in Lebanon. That school seems to have been vindicated by events. It seems, therefore, within the bounds of possibility that a new and less restrictive tacit arrangement could be reached with Syria, over Lebanon, with a certain "territory for peace" content. One version of such an arrangement could include the following:

On Israel's side:

(a) Israel to withdraw all its troops from all of Lebanon.

(b) Israel to agree secretly to Syria's hegemony over all of Lebanon, to be assured by means of Syria's own Machiavellian devising.[10]

On Syria's side, and in exchange for (a) and (b):

(c) Syria to undertake to see that there will be no P.L.O. in Lebanon, other than forces of that name under complete Syrian control, and that those forces will not be allowed to take part in any *fedayeen* activity.

(d) Syria to guarantee the safety of the Maronite population in its own areas, as well as the safety of those elements on Israel's border who have cooperated with Israel.[11]

And finally:

(e) If these arrangements hold, and peace prevails, over a stipulated period, Syria to get back the Golan Heights.

By the summer of 1985, progress in the direction of an Israeli-Syrian understanding on those general lines seemed possible, but problematic. Israel was withdrawing *almost* all its own armed forces from *almost* all of Lebanon, without insisting on its previous precondition: that the Syrians must also withdraw from all of Lebanon. But—and it is a big but—Israel seemed intent on continuing to support the so-called "South Lebanon Army"—a Christian-led militia—on the border strip in the extreme south of Lebanon. As long as this policy is maintained, it seems certain to keep Israel still embroiled in the Lebanese factional fighting, at odds with the powerful Syrian-backed Shi'ite militia, Amal, and therefore in continuing friction with Syria itself. This seems a further illustration of the evils accruing to Israel from having, in Moshe Dayan's words, "no foreign policy, only a defense policy."

The Syrians, for their part, were demonstrating, in characteristic fashion, in June 1985, their determination not to allow the Palestinians, in a Lebanon falling increasingly under Syrian control, to renew *fedayeen* raids, and so provoke Israeli retaliation. Amal, with discreet Syrian support, attacked the Palestinian camps, including Sabra and Chatila, killing hundreds of Palestinians, and supplying one more bloody chapter in Assad's cynical rendition of "the Shirt of Uthman." To the Israelis, Assad seemed to be signaling that some kind of deal over Lebanon is possible. That would require not only that Syria finally drop the Palestinian *fedayeen,* but also that Israel drop its "South Lebanon Army."

If some such arrangements as those outlined above could eventually be worked out with Syria—building on the 1976 precedent—Israel would then at last have peace with all its neighboring states: peace by treaty with Egypt; peace by tacit understanding with Jordan (see below) and with Syria, and, through Syria, with Lebanon.

That seems the nearest thing to a comprehensive Middle Eastern settlement that is actually available in the real world.

IX

Even so, the problem of the West Bank, and of Israel's incapacity to get out of it, will still remain. There, the best that can realistically be hoped for—and even that cannot be taken for granted—would be a return to the noninterventionist attitudes of the Dayan years. That is made more difficult by the existence of the "Begin settlements"—which are not going to be uprooted—but at least there could be a return to the policy of "no new settlements near centers of Arab population," and even an enhancement of the famous adversarial partnership with Jordan. There could be—as there was under Dayan, and was not under Begin—a regime based on the principles of minimum interference and avoidance of provocation. The example of Teddy Kollek, as mayor of Jerusalem, has shown that even under siege conditions a potentially hostile population can be treated with consideration and respect, and that this policy can be rewarding for all concerned. Unfortunately, there are not many Teddy Kolleks around, inside or outside Israel. But the example is there, and Shimon Peres is known to admire the Kollek achievement.

"There is no Jordanian option," a Jordanian Minister has said, "but there is a Jordanian *role*." That sounds like a hint. It seems possible that some kind of *tacit* agreement could be reached with Jordan over certain areas of the West Bank, resembling in some respects the Allon Plan, but reached without fanfare or the signature of any treaty.

Both the situation and the mood of Israel in the wake of the Lebanon War, and of the retreat from Lebanon, seem fairly propitious for such a tacit agreement. With a grave economic crisis and severe measures needed to reduce inflation, Shimon Peres could and did inform his Likud colleagues that there is simply no money for more settlements in the West Bank. Both Likud and the country seem to accept that. This could lead to an abandonment—again a tacit one—of the attempt to make Judea and Samaria Jewish, and a return to the old Dayan policy of maximum noninterference with the Arab population. Such a policy shift could open the way to closer, unavowed cooperation between Israel and Jordan, with both parties encouraging the West Bankers to put up with their anomalous but not necessarily intolerable status of Jordanian subjects, in civil matters, living in a territory under Israel's military control. And deep down—despite the verbal deference accorded by Hussein and the West Bank mayors to the P.L.O.—Israel, the West Bank population and Jordan share a common interest in continuing not to allow the *fedayeen* to implant themselves in the West Bank.

Arrangements of this type seem about the best available, within the bounds of realistic assessment. But all such arrangements will remain precarious and vulnerable. That is obvious in the case of the tacit understandings: the actual (and improvable) one with Jordan, and the possible one with Syria. But even the formal peace treaty between Israel and Egypt could be denounced—in the event, for example, of a seizure of power in Cairo by a group of extreme nationalist or Muslim fundamentalist officers. In that case, Israel would have surrendered territory in Sinai *without* securing lasting peace.

For ordinary Israelis, the siege remains a fact of daily life. On March 21, 1985, in Jerusalem, I watched a bunch of schoolchildren—boys and girls, about nine years old—coming down the steps of Yemin

Moshe Street to take a look at one of Jerusalem's jollier landmarks, the Montefiore Windmill. Just behind the children were two men in civilian clothes carrying submachine guns. As Israeli schools and children have been targets of *fedayeen* attack, Israeli parents, as a matter of routine, take turns to maintain guard over the schools and the children.

Outsiders often refer to Israel's "siege mentality." The phrase is quite accurate, except when it is used to imply that the siege exists in the mind alone. The siege is a reality now in the Middle East, as it was in the past in Europe. The fusion of the two sieges into one—a fusion that was at the core of Menachem Begin's vision of the world—is indeed a historically formed phenomenon of the mind. But it is so powerful and so haunting a phenomenon of the mind that it is now also a large part of the political realities of the Middle East.

It has become commonplace to call Israel a militaristic State, a new Prussia or a new Sparta. But Israel is not at all like that. Spartan and Prussian militarism, and other militarisms—Napoleon's, for example—were based on sustained willingness to accept high casualties. Israel's policies are shaped, to an extent unparalleled in the history of any other major military power, by a desire to avoid loss of life among its soldiers. Anyone who has been in Israel during a period of victorious war—as I was in June 1982—knows that there is at such times nothing remotely resembling a "Mafeking spirit": only a universal apprehension and sorrow about Israeli casualties.

It is the very intensity of this concern about the need to save Jewish lives—a concern that has the Holocaust at the back of it—that produces the pattern of military behavior which shocks outside observers. Israel refuses to accept a conflict of attrition—"one for one"—which Israel must inevitably lose because of its inferiority in numbers. Israel has therefore consistently applied the doctrine of "asymmetrical response," hitting back with far greater force at the quarter from which it is attacked.

Israel started to withdraw from Lebanon in the spring of 1985 because of the unacceptably high casualties—more than 650 since June 1982—which remaining in Lebanon involved. And when the Shi'ite militia inflicted further casualties on the retreating Israeli forces, those forces hit back with their accustomed increment of violence. It was the level of Israeli casualties that determined both the retreat and the reprisals.[12]

For some outside observers, the reprisals tended to obscure, in the spring and summer of 1985, the fact of the retreat, and the mood that dictated that retreat. That mood, in my belief, remained in 1985 that described by Eric Silver in the immediate aftermath of Begin's retirement:

> The Israel Menachem Begin created in his own image was more narrowly Jewish, more aggressive and more isolated. Social and religious tensions were closer to the surface. But as the Kahan Commission demonstrated, government was still accountable to the people, democracy and the rule of law were live and kicking. The press was not silenced by appeals to patriotism. In the autumn of 1983, the disengagement from the problems of Lebanon showed Israelis soberly aware of their limitations as well as their strengths. That was not the legacy the sixth Prime Minister had meant to leave his people, but it was one worth cherishing.

Shimon Peres's style as Prime Minister reflects that mood. He is, today, modest and judicious, and free—as is also Shamir—from the contagious and intoxicating shrillness of Begin. The Government of National Unity has done a little better than most people thought it might, and Peres's own stature has risen accordingly.[13] There are chances of improved accommodations and relaxing of tensions. But neither the Government of National Unity nor any probable successor is likely to be able altogether to lift the siege.

Israel is obliged, by the nature of its predicament, to remain on its guard, and to be the judge of its own security. And those who condemn Israel should reflect that Israel's predicament is not the creation of Israelis only, but is also the creation of all the rest of us— those who attacked and destroyed the Jews in Europe, and those in Europe and America who just quietly closed our doors.

Against that background, the statesmen of Europe might have the grace to be more sparing in their admonitions addressed to Israel, bearing in mind that so many of the people those statesmen represent did so much, over so many years, and in so many ways, to impress upon Jews the necessity of creating the Jewish State.

The Palestinian Arabs have every right to say that they are the indirect and innocent victims of what happened to the Jews in Europe. They are. They are also the victims of the vanity and fantasies of their own leaders; victims also of the Machiavellian Arab rulers who use them as the Shirt of Uthman, and of illusions prompted by the hollow and far-from-disinterested sympathy of European leaders. The best hope of the West Bankers is in ceasing to rely on Palestinian émigrés or professions of sympathy whose cruel unreliability has been demonstrated on countless occasions. They have to face Israel, on their own, with nothing serious going for them except their lifeline to Jordan. Their best hope for the future lies not in the illusory and ever-receding perspective of "territory for peace," but in the strengthening of the "tacit condominium" described above. In practice, West Bankers have shown themselves willing to exercise that condominium, over the years, to the extent that it was available. Events in Lebanon, from 1982 to 1985, have surely been of a nature to suggest to West Bankers that the people who are most clamorous about the absolute need to secure "full Palestinian rights" are no friends to the Palestinians. It was not only Christian Arabs, allied with Israel, who massacred Palestinian Arabs at Sabra and Chatila (in 1982); it was also Muslim Arabs, allied with Syria, who carried out such massacres (in 1985). There was a world outcry about the first massacres; remarkably little was heard about the second. But Palestinians were equally victims in both cases.

Israeli leaders, as Eric Silver suggests, have been, at least to some extent, sobered and chastened by some of the results, for Israel, of Sharon's Hubris over Lebanon. It may be that a similar process is going on among Palestinian leaders, where it matters most: in the West Bank itself. If so, the illusory and highly publicized pursuit of "territory for peace" is likely to be paralleled by quieter talks about how to make the sharing of the territory somewhat less uncomfortable and less dangerous for Israelis and Palestinians alike. In such a case— and on the other *relatively* optimistic hypotheses discussed above—we would witness a considerable abatement of the siege, as the century draws to a close. But the possible abatement depends on Arab recognition of superior Israeli military strength, and adjustment to that fact, which is not likely to be accepted as necessarily a permanent fact. And so "abatement" implies suspension, not necessarily an approaching termination. What is not in sight is an end to the siege.

NOTES

PROLOGUE: How This Book Came to Be Written

1. Rafael later became director-general of the Israeli Foreign Office.
2. In circumstances faithfully set out in my book *To Katanga and Back* (New York: Simon and Schuster, 1962).
3. The P.L.O. itself had not yet come into existence at that time, but Ahmed Shugeiri, who was to be its first secretary-general, was already one of the General Assembly's most indefatigable orators, always on the theme of "the Zionist entity."
4. See the end of Chapter 6.
5. But see also the end of the Epilogue.

1: THE STRANGER

1. Chaim Weizmann, *Trial and Error*, p. 290.
2. Unless we restrict the category of "real opponents" to the anti-semitic opponents, in which case the statement becomes what logicians call an "analytical proposition."
3. Dugdale, *Arthur James Balfour*, Vol. II, p. 214. Balfour (1848–1930) was Foreign Secretary in David Lloyd George's Coalition Government in 1917. He had been Prime Minister from 1902 to 1906.
4. Quoted in Dubnov, *History of the Jews*, Vol. V, p. 433.
5. The Arab enemies of modern Israel are also strongly attached to this view of the matter.
6. Weizmann calls Montefiore "a high-minded man who considered nationalism beneath the religious level of Jews—except in their capacity as Englishmen." (*Trial and Error*, p. 124.) Herzl had called him "a stupid ass who affected English correctness." (*Diaries*, III, p. 1165.)
7. Quoted in Stein, *Balfour Declaration*, p. 526.
8. Chesterton, *New Jerusalem*, p. 283. That Chesterton's pro-Zionism was *partly* genuine, and not entirely a mask for anti-semitism, appears from the following: "It is true that for anyone whose heart is set on a particular home or shrine, to be locked out is to be locked in. The narrowest possible prison for him is the whole world."
9. Stein, *Balfour Declaration*, p. 129.
10. As was pointed out by C. P. Trevelyan during the Second Reading

of the Aliens Bill, conscription in Russia bore particularly heavily on Jews. "The family of the ordinary Russian soldier in case of his death gets a pension of forty roubles, but a Jew's family gets nothing." (*Hansard*, Vol. 145, Col. 705, May 2, 1905.)

11. *Hansard*, Vol. 145, Col. 795, May 2, 1905.

12. Supported by public opinion in Britain. The Liberal opposition to the bill was tepid, suggesting that Liberals did not want to make themselves conspicuous in a cause unpopular with their constituents. But the Liberals who did oppose included the young Winston Churchill.

13. In the Commons debate, speakers spoke of "stringent restrictions in America" as if these had already been introduced. In fact they were only being advocated. Beginning early in the century there arose an insistent demand for some plan designed to reduce the total number who would be admitted and to select those thought to be best. In practice, mass immigration of Jews, mainly from Russia, continued unchecked up to the outbreak of the First World War. The bars did not go up against mass immigration until the Immigration Acts of 1921 and 1924 introduced and extended the quota system.

14. That he didn't want more Jews in Britain is plain from the Aliens Bill. His not caring for British Jews has to be inferred from small indices. In 1917, for example, in arguing in favor of the Balfour Declaration in Cabinet, he referred to "a continuity of religious and social tradition that make the unassimilated Jew a great conservative force in world politics." (Dugdale, Vol. II, p. 216.) As a principal opponent of the Declaration in Cabinet was an assimilated Jew, Edwin Montagu, this testimonial (as it was, coming from a Conservative) to the *unassimilated* Jews must have caused an intake of breath around the Cabinet table.

15. See *The Letters and Papers of Chaim Weizmann*, Series A, Vol. IV, Jan. 1905–Dec. 1906, pp. 216, 220–221.

16. Dugdale, *Arthur James Balfour*, Vol. I, p. 433. This biography makes no mention of any form of anti-semitism in its subject, but then it makes no mention of the Aliens Bill either.

17. Churchill, *Winston S. Churchill*, Vol. II, p. 80.

18. Chaim Weizmann, *Trial and Error*, pp. 142–145. Weizmann's contemporary account is much balder, mentioning a long and interesting talk with Balfour about Zionism. "We talked about territorialism, African and other alternatives to Palestine. I explained to him why this was not possible." (To Vera Khatzman, Jan. 9, 1906, in *Letters and Papers*, Series A, Vol. IV, p. 219.) Jehuda Reinharz, in *Chaim Weizmann*, p. 271, infers that Weizmann's contemporary account was "no doubt more accurate" than his retrospective one. But the two accounts are not incompatible. Weizmann's fiancée did not have to be told what arguments he used. See also Dugdale, *Arthur James Balfour*, pp. 433–435.

19. There were of course other reasons for the Declaration besides Balfour's interest. See Chapter 2.

20. Dugdale, *Arthur James Balfour*, Vol. II, p. 221.

21. C. C. Aronsfeld in preface to his edition of *Israel in Europe*, by G. F. Abbott.

22. *Aliyah*, Hebrew for "ascent." The term means more than immigration. "It implies personal participation in the rebuilding of the Jewish homeland and the elevation of the individual to a higher plane of self-fulfillment as a member of the renascent nation." (*Encyclopaedia Judaica:* "Aliyah.")

23. One of the six sentenced to death for taking part in the conspiracy to kill Alexander II was a Jewish woman, Hessia Helfman (1855–1882).

24. Anti-semitism itself is older than established Christianity and appears in Tacitus and Juvenal. According to the *Encyclopaedia Judaica* ("Anti-Semitism") it first appeared among the Gentiles of Eretz Israel, stimulated by Jewish exclusivity. "In the eyes of the Jews, as these Gentiles knew, their pagan religion and practices rendered them 'unclean'; intermarriage with them was forbidden and, as a consequence of the dietary laws, no real social intercourse was possible." The friction between Jewish exclusivity and Gentile anti-semitism eventually led to the Roman repression of the Jews and the *galut*, or forced dispersion. The term "Diaspora" is reserved, in strict Jewish use, for voluntary migration.

25. Baron, *Russian Jew*, p. 3.

26. Ibid., p. 27.

27. Dubnov, *History of the Jews*, Vol. IV, p. 733.

28. Quoted in Baron, *Russian Jew*, pp. 36–37, and often by other writers. The great modern Russian writer Nadezhda Mandelshtam was a descendant of one of these children. She died a devout member of the Russian Orthodox Church.

29. See Dubnov, *History of the Jews*, Vol. V, Chapter 3, "The Epoch of Great Reforms."

30. There had been a pogrom at Odessa in 1871, but that was an isolated case.

31. Used here to mean educated in a European Gentile sense. Many Jews who had no such education were profoundly versed in Jewish religious tradition and in Talmudic dialectics.

32. A contemporary estimate from a Yiddish source, cited in Vital, *Origins of Zionism*, p. 52. This whole chapter is deeply indebted to this splendid book, with many quotations from Hebrew and other sources which would otherwise be closed to the present writer.

33. From the fewness of the murders in the course of the pogroms of the 1880s I would infer that the word to the peasants, from their betters, was that they could get away with anything done to Jews short of murder. But drunken peasants sometimes lost sight of this fine distinction.

34. Dostoevski was employed in the early seventies as editor of a right-wing organ called *Grazhdanin* (*The Citizen*) to which Pobedonostsev contributed anonymously, and which he used for knifing some of his colleagues. Dostoevski thought Pobedonostsev had "an enormous mind" and shared his views. Dostoevski's biographer Ernest Simmons writes of "the strange and unequal friendship" between the two men. Dostoevski died in January 1881, before his friend and correspondent came into the fullness of his power. Pobedonostsev was his executor and the guardian of his children.

35. Quoted in Byrnes, *Pobedonostsev*, p. 205.

36. Byrnes, *Pobedonostsev*, p. 207.

37. Ibid., p. 209. See Glossary under "Blood Libel."

38. Baron, *Russian Jew*, p. 59.

39. Vital, *Origins of Zionism*, p. 57.

40. That gorgeous thank offering does not of course celebrate Alexander as the persecutor of the Jews, but as the ally of France. But the bridge does stand as a baroque symbol of the capacity of a great civilized country to ignore the persecution of the Jews, and glorify the persecutor, in his role as an ally.

41. Figures from Baron, *Russian Jew,* pp. 87–88. These high figures are not due solely to persecution. They are due to the general poverty of the Jews in Russia (and Eastern Europe), to good reports of life in America and to the expansion of the Jewish population, as well as to pogroms, conscriptions and restrictions.

42. The Land of Israel.

43. Menachem Ussishkin's account from the Hebrew original; quoted in Vital, *Origins of Zionism,* pp. 75–76.

44. Even Herzlian Zionism did not *unambiguously* proclaim a political objective.

45. Vital, *Origins of Zionism,* p. 85. The opening sentences are also quoted by David Ben-Gurion (*Israel,* p. 26). The translations are different, Ben-Gurion's being the more vigorous. Where Vital has "to take possession in due course of Palestine" Ben-Gurion has to "seize the land of Israel in the course of time."

46. See Berlin, *Moses Hess.*

47. In the West, that is. What hit the Eastern Jews, from 1881 on, was the ancient Christian anti-semitism, in its Holy Russian form, but modernized and organized by the State.

48. Laqueur, *History of Zionism,* p. 30.

49. Racism was inescapable, but not in itself necessarily lethal. When it became associated, in the late-nineteenth century, with a radically *anti-Christian* ethic, of Nietzschean inspiration, it acquired genocidal potential. The conditions of Germany in the wake of the First World War brought that potential to fruition.

50. There were a number of other precursors of Herzl, but these were the outstanding names.

51. Vital, *Origins of Zionism,* p. 123.

52. Baron, *Russian Jew,* p. 61. The petition was not, in any case, altogether typical. Russian nineteenth-century literature, from Pushkin and Gogol to Turgenev and Dostoevski and even Chekhov, is rich in anti-semitic references. But so, of course, was the literature of other countries.

53. Vital, *Origins of Zionism,* p. 130.

54. Article in the Russian-language Jewish publication *Razsvyet* for Oct. 9, 1881 (O.S.); quoted in Vital, *Origins of Zionism,* p. 119.

55. Avineri, *Making of Modern Zionism,* p. 57.

56. A Yiddish derivative from *shtot,* meaning "town." A *shtetl* could vary in size from much less than 1,000 to 20,000 or more. (*Encyclopaedia Judaica:* "Shtetl.")

57. "The Road from Motol," by Maurice Samuel, in *Chaim Weizmann,* Weisgal and Carmichael (eds.). Samuel adds: "The *Shtetl* was something of a freak, the life of its inhabitants correspondingly freakish."

58. Greenberg, *Jews in Russia,* p. 161.

59. Avineri, *Making of Modern Zionism,* p. 51.

60. See the important chapter "The Dialectics of Redemption," in Avineri, *Making of Modern Zionism,* pp. 187–197.

61. Pulzer, *Rise of Political Anti-semitism,* p. 70. "Logical conclusion" may be a misnomer; see note 49, above.

62. Byrnes, *Antisemitism in Modern France,* p. 80.

63. Pulzer, *Rise of Political Anti-semitism,* p. 52.

64. Ibid., p. 249.

65. Ibid., p. 126.

66. *Encyclopaedia Judaica:* "Anti-semitism."

67. The long entry on anti-semitism in the *Encyclopaedia Judaica* does not mention Nietzsche, and the encyclopedia's article on Nietzsche is written from a "gentle Nietzschean" point of view ("gentle Nietzscheans"—a coinage of Crane Brinton's—being those scholars who like to explain away the more ferocious aspects of the philosopher's writings). The historian of German anti-semitism for this period believes that Nietzsche's "hatred of modern vulgarity made him also hate anti-semitism and racialism." (Pulzer, p. 302.) But what Nietzsche hated in vulgar anti-semitism was its limiting Christianity.

68. See Herzberg, *French Enlightenment*. Herzberg's demonstration of the anti-Jewish current in Voltaire's writing has been challenged, but rests on solid ground.

69. See the present writer's "Nietzsche and the Machiavellian Schism" in *The Suspecting Glance* (London: Faber and Faber, 1972).

70. See, for example, the last pages of Hitler's recorded *Table Talk*.

71. Pulzer, *Rise of Political Anti-semitism*, p. 10.

72. The speech, delivered on Oct. 2, 1887, is quoted in full in Pulzer, *Rise of Political Anti-semitism*, Appendix III.

73. Kann, *Hapsburg Empire, 1526–1918*, p. 435.

74. Macartney, *Hapsburg Empire*, p. 672.

75. Pulzer, *Rise of Political Anti-semitism*, p. 157.

76. Hitler *Table Talk*, p. 146.

77. See Hitler, *Mein Kampf* (New York, 1939), pp. 125–130, 140.

78. Chapman, *Dreyfus Case*, p. 28.

79. Byrnes, *Anti-semitism in Modern France*, p. 142.

80. "Beautifully executed," according to Byrnes (*Anti-semitism in Modern France*, p. 139), "magnificent invective." Obviously many readers agreed. Herzl seems indeed to have been one of them. "I owe to Drumont a great deal of the freedom of my concepts—because he was an artist." (*Diaries*, II, p. 509.) The admiration was mutual. Herzl noted in his diary, in January 1897, "a highly flattering editorial" about *The Jewish State* by the author of *La France Juive*. This is perhaps the most startling example of anti-semitic support for Zionism.

81. Quoted in Chapman, *Dreyfus Case*, p. 76. *La Libre Parole* was not the first with the *news* in this matter. But it was the first to hint at it.

82. *La Libre Parole*, Dec. 26, 1894.

83. Chapman, *Dreyfus Case*, p. 228.

84. Herzl, *Diaries*, I, p. 97. This was Herzl's thinking as late as 1893.

85. Vital, *Origins of Zionism*, p. 244. Vital does, however, acknowledge that the degradation "may have helped precipitate the change. . . ." A biographer of Herzl, Desmond Stewart, says: "In retrospect, the Dreyfus Case has little logical connection with the views to which Herzl became committed immediately after the trial." (*Theodor Herzl*, pp. 63–68.) True, if we look at the Dreyfus case as a whole, including the rehabilitation (which Herzl did not live to see). But there is a connection, both logical and emotional, between the rejection of assimilation *and the spectacle in the École Militaire*.

86. Article "Zionism," offered to the *North American Review* (Fall 1899) in *Zionist Writings: Essays and Addresses* (translated from the German by Harry Zohn), Vol. II, pp. 112 and 114.

87. These words were addressed specifically to the group in which

Herzl and Barrès were both standing. They do not occur in Chapman's description of the degradation ceremony, but Herzl's report of the occasion to his newspaper gives the words precisely as Barrès gives them, and specifies that they were addressed to the group of journalists.

88. Herzl's reports, as published in the *Neue Freie Presse* (Saturday, January 5, and Sunday, January 6, 1895), are factual, with no direct expression of opinion. But Herzl's first report ends with the words, "The witnesses of the degradation went away in the grip of a bizarre emotion. The strikingly firm attitude of the man who had just been dishonored had made a deep impression on some amongst them." The dispatches contain no mention of Jews, although Herzl later recalled what is generally known, that the crowd outside the École Militaire was shouting "Death to the Jews!" It was the policy of the paper to play down the existence of anti-semitism, for fear of stimulating it. From the end of October 1894 to January 5, 1895, Herzl is known to have filed seventeen reports on the evolution of the Dreyfus case. In the reports as published in the *Neue Freie Presse*, there is only one reference to Dreyfus's Jewishness—a quotation of Dreyfus's own words: "I am being persecuted because I am a Jew." (December 27, 1894.) Herzl's reports to the *N.F.P.* (and other German-language papers) on the Dreyfus case have been collected in pamphlet form by the Fédération Sioniste de France (translated by Leon Vogel; Paris, n.d.).

89. Barrès, *Scènes et doctrines du nationalisme* (1902), Vol. I, pp. 136–141. Pulzer quotes the passage (*Rise of Political Anti-semitism*, pp. 62–63), and calls it "a refined example of literary anti-semitic sadism." There is more than that to it, though. There is fear along with hate.

90. Herzl was born in Budapest, but regarded himself—before his conversion to Zionism—as a German-Austrian.

91. Herzl, *Diaries*, I, p. 273.

92. Preface to Herzl's *The Jewish State*.

93. Eliot, *Daniel Deronda*, p. 529.

94. Herzl, *Diaries*, I, p. 248. It is an isolated entry. I had not seen it when I introduced the comparison in the original draft of this chapter.

95. Ibid., p. 368.

96. Ibid., p. 402.

97. Ibid., p. 421.

98. *Encyclopaedia Judaica:* "Messianic Movements."

99. Reuben Brainin, *Life of Herzl* (Hebrew, New York, 1919); quoted in Nedava, "Herzl and Messianism," in Patai (ed.), *Herzl Year Book*.

100. Joseph Nedava, "Herzl and Messianism," in Patai (ed.), *Herzl Year Book*, Vol. VII. The adviser was Joseph Bloch (1850–1923), editor of an Austrian weekly and founder of the Union of Austrian Jews to Combat Anti-Semitism.

101. Ben-Gurion was speaking over the Israel Broadcasting Service on July 1, 1966. Quoted by Joseph Nedava.

102. Herzl, *Diaries*, I, p. 331.

103. Vital, *Origins of Zionism*, p. 363.

104. Quoted in Vital, *Origins of Zionism*, p. 356, and in Joseph Nedava, "Herzl and Messianism," in Patai (ed.), *Herzl Year Book*, Vol. VII, p. 18. The last sentence, with specific reference to the Messiah, is quoted by Nedava, not by Vital.

105. Can the "white" ritual drama Herzl staged in Basel have been his psyche's answer to the "black" ritual drama he had witnessed in Paris on

a January day two years before? I am tempted to think so, but my imagination may be overheating.

106. Dubnov was a Jewish nationalist but a non-Zionist; he did not support the Return.

107. Zionists, no doubt for related reasons, long offered internationalization of the Holy Places. In 1903, Herzl tried to convey this message to the Pope: "We have no intention of touching the Holy Places, even from afar. The Holy Places must be permanently extra-territorialized. . . ." (Quoted in Vital, *Zionism: The Formative Years*, p. 337.)

108. Twenty years later, the Balfour Declaration was to retain the "home," prefixing it with "national." The Zionist aim—a Jewish State—remained the same throughout. By 1917 the old reasons for dissimulation—the Tsar and the Sultan—had disappeared, but new reasons had arisen, which were no less pressing.

109. Herzl, *Diaries*, II, p. 581.

2: A HOME? (1897–1917)

1. Also partly because of the Capitulations system, under which European nationals were immune from local jurisdiction within the Ottoman Empire.

2. Laqueur, *History of Zionism*, p. 135.

3. Vital, *Zionism: The Formative Years*, p. 67.

4. Ibid., p. 65.

5. Ibid.

6. See Rabinowicz's detailed critique, in *Fifty Years of Zionism*, of Weizmann's autobiography, *Trial and Error*.

7. Vital, *Origins of Zionism*, p. 190. But even Ahad Ha'am had long been in doubt as to whether turning Hebrew into a modern spoken language was practicable.

8. Ibid., p. 188.

9. Herzl, *Diaries*, II, p. 577.

10. Vital, *Origins of Zionism*, p. 189.

11. In 1886, Pobedonostsev's May Laws prevented the renewal by Ahad Ha'am's father of the lease of the estate he had farmed continuously for eighteen years. (Vital, *Origins of Zionism*, p. 188.)

12. Klausner, *Menachem Ussishkin*, pp. 30–31.

13. Chaim Weizmann, *Trial and Error*, p. 59.

14. *Ha-Shiloah*, Sept. 1897; quoted in Vital, *Zionism: The Formative Years*, p. 24.

15. Quoted in Elon, *Herzl*, p. 186. Ussishkin was the first Russian Zionist to meet Herzl. Although skeptical about Herzl's promises, he was temperamentally more attracted to Herzlian dynamism than to Ahad Ha'am's approach. ". . . there was more to be hoped for," he wrote to Ahad Ha'am, "from some movement, however egregious, than from the despair which you and your friends on *Ha-Shiloah* offer." (Vital, *Origins of Zionism*, p. 343.)

16. Kaiser to Grand Duke of Baden; quoted in Vital, *Zionism: The Formative Years*, p. 85.

17. Herzl, *Diaries*, II, pp. 693–695.

18. Ibid., p. 734.

19. Von Bülow, *Memoirs*, Vol. I, pp. 249–250.

20. Herzl, *Diaries*, III, p. 981; Oct. 5, 1900.

21. The Grand Duke of Baden; quoted in Friedman, *Germany, Turkey and Zionism*, p. 76.

22. Aide-memoire of Jan. 26, 1904; quoted in Vital, *Zionism: The Formative Years*, p. 93.

23. Gooch, *Before the War*, Vol. I, p. 190.

24. Von Bülow, *Memoirs*, Vol. I, pp. 249–250.

25. See Cowles, *The Kaiser*, p. 162; Liddell Hart, *History of the World War*, p. 24.

26. Herzl, *Diaries*, II, p. 704; Oct. 1898.

27. Letter of Dec. 22, 1898; quoted in Vital, *Zionism: The Formative Years*, p. 98.

28. Mandel, *Arabs and Zionism*, Chapter 1.

29. Herzl, *Diaries*, I, p. 378.

30. Vital, *Zionism: The Formative Years*, p. 110.

31. Vambery, *Story of My Life*.

32. Herzl, *Diaries*, III, p. 1128.

33. To Tevfik Pasha (Foreign Minister), Aug. 31, 1903; quoted in Vital, *Zionism: The Formative Years*, p. 125.

34. Wittlin, *Abdul Hamid*, p. 113.

35. Ibid.

36. Ambassador Marschall von Biberstein to Foreign Minister von Bülow, Mar. 19, 1902; in Vital, *Zionism: The Formative Years*, p. 94. Mandel (*Arabs and Zionism*, p. 3) gives "two main reasons" for Ottoman resistance to Zionism: fear of creating another "national problem" and fear of increasing "the number of foreign subjects." But Palestine was special, and Jews, in relation to Palestine, were no ordinary foreign subjects. As Mandel acknowledges (p. 17): "With an eye to his Arab subjects as the would-be Caliph of all Muslims, Abdulhamid could scarcely deliver Jerusalem, the third city of Islam, to the Jews."

37. Herzl, *Diaries*, II, pp. 623–624, 644.

38. Ibid., IV, p. 1344.

39. Vital, *Zionism: The Formative Years*, p. 143.

40. Ibid., p. 240.

41. Witte had asked how far from the Holy Places Herzl would have his settlement. Herzl told him the settlement would be in the north, far from Jerusalem. (*Diaries*, IV, p. 1532.)

42. Vital, *Zionism: The Formative Years*, p. 264.

43. Ibid., pp. 262–263.

44. Schechtman, *Rebels and Statesmen*, p. 89.

45. Chaim Weizmann, *Trial and Error*, p. 87.

46. Ussishkin himself was Orthodox. But the significant aspect is Ussishkin's ascendancy over the "secular" Russian Jews at this most critical moment.

47. Vital, *Zionism: The Formative Years*, p. 345.

48. Herzl, *Diaries*, IV, p. 1599.

49. Ibid., p. 1606.

50. Elon, *Herzl*, pp. 401–402.

51. Quoted in Elon, *Herzl*, p. 402. Another who mourned for Herzl was David Ben-Gurion. Forty-five years later, Ben-Gurion, as Premier of the newly founded State of Israel, acted on Herzl's wish and removed his

remains to Israel. Herzl is buried on Mount Herzl, west of Jerusalem, within sight of Yad Vashem, the memorial to the Holocaust.

52. As soon as the British settlers in East Africa learned of the plan for Jewish colonization there, they began to agitate against it. If Jews had settled in East Africa they would have had to face the combined hostility of the dominant settlers and the black Africans, egged on by the settlers, as the Russian peasants were egged on by the rulers of Russia. Rather similar things were to happen in Palestine also.

53. Quoted in Vital, *Zionism: The Formative Years,* p. 384.

54. Vital, *Zionism: The Formative Years,* p. 83.

55. Mandel, *Arabs and Zionism,* pp. 39–40.

56. Vital, *Origins of Zionism,* p. 196.

57. *Yishuv* means "settlement." There was the Old Yishuv, of religious, nonpolitical Jews, and the New Yishuv, of secular Zionists, and much tension between the two Yishuvs.

58. For example, the earliest Arab anti-Zionist organization, Nagib Azouri's *Ligue de la Patrie Arabe* (1904), consciously imitated Drumont's *Ligue de la Patrie Française.*

59. That particular message was reinforced by the attitude of the Ottoman authorities, who were prompt, generally, in coming to the aid of attacked Europeans, but less prompt when those attacked were Jews.

60. This was a paper, edited by Lebanese Christians, that had moved from Beirut to Cairo to escape the Ottoman censorship.

61. Mandel, *Arabs and Zionism,* p. 45.

62. Elie Kedourie, by no means a gushing author, calls Rashid Rida "a man of stout intelligence, sober understanding and undoubted integrity." (*England and the Middle East,* p. 38.)

63. Mandel, *Arabs and Zionism,* p. 46.

64. Ibid., p. 48; Vital, *Zionism: The Formative Years,* p. 380.

65. Herzl to al-Khalidi, Mar. 19, 1899; quoted in Vital, *Zionism: The Formative Years,* p. 381.

66. See, on that aspect, Herzl's account of his 1902 conversation with Chamberlain (*Diaries,* IV, p. 1363). It is quite clear that neither Chamberlain nor Herzl takes "assurances to the Sultan" seriously.

67. It wasn't all as bleak as that. Jabotinsky, born in 1880, seems to have had a happy enough childhood. But that was in Odessa, an exceptional and remarkably un-Russian city.

68. Vital, *Zionism: The Formative Years,* pp. 392–393. Ben-Zvi was to become Israel's second President.

69. Lucas, *Modern History of Israel,* pp. 62–66.

70. "Socialist" is, of course, one of the most Protean of all political terms. These particular socialists were people strongly affected by the Russian revolutionary ferment of ideas. Their common, relevant characteristics included a radical puritanism, and a kind of regenerative milliennalism, affected by Marxism in its rhetoric, but probably emotionally much more intimately affected by the messianic strain in Judaism and in Zionism itself.

71. Mandel, *Arabs and Zionism,* pp. 55 and 38.

72. Schechtman, *Rebels and Statesmen,* Chapter 8, "Assignment to Turkey."

73. Most Arabs at this time, and after, were illiterate. But ideas are quite readily communicated from the press to an illiterate population through a few literate people in each district.

74. *Al-Asali;* quoted in Mandel, *Arabs and Zionism,* p. 81.

75. Quoted in Mandel, *Arabs and Zionism,* p. 89.

76. Thus a cartoon, reproduced by Mandel (p. 91), shows an elderly Jew with a moneybag, confronted by an Arab hero, Saladin, brandishing a sword.

77. Mandel, *Arabs and Zionism,* Chapter 8, "Apropos of a Muslim-Jewish Alliance, 1913–1914"; Chapter 9, "Apropos of an Arab-Zionist *Entente,* 1913–1914." The idea of this alliance was floated off by Arab émigrés in Cairo, which was under British control at the time. Mandel ignores the possibility that the idea may have been of British rather than Arab inspiration. Some British already had an eye on Palestine.

78. Quoted in Mandel, *Arabs and Zionism,* pp. 213–214.

79. Ibid., p. 221.

80. Christian anti-Zionism was cooling at this time, and some Christians already realized some common interest with Jews, as minorities within an Islamic regime.

81. Albert Antebi quoted in Mandel, *Arabs and Zionism,* p. 121. The date was June 1911.

82. Sachar, *History of Israel,* p. 88.

83. To Judah Magnes, Sept. 8, 1914. All references to Weizmann letters here are taken from *The Letters and Papers of Chaim Weizmann,* Series A, Vol. VII, Aug. 1914.

84. To Israel Zangwill, Oct. 19, 1914.

85. To C. P. Scott, Nov. 12, 1914.

86. To Ahad Ha'am, Dec. 1914.

87. Weizmann's italics.

88. Habitual self-description of assimilated German Jews.

89. Weizmann's italics.

90. Rothwell, *British War Aims,* p. 128.

91. Quoted in Sanders, *High Walls of Jerusalem,* p. 330.

92. Monroe, *Britain's Moment,* p. 43.

93. Letter of Feb. 3, 1914; quoted in Gwynn, *Letters and Friendships,* Vol. II, p. 201.

94. Nov. 13, 1914; Gwynn, *Letters and Friendships,* p. 245.

95. Curiously, Sir Cecil Spring-Rice disparaged the Balfour Declaration when it came, alleging: "You would not conciliate all the Irish by making Carson a Viscount and the situation is rather similar." (Gwynn, p. 421.) It wasn't in the least similar. But Spring-Rice's judgment was probably not at its best at this particular moment. The ambassador had just learned that he was to be replaced by a Jew, Lord Reading (Rufus Isaacs). By his insistence on the need to conciliate the American Jews, Sir Cecil had dug his own diplomatic grave.

A modern writer, Ronald Sanders, in *The High Walls of Jerusalem,* also takes the view that the Declaration failed in its purposes. Having shown that the "Russian" argument for the Balfour Declaration had become irrelevant by the time the Declaration was issued, Sanders goes on: "The argument for winning American-Jewish support for the Entente had also become irrelevant." (*High Walls,* p. 615.) But had it? The British Cabinet clearly didn't think that America's entry into the war (the previous April) had made the winning of American-Jewish appeal for the war effort irrelevant. American public opinion—of which the Jews were a significant part—remained very important. America had not yet committed forces of its own to the war in Europe. See my review of Sanders's otherwise excellent book, *New York Review of Books*, March 15, 1984; and subsequent correspondence in *New York Review of Books*.

96. See Friedman, *Germany, Turkey, and Zionism*, Chapter 11, "Germany Protects the Jews in Palestine," and the conclusion. The "pro-Jewish" attitudes of the German Government during the First World War were bitterly resented by the German far Right, whose spokesman on this and other matters was the eminent anti-semitic English-born intellectual Houston Stewart Chamberlain, later a warm admirer of Adolf Hitler.

97. Although France had issued its own pro-Zionist statement, the Cambon Declaration, as early as June 1917. But that was not made public at the time.

98. Friedman, *Question of Palestine*, p. 285.

99. Chaim Weizmann, *Letters and Papers*, Series A, Vol. I, p. 351, n. 6 (quoting Cabinet papers).

100. Quoted in Stein, *Balfour Declaration*, p. 504.

101. Ibid., p. 505.

102. Ibid., p. 507.

103. Stein, *Balfour Declaration*, pp. 510–511.

104. Oct. 13, 1917; Stein, *Balfour Declaration*, p. 509.

105. Stein, *Balfour Declaration*, p. 530.

106. Ibid., p. 545.

107. Text on p. 81.

108. Koestler, *Promise and Fulfilment*, p. 6.

109. Gilbert, *Winston Spencer Churchill*, Vol. 4, p. 847.

110. Words used in a different context by the pro-British Jewish anti-Zionist Lucien Wolf.

111. A memorandum (prepared by Sir Mark Sykes) submitted by the Foreign Office to the Government stated flatly: "The Zionists do not want . . . to set up a Jewish Republic or other form of State in Palestine or any part of Palestine."

Balfour himself, in his statement to the Cabinet, on the day of decision, was much more cautious. The National Home, he said, "did not necessarily involve the early establishment of an independent Jewish State, which was a matter for gradual development in accordance with the ordinary laws of political evolution." (Stein, p. 547.) That sounds like a formula worked out between Balfour and Weizmann.

3: A HOME CONTESTED (1917–1933)

1. Polk, *The Arab World*, p. 49. "Dreamed" may be Polk, rather than Omar.

2. Report to the Foreign Office by Sir Gilbert Clayton; quoted in Ingrams, *Seeds of Conflict*, pp. 43–44.

3. It was not as propaganda that he himself wanted the Declaration: he was himself a convinced Zionist. But it was for its propaganda value that he commended it to his colleagues.

4. Ingrams, *Seeds of Conflict*, p. 19. As the propaganda in question was in Yiddish, the Foreign Office may not have followed the details, or even have wanted to.

5. Letter quoted in Wasserstein, *British in Palestine*, pp. 42–43, n. 4.

Ussishkin read this story in the Russian press. Klausner, *Menachem Ussishkin*, p. 111.

6. "Balfour sent Allenby a vast quantity of pamphlets publicizing the Balfour Declaration. These were to be distributed in Jerusalem in advance of Allenby and his triumphant army. But at this time the population of Jerusalem was made up mostly of Arabs. Allenby took the decision to reject the order from the Foreign Office, and Balfour's pamphlets were put to other uses." (Beaverbrook, *Men and Power*, pp. 187–188.) Beaverbrook was wrong about Jerusalem—mostly Jewish since 1890—but he would have been right if he had made it "Palestine."

7. Text in *Peel Commission Report*, Chapter II, para. 23. The Declaration is also included as an Appendix in Antonius, *Arab Awakening*. For the Arabs, the Joint Declaration was the answer to the Balfour Declaration.

8. "Sykes-Picot," wrote Balfour, "was quite contrary to those modern notions of nationality which are enshrined in the Covenant and proclaimed in the [Anglo-French Joint] Declaration." (Memorandum of Aug. 11, 1919; *Documents on British Foreign Policy* [1919–1939], First Series, Vol. IV, p. 343.)

9. It also embarrassed the British, in their relations with the Arabs; and the Arab leaders, in their relations with their followers. The Hashemite leaders probably already knew about the substance of Sykes-Picot. See Kedourie, *England and the Middle East*, "The Making of the Sykes-Picot Agreement." The Turkish authorities published Sykes-Picot, in their Arab provinces, immediately after the Bolsheviks had released it.

10. Kedourie, *England and the Middle East*, p. 41.

11. Adelson, *Mark Sykes*, p. 268. Sykes had a robust sense of humor, and must have enjoyed overdoing the *mauvaise foi britannique* bit, and watching Picot suffer.

12. Monroe, *Britain's Moment*, p. 48.

13. Lord Hardinge to Gertrude Bell, Mar. 29, 1917.

14. *Documents on British Foreign Policy* (1919–1939), First Series, Vol. IV, p. 344.

15. Wasserstein, *British in Palestine*, p. 33. (Storrs to O.E.T.A. headquarters, Nov. 4, 1918.)

16. Chaim Weizmann, *Letters and Papers*, Series A, Vol. IX, p. xxviii; Letter of Nov. 12, 1918.

17. Wasserstein, *British in Palestine*, p. 48.

18. Quoted (by Helen Bentwich) in Bentwich, *Mandate Memories*, p. 57.

19. Sykes, *Crossroads to Israel*, p. 39.

20. Sanders, *High Walls of Jerusalem*, p. 14.

21. Bentwich, *Mandate Memories*, p. 37.

22. Published in 1943. Storrs died in 1955. He had been invalided out of the Colonial Service (Northern Rhodesia) in 1934 "in circumstances which remain obscure." (Wasserstein, p. 244.)

23. Storrs, *Orientations*, p. 397.

24. Storrs to O.E.T.A. headquarters, Nov. 19, 1918.

25. Sykes, *Crossroads to Israel*, pp. 39–40. Yet the *Encyclopaedia Judaica* entry on Storrs is not unfriendly.

26. Wasserstein, *British in Palestine*, p. 42.

27. "Behind the scenes there is no doubt that [the Military Administration] were attempting to influence the nature of the future political settle-

ment and to persuade the British Government to abandon the policy of the Balfour Declaration." (Marlowe, *Seat of Pilate*, p. 71.)

28. Wasserstein, *British in Palestine*, p. 41. The King-Crane Report itself was strongly anti-Zionist and recommended that Palestine be mandated to the United States, but none of the Powers took notice of it, not even the U.S., which suppressed it. Wilson's grounds for selecting King and Crane may be relevant: "The President felt that these two men were particularly qualified to go to Syria because they knew nothing about it." (Kedourie, *England and the Middle East*, p. 141.)

29. *Documents on British Foreign Policy* (1919–1939), First Series, Vol. IV, p. 345. See the commentary on this by Sykes (*Crossroads to Israel*, pp. 16–17).

30. Colonel French, a British intelligence officer in Egypt, wrote to Lord Curzon (Aug. 26, 1918): "Dr. Weizmann's agreement with Emir Faisal is not worth the paper it is written on, or the energy wasted on the conversation to make it." (Chaim Weizmann, *Letters and Papers*, Series A, Vol. IX, p. xviii).

31. Wasserstein, *British in Palestine*, pp. 34–35; Sykes, *Crossroads to Israel*, pp. 50–51.

32. Kedourie, *England and the Middle East*, pp. 122–132.

33. See Monroe, *Britain's Moment*, p. 165.

34. Wasserstein, *British in Palestine*, pp. 58–62; citing Foreign Office and Wingate papers.

35. This curious adventure in unauthorized military diplomacy is documented in Wasserstein, *British in Palestine*, pp. 60–62. The officer who negotiated with Faisal was Colonel B. H. Waters-Taylor (1870?–1946), Chief of Staff of O.E.T.A. under General Louis Bols, the last military Chief Administrator of Palestine. Faisal was to be overlord of the entire Fertile Crescent (Syria, Lebanon, Palestine and Mesopotamia—the latter now Iraq) but with British military administrators in Mesopotamia and Palestine. Bols would have been Governor-General of Palestine, with Waters-Taylor as his Chief Secretary. These arrangements would have effectively aborted the Balfour Declaration.

36. Wasserstein, *British in Palestine*, p. 60.

37. The Jerusalem police at the time consisted of 20 percent Jews, 20 percent Christians and the rest Muslims. (Evidence of Ronald Storrs to the Court of Enquiry into the 1920 Jerusalem riots; *Palestine Weekly*, June 25, 1920.)

38. Troops were forbidden to enter the Old City while the riots went on. The troops just held the city walls, and looked on. It was argued that it was undesirable to disperse troops among the "tortuous alleys" in the Old City. As an argument for military refusal to disperse a mob of civilians, this is not impressive.

39. Central Zionist Archives: L/3/256; Apr. 13, 1920.

40. Even the low death toll in the Jewish Quarter fits the pogrom pattern. "Teaching the Jews a lesson" was the idea.

41. Although the U.S. Government, in 1925, formally recorded its approval of the terms of the Mandate.

42. *Peel Commission Report* (1937), Vol. II, p. 42.

43. Curzon to Allenby, Apr. 26, 1920, in Ingrams, *Seeds of Conflict*, pp. 91–92. Curzon's choice of words distances the Declaration from the War Cabinet of 1917.

44. Stoyanovsky (*Mandate for Palestine*, p. 41, n. 4) says that "historical right"—instead of "connection"—was considered but not used "probably because of the disrepute into which it fell owing to the abuse made of it in the course of history." "Probably" seems a bit strong.

45. United Kingdom, *1922 White Paper*, Cmd. 1700 (1922). Correspondence with the Palestine Arab Delegation and the Zionist Organization.

46. Stein, *Balfour Declaration*, p. 556.

47. Ronald Graham to Ronald Storrs, May 24, 1920; in Wasserstein, *British in Palestine*, p. 55. Graham, in 1917, had done more than most to clinch the sale in question to the War Cabinet.

48. Wasserstein, *British in Palestine*, p. 55.

49. Stein, *Balfour Declaration*, p. 555. Non-Zionists have had the same impression. Thus D. G. Hogarth, of the Arab Bureau, said that the Balfour promise was redeemed "in depreciated currency" in 1922. I can see no such depreciation.

50. Unless you count the Department of Information's wartime leaflets in Yiddish.

51. Ingrams, *Seeds of Conflict*, Chapter 9, "Drafting the Mandate," pp. 96–97. The remaining quotations in the text, on Curzon and drafting, are taken from the same source.

52. Letter to Lord Hardinge (Under-Secretary of State at the Foreign Office), Sept. 1920. Balfour was trying to distance himself a little from Weizmann and in general from "our Jewish friends, who are not always easy to deal with," while giving them effective support.

53. Jezebel to her daughter, Athalie, in a dream. Racine, *Athalie*, Act II, Scene V.

54. Some explanations, based on "British interests," were offered. Thus *The Times* argued (Nov. 30, 1922) that, in view of current troubles in Egypt, "it is, to put it no higher, wise strategy to have in Palestine a state that owes us thanks for its birth and early development." Strangely speculative "strategy" for 1922, twenty-six years before the actual—and thankless—birth of the state in question.

55. The historian Noah Lucas also stresses the strategic factor: "It is probably easier to determine the reasons for the growing firmness of London Zionism at this time than for the Balfour Declaration itself. It is at least probable that strategic imperial considerations and especially French rivalry had come to supplant the tactical considerations of wartime." (*Modern History of Israel*, pp. 96–97.) Strategic Imperial considerations may have required holding on to Palestine, but the British Army at all levels thought that Zionism was a strategic *liability*, in relation to both Palestine and the region generally. "French rivalry" in relation to Palestine was no longer a serious factor by the spring of 1920, when the drafting of the Mandate was being completed. Neither factor can serve to explain the *reinforcement* of the Balfour commitment in the Mandate itself.

56. Chaim Weizmann, *Letters and Papers*, Series A, Vol. IX, p. xx; Letter 44 of Nov. 29, 1918.

57. Ibid., Letter 123, Feb. 28, 1919, p. xxl.

58. "L.G. and A.J.B. both said that by the Declaration they always meant an eventual Jewish State." ("Notes of a conversation at Mr. Balfour's house on July 22, 1921." Meinertzhagen, *Middle East Diary*, pp. 103–104.) See Sykes, *Crossroads to Israel*, pp. 79–81.

59. Palestine was transferred to the Colonial Office in 1921.

60. Sykes, *Crossroads to Israel*, p. 54.

61. Lord Ronaldshay (alias Lord Zetland), the author of the three-volume *Life of Lord Curzon*, records at length Curzon's memoranda of October 1917 opposing the National Home, but altogether fails to mention Curzon's share in the preparation of the Mandate. But Ronaldshay (Vol. III, p. 260) does say that by the time he became Foreign Secretary, Curzon was already "imbued with the belief that what he regarded as the rightful position of the Foreign Office had already been forfeited by default." Harold Nicolson, the author of the Curzon biography in the *Dictionary of National Biography*, indicates that Curzon's "firmness of decision" did not always live up to the expectations raised by his "rigid manner."

62. Anti-Zionists of the vulgar sort will find the emphasis on the power of *an idea* absurdly highfalutin. They habitually locate the source of Zionist power in Jewish finance, the Jewish vote in the United States, etc. But no financial pressures were exerted, no significant Jewish voting bloc exists in Britain, and the United States was not particularly interested, in the 1920s. The importance and relevance of Britain's financial links with American Jews would no doubt have been weighed, if the British Government, in this period, had seriously considered extricating itself from the Balfour Declaration, which it did not. But these considerations do not explain the *deepening* of the commitment.

63. Bowle, *Viscount Samuel*, p. 195.

64. Storrs, *Orientations*, p. 394.

65. Bowle, *Viscount Samuel*, p. 191. Allenby by now was High Commissioner in Cairo, where he was trying at this time to conciliate Egyptian nationalists. Allenby's letter was a redraft of a much stronger draft from General Sir Louis Bols, outgoing head of O.E.T.A.

66. Wasserstein, *British in Palestine*, p. 89.

67. Report by Weizmann, Jan. 7, 1917; quoted in Wasserstein, *British in Palestine*, p. 75, from the Ahad Ha'am papers.

68. Minutes of first meeting of Advisory Council, Oct. 6, 1920; Wasserstein, *British in Palestine*, p. 93.

69. Wasserstein, *British in Palestine*, p. 96.

70. For Richmond, see Wasserstein, *British in Palestine*, pp. 143–145, and the essay "Samuel and the Government of Palestine" in Kedourie, *Chatham House Version*, pp. 63–67. On Richmond's resignation four years later, he told Samuel that the spirit of his (Samuel's) administration was "not merely unwise and impolitic but evil."

71. Letter of Jan. 9, 1921, in Bowle, *Viscount Samuel*, p. 211. Bowle calls Curzon's letter "characteristic."

72. Sykes, *Crossroads to Israel*, pp. 64–65.

73. The elections, according to Sykes (p. 63), "could be harshly but not inaccurately described as 'rigged.'"

74. Sachar, *History of Israel*.

75. See Lucas, *Modern History of Israel*, Chapter 4, "Founding Fathers: Third Immigration (1914–24)."

76. Posters in the Old City of Jerusalem, Apr. 19–20, 1921. Wasserstein, *British in Palestine*, p. 99.

77. United Kingdom. Commission of Enquiry. *Palestine: Disturbances in May 1921* (Haycroft Report). Cmd. 1540, 1921.

78. Ibid.

79. Wasserstein, *British in Palestine*, p. 107.

80. Copy of circular sent to Lloyd George by Weizmann in Lloyd George papers, House of Lords Records Office, London (F86/8/4); cited in Wasserstein, *British in Palestine*, p. 107. Weizmann commented: "I am grieved to say that this text reminds me painfully of orders issued under similar circumstances by Russian pogrom-making generals." (*Letters and Papers*, Series A, Vol. IX, pp. 325–330; Letter 323, to Zionist Executive.)

81. Not yet, technically speaking, since the Mandate did not come into force until September 1923. But the principle was already well established.

82. *Peel Commission Report*, Vol. II, p. 52. The Peel Commission acknowledged a permanent contradiction between the Mandate system and the terms of the Mandate for Palestine. "The Mandate system involved certain general obligations, mainly toward the Arabs. The Mandate itself involved certain specific obligations, mainly toward the Jews."

83. Samuel to Churchill, May 8, 1921; Wasserstein, *British in Palestine*, p. 109.

84. Speech at Government House, June 3, 1921; Wasserstein, *British in Palestine*, p. 109.

85. Wasserstein, *British in Palestine*, p. 116, n. 6.

86. *The Future of Palestine* (draft report of Cabinet Committee by Lord Curzon, n.d., July 1923; PRO CO 733/54/455). See Wasserstein, *British in Palestine*, p. 127, and Sykes, *Crossroads to Israel*, pp. 94–96. The Cabinet Committee was set up following the debate of an anti-Zionist motion in the House of Lords (March 1923). Porath (*Palestinian-Arab National Movement*, p. 167) dismisses "all the assumptions" on which the report is based. This judgment seems a bit sweeping—Porath notes the recommendation of the Army, but ignores those of the Air Force and the Navy—but one may agree with his conclusion: "It appears that what won out in the end was the convenience of continuing a policy which had already been formulated and the recognition that the Balfour Declaration was an explicit commitment which had received international approval and which could not be abandoned without risking a loss to Britain's prestige and status as a world power." That is very close to what Curzon said.

87. Wasserstein, *British in Palestine*, p. 120.

88. *Encyclopaedia Judaica*: "Hagana."

89. Lucas, *Modern History of Israel*, p. 86.

90. The Arab Christians of Palestine at this period were not politically distinguishable from the Muslim majority.

91. Simson, *British Rule in Palestine*, pp. 168–169.

92. *Population of Israel*, by Roberto Bachi.

93. Sachar, *History of Israel*, p. 154.

94. Ibid., p. 155.

95. Sykes, *Crossroads to Israel*, p. 104, rejects the theory of "Zionist spokesmen" that the Arabs of Palestine had in reality no hostility to Zionism but concedes that "the propagandists" have "one very striking piece of evidence in their favour. The mass immigration of 1925 had no political repercussions either in Palestine or in the neighbouring countries." Sykes calls this "very curious," and so it remains.

96. As Sykes writes: "Neither the National Congress of the Arabs nor the Muslim-Christian Association were moved to action."

97. Wasserstein, *British in Palestine*, p. 31, calls this "the first sign of violent conflict which was in the making."

98. Sykes, *Crossroads to Israel*, p. 96; Wasserstein, *British in Palestine*, p. 149.

99. Sykes, *Crossroads to Israel*, p. 96. It is interesting that Balfour had a much rougher time in Damascus, which he ill-advisedly visited after Jerusalem. There, a yelling mob assembled outside his hotel, his life was supposed to be in danger—according to Storrs—and "the French authorities forcibly hurried him out of Syria and confined him for three days to the safety of his boat." (Sykes, p. 97.) No doubt, some Syrian Arabs would have resented the letting down of Faisal, as well as the Balfour Declaration. But it is hard to see why Syrian Arabs should show themselves so much more hostile to Balfour than Palestinian Arabs were, unless prevailing *official* attitudes were determinant. The French had good French reasons for detesting Britain's wartime Foreign Secretary (welshing on the Palestine part of Sykes-Picot, and trying to welsh on the Syrian part as well). So I suspect that Balfour was here a victim not so much of spontaneous Arab indignation as of a *mauvaise plaisanterie* on the part of his old allies.

100. John Higham, "Emma Lazarus, the New Colossus," in Boorstin (ed.), *American Primer*. However, Emma Lazarus's biography in the *Dictionary of American Biography* says her sonnet was placed on the pedestal in 1886.

101. See Caplan, *Palestine Jewry*, concluding section.

102. Ibid., p. 190. The speaker was Meir Dizengoff (1861–1937). He was mayor of Tel Aviv at the time. One comment on his remark was: "Since when are we so sensitive that we don't deal with those who take baksheesh?"

103. Report, "The Situation in Palestine, August 1921"; quoted in Caplan, *Palestine Jewry*, p. 101. As it happens, Lloyd George had earlier suggested bribery as the solution to Zionism's Arab problem. Weizmann had rejected this as "neither moral nor rational." (Sykes, p. 81.)

104. Since Berit Shalom was clearly an idealistic body—even verging on the Quixotic—it is somewhat surprising to find, among its founder members, the name of the pragmatist Kalvaryski. No doubt Kalvaryski was willing to try anything, even idealism, while idealists like Dr. Magnes may not have fully realized what Kalvaryski's pragmatism had involved.

105. Quoted in Laqueur, *History of Zionism*, p. 253.

106. Caplan, *Palestine Jewry*, p. 29.

107. Jabotinsky's address to the Zionist Actions Committee in July 1921. (Caplan, p. 113.)

108. This argument was developed in two seminal articles, "About the Iron Wall" and "The Ethic of the Iron Wall," published in Jabotinsky's Russian-language paper *Razsvyet*, on Nov. 4 and 11, 1923. Laqueur, in *History of Zionism* (pp. 256–257), comments: "In their transfer to Palestine, Jabotinsky's views lost much of their sophistication and served as the ideological justification for primitive and charismatic slogans which helped to poison Arab-Jewish relations during the 1930s and 1940s." The followers were certainly cruder, but moderation is hardly what the master preached, or can have expected to inspire.

109. Bentwich, *Mandate Memories*, p. 121.

110. Basic population in Bachi, Table A. 12. There were also, by 1931, nearly 100,000 "others" (about 90,000 of whom were Christians), most of whom were unfavorable to the Jewish National Home.

111. *Encyclopaedia Judaica:* "Weizmann."

112. See Urofsky, *American Zionism*, Chapters 7 and 8.

113. Ibid., Chapter 9. The least contestable positive material achievement during the Mandate period was the spectacular improvement in public health, as compared with the Ottoman and immediate post-Ottoman period. The average death rate, in the whole population, fell from 23.8 per thousand in the early twenties to 12.3 in 1946. In the sixteen years from 1929 to 1944, the child mortality rate fell among Muslims by 39 percent, among Jews by 60 percent and among Christians by 51 percent. The general life expectancy, for Muslims and Jews together, rose by 16.5 years in the same period. Much of the credit for this achievement belongs to the Mandatory and its Department of Health, but much also belongs to Hadassah. (Hyamson, *Palestine under the Mandate*, p. 43. Hyamson, himself Jewish, was an official under the Mandate, and is concerned to rebut criticism of the Mandatory. As much of the most relevant criticism came from America, his acknowledgment of this positive American contribution is significant.) Hadassah's doors were open to all creeds and its funds were plentiful. In America itself, Hadassah flourished to the point where it became the largest Zionist organization in the world.

114. Marlowe, *Seat of Pilate*, p. 113.

115. Laqueur, *History of Zionism*, p. 245.

116. Sykes, *Crossroads to Israel*, p. 129.

117. Bentwich, *Mandate Memories*, p. 130.

118. Wasserstein, *British in Palestine*, p. 155. Unlike Storrs, however, Luke was a bore, as he proves in lengthy volumes of reminiscences. Luke also wrote Storrs's entry in the *Dictionary of National Biography*. Storrs had written T. E. Lawrence's. It is a kind of apostolic succession.

119. Luke, *Cities and Men*, Vol. II, p. 15.

120. It may be marginally relevant here that Luke was partly of Jewish origin and tried to conceal the fact. (Wasserstein, p. 156.) Bentwich (p. 76) mentions his "gentle apprehension of Zionism."

121. Jeffery's *Reader on Islam* contains (pp. 621–639) an English translation of a sixteenth-century version of this journey: "The Story of the Night Journey and the Ascension," by the Egyptian Imam Najm ad-Din al-Ghaiti. Buraq is described as "a large white riding-beast, standing somewhat higher than an ass but not so high as a mule, who at every step travels as far as its eye can reach. It has constantly moving ears. . . . It was Abraham's riding-beast on which he used to ride to the Inviolable House [i.e., the Ka'ba at Mecca]."

122. Sykes, *Crossroads to Israel*, p. 127, quoting Duff, *Sword for Hire* and *May the Winds Blow*.

123. Ibid., p. 128.

124. Marlowe, *Seat of Pilate*, p. 4.

125. Bentwich, *Mandate Memories*, p. 129.

126. Wasserstein, *British in Palestine*, p. 155.

127. Ibid., p. 156. Before coming to Palestine, Chancellor had been opposed to any move toward self-government. But once in Palestine, he fell in with the views of Luke, which were representative of British officialdom on the spot.

128. See Porath, *Palestinian-Arab National Movement*, pp. 250–257.

129. Ibid., p. 256.

130. Ibid., p. 257.

131. Ann Lesch, *Arab Politics in Palestine,* suggests that an improvement in the economy in Palestine and an increase in immigration, by the end of 1928, "lent urgency to the Arab Executive's negotiations with the British administration." This is similar to Marlowe's interpretation to the effect that the Arabs were quiet when Jewish immigration was low. Again, this doesn't seem to fit the facts. Nineteen twenty-eight, the nadir year for Jewish immigration (2,178, exceeding *emigration* that year only by ten persons), was the year in which the Arab interest in representative institutions was at its height, and it was at the end of that same year that Haj Amin began his campaign of violent incitation.

132. Sykes, *Crossroads to Israel,* p. 159.

133. Laqueur, *History of Zionism,* p. 256.

134. Marlowe, *Seat of Pilate,* p. 115.

135. Sykes, *Crossroads to Israel,* p. 137.

136. Ibid.

137. Stewart Perowne's entry on Luke in the *Dictionary of National Biography* says: "By his promptness and resolution in summoning British troops from Egypt, Luke prevented a major catastrophe." If he had summoned some troops during the months of incitement that led up to the outbreak of violence, he might have avoided any catastrophe at all.

138. Quoted in Laqueur, *History of Zionism,* p. 230.

139. *Encyclopaedia Judaica:* "Hagana."

140. Porath, *Palestinian-Arab National Movement,* p. 271.

141. Ibid., p. 272.

142. The relative ease with which Arabs were able to slaughter Jews on this occasion was probably due to Haj Amin's emphasis on the Holy Places, and the fact that the Jews to be found around there were mainly pious and defenseless people of the Old Yishuv.

143. Chaim Weizmann, *Trial and Error,* p. 331. I find it hard to believe that even Beatrice Webb actually used those words. Weizmann's reminiscences are not invariably reliable, and he was not above touching up an anecdote. But I have no doubt that she was utterly unsympathetic. Her letters show her to have been strongly anti-Zionist, and at least somewhat anti-semitic. "Why is it," she asks in a 1930 letter, "that everyone who has dealing with Jewry ends up by being prejudiced against the Jews?" (*Letters of Sidney and Beatrice Webb,* p. 334.)

144. Sykes, *Crossroads to Israel,* p. 143.

145. Sachar, *History of Israel,* p. 175.

146. Cmd. 3582 of 1932.

147. Marlowe, *Seat of Pilate,* p. 119.

148. Chaim Weizmann, *Letters and Papers,* Series A, Vol. XIV; Letter 187 of Jan. 17, 1930. The "fundamental change" came exactly three years and two weeks later.

149. "The position of the Government is steadily getting worse. With blunders like Palestine, I can do nothing." Memorandum of Nov. 9, 1930 (quoted in Marquand, *Ramsay MacDonald,* p. 577). This was a week before the debate on the White Paper. The Prime Minister had Weizmann to lunch three days before and had promised that the "errors" in the White Paper would be "put right" in a letter from him to Weizmann. (Sachar, *History of Israel,* p. 177.)

150. *Hansard,* Vol. 248, Cols. 751–757, Feb. 13, 1931.

151. Ibid., Col. 599, Feb. 12, 1931. A moment later (Col. 600) he said he had misheard the question and there had been "no change of policy." But there had been one.

152. *Encyclopaedia Judaica:* "Germany."

153. Shirer, *Third Reich,* p. 138.

154. Interview with Jacob Landau of the Jewish Telegraphic Agency; quoted in Chaim Weizmann, *Letters and Papers,* Series A, Vol. IX, p. xxi. When challenged about this interview, Weizmann said that his words had been given "an unfortunate formulation," but he did not repudiate the substance.

155. Chaim Weizmann, *Letters and Papers,* Series A, Vol. XV, p. xxi, p. 174; Letter 170 of July 25, 1931.

156. Chaim Weizmann, *Trial and Error,* p. 420. Weizmann may not have known that Herzl too had compared himself to Moses.

4: DEATH AND BIRTH (1933–1948)

1. Patai (ed.), *Encyclopedia of Zionism and Israel:* "Ha'avara."

2. See Krikler, "Boycotting Nazi Germany."

3. *Jewish Chronicle,* Mar. 17, 1933.

4. Krikler, "Boycotting Nazi Germany," pp. 29–30.

5. Article in *Jüdische Rundschau*—organ of the German Zionists—in May 1933; quoted in Gelber, "Zionist Policy."

6. See the section "The Ordeal of the Eighteenth Congress" in Schechtman, *Fighter and Prophet,* pp. 181–197.

7. A follower of Jabotinsky's charged with the crime had been identified by Arlosoroff's wife. He was later acquitted on a technicality.

8. Jabotinsky himself, a little later, tried to negotiate with the antisemitic Polish authorities an emigration agreement comparable to Ha'avara.

9. Plehve's international reputation in 1903 was bloodier than Hitler's was in 1933.

10. Gelber, "Zionist Policy." Presumably the persuasion was to be indirect, through the Zionist Executive. The demonstration was not canceled.

11. David Yisraeli, "The Third Reich and Palestine," in Kedourie and Haim (eds.), *Palestine and Israel,* pp. 106–113.

12. Ibid. Drawing on the files of the German Near Eastern Division, in the Political Archive in Bonn.

13. Hitler, *Mein Kampf* (London, 1969), Chapter II, "Nation and Race."

14. After his first meeting with Weizmann, Money noted in his diary for April 23, 1918: "The trouble about all these Jewish schemes is that . . . they are rather open to the suspicion of having some financial end in the background, as the Jew is not in the habit of going to out-of-the-way points of the world solely for the sake of his health." (Quoted in Wasserstein, *British in Palestine,* p. 215.)

15. Memorandum of June 1, 1937; quoted in R. Melka, "Nazi Germany and the Palestine Question," in Kedourie and Haim (eds.), *Palestine and Israel,* pp. 89–95. Curiously, Neurath's "Vatican State" concept is not very far (except in feeling) from Ahad Ha'am's idea of Israel as a cultural center for world Jewry.

16. *Peel Commission Report* (1937), Vol. X, p. 2. There are reckoned

to have been, in addition, about 25,000 illegal immigrants, from 1933 to 1939.

17. Ibid., p. 3; Hyamson, *Palestine under the Mandate,* p. 67.

18. Esco Foundation, *Palestine,* Chapter X, "Development During the Second Decade: 1930–1939," p. 680.

19. Quoted in Lucas, *Modern History of Israel,* p. 148.

20. Ambivalence ran in the family. His father, Sir Mark Sykes, was eponymous coauthor, and then chief dismantler, of the Sykes-Picot agreement, and then an enthusiast for the Balfour Declaration, which, however, he interpreted as *not* opening the way for a Jewish State.

21. Sykes, *Crossroads to Israel,* pp. 167–168.

22. Ibid., p. 168.

23. Polk, *The Arab World,* pp. 118–119, 126.

24. If so, it was a fortuitous effect. There seems to be no evidence that the Mandatory intended anything so Machiavellian—and so coherently purposeful.

25. Compare, in our own time, Sir Harold Wilson's policy of enforcing sanctions against Rhodesia while avoiding sanctions against South Africa, which supplied Rhodesia.

26. Walters, *League of Nations,* p. 663. Walters was the (British) Deputy Secretary-General of the League of Nations at the time.

27. *Al-Difa,* Sept. 30, 1935. Quoted by Shai Lachman, "Arab Rebellion and Terrorism in Palestine," in Kedourie and Haim (eds.), *Zionism and Arabism,* p. 68. Lachman cites other examples from the Arabic press for the summer and autumn of 1935.

28. *Survey,* 1936, p. 24.

29. Hyamson, *Palestine under the Mandate,* p. 143.

30. Michael J. Cohen, "Sir Arthur Wauchope, the Army and the Rebellion in Palestine," *Middle Eastern Studies.*

31. Sykes, *Crossroads to Israel,* p. 166, n. 2.

32. A similar phenomenon appeared among the Catholic population of Northern Ireland, after a similar period of time had elapsed following the broadening of educational opportunities after the Second World War.

33. See Shai Lachman, "Arab Rebellion and Terrorism in Palestine," in Kedourie and Haim (eds.), *Zionism and Arabism,* pp. 52–99.

34. Sykes, *Crossroads to Israel,* p. 175. Sykes perhaps exaggerates somewhat here. But British eagerness on the point must have been suggestive of fear, and so exciting to the political rebels.

35. Porath, *Palestinian Arab National Movement,* p. 156.

36. I.e., largely Arab police.

37. Text in Schechtman, *Fighter and Prophet,* p. 300. The Colonial Office dismissed Jabotinsky's warning.

38. Sykes, *Crossroads to Israel,* pp. 183–185; Porath, *Palestinian Arab National Movement,* pp. 163–178.

39. In the postwar period, Ben-Gurion's position as head of the official Jewish Agency and also of the Jewish revolt was to become oddly symmetrical to Haj Amin's prewar position.

40. Porath, *Palestinian Arab National Movement,* p. 193.

41. Ibid., p. 194.

42. Porath suggests that the Mufti's fear of the ambitions of Emir Abdullah of Transjordan may have been at work.

43. *Hansard,* Vol. 311, Cols. 1732–1741, May 6, 1936.

44. Simson, *British Rule and Rebellion,* p. 239.
45. Ibid., p. 205.
46. See Kedourie, "'Great Britain and Palestine: The Turning Point," in his *Islam in the Modern World,* pp. 93–170. Also Rubin, *Arab States,* Chapter 3, "Entrance of the Arab Kings." Norman Anthony Rose, "Arab Rulers and Palestine," Aaron S. Klieman, "The Arab States in Palestine," and Shai Lachman, "Arab Rebellion and Terrorism in Palestine," in Kedourie and Haim (eds.), *Zionism and Arabism.*
47. The name of a fourth ruler, the Imam of Yemen, was made use of, but he does not seem to have played an active part.
48. See Kedourie, "Ibn Saud on the Jews," in his *Islam in the Modern World.*
49. Kedourie, "Great Britain and Palestine," in his *Islam in the Modern World,* p. 150.
50. Ibid. This article amply documents this point. Citing the Eastern Department's apocalyptic predictions, he calls Rendel, "this sybil, this pythoness."
51. Simson, *British Rule and Rebellion,* p. 224.
52. Porath's phrase in *Palestinian Arab National Movement,* p. 197.
53. Porath, *Palestinian Arab National Movement,* p. 214.
54. Ibid., p. 215; citing a text (of before October 20) preserved in the Zionist Archives. No agreements were concluded, but there may well have been verbal promises.
55. Texts in Schechtman, *Fighter and Prophet,* pp. 302–304. Jabotinsky had been quite strongly pro-British, though the British were never particularly pro-Jabotinsky.
56. Quoted in Rose, *Gentile Zionists,* p. 133.
57. Marlowe, *Seat of Pilate,* p. 158.
58. Bauer, *From Diplomacy to Resistance,* pp. 41–42.
59. Cowling, *Impact of Hitler,* p. 269. Cowling adds: "Some Conservatives did, most did not, believe in the international Jewish conspiracy. British anti-semitism was always far milder than the various continental sorts, but it was rising in the thirties, often combining with some degree of sympathy with the Jews in Germany." (See for example, Harold Nicolson, *Diaries and Letters.*) There was very little overt anti-semitism in the press, but there was a general tendency (with exceptions) to play down the sufferings of the Jews, and to stress the purely German-internal character of the Nazi phenomenon. (See Gannon, *British Press and Germany,* pp. 226–228.) The mood of official circles was interpreted by Angus Calder as follows: "A morbid fear of anti-semitism especially in Arab countries but also at home in Britain and America . . . resulted in virtual anti-semitism." (*The People's War,* pp. 498–501.) It is not always easy to distinguish between anti-semitism and fear of anti-semitism.
60. Feiling, *Neville Chamberlain,* p. 285.
61. Ibid., Bar-Zohar, *Ben-Gurion,* p. 79.
62. Ibid., pp. 77–78.
63. Peel Commission Minutes.
64. Ibid. The words "in Hebrew" touched the commission on a sensitive spot. A witness had referred to the "non-Hebrew languages" in Palestine. A commission member asked what languages these were. The witness replied "English and Arabic." The member protested, "But English is not a non-Hebrew language! English is English!" No answer to that.

65. Ibid., Jan. 12, 1937.

66. Ibid., Jan. 18, 1937.

67. *Peel Commission Report,* Chapter XX, p. 370.

68. Ibid., p. 375.

69. Ibid., Chapter XXII, p. 381.

70. Parliamentary Papers, 1936–1937: Cmd. 5513.

71. *Peel Commission Report,* Vol. V, p. 2.

72. Hurewitz, *Struggle for Palestine,* p. 77.

73. Peel Commission Minutes.

74. Ibid.

75. Letter to Mrs. A. Paterson, July 7, 1937; text in Rose, *Gentile Zionists,* p. 138.

76. *D. Ben-Gurion, Letters to Paula and the Children* (Tel Aviv, 1968), pp. 210–213 (Hebrew). English translation in Sheffer, *Resolution vs. Management,* p. 26. Those who think that Ben-Gurion would have been more "reasonable" than Begin, about the West Bank, etc., should consider the above passage.

77. Porath, *Palestinian Arab National Movement,* p. 231; also Rubin, *Arab States,* p. 94.

78. *Peel Commission Report,* Vol. 5, p. 55.

79. Porath, *Palestinian Arab National Movement,* p. 235.

80. Ibid., Chapter Nine, "The Revolt."

81. Chamberlain's guiding principle may already have been that communicated by him to the Cabinet in April 1939: "If we must offend one side, let us offend the Jews rather than the Arabs." (Quoted in Michael Cohen, p. 84.)

82. See Michael Cohen, *Retreat from the Mandate,* Chapters 3 and 5.

83. With something of Jabotinsky in his Zionism, according to Christopher Sykes.

84. Sykes, *Crossroads to Israel,* p. 222.

85. Hurewitz, *Struggle for Palestine,* p. 92.

86. Sykes, *Crossroads to Israel,* p. 219.

87. Ibid., p. 221.

88. Memorandum of Sept. 1936; quoted in Kedourie, *Islam in the Modern World,* pp. 114–115.

89. Hanna, *British Policy in Palestine,* p. 138.

90. Which Egypt entered in 1937.

91. Hurewitz, *Struggle for Palestine,* p. 90.

92. Rubin, *Arab States,* p. 94, speaks of 200–300 volunteers a month, mainly from Iraq and Syria.

93. Porath, *Palestinian Arab National Movement,* pp. 275–276.

94. Hirszowicz, *Third Reich,* passim. Also David Yisraeli, "The Third Reich and Palestine," and R. Melka, "Nazi Germany and the Palestine Question," both in Kedourie and Haim (eds.), *Palestine and Israel.*

95. *Documents on German Foreign Policy,* July 9, 1937. After the war, Hentig became an adviser to Ibn Saud: so it looks as if he got it about right. Rubin, *Arab States,* p. 250, n. 9.

96. Porath, *Palestinian Arab National Movement,* p. 277; Rubin, *Arab States,* p. 101.

97. Sykes, *Crossroads to Israel,* pp. 238–239. The weakness in this seems to be that if the ruthless crushing of the Arab Revolt, in 1937–1938, had not opened up "a major quarrel," perhaps to explode later, the mere

failure to produce a promissory White Paper in 1939 would hardly have done so, nor could a mere White Paper do much to abate emotions stirred by the crushing of a revolt. Kedourie's argument tends to the conclusion that the attitude of the Arab rulers to Nazi Germany would be less affected by thoughts of Palestine than by the realities of power, both internationally and in the region. Also the Arab leaders, remembering the fate of—among other documents—the Joint Declaration of 1918 and the White Paper of 1930, were unlikely to allow just a new White Paper to affect their course of action to any great extent.

98. In the last stages of the Arab Revolt, then sputtering out, the most frequent victims were Arabs, considered to have betrayed the Arab cause, of which the Mufti was the standard-bearer.

99. Michael Cohen, *Retreat from the Mandate*, p. 80.

100. Cmd. 6019 of 1939.

101. Hanna, *British Policy in Palestine*, p. 149.

102. *Lords Debates*, Vol. 113, Col. 104, May 23, 1939.

103. Porath, *Palestinian Arab National Movement*, p. 286.

104. This proceeding has sometimes more legitimacy in it than its critics allow. Not many of the critics of Britain's rule in India predicted the slaughter that would ensue when Britain left.

105. Hurewitz, *Struggle for Palestine*, pp. 105–106.

106. Letter of June 5, 1939; quoted in Schechtman, *Fighter and Prophet*, p. 365.

107. Porath, *Palestinian Arab National Movement*, p. 290.

108. Rubin, *Arab States*, p. 115.

109. Except Transjordan.

110. Sykes, *Crossroads to Israel*, pp. 239–240.

111. Hurewitz, *Struggle for Palestine*, p. 106.

112. Ibid., p. 109. The Jewish Agency was not, however, officially involved in illegal immigration, and indeed in 1938–1939 many members of the agency opposed this (especially Weizmann).

113. The Jewish Agency at this time contained both official Zionists and non-Zionists.

114. Report of July, 1939; quoted in Bethell, *Palestine Triangle*, p. 73.

115. *Survey of International Affairs 1938*, Vol. I, p. 479.

116. *Ibid.*, pp. 469–470.

117. Weizmann speaks as if Britain is already at war.

118. Bauer, *From Diplomacy to Resistance*, p. 94.

119. Hurewitz, *Struggle for Palestine*, pp. 119, 127.

120. Bauer, *From Diplomacy to Resistance*, p. 101.

121. Ibid., p. 132. Bauer adds: "Understandably the mission ended unsuccessfully."

122. Ibid., p. 312.

123. Ibid., p. 78.

124. Professor Bauer's definition.

125. Bauer, *From Diplomacy to Resistance*, Chapter 5, "The Danger of German Invasion."

126. Birdwood, *Nuri Said*, p. 17.

127. Mortimer's definition in Glossary to *Faith and Power*.

128. Schechtman, *Mufti and the Fuehrer*, pp. 110–122, has the *fatwa* in full, in English translation, citing Arabic newspaper sources, as well as the broadcast.

129. Glubb, *Arab Legion*.

130. Schechtman, *Mufti and the Fuehrer*, pp. 306–308.

131. Ibid., p. 308.

132. Hitler, *Table Talk*, p. 547. One of the Reich's advisers on racial science had found—after the Mufti's meeting with Hitler—that the Mufti was not really an Arab, but more of a Circassian, and that "Caucasian or Aryan blood enables us to expect from the Mufti in future the faithfulness of an ally of which pure Arab blood would be incapable." (Quoted in Hirszowicz, p. 263.)

133. The interpreter, John Eppler, was an Egyptian-born German. He annoyed Hitler by protesting about the coffee. (Schechtman, *Mufti and the Fuehrer*, p. 123.)

134. Weisgal and Carmichael (eds.), *Chaim Weizmann*, p. 259.

135. Urofsky, *American Zionism*, p. 394. Urofsky offers some qualifications of this picture, but it remains convincing.

136. Bauer, *From Diplomacy to Resistance*, p. 92.

137. Bar-Zohar, *Ben-Gurion*, p. 107.

138. Ibid., p. 110.

139. Ibid., p. 111.

140. Bauer, *From Diplomacy to Resistance*, p. 273.

141. Morse, *While Six Million Died*, pp. 16–17.

142. Hurewitz, *Struggle for Palestine*, p. 196.

143. Bauer, *From Diplomacy to Resistance*, p. 273; Morse, *While Six Million Died*, p. 52.

144. Hurewitz, *Struggle for Palestine*, p. 198.

145. Bethell, *Palestine Triangle*, p. 151.

146. Not Lehi—curiously enough, though Lehi had actually committed the murders. Lehi seems to have agreed to suspend operations at this time.

147. Bethell, *Palestine Triangle*, p. 197.

148. Crossman, *Palestine Mission*, p. 62.

149. Ibid., p. 149.

150. Williams, *Prime Minister Remembers*, p. 189.

151. Ibid.

152. Bar-Zohar, *Ben-Gurion*, p. 129.

153. Kirk, *Survey of International Affairs*, p. 4.

154. In fact the precedent seems either to have been forgotten, or simply not to have registered. Ernest Bevin's biographer describes the British forces in Palestine in the 1940s as "facing a war of liberation for the first time." (Bullock, p. 166.)

155. Bethell, *Palestine Triangle*, pp. 241, 267.

156. Ibid., pp. 170–171.

157. For a discussion of Bevin's growing anti-Jewishness see the chapter "The End of the Mandate; Ernest Bevin" in Crossman, *A Nation Reborn*.

158. Crossman, *Palestine Mission*, p. 158. Crossman himself was pro-Zionist because "they needed a land of their own where they could rid themselves of the persecution complex which was their undoing in the West." It seems an odd formula in 1946.

159. Hurewitz, *Struggle for Palestine*, p. 253. Eleanor Roosevelt, for one, thought that Bevin had a point. "It is not fair," she commented, "to ask of others what you are not willing to do yourself." (Pp. 116–117.)

160. Bar-Zohar, *Ben-Gurion*, p. 129.

161. See Bullock, *Ernest Bevin*, p. 293.

162. Hurewitz, *Struggle for Palestine*, p. 255.

163. Ibid.

164. See Snetsinger, *Truman*, pp. 44–47. Truman's speech was delivered on Yom Kippur, and a month before the midterm congressional elections. Ernest Bevin was understandably furious at this electioneering use of what Bevin called "my problem." But Jewish votes in America were no less important a part of the international context in which Bevin had to work than Arab oil was. Bevin's biographer acknowledges that Bevin's anger at the influence of Jewish votes was "naïve" and "clouded his judgment." (Bullock, p. 175.) But he also shows that Bevin himself took the American factor more seriously than his officials did.

165. Hurewitz, *Struggle for Palestine*, p. 265.

166. Weisgal and Carmichael (eds.), *Chaim Weizmann*, "Tragedy and Triumph."

167. Weizmann was in fact ambivalent about Irgun's actions. Richard Crossman (*A Nation Reborn*, p. 77) records a visit to him shortly after the King David Hotel explosion: "When I mentioned the King David Hotel I saw that he was crying. As the tears streamed down his cheeks he said to me: 'I can't help feeling proud of our boys. If only it had been a German headquarters, they would have got the V.C.'" Crossman adds: "This remark illuminates not only his attitude to the use of force but his complex feelings about Britain."

168. These had declared war on the Axis in the final months of the war—thus qualifying as founding members of the United Nations.

169. Cabinet Office 129/16; quoted in Bethell, *Palestine Triangle*, p. 292.

170. See Bullock, *Ernest Bevin*, p. 496.

171. Bethell, *Palestine Triangle*, p. 312.

172. U.N. General Assembly, 1st Special Session I 127.35; Hurewitz, *Struggle for Palestine*, p. 288.

173. Bethell, *Palestine Triangle*, p. 313.

174. Ibid., p. 333.

175. Up to 1958, with considerable, but steadily lessening, influence thereafter, as far as voting patterns were concerned.

176. "The G.O.C. was quite explicit that Haganah would be able without difficulty to hold any area allocated to the Jews under partition, whereas large British reinforcements would be required to police any pro-Arab solution which required the suppression of the Haganah. The Labour Government, however, insisted that our Report could only be accepted if the Haganah was suppressed. I was later to learn their main reason for doing so was the advice proffered to them by the Chiefs of Staff that otherwise two extra divisions would be required to implement the report." (Crossman, *A Nation Reborn*, p. 71.) As A. J. P. Taylor says (in a different context): "Every expert is a human being, and technical opinions reflect the political views of the people who give them." (*Origins of the Second World War*, pp. 92–93.)

177. Weisgal and Carmichael (eds.), *Chaim Weizmann*, p. 302.

178. Lash, *The Years Alone*, p. 123. Niles was a convinced Zionist; Henderson a convinced *anti*-Zionist. See Snetsinger, *Truman*, pp. 35–39. Snetsinger (pp. 68–69) thinks that the U.S. delegation did not really twist arms on this occasion. He seems to be relying on the testimony of delegates

whose arms were successfully twisted. Truman, in his memoirs, expresses pious horror at Zionist suggestions that the U.S. should apply pressure to other U.N. delegates. "Some were even suggesting that we pressure sovereign states into favorable votes in the General Assembly. . . . No American policy worthy of the name will ever treat any other nation as a satellite." (*Memoirs*, II, p. 132.) "You could have fooled me" has to be the reaction of anyone who has ever represented a small nation at the U.N.

179. Quoted in Lucas, *Modern History of Israel*, p. 248. [X] may be Moshe Sharett, soon to be Israel's first Foreign Minister.

180. Golda Meir complained (December 17, 1947): "The main activity of the Government has been directed at weakening the standing force of the Jews through searches of arms and almost daily arrests. . . ." (Bethell, p. 352.)

181. This does not require us to assume that the Government in question either intended, or would have acquiesced in, the physical destruction of the Palestine Jewish community. On the above hypothesis, some form of British intervention, to save the defeated Jews, concentrated in the coastal strip, would seem a probable prelude to a "White Paper" solution: a Palestinian State, tied by treaty to Britain, with guarantees for the Jewish community. What the guarantees would have been worth is another matter. However, the political leaders (as distinct from officials) may not have entertained any such ideas. As far as Bevin is concerned, his biographer states that "the last thing Bevin wanted" was for the British "to have to rescue the country on their own terms." (Bullock, p. 560.)

182. Bethell, *Palestine Triangle*, p. 353.

183. Begin, *The Revolt*, pp. 225–227.

184. "Probably with truth," says Sykes (*Crossroads to Israel*, p. 416), as far as the advance warning is concerned.

185. Kirk, *Survey of International Affairs: The Middle East, 1949–50*, p. 263.

186. Sykes, *Crossroads to Israel*, p. 417.

187. Weisgal and Carmichael (eds.), *Chaim Weizmann*, p. 304.

188. Truman, *Years of Trial and Hope*, pp. 171–172.

189. See Schlesinger and Israel (eds.), *American Presidential Elections*, pp. 3110–3111. Truman's problem was not so much how to attract Jewish votes as to how to stop losing them to rivals—Wallace and Dewey—who were competing for them with a vigor uninhibited by the responsibilities of office. In the event, Truman lost in the state—New York—where there were most Jewish votes. But Truman is believed to have held 60–75 percent of the Jewish vote. If he had held significantly less—especially in the three key states of Ohio, California and Illinois, all with large Jewish communities—he could hardly have achieved his very narrow victory over Dewey. It looks therefore as if he would have lost if he had stuck much longer to "trusteeship" as against partition in Palestine. Weizmann's call may have come in the nick of time, for Truman. See Snetsinger, *Truman*, p. 133.

190. Truman, ibid.

191. According to Margaret Truman (*Harry S. Truman*, p. 388), "the President scrawled on his calendar for March 19 the complaint that 'the State Department has reversed my Palestine policy' "—that is, the policy he had himself adopted under Weizmann's influence the day before, reversing his

previous policy. But the scrawl is of great interest, as contemporary evidence of Weizmann's mesmeric powers over a President's conception of what his own policy was.

192. Weisgal and Carmichael (eds.), *Chaim Weizmann*, p. 307.

193. On the same day, Eleanor Roosevelt offered her resignation from the U.S. delegation to the U.N. over the Palestine trusteeship question. This move must have reinforced Weizmann's diplomacy.

194. Weisgal and Carmichael (eds.), *Chaim Weizmann*, p. 310.

195. Ibid.

196. The U.S. delegation at the U.N., along with the other delegates, learned of this decision from the public ticker tape of the wire services.

5: THE YEAR ONE

1. Glubb, *Soldier with the Arabs*, p. 66.

2. Kirkbride, *Crackle of Thorns*, p. 2.

3. Kimche, *Both Sides of the Hill*, p. 107. The Kimche account is, however, questioned by some other authorities.

4. Kenneth Harris, *Attlee*, p. 390. This may be something of an overstatement, but the general trend of official advice seems to have been in that direction.

5. Sharef, *Three Days*, p. 289. Strangely, Ahad Ha'am had used almost the same phrase about his own feelings amid the exaltation of the First Zionist Congress, fifty years before.

6. Lorch's *Edge of the Sword* is a very full account by a military historian. There is a shorter, but still detailed, account in *Arab-Israeli Wars*, by Chaim Herzog.

7. Nasser, *The Truth about the Palestine War* (Cairo, 1956); quoted in Sachar, *Europe Leaves*, p. 337. Nasser had, however, an interest in stressing Egypt's unpreparedness under a predecessor regime.

8. "The Arab side" is, however, something of an oversimplification. Britain did not want to offend any of the Arab states, but this was difficult, since the objectives of the states in question were different, and sometimes incompatible.

9. See the article "The United Nations and Palestine," by J. C. Hurewitz, in Frye (ed.), *Near East*.

10. These did not include Glubb himself, who had retired from the British Army.

11. Kurzman, *Genesis 1948*, pp. 457–486. This account is confirmed by an Israeli authority on the period (in a private communication to the author).

12. Quoted in Bell, *Terror out of Zion*, p. 326.

13. There are interesting parallels and divergences between the shelling of the *Altalena* and the shelling of the Four Courts in Dublin in 1922, the incident with which the Irish Civil War (1922–1923) began. In both cases, the Government of a new State was trying to assert its authority against a section of those who had fought to bring the State into being, but who now rejected the form taken by the new State, and particularly its boundaries. But unlike Begin, Eamon de Valera, the most prominent figure on the dissident side, threw in his lot with those who continued to resist the Government, in arms, after the shelling of the Four Courts. It would be

unwise to conclude that Begin was more moderate than de Valera—whom, incidentally, Begin greatly admired. The basic difference lay in the situation of the two countries. The Irish Free State, unlike the State of Israel, did not lie, at the time, under any grave *external* threat to its existence.

14. Bernadotte, *To Jerusalem*.

15. Truman's ambassador to Israel, James G. McDonald, described Bernadotte as "charming, public-spirited, wholly devoted but not unusually able or perceptive." (*Mission in Israel,* p. 65.)

16. Bernadotte, *To Jerusalem*, p. 209. Actually, Sharett was a gentle and long-suffering person. Bernadotte should have met Ussishkin!

17. See my *To Katanga and Back*. It was Dr. Bunche who (in effect) fired me from U.N. service, in December 1961. But I bore him no hard feelings; in his shoes, I would have fired me too.

18. Glubb, *Soldier with the Arabs,* p. 152.

19. The article from which this passage is taken first appeared in the Beirut periodical *al-Manaqif*. The English translation appeared in the *Jerusalem Quarterly* (no. 4, Summer 1977) under the title "Alienation and Revolution in Arab Life."

20. For example, in the stylish polemic of Said, *Question of Palestine,* the refugees are all invariably "driven out." For the subsequent fate of the refugees, see below, Chapter 9.

21. Lucas, *Modern History of Israel,* p. 253.

22. Quoted in Sachar, *Europe Leaves,* p. 554.

23. As Jerusalem was not among the "areas allotted to the Jews," under the General Assembly resolution, it was not internationally considered part of the new State, and Ben-Gurion had up to this point been sufficiently sensitive to international opinion to refrain from asserting jurisdiction even over that part of Jerusalem held by the Jews.

24. The Negev also attracted Ben-Gurion because he dreamed of making it bloom, and because it was sparsely populated.

25. Kirk, *Middle East, 1945–1950,* pp. 143–147 and 292–293.

26. Richard Crossman states that Bevin "personally ordered" these planes "into combat." (*A Nation Reborn,* p. 72.) Bevin's biographer finds "no evidence" for this assertion. (Bullock, *Ernest Bevin,* p. 650.) Whatever the truth about "combat," recent scholarship makes it clear that Bevin was involved in military activity to an extent unusual for a Foreign Secretary. According to Louis, *British Empire,* p. 565, Bevin "had been supervising the reconnaissance flights as a quasi-commander-in-chief."

27. Crossman, *A Nation Reborn,* p. 72.

28. *Hansard,* Vol. 460, Col. 926, Jan. 26, 1949.

29. This reflection seems all the more untimely in that Truman had just been re-elected President, contrary to Bevin's hope and expectation. In the course of the debate, Richard Crossman took up the point Bevin was hinting at: "The point that there are so few Jews here that they can be safely disregarded, electorally, does not make us moral and the Americans immoral, for having regard to the Jewish vote." (Col. 957.)

30. Churchill's revulsion against the Jews, after the murder of Lord Moyne, and his subsequent acquiescence (in opposition) to the Government's course contributed in some degree to the "astounding mishandling" of which he now complained.

31. Kurzman, *Genesis 1948,* p. 687.

32. Tibouri, *Modern History of Syria,* p. 382.

6: HOLOCAUST IN MIND

1. Vera Weizmann, *Impossible Takes Longer*, p. 245; diary entry for Jan. 29, 1949.

2. Quoted in Wallenrod, *Literature of Modern Israel*, p. 213.

3. Quoted by Ben-Ezer in "War and Siege in Israeli Literature," in *Jerusalem Quarterly*, no. 2 (Winter 1977), p. 103.

4. Oz, in the collection *Where Jackals Howl*.

5. "Hirbeth Hiz'eh"; passage translated in Ben-Ezer, "War and Siege in Israeli Literature," in *Jerusalem Quarterly*, no. 2 (Winter 1977), p. 95.

6. Translated in Ben-Ezer, "War and Siege in Hebrew Literature," in *Jerusalem Quarterly*, no. 9 (Fall 1978).

7. Applefeld, "1946"; English translation in *Jerusalem Quarterly*, no. 7 (Spring 1978).

8. Phrase quoted by J. L. Talmon in *Jerusalem Quarterly*, no. 3 (Spring 1977), p. 4. I take the feminine form, in the French, to be required by the gender of French *nation*.

9. Alexander, commenting on Abba Kovner's "My Little Sister," in *Midstream*, October 1977.

10. Gertz, "Israeli Novelists," in *Jerusalem Quarterly*, no. 17 (Fall 1980), p. 77.

11. Sperber, "The Ending Aftermath," in *Wiener Library Bulletin*, Vol. XXV; new series, nos. 24/25; 1972.

12. It was a matter of prominence—or salience or "visibility"—rather than power and influence. Jews had no influence in German banking and heavy industry, for example, though anti-semites said they had.

13. See Talmon, "Seedbed of the Holocaust," in *Yad Vashem*. Among other instances of left-wing anti-semitism, Professor Talmon quotes a Socialist member of the Reichstag on Jewish smugglers: "These parasites . . . must be wiped off the face of the earth."

14. Herman, "In the Shadow of the Holocaust," in *Jerusalem Quarterly*, no. 3 (Spring 1977). Those who said "some countries" had in mind principally the Arab countries and the Soviet Union.

15. Ibid.

16. University training follows a long period of military service.

17. It was Imperial Germany that saved the Jews of Palestine during the First World War. But anti-semitism was already very strong in Germany, especially in the last year of the war.

18. Oz, *Touch the Water*.

19. Gertz, "Israeli Novelists," in *Jerusalem Quarterly*, no. 17 (Fall 1980).

20. Kovner, "My Little Sister," in *Canopy in the Desert*.

21. Alexander, "Abba Kovner, Poet of Holocaust and Rebirth," in *Midstream* (October 1977).

22. Gilboa, *Songs* (1953); translated and quoted by Dan Laor, "Vehicle of Parody," in *Jerusalem Quarterly*, no. 5 (Fall 1977).

23. Vinner, "Jerusalem" and "In the Wardrobe"; translated in *Jerusalem Quarterly*, no. 10 (Winter 1979).

24. Shahar, the last story in the collection *Stories from Jerusalem*.

25. Stern, "Stopgap Litter," in Dennis Silk (ed.), *Fourteen Israeli Poets*.

26. Oz, *Elsewhere, Perhaps.*

27. Oz, *Unto Death.*

28. Oz, *Hill of Evil Counsel.*

29. Ben-Ezer, "War and Siege in Israeli Literature," in *Jerusalem Quarterly,* no. 2 (Winter 1977).

30. Treinin, "Gates," in *Jerusalem Quarterly,* no. 17 (Fall 1980).

31. Alexander, "Abba Kovner," in *Midstream* (October 1977). This is a valuable explication of what is—to an outside, Gentile reader like myself especially—some very difficult poetry.

32. Gertz, "Israeli Novelists," in *Jerusalem Quarterly,* no. 17 (Fall 1980), referring specifically to the stories "The Battle of Fort William," by Eitan Notev, and "Late Love," by Amos Oz.

33. One of the two stories which make up the volume *Unto Death.*

34. But see Chapter 7.

35. Said, *Question of Palestine;* Hadawi, *Bitter Harvest.*

36. Israelis of European origin are more inclined to accept this than Oriental Jews.

37. For Arab writers, writing for Western audiences, Haj Amin has become a nonperson. Said and Hadawi both leave him out, though they include people of vastly less significance in the history of Arab Palestine.

38. Whether this is true of "most Arabs" would be hard to say. But certainly those (other than certain intellectuals and propagandists) who are most hostile to the Jewish State are equally hostile to its inhabitants, naturally enough.

39. Herman, "In the Shadow of the Holocaust," in *Jerusalem Quarterly,* no. 3 (Spring 1977).

40. Perhaps as a result of European efforts to placate Arab opinion in the wake of the Yom Kippur War of 1973.

41. See Ben-Ezer, "War and Siege in Hebrew Literature," in *Jerusalem Quarterly,* no. 9 (Fall 1978).

42. Ben-Ezer, ibid., summarizing Yaoz-Kest, in *Jerusalem Quarterly,* no. 9 (Fall 1978).

43. A reader may wonder where the citizens of the Republic of Ireland fit in, in relation to the Palestinian Arab–Northern Irish comparison. I think the people of the Republic are rather like Israel's Arab neighbors. In principle, and rhetoric, they sympathize with the Northern Catholics (Palestinians). In practice, they generally put their own interests first, but with flickers to the contrary whenever that film is rerun.

7: THE SECOND ISRAEL

1. The two sets of people are often referred to as Ashkenazim and Sephardim, after the branches of Judaism to which most of them belonged. As some of the European Jews belong to the Sephardic branch, by their traditions, and as the present perceived differences between the two main groups have much more to do with the social and cultural context of their regions of origin than with any difference in forms of religious observance, I prefer the "geographical" terms—even though "Oriental" is a bit strained by the inclusion of the Maghreb. I am following the usage which applies "Oriental" to all Jews from Muslim countries.

2. Before the Common Era.

3. But there was also an ancient and numerous settled Jewish community in Spain, at least since Roman times.

4. Raphael Patai, "Western and Oriental Culture in Israel," in Curtis and Chertoff (eds.), *Israel*.

5. Hadawi, *Bitter Harvest*, pp. 12–13.

6. *Encyclopaedia Britannica*, 11th ed.: "Turkey."

7. See Littman, "Jews under Muslim Rule in the Late Nineteenth Century," in *Wiener Library Bulletin*, 28 (n.s. 35/36), 1975.

8. Landshut, *Jewish Communities*, p. 18.

9. Ibid. In relation to a Western-inspired injunction of the Sultan of Morocco in 1902, "to treat the Jews with justice," Landshut describes Muslim reaction as "both bewildered and haughtily resentful."

10. It may be worth noting that the Almoravides were not Arabs but Berber Muslims. Other Muslims who persecuted Jews and Christians—the Mameluke rulers of late-medieval Egypt—were themselves the descendants of Christians, forcibly converted to Islam.

11. Lewis, *"L'Islam et les Non-Musulmans,"* in *Annales: Économies, Sociétés, Civilisations*.

12. Ibid.

13. The Ottoman Sultan had earlier decreed equal rights, but the Sultan's writ did not run in Northern Africa.

14. *Encyclopaedia Judaica:* "Purim" and "Purims."

15. Ibid.: "Morocco."

16. Luks, "Iraqi Jews during World War II," in *Wiener Library Bulletin*, (No. XXX (43/44).

17. *Encyclopaedia Judaica:* "Morocco." "Fanaticized" or not, the Moroccans were right about the Jews being agents of European influence. However, see David Littman's recent article "Mission to Morocco (1863–64)," in Lipman (eds.), *Sir Moses Montefiore*.

18. See Lewis, *"L'Islam et les Non-Musulmans,"* in *Annales: Économies, Sociétés, Civilisations*, p. 797.

19. See Littman, "Jews under Muslim Rule, Morocco 1903–1912," in *Wiener Library Bulletin*, 29 (37/38), 1976. V. D. Segre, in *Israel*, writes (p. 124): "No one can compare the Arab violence against the Jews in the Arab world to even the mildest Russian pogroms." But these words were written some years before the publication of the results of Dr. Littman's researches in the archives of the Alliance Israelite Universelle. Dr. Littman's documents show that one of the Moroccan massacres (Settat) was as bad as, and another (Fez) worse than, even the worst of all the Russian pogroms, that at Kishinev in 1903.

20. Landshut, *Jewish Communities*, p. 23.

21. Or "Regions of War."

22. Rahman, *Islam*, introduction.

23. O.S.S. Report of Feb. 3, 1945; quoted in Luks, "Iraqi Jews during World War II," in *Wiener Library Bulletin*, No. XXX (43/44), 1977.

24. Ye'or, "Aspects of the Arab-Israeli Conflict," in *Wiener Library Bulletin*, No. XXXII (49/50), 1979.

25. Only 5,000 to Israel.

26. It may be asked why, if so, the Moroccan Jews did not leave earlier. The answer appears to be that once the French protectorate was established (1912), Jews felt safe in the settled areas of Morocco. After the

Second World War, however, French influence was clearly on the wane. The Sultan had demanded independence in 1947. He got it nine years later.

27. Orthodox Russian resentment of the West centered on Imperial Germany, the nearest and most obnoxious of the Western countries, the one to which Russian Jews looked for education and social advancement, the one of whose language they spoke a dialect (Yiddish) and the protector of the Russian (and Oriental) Jews during the First World War. Muslim resentment was primarily directed at Britain and France. But "the West" in both cases stood for the same value system: congenial to many Jews—sometimes in itself, sometimes simply because of its social and political consequences—and profoundly uncongenial to Orthodoxy and Islam, both in itself and because of its consequences.

28. Eisenstadt, *Absorption of Immigrants.*

29. The fifth *aliyah,* or at least its German component, constituted a separate elite of its own. Probably the most "cross-representative" and least elite was the fourth *aliyah,* mainly from Poland.

30. Ye'or, "Zionism in Islamic Lands, the Case of Egypt," in *Wiener Library Bulletin,* No. XXX (43/44), 1977.

31. Herzl was almost comically dejudaized in the eyes of Eastern European intellectual Zionists, yet he had an appeal to the fundamentalist masses that was never matched by any of the Eastern European intellectuals.

32. Quoted in Smooha, *Israel,* p. 89. Professor Smooha is quoting from "a respectable Hebrew daily" which he does not otherwise identify.

33. Smooha, *Israel,* p. 88; quoting "one well-meaning Ashkenazi apologist for the Orientals."

34. Ibid.

35. Actually Mrs. Meir, who was talking to Eastern European Jews at the time, doesn't seem to have been thinking about the Orientals at all. "I didn't mean that for every Jew," she explained later. "I meant it for the Ashkenazi." She was contributing to a long-standing family dispute, among Zionists of European origin, about the use of Yiddish. But the ease with which she forgot about the Orientals, while generalizing about Jews, was in itself significant. See Henry Toledano, "Time to Stir the Melting Pot," in Curtis and Chertoff (eds.), *Israel.*

36. Celia S. Heller writes: "In Israel the European Jews are increasingly rationalizing and justifying their behavior toward the Oriental Jews by invoking 'culturalism,' to coin a phrase, the idea of culturally inherited superiority and inferiority. It differs from racism, which invokes biologically inherited superiority and inferiority." ("The Emerging Consciousness of the Ethnic Problem among the Jews of Israel," in Curtis and Chertoff [eds.], *Israel,* p. 320.

37. Peres, "Ethnic Relations in Israel," in *American Journal of Sociology,* Vol. 46, No. 6. Actually the figures cited generally suggest that the prejudice in question is slightly *higher* among Orientals. Thus a question put was: "Some people say that for prejudice to be abolished, Orientals must rid themselves of their shortcomings. What's your opinion?" Of the Oriental respondents, 25 percent "definitely agreed" as against 23 percent of the Europeans. Thirty-four percent of Orientals and thirty-nine percent of Europeans "disagreed."

38. There is the view that they would not have had to take refuge at all if the fortress had not been established. But see above, Section III.

39. Smooha, *Israel,* pp. 228–229.

40. Quoted in Celia S. Heller, "The Emerging Consciousness of the Ethnic Problem among the Jews of Israel," in Curtis and Chertoff (eds.), *Israel*. Dr. Heller disagrees, saying, ". . . I think that real peace would not lead to civil war or an eventual split but would lead to structural integration through the destruction of ethnic stratification." Before that proposition can be put to the test, structural integration seems likely to be far advanced, if not completed.

41. Erik Cohen, "The Black Panthers and Israeli Society," in *The Jewish Journal of Sociology*. This is my source for the epigraph to this chapter, for which I thank Professor Cohen.

42. Ibid.

43. Isaac, *Party and Politics*, Chapter 7, "The Nonideological Challenge," p. 291.

44. Ibid., p. 194.

45. Shlomo Avineri, "Israel: Two Nations?" in Curtis and Chertoff (eds.), *Israel*.

46. Isaac, *Party and Politics*, p. 195.

47. Ibid. It is only fair to add that Mr. Isaac is a well-known supporter of Likud.

48. Diary entry quoted in Kurzman, *Ben-Gurion*, p. 430.

49. Peres, "Ethnic Relations in Israel," in *American Journal of Sociology*. Table 12: "Prejudice against Arabs: A Comparison between Oriental and European Respondents." Oddly enough, on one important matter, Orientals showed themselves more "pro-Arab" than Europeans. Very few Jews of either group asserted willingness to marry an Arab, but more Orientals (11 percent) did so than Europeans (9 percent).

50. Dutter, "Eastern and Western Jews: Ethnic Divisions in Israeli Society," in *Middle East Journal*. The size of the gap may partly be accounted for by cultural linguistics. The Europeans would be inhibited, culturally, from sounding "aggressive" but Orientals would not.

51. Smooha, *Israel*, p. 104.

52. Peres, "Ethnic Relations in Israel," in *American Journal of Sociology*. Peres offers a table—Table 14—showing that the more Orientals look and sound like Arabs, the more extreme the anti-Arab sentiments they are likely to express.

53. Shlomo Avineri, "Israel: Two Nations?" in Curtis and Chertoff (eds.), *Israel*.

54. Peres, "Ethnic Relations in Israel," in *American Journal of Sociology*. Table 12.

55. And Orientals joined enthusiastically in the welcome for Sadat when he came to Jerusalem.

56. See Chapter 10.

8: DIPLOMACY AND WAR (1948–1967)

1. Interview with a German journalist; quoted in Safran, *From War to War*, p. 39.

2. The formula became familiar only at a later date, but the idea itself was inherently present from the time of the creation of the State.

3. It did produce a thing called the Lausanne Protocol (May 12, 1949), subsequently invoked, by participants, for various debating pur-

poses. But the protocol was no more than an agenda and "basis for discussion," and remained without practical sequel. The main interest of the protocol today is that it shows the extreme anxiety of Israel's negotiators, at this time, to get a settlement with Israel's neighbors. Israel, as well as the Arabs, "agreed to accept the United Nations partition resolution [of November 1947] as a basis for discussing the boundaries question, after Israel had undertaken to take back 100,000 refugees as a good-will gesture prior to any negotiation of the refugee question." (Safran, *From War to War*, p. 36.) If the Arab states had taken that up, and Israel had stuck to it, the subsequent "basis for discussion," within Israel, might have caused trouble for Ben-Gurion's Government. But once more, the Arabs let Israel off the hook.

4. Moshe Dayan, *Story of My Life*, pp. 114–115. However, I am informed by Yehoshua Freundlich, assistant general editor of the *Documents of the Foreign Policy of Israel*, Israel State Archives, that archival material recently declassified shows that the British actively supported the Israeli-Jordanian negotiations.

5. *Jerusalem Post*, Dec. 12, 1949; quoted in Brecher, *Israel's Foreign Policy*, p. 31. If Ben-Gurion had made such a declaration at any time before Nov. 29, 1947, the historic resolution legitimizing the Jewish State could not have had a majority.

6. There was also a Catholic lobby—headed by Cardinal Spellman—to be thought about. But such a lobby gets results only if people really care about the subject of its exertions. In comparison with the intensity of Jewish emotional commitment to Jerusalem, Catholic concern for that city is a pretty pale, theoretical thing. No American President would be left long in doubt about that. The U.S. Catholic lobby is formidable in certain areas—in relation to Communist regimes in particular—but not in relation to Palestine.

7. The stages of its withering may be followed in Brecher, *Israel's Foreign Policy*, pp. 33–34. Israel did not transfer its Foreign Office to Jerusalem until it was satisfied that the withering had reached a sufficiently advanced stage: July 13, 1953.

8. As indicated elsewhere, this is not a history of Israel but an outline account of a siege. The distinction would not be tenable, in the case of anything more than an outline, since the whole history of Israel, in both its internal and external relations, cannot be understood except in the context of a siege. I am trying here to establish the general pattern of that siege, in terms of external relations, taking no more account of internal relations and developments than seems strictly necessary for a consideration of the external aspects.

9. On independence, the State of Israel modeled its democracy mainly on the British parliamentary system: the only form with which the founders, born within the Empire of the tsars, had had much personal contact. But Ben-Gurion's personal authority was of presidential, rather than prime-ministerial, order.

10. It was not in the power of Israel to avert the passage of a resolution, in the circumstances. That was possible only if the United States was prepared to "twist arms" of Latin-American and other delegates, as in November 1947. But no American President, with Catholic voters to think about, would try to twist Catholic arms at the U.N. on a religious issue, with the Pope twisting them the other way.

11. Brecher, *Israel's Foreign Policy*, p. 30.

12. I am informed by Yehoshua Freundlich that "in spite of many Israeli scholars' efforts to trace this expression in Ben-Gurion's writings and speeches, nobody to date has been able to furnish the source." Hardly surprising—it sounds like the sort of off-the-cuff comment that gets remembered without being written down or publicly proclaimed.

13. In Ben-Gurion's attitude to Sharett there seems to have been a trace—no more—of the attitude of Amos Oz's superhawk "Z" toward his dovish interlocutor. "I'll wipe out the Arab villages and you can hold protest demonstrations and write the epitaphs. You'll be the family's honor and I'll be the stain on the family's honor. Be my guest. Is it a deal?" (*In the Land of Israel*, p. 98.)

14. He was of course disappointed in that last hope, and his eagerness for the promotion of his young favorites—who included, as well as Dayan, Shimon Peres, later leader of the Labor Party and now Prime Minister—may not have helped his protégés as much as he hoped it would.

15. "There are hawks in dove's feathers," wrote Abba Eban, "and there are doves in hawk's feathers." Eban was hinting at his own inclusion in the first class, and he may have meant to include Dayan in the second. In reality these two brilliant men were very much alike, in quality of mind and in outlook, though not in style or appearance. That ornithological metaphor is often unhelpful. `

16. The Oriental children in the classrooms of Israel would have known that manner all too well.

17. Dayan, *Story of My Life*, p. 109.

18. Nasser is said to have told an emissary of Ben-Gurion's that "he did not want what happened to Abdullah to happen to him: and the only charge against Abdullah had been that he had held negotiations. . . . Four times . . . he mentioned the murder of Abdullah. . . ." (Ben-Gurion, *Talks with Arab Leaders*, pp. 298, 313.)

19. Dayan, *Story of My Life*, p. 134.

20. Brecher, *Israel's Foreign Policy*, p. 113.

21. Ibid.

22. Safran, *From War to War*, p. 48; Brecher, *Israel's Foreign Policy*, p. 219. Meir Avidan, in his essay "Main Facets of American-Israeli Relations in the 1950s," lists a number of examples of "nonaligned" voting by Israel at the U.N. during the Korean War. But it is clear that these voting positions were essentially vestiges of a *previous* nonaligned policy: rays from a dead star.

23. The decision to send in forces to South Korea, to resist the North Korean invaders, was made in Washington, D.C., the only place where such a decision could be made. The United States then took advantage of a temporary Soviet absence from the Security Council to get the Council's blessing for its war, and then—when the Soviets returned and challenged the legality of that procedure—got their blessing from the General Assembly, where the United States, at that time, could control a safe two-thirds of the vote. All this enabled the United States to present itself as acting "at the behest" of the world body, which had in fact acted at the behest of the United States. The United Nations may well owe its survival to its almost infinite capacity for making something look like something quite different.

24. Israel did make a rather feeble effort to reassure the Soviets that "nonidentification" was still in being. The assurance was conveyed, in Feb-

ruary 1952, that Israel "would not join any aggressive bloc against the Soviet Union." But the Soviet Union well knew that the reason Israel would not join the "aggressive bloc" they had in mind was that the aggressive bloc in question would not let Israel in. Any regional bloc would have to be composed mainly of Arabs.

25. The "friends of Ireland" have a particular problem, since 1922, in that they tend to be alienated, by pro-I.R.A. sentiment, from the actual Government of the Republic of Ireland. The "friends of Israel," on the other hand, have remained close to the Government of Israel. On the other hand, in the period 1946–1948, Zionists were powerfully conscious of the precedent of American support for Ireland in 1919–1921—a precedent which the British appear to have forgotten.

26. Tillman, *United States in the Middle East,* Chapter Two, "American Interests and the American Political System," p. 54. This chapter also contains (p. 65) an account of the manifold "operating arms" of the pro-Israel lobby. Tillman lists these, including the American Israel Public Affairs Committee (AIPAC); the Conference of Presidents of Major Jewish Organizations, "which tends to concentrate its efforts on the White House and the State Department while AIPAC works on Congress"; the American Jewish Committee; the Anti-Defamation League of B'nai B'rith; "and not least the Israeli Embassy." ("Embassy lobbying," previously discouraged, was successfully pioneered by the Washington embassies of Israel and of the Republic of China, from 1948 on.) "Associated with these collective efforts is the individual work of myriads of dedicated individuals, including well-placed congressional aides."

27. Some reservations are expressed about this phenomenon. At a conference on anti-semitism (at Rutgers University, New Brunswick, New Jersey, in November 1983), a rapporteur said that the "traditional indices"—based on neighborhood, employment, intermarriage, etc.—may not pick up the growth of an anti-semitism which is professedly and even fastidiously *anti*-anti-semitic, and which operates under the guise of the "anti-Zionism" of, for example, the student Left. This seems overanxious, as far as America is concerned. Anti-Zionism, coming from the Left—and with vociferous Soviet agreement—may actually be a bonus for the pro-Israel lobby, and a reducer of anti-semitism.

28. Tillman, *United States in the Middle East,* p. 64.

29. The commitment to partnership with the United States has led Governments of Israel to involve themselves in "aid programs" to unsavory regimes favored by the United States in Latin America and elsewhere. Such programs have increased Israel's unpopularity in the Third World.

30. The Poles and the Irish acquired States of their own after the mass migrations to America, but they never ceased to hold a *national territory* ("old country") of their own even under foreign rule. But the "old country" of the Jews was not among the countries from which they streamed to America.

31. For a careful statement of the gentlemanly view, see Tillman, *United States in the Middle East,* passim.

32. Eban, *Autobiography,* p. 161.

33. Tillman, *United States in the Middle East,* p. 69. An Arab writer concurs: "The oil companies do not exert any significant pressure or have any significant effect on U.S. Middle East policy." (Shadid, *United States and the Palestinians,* p. 165, n. 1.)

34. Seale, *Struggle for Syria*, p. 191.

35. Brecher, *Israel's Foreign Policy*, p. 229.

36. Ibid., p. 246.

37. Eban, *Autobiography*, p. 173.

38. This was the so-called "Lavon Affair." Whether the eponymous Minister for Defense actually knew about it all, or whether it was ordered by Moshe Dayan, or carried out by Dayan's subordinates without his knowledge, never became clear. The "Affair" gave rise to many years of reverberations and recriminations in the internal politics of Israel. Fortunately, these do not concern us here. What seems surprising, in retrospect, is that this operation did so *little* damage to relations between Israel and America. Perhaps there is an unsung triumph here for the "pro-Israel lobby" in relation to the media.

39. Quoted in Eban, *Autobiography*, p. 183.

40. Vatikiotis, *Conflict*, p. 138.

41. Dayan, *Story of My Life*, p. 146.

42. Eban, *Autobiography*, p. 205. The people who opposed "for other reasons" included congressmen from the southern "cotton belt who objected to proposals which would have the effect of increasing a competitor's production."

43. Ibid.

44. The near-paranoid mood of French opinion on this point is reflected in the fact that even Albert Camus attributed France's Algerian troubles to "the imperialism of Cairo."

45. Dayan, *Story of My Life*, p. 149.

46. Ibid., p. 175.

47. Quoted in Brecher, *Israel's Foreign Policy*, p. 248.

48. Brecher, *Israel's Foreign Policy*, p. 277.

49. Ireland had been admitted to the United Nations in the previous year.

50. Dayan, *Story of My Life*, p. 209.

51. Brecher, *Israel's Foreign Policy*, pp. 285–286.

52. Ibid., p. 285.

53. Ibid., p. 282.

54. Ibid., p. 286.

55. Ibid., p. 287.

56. And with no reward in terms of Arab goodwill. Rafik Halabi, writing more than twenty years later, provides a sample of the impression left in the Arab folk memory by America's role at Suez. "The Americans arrange everything," a Jerusalem Arab told Halabi. "In '56 they sent the British and the French to wallop Egypt." (*West Bank Story*, p. 97.)

57. Arab Governments sometimes claimed that they had no control over the *fedayeen*, but this does not seem to have been true, at least as far as Nasser's Egypt is concerned. Robert Stephens, Nasser's sympathetic English biographer, uses the revealing words (referring to the immediate aftermath of the nationalization of the Suez Canal Company): "[Nasser] tried to keep the border with Israel quiet. The *fedayin* were called off for the time being." (*Nasser*, p. 209.) What can be called off can be called on.

58. Sachar, *History of Israel*, pp. 622–623.

59. The same principles apply to the closure of the Suez Canal. But Israel was not in possession of the Canal, and so could not make its re-

opening a condition of withdrawal. "One thing at a time" has been Israel's guiding principle.

60. Eban, *Autobiography*, p. 250.

61. Meir, *My Life* (Dell paperback ed.), p. 295. Abba Eban in his *Autobiography* (p. 258) has a detailed, positive—and objective—assessment of the same arrangements. The experienced memoir reader will infer that it was the then ambassador, and not the then Foreign Minister, who did the work, and deserves the credit.

62. In Israel itself, Eban has been a victim of that form of detraction which superficially looks like praise. Golda Meir spoke of his "eloquence"; Ben-Gurion, at a Mapai rally in Tel Aviv, called Eban "the greatest spokesman for our nation's cause since Weizmann." Eban's biographer, Robert St. John, tells us that Eban "silently suffered" on learning of this tribute. He recognized it as a double belittlement, downgrading Israel's two great diplomatists into mere "spokesmen": Ben-Gurion's barkers.

63. Laqueur, *History of Israel*, p. 528.

64. See Schueftan, "Nasser's 1967 Policy Reconsidered," in *Jerusalem Quarterly*, p. 129. Nasser played a leading role in the initiative in 1964 to set up the P.L.O. (which was structured from the start so as to insure full Egyptian supervision) with the aim of insuring the neutralization of any independent Palestinian action. See below, Chapter 9.

65. Brecher, *Israel's Foreign Policy*, p. 310. Professor Brecher prefers the earlier policy of nonalignment, *ee-hizdahut*.

66. Sachar, *History of Israel*, p. 558.

67. Brecher, *Israel's Foreign Policy*, p. 67.

68. Sachar, *History of Israel*, p. 560.

69. Dan Schueftan's useful concept. Of the workings of the system, from the mid-fifties on, P. J. Vatikiotis has this to say. "Even though individual Arab governments and their leaders were primarily concerned with the pursuit of state interests, they found it necessary to express their policies in terms of the nonexistent framework of the Arab nation." (*Conflict*, p. 89.) Among the results of this pursuit, thus expressed, Vatikiotis numbers "ideologically induced paralysis," subversion and unbridled propaganda, of which the Arabs "became the prisoner."

70. As Safran puts it, Syria at this time "became a vested interest for those [Soviet officials] who had staked their reputations on the policy of large-scale assistance." (*From War to War*, p. 276.)

71. Ibid., p. 274.

72. Brecher, *op. cit.*, p. 366, calls it "a serious blunder, of explosive proportions."

73. Safran, *From War to War*, p. 268.

74. Ibid., p. 308.

75. Brecher, *Israel's Foreign Policy*, p. 379.

76. Ibid., p. 380.

77. Ibid., p. 390.

78. As Prime Minister and Minister for Defense from 1963.

79. Brecher, *Israel's Foreign Policy*, pp. 414–417.

80. Ibid., p. 417.

81. In New York, the representative of Israel informed the president of the Security Council "that Egyptian land·and air forces had moved against Israel, whose armed forces were engaged in repelling the attack."

(*United Nations Yearbook, 1967*, p. 175.) No trace of this fiction now remains, except in United Nations records.

82. For a detailed account and analysis of the Six-Day War, see Herzog, *Arab-Israeli Wars*.

83. *United Nations Yearbook, 1967*, p. 191.

84. A resolution was passed calling on Israel not to "alter the status of Jerusalem," but did not specifically call on Israel to withdraw from East Jerusalem.

85. The nonpermanent members of the Council are elected by the Assembly; but the United States can exercise much more influence in the Assembly over practical and "silent" matters like elections than it can over public declarations. In 1967, there were no Arab members in the Council.

86. *United Nations Yearbook, 1967*, p. 254. Neither Israel nor Syria was a member of the Council; both were invited to address it.

9: THE SHIRT OF UTHMAN

1. The Israeli is David Glass, a contributor to the Jerusalem symposium *Every Sixth Israeli*, edited by Alouph Hareven. For "Uthman's Shirt," see the end of this chapter.

2. There is a small fourth group: the Arabs of East Jerusalem. Internationally, East Jerusalem is classed as part of the occupied territory. Under Israeli law, however, it is part of Israel, although its Arab inhabitants are citizens of Jordan.

3. Because the framing of such a constitution would have involved impossibly exhausting and unsettling debate between the religious and the secular components of the Jewish population.

4. For the tenuous—but significant in context—distinction between "State of Israel" and "the Jewish State," see pp. 421 ff.

5. Teddy Kollek, mayor of Jerusalem, has raised some funds among the Jewish Diaspora to be used for the benefit of Jerusalem Arabs.

6. Apparently this support went to Mapai as the principal governing party. Arab voters—like Oriental Jewish voters—had no previous experience of either democracy or the concept of "loyal opposition."

7. Quoted in Lustick, *Arabs in the Jewish State*, p. 66. A recent study shows that Ben-Gurion in the Mandate period devoted much time to exploring possibilities of a settlement with the Palestinian Arabs. But the talks led to nothing. By the time of the Arab Revolt (1936), Ben-Gurion was led by circumstances to adopt the language of force. (Teveth, *Ben-Gurion and the Palestinian Arabs*, p. 186.)

8. Quoted in Jiryis, *Arabs in Israel*, p. 45.

9. For Military Government generally, see Lustick, *Arabs in the Jewish State*, pp. 123–128; Sayigh, *Arabs in Israel*, pp. 9–29.

10. Lustick, *Arabs in the Jewish State*, p. 126, quoting an article in the newspaper *Davar*.

11. Jiryis, *Arabs in Israel*, p. 29.

12. Ibid., p. 79.

13. The story is told in ibid., p. 73.

14. The total amount of absentee land transferred under this law was about a quarter of a million acres. This included the *waqf* land.

15. In Hareven (ed.), *Every Sixth Israeli*, p. 93.

16. Landau, *Arabs in Israel*, p. 8. This historian does not mention the seizure of the assets of the *waqf* at all, though the transaction falls within the period of his study and has highly significant bearing on his subject. This is the first time the present writer has observed such a major omission of pertinent fact in the work of an Israeli historian. Generally speaking, Israel's historians, like its journalists, are publishers of inconvenient facts, and have therefore had to supply a certain amount of ammunition to hostile critics of Israel.

17. Lustick, *Arabs in the Jewish State*, p. 202.

18. Figures in Zureik, *Palestinians in Israel*, p. 108. There seems to be some doubt about the exact figures. Alouph Hareven, of the Van Leer Foundation, Jerusalem, gives a significantly smaller figure—156,000—for Arabs *remaining* than seems to follow from Zureik's figures.

19. Figures in Nakhleh and Zureik (eds.), *Sociology of the Palestinians*, p. 7. Presumably "Jerusalem" here is Jewish Jerusalem, not including East Jerusalem, in Jordanian hands from 1948 to 1967.

20. Quoted in Lustick, *Arabs in the Jewish State*, p. 48. One of Ben-Gurion's advisers on Arab affairs recalled that he received a lot more advice on that subject from the Prime Minister than he was allowed to offer.

21. Lustick, *Arabs in the Jewish State*, p. 121.

22. Quoted in Lustick, *Arabs in the Jewish State*, pp. 118–119.

23. Lustick, *Arabs in the Jewish State*, pp. 118–119.

24. Hareven (ed.), *Every Sixth Israeli*, p. 139.

25. Jiryis, *Arabs in Israel*, p. 169. The reference is to Herzl's Utopian Zionist novel, *Altneuland*.

26. Quoted in Zureik, *Palestinians in Israel*, p. 185. Husain had once been a moderate himself. He later became a P.L.O. official and was working for them in New York when he died, in 1971.

27. Lustick, *Arabs in the Jewish State*, pp. 244–250.

28. Hareven (ed.), *Palestinian Problem*, p. 185.

29. There also appear to be conflicting computations. According to a table in Zureik (*Palestinians in Israel*, p. 109), Arabs were 14.1 percent of the population in 1948, 15.1 percent in 1974: a rise of one percentile point in twenty-six years. According to contributors to the Van Leer Symposium, Hareven (ed.), *Every Sixth Israeli* (pp. 4, 18), the Arab proportion of the total population actually *fell* between 1948 and 1982, from 18 percent to 16 percent, though it then rose steeply. According to Professor Shmuel Toledano, Israeli Arabs were 12.2 percent of the population of Israel in 1948, 12.8 percent in 1982. Professor Toledano's reckoning excludes the Arabs of East Jerusalem, who are residents, but not citizens, of the State of Israel.

30. Hareven (ed.), *Every Sixth Israeli*.

31. Zureik, *Palestinians in Israel*, p. 153.

32. Hareven (ed.), *Every Sixth Israeli*, p. 22. Some critics allow Israel no credit for this development, which indeed is implicitly denied. Thus David Hirst, in the section "The Arabs Who Stayed Behind" of his book *The Gun and the Olive Branch*, has only this to say about Arab education in Israel: "Nor could parents, miserable though their own plight might be, look forward to a brighter future for children. The deliberate stunting of Arab education meant that there were about nine Jewish university graduates, *per capita* [*sic*], for every one Arab." (P. 193.) But the high propor-

tion of Jewish to Arab graduates does not have to be accounted for on the malign hypothesis of "deliberate stunting." When the State of Israel came into existence, Jewish education was already advanced while Arab education had not gotten beyond its original Ottoman levels. As the figures in the preceding paragraph indicate, the Israeli authorities, far from "deliberately stunting" Arab education, greatly stimulated its growth. It still lags far behind Jewish education, but there are signs of catching up.

33. Ibid., p. 136.

34. Fouzi el-Asmar; quoted in Lustick, *Arabs in the Jewish State*, p. 136.

35. Hareven (ed.), *Every Sixth Israeli*, pp. 75–76.

36. Ibid., pp. 114–115.

37. Baranski, "Story of a Palestinian," in *Journal of Palestinian Studies*.

38. Quoted in Zureik, *Palestinians in Israel*, p. 184.

39. Hareven (ed.), *Every Sixth Israeli*, p. 123.

40. Saad Sarsour, "Arab Education in a Jewish State," in Haleven (ed.), *Every Sixth Israeli*, p. 119.

41. Lustick, *Arabs in the Jewish State*, p. 23.

42. Hareven (ed.), *Every Sixth Israeli*, p. 45.

43. Jiryis gives the number at forty-nine, elsewhere at forty-seven; Lustick at forty-three; Landau says "a few."

44. This was brought out at the trials, by an Israeli Military Court, in 1959, of the officers and men involved. The report is quoted at length by Jiryis in a chapter, "From Deir Yasim to Kfar Kassim" (pp. 137–157), of his book *Arabs in Israel*.

45. Jiryis, *Arabs in Israel*, p. 67, does not suggest that the Israeli authorities were "overreacting" in this period. Indeed the chapter in question is entitled "The Velvet Glove."

46. Jalal Abu-Ta'ama, "Testimony of an Inhabitant of Baqa al-Gharbiya," in Hareven (ed.), *Every Sixth Israeli*.

47. Rafi Israeli, "Arabs in Israel: The Surge of a New Identity," in Hareven (ed.), *Every Sixth Israeli*.

48. Sammy Smooha, "Issues in Arab-Jewish Relations in Israel," in Hareven (ed.), *Every Sixth Israeli*, p. 109. Professor Smooha's remarks are based on an opinion survey conducted among Israeli Arabs in the summer of 1976. His optimistic interpretation of rather ambiguous data hardly seems to be borne out by the political manifestations which took place contemporaneously with the survey.

49. Lustick's phrase.

50. Jiryis, *Arabs in Israel*, p. 221.

51. Ibid., p. 69.

52. Halabi, *West Bank Story*, Chapter 11, "The Nazareth-Nablus Axis," p. 242. This chapter describes a fusion of feeling between Israeli Arabs and West Bank Arabs, setting in from 1973 on, and manifesting itself in open and combined defiance in 1976.

53. Hareven (ed.), *Every Sixth Israeli*, p. 109.

54. Ibid.

55. Ibid., p. 110.

56. Ibid., p. 202.

57. See the present writer's *Parnell and His Party*.

58. Hareven (ed.), *Every Sixth Israeli*, p. 176.

59. Ibid.

60. Moshe Arens, "A Jewish Problem," in Haleven (ed.), *Palestinian Problem*, pp. 181–186.

61. Hareven (ed.), *Every Sixth Israeli*, p. 206.

62. Ibid., p. 211. The remainder of Professor Porath's statement is directed to relations between Finns and Swedes in Finland: relations which he seems—or tries—to hope may provide a model for relations between Jews and Arabs in Israel. A weakness of Israel's doves is a tendency to lapse into wishful thinking.

63. For the status of this politicization in the mid-eighties, see Epilogue.

64. Benvenisti, "Jerusalem: Study of a Polarized Community," p. 36. The Data Project has published a valuable series of papers, some of which are cited below. Its publications are often highly critical, both implicitly and explicitly, of governmental policy and practice.

65. Various reasons could be assigned for this—e.g., absence of the "Irgun factor," speed and character of the military operation, lack of belief in Arab victory and of expectation of return—but these must remain speculative.

66. Gabatello, "The Population of the Administered Territories," West Bank Data Project, p. 9, Table 1. The population of Gaza was about the same as before the war; that of the West Bank had fallen by about 20 percent.

67. Halabi, *West Bank Story*, p. 77.

68. Ibid., p. 80.

69. See below, Chapter X, Section VIII.

70. Susser, "Jordanian Influence in the West Bank," in *Jerusalem Quarterly*, no. 8 (Summer 1978).

71. Ibid., p. 57.

72. Shehadeh, *The Third Way*.

73. Israeli statistics do not have an "Arab" category but distinguish "Jews" and "non-Jews"—and among non-Jews, Muslims, Christians and Druze.

74. Benvenisti, "The West Bank and Gaza Data Base Project Interim Report No. 1," p. 1.

75. Ibid., pp. 17–18.

76. Ibid., p. 12.

77. Ibid., p. 11.

78. Tamari, "Building Other People's Homes," in *Journal of Palestine Studies*, Vol. XI, no. 1 (Autumn 1981).

79. Halabi, *West Bank Story*, p. 88.

80. O'Neill, *Armed Struggle in Palestine*, p. 6.

81. Kampf, "Israeli Administration of the West Bank," in *International Problems* 16 (Spring 1977).

82. Ibid.

83. Harris, *Taking Root*, p. 36.

84. Quoted in Harris, *Taking Root*, p. 38.

85. Silver, *Begin*, p. 140.

86. Newman, *Jewish Settlement*, p. 28.

87. Ibid., p. 30.

88. Yaniv and Pascal, "Doves, Hawks and Other Birds of a Feather," in *British Journal of Political Science*, Vol. 10, 1980.

89. By this definition, Menachem Begin was a Militant Hawk; those to the right of him, Unconditional Hawks.

90. For the status of Allon Plan ideas in the mid-1980s, see Epilogue.

91. David Glass. "The Attitude of Judaism," in Hareven (ed.), *Every Sixth Israeli*, pp. 187–194. Glass's point is that the attitude of these settlers is *contrary* to true Judaism.

92. Figures (for 1975) in George Kossaifi, "Demographic Characteristics of the Palestinian People," in Nakhleh and Zureik (eds.), *Sociology of the Palestinians*, p. 27.

93. Turki, *The Disinherited*, p. 8.

94. Ibid., p. 41.

95. Ibid., pp. 53, 153.

96. Ibid., p. 77.

97. Sayigh, *Palestinians*, p. 10.

98. Ibid., p. 124.

99. Ibid., pp. 126–127.

100. Kiernan, *Yasser Arafat*.

101. Johnson, *Politics of Meaning*, pp. 80–81.

102. Gilmour, *Dispossessed*, p. 144.

103. Ibid.

104. See Kiernan, *Yasser Arafat*, p. 242; also Hirst, *Gun and the Olive Branch*, p. 275; Quandt, Jabber and Lesch, *Politics of Palestinian Nationalism*, p. 173. Kiernan discusses the Syrian connection at length (pp. 195–200). Some writers play down the Syrian connection; Gilmour ignores it completely, presenting the emergence of Fatah as primarily a Palestinian phenomenon, with only some encouragement from distant Algeria. (*Dispossessed*, p. 144.) But there seems to be no doubt that it was Syria which launched Fatah in its paramilitary role. Fuad Jabber writes that in this period the "practically complete dependence of [Fatah's] commandos on one regime [Syria] necessarily entailed a considerable surrender of their autonomy." (In Quandt, Jabber and Lesch, p. 173.) Kiernan's informants, members of Fatah at the time, stress the importance of the relationship, and give details.

105. Quandt, Jabber and Lesch, *Politics of Palestinian Nationalism*, p. 184.

106. Sayigh here (*Palestinians*, p. 144) ignores what Fuad Jabber calls "the Syrian exception" (before 1967). Like Gilmour, Sayigh has some romantic tendencies.

107. Yodfat and Arnon-Channa, *P.L.O. Strategy and Tactics*, p. 32.

108. Naseer H. Aruri and Samih Farsoun, "Palestinian Communities and Arab Host Countries," in Nakhleh and Zureik (eds.), *Sociology of the Palestinians*, p. 126.

109. Quandt, Jabber, and Lesch, *Politics of Palestinian Nationalism*, p 124.

110. That Black September was an arm of Fatah is accepted even by sources sympathetic to the P.L.O. See Hirst, *Gun and the Olive Branch*, pp. 309–310.

111. Ibid., p. 315.

112. Quoted in Yodfat and Arnon-Channa, *P.L.O. Strategy and Tactics*, p. 36.

113. The buffer zone was not entirely Assad's idea. Israel warned Syria to keep out of the border area. This may well have been a mistake on Israel's part.

114. In Quandt, Jabber and Lesch, *Politics of Palestinian Nationalism*, pp. 155–216.

115. Johnson, *Politics of Meaning*, p. 50.

10: DOING WITHOUT DIPLOMACY (1967–1973)

1. Rabin, *Rabin Memoirs*, p. 105.

2. See Kerr, *Arab Cold War*, pp. 137–140.

3. Ajami, *The Arab Predicament*, p. 149.

4. Rabin, *Rabin Memoirs*, pp. 118–119.

5. Ibid., pp. 120–121.

6. Eban, *Autobiography*, p. 465.

7. Ibid.

8. But the new position had been revealed in Israel itself, notably at the Labor Party conference of August 1969.

9. Rabin, *Rabin Memoirs*, p. 129.

10. Heikal, *Road to Ramadan*, pp. 86–87. Heikal, who was Nasser's closest confidant, was with him on this momentous and dramatic occasion. It is possible that Heikal touches up the drama a bit, but perhaps not.

11. Rafael, *Destination Peace*, p. 209. All the quotations in this section are from Chapter 23 of this book. *Destination Peace*—despite its rather off-putting title—is among the classical memoirs of the twentieth century: wise, wryly witty and full of that which Edmund Burke so valued: "the late, ripe fruit of mere experience."

12. During 1968 Israel's Foreign Office had on several occasions publicly reiterated Israel's acceptance of Security Council Resolution 242 (and of the Jarring mission, based on 242). See the section "Attitude to the S.C. Resolution and the Jarring Mission" in the chapter on Israel of *Middle East Record* (Tel Aviv), Vol. IV, pp. 246–249.

13. In June 1968, Dayan suggested "refraining from announcing that Israel accepts the S.C. Resolution as basis for any solution, because it means withdrawal to the June 4 boundaries and because we are in conflict with the S.C. on that resolution." Foreign Minister Eban strongly objected to Dayan's statement and Eshkol upheld Eban. (*Middle East Record*, Vol. IV, p. 247.)

14. Rafael, *Destination Peace*, p. 219.

15. Sadat, *In Search of Identity*, p. 263. I am informed that he did not make the reference to a peace treaty on February 4, but he did make it eleven days later.

16. Rafael, *Destination Peace*, p. 193.

17. Slater, *Rabin of Israel*, p. 154.

18. Rabin, *Rabin Memoirs*, p. 123. Referring to the briefing given by the Foreign Minister to his new ambassador, Rabin said that "dialogues with Eban have a way of turning into soliloquies."

19. Rafael, *Destination Peace*, p. 203.

20. Ibid., p. 198.

21. Sachar, *History of Israel*, p. 680.

22. Heikal, *Road to Ramadan*, p. 22.

23. Quoted in Eban, *Autobiography*, p. 487.

24. Quoted in Rafael, *Destination Peace*, p. 256.

25. Rafael, *Destination Peace*, p. 253.

26. Ibid.
27. Ibid., p. 257.
28. Ibid., p. 277.
29. Eban, *Autobiography*, p. 479.
30. Rafael, *Destination Peace*, p. 277.
31. Heikal, *Autumn of Fury*, pp. 49–50.
32. Ibid., p. 64.
33. Sadat, *In Search of Identity*, p. 238. Sadat gives the place of this meeting as Paris, but Kissinger, who was there, places it in Washington.
34. Ibid., p. 343.
35. Kissinger, *Years of Upheaval*, p. 206.
36. Ibid.
37. Ibid., p. 212.
38. Ibid., p. 227.
39. Heikal, *Road to Ramadan*.
40. Ibid., p. 155.
41. In a long and unfavorable review of *Autumn of Fury* (*New York Review of Books*, May 31, 1984), Professor Bernard Lewis taxes Heikal with (among other things) "a somewhat high-handed selection and treatment of the historical record," and illustrates this with various errors and strained judgments. None of these, however, appears to be in the category of "flat lies." Professor Lewis makes no reference at all, in this review, to Heikal's allegations about Kissinger, the C.I.A. and "heating up."
42. Rabin, *Rabin Memoirs*, pp. 153–156.
43. Not that Sadat had decided on war so early as summer 1972, but he seems to have been considering the possibility.
44. Golan, *Secret Conversations*, p. 145.
45. Rafael, *Destination Peace*, pp. 284–285.
46. Quandt, *Decade of Decisions*, p. 168.
47. Ibid.
48. Ibid., n. 7.
49. Herzog, *Arab-Israeli Wars*, p. 316.
50. Ibid., p. 241.
51. Ibid., p. 243.
52. Ibid., p. 255.
53. Eban, *Autobiography*, pp. 514–515.
54. Herzog, *Arab-Israeli Wars*, p. 259.
55. Golan, *Secret Conversations*, p. 51.
56. Quandt, *Decade of Decisions*, p. 175.
57. Golan, *Secret Conversations*, p. 51.
58. Quandt, *Decade of Decisions*, pp. 181–182.
59. Ibid., p. 181; quoting *Department of State Bulletin*, Oct. 29, 1973.
60. Ibid., p. 182.
61. Ibid., p. 183.
62. Heikal, *Road to Ramadan*, p. 224.
63. Quandt, *Decade of Decisions*, p. 191.
64. Ibid., p. 198, n. 71.
65. Kissinger, *Years of Upheaval*, p. 607.

11: STEP BY STEP (1973–1977)

1. See Aronson, *Conflict and Bargaining*, p. 212. As for Portugal, it also wanted to deny facilities, and provided them only after receiving what Kissinger calls "a Presidential letter of unusual abruptness," drafted by Kissinger. (*Years of Upheaval*, p. 520.)

2. See Eban, *Autobiography*, p. 558.

3. Aronson, *Conflict and Bargaining*, p. 248.

4. Kissinger, *Years of Upheaval*, p. 742.

5. Eban, *Autobiography*, p. 555.

6. Sadat, *In Search of Identity*, p. 315. Sadat had never claimed that his objective was the destruction of the Jewish State, but the Arab public assumed that that would be the result of victory.

7. Quandt, *Decade of Decisions*, p. 220.

8. Kissinger, *Years of Upheaval*, pp. 484 and 1037.

9. Rabin, *Rabin Memoirs*, p. 185.

10. See ibid.; Eban, *Autobiography*, p. 544; Dayan, *Story of My Life*, p. 490.

11. Aronson, *Conflict and Bargaining*, p. 236.

12. Slater, *Rabin of Israel*, p. 203; Silver, *Begin*, p. 150.

13. Rabin, *Rabin Memoirs*, p. 190.

14. Ibid., p. 46.

15. Ibid., p. 189. There are other references in the same vein. Fortunately or unfortunately, Peres has not published his own memoirs.

16. For the question of non-Jews, in relation to Jewish democracy, see Chapter 9, Section A.

17. Aronson, *Conflict and Bargaining*, p. 256.

18. Ibid., p. 258.

19. Quandt, *Decade of Decisions*, p. 233.

20. *Al-Ahram*, Nov. 16, 1973. This long article—favorable to Kissinger—was translated for me by Robert Jones.

21. Kissinger, *Years of Upheaval*, p. 111 and passim.

22. Safran, "Engagement in the Middle East," in *Foreign Affairs*.

23. Nixon, *Memoirs*, p. 1021.

24. Sicherman, *Broker or Advocate?*, Chapter I. The appearance of "hinging recognition" was misleading, at least in the case of Egypt.

25. Quandt, *Decade of Decisions*, p. 264.

26. Golan, *Secret Conversations*, p. 291.

27. Ibid.

28. Quandt, *Decade of Decisions*, p. 270.

29. Rabin, *Rabin Memoirs*, p. 207.

30. Safran, "Engagement in the Middle East," in *Foreign Affairs*.

31. Muhammad Y. Muslih, "Moderates and Rejectionists within the Palestine Liberation Organization," in *Middle East Journal*.

32. Hoffman, "A New Policy for Israel," in *Foreign Affairs*.

33. Quandt, *Decade of Decisions*, pp. 269–270; n. 21.

34. Ibid., p. 270.

35. Ibid., p. 275.

36. *New York Times*, Sept. 1975. After the secret memorandum was published, the State Department Legal Council said the document was "not legally binding." Kissinger, with masterly ambiguity, defined the mem-

orandum—before the Senate Committee on Foreign Relations on Oct. 7, 1975—as "an important statement of diplomatic policy which will engage the good faith of the U.S. so long as the circumstances which gave rise to it continue." (See Ran Marom, *The Development of U.S. Policy in the Palestine Issue, October 1973–November 1976*; Shiloah Center, Tel Aviv; March 1978; p. 6.)

37. See Quandt, *Decade of Decisions*, p. 282; Aronson, *Conflict and Bargaining*, p. 316.

38. Aronson, *Conflict and Bargaining*, pp. 317–318.

39. Quandt, *Decade of Decisions*, p. 284.

40. Rabin, *Rabin Memoirs*, p. 227.

41. Ibid.

42. Slater, *Rabin of Israel*, p. 270.

43. Rabin, *Rabin Memoirs*, p. 234.

44. Likud was probably also helped by a monumental Rabin social gaffe (recorded by Brzezinski in his memoirs): "Carter tried to engage him as a human being by inviting Rabin, after the State Dinner, to look in on Carter's special pride and joy, his daughter Amy, asleep in her White House bedroom. Rabin declined the offer with a curt, 'No, thank you,' thereby ending his chance of establishing a personal rapport with a proud father."

45. Rabin, *Rabin Memoirs*, p. 243.

46. Slater, *Shimon Peres*, p. 192.

47. Silver, *Begin*, p. 153.

48. Ibid., p. 154.

49. Ibid., p. 157.

50. Ibid.

51. Quoted in Silver, *Begin*, p. 159.

52. Dayan had broken with his party in September 1975 over Second Sinai. He condemned territorial concessions not requited by peace with Egypt.

53. Quoted in Silver, *Begin*, p. 167.

12: PEACE AND WAR (1977–1982)

1. Brzezinski, *Power and Principle*, pp. 85–86, n. 1.

2. Aronson, *Conflict and Bargaining*, pp. 331–332.

3. Legum (ed.), *Middle East Contemporary Survey*, Vol. I, pp. 26–28. The annual volumes of this survey contain vast quantities of useful material for the late seventies and early eighties. Cited from now as *MECS*.

4. Ibid. Carter had used the term "Palestinian entity" at a press conference on March 8, 1977, and on March 16, at a public meeting he first used the phrase "a homeland for the Palestinans."

5. Brzezinski, *Power and Principle*, p. 105.

6. Interview with Patrick Seale, in *The Observer*, Mar. 6, 1977.

7. Legum (ed.), *MECS*, Vol. I, p. 216. The venue—Geneva, not Washington—itself enhanced Assad's prestige. The American mountain had come to the Syrian Mahomet.

8. "To the Jordan" represented a relatively moderate position, for Begin's Likud. Its mentor, Jabotinsky, had demanded all of Palestine, both banks of the Jordan.

9. Carter, *Keeping Faith*, p. 286.

10. Ibid., p. 287.

11. Ibid., p. 288.

12. Ibid.

13. Weizman, *Battle for Peace*, p. 76.

14. Carter, *Keeping Faith*, p. 290; *Israel's Foreign Relations: Selected Documents, 1977–1979*, Vol. IV, Ministry for Foreign Affairs, ed. by Meron Medzini, pp. 38–55.

15. Legum (ed.), MECS, Vol. I (B. Reich).

16. Dayan, *Breakthrough*, p. 60.

17. Ibid., pp. 63–64.

18. Legum (ed.), MECS, Vol. I, p. 29.

19. Text in ibid.

20. Brzezinski, *Power and Principle*, p. 108.

21. Legum (ed.), MECS, Vol. I, p. 30.

22. Ibid., pp. 30–31.

23. Ibid., pp. 76–77.

24. Carter, *Keeping Faith*, p. 294.

25. Sadat, *In Search of Identity*, p. 364.

26. Dayan, *Breakthrough*, p. 75.

27. Ibid., p. 76; Weizman, *Battle for Peace*, p. 23.

28. Quoted in Dayan, *Breakthrough*, p. 76.

29. Dayan, *Breakthrough*, p. 76.

30. Ibid., p. 77 (quoting Sadat's Minister of State for Foreign Affairs, Boutros Ghali).

31. Sadat's first specific reference to signing a peace treaty had come some days after the February 4 speech.

32. Full texts of the speech and Begin's reply in Legum (ed.), MECS, Vol. II, pp. 134–142.

33. Legum (ed.), MECS, Vol. II, p. 90.

34. Brzezinski, *Power and Principle*, p. 113.

35. Ibid.

36. Dayan, *Breakthrough*, p. 99. Dayan was in Washington at the time.

37. Legum (ed.), MECS, Vol. II, pp. 98–99.

38. Quoted in Legum (ed.), MECS, Vol. II, p. 94.

39. Legum (ed.), MECS, Vol. II, p. 93. Begin first publicly presented the autonomy plan at the Ismailia Conference on December 26, 1977, and then two days later in the Knesset.

40. Ibid., p. 20.

41. Weizman, *Battle for Peace*, p. 104.

42. Ibid., pp. 142–143.

43. Ibid., p. 147.

44. Legum (ed.), MECS, Vol. II, p. 110.

45. Weizman, *Battle for Peace*, p. 233.

46. *Israel's Foreign Relations: Selected Documents, 1977–1979*, Vol. V, pp. 372–391.

47. Legum (ed.), MECS, Vol. II, p. 115.

48. Dayan, *Breakthrough*, pp. 171–172.

49. Carter, *Keeping Faith*, p. 308.

50. Ibid., p. 396.

51. Ibid.

52. Dayan, *Breakthrough*, p. 192.

53. Ibid., pp. 191–192.

54. Ibid., p. 193.

55. Ibid.

56. Quoted in Dayan, *Breakthrough*, p. 193.

57. Dayan, *Breakthrough*, p. 194.

58. Legum (ed.), MECS, Vol. II, p. 214.

59. In MECS, Vol. II.

60. Legum (ed.), MECS, Vol. II, p. 24.

61. *New York Times,* June 1, 1980; quoted in Legum (ed.), MECS, Vol. IV, p. 74.

62. Brzezinski, *Power and Principle*, p. 278.

63. Ibid.

64. A similar error was made by the State Department in 1948, in clinging to "trusteeship" while the President had gone back to "partition."

65. Legum (ed.), MECS, Vol. IV, p. 557.

66. Ibid., Vol. V, p. 124.

67. Ibid., Vol. IV, p. 282.

68. The term "Phalanges" is in general use. I think it should be treated with reserve because of its ideological and European connotations, misleading in the local context. The same applies to the appellation of "left-wing," habitually bestowed by the media on the Druze clans who follow their hereditary leader, the moody patrician Walid Jumblatt.

69. See Schiff and Ya'ari, *Israel's Lebanon War*, pp. 75–76.

70. Legum (ed.), MECS, Vol. V, Chapter "Israel," p. 617.

71. *Newsweek,* June 22, 1981.

72. Legum (ed.), MECS, Vol. V, Chapter "The Israeli Raid of Osirak," pp. 182–207.

73. Ibid., p. 199.

74. *Jerusalem Post,* June 26, 1981.

75. Caspi, Diskin and Gutmann (eds.), *Begin's Success*, p. 61.

76. Yochanan Peres and Sara Shemer, "The Ethnic Factor in Elections," in Caspi *et al.* (eds.), *Begin's Success,* pp. 89–111.

77. Avraham Diskin, "Polarization and Volatility among Voters," in Caspi *et al.* (eds.), "Begin's Success," pp. 113–139.

78. Herzog, *Arab-Israeli Wars,* p. 120.

79. Legum (ed.), MECS, Vol. V, "The West Bank and the Gaza Strip," p. 336.

80. Ibid., Vol. VI, p. 362.

81. *Jerusalem Post,* May 15, 1982.

82. Interview with the Saudi Press Agency, Aug. 7, 1981; text in Legum (ed.), MECS, Vol. V, pp. 163–164.

83. See Meiring, *Fire of Islam,* pp. 159–164.

84. *The Observer,* May 9, 1982.

85. Rabinovich, *War for Lebanon,* p. 149.

86. Ibid., p. 125.

87. Ibid., p. 122.

88. Ibid., p. 126.

89. Schiff and Ya'ari, *Israel's Lebanon War*, pp. 75–76.

90. Ibid. Haig stipulated that Israel's attack had to "fit the provocation," but the I.D.F. has its own doctrine on that matter.

91. Chomsky, *The Fateful Triangle,* p. 78. The *sic* is mine, not Chomsky's.

92. *Le Monde,* August 12, 1982.

93. The account of Abu Nidal is based on a biographical article on him in *Le Monde* (August 12, 1982). I am indebted, for this reference, to my colleague at Dartmouth College (1984–1985) Ian Lustick. Schiff and Ya'ari (*Israel's Lebanon War*) believe that in the summer of 1982, Abu Nidal was working for Baghdad, with the object of embarrassing and ensnaring Syria, as well as Arafat's P.L.O.

94. As may be seen from the above, *fedayeen* politics are extremely complex. Those who are the object of such attacks tend to hit back at whichever branch of the *fedayeen* it seems most useful to hit at a given moment, rather than attempt a judicial investigation into responsibility for a particular act.

95. Legum (ed.), MECS, Vol. VI, pp. 641–642.

96. Ibid., p. 142.

97. Ibid., p. 143.

98. Gabriel Ben-Dor, "The Middle East in 1982," in Legum (ed.), MECS, Vol. VI, p. 6.

99. Legum (ed.), MECS, Vol. VI, pp. 248, and 340.

100. Ibid., p. 41.

101. Radio Damascus, July 26; quoted in ibid., p. 719. That was just after Bashir had declared his candidacy.

102. Government Press Office, Sept. 15; quoted in Legum (ed.), MECS, Vol. VI, p. 151.

103. Legum (ed.), MECS, Vol. VI, p. 664.

104. *New York Times,* Sept. 26, 1982.

105. Legum (ed.), MECS, Vol. VI, p. 648.

106. Conspicuous because Sharon is conspicuous by nature, rather than because the Likud leadership wished him to be so. Likud's new leader, Yitzhak Shamir, after all, had been among those who had voted Sharon out of the Ministry of Defense.

107. In all that follows, I am considering reactions to the war before Sabra and Chatila.

108. At Sidon, for example, most of the civilian population, warned by Israeli leaflets in Arabic, had taken refuge on a neighboring beach before the bombardment of the town. Early casualty reports, based on the number of dwellings destroyed, assumed that the inhabitants were destroyed too, though most of them had escaped. But in other places, and especially in Beirut, that was not the case. The risk to civilians was enhanced by the P.L.O. as a matter of deliberate policy, as Robert Fisk attests: "The Palestinians, as they now admit, had used schools and hospitals and civilian houses as cover for their anti-aircraft guns." (*The Times,* July 24, 1982.)

109. It is true that Arafat, in interviews with *Le Monde,* etc., no longer spoke of the destruction of Israel. But ordinary P.L.O. militants, in Lebanon itself, made clear that that remained their ultimate objective. I heard them, in September 1981.

110. A provocation of course which was itself provoked, originally, by the Return itself. But Israel cannot be expected either to revoke the Return or to acquiesce in attacks on itself.

111. One aspect of the difference is that higher ethical standards are supposed to be expected from Israel than from other states. This expectation is legitimized by a great deal of Zionist rhetoric (and indeed Zionist expectation). As Edward Alexander neatly puts it: "Jews, in their folly"

have persuaded others that they ought to be judged by higher standards than other peoples. ("The Journalists' War Against Israel," in *Encounter*. A variant on this theme is the proposition that contemporary Zionists are unworthy of their high-minded predecessors, such as David Ben-Gurion. But it would be hard to see in what way "Lebanon 1982" was less ethical than "Suez/Sinai 1956." The real difference is that Israel had company in 1956, but was alone in 1982. But the concept that Jews were *once* very holy, and are *now* very much not, has deep roots in the Christian tradition.

112. When I publicly objected to that metaphor, a friend reminded me that Begin often identifies Israel's Arab enemies with the Nazis. True, but heated language is excusable enough among the *parties* to one of the bitterest conflicts of modern times. What I found disturbing was to see such a monstrously exaggerated comparison appearing in the language of people who were *not* parties to the conflict, but supposedly disinterested commentators on it.

113. "Epilogue: Territory for Peace?"

114. Acceptance qualified by having Sharon as Minister Without Portfolio.

115. Though the resemblance to General Patton, noted by Herzog, is much closer.

116. The President never actually signed this agreement, but it was widely assumed to exist.

117. Compare the impact of the Fahd Plan and the Camp David peace process in stirring up additional trouble in the West Bank. Also, actual peace agreements have started wars in other places. Thus the cease-fire between Israel and Egypt in 1970 precipitated a war in Jordan, and the peace "step" at Second Sinai precipitated a war in Lebanon.

118. The Shi'i branch of Islam is noted for its ancient cult of martyrdom and martyrs, a cult favorable to the formation of volunteers for suicidal missions.

119. But see "Epilogue: Territory for Peace?"

EPILOGUE: TERRITORY FOR PEACE?

1. Ex-President Carter seemed to be envisaging such a development in an interview in New York, promoting his book *The Blood of Abraham* ("Carter Sees Hope for Mideast Peace," *The New York Times*, April 1, 1985). Carter called for more U.S. "follow-up" in the Reagan Plan and for a display of "political resolve and courage" on the part of Israeli leaders, comparable to the qualities displayed by Sadat in 1977. But Sadat was engaged in *recovering* territory; Israel is required to *sacrifice* territory. That calls for a different type of resolve and courage, and more of both than is likely to be forthcoming.

2. The following dispatch appeared in *The New York Times* on Feb. 24, 1985:

Amman, Jordan, February 23 (AP)—Following is the text of an agreement reached Feb. 11 by King Hussein of Jordan and Yasir Arafat, leader of the Palestine Liberation Organization, as made public in translation today by Jordan's Acting Information Minister, Taher Hikmat:

Emanating from the spirit of the Fez summit resolutions, approved by Arab states, and from United Nations resolutions relating to the Palestine question,

In accordance with international legitimacy, and

Deriving from a common understanding on the establishment of a special relationship between the Jordanian and Palestinian peoples,

The Government of the Hashemite Kingdom of Jordan and the Palestine Liberation Organization have agreed to move together toward the achievement of a peaceful and just settlement of the Middle East crisis and the termination of Israeli occupation of the occupied Arab territories, including Jerusalem, on the basis of the following principles:

1. Total withdrawal from the territories occupied in 1967 for comprehensive peace as established in United Nations and Security Council resolutions.

2. Right of self-determination for the Palestinian people: Palestinians will exercise their inalienable right of self-determination when Jordanians and Palestinians will be able to do so within the context of the formation of the proposed confederated Arab states of Jordan and Palestine.

3. Resolution of the problem of Palestinian refugees in accordance with United Nations resolutions.

4. Resolution of the Palestine question in all its aspects.

5. And on this basis, peace negotiations will be conducted under the auspices of an international conference in which the five permanent members of the Security Council and all the parties to the conflict will participate, including the Palestine Liberation Organization, the sole legitimate representative of the Palestine people, within a joint delegation (joint Jordanian-Palestinian delegation).

3. But it is of interest that the Hussein-Arafat pact of Feb. 23, 1985, makes no mention of a Palestinian State except in the ambiguous phrase "the proposed confederated Arab states of Jordan and Palestine."

4. It should be noted, however, that there is *also* more support among Israeli soldiers for the dovish party Shinui than there is among the population at large. See Goldberg, "The I.D.F. at the Polls," in *Jerusalem Quarterly*, pp. 59–67.

5. Title of a book of essays published after the Yom Kippur War. (Edited by Ehud Ben-Ezer; Jerusalem and New York, 1974.)

6. There are, however, some counteracting factors tending, in the long term, to close the divisions. The most significant of those is the fairly high rate of intermarriage between Ashkenazim and Orientals.

7. With the major exception of the rule of Islamic law in Muslim fundamentalist states. But this is something widely different from the rule of law as understood in the West.

8. The appeal can be addressed to the West with some confidence today since the Western countries, after the decolonization following the Second World War, habitually treat Consent of the Governed as a universally applicable principle. But the English and the Americans, who—in their seventeenth- and eighteenth-century revolutions—gave the concept its

first impulsions, originally took it as inapplicable to peoples considered as "backward," such as the Irish and the Red Indians.

9. The *Tractatus Theologico-Politicus*, published anonymously in 1670, and written by the excommunicated Jew Baruch Spinoza, has a strong claim to be the foundation document of the Enlightenment.

10. Some readers might feel that this would be a betrayal of Lebanon's sovereign independence. It seems probable, however, that most Lebanese—with the exception of many Maronites and Druze—would settle for some version of a Pax Syraica. "Independent Lebanon" was a French invention which collapsed.

11. Alternatively Israel, having shed its philo-Maronite illusions of the Sharon period, might leave that community to its own devices. In March 1985, when the Maronite "rebels" of the Forces Libanaises were under threat from Syria, Shimon Peres indicated that this dispute was no concern of Israel's.

12. The most avoidable of all Israel's mistakes in Lebanon was remaining too long. In southern Lebanon, in July 1982, I heard Shi'ites say: "We are glad the Israelis kicked out the Palestinians. But we want the Israelis to go soon." If Israel had gotten right out of Lebanon after the departure of the P.L.O. from Beirut, it could have left behind a well-disposed population in southern Lebanon. As it is, it leaves an embittered population on its border, a potential increment to the siege.

13. The feud with Rabin, so long destructive to both men and to their party, was dropped before the 1984 elections, with Rabin apparently abandoning his ambition to lead the party. And Peres is no longer doing things like condoning illegal settlements, as he was in 1977.

BIBLIOGRAPHY

[*What follows is basically a list of books, articles, reports, etc., cited in the text and notes, plus a few other works of value for background.*]

Abbott, George Frederick. *Israel in Europe*. New York: Humanities, 1972.

Adelson, Roger. *Mark Sykes: Portrait of an Amateur*. London: Cape, 1975.

Ajami, Fouad. *The Arab Predicament: Arab Political Thought and Practice Since 1967*. Cambridge: Cambridge University Press, 1981.

Alexander, Edward. "Abba Kovner: Poet of the Holocaust and Rebirth." *Midstream* (October 1977).

————. "The Journalists' War Against Israel." *Encounter* (September-October 1982).

Amichai, Yehuda. *Not of This Time, Not of This Place*. London: Vallentine, Mitchell, 1973.

Antonius, George. *The Arab Awakening*. London: Hamish Hamilton, 1955.

Appelfeld, Aharon. "1946." *Jerusalem Quarterly* 7 (Spring 1978).

Aronson, Shlomo. *Conflict and Bargaining in the Middle East: An Israeli Perspective*. Baltimore: Johns Hopkins University Press, 1978.

Avineri, Shlomo. *The Making of Modern Zionism: The Intellectual Origins of the Jewish State*. London: Weidenfeld and Nicolson, 1981.

Bachi, Roberto. *The Population of Israel*. Jerusalem: Institute of Contemporary Jewry, Hebrew University of Jerusalem, 1974.

Barakat, Halim. "Alienation and Revolution in Arab Life." *Jerusalem Quarterly* 4 (Summer 1977).

Baranski, Salih. "The Story of a Palestinian." *Journal of Palestine Studies* 11, No. 1 (Autumn 1981).

Baron, Salo Wittmayer. *The Russian Jew Under Tsars and Soviets*. London: Collier-Macmillan, 1964; New York: Macmillan, 1965.

Bar-Zohar, Michael. *Ben-Gurion*. London: Weidenfeld and Nicolson, 1978.

Bauer, Yehuda. *From Diplomacy to Resistance: A History of Jewish Palestine, 1939–1945*. New York: Atheneum, 1973.

Beaverbrook, Lord: *Men and Power*, new ed. London: Collins, 1966.

Becker, Jillian. *The Rise and Fall of the Palestine Liberation Organization*. London: Weidenfeld and Nicolson, 1984.

Begin, Menachem. *The Revolt*, rev. ed. New York: 1977.

Bell, J. Bowyer. *Terror out of Zion: Fight for Israeli Independence*. Dublin: Academy Press, 1979.

Ben-Ezer, Ehud. "War and Siege in Israeli Literature 1948–1967." *Jerusalem Quarterly* 2 (Winter 1977).

———. "War and Siege in Israeli Literature After 1967." *Jerusalem Quarterly* 9 (Fall 1978).

Ben-Gurion, David. *Israel: A Personal History.* Translated by Nechemia Meyers and Uzy Nystar. New York: Funk and Wagnalls, 1971.

———. *My Talks with Arab Leaders.* Translated by Aryeh Rubinstein and Misha Louvish. Jerusalem: Keter Books, 1972.

Bentwich, Norman and Helen. *Mandate Memories.* London: Hogarth Press, 1965.

Benvenisti, Meron. "Jerusalem: Study of a Polarized Community." Research Paper No. 3 of the West Bank Data Project, Jerusalem, 1983.

———. "The West Bank and Gaza Data Base Project Interim Report No. 1." Jerusalem, 1982.

Berlin, Sir Isaiah. *Chaim Weizmann.* London: Weidenfeld and Nicolson, 1958.

———. *The Life and Times of Moses Hess.* Cambridge: W. Heffes, 1959.

Bernadotte, Count Folke. *To Jerusalem.* London: Hodder and Stoughton, 1951.

Bethell, Nicholas. *The Palestine Triangle.* London: Deutsch, 1979.

Birdwood, Christopher B. *Nuri Said: A Study in Arab Leadership.* London: Cassell, 1959.

Boorstin, Daniel J. (ed.). *An American Primer.* Chicago and London: University of Chicago Press, 1966.

Bowle, John. *Viscount Samuel: A Biography.* London: Gollancz, 1957.

Brecher, Michael. *Decisions in Israel's Foreign Policy.* London: Oxford University Press, 1974; New Haven: Yale University Press, 1975.

British Institute of International Affairs. *Surveys of International Affairs 1920–1923* and *1924.* Oxford, Oxford University Press, 1925 and 1926.

Brzezinski, Zbigniew. *Power and Principle: Memoirs of the National Security Adviser 1977–1981.* New York: Farrar, Straus and Giroux, 1983; London: Weidenfeld and Nicolson, 1983.

Bullock, Alan. *The Life and Times of Ernest Bevin;* Vol. 3, *Foreign Secretary, 1945–1951.* London: Heinemann, 1983.

Bülow. See Von Bülow, Prince.

Byrnes, R. F. *Antisemitism in Modern France.* New Brunswick, N.J.: Rutgers University Press, 1950.

———. *Pobedonostsev.* Bloomington, Ind.: Indiana University Press, 1968.

Caplan, Neil. *Palestine Jewry and the Arab Question.* London: Cass, 1978.

Calder, Angus. *The People's War: Britain 1939–45.* London: Cape, 1969.

Carter, Jimmy. *Keeping Faith.* London: Collins, 1982.

Caspi, Dan, Abraham Diskin and Emanuel Gutmann (eds.). *The Roots of Begin's Success.* London: Croom Helm; New York: St. Martin's, 1984.

Chapman, Guy. *The Dreyfus Case.* London: Hart-Davis, 1955.

Chesterton, G. K. *The New Jerusalem.* New York: George H. Doran, 1921.

Chomsky, Noam. *The Fateful Triangle: The United States, Israel and the Palestinians.* Boston: South End Press, 1983.

Churchill, Randolph S. *Winston S. Churchill,* Vol. 2, *Young Statesman.* London: Heinemann, 1967.

Cohen, Erik. "The Black Panthers and Israeli Society." *Jewish Journal of Sociology* 14, No. 1.

Cohen, Michael J. *Palestine: Retreat from the Mandate: The Making of British Policy 1936–45.* New York: Holmes and Meier, 1978.

Cowles, Virginia. *The Kaiser.* London: Collins, 1963.

Cowling, Maurice. *The Impact of Hitler: British Politics and British Policy, 1933–1940.* Chicago and London: University of Chicago Press, 1975.

Crossman, Richard. *A Nation Reborn.* London: Hamish Hamilton, 1960; New York: Atheneum, 1960.

———. *Palestine Mission: A Personal Record.* London: Hamish Hamilton, 1947.

Curtis, Michael (ed.). *Religion and Politics in the Middle East.* Boulder, Colo.: Westview Press, 1981.

Curtis, Michael, and Mordecai S. Chertoff (eds.). *Israel: Social Structure and Change.* New Brunswick, N.J.: Transaction Books, 1973.

Dayan, Moshe. *Breakthrough: A Personal Account of the Egypt–Israel Peace Negotiations.* London: Weidenfeld and Nicolson, 1981; New York: Knopf, 1981.

———. *Story of My Life.* London: Weidenfeld and Nicolson, 1966.

Documents on British Foreign Policy, etc. *See* United Kingdom, H.M. Stationery Office.

Drumont, Edouard. *La France Juive.* Paris: Flammarion, 1886.

Dubnov, Simon. *History of the Jews,* 4th ed. Translated from the Russian by Moshe Spiegel. New York and London: Thomas Yoseloff, 1967.

Dugdale, Blanche. *Arthur James Balfour,* 2 vols. London: Hutchinson, 1936; New York: Putnam, 1937.

Dundas. *See* Ronaldshay.

Dutter, Lee E. "Eastern and Western Jews: Ethnic Divisions in Israeli Society." *Middle East Journal* 31, No. 4 (Autumn 1977).

Eban, Abba. *Abba Eban: An Autobiography.* London: Weidenfeld and Nicolson, 1978.

Eisenstadt, Shmuel N. *The Absorption of Immigrants.* London: Routledge and Kegan Paul, 1954.

Eliot, George. *Daniel Deronda.* London: Penguin Books, 1979.

Elon, Amos. *Herzl.* London: Weidenfeld and Nicolson, 1976.

Encyclopaedia Judaica. Jerusalem: Keter Books, 1972.

Encyclopaedia of Zionism and Israel. See Patai, Raphael.

Esco Foundation for Palestine, Inc. *Palestine: A Study of Jewish, Arab and British Policies.* Yale and Oxford: Yale University Press, 1947.

Feiling, Keith. *The Life of Neville Chamberlain.* London: Macmillan and Co., 1946.

Friedman, Isaiah. *Germany, Turkey, and Zionism: 1897–1918.* Oxford: Oxford University Press, 1977.

———. *The Question of Palestine, 1914–18: British-Jewish-Arab Relations.* London: Routledge and Kegan Paul, 1973.

Frye, R. N. (ed.). *The Near East and the Great Powers.* Cambridge, Mass.: Harvard University Press, 1951.

Gabatello, Eitan. "The Population of the Administered Territories: Some Demographic Trends and Implications." West Bank Data Project, Jerusalem, 1983.

Gannon, Franklin R. *The British Press and Germany 1936–39.* Oxford: Clarendon Press, 1971.

Gelber, Yoau. "Zionist Policy and the Transfer Agreement." *Yalkut Moreshet* 17 (January 1974).

Gertz, Nurith. "Israeli Novelists." *Jerusalem Quarterly* 17 (Fall 1980).

Gilbert, Martin. *Winston Spencer Churchill*, Vol. 4. London: Heinemann, 1975.

Gilboa, Amir. *Songs in the Early Morning*. Translated by Dan Laor. "The Vehicle of Parody." *Jerusalem Quarterly* 5 (Fall 1977).

Gilmour, David. *Dispossessed: The Ordeal of the Palestinians*. London: Sidgwick and Jackson, 1980.

Glick, Edward B. *The Triangular Connection: America, Israel and American Jews*. London: George Allen and Unwin, 1982.

Glubb, Sir John Bagot. *A Soldier with the Arabs*. London: Hodder and Stoughton, 1957; New York: Harper, 1957.

Golan, Matti. *The Secret Conversations of Henry Kissinger: Step-by-Step Diplomacy in the Middle East*. Translated by Ruth Geyra Stern and Sol Stern. New York: Quadrangle/New York Times Books, 1976.

——. *Shimon Peres: A Biography*. London: Weidenfeld and Nicolson, 1982.

Goldberg, Giora. "The I.D.F. at the Polls." *Jerusalem Quarterly* 34 (Winter 1985).

Gooch, George Peabody. *Before the War: Studies in Diplomacy*, Vol. 1. London and New York: Longman, Green, 1936.

Greenberg, Louis. *The Jews in Russia: The Struggle for Emancipation*. New Haven: Yale University Press, 1965.

Gwynn, Stephen (ed.). *The Letters and Friendships of Sir Cecil Spring-Rice*, Vol. II. London: Constable, 1929; New York: Houghton Mifflin, 1929.

Hadawi, Sami. *Bitter Harvest: Palestine Between 1911 and 1967*. New York: New World Press, 1967.

Halabi, Rafik. *The West Bank Story: An Arab's View of Both Sides of a Tangled Conflict*. Translated from the Hebrew by Ina Friedman. New York and London: Harcourt Brace Jovanovich, 1982.

Halpern, Ben. *The Idea of the Jewish State*, 2nd ed. Cambridge, Mass., and London: Harvard University Press, 1961, 1969, 1976.

Hanna, Paul. *British Policy in Palestine*. Washington, D.C.: American Council on Public Affairs, 1942.

Hansard Parliamentary Debates. *See* United Kingdom, H.M. Stationery Office.

Hareven, Alouph (ed.). *Can the Palestinian Problem Be Solved? Israeli Positions*. Jerusalem: Van Leer Foundation, 1983.

——. *Every Sixth Israeli: Relations Between the Jewish Majority and the Arab Minority in Israel*. Jerusalem: Van Leer Foundation, 1983.

Harkabi, Yehoshafat. *Arab Attitudes to Israel*. Jerusalem : Keter, 1972.

Harris, Kenneth. *Attlee*. London: Weidenfeld and Nicolson, 1982.

Harris, William Wilson. *Taking Root: Israeli Settlement in the West Bank, the Golan and Gaza-Sinai: 1967–1980*. Chichester and New York: Research Studies Press, 1980.

Heikal, Mohamed. *Autumn of Fury: The Assassination of Sadat*. London: Deutsch, 1983; New York: Random House, 1984.

——. *The Road to Ramadan*. London: Collins, 1975; New York: Quadrangle/New York Times Books, 1975.

Herman, Simon. "In the Shadow of the Holocaust." *Jerusalem Quarterly* 3 (Spring 1977).

Herzberg, Arthur. *The French Enlightenment and the Jews* (New York: Columbia University Press, 1968).

Herzl, Theodor. *Der Judenstaat, Versuch einer Modernen Lösung Der Judenfrage*. Vienna: M. Breitenstein, 1896. Translated as *The Jewish State*.

―――. *Diaries*. See Patai, Raphael (ed.).

―――. *Herzl Year Book*. See Patai, Raphael (ed.). *See also under* Elon, Amos; Nedava, Joseph; Stewart, Desmond.

Herzog, Chaim. *The Arab–Israeli Wars*. London: Arms and Armour Press, 1982.

Hirst, David. *The Gun and the Olive Branch*. London: Faber and Faber, 1977; New York: Harcourt Brace Jovanovich, 1977.

Hirszowicz, Lukasz. *Third Reich and the Arab East*. London and Toronto, 1966.

Hitler, Adolf. *Hitler's Table Talk: His Private Conversations 1941–44*, Roper ed. London: Weidenfeld and Nicolson, 1973.

―――. *Mein Kampf*. London: Hutchinson, 1939, 1969; Boston: Houghton Mifflin, 1943.

Hoffman, Stanley. "A New Policy for Israel." *Foreign Affairs* 53, No. 31 (April 1975).

Hurewitz, Jacob Coleman. *The Struggle for Palestine*. New York: Norton, 1950.

―――. *The Middle East and North Africa in World Politics*, 2nd ed., rev. and enl., Vol. 2, *British-French Supremacy 1914–1945*. New Haven and London: Yale University Press, 1979.

Hyamson, Albert Montefiore. *Palestine Under the Mandate*. London: Methuen, 1950.

Ingrams, Doreen. *Seeds of Conflict: Palestine Papers*. London: John Murray, 1972.

Isaac, Rael Jean. *Party and Politics in Israel*. New York and London: Longman, 1981.

Jeffery, Arthur. *Reader on Islam*. Columbia University Publications in Near and Middle East Studies, Series A, 2. 'S-Gravenhage: Mouton, 1962.

Jiryis, Sabri. *The Arabs in Israel*. Translated by Inea Bushnaq. New York and London: Monthly Review Press, 1976.

Johnson, Nels. *Islam and the Politics of Meaning in Palestinian Nationalism*. London: Kegan Paul, 1982.

Kampf, H. A. "Israeli Administration of the West Bank: The Arab View." *International Problems* (The Journal of the Israeli Institute for the Study of International Affairs) 16 (Spring 1977).

Kann, Robert A. *History of the Hapsburg Empire, 1526–1918*. Berkeley and London: University of California Press, 1974.

Kedourie, Elie. *The Chatham House Version*. London: Weidenfeld and Nicolson, 1970.

―――. *England and the Middle East*. London: Bowes and Bowes, 1956.

―――. *Islam and the Modern World and Other Studies*. London: Mansell Publishing, 1980.

――― and Sylvia G. Haim (eds.). *Palestine and Israel in the 19th and 20th Centuries*. London: Cass, 1982.

―――. *Zionism and Arabism in Palestine and Israel*. London: Cass, 1982.

Kenen, I. L. *Israel's Defense Line: Her Friends and Foes in Washington*. Buffalo, N.Y.: Prometheus Books, 1981.

Kerr, Malcolm H. *The Arab Cold War: Gamal Abd al-Nassir and His Rivals, 1958–1970*, 3rd ed. London and New Lork: Royal Institute of International Affairs/Oxford University Press, 1971.

Kiernan, Thomas. *Yasir Arafat: The Man and the Myth*. London: Sphere Books, 1976; New York: Norton, 1976.

Kimche, Jon and David. *Both Sides of the Hill*. London: Secker and Warburg, 1960.

Kirk, George. *See* Royal Institute of International Affairs.

Kirkbride, Alec Seath. *A Crackle of Thorns: Experiences in the Middle East*. London: John Murray, 1956.

Kissinger, Henry. *Years of Upheaval*. Boston: Little, Brown, 1982; London: Weidenfeld and Nicolson and Michael Joseph, 1982.

Klausner, Joseph. *Menachem Ussishkin: His Life and Work*. New York: Scopus Publishing, 1942.

Koestler, Arthur. *Promise and Fulfillment: Palestine, 1917–1949*, new ed. London: Papermac, 1983.

Kohn, Hans (ed.). *Nationalism and the Jewish Ethic: Basic Writings of Ahad Ha'am*. New York: Herzl Press, 1962.

Kovner, Abba. "My Little Sister." In *A Canopy in the Desert: Selected Poems*. Translated by Shirley Kaufman. Pittsburgh: University of Pittsburgh Press, 1973.

Krikler, Bernard. "Boycotting Nazi Germany." *Wiener Library Bulletin* 1969, Vol. xxiii, No. 4 (new series No. 17).

Kurzman, Dan. *Ben-Gurion: Prophet of Fire*. New York: Simon and Schuster, 1983.

———. *Genesis, 1948: First Arab–Israeli War*. London: Vallentine, Mitchell, 1972.

Landau, Jacob M. *The Arabs in Israel: A Political Study*. London: Royal Institute of International Affairs, 1969.

Landshut, Siegfried. *Jewish Communities in the Muslim Countries of the Middle East: A Survey*. London: Jewish Chronicle, 1950.

Langer, Lawrence L. *The Holocaust and the Literary Imagination*. New Haven and London: Yale University Press, 1975.

Laqueur, Walter. *A History of Zionism*. London: Weidenfeld and Nicolson, 1972.

Lash, Joseph P. *Eleanor: The Years Alone*. New York: Norton/London: Deutsch, 1973.

Legum, Colin (ed.). *Middle East Contemporary Survey*, Vol. 1, 1976–1977, and annually. New York and London: Holmes and Meier for the Shiloah Center for Middle Eastern and African Affairs, Tel Aviv University.

Lesch, Ann. *Arab Politics in Palestine*. Ithaca N.Y.: Cornell University Press, 1979.

Lewis, Bernard. "L'Islam et les Non-Musulmans." *Annales: Economies, Sociétés, Civilisations* 3, 4 (Mai, Août 1980).

———. *Islam in History: Ideas, Men and Events in the Middle East*. London: Alcove Press, 1973.

———. *The Middle-East and the West*. London: Weidenfeld and Nicolson, 1968.

———. Review of *Autumn of Fury: The Assassination of Sadat*, by Mohamed Heikal. *New York Review of Books*, May 31, 1984.

Liddell Hart, B. H. *A History of the World War 1914–1918.* London: Faber and Faber, 1934; Boston: Little, Brown, 1935.

Littman, David. "Jews Under Muslim Rule in the Late Nineteenth Century," Parts 1, 2. *Wiener Library Bulletin* 28 (new series No. 35–36) (1975).

———. "Jews Under Muslim Rule: Morocco 1903–1912." *Wiener Library Bulletin* 29.

Lorch, Netanel. *The Edge of the Sword: Israel's War of Independence, 1947–1949.* London and New York: Putnam, 1961.

Louis, William Roger. *The British Empire in the Middle East, 1945–51.* Oxford: Oxford University Press, 1984.

Lucas, Noah. *The Modern History of Israel.* London: Weidenfeld and Nicolson, 1974.

Luke, H. C. *Cities and Men: An Autobiography.* 3 vols. London: Bles, 1953–1956.

Luks, Harold Paul. "Iraqi Jews during World War II." *Wiener Library Bulletin* xxx (1977).

Lustick, Ian. *Arabs in the Jewish State: Israel's Control of a National Minority.* Austin and London: University of Texas Press, 1980.

Macartney, C. A. *The Hapsburg Empire: 1790–1918.* London: Weidenfeld and Nicolson, 1971.

McDonald, James G. *My Mission in Israel: 1948–51.* London: Gollancz, 1951; New York: Simon and Schuster, 1951.

Mandel, Neville J. *The Arabs and Zionism Before World War I.* Berkeley: University of California Press, 1976.

Marlowe, John. *The Seat of Pilate.* London: Cresset Press, 1959.

Marom, Ran. *The Development of U.S. Policy in the Palestine Issue: October 1973–November 1976.* Tel Aviv: Shiloah Center, 1978.

Marquand, David. *Ramsay MacDonald.* London: Jonathan Cape, 1977.

Meinertzhagen, Richard. *Middle East Diary, 1917–56.* London: Cresset Press, 1959.

Meir, Golda. *My Life.* New York: Putnam and Dell Paperback, 1975.

Meiring, Desmond. *Fire of Islam.* London: Wildwood House, 1982.

Monroe, Elizabeth. *Britain's Moment in the Middle East.* London: Chatto and Windus, 1981.

Moore, John Norton (ed.). *The Arab–Israeli Conflict: Readings and Documents,* abr. and rev. ed. Princeton, N.J.: Princeton University Press, 1977.

Morse, Arthur D. *While Six Million Died.* New York: Random House, 1968.

Mortimer, Edward. *Faith and Power.* London, Faber and Faber, 1983; New York: Random House, 1982.

Muslih, Muhammad Y. "Moderates and Rejectionists Within the Palestine Liberation Organization." *The Middle East Journal* 30 (Spring 1976).

Nakhlek, K., and E. Zureik (eds.). *The Sociology of the Palestinians.* London: Croom, Helm, 1980.

Nedava, Joseph. "Herzl and Messianism." *Herzl Year Book* (*see* Patai, Raphael), Vol. VII. New York: Herzl Press, 1971.

Newman, David. *Jewish Settlement in the West Bank: The Role of Gush Emunim.* Durham: University of Durham Centre for Middle Eastern and Islamic Studies, 1982.

O'Neill, Bard E. *Armed Struggle in Palestine.* Boulder, Colo.: Westview Press, 1978.

Oz, Amos. *Elsewhere, Perhaps*. Translated by N. De Lange. New York: Harcourt Brace Jovanovich, 1973.

———. *The Hill of Evil Counsel*. London: Fontana Books, 1981.

———. *In the Land of Israel*. Translated by M. Goldberg-Bartura. London and New York: Hogarth Press, 1983.

———. *Touch the Water, Touch the Wind*. Translated by N. De Lange. London: Chatto and Windus, 1975.

———. *Unto Death*. Translated by N. De Lange. London: Chatto and Windus, 1976.

———. *Where Jackals Howl*. Translated by N. De Lange and P. Simpson. London: Chatto and Windus, 1981.

Patai, Raphael (ed.). *The Complete Diaries of Theodor Herzl*. Translated by Harry Zohn. New York: Herzl Press and Thomas Yoseloff, 1960.

———. *Encyclopaedia of Zionism and Israel*. New York: Herzl Press, 1971.

———. *Herzl Year Book*, Vol. 1, 1958, and annually. New York: Herzl Press. *See also* Nedava, Joseph.

Peel Commission Report. *See* United Kingdom, H.M. Stationery Office, *Sessional Papers*.

Peres, Yochanan. "Ethnic Relations in Israel." *American Journal of Sociology* 76 (July 1970–May 1971).

Peri, Yoram. *Between Battles and Ballots: Israeli Military in Politics*. Cambridge: Cambridge University Press, 1983.

Polk, William R. *The Arab World*, 4th. ed. Cambridge, Mass., and London: Harvard University Press, 1980.

Poliakov, Leon. *The History of Anti-Semitism*, Vol. III, *From Voltaire to Wagner*. London: Routledge and Kegan Paul, 1968.

Porath, Yehoshua. *The Emergence of the Palestinian-Arab National Movement: 1918–1929*. London: Cass, 1974.

Prittie, Terence: *Eshkol of Israel*. London: Museum Press, 1969.

Pulzer, P. G. J. *The Rise of Political Anti-Semitism in Germany and Austria*. New York: Wiley, 1964.

Quandt, William B. *Decade of Decisions: American Policy Toward the Arab–Israeli Conflict*. Berkeley and Los Angeles: University of California Press, 1977.

Quandt, William B., Fuad Jabber and Ann Lesch. *Politics of Palestinian Nationalism*. Berkeley: University of California Press, 1973.

Rabin, Yitzhak. *The Rabin Memoirs*. London: Weidenfeld and Nicolson, 1979; Boston: Little, Brown, 1979.

Rabinovich, Itamar. *The War for Lebanon, 1970–1983*. Ithaca, N.Y., and London: Cornell University Press, 1984.

Rabinowicz, Oskar. *Fifty Years of Zionism*. London: R. Anscombe, 1950.

Rafael, Gideon. *Destination Peace*. London: Weidenfeld and Nicolson, 1981; New York: Stein and Day, 1981.

Rahman, Fazlur. *Islam*. Chicago: University of Chicago Press, 1979.

Reinharz, Jehuda. *Chaim Weizmann: The Making of a Zionist Leader*. London and New York: Oxford University Press, 1985.

Rodinson, Maxime. *Israel and the Arabs*, 2nd ed. London: Penguin Books, 1968, 1982.

Rose, Norman Anthony. *The Gentile Zionists: A Study in Anglo-Zionist Diplomacy 1929–1939*. London: Cass, 1973.

Ronaldshay, Lord (John Lawrence Dundas, later Marquis of Zetland). *The Life of Lord Curzon*. 3 vols. London: Ernest Benn, 1928.

Rothwell, V. H. *British War Aims and Peace Diplomacy, 1914–18*. Oxford: Oxford University Press, 1971.

Royal Institute of International Affairs. *Documents on International Affairs*, Vol. 1, 1928, and annually. London: Oxford University Press.

———. *Survey of International Affairs*, Vol. 1, 1925, and annually. See especially the 1954 volume, by George Kirk, *The Middle East 1945–1950*. See also under British Institute, etc. (predecessor of the Royal Institute).

Rubin, Barry M. *The Arab States and the Palestine Conflict*. Syracuse, N.Y.: Syracuse University Press, 1982.

Sachar, Howard M. *Europe Leaves the Middle East*. London: A. Lane, 1974.

———. *A History of Israel from the Rise of Zionism to Our Time*. Oxford: Blackwell, 1977.

Sadat, Anwar. *In Search of Identity: An Autobiography*. London: Collins and Fontana, 1978; New York: Harper and Row, 1978.

Safran, Nadav. "Engagement in the Middle East." *Foreign Affairs* 52, No. 1 (October 1974).

———. *From War to War: The Arab–Israeli Confrontation, 1948–1967*. New York: Pegasus, 1969.

Said, Edward W. *The Question of Palestine*. London: Routledge and Kegan Paul, 1981.

Sanders, Ronald. *The High Walls of Jerusalem*. New York: Holt, Rinehart and Winston, 1983.

Sayigh, Rosemary. *Palestinians: From Peasants to Revolutionaries*. London: Zed Press, 1979.

Sayigh, Yusif A. *Arab Oil Policies in the 1970s: Opportunity and Responsibility*. London and Canberra: Croom Helm, 1983.

Schechtman, J. B. *Fighter and Prophet: The Vladimir Jabotinsky Story. The Last Years*. New York and London: Thomas Yoseloff, 1961.

———. *Rebels and Statesmen: The Vladimir Jabotinsky Story. The Early Years*. New York: Thomas Yoseloff, 1956.

———. *The Mufti and the Fuehrer*. New York: Thomas Yoseloff, 1969.

Schiff, Ze'ev, and Ehud Ya'ari. *Israel's Lebanon War*. New York: Simon and Schuster, 1984.

Schlesinger, Arthur M., Jr., and Fred Israel (eds.). *History of American Presidential Elections*, Vol. IV, 1940–1968. New York and London: Chelsea House in association with McGraw-Hill, 1971.

Schueftan, Dan. "Nasser's 1967 Policy Reconsidered." *Jerusalem Quarterly* No. 3 (Spring 1977).

Seale, Patrick. *The Struggle for Syria: A Study of Post-War Arab Politics, 1945–1958*. London and New York: Oxford University Press, 1965.

Segre, V. D. *Israel: A Society in Transition*. London: Oxford University Press, 1971.

Shadid, Mohammed K. *The United States and the Palestinians*. London: Croom, Helm, 1981; New York: St. Martin's, 1981.

Shahar, David. "The Death of the Little God," in *Stories from Jerusalem*. London: Elek, 1976.

Shaked, Haim, and Itamar Rabinovich (eds.). *The Middle East and the United States: Perceptions and Policies*. New Brunswick, N.J.: Transaction Books, 1980.

Sharef, Ze'ev. *Three Days*. Translated by Julian Louis Meltzer. London: W. H. Allen, 1962.

Sheffer, Gabriel. *Resolutions vs. Management of the Middle East Conflict*. Jerusalem: 1980.

Shehadeh, Raja. *The Third Way: A Journal of Life on the West Bank*. London and New York: Quartet Books, 1982.

Shirer, William E. *The Rise and Fall of the Third Reich*. New York: Simon and Schuster, 1960; London: Secker and Warburg, 1963.

Sicherman, F. Harry. *Broker or Advocate? The U.S. Role in the Arab–Israeli Dispute 1973–1978*. Philadelphia: Foreign Policy Research Institute, 1978.

Silver, Eric. *Begin: A Biography*. London: Weidenfeld and Nicolson, 1984.

Simson, H. J. *British Rule in Palestine*. Edinburgh and London: Blackwood, 1937.

Slater, Robert. *Rabin of Israel*. London: Robson Books, 1977.

Smooha, Sammy. *Israel: Pluralism and Conflict*. London: Routledge and Kegan Paul, 1978.

Snetsinger, John. *Truman, the Jewish Vote and Israel*. Stanford, Calif.: Hoover Institution Press, 1974.

Snow, Peter. *Hussein: A Biography*. London: Barrie and Jenkins, 1972.

Sperber, Manes. "The Ending Aftermath: Thirty Years after the Wannsee Conference." *Wiener Library Bulletin* 25 (new series 24–25) (1972).

Stein, Leonard. *The Balfour Declaration*. London: Vallentine Mitchell, 1961.

Stephens, Robert. *Nasser: A Political Biography*. London: Allen Lane, 1971.

Stern, Noah. "Stopgap Litter," in Dennis Silk (ed.), *Fourteen Israeli Poets*. London: Deutsch, 1976.

Stewart, Desmond. *Theodor Herzl*. London: Hamish Hamilton, 1974.

Storrs, Ronald. *Orientations*. London: Nicholson and Watson, 1937.

Stoyanovsky, Jacob. *Mandate for Palestine*. London and New York: Longman, Green, 1928.

Susser, Asher. "Jordanian Influence in the West Bank." *Jerusalem Quarterly* No. 8 (Summer 1978).

Sykes, Christopher. *Crossroads to Israel*. Bloomington, Ind.: Indiana University Press, 1973.

Talmon, J. L. *Yad Vashem: Holocaust and Rebirth*. Jerusalem: 1974; London: Secker and Warburg, 1981.

Tamari, Salim. "Building Other People's Homes: The Palestinian Peasant's Household and Work in Israel." *Journal of Palestine Studies* 11, No. 1 (Autumn 1981).

Teveth, Shabtai. *Ben-Gurion and the Palestinian Arabs: From Peace to War*. London and New York: Oxford University Press, 1985.

Tibawi, A. L. *A Modern History of Syria, Including Lebanon and Palestine*. London: Macmillan, 1969; New York: St. Martin's, 1970.

Tillman, Seth P. *The United States in the Middle East: Interests and Obstacles*. Bloomington, Ind.: Indiana University Press, 1982.

Treinin, Avner. "Gates." *Jerusalem Quarterly* 17 (Fall 1980).

Truman, Harry S. *Memoirs*, Vol. II, *Years of Trial and Hope, 1946–1953*. New York: Doubleday/London: Hodder and Stoughton, 1956.

Truman, Margaret. *Harry S. Truman*. New York: Morrow, 1973.

Turki, Fawaz. *The Disinherited: Journal of a Palestinian Exile*. London and New York: Monthly Review Press, 1972.

United Kingdom, H.M. Stationery Office, Official Publications. *Documents* on British Foreign Policy, 1919–1939 (published 1947 to 1955): First Series, Vols. I to XXV (1919–1925); Series 1A, Vols. I to VII (1925–1930); Second Series, Vols. I to XXI (1930–1938); Third Series, Vols. I to IX (1938–1939).

――――. Documents on German Foreign Policy, 1933–1941 (published by Britain at intervals—1954 to 1983—after World War II).

――――. Sessional Papers, presented to Parliament by Royal Command Command Papers):

Cmd. 1500 (1921). Final Drafts of the Mandates for Palestine and Mesopotamia as Submitted for the Approval of the League of Nations.

Cmd. 1540 (1921) Palestine: Disturbances in May, 1921 [report of the Haycroft Commission].

Cmd. 1700 (1922). Correspondence with the Palestine Arab Delegation and the Zionist Organization [the "1922 White Paper"].

Cmd. 1785 (1923) Mandate for Palestine, Together with a Note by the Secretary-General of the League of Nations, Relating to Its Application to the Territory Known as Trans-Jordan Under the Provisions of Article 25 [Author's note: The effect was to make those provisions of the Mandate which embodied the Jewish National Home inapplicable in Mandate Palestine east of the Jordan in what is now the Hashemite Kingdom of Jordan.]

Cmd. 3686 (1930–31) Palestine: Report on Immigration, Land Settlement and Development, by Sir John Hope Simpson.

Cmd. 3692 (1930–35). Palestine: Statement of Policy by His Majesty's Government in the United Kingdom. [the "Passfield White Paper"].

Cmd. 5479 (1936–37). Report by the Royal Commission on Palestine [the "Peel Commission Report"].

Cmd. 5513 (1936–37) Statement of Policy by His Majesty's Government on Palestine [endorsing the Peel Commission Report and "supporting a solution of the Palestine problem by means of partition"].

Cmd. 5584 (1936–37). Report of the Palestine Partition Commission [the "Woodhead Report," preparing the way for a reversal of the Statement of Policy in Cmd. 5513].

Cmd. 6019 (1938–39) Palestine: Statement of Policy. [The "White Paper of May, 1939" abandoning partition, and so rejecting the Jewish State. This remained, at least formally, the basis of British policy up to the end of the Mandate.]

United Nations, Department of Public Information, United Nations, New York. Yearbooks of the United Nations, 1946–1980. [Author's note: This series forms an indispensable clue to the labyrinth of U.N. documentation.]

Urofsky, Melvin I. American Zionism from Herzl to the Holocaust. Garden City, N.Y.: Anchor Press, 1975.

Vambery, Arminius. Story of My Life, 2 vols. London: Fisher Unwin, 1905.

Vatikiotis, P. J. Conflict in the Middle East. London: Allen and Unwin, 1971.

Vinner, Shlomo. "Jerusalem" and "In the Wardrobe." Jerusalem Quarterly 10 (Winter 1979).

Vital, David. The Origins of Zionism. Oxford: Clarendon Press, 1975.

————. *Zionism: The Formative Years*. New York: Oxford University Press, 1982.

Von Bülow, Prince, *Memoirs 1903–1909*. Translated by F. A. Voigt. London and New York: Putnam, 1931.

Wallenrod, Reuben. *The Literature of Modern Israel*. New York and London: Abelard-Schuman, 1956–1957.

Walters, L. P. *A History of the League of Nations*. London: Royal Institute of International Affairs, 1952.

Wasserstein, Bernard. *The British in Palestine: the Mandatory Government and the Arab–Jewish Conflict, 1917–29*. London: Royal Historical Society, 1979.

Webb, Sidney and Beatrice, *Letters*, 3 vols. Edited by Norman Mackenzie. Cambridge: Cambridge University Press, 1978.

Weisgal, Meyer W., and Joel Carmichael (eds.). *Chaim Weizmann*. London: Weidenfeld and Nicolson, 1962.

Weizman, Ezer. *The Battle for Peace*. London and New York: Bantam, 1981.

Weizmann, Chaim. *The Letters and Papers of Chaim Weizmann*. Edited by Meyer W. Weisgal *et al*. English ed., Vols. 1–3, Series A. London: Oxford University Press and Yad Chaim Weizmann, 1968–1972; Vols. 4–7, Series A. Jerusalem: Israel Universities Press, 1973–75.

————. *Trial and Error: Autobiography*. London: Hamish Hamilton, 1949. *See also* Berlin, Isaiah, and Reinharz, Jehuda.

Weizmann, Vera. *The Impossible Takes Longer*. London: Hamish Hamilton, 1967.

White Papers, British. *See* United Kingdom, H.M. Stationery Office.

Williams, Francis (ed.) *A Prime Minister Remembers: The War and Post-War Memoirs of the Rt. Hon. Earl Attlee*. London: Heinemann, 1961.

Wittlin, Alma. *Abdul Hamid: The Shadow of God*. London: John Lane, 1940.

Yaniv, Avner, and Fabian Pascal. "Doves, Hawks and Other Birds of a Feather: The Distribution of Israeli Parliamentary Opinion on the Future of the Occupied Territories, 1967–1977." *British Journal of Political Science* (Cambridge University Press) 10 (1980).

Yehoshua, A. B. *The Lover*. Translated by P. Simpson. London: Heinemann, 1979.

Ye'or, Bat. "Aspects of the Arab–Israeli Conflict." *Wiener Library Bulletin* 32 (1979).

————. *The Dhimmi: Jews and Christians Under Islam*. London and Toronto: Associated University Press, 1985.

————. "Zionism in Islamic Lands: The Case of Egypt." *Wiener Library Bulletin* 30 (1977).

Yodfat, A. Y., and Y. Arnon-Channa. *P.L.O. Strategy and Tactics*. London: Croom Helm, 1981.

Zetland. *See* Ronaldshay, Lord.

Zureik, Elia T. *The Palestinians in Israel*. Boston and London: Routledge and Kegan Paul, 1979.

CHRONOLOGICAL TABLE

FROM EMANCIPATION TO HOLOCAUST

1775–1791
American and French revolutions.
First emancipations of Jews, as a consequence of emergence of secular states.

1807
Great Sanhedrin of Paris, convened by Napoleon, declares Jews to be a religious group, and not a nation. This definition is generally accepted by the leaders of the Western Jewish communities, and becomes a principle of further emancipation in the Napoleonic and post-Napoleonic periods.

1850
Richard Wagner's *Das Judentum in der Musik*. First major manifesto of modern anti-semitism: hostile to Jews, as foreigners, irrespective of religion.

1853
Gobineau's *Essai sur l'Inégalité des Races Humaines*. First systematic presentation of racist general theory.

1862
Moses Hess's *Rome and Jerusalem*. First manifesto of modern Jewish nationalism.

1865
Eugen Duehring's *Der Wert des Lebens*. First suggestion of genocide as a solution for the Jewish question.

1871
Newly founded German Empire emancipates Jews throughout its territory, thus completing the process of Jewish emancipation in Western Europe.

1873
Jews widely blamed for German stock-market crash.

1881
Assassination of Tsar Alexander II followed by the revival of persecution of the Jews throughout the Russian Empire.

1881–1914
2,600,000 Jews from Russia and Eastern Europe emigrate to the United States.

1882
Leon Pinsker, in *Autoemancipation!*, argues the case for a Jewish State.
Beginning of first *aliyah:* migration/"ascension" of Zionist Jews from Russian Empire to Palestine.

1882–1889
Major writings of Friedrich Nietzsche. Effort to rehabilitate an Aryan morality of fierceness, superseding the corrupting Christian ideology of compassion foisted by the Jews on the Aryans.

1886
Success of Édouard Drumont's *La France Juive* reflects widespread anti-semitism in France.

1889
Nietzsche goes mad.
Hitler is born.

1891
First Arab protests against Zionist settlements in Palestine.

1894–1895
Conviction and ceremonial degradation in Paris of the Jew Alfred Dreyfus, falsely charged with espionage.
Karl Lueger, head of the anti-semitic Christian Social Party, elected mayor of Vienna.

1896
Theodor Herzl: *Der Judenstaat.*

1897
Basel, August 29–31, First International Congress of Zionists.

1898
Kaiser Wilhelm II visits Palestine.

1900
Publication of Houston Stewart Chamberlain's *Foundations of the Nineteenth Century.* Effectively blending German romantic nationalism, general racist theory and obsessive anti-semitism, this work won the admiration both of Kaiser Wilhelm II and of Adolf Hitler (as well as of George Bernard Shaw and others).

1903
Major pogrom at Kishinev, in Bessarabia.

1904
Beginning of second *aliyah.*
Death of Herzl.

1905
Aliens Bill in Britain seeks to avert mass immigration, mainly Jewish, from Russia.

1905

Seventh Zionist Congress (Basel) rules out any alternative to Palestine as the objective of the Zionist enterprise.

1908–1909

Revolution in Ottoman Empire.
Intensification of Arab opposition to Zionist settlements.

1909

Tel Aviv founded.

1914–1918

The First World War can be seen in retrospect as the decisive period not merely for Zionism but for the fate of the Jews of the Old World.

1917

November 2   The Balfour Declaration.
December   British conquest of Palestine.

1918–1919

The *Dolchstosslegende* (legend of the stab in the back). The Jews identified by the German Army leadership, and the German Right as a whole, as principally responsible for Germany's defeat, and standing in the way of German recovery.

1919

Chaim Weizmann leads Zionist delegation at Peace Conference at Versailles.
Treaty of Versailles.
German military prepare to undermine the provisions of the treaty, and reverse the outcome of First World War.
Adolf Hitler recruited in Munich by the Army's political branch as a propagator of the *Dolchstosslegende*.

1919–1923

The third *aliyah*.

1919 and 1921

Anti-Jewish Arab riots in Palestine.

1920

British Mandate over Palestine; Sir Herbert Samuel appointed High Commissioner.

1921–1924

Closing of America to mass immigration.

1922

White Paper separates Transjordan from the area to be affected by the "Jewish national home" provisions of the Balfour Declaration and Mandate.

1923

Beer Hall Putsch in Munich.

1924

Adolf Hitler, a prisoner in Landsberg, writes *Mein Kampf*.

1924–1932
Fourth *aliyah* (mainly from Poland).

1929
August   Arabs riot in Jerusalem; massacres of Jews in Hebron and Safed.
October   Wall Street crash begins the process leading to worldwide economic depression.

1930
September   Sensational advance in German elections by Hitler's National Socialist Party, which becomes the second-largest party in the Reichstag.
October   The Passfield/White Papers, first attempt at British disengagement from the "Jewish national home" aspects of the Declaration and the Mandate.

1931
February   Passfield implicitly disavowed by Prime Minister Ramsay MacDonald. Britain recommitted to Jewish National Home in Palestine.
Spring   Irgun Zvai Leumi founded.

1933
January   Adolf Hitler becomes Chancellor of the Reich.

1933–1939
Fifth *aliyah:* emigration from Germany and German-controlled territories to Palestine.

1935
October   Mussolini invades Ethiopia.

1936
March   German Army reoccupies the demilitarized Rhineland.
April   Outbreak of Arab Revolt in Palestine.
May   Italian forces enter Addis Ababa; Emperor Haile Selassie comes to Jerusalem as a pilgrim.
July   Arab princes appear as mediators in relation to the Arab Revolt in Palestine.

1937
July   The Peel Commission recommends the partition of Palestine between Arabs and Jews. The British Government accepts this recommendation in principle.

1937–1938
Repression of Arab Revolt.

1938
March   Nazis take over Austria. Pogrom in Vienna.
July   Evian Conference on "refugee problems" gives few positive results, being based on the principle "that no country will be expected or asked to receive a greater number of immigrants than is permitted by its existing legislation." Palestine excluded from the Evian agenda.
September 29–30   The Munich crisis and agreement, resulting in annexation of the Sudetenland.
November   The *Kristallnacht.* Officially sponsored attacks on Jews and Jewish-owned premises throughout the Reich.
British Government hedges its commitment to the partition of Palestine.

1939

January–February Conference at St. James's Palace, London, on Palestine. Deadlock.

March Hitler occupies Prague.

May British White Paper repudiates partition and envisages an independent Palestinian State.

August 16–24 Twenty-first Zionist Congress meets in Geneva.

August 23 Hitler-Stalin Pact announced.

September Second World War. "We shall fight the war as if there were no White Paper, and the White Paper as if there were no war."—David Ben-Gurion

1939–1942

Period of close military cooperation between British and Jews in Palestine.

1942

January 20 Conference at Wannsee, Berlin, coordinates the Final Solution (*Endlösung*).

February Loss of the *Struma* with 767 Jewish refugees refused admission to Palestine.

May 9–11 Biltmore Conference of American Jews demands "that the gates of Palestine be opened."

November News of the Holocaust reaches the Jews of Palestine.

HOLOCAUST TO JEWISH STATE

1943

April 19–30 Anglo-American Conference at Bermuda on refugees. Same negative result as at Evian, in 1938.

1944

November 6 Assassination of Lord Moyne in Cairo.

1945

April Death of Roosevelt; Truman becomes President.

July Labour in power in postwar Britain.

July–September Truman supports demand for admission of larger numbers of Holocaust survivors to Palestine. British replies are negative. Illegal immigration is organized.

1946

April 30 Truman publicly endorses demand for immediate admission of 100,000 Jewish refugees to Palestine. British refusal.

June 16 Major sabotage operations organized throughout Palestine by all Jewish paramilitary organizations under political leadership of David Ben-Gurion.

June 29 British Government orders arrest of Jewish leaders. Ben-Gurion escapes net.

July 22 Irgun blows up King David Hotel in Jerusalem, killing ninety-one people.

October 4 Truman's "Yom Kippur speech," endorsing the partition of

Palestine and the creation of a Jewish State, as well as reiterating the demand for the admission of the 100,000 refugees.

1947
February 18   British Foreign Secretary Ernest Bevin declares his Government's intention to refer the Palestine Mandate back to the United Nations without specific recommendation.

July   Steamer *Exodus* turned back by force from Palestine to Europe, with 4,500 survivors of the Holocaust.

Two British sergeants hanged by Irgun in reprisal for the executions of three Jewish terrorists.

November 29   United Nations General Assembly votes for the partition of Palestine and a Jewish State.

December 11   British Government announces its intention to terminate, on May 15, 1948, its responsibility under the Mandate.

1947–1948
Britain supplying arms to Arab States; Eastern bloc supplying Jews in Palestine.

Fighting between Jews and Arabs inside Palestine.

United States swinging away from partition and toward trusteeship.

1948
March 18   Meeting between Truman and Weizmann. Truman swings back toward partition.

April   Massacre by Irgun of Arab villagers at Deir Yassin, followed by Arab reprisals against a Jewish hospital convoy near Jerusalem.

May 14   Ben-Gurion proclaims State of Israel.

May 15   Expiration of the British Mandate. Truman extends *de facto* recognition to State of Israel. Soviet *de jure* recognition follows three days later.

THE ARAB-ISRAELI CONFLICT

1948
May 15–16   Arab armies invade Israel.

May 21   U.N. appoints mediator, Count Folke Bernadotte.

June 11–July 7   Truce between Israel and Arab states.

July 8–18   Renewed war; Arab forces beaten back in most of Palestine.

September 17   Bernadotte assassinated in Jerusalem.

October–December   Renewed fighting between Israel and Egypt. Egyptian forces driven out of Negev.

1949
January   De facto recognition of Israel by Britain.

February–July   Israel concludes armistice agreements with Egypt, Lebanon, Jordan and Syria.

December   United Nations General Assembly votes in favor of the internationalization of Jerusalem. Ben-Gurion's Government declares Jerusalem the eternal capital of Israel.

1950
May   Tripartite Declaration (Britain, France and the United States) "regulating" supply of arms to the Middle East, etc.

1950–1953

Korean War. Israel tacitly abandons its announced policy of "nonidentification" as between the superpowers.

1950–1970

Massive immigration to Israel by the Jewish populations of Arab lands. Before the end of this period Oriental Jews make up more than half the population of Israel.

1951

July 20   King Abdullah of Jordan assassinated.

1952

Overthrow of King Farouk of Egypt. Beginning of Nasser's rise to power.

1953

Eisenhower becomes President of the United States (*January*).
U.S.S.R. breaks off relations with Israel.
Temporary retirement of David Ben-Gurion.
Moshe Sharett becomes Prime Minister; Pinchas Lavon Minister for Defense.

1954

Nasser in charge in Egypt.
Britain preparing to leave the Canal Zone.
Increasing *fedayeen* attacks on Israel.
Israeli agents caught and hanged in Cairo. Beginning of "the Lavon Affair."

1955

Ben-Gurion replaces Lavon as Defense Minister; Israel launches major raid against Egyptians in Gaza.
Major American and British anti-Soviet diplomatic activity results in the Baghdad Pact. Nasser reacts by concluding a large arms deal with the Soviet bloc.
September   Military pact between Egypt and Syria.
November   Ben-Gurion again Prime Minister of Israel.

1956

U.S. cancels support for Aswan Dam project.
July   Nasser announces the nationalization of the Suez Canal Company. Britain, France and Israel begin planning concerted attacks on Egypt.
October 29   Israel attacks in Sinai.
October 30   United States resolution in Security Council calling for Israeli withdrawal from Sinai vetoed by Britain and France.
November 5   British and French attack in Canal Zone, but Anglo-French military initiative quickly collapses under pressure from the superpowers, leaving Israel isolated and under heavy pressure to withdraw from Sinai.

1957

Israel announces its intention to withdraw from Sinai on certain stated assumptions (*March*) and following the stationing of a United Nations Expeditionary Force (U.N.E.F) in Sinai.

1958

Revolution in Iraq (*July*). Strengthening of relations between Israel and U.S.

1958–1959

Fatah founded. Yasser Arafat's career begins.

1961

Trial of Adolf Eichmann in Jerusalem.

1963

Final retirement of Ben-Gurion (*June*). Levi Eshkol becomes Prime Minister and Minister for Defense.

1964

P.L.O. founded under Nasserite auspices.

1966

Left-wing coup in Syria. Hafez al-Assad Minister for Defense. Increased *fedayeen* activity against Israel, by both Fatah and P.L.O.

1967

May 13   Soviet Union warns Egypt of impending Israeli attack on Syria.
May 17   Nasser declares alert, sends combat troops into Sinai.
May 18   Nasser "terminates" the U.N.E.F. presence in Sinai.
May 22   Nasser closes the Gulf of Aqaba to Israeli shipping.
May 23   Israeli Government declares Nasser's blockade an act of aggression against Israel. U.S. reaffirms "right of free and innocent passage."
June 1   Moshe Dayan replaces Eshkol as Minister for Defense. Menachem Begin enters Government of National Unity.
June 5–10   Six Day War.
August   Arab Summit at Khartoum: "the three noes."
November 22   Security Council Resolution 242.

1968–1969

Reorganization of P.L.O., around Fatah, with Arafat as chairman. Lebanon and Jordan bases for P.L.O. and *fedayeen* activity.

1969

Death of Levi Eshkol; Golda Meir becomes Prime Minister.
Egypt's "War of Attrition" against Israel. Israel replies with "deep penetration" raids against Egypt.

1970

Soviets begin a program of massive military aid to Egypt.
American pressure on Israel to end "deep penetration" raids.
August 4   Following success of this pressure, Begin and his colleagues withdraw support from Golda Meir, bringing the Government of National Unity to an end.
September   Fedayeen hijack airliners to Jordan, and Hussein moves against P.L.O.
September 28   Death of Nasser.
Nasser succeeded by Anwar Sadat.

1971

February Sadat makes first peace overture to Israel. Overture rebuffed by Israel.

Hussein completes eviction of P.L.O. forces from Jordan.

September Assassination of Jordanian Prime Minister Wasfi al-Tal.

1972

July Sadat expels Soviet military advisers.

September Black September organization—a cover name for Fatah—kidnaps eleven Israeli athletes at Munich Olympics.

Israeli air attacks on Lebanon, now the principal base of *fedayeen* operations.

1973

October 6 Yom Kippur. Egypt and Syria launch surprise attack on Israel.

October 6–25 Yom Kippur War. Soviet airlifts to Egypt and Syria; American airlift to Israel.

October 17 Arab oil embargo and cutbacks.

October 22 Security Council Resolution 338 urges direct negotiation between Arab states and Israel.

October 25 Belligerents accept cease-fire.

December 21 Geneva Peace Conference. U.S. Secretary of State Henry Kissinger in role of Middle East mediator.

1974

January 18 First Sinai (agreement on disengagement of forces).

April 11 Golda Meir announces resignation.

May 31 Disengagement agreement between Israel and Syria mediated by Kissinger.

June Yitzhak Rabin becomes Prime Minister of Israel; Shimon Peres Minister for Defense.

October 26–29 Arab Summit at Rabat recognizes P.L.O. as "sole legitimate representative of the Palestinian people."

November 13 Yasser Arafat addresses the General Assembly of the U.N.

1975

September 4 Second Sinai. Israel agrees to further withdrawals, in exchange for U.S. assurances, including assurances on P.L.O.

1976

January Jimmy Carter becomes President of the United States.

June Syria moves forces into Lebanon.

December Resignation of Rabin Government.

1977

May General Elections in Israel. Likud gains and Labor loses.

June Menachem Begin forms Government. Ezer Weizman, Minister for Defense; Moshe Dayan, Foreign Minister.

September 12 U.S. State Department calls for "a comprehensive Arab-Israeli agreement."

October 1 Joint Statement by United States and Soviet Union calls for renewed Geneva negotiations including representatives "of the Palestinian people."

November 9   Sadat, addressing the Egyptian Parliament, declares his willingness to go to Israel and talk to the Knesset.

November 14   Begin invites Sadat to Jerusalem.

November 19–20   Sadat in Jerusalem.

December 2–5   Arab Front of Steadfastness and Opposition (to Egypt) meets in Tripoli.

1978

January 18   Israel-Egypt negotiations stall (over settlements in Sinai).

March 11   Fatah *fedayeen*, arriving by boat from Lebanon, massacre thirty-seven Israeli civilians.

March 14   Israel launches punitive offensive, Operation Litani, into southern Lebanon.

March 19   Security Council Resolution 425, actively supported by the U.S., calls upon Israel to withdraw its forces from Lebanon, and calls for the establishment of a U.N. force (U.N.I.F.I.L.).

September 6–18   Camp David talks (Egypt, Israel, U.S.) result in a Framework for a Peace Treaty between Egypt and Israel and a more nebulous Framework for Peace (Palestine).

September 25   Knesset ratifies Camp David Accords by 84 votes to 19, with 17 abstentions.

November 2–5   Arab Summit at Baghdad denounces the Camp David Accords.

1979

January–February   Iranian Revolution.

March 26   Treaty of Peace between Egypt and Israel signed in White House.

March 31   Second Baghdad Summit condemns the treaty.

November 4   Seizure of American Embassy in Teheran, and of American hostages.

1980

January   U.N. General Assembly condemns Soviet invasion of Afghanistan.

May–June   Violent incidents in West Bank.

June 13   Venice Summit of E.E.C. heads of Governments issues declaration on necessity to associate the P.L.O. in future Middle East negotiations.

September   Outbreak of war between Iraq and Iran.

November–December   Riots and anti-Israeli demonstrations in West Bank.

December   Treaty of cooperation between the Soviet Union and Syria.

1981

January   Ronald Reagan becomes President of the United States.

April   Israeli-Syrian clashes in Lebanon.

June   Israel's Air Force destroys Iraq's nuclear reactor, Osirak.

Israel's General Elections again provide Begin with a parliamentary majority. Begin forms new Government with Ariel Sharon as Minister for Defense.

August   Saudi Arabia's Crown Prince Fahd calls for "an independent Palestinian State with Jerusalem as its capital."

October Sadat assassinated in Cairo. Hosni Mubarak becomes President of Egypt.

November Renewed disturbances in West Bank.

1982

February Syrian Government forces crush revolt at Hama, killing an estimated 25,000 people.

March–May Thirteen Arab civilians in West Bank killed by Israeli fire, in the course of riots and repression.

June 3 Shlomo Argov, Israel's ambassador in London, shot and seriously wounded by Arab gunmen.

June 6 Israel invades Lebanon.

June 9 Israeli Air Force destroys Syrian air defense system in Lebanon.

Mid-June Israeli forces enter Christian East Beirut and cut off P.L.O. and Syrian forces in West Beirut.

July–August Israeli bombardment of Palestinian and Syrian positions in West Beirut.

August 21– September 1 Evacuation of Beirut by the P.L.O. and Syrian forces.

August 23 Bashir Gemayel elected President by the Parliament of Lebanon.

September 14 Assassination of Bashir Gemayel.

September 15 Israelis occupy West Beirut.

September 17–18 Massacre of Palestinians by Maronite militia, at Sabra and Chatila, West Beirut.

September 21 Amin Gemayel elected President of Lebanon.

September 25 Massive protest demonstration in Israel over the Sabra and Chatila massacres.

September 28 Begin agrees to full and independent inquiry: the Kahan Commission.

1983

February Kahan Commission report precipitates Government crisis. Sharon resigns as Minister for Defense and becomes Minister without Portfolio.

August Israeli forces retreat to the line of the Awali river in southern Lebanon.

September Begin retires. Yitzhak Shamir becomes leader of Likud.

October Syrians crush pro-Arafat forces in northern Lebanon. Shamir succeeds Begin as Prime Minister.

1984

July–August "Hung" elections in Israel result in the formation of a Government of National Unity, with Shimon Peres as Prime Minister and Yitzhak Shamir as Deputy Prime Minister and Foreign Minister.

1985

February Joint proposals by Hussein and Arafat on Framework for Peace. President Mubarak of Egypt praises Hussein-Arafat statement and calls for talks.

June–July Israel completes withdrawal from Lebanon except for continuing support for the South Lebanon Army on Israel's border. Under attack from Shi'ite militia, retreating Israeli forces take and hold Shi'ite hostages. Shi'ites hijack U.S. airplane and take American hostages. Syrian mediation secures release of American hostages. Israel releases about half its Shi'ite hostages. Murders of Jews by Arabs in Israel lead to anti-Arab violence and increasing support for Jewish extremist groups.

GLOSSARY

HEBREW TERMS

AHDUT HA'AVODA "Unity of Labor." Formerly an independent left-wing party; part of the Labor Alignment since 1965. Retains strong support in the kibbutz movement. See *Mapai*.

ALIYAH (pl. ALIYOT) "Ascent." The coming of Jews to the Land of Israel for permanent residence. As used by Zionists, "implies personal participation in the rebuilding of the Jewish homeland and the elevation of the individual to a higher plane of self-fulfillment as a member of the renascent nation" (*Encyclopaedia Judaica*).

First *Aliyah*,	1882–1903
Second *Aliyah*,	1904–1914
Third *Aliyah*,	1919–1923
Fourth *Aliyah*,	1924–1928
Fifth *Aliyah*,	1929–1939

ASHKENAZ, ASHKENAZI Jews of northern Europe and their cultural complex and legacy. Used in contradistinction to *Sepharad* (adj. Sephardic *q.v.*), the Jewish cultural complex originating in Spain. In Israel, "Ashkenazic" is often used in contrast to "Oriental" (*q.v.*), although the term "Sephardic" is also used in relation to Oriental Jews generally.

BERITH SHALOM (also *Brit Shalom*) "Covenant of Peace." Founded in Jerusalem in 1925 to foster amicable Arab–Jewish relations. Favored a bi-national Arab-Jewish State in Palestine. Faded out in 1930s. See *Ihud*.

BETAR Activist Zionist youth movement founded in 1923 in Riga, Latvia. Often accused of fascist tendencies by Zionist Socialists. Vladimir Jabotinsky became *Rosh Betar*, "head of Betar," in 1931. See also "Revisionism."

BILU Acronym signifying "House of Jacob, come and let us go." First organized group of pioneers to go to Palestine (*Eretz Israel*) in the First *Aliyah* (1882).

CHALUTZIM "Pioneers." Used of Zionist settlers in "frontier" situations.

EE-HIZDAHUT "Non-identification," or "non-alignment," as between the blocs led by the superpowers. *Ee-Hizdahut* was proclaimed as a basic policy principle of the State of Israel in the first year of its independence. It was tacitly abandoned during the Korean War and eventually succeeded (especially after June 1967) by a policy of identification with the United States.

741

ERETZ ISRAEL (and variant transliterations) The "Land of Israel" (Biblical). Became "the official designation of the area governed by British mandate after World War I until 1948" (*Encyc. Jud.*).

GAHAL "The Herut-Liberal Bloc." Political alliance formed before the 1965 elections. See *Herut* and *Likud*.

GALUT "Exile." The Hebrew term "expresses the Jewish conception of the condition and feeling of a nation uprooted from its homeland and subject to alien rule" (*Encyc. Jud.*). Used for the "forced dispersion" of the Jewish people, insofar as distinguishable from their "voluntary dispersion" ("Diaspora").

GUSH EMUNIM "Bloc of the Faithful." Religious-political group founded in 1974 for the purpose of Judaizing the Occupied Territories through illegal settlement (*Hitnahalut*).

HA'AVARA A company for the transfer of Jewish property from Nazi Germany to Palestine. Made possible the immigration of about 60,000 German Jews to Palestine in the years 1933–1939.

HADASSAH The Women's Zionist Organization of America, largest Zionist organization in the world. Grew out of the "Daughters of Zion" movement, which changed its name to "Hadassah" in 1914. Organized medical aid and medical education on a large scale in Mandate Palestine and later in Israel.

HAGANA "Defense." The underground military organization of the *Yishuv* (*q.v.*). from 1920 to 1948. Became the regular army of the State of Israel on May 31, 1948.

HALUKKAH "Division." Financial support for religious Jews choosing to live in Palestine from the contributions of congregations in the Diaspora. The practice, of ancient origin, was challenged by the Hovevei Zion (*q.v.*) and by the Zionist movement generally and ceased to be of public importance after World War I.

HAMTANA The "waiting period" on the eve of the Six Day War.

HA-SHILOAH Hebrew periodical published in Russia (1896–1914) and originally edited by Ahad Ha'am. Organ of cultural Zionism and (under Ha'am) strongly critical of Herzl's version of Political Zionism.

HA-SHOMER "The Watchman." Self-defense organization of Zionist pioneers, 1909–1920. The nucleus of the *Hagana* (*q.v.*) and so ultimately of the Israel Defense Forces.

HASKALA Hebrew term for "the Enlightenment movement and ideology which began within Jewish society in the 1770's" (*Encyc. Jud.*). Assimilationist in tendency, especially in linguistic and cultural terms. See also *Maskil*.

HATIKVAH "The Hope." Anthem of the Zionist movement and national anthem of the State of Israel. Written by Naphtali Herz Imber (1856–1909) under the influence (according to *Encyc. Jud.*) of "Die Wacht am Rhein."

HAVLAGA "Restraint." *Hagana* (*q.v.*) policy (esp. in period 1936–1939) of refraining from retaliation against Arabs generally for acts of Arab terrorism. The *Irgun* (*q.v.*) rejected *Havlaga*.

HERUT "Freedom." Political movement established in July 1948 by the *Irgun* (*q.v.*) "with the aim of continuing as a parliamentary party in the State of Israel in accordance with the ideals of Vladimir Jabotinsky." See also *Likud*.

HISTADRUT The General Federation of Labor in Israel, founded in 1920. The largest labor union and the largest voluntary organization in Israel.

HITNAHALUT See *Gush Emunim*.

HOVEVEI ZION "Lovers of Zion." Participants in a movement (known as *Hibbat Zion*) for Zionist settlement (*aliyah*) among the Jews of the Russian Empire, esp. in the period 1882–1897.

IHUD Palestinian Jewish-Arab group, founded in 1942, advocating (like *Berith Shalom*, *q.v.*) an Arab-Jewish bi-national state in Palestine. Its Arab members were murdered by other Arabs, and its influence in the Jewish community was very limited.

IRGUN ZVAI LEUMI Palestinian Jewish military organization founded in 1931. Adhered to doctrine of retaliation against Arab violence. Declared a state of war against Britain in 1944. Units disbanded and merged with Israel Defense Forces in 1948. Tradition continued, in political and parliamentary form, by *Herut* (*q.v.*)

K'FAR Hebrew for "village."

KIBBUTZ "A voluntary collective community, mainly agricultural, in which there is no private wealth and which is responsible for all the needs of the members and their families" (*Encyc. Jud.*). The first such community was founded in 1909 at Deganyah. The *kibbutzim* have supplied many of the leaders of Israel, both civil and military, and have been increasingly identified with the Ashkenazic and especially *Mapai* (*q.v.*) establishment. See *Moshav*.

KIRYAT Hebrew for "city."

KNESSET "Assembly." The parliament of Israel. The name is derived from the *K'nesset Hag'dola* (Great Assembly), the legislative body of the Jewish people at the beginning of the Second Commonwealth in Palestine. The modern Knesset met for the first time, as parliament of the newly independent State of Israel, in February 1949.

LEHI Acronym for *Lohame Herut Israel* (Fighters for the Freedom of Israel). Jewish underground fighting force in Palestine formed by Avraham Stern in 1940, after a split in the *Irgun* (*q.v.*). Known to the British as "the Stern Gang." Banned and disbanded in 1948.

LIKUD "Unity." Political bloc, formed in 1973, of *Gahal* (*q.v.*) and smaller groups. The dominant group within Likud remained Begin's *Herut* (*q.v.*).

MA'ABARA (pl. *Ma'abarot*) Temporary accommodation (transit camps) provided by the State of Israel for mass immigration between 1950 and 1954.

MAPAI (Acronym) Israel Labor Party. Founded in 1930 as "a Zionist-Socialist Party faithful to the ideal of national redemption and the ideal of socialism in the homeland." Merged with *Ahdut Ha-Avoda* (*q.v.*) into the Labor Alignment in 1965.

MAPAM (*Acronym*) United Workers Party. Left-wing, and at one time strongly pro-Soviet, party. Adhered to Labor Alignment in 1969.

MASKIL A person of the Enlightenment (*Haskala, q.v.*).

MIZRACHI Abbreviation of *Merkaz Ruhani,* "Spiritual Center." "Religious Zionist movement whose aim was expressed in its motto "The Land of Israel for the people of Israel according to the Torah of Israel" (*Encyc. Jud.*). Founded in 1902 at Vilna.

MIZZUG GALUYOT "Merging of the Exiles." "Sociocultural concept forming one of the major basic tenets of Zionism and the reconstituted Jewish State of Israel" (Patai, *Encyclopaedia of Zionism and Israel*).

MOSHAV (pl. *moshavim*) "Workers' settlement." "Co-operative smallholders village, combining some of the features of both co-operative and private farming." The first *moshavim* were established in 1921. After 1948, the *moshavim* expanded greatly, as instruments for the settlement of Oriental immigrants on the land.

PALMAH (also *Palmakh*) Abbreviation for *Peluggot Mahaz,* "assault companies." The permanently mobilized striking force of the *Hagana* (*q.v.*) and later, until its dissolution, part of the [Israel Defense Forces]" (*Encyc. Jud.*). Founded in 1941; merged with other I.D.F. units in 1949.

PANTERIM SHEHORIM "Black Panthers." Militant movement of Oriental Jews in Israel (1971).

PURIM Feast instituted, according to the book of Esther (9:20–28), by Mordecai "to celebrate the deliverance of the Jews from Haman's plot to kill them" (*Encyc. Jud.*). PURIMS, Special. Custom for "Jewish communities or families to celebrate the anniversary of their escape from destruction by reciting special prayers and with a ritual similar to that of Purim." The *Encyclopaedia Judaica* lists 100 such special community Purims, from 1191 to 1891, in various parts of Europe, North Africa and the Middle East.

RAKAH "New Communist List." Party supported mainly by Israeli Arabs.

SANHEDRIN "Great Sanhedrin usually means the supreme political, religious and judicial body in Palestine during the Roman period" (*Encyc. Jud.*). The French *Sanhedrin* was a "Jewish Assembly of 71 members convened in Paris during February–March 1807 on the request of Napoleon Bonaparte" (*Encyc. Jud.*). The 1807 Sanhedrin laid down a number of regulations of which the most significant, socially and politically, was that "Jews who have become citizens of a state must regard that country as their fatherland."

SEPHARDIM Term denoting those Jews whose ancestors lived in Spain and Portugal; derived from the traditional medieval Hebrew name for Spain (*S'pharad*). Sometimes applied to the Oriental element in the population of Israel, in contradistinction to *Ashkenazim* (*q.v.*).

VA'AD LEUMI (also *Leummi*) "National Committee." The National Council of Jews of Palestine, 1920–1948. Representative body of the *Yishuv* in its dealings with such bodies as the Mandates Commission.

YAD VASHEM "Martyrs' and Heroes' Remembrance Hall." "An Israeli national institution, dedicated to perpetuate the memory of the martyrs of the Holocaust and for research and documentation" (*Encyc. Jud.*).

YESHIVA (pl. *Yeshivot*) Institution of Talmudic learning.

YISHUV Jewish population of Palestine. After the arrival of the first Zionist pioneers in 1882, a distinction was made between "the old *Yishuv*," consisting of pious Jews without political intentions, and "the new *Yishuv*," formed by the Zionists.

ARABIC AND TURKISH TERMS

AL-ARD Arab nationalist party, set up in Israel in 1959 and soon suppressed by the authorities.

AL-BURAQ In Muslim tradition, the Prophet's magic steed. Also applied to the area of the Temple Mount in Jerusalem where the Prophet is believed to have tethered his steed before his ascent to Heaven.

DHIMMI A term of public law applicable under Islamic law to Christians and Jews, as vanquished and tolerated communities.

FATAH "Palestinian National Liberation Movement." The term is an Arabic acronym-in-reverse; also, *fatah* is an Arabic word meaning the opening up of a land, by conquest, to Islam. *Fatah* was founded in Kuwait in the late 1950s by a group of Palestinian students who included Yasser Arafat. It was originally a propaganda organization, but was encouraged by Syria to engage in *fedayeen* (*q.v.*) activity from the mid-1960s on. After the Six Day War, Arafat's *Fatah* became the principal component in the reconstituted *Palestine Liberation Organization* (*q.v.*). See also *Black September*.

FATWA A formal answer to a question on Islamic law submitted by a judge, an official body or a private individual to a *Mufti* (*q.v.*).

FEDAYEEN (also *Fidayin*) Arabic for "self-sacrificers." In its modern connotation, the term was first applied to Egyptian guerrilla volunteers attacking British troops in the Suez Canal Zone from 1950 on. Later applied to armed Palestinians attacking Israel and Israelis.

HAMULA Group of Arabs claiming descent from a common ancestor; "usually a territorial group whose members cooperate politically and economically" (*Encyclopaedia of Islam*).

HARAM ESH-SHARIF (or *al-Sharif*) The third sacred place of Islam (after Mecca and Medina), consisting of the surroundings of the Dome of the Rock and the Mosque of Al-Aqsa in Jerusalem (on the Jewish Temple Mount).

HASHEMITES Families claiming descent from the clan of the Prophet. Title of the dynasties established by the British in the 1920s in Transjordan (later Jordan) and Iraq. The Iraqi branch was wiped out in the Revolution of 1958. Hussein's Hashemite Kingdom of Jordan has endured.

IKHWAN See Muslim Brotherhood.

JIHAD An Arabic word meaning "effort" or "striving"; the holy war for Islam, a religious duty prescribed by the faith. A soldier in the *Jihad* is a *Mujahid*.

JIZYAH Arabic word meaning "ransom"; a head tax levied in the Islamic world on *Dhimmi* (*q.v.*) peoples, mainly Christians and Jews.

KATAEB/PHALANGES Names assumed by the Maronite politico-sectarian movement in Lebanon and its militia.

KUSHAN TABO Title deeds under the Ottoman Empire. Adapted to Israeli use in the phrase "We have the *Kushan* [*Tabo*] of the land from Beersheba to Eilat."

MUFTI An official Muslim expert in Islamic jurisprudence. See *Fatwa*.

MUJAHID See *Jihad*.

MUKHTAR A village headman.

AL-NAKBA "The Catastrophe." Used with reference to the defeat of the Arab armies in 1948.

QADI Muslim magistrate or judge.

SANJAK (also *Sandjak*) Administrative sub-division in the Ottoman Empire.

SUMUD, SAMID The quality of steadfastness; a steadfast person. Applied to Arabs of the Occupied Territories.

TANZIMAT "Beneficent Legislation." Term for the reforms introduced in the Ottoman Empire, under Western pressure, in the nineteenth century.

VILAYET Largest administrative division in the Ottoman Empire.

WAQF (also *Wakf*) Pious endowment under Muslim law.

OTHER TERMS

BLACK SEPTEMBER The Arab organization which claimed responsibility for various acts of terrorism in the early 1970s, including the attack on the Israeli Olympic Team at Munich in 1972. "Black September" was in fact a flag of convenience for a section of *Fatah* (*q.v.*).

BLOOD LIBEL The allegation that Jews murder Christians in order to obtain blood for the Passover or other rituals. Jews were persecuted on this ground in the Middle Ages, and in Eastern Europe, into the twentieth century.

ENDLÖSUNG "Final Solution"; Nazi euphemism for the mass murder of the Jews during the Second World War, from 1942 on.

ENDZIEL The "final goal" of Zionism: the Jewish State. Not publicly proclaimed by Zionist gatherings before 1942.

JUDENSTAAT, DER Title of Theodor Herzl's principal Zionist book (1896). Usually translated *The Jewish State*, though "the Jew State" would be nearer to the German.

MUSLIM BROTHERHOOD (*Ikhwan al-Muslimin*) Politico-religious society founded in Egypt in 1929; fundamentalist, terrorist and anti-Western.

PALESTINE LIBERATION ORGANIZATION (P.L.O.) Founded in 1964 as an Egyptian-sponsored counterweight to the Syrian-backed *Fatah* (*q.v.*). Reconstituted in 1968 with *Fatah* as its principal component and Arafat as its chairman. Recognized in 1974 by the Arab Summit at Rabat as "sole legitimate representative of the Palestinian people."

PALESTINIAN NATIONAL COVENANT   Basic document of the *Palestine Liberation Organization* (*q.v.*). First issued in 1964 and revised in 1968, the Covenant declares that "Armed struggle is the only way to liberate Palestine. Thus it is the overall strategy, not merely a tactical phase" (Article 9). "Palestine, with the boundaries it had during the British Mandate, is an indivisible unit" (Article 2). "The liberation of Palestine . . . aims at the elimination of Zionism in Palestine" (Article 15). "The Jews who had normally resided in Palestine before the beginning of the Zionist invasion will be considered Palestinians" (Article 6). As "the beginning of the Zionist invasion" was in 1882, the Jewish beneficiaries of Article 6 are now all centenarians.

PHALANGES   See *Kataeb*.

POGROM   "Devastation; desolation"; Russian diminutive of *grom*, meaning "thunder." Organized attacks on Jews in Russia, esp. in the late nineteenth and early twentieth centuries. The *pogrom*-makers were called *pogrom-shchiki*.

PROTOCOLS OF THE ELDERS OF ZION   Anti-semitic forgery originating in Russia, circa 1902, widely circulated in Europe between the two World Wars and in the Arab world today. It is an account of a plan for world domination by a secret Jewish Government. Ezra Pound believed that the Protocols were true, even if they were forged.

REKRUTCHINA   Russian term for conscription, applicable to young Jewish boys and accompanied by pressure toward Christianization.

REVISIONISTS   Hard-line Jewish nationalists; followers of Vladimir Jabotinsky, and precursors of Menachem Begin's *Herut* (*q.v.*). See also *Betar*.

SAISON   The code word for the cooperation of *Hagana* with the British authorities against *Irgun*, in the period immediately following the assassination of Lord Moyne. The *Saison* lasted from November 1944 to May 1945.

SHTETL   Jewish town or village in the Russian Empire.

UMWERTUNG DES WERTES   "Transvaluation of Values." A concept of Friedrich Nietzsche's, according to which the proper Aryan values, based on fierceness, had been corrupted by the Jews through the Christian ethic and needed to be reasserted.

UNIFIL   United Nations Force in Lebanon. A truce-supervising body on the Lebanese side of the Lebanon–Israel frontier.

INDEX

Abd al-Malik, 338

Abd al-Mujid, 335

Abdul Hamid II, Sultan, 112
Herzl and, 92-94
after Revolution of 1908, 116
Zionist immigration opposed
by, 78-79, 87-88, 89, 90-91,
92-94, 96, 99, 100

Abdullah ibn Hussein, King of
Transjordan, 158, 215, 216,
227, 235, 289-90, 291, 293,
300, 303, 304, 308, 363
Haj Amin vs., 289-90, 303, 304,
368-69
internationalization of Jerusalem opposed by, 364, 365
Israeli negotiations with, 363,
364, 365-66, 367-68
murder of, 368

Abraham, 186, 577, 578, 602

Absentees' Property Law (Israel,
1950), 425

Abu-Hana, Hana, 436

Abu Nidal, 622-23

Acre, 423

Adenauer, Konrad, 406

Adhem, Kamal, 512-13

"Admission of Guilt" (Kovner),
323-24

Afghanistan, Soviet invasion of
(1979), 599, 605

Africa:
East, Zionists offered land in,
29-30, 101-2, 103, 105
influence of oil-rich Arab countries in, 403

Israel's isolation from, 530-31
North, Oriental Jews in, 334,
337, 338, 339

Agranat Commission of Inquiry
report (1974), 537

Agudat Party, Israeli, 612

Ahad Ha'am (Asher Ginsberg),
84-85, 86, 90, 104, 109, 113,
174, 376

Ajami, Fouad, 492

Al-Ard Party, 438

Alawi Muslims, 618, 619, 655

al-Ba'ath (Damascus), 628, 629

Alexander, Edward, 320-21, 324

Alexander I, Tsar of Russia, 32,
33, 37

Alexander II, Tsar of Russia, 31,
34, 37, 44, 113
assassination of, 34-35

Alexander III, Tsar of Russia, 51,
98
anti-semitic policies of, 33-34,
36, 37, 39, 45, 372
French support of, 40
second *aliyah* and, 113

Alexandria, 339, 386

Algeria, 206, 338, 339, 340, 342,
384, 387, 473, 580, 602

Algiers, 338, 473

Aliens Act (Great Britain, 1904),
27-30, 95

aliyah, first (1882-1903), 42, 51,
52, 107, 114-15
Arabs and, 114
origins of, 31, 113

aliyah, second (1904-1914), 107,

Eastern European Jews, 28, 29,
31-52, 192
as beneficiaries and victims of
Enlightenment, 343
Nazi annihilation of, *see* Holocaust
see also Ashkenazim; *and
specific countries*
Eban, Abba, 270, 273, 279, 283,
284, 377, 382, 490, 511
in Eshkol Government, 406,
407, 411-12, 414, 506
in Meir Government, 506-8, 509
Rabin and, 495, 506, 538
response to Sadat initiative by,
509, 510
Six Day War and, 411-12, 414
Suez Crisis and, 386, 391-92,
394-96, 398
Eden, Sir Anthony, 212, 257, 258,
388, 396, 500
on British Middle Eastern interests, 259
reliance on Eastern Department by, 216-17
Suez Canal nationalization and,
386-87
ee-hizdahut (nonidentification
policy), 370-72, 405
Egypt, 93, 95, 96, 206, 235, 237
Arab nationalists in, 264
British arms supplied to, 373
British treaty with (1936), 238,
304, 379
Czechoslovakia and, 384-85,
386, 387
effect of 1948 War on, 308
fedayeen and, 381-82, 383, 389,
390, 395, 396, 397, 492
France and, 380, 385, 387
Gaza Strip as strategically important to, 448-49
Gaza Strip residents not citizens of, 448
at Geneva Conference (1973),
533-34, 543
Great Britain and, 121-22, 137,

238, 294, 304-5, 307, 378-79,
385, 386-87, 401
growth of nationalism in, 236,
339
Haj Amin backed by, 364,
369
independence of, 341
Israeli armistice with (1949),
304, 307
Israeli "deep penetration"
bombing of (1970), 495, 496-
497
Jews in, 338
Jordan and, 408, 413, 550, 593-
594
at Lausanne Conference, 363
Lebanon and, 553, 621, 626
military coup in (1952), 308
neutralization of, after Suez
Crisis, 399-400
in 1948 War, 291, 292, 293, 300-
301, 303, 304, 306
Open Bridges on West Bank
opposed by, 453
Palestinian Arabs in, 302, 469,
478-79
and partition of Palestine, 289
P.L.O. and, 475-76, 477, 478-79,
481, 502, 504, 544, 550-52,
553, 556, 574, 579-80, 595-96
and proposed Jewish colony in
Sinai (1902), 96
Saudi Arabia and, 408, 492
in Six Day War, 409-16
after Six Day War defeat, 489-
493
Soviet Union and, 384-85, 401-
403, 408, 409, 494-501, 502,
511-12, 518, 520, 524, 527,
533, 534, 543, 571-72, 573
strategic importance of, 236
in Suez War, 14, 380, 386-87
Syria and, 407-8, 474, 549, 550-
552, 554, 566, 580
U.N. delegation of, 15
U.N.E.F. ousted by (1957),
409-10